Fodor's

PERU

4th Edition

D0770039

Fodor's Travel Publications   New York, Toronto, London, Sydney, Auckland
www.fodors.com

Eugene Fodor:
The Spy Who Loved Travel

As Fodor's celebrates our 75th anniversary, we are honoring the colorful and adventurous life of Eugene Fodor, who revolutionized guidebook publishing in 1936 with his first book, *On the Continent, The Entertaining Travel Annual.*

Eugene Fodor's life seemed to leap off the pages of a great spy novel. Born in Hungary, he spoke six languages and graduated from the Sorbonne and the London School of Economics. During World War II he joined the Office of Strategic Services, the budding spy agency for the United States. He commanded the team that went behind enemy lines to liberate Prague, and recommended to Generals Eisenhower, Bradley, and Patton that Allied troops move to the capital city. After the war, Fodor worked as a spy in Austria, posing as a U.S. diplomat.

In 1949 Eugene Fodor—with the help of the CIA—established Fodor's Modern Guides. He was passionate about travel and wanted to bring his insider's knowledge of Europe to a new generation of sophisticated Americans who wanted to explore and seek out experiences beyond their borders. Among his innovations were annual updates, consulting local experts, and including cultural and historical perspectives and an emphasis on people—not just sites. As Fodor described it, "The main interest and enjoyment of foreign travel lies not only in 'the sites,' ... but in contact with people whose customs, habits, and general outlook are different from your own."

Eugene Fodor died in 1991, but his legacy, Fodor's Travel, continues. It is now one of the world's largest and most trusted brands in travel information, covering more than 600 destinations worldwide in guidebooks, on Fodors.com, and in ebooks and iPhone apps. Technology and the accessibility of travel may be changing, but Eugene Fodor's unique storytelling skills and reporting style are behind every word of today's Fodor's guides.

Our editors and writers continue to embrace Eugene Fodor's vision of building personal relationships through travel. We invite you to join the Fodor's community at fodors.com/community and share your experiences with like-minded travelers. Tell us when we're right. Tell us when we're wrong. And share fantastic travel secrets that aren't yet in Fodor's. Together, we will continue to deepen our understanding of our world.

Happy 75th Anniversary, Fodor's! Here's to many more.

Tim Jarrell, Publisher

FODOR'S PERU

Editor: Molly Moker

Editorial Contributor: Kelly Kealy
Writers: David Dudenhoefer, Nicholas Gill, Michelle Hopey, Marlise Elizabeth Kast, Katie Tibbetts, Jeffrey Van Fleet

Production Editors: Carolyn Roth, Emily Cogburn
Maps & Illustrations: David Lindroth and Mark Stroud, *cartographers*; Bob Blake, Rebecca Baer, *map editors*; William Wu, *information graphics*
Design: Fabrizio La Rocca, *creative director*; Guido Caroti, Siobhan O'Hare, *art directors*; Tina Malaney, Nora Rosansky, Chie Ushio, Jessica Walsh, Ann McBride, *designers*; Melanie Marin, *senior picture editor*
Cover Photo: Machu Picchu: Caroline Webber/age fotostock
Production Manager: Angela McLean

4th Edition

ISBN 978-1-4000-0531-4

ISSN 1542–3433

SPECIAL SALES

This book is available at special discounts for bulk purchases for sales promotions or premiums. Special editions, including personalized covers, excerpts of existing books, and corporate imprints, can be created in large quantities for special needs. For more information, write to Special Markets/Premium Sales, 1745 Broadway, MD 6-2, New York, NY 10019, or e-mail specialmarkets@randomhouse.com.

AN IMPORTANT TIP & AN INVITATION

Although all prices, opening times, and other details in this book are based on information supplied to us at press time, changes occur all the time in the travel world, and Fodor's cannot accept responsibility for facts that become outdated or for inadvertent errors or omissions. So **always confirm information when it matters**, especially if you're making a detour to visit a specific place. Your experiences—positive and negative—matter to us. If we have missed or misstated something, **please write to us**. Share your opinion instantly through our online feedback center at fodors.com/contact-us.

PRINTED IN COLOMBIA

10 9 8 7 6 5 4 3 2 1

CONTENTS

1 **EXPERIENCE PERU** 8
   What's Where. 10
   Peru Planner 12
   FAQs 14
   What's New in Peru 16
   Peru Today. 18
   Quintessential Peru 20
   Peru Top Attractions. 22
   If You Like 24
   Packing and Preparations 26
   When to Go. 27
   Tour Operators 28
   Great Itineraries 32

2 **LIMA** 47
   Welcome to Lima 48
   Planning 51
   Exploring Lima 54
   Where to Eat 70
   Shopping. 98

3 **THE SOUTHERN COAST** 101
   Welcome to
   The Southern Coast 102
   Planning 105
   North of Pisco 107
   Pisco and the Paracas
   Peninsula 113

4 **THE SOUTHERN ANDES AND
   LAKE TITICACA** 145
   Welcome to The Southern Andes
   and Lake Titicaca. 146
   Planning 148
   The Far Southern Coast. 151
   Canyon Country 155
   Arequipa 167
   Puno and Lake Titicaca 186

Fodor's Features

Visible History. 39
Food in Peru. 71
Nazca Lines 135
The Islands of Lake Titicaca 197
Touring the Sacred Valley 257
Journey to Machu Picchu. 278
The Jungle Life. 315
Big Mountains. 409

5 **CUSCO AND THE
   SACRED VALLEY** 209
   Welcome to Cusco and the
   Sacred Valley 210
   Planning 213
   Cusco. 215
   Side Trips from Cusco 246
   Sacred Valley of the Inca. 252

6 **MACHU PICCHU AND
   THE INCA TRAIL** 271
   Welcome to Machu Picchu and
   the Inca Trail 272
   Planning 274
   Aguas Calientes 276

7 THE AMAZON BASIN 303
   Welcome to
   The Amazon Basin 304
   Planning 307
   Madre de Dios 309

8 THE CENTRAL HIGHLANDS . . 339
   Welcome to
   The Central Highlands. 340
   Planning 343
   Huánuco South to Tarma 345
   Tarma South to Ayacucho 356

9 THE NORTH COAST AND
   NORTHERN HIGHLANDS 375
   Welcome to The North Coast
   and Northern Highlands 376
   Planning 380
   The North Coast 383
   Huaraz and the Cordillera
   Blanca 408

10 BOLIVIA 435
   Welcome to Bolivia 436
   Planning 439
   La Paz 447
   Lake Titicaca. 471
   Central Bolivia 485

   UNDERSTANDING PERU 511
   Spanish Vocabulary 512

   TRAVEL SMART PERU 529

   INDEX 547

   ABOUT OUR WRITERS 556

MAPS

El Centro 56
San Isidro 61
Miraflores 64
Barranco 67
Where to Eat and Stay
in Barranco 77

Where to Eat and Stay in
El Centro 78
Where to Eat and Stay
in Miraflores 80
Where to Eat and Stay in
San Isidro. 85
Pisco. 115
Paracas Peninsula. 121
Ica 125
Ica Valley Wineries 128
Nazca 140
Colca Canyon and
Cotahuasi Canyon. 159
Arequipa 168
Where to Eat and Stay
in Arequipa. 177
Lake Titicaca 187
Puno. 189
Cusco 217
Where to Eat and Stay in Cusco . . 232
Side Trips from Cusco 247
Pisac 255
Ollantaytambo. 269
Aguas Calientes 277
Madre de Dios 312
Iquitos. 327
Iquitos Environs 335
Huanuco. 348
Huancayo 358
Ayacucho 367
Outside Trujillo. 382
Trujillo 392
Huaraz. 417
Cajamarca 427
La Paz 450–451
Lake Titicaca 472
Central Bolivia. 484
Sucre. 497
Potosí 501

ABOUT THIS BOOK

Our Ratings

Sometimes you find terrific travel experiences and sometimes they just find you. But usually the burden is on you to select the right combination of experiences. That's where our ratings come in.

As travelers we've all discovered a place so wonderful that its worthiness is obvious. And sometimes that place is so unique that superlatives don't do it justice: you just have to be there to know. These sights, properties, and experiences get our highest rating, **Fodor's Choice,** indicated by orange stars throughout this book.

Black stars highlight sights and properties we deem **Highly Recommended,** places that our writers, editors, and readers praise again and again for consistency and excellence.

By default, there's another category: any place we include in this book is by definition worth your time, unless we say otherwise. And we will.

Disagree with any of our choices? Care to nominate a place or suggest that we rate one more highly? Visit our feedback center at www.fodors.com/feedback.

Budget Well

Hotel and restaurant price categories from ¢ to $$$$ are defined in the opening pages of each chapter. For attractions, we always give standard adult admission fees; reductions are usually available for children, students, and senior citizens. Want to pay with plastic? **AE, DC, MC, V** following restaurant and hotel listings indicate whether American Express, Diner's Club, MasterCard, and Visa are accepted. The Discover card is accepted almost nowhere in South America.

Restaurants

Unless we state otherwise, restaurants are open for lunch and dinner daily. We mention dress only when there's a specific requirement and reservations only when they're essential or not accepted—it's always best to book ahead.

Hotels

Hotels have private bath, phone, and TV and operate on the European Plan (aka EP, meaning without meals), unless we specify that they use the Continental Plan (CP, with a continental breakfast), Breakfast Plan (BP, with a full breakfast), or Modified American Plan (MAP, with breakfast and dinner) or are all-inclusive (including all meals and most activities). We always list facilities but not whether you'll be charged an extra fee to use them, so when pricing accommodations, find out what's included.

Listings

★	Fodor's Choice
★	Highly recommended
✉	Physical address
⊹	Directions or Map coordinates
⌂	Mailing address
☎	Telephone
🖷	Fax
⊕	On the Web
✍	E-mail
☞	Admission fee
☉	Open/closed times
Ⓜ	Metro stations
▭	Credit cards

Hotels & Restaurants

☒	Hotel
↳	Number of rooms
⚙	Facilities
⦿	Meal plans
✕	Restaurant
⟲	Reservations
🏛	Dress code
⌇	Smoking
⛾	BYOB

Outdoors

⚐	Golf
⛺	Camping

Other

☾	Family-friendly
⇨	See also
✉	Branch address
☞	Take note

Experience Peru

WHAT'S WHERE

The following numbers refer to chapters in the book.

2 Lima. In Peru's cultural and political center, experience some of the best dining in the Americas, vibrant nightlife, and great museums and churches. See the Catedral and the catacombs at the Iglesia de San Francisco, and stroll about Miraflores for shops and eats.

Fishing boats.

3 The Southern Coast. Head south for wines and piscos around Ica, dune-boarding in Huacachina, the mysterious Nazca Lines, the marine life of Paracas National Preserve, and tranquil fishing villages at Pucusana and Cerro Azul. The inland area, particularly Pisco, was devastated by an earthquake in 2007, but is rebuilding.

4 The Southern Andes and Lake Titicaca. Colca and Cotahuasi canyons are the world's two deepest canyons. Peru's "second city"

Pisac.

Arequipa may also be its most attractive. Lake Titicaca is the world's highest navigable lake and home to the floating Uros Islands.

5 Cusco and the Sacred Valley. Cusco (11,500 feet above sea level) is a necessary stop on your journey to Machu Picchu. The former Inca capital is gorgeous, and packed with fine restaurants, hotels, churches, and museums. Visit the nearby Inca ruins of Sacsayhuamán, take a day trip to the Pisac market and Ollantaytambo, or spend a night in the Sacred Valley.

6 Machu Picchu. The great Machu Picchu, crowded or not crowded, misty rains or clear skies, never ceases to enthrall, and the Inca Trail is still the great hiking pilgrimage. Stay in Aguas Calientes for the best access.

7 Amazon Basin. Peru's vast tract of the Amazon may contain the world's greatest

biodiversity. Fly into Iquitos or Puerto Maldonado for the wildlife preserves, jungle lodges, rain-forest hikes, and boat excursions.

8 The Central Highlands. Festivals and market towns dominate Huancayo and the Mantaro Valley, while the passionate Semana Santa celebrations are the rage in Ayacucho. From Lima to Huancayo, the world's highest railroad tops out at 15,685 feet.

9 The North Coast and the Northern Highlands. Go up the coast for some of South America's best beach life and inland to the Cordillera Blanca for some of the world's highest mountains. Many of Peru's greatest archaeological discoveries were made in the north.

Camp near Laguna Satuna, Cordillera Blanca.

PERU PLANNER

Time

Peru shares the Eastern Standard Time zone with New York and Miami when the U.S. East Coast is not on daylight saving time. So when it's noon in Lima it will be 11 AM in Dallas and 9 AM in Los Angeles.

Connectivity

Cell phone coverage and wireless Internet access are increasingly common in Peru, which means you can take your smart phone and laptop with you, if you want to. Check with your carrier to see if your cell phone will work in Peru, and what the rates are. It is probably expensive, so keep in mind that there are *locutorios* (phone centers) all over Lima and other cities, and calling cards for sale at most convenience stores and pharmacies, which means you can call home for pennies a minute. All but the cheapest hotels—even some of the jungle lodges—have Wi-Fi, which is usually free. If you don't want to carry a laptop, most hotels also have computers for guest use and there are Internet cafés all over the country that charge S/1 or S/2 an hour.

Health and Safety

Peru is safer than it has been in years, but standard travel precautions apply. Remember: you represent enormous wealth to the typical person here; the budget for your trip might exceed what many Peruvians earn in a year. Conceal your valuables, watch your things, avoid deserted streets, walk purposefully, take taxis at night, and be vigilant if somebody invades even your personal space, or if there is a scene of commotion, either of which may be done to distract you. Bag slashers and pickpockets tend to work in markets and on buses; keep track of your valuables in any crowded place.

In terms of health and sanitation, few visitors experience anything worse than a bout of traveler's diarrhea. If you stick to upscale eateries in well-trodden destinations, you may minimize even those problems. Be wary of raw foods (peel your fruit!), and don't drink tap water or ice cubes. Check with your physician about any pre-travel immunizations or medications at least a month before you leave, since some vaccines require multiple injections.

High Altitude

Peru's lofty heights present you with both majesty and menace. The Andes, the country's signature geographic feature, provide a glorious backdrop. The 6,768-meter (22,204-feet) Huascarán tops Peru's peaks, and much of the center north–south band of the country sits at 3,000–4,000 meters (9,800–13,000 feet) altitude.

Treat that altitude with respect. Its consequences, locally known as *soroche*, affect many visitors. For most, it's little more than a shortness of breath, which can be minimized by taking it easy the first couple of days and a good intake of nonalcoholic liquids. It occasionally requires immediate descent to lower altitudes. Peruvians swear by tea brewed from coca leaves, a completely legal way (in Peru, at least) to prevent symptoms. We recommend a pre-trip check with your doctor to see if any underlying conditions (hypertension, heart problems, pregnancy) might preclude travel here.

First-timer?

While Cusco and Machu Picchu are obligatory destinations for a first trip to Peru, the country has much more to offer, as the pages of this guide attest. There is too much to see and do in one trip, so plan your itinerary according to your interests and the season.

Wherever you go, build some downtime into your itinerary, especially your first day in the Andes, when you may feel weak or ill. Don't let all those churches, ruins, convents, and museums blur together. Give yourself enough time to stop and smell the pisco sours.

For years, travelers avoided Lima, which is increasingly a mistake. The country's capital is a sprawling metropolis with horrible traffic and more than its share of slums, but the plazas and colonial churches of the historic El Centro are impressive, Barranco is charming, and the metropolitan area has the country's best museums and restaurants.

Postpone that diet. "Amazing" is the only way to describe what we think is the hemisphere's best food. A mix of European, Indigenous, Asian, and African influences make Peruvian cuisine remarkably varied and delicious. The seafood is excellent, and the best is found in Lima and other coastal cities, but Cusco and Arequipa have ample selections of restaurants that serve up some tasty regional dishes.

Shopping is another popular distraction from exploring, and the handicraft selection is impressive, especially in Cusco. In the market and all but the fanciest shops in the Andean cities you are expected to bargain, so don't be shy.

Try to learn a few words of Spanish. Outside the tourist industry, few people speak much English. Learning some common words and phrases can simplify life, and make your trip more pleasant. (Spanish is a second language for many Peruvians, too.)

Pack reserves of patience. Peru offers a polished tourism product, but schedules occasionally go awry, traffic in the cities is chaotic, and street hawkers or beggars can get on your nerves.

Tipping

A 10% tip suffices in most restaurants unless the service is exceptional. Porters in hotels and airports expect S/2 per bag. There's no need to tip taxi drivers, although many people round up the fare. At bars, tip about S/1 a drink. Bathroom attendants get 20 céntimos; gas-station attendants get 50 céntimos for extra services such as adding air to your tires. Tour guides should get S/20 and bus drivers S/10 each per day.

Electricity

Electrical outlets in Peru are like the ones in the United States and Canada, but the electrical grid runs 220 volts, which will destroy an electronic device made for the 110-volt system of North America unless it has a power adapter. Laptop computers and many other electronic goods have power adapters built into their cords, but if you have any doubts, check before you plug in. Many hotels have a 110-volt outlet in the bathroom for electric shavers and other devices. Unless it is marked otherwise, you can assume that every outlet in Peru is 220.

FAQS

How difficult Is Peru to Get Around?

Thanks to more domestic flights, Peru is much easier to move about these days. Almost every worthwhile destination is within a two-hour flight from Lima. Train travel is limited, but fun and easy. Traveling by car is trickier—roads are improving, but signs aren't well posted. Buses go everywhere, and the most expensive seats are quite comfortable; only travel with big companies such as Cruz del Sur and Junin. In cities, cabs are abundant and cheap, but check for an official license.

Is Machu Picchu Hard to Get To?

Travel to Machu Picchu is almost too easy. Most people do the trip in a day out of Cusco, but it is worth two or three days, with overnights in Aguas Calientes and the Sacred Valley. The most common method is to hop on a train from Cusco or Ollantaytambo to Aguas Calientes, which is a 20-minute bus trip from the ruins. Or you can do as the Incas did and walk the trail, which is a two- to four-day jaunt and a highlight for those who do it. Either option is likely to be the most expensive thing you do in Peru, but Machu Picchu is also one of the most amazing things you're likely to ever see.

What Languages Do People Speak?

The official language is Spanish and nearly everyone speaks it. But in the highlands the language the Incas spoke, Quechua, is still widely used. Older people in indigenous communities often don't know Spanish, but younger generations do. Aymara, a pre-Inca language, is spoken in the towns around Lake Titicaca and dozens of native tongues are spoken in the Amazon Basin. And a growing number of Peruvians speak English.

Will I Have Trouble if I Don't Speak Spanish?

No problem. Although it's helpful to know some Spanish, it's not a necessity, especially on an organized tour or in tourist areas. There's a strong push for tourist professionals to learn English, but cab drivers or store clerks aren't likely to know a lick. We suggest learning a few simple phrases. *Cuánto cuesta?* (How much?) is a good one to start with.

Was Machu Picchu Damaged by Floods?

Flooding destroyed part of the railroad between Cusco and Machu Picchu in January of 2010, but the ruins and nearby town of Aguas Calientes escaped damage. The tracks were repaired within a matter of months and Machu Picchu was promptly reopened.

Is the Water Safe to Drink?

Nope. But bottled water is cheap and sold nearly everywhere. Drink as much as you can, it'll help you beat altitude sickness.

Will I get sick?

Stomach bugs are a frequent problem for visitors, but if you avoid salads and only eat fruits that you peel, you should be okay. Cebiche and other "raw" seafood dishes popular in Lima also carry a risk, but are so tasty that it would be a shame to avoid them. Bring anti-diarrhea medicines and play it by ear, or tummy.

What Are the Safety Concerns?

Petty crime is the primary concern. If you're "gringo," you probably have a camera, iPod, watch, jewelry, credit cards, cash—everything a thief wants. Pickpocketing and bag slashing are the most common methods. Thieves are fast and sneaky so be alert, especially in crowded markets and bus stations, and never walk

on deserted streets. In the last couple years there have been "strangle muggings," when several robbers strangle the traveler until they're unconscious, making for an easy steal, so stick to the busy streets in Lima's Centro. Taxi kidnappings, in which people are forced to withdraw money from ATMs at gunpoint, are also a problem, albeit rare. Use official taxis.

Should I Worry About Altitude Sickness?

Yes and no. If you have health issues, you should check with your doctor before heading to high altitudes. Otherwise, don't worry too much because nearly everyone experiences a little altitude sickness. The lucky ones may have a headache for the first 24 hours, while others may endure several days of intense fatigue and headaches. When up high, lay off the booze, limit physical activity, hydrate, drink lots of coca tea, suck coca hard candy, or chew coca leaves. If the headache persists, take an ibuprofen, hydrate some more, and sleep it off. Many hotels have oxygen so don't hesitate to ask for it.

Do I Have to Pay Any Fees to Get into the Country?

No. But you pay to get out. The departure tax system (which nearly every South American country embraces) is alive and well in Peru. Be prepared to fork over $31 USD, or the equivalent in soles, when you leave Lima for any international destination. Every time you fly domestically, you also get hit with a departure tax, but it's only $6.82 USD. Warning: you can only pay with cash—soles or dollars.

What's in a Pisco Sour?

A smooth sipper, pisco sours are made with 2 ounces of pisco, (a white-grape brandy made from locally-grown grapes), ¾ ounce of freshly squeezed lime juice, a half-ounce of simple sugar syrup, 1 whipped egg white, and a dash of Angostura bitters. They're so tasty it's no wonder Peruvians are proud of their mildly tangy, national cocktail (and so are Chileans, who also claim the pisco sour as their national drink). Beware, they're quick to sneak up on you.

Are There Cultural Sensitivities I Should Be Aware Of?

Peruvians are very polite, and it's customary to be the same. You'll notice that men and women kiss each other on the cheek when saying hello, and the same goes for women to women. It's nonsexual and a sign of friendliness. There's no 6 inches of personal space in Peru, it's more like 2: people talk, walk, and sit close in general, so don't be alarmed. Peruvians, like many South American countries, are also on "Latin Time," meaning, arriving an hour late for a social engagement is considered customary. Finally, there's actually bathroom etiquette in Peru. It's polite not to throw toilet paper down the toilet and instead place it in the bin provided. Plumbing is not super-sophisticated and pipes clog frequently.

WHAT'S NEW IN PERU

Economic Powerhouse

For much of the past decade, Peru has experienced some of the highest economic growth in Latin America, averaging nearly 7% annually. Driven by high mineral prices and steady demand from China, the boom has also included growth in exports of agricultural products such as asparagus, coffee, seafood, and textiles, as well as tourism. Per capita income has doubled since 2003, and though much of that increase has gone to the upper echelons, the percentage of Peruvians living in poverty has dropped from 50% to 35%. Tax revenues have likewise grown, which is reflected in the refurbished buildings, new infrastructure, and a bigger police force. For travelers, this means more hotels and restaurants to choose from and safer, cleaner cities, but also higher prices.

Change and Continuity

At press time, Peru was preparing for presidential elections in April 2011, with a likely second round in May, if no candidate topped 50% of the vote. The leading contenders, which included a former mayor of Lima, ex-president Alejandro Toledo, and the daughter of jailed ex-president Alberto Fujimori, all represented center-right parties likely to continue the pro-business policies of recent administrations. It would seem that despite a third of the country living in poverty and sporadic social conflicts, the majority of Peruvians want stability and have faith in the current economic model.

Planes, Trains and Buses

A combination of public infrastructure and private investment has made Peru an easier country to explore than ever before. In Lima, a new express bus called the Metropolitano provides quick and inexpensive transportation between the neighborhoods of Barranco, Miraflores, and the historic El Centro. The addition of Peruvian Airlines to the list of domestic carriers and an expansion of routes flown by Star Peru and Lan means more options for flying between Lima and other Peruvian cities. This is especially good news if you're on a tight budget, since Peruvian Airlines and Star Peru charge foreigners considerably less than LAN, the country's main domestic airline. A comparable development in Cusco, where two new companies—Inka Rail and Andean Railway—now run trains to Machu Picchu, means there are more options for getting to Peru's top attraction. For years, one company, PeruRail, departed Cusco for Machu Picchu early in the morning and returned in the evening. Trains now run between the Sacred Valley towns of Ollantaytambo and Urubamba and Machu Picchu every hour or two, though PeruRail still offers early-morning departures from the Poroy station, near Cusco.

Peru's Nobel Laureate

Peruvian writer Mario Vargas Llosa, one of Latin America's most popular authors, won the Nobel Prize for Literature in 2010. The award's announcement sparked widespread celebration in Peru and renewed interest in his work throughout the world. The author of more than a dozen novels and numerous plays, Vargas Llosa is also a respected journalist and essayist; his weekly opinion column is published on Sundays by the principal Spanish-language newspapers. Though he has set novels in other countries, Vargas Llosa primarily writes about Peru, which makes him a good author to read before or during a Peru trip. *The Story Teller* and *The Green House* are two of his most Peruvian novels, though the comic *Aunt Julia and the Script Writer* and *Captain*

Pandora and the Special Services are also set in the country. More intense novels include *The Time of the Hero*, based on the author's years in a Lima military academy, and *Death in the Andes* and *Who Killed Palomino Molero?*, both of which chronicle the violence that wracked the country in the 1980s and early '90s, when the military struggled to defeat the Shining Path guerrillas.

Machu Picchu Centennial

July 7, 2011 marks the 100th anniversary of American adventurer Hiram Bingham's rediscovery of Machu Picchu. Bingham reached the Incan citadel on an expedition funded by Yale University, which became the owner of all the artifacts his team unearthed. The Peruvian government is organizing a centennial celebration at Machu Picchu, promising participation by international celebrities. The centennial is sweetened by Yale's announcement in December 2010 that it would finally return the artifacts that Bingham removed from Machu Picchu back to Peru; they will be housed in a new Cusco museum.

Mother Nature's Fury

Peru suffers more natural disasters than any other country except Bangladesh. This includes periodic tremors and quakes, such as the 8-magnitude earthquake that shattered the southern coastal cities of Pisco, Ica, and Chincha Alta on August 15, 2007. That quake flattened entire city blocks, and killed more than 500, but the region's hotels and other tourist services reopened quickly and the southern coast remains a popular destination. More frequent disasters are the mudslides and flash floods, known as *huaicos* (pronounced "whycos"), that destroy homes, roads, bridges, and lives in the eastern Andes during each December–May rainy season.

The most newsworthy huaico in recent years roared down the Vilcabamba River Valley in January of 2010, tearing out several kilometers of the railway between Ollantaytambo and Machu Picchu and leaving thousands of tourists stranded in the town of Aguas Calientes until they could be rescued by helicopter. The tracks were replaced in a matter of months, during which time the country lost more than $1 million per day. According to scientists, such extreme weather events will happen more frequently due to climate change.

Protests

Protests, marches, and road barricades are part of Peruvian political life as communities, unions, and other groups periodically take to the streets to stop projects or policies they don't like, or to demand government help. The protests usually end peacefully, but under the government of Alan Garcia, police fired on several protests, resulting in numerous deaths. Cusco residents staged various strikes in 2010 that stranded travelers for a couple of days and halted train service to Machu Picchu. Unfortunately, many of that region's residents perceive no benefit from tourism and don't hesitate to disrupt transportation to pressure the government. The likelihood of having a protest interfere with your travels is small, but keep an eye on the local news nevertheless.

PERU TODAY

Government

Peru gets a new president in 2011, which marks a bit of continuity after decades on a political roller coaster. The military ran Peru from 1968 to 1980, and once the country returned to democracy, a ruthless guerrilla group called the Shining Path began sowing terror in the countryside. In 1985, a 36-year-old socialist named Alan Garcia won the presidency and oversaw what many consider the worst five years in the country's history. His presidency was marked by increased violence by the Shining Path and the military, hyperinflation, a banking crisis, capital flight, and a wave of emigration.

Garcia was followed by Alberto Fujimori (elected 1990), who instituted an austere financial reform program and authoritarian policies—shutting down Congress, suspending the constitution—but he got the economy back on track, and virtually defeated the Shining Path. Fujimori arranged a constitutional reform that allowed him to run for consecutive reelection, and he handily won another five years in office in 1995. A combination of Fujimori fatigue and growing corruption weakened his support, but he was declared the winner of the 2000 elections, while his challenger, Alejandro Toledo, claimed fraud. Subsequent revelations about the degree of corruption in his administration led Fujimori to resign later that year.

New elections were held in 2001, which Toledo won, beating out Garcia who had the audacity to run for president again. Toledo, Peru's first indigenous president, oversaw modest economic growth, but his presidency was rife with scandals. Garcia gave the office another shot in 2006, going up against the leftist Ollanta Humala, who many Peruvians feared was too close to Venezuelan president Hugo Chavez. They consequently gave Garcia another chance, voting for "the lesser of two evils," and he rehabilitated his name, overseeing five years of record economic growth, infrastructure improvements, and a steady reduction of poverty. Fujimori, who tried to return to Peru from exile to run for president again, was arrested, tried, and found guilty of corruption and human rights violations, based on murders committed by a death squad. At press time, the leading contenders for the 2011 elections included Fujimori's daughter, Keiko, former mayor of Lima Luis Castañeda, and ex-President Alejandro Toledo.

Economy

Driven mainly by mining, textile, agricultural, and seafood exports, the Peruvian economy has flourished during the past two decades, experiencing some of the highest growth in Latin America in 2009 and 2010. Fujimori brought the economy back from the brink by stabilizing the currency and privatizing government mines and the electric and telecommunications industries. Toledo took over during a slump, but oversaw modest economic growth and a 60% increase in agricultural exports. Garcia oversaw booms in mining and natural gas extraction and growth in various exports, as well as tourism, which helped the country fare the global recession remarkably well.

Religion

As a result of Spanish conquest, Peru remains predominantly Roman Catholic, with more than 80% of the population identifying themselves this way. Catholicism has a heavy influence in the daily life of the average Peruvian, as well as in state affairs. The newly elected president's

inauguration ceremony begins with a mass in Lima's Cathedral, for example. Despite this overwhelming presence, many Peruvians have moved toward Protestantism and Evangelicalism, which currently represent about 12% of the population. Indigenous Peruvians fused Catholicism with their pre-conquest religion, with Pachamama (Mother Earth) representing the Virgin Mary.

Sports

As with most of South America, *fútbol* (soccer) is Peru's second religion. The country's best teams are Universitario de Deportes and Alianza Lima, and a game between Universitario and Alianza is considered a "clasico." Peru's national team hasn't managed to qualify for the World Cup in more than two decades, which causes much frustration and debate. The country's female athletes are its greatest source of pride; boxer Kina Malpartida and surfer Sofía Mulanovich have both been world champions in recent years and the women's volleyball team won a silver medal in the 1988 Olympics. Although some people may not consider it a sport, bullfighting is still popular in Lima, where the season runs from October to December at Plaza de Acho.

Literature

Peru's most famous writer is the Nobel Laureate Mario Vargas Llosa. The novelist, who once ran for president but was defeated by Alberto Fujimori, is celebrated as a member of the Latin American literary boom of the 1960s. The country's second most famous author is Alfredo Bryce Echenique, who has written more than a dozen comic novels and short story collections, though he has recently faced accusations of plagiarism. Other important 20th-century writers are José María Arguedas, Ciro Alegría, and Manuel Scorza, all of who wrote about the country's indigenous culture. Daniel Alarcón, who was born in Peru but raised in the United States, sets his fiction in the country. Peru's most famous poet is Cesar Vallejo, who only published three books of his poetry, but is considered one of the most innovative poets of the 20th century.

Music

Peruvian music can be split by regions: the sounds of the Andes and the sounds of the coast. "Huayno," the music of the Andes, is traditionally played on acoustic guitars, a small stringed instrument called the charango, and a panpipe called the zampoña, but its more popular form now relies on synthesizers and electric guitars. Coastal "música criolla" has Spanish, Gypsy, and African roots and is played on acoustic guitars and a percussion instrument called the *cajón*—a large wooden box. The late Chabuca Granda popularized this genre, and singers such as Susana Baca, Tania Libertad, and Eva Allyón continue the tradition. Peru's most popular music is probably Cumbia, a Colombian genre popular throughout Latin America, played here with a distinctive Peruvian touch.

Film

Though the film industry in Peru lags well behind that of Argentina, Brazil, or Mexico, Peruvian directors have won important prizes in recent years. Claudia Llosa, a niece of writer Mario Vargas Llosa, won a Golden Bear award at the 2009 Berlin Film Festival for her second film, *The Milk of Sorrow*, which was also nominated for an Academy Award in the Best Foreign Film Category in 2010. The film *Undertow*, directed by Javier Fuentes-León, won an audience award at the 2010 Sundance Film Festival.

QUINTESSENTIAL PERU

Exploring the Past

Machu Picchu is great, but there's more to see of Peru's fascinating past. Stand at Cajamarca where Inca Atahualpa was captured by Spanish leader Francisco Pizzaro. Explore the ancient Moche culture by walking about its adobe pyramids. Puzzle over the mysterious Nazca Lines from the sky. Then enjoy city life in Spanish-influenced Lima, Trujillo, and Arequipa, with their colonial-era mansions, churches, monasteries, and museums.

Peruvian history is best understood by visiting its people and experiencing its cultures. The islands of Lake Titicaca reveal a slice of raw ancient Andean culture. It's as if time has frozen while Quechua and Aymara families live and work off the land, eating and dressing as they did in the 16th century. It's not much different in the highlands around Cusco, where Quechua-speaking folks farm terraces thousands of years old.

Festival Time

Clanging bells, chanting, and wafting incense rouse you before dawn. You peer out your window: scores of people draped in bright colorful costumes walk down the street carrying a saint's figure.

Catholic observances, a strong indigenous tradition, and history pack the calendar with fiestas—from Lima's birthday in January, to the nationwide Semana Santa in spring, to the Inca ritual Inti Raymi on June 24. In Puno each November, citizens reenact the birth of the first Inca emperor, Manco Capac, who, legend has it, rose out of Lake Titicaca.

Among the crosses, saints, and colorful costumes, townspeople try their luck at bingo, beauty queens compete for the crown, Huayno music blasts from speakers, and the Pilsen and Cristal beer flows freely.

High Living

Life in the Andes, the altiplano, has changed little through the centuries. In many villages Quechua is still the only language spoken. There are few cars and computers, no ATMs, and no restaurants, though you will see locals carrying cell phones. Families live in stone and adobe huts and plumbing is a hole in the ground.

Nearly every family raises animals for food and transport. Parents harvest crops from the ancient terraces while children attend school. Cold temperatures call for hearty foods like soup, potatoes, bread, quinoa, and meats.

When it comes to fiestas, these villagers know how to let loose. No major floats needed. Parades consist of local instruments, traditional folk dances that reenact Peruvian history, hand-sewn clothing embroidered with bright colors, a crowd, and lots of alcohol.

Rituals of the Dance

Peruvian folkloric dances vary dramatically between coast and mountains.

The coastal *marinera* is performed to the music of a brass band by a courting couple who execute elegant, complex movements while holding a handkerchief, but never touch. Trujillo is the city best known for marinera festivals and performances. Afro-Peruvian dance is more sensual, performed to the music of guitars and the rhythm of a cajón, a sonorous wooden box on which the percussionist sits.

The most spectacular dance is the Andean *danza de tijeras* (scissors), which involves gymnastic leaps to the strains of harp and violin. Colonial-era priests claimed that a pact with the devil enabled dancers to swallow swords; stick pins in their faces; and eat insects, frogs, and sometimes snakes. The dance has toned down since then.

PERU
TOP ATTRACTIONS

Machu Picchu and the Inca Trail

(A) This "Lost City of the Incas" is the main reason why people come to Peru. The Machu Picchu ruins were built around the 1450s, only to be abandoned a hundred years later. Spanish conquistadors never found it, and for centuries it stayed hidden. But in 1911, it was rediscovered by an American historian. If you're adventurous, and in good shape, the four-day Inca Trail is the classic route to Machu Picchu.

Colca Canyon

(B) Twice as deep as Arizona's Grand Canyon, Colca Canyon is typically a side trip from Arequipa, which is a three-hour drive away. Adventure enthusiasts head for the Canyon's Colca River for whitewater rafting, while those less inclined toward danger hike along the canyon for gorgeous vistas. The highlight is the Cruz del Condor, a mirador where lucky

visitors might spot the Andean condor in flight.

Chan Chan

(C) A UNESCO World Heritage Site since 1986, this archaeological site was home to the second largest pre-Columbian society in South America: the Chimú. The estimated 30,000 Chimú residents built the mud city between 850 and 1470. You can roam the ruins—which contain 10 walled citadels that house burial chambers, ceremonial rooms, and temples—on a day trip from the charming northern city of Trujillo.

Lake Titicaca

(D) At 3,812 meters (12,500 feet), Puno's Lake Titicaca is the highest navigable lake in the world. More than 25 rivers empty into it, and according to Inca legend, it was the birthplace of the Sun God who founded the Inca dynasty. On Isla Taquile and other islands here, Quechua-speak-

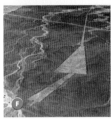

ing people preserve the traditions of their ancestors.

Baños del Inca

(**E**) Six kilometers (3.7 mi) from the northern city of Cajamarca, Baños del Inca (Inca Baths) hot springs were once used by Atahualpa, the last sovereign Inca emperor. Supposedly, the emperor was relaxing in one of the mineral-rich baths when Spanish conquistadors arrived in Cajamarca. While visitors can only view the older pools that have been preserved intact, they can bathe in the newer pools built specifically for tourists.

Nazca Lines

(**F**) It's thought that between 900 BC and AD 600, the Nazca and Paracas cultures constructed the Nazca Lines: geometric figures drawn into the Pampa Colorado (Red Plain) near Nazca, a city south of Lima. Three hundred geoglyphs and 800 straight lines make up these mysterious figures. No one knows why these massive drawings—which include representations of a lizard, monkey, condor, and spider—were created. The only way to get a good view is to take a flight-seeing tour.

Sacsayhuamán

(**G**) Machu Picchu isn't the only must-see Inca ruin to visit from Cusco. Used as a fortress during Pizarro's conquest, the military site of Sacsayhuamán is made of huge stone blocks; the largest is 8.5 meters (28 feet) high and weighs more than 300 tons (600,000 pounds). It's believed that some 20,000 men worked on the site.

Cordillera Blanca

(**H**) Part of the Andes, Cordillera Blanca (White Range) has more than 50 peaks that reach 5,500 meters (18,000 feet) or higher and stretches 20 kilometers (12.5 miles) wide and 180 km (112 miles) long. Mountain climbers and hikers of all skill levels can enjoy this majestic range, which is part of the Huascarán National Park.

IF YOU LIKE

Sun, Surf, and Seafood

During the summer months (December–April), beach lovers around Peru head west to enjoy a day of surfing the Pacific Ocean waves, sunbathing, and devouring the country's freshest seafood.

Máncora. This fishing town on Peru's northern coast is the country's worst-kept secret. Ask any Peruvian which is the best beach in Peru and they will all mention this stretch of pale-gray sand lined with coconut palms and hotels. Máncora is sunny year-round and visited by beach lovers from Lima and abroad.

Puerto Chicama. This fishing outpost north of Trujillo claims to have the world's longest left-hand point break. Surfers of all skill levels can find suitable waves year-round, but the biggest swells roll in between March and August.

Lima. While the ocean views from Miraflores and Barranco are impressive, the capital's greatest marine asset is the food. Lima has restaurants that specialize in everything, but *cebicherías* (restaurants dedicated to seafood) are the place to head for lunch. Check out Punta Sal, Segundo Muelle, and Chef Gaston Acurio's upscale "Cebichería La Mar."

South of Lima. Urbanites from Lima flock southward from December to April to beach resorts such as San Vicente de Cañete, a couple of hours from the capital. Cerro Azul, a small beach town in Cañete, is a tranquil alternative to the beaches closer to Lima. In contrast, Asia, also in Cañete, is where the wealthiest Limeños summer.

Ancient Archaeological Sites

The main reason most travelers visit Peru is to see the ancient ruins left by the Inca and older civilizations. Machu Picchu is the biggie, but don't stop there. Here are a few archaeological sites that are worth the trip.

Caral. Four hours north of Lima, the archaeological ruins of Caral in the Supe Valley shocked the world when their origins were discovered to date back to 2627 BC—1,500 years earlier than what was believed to be the age of South America's oldest civilization. Growing numbers of visitors make the day trip to Peru's most recently discovered ancient wonder.

Chan Chan. This capital of the pre-Inca Chimu empire was the largest pre-Columbian city in the Americas and the largest adobe city in the world. A 5-km (3-mi) trip from the northern city of Trujillo, Chan Chan is a UNESCO World Heritage Site. It's threatened by erosion because of its close proximity to the coast, which experiences heavy seasonal rains.

Choquequirau. The Inca ruins of Choquequirau, in Cusco province, is the ideal destination for hikers who want to stray from the beaten trail. Five-day trekking tours are available to this remote site, which has been called "Machu Picchu's sacred sister" because of the similarities in architecture.

Ollantaytambo. Sixty kilometers (37 miles) northwest of Cusco, the extensive Inca fortress of Ollantaytambo is one of the few locations where the Incas managed to defeat Spanish conquistadors. The fort held a temple, with a ceremonial center greeting those who manage to get to the top.

Natural Beauty

With more than 50 natural areas or conservation units—in the forms of national parks, reserves, sanctuaries, and protected rain forests—Peru is a great place to experience tropical nature.

Colca Canyon and Cotahuasi Canyon. The two deepest canyons in the world are in Peru's dry, southern Andes. Dipping down 10,600 feet and 11,000 feet respectively, they are skirted by hiking trails, whereas the rivers that flow through them offer intense kayaking and rafting. Near this exceptional geology are villages offering glimpses into the indigenous culture.

Huascarán National Park. Towering over the town of Huaraz, this park was established to protect the flora and fauna and landscapes of the Cordillera Blanca, or "White Mountain Chain." A UNESCO World Heritage Site, it is home to such rare species as the spectacled bear and the Andean condor.

Rio Abiseo National Park. The lush jungle of this remote park is home to such rare species as the yellow-head parrot and "mono choro de cola amarilla" (yellow-tailed Woolly Monkey). It also protects the archaeological site Gran Pajaten of the Chachapoyas Culture, an impressive monument complex.

Tingo María National Park. While the park is home to an array of flora and fauna, most people are happy to admire the chain of mountains called La Bella Durmiente because its silhouette resembles a sleeping woman, or visit the Cueva de las Lechuzas, a cave where owls are known to sleep.

Museums

It could be argued that Peru is one big open-air museum. However, a little background information before you head to the ruins is always helpful. Museums in Peru do an excellent job of documenting the history and culture of a country overflowing with both.

Museo de Arte de Lima. This 19th-century gem on the Parque de la Exposicion is called the MALI by Limeños. It has the best collection of Peruvian art, from historical paintings depicting colonial Peru to works by modern artists such as Fernando de Szyszlo.

Museo Nacional Sicán. Twenty kilometers (12.5 miles) north of Chiclayo, this modern museum focuses on the ancient Sicán civilization, which originated in AD 750. Learn about the life and death of one of their leaders, the Lord of Sicán, who represented the "natural world" in their culture.

Museo Rafael Larco Herrera. Recently refurbished, Lima's finest museum was constructed on the site of a pre-Columbian pyramid. It's most famous for its titillating collection of erotic ceramics, but it has more than 40,000 other ceramic pieces, textiles, and gold work on display.

Museo Santury. Home to the famed "Juanita, the Inca princess" mummy, the Museo de la Universidad Católica de Santa María, as it's formally known, is an obligatory stop for anyone visiting the city of Arequipa. Juanita was discovered in southern Peru and is now kept in a cold glass box to preserve her body so that future visitors can learn about her sacrificial death.

PACKING AND PREPARATIONS

What you pack depends on where and when you travel. If you're heading to several regions, you'll need a good variety of clothing. If you visit the Amazon Basin or Andes between November and May, pack rain gear and a few plastic bags to protect cameras and other items. Good walking shoes or boots are essential everywhere, as are sunblock and insect repellent.

Clothing

Peru's varied geography means a diversity of climates, with the major climate regions being the Costa (coast), the Sierra (mountains) and the Selva (Amazon rain forest). Add to this the fact that southern Peru experiences distinct summer and winter, which are the opposite of the northern hemisphere's seasons, whereas northern Peru has less seasonal variation. When it's torrid in Manhattan, Lima is chilly and gray, but when New Yorkers are bundling up, Lima is hot and sunny. It can get quite cool in the mountains at night, with frequent freezes between June and September, but it is warm and sunny during the day then. The coast is a desert, but it rains most afternoons in the mountains from October to May and pretty much year round in the Amazon Basin, though more between October and May. If you visit then, you'll need rain gear. However, the mountains don't get as cold at night during the rainy months, so you won't need that down jacket.

The best policy is to bring a good mix of clothes that go well together so that you can layer, since a mountain day begins brisk, but quickly warms. Once the clouds roll in, or the sun gets low, you'll need a raincoat or a jacket. Rather than packing a sweater, hat, and gloves, you may want to buy them in Lima or Cusco, where the shops and markets hold a kaleidoscopic selection of sheep and alpaca wool clothing.

You'll want light clothing, a hat, and rain gear for the Amazon Basin, where it is usually scorching. Long pants and sleeves will help you avoid mosquito bites and sunburn. Keep in mind that the Madre de Dios region gets little rain from May to September, when it gets hit by occasional cold fronts that can make you break out your mountain clothes.

Toiletries

Sunblock is essential everywhere, and can be purchased at any Peruvian pharmacy. Insect repellent, preferably with DEET, is essential in the Amazon Basin and eastern Andes (Machu Picchu), but the local brands aren't as good as what you can buy at home. Pack an anti-diarrhea medicine, such as Imodium, just in case, and always carry a small packet of tissues, since bathrooms don't always have toilet paper. You'll want a skin moisturizer if you spend much time in the mountains between May and October. If your camera, travel alarm, or other electronic goods use unusual-sized disposable batteries, pack extras.

Vaccines

The Centers for Disease Control and Prevention recommend that travelers to Peru be up to date on routine shots and consult their doctor about getting vaccinated against hepatitis A and B and typhoid. Travelers heading to the Amazon basin should get a yellow fever vaccine and consider taking an antimalarial drug other than chloroquine. However, diligent use of insect repellent, long pants, and long sleeve shirts is the best policy in the jungle, since it can protect you against various mosquito-borne diseases.

WHEN TO GO

Most people visit Peru between June and September, which is the dry season in the Sierra (mountains) and the Selva (Amazon Basin), but that is by no means the only time to visit. The best time to go depends on your primary interest, or what regions you want to explore. If you prefer to avoid the crowds, high prices, and the cold, consider doing your Cusco–Machu Picchu trip in late April, May, October, or November.

The seasons are flipped in the southern hemisphere, but since northern Peru is practically on the equator, "summer" and "winter" mean less there than in the country's southern half. The dry season, from May to September, is winter in the southern Andes, where it often freezes at night, but the days are sunny. Lima is enveloped in a chilly fog called the *garúa* for the better part of those months. You may get some rain in the Andes in April and May, but the highland landscapes are a beautiful shade of green then, and there are fewer tourists.

The dry months are the best time to visit the Madre de Dios portion of the Amazon Basin, but you are better off visiting Iquitos and the Amazon River during the "rainy" season, because the water is high then, facilitating access to streams and lakes for wildlife watching, and it doesn't rain that much more than the during "dry" months.

You'll want to make your reservations far in advance for travel anywhere in Peru during the second half of July, or first week of August, when local school vacations add Peruvian tourists to foreign masses.

If you're a surfer and want to spend more time in Lima and the coast, or simply want a break from winter, the December-to-May southern summer is a great time to visit Peru. It may be raining in the Andes and Amazon, but the weather is lovely in Lima and such coastal sites as the Nazca Lines, Paracas, and the pre-Incan ruins near Trujillo and Chiclayo.

Festivals and Celebrations

Fireworks and colorful processions honor the **Virgen de la Candelaria** during the first half of February in Puno, on Lake Titicaca. The faithful follow images of the Virgin Mary through the streets as colorful dancers depict the struggle between good and evil. (The demons always lose.)

Carnaval (February or March) is celebrated with parades and folk dancing in most highland towns, though especially in Cajamarca, Ayacucho, and Huarás.

Semana Santa (March or April) is marked by Holy Week processions countrywide, though Ayacucho's celebrations are the most elaborate.

Thousands flock to the Ausangate Glacier for **Qoyllur Rit'i** (June 9), a religious festival that mixes Incan and Christian rites in Sinakara, Cusco department.

Cusco's spectacular **Inti Raymi** (June 24) marks the winter solstice with a reenactment of an Inca ritual that beseeches the sun to return. The fortress ruins of Sacsayhuamán form the stage for that proverbial cast of thousands.

Firecrackers may rouse you out of bed during Peru's two-day **Fiestas Patrias** (July 28–29), which celebrate the country's independence from Spain in 1821.

Lima and the Central Highlands revere the **Señor de los Milagros** (October 18–28), a colonial-era, dark-skinned Christ statue that survived a 1655 earthquake that destroyed much of the capital.

TOUR OPERATORS

Who's Who

There is no shortage of companies selling tours to Peru, but not all of them have the same level of experience and reputation. Most U.S., Canadian, and British tour companies offering trips to Peru merely sell tours that are designed and run by Peruvian operators. However, there are international companies that run their own shows in Peru, notably Orient Express. Others send a trip leader to accompany each group, who will often team up with a Peruvian guide. However, many simply sell tours that are operated by one or more Peruvian companies.

If you've traveled with a company to other destinations and had good experiences, you have good reason to use them in Peru. Though you may be reluctant to buy a package directly from a Peruvian company, keep in mind that you may get the same tour you would buy from a U.S. company for considerably less money. If you want to stray from the beaten path, you may have no choice but to book directly with a Peruvian company. Rest assured that the local operator's included in this section have decades of experience and good reputations.

Where to Go

While every company offers trips to Machu Picchu—Peru's must-see attraction—the country has much more to offer, including the Amazon wilderness, vibrant indigenous cultures, colonial cities, and jaw-dropping mountain landscapes. The great thing is that many of those attractions are easy to combine with Machu Picchu.

Nearly all first-time visitors do some sort of a Cusco/Sacred Valley/Machu Picchu combination, a tour that every company offers. Whether you hike there on a four-day Inca Trail trek, or roll in luxuriously on Orient Express's classic Hiram Bingham train, Machu Picchu is all that it is cracked up to be. There is enough to see between that ancient citadel, the Sacred Valley and Cusco to fill a week, though many people cover the area in a few days. Many tours combine Machu Picchu and Cusco with the rain forest of nearby Madre de Dios, whereas others combine it with southern attractions such as Lake Titicaca, or Arequipa and the Colca Canyon. A longer extension or second trip is needed to include the ancient sites and impressive landscapes of northern Peru.

What to Do

Peru's combination of culture, history, scenery, and biodiversity make it a great place to visit, and you get exposure to all of the above on the classic Cusco–Machu Picchu trip. It is also a world-class destination for people who want to concentrate their vacations on one thing, be it bird-watching (Peru is the number-two country for avian diversity), surfing (the swells are sometimes as big as Hawaii's), or trekking (countless highland trails). Travelers with that kind of focus will want to book their tour with an outfitter that specializes in their passion, and we've included experts in each of those activities here.

The following list features some of the best international and local tour outfitters that offer trips in Peru, ranging from companies that accommodate thousands of tourists per month, to smaller operations that specialize in custom tours. While nearly all of them offer Cusco–Machu Picchu tours, some have expertise, or hotels in certain regions, while others focus on activities such as bird-watching or trekking.

Tour Company	Location	Telephone	Website	Specialties
Abercrombie & Kent	USA	900/554–7016	www.abercrombiekent.com	Popular sites, family trips
Adventure Life	USA	800/344–6118	www.adventure-life.com	Outdoor adventures
Andean Treks	Peru & USA	800/683–8148	www.andeantreks.com	Trekking, traditional tours
Auqui Mountain Spirit	Peru	5184/261–517	www.auqui.com.pe	Customized trips, expert guides
Birding in Peru	Peru	5184/225–990	www.birding-in-peru.com	Tours for serious bird watchers
Condor Travel	Peru & USA	877/236–7199	www.condortravel.com	Traditional and specialty tours
Earthwatch	USA & UK	800/776–0188	www.earthwatch.org	Participation in research, conservation
Field Guides	USA	800/728–4953	fieldguides.com	Bird-watching specialists
GAP Adventures	USA	416/260–0999	www.gapadventures.com	Traditional, moderately priced tours
InkaNatura Travel	Peru	511/440–2022	www.inkanatura.com	Ecotourism,birding, Inca sites
Inkaterra	Peru	800/442–5042	www.inkaterra.com	Machu Picchu, rain forest
Olas Peru Surf Travel	Peru	511/9891–39203	www.olasperusurftravel.com	Surfing Tours
Orient Express	UK & USA	800/524–2420	www.orient-express.com	Luxury travel
Overseas Adventure Travel	USA	800/493–6824	www.oattravel.com	Moderately priced, standard tours
Setours	Peru	511/446–9229	www.setours.com	Traditional tours
Solmartour	Peru	511/444–1313	www.solmar.com.pe	Unique destinations and activities

TOUR OPERATORS

Abercrombie & Kent (✉ *USA* ☎ *900/554–7016* ⊕ *www.abercrombiekent.com*). Established in 1962, this respected company offers a selection of Peru itineraries that includes such emblematic attractions as Machu Picchu and the Amazon River as well as less-visited sites such as the Colca Canyon and the pre-Inca sites of the northern coast. The company also runs tours that combine Peru with Ecuador's Galapagos Islands and trips specifically for families or women.

Adventure Life (✉ *USA* ☎ *800/344–6118* ⊕ *www.adventure-life.com*). The South and Central America specialist Adventure Life has a good mix of Peru options for active travelers, including treks on the Inca Trail and less-hiked routes such as Ausangate Glacier and the Cordillera Blanca, white-water rafting, and trips into the rain forest of Manu and Tambopata. They also offer the standard Cusco-Machu Picchu tour and a trip that combines it with the pre-Incan sites of northern Peru, or an Amazon nature cruise.

Andean Treks (✉ *Peru & USA* ☎ *800/683–8148, or 617/924–1974* ⊕ *www.andeantreks.com*). Pioneers in outfitting Inca Trail treks, Andean Treks was also one of the first companies to organize treks to less-visited areas such as Choquequirao and Ausangate. They also offer non-hiking trips to Cusco, Machu Picchu, and the Amazon Basin, as well as tours to Argentina, Bolivia, Chile, and Ecuador.

Auqui Mountain Spirit (✉ *Peru* ☎ *5184/261–517* ⊕ *www.auqui.com.pe*). This small, Peruvian company specializes in custom trips that range from trekking and mountaineering to luxury travel, with expert guides and personalized service. They also offer trips to the Amazon Basin, coastal sites, and the Galapagos Islands.

Birding in Peru (✉ *Peru* ☎ *5184/225–990* ⊕ *www.birding-in-peru.com*). Run by British birder Barry Walker, this Peruvian company runs one- to three-week trips to the country's varied ecological regions led by local and foreign guides, and runs a nature lodge in Manu. Most of their tours are for dedicated birders.

Condor Travel (✉ *Peru and USA* ☎ *877/236–7199* ⊕ *www.condortravel.com*). One of Peru's largest tour companies, Condor Travel operates many tours sold by U.S. and European companies. They offer one of the most complete selections of tours and destinations in Peru, as well as golf, trekking, bird watching, adventure, and family tours.

Earthwatch (✉ *USA & UK* ☎ *800/776–0188, or 44/1865–318–838* ⊕ *www.earthwatch.org*). A nonprofit organization that uses tourism revenues to support scientific research and conservation, Earthwatch runs expeditions in the Amazon Basin that let travelers participate in wildlife surveys in Pacaya-Samiria National Reserve, or study macaws in the Madre de Dios region.

Field Guides (✉ *USA* ☎ *800/728–4953* ⊕ *www.fieldguides.com*). The international bird-watching specialist Field Guides offers half a dozen tours to different regions of Peru led by expert birding guides, who help their clients spot as many of the country's more than 1,800 bird species as possible.

GAP Adventures (✉ *USA* ☎ *416/260–0999* ⊕ *www.gapadventures.com*). You can choose from eight competitively priced Peru adventure itineraries with GAP Adventures, most of which include a four-day Inca Trail trek, which can be combined with Lake Titicaca, Arequipa, the Nazca Lines, or an Amazon River cruise.

InkaNatura Travel (✉ *Peru* ☎ *511/440–2022* ⊕ *www.inkanatura.com*). One of the country's premier ecotourism companies, InkaNatura runs trips to its four lodges—in the cloud forest, Manu and Tambopata regions of the Amazon Basin—as well as Machu Picchu and the archaeological sites of northern Peru.

Inkaterra (✉ *Peru* ☎ *800/442–5042, 511/610–0400* ⊕ *www.inkaterra.com*). The tour division of this small Peruvian company offers various trips that combine access to the rain forest of Madre de Dios with the classic Cusco–Machu Picchu route using three of the country's best hotels.

Olas Peru Surf Travel (✉ *Peru* ☎ *511/9981–39203* ⊕ *www.olasperusurftravel.com*). This company is dedicated to one thing only: helping foreign surfers enjoy Peru's massive waves. Tours range from three days at one of the breaks south of Lima, to a week at Chicama, to longer trips to northern Peru's breaks.

Orient Express (✉ *UK & USA* ☎ *800/524–2420, 44/207–921–4010* ⊕ *www.orient-express.com*). This venerable company offers a selection of eight luxury itineraries in Peru using its own trains and hotels, which are some of the country's best. Tours range from the classic Cusco–Machu Picchu trip to visits to Lake Titicaca and Colca Canyon. They also have a tour that combines Machu Picchu with Brazil's Iguazú Falls.

Overseas Adventure Travel (✉ *USA* ☎ *800/493–6824* ⊕ *www.oattravel.com*). This popular company offers moderately priced tours with small groups and knowledgeable guides to Cusco, the Sacred Valley and Machu Picchu, Amazon River cruises, and trips that combine Machu Picchu with Ecuador's Galapagos Islands.

Setours (✉ *Peru* ☎ *511/446–9229* ⊕ *www.setours.com*). The Peruvian tour operator Setours has been in business since 1977, and in recent decades it has expanded to compile one of the most extensive offerings of Peru tours. In addition to Peru's most popular attractions, they offer trips to the archaeological sites of northern Peru, overland trips into Bolivia, and longer itineraries that combine some of South America's greatest attractions.

Solmartour (✉ *Peru* ☎ *511/444–1313* ⊕ *www.solmar.com.pe*). One of Peru's most established tour operators, Solmartour has offices in four cities and is able to set up trips to areas that few companies work in, though they also take plenty of travelers to the country's most popular attractions. They offer stays in traditional indigenous communities that would otherwise receive no benefit from tourism, plus an array of outdoor tours that include trekking, white-water rafting, horseback riding, sand-boarding, and bird-watching.

GREAT ITINERARIES

If this will be your first trip to Peru, Cusco and Machu Picchu are practically obligatory. The question is "what else?", and the answer depends on how much time you have, and what your interests are. You can combine Machu Picchu with a number of other Andean attractions, the Amazon rain forest, or pre-Inca archaeological sites on the coast. If this is not your first trip to Peru, the last itineraries in this section offer you something a little different.

ESSENTIAL PERU

The former Inca capital of Cusco and citadel of Machu Picchu are two of the most impressive places in South America and the reasons that most people visit Peru. If you only have a week, this is where you head, but it is easy and highly recommended to combine a Machu Picchu pilgrimage with a visit to the rain forest, either in the nearby Madre de Dios province or on the Amazon River proper.

Day 1: Lima

Lima has more to see than you could possibly pack into a day. You should definitely take a three-hour tour of Lima's historic Centro, or give yourself that much time to explore it on your own. In the afternoon, head to Pueblo Libre to visit the Museo Nacional de Antropología y Arqueología and the Museo Rafael Larco Herrera, or take a taxi out to the suburb of Monterrico to visit the Museo de Oro (Gold Museum). In the evening, stroll around historic Barranco and have a drink, and perhaps dinner, there or at the Huaca Pucllana, where you have the option of exploring a pre-Inca site before you eat. ⇨ *Lima, Chapter 2.*

Day 2: Cusco

From Lima, take an early-morning flight to the ancient Inca capital of Cusco. Try to get seats on the left side of the plane for an amazing view of snow-draped peaks toward the end of the flight. You'll want to take it easy upon arriving in Cusco, which is perched at almost 11,000 feet above sea level. Take a half-day tour, or visit such sights as the Cathedral, Qorikancha, the Museo de Arte Precolombino, and the Museo Hilario Mendivil on your own. Be sure to visit the Plaza de Armas at night, before dining at one of the city's many excellent restaurants. ⇨ *Cusco and the Sacred Valley, Chapter 5.*

Day 3: Sacred Valley

Dedicate this day to the sights of the surrounding highlands, starting with Sacsayhuamán, the Inca ruins outside of town. You could do a day trip to the Sacred Valley, or spend this night at one of the many hotels located there. The Valley holds an array of interesting sites, such as the market town of Pisac, Chinchero, and the massive Inca fortress at Ollantaytambo. It is also lower, and thus warmer, than Cusco, and lies on the route to Machu Picchu, which means you can catch a later train there. ⇨ *Cusco and the Sacred Valley, Chapter 5.*

Days 4 and 5: Machu Picchu

Start this day with the train trip to Machu Picchu, which winds its way past indigenous villages, snowcapped mountains, Inca ruins, and luxuriant forest to the town of Aguas Calientes. Check into your hotel, then spend the afternoon exploring Machu Picchu, the majestic citadel of the Incas. Head up the steep trail on the left shortly after entering the park and climb to the upper part of the ruins for a

panoramic view before you start exploring. Before it gets dark, stroll up to the hot springs in the valley above Aguas Calientes, which is a lovely spot even if you don't get in the water.

On Day 5, get up early to explore a bit of Machu Picchu before it gets crowded. If you're up for a tough hike up a steep, slightly treacherous trail, climb Huayna Picchu, the backdrop mountain, for vertiginous views of the ruins and surrounding jungle. Or take the longer hike through the forest to the Temple of the Moon (be sure to slather on the insect repellent first). After all the hiking, you should be ready for a leisurely three-course lunch at the Fodor's Choice Indio Feliz, in Aguas Calientes. In the afternoon or evening, take the train back to Cusco. ⇨ *Machu Picchu and the Inca Trail, Chapter 6.*

Day 6: Cusco to Lima
Take advantage of the morning to visit a site you missed on your first day in Cusco, or to visit a few of the city's countless shops and markets. Fly to Lima (one hour) early enough to have lunch at one of the city's cebicherías. Use the afternoon to visit a museum or another attraction you missed on your first day there. You may want to catch a folklore show with dinner, or sample the nightlife in Miraflores or Barranco.

MADRE DE DIOS EXTENSION

The Essential Peru tour can easily be combined with a visit to the Amazon Basin by taking a short flight from Cusco to the adjacent Madre de Dios region on Day 6.

Days 6–9: Manu or Tambopata

Take an early-morning flight from Cusco to Puerto Maldonado, where someone from your lodge will meet you and take you to your lodging by boat. Your next three days will be filled with constant exposure to tropical nature on rain-forest hikes, boat trips on oxbow lakes, and wildlife observation at *collpas* (clay licks), from towers that let you ascend into the rain-forest canopy, or from the porch of your bungalow. Some lodges also offer contact with local indigenous peoples. ⇨ *The Amazon Basin, Chapter 7.*

Day 10: Lima

Travel by boat and air back to Cusco and/or Lima. Follow Day 6 of the Essential Peru itinerary.

AMAZON RIVER EXTENSION

An alternative to the nature lodges of Madre de Dios is to visit the Amazon River proper, with a three-night river cruise and some time in the port city of Iquitos.

Day 6: Cusco

Take advantage of an additional day in Cusco to visit some of the sites you missed on your first day there and spend more time in the city's shops and markets. ⇨ *Cusco and the Sacred Valley, Chapter 5.*

Days 7–10: Iquitos and Amazon Cruise

Fly to Lima early and catch a flight to Iquitos, a historic Amazon port city in the northeast corner of the country. Board a riverboat for a three-day cruise up the Amazon River to the Pacaya Samiria Reserve, where you'll explore Amazon tributaries and oxbow lakes in smaller boats to experience the area's exceptional biodiversity. ⇨ *The Amazon Basin, Chapter 7.*

Day 11: Iquitos to Lima

Disembark in Iquitos and either spend a night there, to visit some of the nearby sites, or fly directly back to Lima. Follow Day 6 of the Essential Peru itinerary.

CLASSIC ANDEAN JOURNEY

Day 1: Lima

Follow Day 1 of the Essential Peru itinerary.

Day 2: Arequipa

From Lima, take an early-morning flight to Arequipa, a lovely colonial city with a backdrop of snowcapped volcanoes. Explore the city's historic center with its rambling Monasterio de Santa Catalina and the Museo Santuarios Andinos, home of a pre-Columbian mummy known as "Juanita." Be sure to enjoy some traditional arequipeña cooking, such as *rocoto relleno* (a hot pepper stuffed with beef), or *chupe de camarones* (river prawn chowder). ⇨ *The Southern Andes and Lake Titicaca, Chapter 4.*

Days 3: Colca Canyon

Rise early for the drive to Colca Canyon, the deepest canyon in the world and one of the best places in Peru to spot an

Andean condor. After lunch, take a hike along the canyon's edge or go horseback riding. ⇨ *The Southern Andes and Lake Titicaca, Chapter 4.*

Days 4 and 5: Puno and Lake Titicaca
Rise early and head to Cruz del Condor, the best place to spot those massive birds. Spend the rest of the day traveling overland through a series of Andean landscapes to Puno, on Lake Titicaca, the highest navigable lake in the world. Puno's 3,830-meter (12,500-feet) altitude can take your breath away, so have a light dinner and rest for the day ahead.

Rise early on Day 5 and take a boat tour of Lake Titicaca, stopping at one of the Uros Islands, man-made, floating islands that hold small communities, and Isla Taquile, a naturally-occurring island whose indigenous inhabitants are famous for their weaving skills. In the afternoon, visit the pre-Inca burial ground and stone *chullpas* at Sillustani. ⇨ *The Southern Andes and Lake Titicaca, Chapter 4.*

Days 6 and 7: Cusco
Catch the early morning train from Puno for a full-day trip across more Andean landscapes to the ancient Inca capital of Cusco, a 330-meter (1,083-foot) drop in altitude. Follow Days 2 and 3 of the Essential Peru itinerary.

Days 8 and 9: Machu Picchu
Follow Days 4 and 5 of the Essential Peru itinerary.

Day 10: Cusco to Lima
Follow Day 6 of the Essential Peru itinerary.

APURIMAC RIVER AND INCA TRAIL

Adventurous travelers in good physical condition can combine two of Peru's top outdoor tours—white-water rafting on the Apurimac River and the hike on the Inca Trail to Machu Picchu—for two weeks of adrenaline, exercise, and phenomenal scenery.

Day 1: Lima
Follow Day 1 of the Essential Peru itinerary.

Day 2: Cusco
Follow Day 2 of the Essential Peru itinerary.

Days 3–6: Apurimac River
Spend the next four days paddling down the legendary Apurimac River (Class III-IV), one of the Amazon's main tributaries and Peru's premier white-water route. The trip begins with a four-hour drive from Cusco to Naihua, where the river trip begins. You'll spend the next three days navigating rapids, admiring the surrounding rain forest, and camping near the riverbank. The last day on the river ends around noon, after which you'll have lunch and be driven to Cusco (five hours).

Day 7: Cusco
You'll probably want to relax this day, but Cusco has plenty of sights to tempt you. Or follow Day 3 of the Essential Peru itinerary.

Days 8–12: Inca Trail and Machu Picchu
Rise early this morning and catch the train to Machu Picchu, but get off at Km 82, where the four-day trek on the Inca Trail begins. You'll start by following the Urubamba River to the ruins of Llactapata, from where you climb slowly

to the first campsite, at 9,691 feet. The next day is the toughest; you'll hike over Warmiwanusca pass (13,776 feet) and camp at 11,833 feet. On Day 3 of the trek, you hike over two passes and visit several small Inca ruins. The last day is short, mostly downhill. You may have the option of rising early to reach Machu Picchu's Inti Punku (sun gate) by sunrise. Spend the morning or day exploring Machu Picchu, then bus down to Aguas Calientes for a hot shower and a sumptuous meal at El Indio Feliz.

Rise early on the morning of Day 12 to explore Machu Picchu before it gets crowded. Be sure to climb Huayna Picchu, if you didn't the day before. Catch an afternoon train to Cusco, where great restaurants and nightlife await. ⇨ *Machu Picchu and the Inca Trail, Chapter 6.*

Day 13: Cusco to Lima
Follow Day 6 of the Essential Peru itinerary.

NORTH COAST AND MACHU PICCHU

This trip lets you trace the development of Lima's indigenous cultures by combining the pre-Inca archaeological sites of Northern Peru with the classic Inca sites of Southern Peru. It also lets you explore several colonial cities and sample Peru's geographic diversity, starting in the coastal desert, moving into the Andes, and then descending to the edge of the Amazon Basin.

Day 1: Lima
Follow Day 1 of the Essential Peru itinerary.

Days 2 and 3: Chiclayo
Catch an early flight to the northern city of Chiclayo, which lies near some of the country's most important pre-Inca sites. A small, pleasant city near several excellent museums and a dilapidated beach town called Pimentel, Chiclayo is noticeably warmer and sunnier than Lima. Spend two days visiting the nearby pyramids at Túcume, the Museo Nacional Sicán, the Museo Brüning, and Museo Tumbas de Sipán. ⇨ *The North Coast and Northern highlands, Chapter 9.*

Days 4 and 5: Trujillo
Catch an early flight (40 minutes) or travel by land (3–4 hours) south to Trujillo, an attractive colonial city near the ancient structures of two other pre-Inca cultures. After checking into your hotel, explore the old city, which holds some well-preserved colonial and 19th-century architecture. In the afternoon, head to the rambling ruins of Chan Chan, with its lovely bas relief adobe walls. On Day 5, visit the archaeological sites of Huaca de La Luna and Huaca del Sol, and the beach/fishing port of Huanchaco, where fishermen still use the tiny, pre-Columbian reed boats called *caballitos de totora.* ⇨ *The North Coast and Northern Highlands, Chapter 9.*

Day 6: Lima
Take a quick flight back to Lima and visit some of the sights you didn't have time for on Day 1. Be sure to hit Barranco, a lovely area for an evening stroll, cocktail, or dinner. ⇨ *Lima, Chapter 2.*

Day 7: Cusco
Follow Day 2 of the Essential Peru itinerary.

Day 8: Sacred Valley
Follow Day 3 of the Essential Peru itinerary.

Days 9 and 10: Machu Picchu
Follow Days 4 and 5 of the Essential Peru itinerary.

Day 11: Cusco to Lima
Follow Day 6 of the Essential Peru itinerary.

SOUTHERN COAST AND CORDILLERA BLANCA

This tour combines cultural and natural wonders and takes you through an array of landscapes—from the desert to offshore islands to snowcapped mountains.

Day 1: Lima
Follow Day 1 of the Essential Peru itinerary.

Days 2 and 3: Ica
Head south on the Pan-American Highway for four hours to Ica. Try to visit the archaeological site of Tambo Colorado en route. After checking into your hotel, head for the *Huacachina* oasis for a dune buggy ride or sand-boarding, or arrange a tour of one of the nearby wineries. ⇨ *The Southern Coast, Chapter 3.*

Day 4: Nazca and Paracas
In the morning, board a small plane for a flight over the enigmatic Nazca lines. Then transfer to Paracas, on the coast. In the afternoon, take a boat tour to the Ballestas Islands, where you'll see thousands of sea lions, birds, and tiny Humboldt penguins, as well as the massive candelabra etched on a hillside. ⇨ *The Southern Coast, Chapter 3.*

Day 5: Lima
The next day, return to Lima, stopping at the pre-Inca site of Pachacamac on the way. Sightsee and shop in the afternoon, then enjoy a memorable meal at one of the city's great restaurants. ⇨ *Lima, Chapter 2.*

Days 6–10: Huaraz
Travel overland to Huaraz, in the country's central Andes, where you'll want to take it easy while you acclimatize. Visit the nearby Wari ruins of Wilcahuaían. If you're up for it, spend the next four days trekking on the Santa Cruz circuit, a gorgeous route into the heart of the Cordillera Blanca. If you aren't up for the trek, spend a couple days doing less strenuous hikes to one of the Cordilleras turquoise lakes and the ruins of Chavín de Huantar. ⇨ *The North Coast and Northern Highlands, Chapter 9.*

Day 11: Huaraz to Lima
Travel overland back to Lima. Follow Day 6 of the Essential Peru itinerary once you arrive.

NORTHERN ANDES AND CULTURES

The Northern Andes have some of Peru's most spectacular landscapes, the second most impressive Inca site after Machu Picchu (Kuelap) and the ancient city of Cajamarca. However, the precipitous terrain and bad roads dissuade some travelers from going there and the big tour companies tend to ignore the region. Peruvian tour operators, on the other hand, can help you explore this remote but fascinating region.

Day 1: Lima
Follow Day 1 of the Essential Peru itinerary.

Day 2: Chiclayo
Catch an early flight to the northern city of Chiclayo, which lies near some of the country's most important pre-Inca sites. Spend the day visiting the nearby Museo Nacional Sicán, the Museo Tumbas de Sipán, and the pyramids at Túcume.

⇨ *The North Coast and Northern Highlands, Chapter 9.*

Days 3 and 4: Chachapoyas

Rise early for a long but impressive overland journey deep into the Andes. You'll wind your way up out of the coastal desert into the mountains and through various semi-arid valleys until you reach the lush Uctubamba Valley. You'll arrive in the picturesque mountain town of Chachapoyas around dusk, as the air grows chilly. Check into your hotel and enjoy a hearty dinner.

After breakfast on Day 4, travel up the beautiful Uctubamba Valley to Karajia and "Pueblo de los Muertos" to see the funerary statues of the Chacapoya culture. Look for birds and other wildlife and enjoy the lush scenery en route. Return to Chachapoyas in the late afternoon and explore its small historic center. ⇨ *The North Coast and Northern Highlands, Chapter 9.*

Day 5: Kuelap and Leymebamba

After breakfast, drive for approximately four hours up the Uctubamba Valley to the massive Inca fortress of Kuelap. Spend several hours exploring that vast site, which contains more than 400 structures and is hemmed by lush vegetation. From Kuelap, continue up the valley to the timeless town of Leymebamba, known for its handicrafts. ⇨ *The North Coast and Northern Highlands, Chapter 9.*

Days 6–8: Cajamarca

Travel to Cajamarca via Balzas, where you can stop at a museum with a large collection of mummies and an orchid garden. From there, you'll head over two cordilleras and through the Marañon Canyon, passing some phenomenal scenery. Early in the evening, you'll arrive in the historic city of Cajamarca, where the Spanish conquistadores captured and killed Atahualpa, the last Inca. Cajamarca is perched at 2,650 meters (8,612 feet), so it is quite cool.

Start Day 7 by climbing to the top of Cerro Santa Apolonia for a panoramic view of the city. Then explore the old part of town, with its colonial churches and other structures. Be sure to visit the rambling Complejo de Belén and the Baños del Inca, where you can soak in the same mineral waters that the Inca enjoyed. On Day 8, visit the pre-Inca site of Cumbe Mayo, and hike a section of the Inca Road, such as the stretch to Combayo. ⇨ *The North Coast and Northern Highlands, Chapter 9.*

Day 9: Lima

Fly back to Lima in the morning. Once there, follow Day 6 of the Essential Peru itinerary.

VISIBLE HISTORY

by Paul Steele

About 15,000 years ago, the first people to inhabit what is now Peru filtered down from Northand Central America. They were confronted by diverse and extreme environments at varying altitudes. An ocean rich in fish contrasts with sterile coastal valleys that are only habitable where rivers cut through the desert. To the east the valleys and high plateau of the Andes mountains slope down to the Amazon rainforest, home to exotic foods, animals, and medicinal plants.

Modern Peru incorporates all of these environmental zones. Long before the centralized state of the Inca empire, people recognized the need to secure access to varied resources and products. Images of animals and plants from coast and jungle are found on pottery and stone monuments in highland Chavin culture, c. 400 BC.

Around AD 500 the Nazca Lines etched out in the desert also featured exotic jungle animals.

In the 15th century the Incas achieved unprecedented control over people, food crops, plants, and domesticated animals that incorporated coast, highlands, and the semitropical valleys. Attempts to control coca leaf production in the warmer valleys may explain Machu Picchu, which guards an important trading route.

When the Spaniards arrived in the 16th century, the search for El Dorado, the fabled city of gold, extended the Viceroyalty of Peru into the Amazon lowlands. Since independence in 1821, disputes, wars, and treaties over Amazon territory have been fueled increasingly by the knowledge of mineral oil and natural gas under the forest floor.

(far left) Moche ceramic, portrait of a priest; (above) Cerro Sechin ca. 1000 BC on Peru coast; (left) Mummified corpse skull.

BIG OLD BUILDINGS

2600–1000 BC

Peru's first monumental structures were also the earliest throughout the Americas. Coastal sites like Aspero and Caral have platform mounds, circular sunken courtyards, and large plazas that allowed public civic-ceremonial participation. At Garagay and Cerro Sechin mud and adobe relief sculptures show images connected to death, human disfigurement, and human to animal transformation. A developing art style characterized by pronounced facial features like fanged teeth and pendant-iris eyes reached its height later in Chavin culture.

■ Visit:
Kotosh (⇨ Ch. 8),
Sechín (⇨ Ch. 9).

CHAVIN CULTURE

900–200BC

Chavin de Huantar, a site not far from Huaraz, was famous for its shamans or religious leaders who predicted the future. A distinctive and complex imagery on carved stone monuments like the Lanzón and Tello Obelisk featured animals and plants from the coast, highlands, and especially the jungle. The decline of Chavin de Huantar coincided with the emergence of other oracle temples such as Pachacamac, south of modern Lima. The distinctive Chavin art style, however, continued to influence later cultures throughout Peru, including Paracas on the south coast.

■ Visit:
Chavin de Huantar (⇨ Ch. 9).

ALL WRAPPED UP IN PARACAS

600–50BC

On the Paracas Peninsula the remains of an ancient burial practice are strewn across the desert. Corpses were wrapped in layers of textiles, placed in baskets, and buried in the sand. Many elaborately woven and embroidered garments that could be tens of meters long were only used to bury the dead and never worn in life. The mummy bundles of high status individuals were often accompanied by offerings of gold objects, exotic shells, and animal skins and feathers.

■ Visit:
Pachacamac (⇨ Ch. 3).

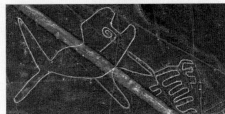

(above) Chavin de Huantar;
(top right) Huaca de la
Luna deity; (bottom right)
Nazca ground picture
of whale.

THE NASCANS

50BC–AD700

On Peru's south coast followed the Nasca, who are famous for the geoglyph desert markings known as the Nazca Lines. Thousands of long straight lines were constructed over many centuries, while around fifty animal outlines date to a more concise period of AD 400–600. An extensive system of underground aqueducts channeled water from distant mountains. In such a barren environment the Nazca Lines were probably linked closely to a cult primarily devoted to the mountain water source.

■ Visit:
Cahuachi (➪ Ch. 3),
Nazca Lines (➪ Ch. 3).

MOCHE KINGDOM

AD100 – 800

On Peru's north coast the Moche or Mochica controlled a number of coastal river valleys. Large scale irrigation projects extended cultivable land. The Temples of the Sun and Moon close to the modern city of Trujillo were constructed from millions of adobe or mud bricks and were some of the largest buildings anywhere in the ancient Americas. The high quality of Moche burial goods for individuals like the Lord of Sipan indicated a wide social gulf not previously seen in Peru. Full-time artisans produced metalwork and ceramics for Moche lords. The pottery in particular is famous for the realistic portrayal of individuals and for the naturalistic scenes of combat, capture, and sacrifice that could have been narrative stories from Moche mythology and history. Some themes like the sacrificing of war captives in the presence of the Lord of Sipan and the Owl Priest were probably reenacted in real life. A number of severe droughts and devastating el niños rains precipitated the decline of the Moche.

■ Visit:
Pañamarca (➪ Ch. 9),
Huaca de la Luna (➪ Ch. 9),
Huaca del Sol (➪ Ch. 9).

Wari Empire begins

Chachapoyas kingdom begins

EXTENSIVE ROAD NETWORK CREATED

550   750   950

(above) Wari face neck jar; (top right) Chan Chan, (bottom right) Kuelap.

WELCOME TO THE WARI EMPIRE

550–950

A new dominant highland group, the Wari, or Huari, originated close to the modern city of Ayacucho. Wari administrative centers, storage facilities, and an extensive road network were forerunners to the organizational systems of the Inca empire. The Wari were influenced by the iconographic tradition of a rival site, Tiahuanaco, in what is now Bolivia, which exerted control over the extreme south of Peru. After Wari control collapsed, regional kingdoms and localized warfare continued until the expansion of the Inca empire.

■ Visit:
Pikillacta (⇨ Ch. 5),
Santuario Histórico Pampas de Ayacucho (⇨ Ch. 8).

CHIMU KINGDOM

900–1470

On the north coast the Chimu or Chimor succeeded the Moche controlling the coastal river valleys as far south as Lima. The capital Chan Chan was a bustling urban sprawl that surrounded at least 13 high-walled citadels of the Chimu lords. The city was built close to the ocean shore and continual coastal uplift meant that access to fresh water from deep wells was a constant problem. An extensive canal network to channel water from rivers never worked properly.

■ Visit:
Chan Chan (⇨ Ch. 9),
Huaca Esmeralda (⇨ Ch. 9).

THE FIGHTIN' CHACHAPOYAS

800–1480

In the cloud forests of the eastern Andean slopes the Chachapoyas kingdom put up fierce resistance against the Incas. The Chachapoyas are famous for their mummified dead placed in cliff-top niches and for high quality circular stone buildings at sites like Kuelap, one of the largest citadels in the world. Kuelap may have been designed as a fortification against the Wari. Later the Incas imposed harsh penalties on the Chachapoyas who subsequently sided with the Spaniards.

■ Visit:
Kuelap (Cuelap) (⇨ Ch. 9).

| | Coastal cultures Ica and Chincha flourish | | Arrival of the Spanish Height of Inca empire | |
| 1150 | | 1350 | | 1550 |

1

IN FOCUS VISIBLE HISTORY

(left) Mama Occlo, wife and sister of Manco Capac, founder of the Inca dynasty, carrying the Moon; (above) Machu Picchu.

C. 1400 INCA ORIGINS

The Inca empire spanned a relatively short period in Peruvian history. The mythical origins of the first Inca Manco Capac, who emerged from a cave, is typical of Peruvian ancestor tradition. Spanish chroniclers recorded at least 10 subsequent Inca rulers although in reality the earlier kings were probably not real people. The famous Inca, Pachacuti, is credited with expansion from the capital Cusco. Inca iconographic tradition that followed geometric and abstract designs left no representational images of its rulers.

■ Visit:
Isla del Sol (⇨ Ch. 4).

1450–1527 INCA EMPIRE

Within three generations the Incas had expanded far beyond the boundaries of modern Peru to central Chile in the south and past the equator to the north. The Amazon basin was an environment they did not successfully penetrate. Although the Incas fought battles, it was a two-way process of negotiation with *curacas*, the local chiefs that brought many ethnic groups under control. The empire was divided into four *suyu* or parts, centered on Cusco. At a lower level communities were organized into decimal units ranging from 10 households up to a province of 40,000 households. Individual work for the state was known as *mit'a*. Communities forcibly resettled to foreign lands were called *mitimaes*. The Incas kept a regular population census and record of all the sacred idols and shrines. The Incas spread the language Quechua that is still spoken throughout most of Peru and in neighboring countries.

■ Visit:
Ollantaytambo(⇨ Ch. 5),
Machu Picchu (⇨ Ch. 6),
Ruins at Pisac (⇨ Ch. 5).

EXTENSIVE DEPOPULATION THROUGHOUT PERU

| 1600 | 1650 | 1700 |

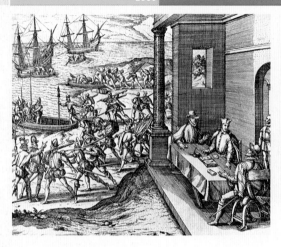

(above) The execution of Tupa Amaru; (left) Francisco Pizarro, Diego de Almagro, and Fernando de Luque planning the conquest of Peru.

ARRIVAL OF THE CONQUISTADORS

1527–1542

The Spanish conquistadors arrived on the coast of Ecuador and northern Peru bringing European diseases like smallpox that ravaged the indigenous population and killed the Inca king. They also introduced the name Peru. In 1532 a small band of conquistadors led by Francisco Pizarro first encountered the Inca ruler Atahualpa in Cajamarca. This famous confrontation of Old and New World cultures culminated with the capture of Atahualpa, who was later strangled. The Spaniards arrived in Cusco in 1533 and immediately took the city residences and country estates of the Inca elite for themselves. The resistance of Manco Inca could not drive the Spaniards out of Cusco, and by the end of the 1530's the Inca loyal supporters had retreated to Ollantaytambo, and then to the forested region of Vilcabamba that became the focus of Inca resistance for the next 30 years. In 1542 the Viceroyalty of Peru was created and a new capital city, Lima, became the political and economic center of Spain's possessions in South America.

■ Visit:
Cajamarca (⇨Ch.9),
Sacsayhuemán (⇨Ch.5).

END OF THE INCAS

1542–1572

A relatively small number of Spaniards overthrew the Incas because of support from many groups disaffected under Inca rule. Native Peruvians quickly realized, however, that these new lighter-skinned people were intent on dismantling their whole way of life. The 1560's nativist movement Taqui Onqoy, meaning dancing sickness, called on native gods to expel the Spaniards and their religion. In 1572 the Inca Tupa Amaru, mistakenly called Tupac Amaru, was captured and executed in public in Cusco.

■ Visit:
Cusco (⇨Ch.5).

(above) Battle of Ayacucho, Bolivar's forces establish Peruvian independence from Spain 1824; (left) Simon Bolivar, aka "The Liberator."

1

IN FOCUS VISIBLE HISTORY

SPANISH COLONIAL RULE

1572–1770

The Spanish crown increasingly sought more direct control over its American empire. A new viceroy, Toledo, stepped up the policy of *reducciones* in which formerly dispersed native communities were resettled into more easily controlled towns. This made it easier to baptize the native population into the Catholic church. The indigenous population was forced to work in mines such as Potosí, which became the biggest urban center in the Americas. Huge quantities of gold and silver were shipped to the Caribbean and then to Europe, and helped fund Spain's wars in Europe. Spanish hacienda estates introduced new food crops such as wheat, and new livestock like pigs and cows. The scale of native depopulation—more acute on the coast—is today reflected by the number of abandoned hillside terraces. The Inca elite and local chiefs started to adopt European dress; some found ways to prosper under new colonial regulations (like avoiding Spanish taxes if demonstrating Inca ancestry).

■ Visit:
Colonial architecture of Arequipa (⇨ Ch. 4), Ayacucho (⇨ Ch. 8), Cusco (⇨ Ch. 5), Lima (⇨ Ch. 2), Trujillo (⇨ Ch. 9).

END OF COLONIAL RULE

1770–1824

The execution of the last Inca ruler in 1572 did not stop continued rebellions against Spanish colonial rule. In the eighteenth century an uprising led by the local chief José Gabriel Condorcanqui, who called himself Tupa Amaru II, foreshadowed the wars of independence that ended colonial rule in Peru and elsewhere in the Americas. Peru declared its independence in 1821 and again in 1824, when Símon Bólivar arrived from Colombia to defeat the remaining royalist forces at the battle of Ayacucho.

■ Visit:
Pampas de Quinua (⇨ Ch. 8).

TIMELINE
| Slavery abolished
Quechua language officially recognized |
⌐POPULATION MIGRATION TO BIG|CITIES⌐
Earthquake devastates
South Peru

| 1900 | 1950 | 2000 | PRESENT |

(above) Former Peruvian President Alberto Fujimori; (right) Lima, Peru.

REPUBLICAN ERA

1824–1900

Despite an initial 20 years of chaos, when every year seemed to bring a new regime, the young republic was attractive to foreign business interests. Particularly lucrative for Peru were the export of cotton and guano—nitrate-rich bird droppings used for fertilizer. Peru benefited from foreign investment such as railroad building, but an increasing national foreign debt was unsustainable without significant industrial development. Disputes with neighboring countries, especially the War of the Pacific against Chile in which Lima was sacked, land to the south ceded, and the country bankrupted, deeply affected the nation.

20TH-CENTURY PERU

1900–2000

For much of the nineteenth century Peru was led by presidents with military backgrounds, and military coups were interspersed with periods of civilian governments. The largest popular political movement, Alianza Popular Revolucionaria Americana, was founded by Victor Raul Haya de la Torre in the 1920s. Democratically elected presidents were rare. Old institutions like the haciendas declined and many are now abandoned ruins. In contrast, Lima's population increased rapidly with the growth of shanty towns called pueblos jóvenes.

RECENTLY . . .

1980–PRESENT

In the 1980s, the Shining Path guerrilla movement characterised a violent time in which thousands were killed. The capture of its leader, Abimael Guzmán, in 1992 has made Peru more attractive to tourism. In 1990 Peru elected as president Alberto Fujimori, who suspended the constitution to force economic reforms, and who now faces corruption and murder charges. He was succeeded by Peru's first president of largely native descent, Alejandro Toledo (2001-06). Alan Garcia, who led the country to economic disaster in the 1980s, won the election in 2006, casting himself as personally reformed and politically reformist. In May 2011, Peruvians will elect a new president who will serve until 2016.

Lima

WORD OF MOUTH

"Central Lima is interesting. Have your taxi driver drop you off at Plaza San Martin, and walk a few blocks up to Plaza Mayor/ Armas. Try to see the changing of the guard at the Presidential Palace. See the cathedral. And definitely take the tour of San Francisco, which is a few blocks away."

—robertino

WELCOME TO LIMA

TOP REASONS TO GO

★ **Neptune's Bounty:** You'll quickly encounter *cebiche*—slices of raw fish or shellfish marinated in lemon juice with onions and hot peppers. Also try the *corvina* (sea bass) and *lenguado* (sole).

★ **Lima Baroque:** In El Centro, Iglesia de San Francisco's facade is considered the height of the "Lima Baroque" style of architecture. The crypt below stores the bones of dearly departed monks.

★ **Cool Digs:** More than 30 archaeological digs are around Lima, such as the pre-Inca temple Pucllana in Miraflores and the Huaca Huallamarca temple in San Isidro.

★ **Handicrafts:** Calle Alcanflores, which runs through Miraflores, has stores selling everything from hand-carved wooden masks to silver-filigree jewelry.

★ **Park Life:** On weekends families and couples fill Lima's parks, especially the ones that line Miraflores' ocean-view *malecones,* such as the incomparable Parque del Amor.

1 El Centro. The Plaza Mayor (the city's main square) and nearby Plaza San Martin are two of the most spectacular public spaces in South America. Nearly every block has something to catch your eye, whether it's the elaborate facade of a church, or the enclosed wooden balconies on centuries-old houses, but unfortunately, much of the neighborhood is dilapidated.

2 San Isidro. The city's nicest residential neighborhood surround's Parque El Olivar, a grove of olive trees, where half-timbered homes are set among the gnarled trunks. Nearby is the city's oldest golf course and an array of banks and businesses, but the main attraction for travelers is its selection of restaurants and hotels.

3 Miraflores. A mix of modern and early 20th-century, Miraflores has the city's best selection of hotels, restaurants, bars, and boutiques, which are a draw for locals, so the neighborhood is always full of people. Visit Parque del Amor and the string of other parks along the malecon, which runs along the coastal cliffs—the view is unforgettable.

4 Barranco. The city's most bohemian, but also most charming, neighborhood,

Barranco combines historic architecture with ocean views. Low-key seafood eateries line the Bajada Los Baños, a cobblestone path leading down to the beach. In the evening, it fills with young people in search of a good time.

5 Pueblo Libre. This neighborhood feels like a village, which is exactly what Pueblo Libre was until the city's borders pushed outward. The city's best museum, the Museo Arqueológico Rafael Larco Herrera, is here.

2

GETTING ORIENTED

Most of Lima's colonial-era churches and mansions are in **El Centro**, along the streets surrounding the Plaza de Armas. From there, a speedy express-way called Paseo de la República (aka Via Espress) or a traffic-clogged thor-oughfare called Avenida Arequipa take you south to **San Isidro** and **Miraflores**, two fairly upscale neighbor-hoods where you'll find the bulk of the city's dining and lodging options. East of Miraflores is **Barranco**, where colonial architec-ture is complemented by a bohemian ambience.

Banco de Credito, Lima.

Updated by David Dudenhoefer

When people discuss great South American cities, Lima is often overlooked. But Peru's capital can hold its own against its neighbors. It has an oceanfront setting, colonial-era splendor, sophisticated dining, and nonstop nightlife.

It's true that the city—clogged with traffic and choked with fumes—doesn't make a good first impression, especially since the airport is in a poor, industrial neighborhood. But wander around the regal edifices surrounding the Plaza de Armas, among the gnarled olive trees of San Isidro's Parque El Olivar, or along the winding lanes in the coastal community of Barranco, and you'll find yourself charmed.

In 1535 Francisco Pizarro found the perfect place for the capital of Spain's colonial empire. On a natural port, the so-called Ciudad de los Reyes (City of Kings) allowed Spain to ship home all the gold the conquistador plundered from the Inca. Lima served as the capital of Spain's South American empire for 300 years, and it's safe to say that no other colonial city enjoyed such power and prestige during this period.

When Peru declared its independence from Spain in 1821, the declaration was read in the square that Pizarro had so carefully designed. Many of the colonial-era buildings around the Plaza de Armas are standing today. Walk a few blocks in any direction for churches and elegant houses that reveal just how wealthy this city once was. But the poor state of most buildings attests to the fact that the country's wealthy families have moved to neighborhoods to the south over the past century.

The walls that surrounded the city were demolished in 1870, making way for unprecedented growth. A former hacienda became the graceful residential neighborhood of San Isidro. In the early 1920s, the construction of tree-lined Avenida Arequipa, heralded the development of neighborhoods like bustling Miraflores and bohemian Barranco.

Almost a third of the country's population of 29 million lives in the metropolitan area, many of them in relatively poor *conos:* newer neighborhoods on the outskirts of the city. Most residents of those neighborhoods moved there from mountain villages during the political violence and poverty that marked the 1980s and '90s, when crime increased dramatically. During the past decade, the country has enjoyed peace, steady economic growth, and decreasing crime, which have been accompanied by many improvements and refurbishment in the city. Residents who used to steer clear of the historic center now stroll along its streets. And many travelers who once would have avoided the city altogether now plan to spend a day here and end up staying two or three.

PLANNING

WHEN TO GO

The weather in Lima is a relative opposite of North America's. Summer, from December to April, is largely sunny with temperatures regularly rising above 80°F, whereas the nights and mornings are cool. From May to November, it is mostly cloudy and cool, sometimes dipping below 60°F, though there are occasional sunny days. The coastal region gets little precipitation, so you'll rarely find your plans ruined by rain, but there are winter days that start with a miserable foggy drizzle.

GETTING HERE AND AROUND

AIR TRAVEL

If you're flying to Peru, you'll touch down at Aeropuerto Internacional Jorge Chávez, in the northern neighborhood of El Callao. Once you're in the main terminal, hundreds of people will be waiting. Do yourself a favor and arrange through your hotel for a transfer. Otherwise, hire a cab from one of the companies that have desks in the corridor outside of customs, such as **CMV** (☎ 01/517–1891) or **Green Taxis** (☎ 01/484–4001).

Various airlines handle domestic flights, so getting to and from the major tourist destinations is no problem. LAN is the carrier with the most national flights, with a dozen flights per day to Cusco and several daily departures to Arequipa, Chiclayo, Iquitos, Juliaca (Puno), Puerto Maldonado, and Trujillo. It is the most convenient airline, but also the most expensive. Peruvian Airlines offers the best deals, with daily flights to Arequipa, Cusco, Iquitos, and Tacna, on the border with Chile. Star Peru is relatively inexpensive and flies to Ayacucho, Chiclayo, Cusco, Huanuco, Iquitos, Juliaca, Puerto Maldonado, and Trujillo. Taca Peru has two flights per day to Cusco.

Airport Information Aeropuerto Internacional Jorge Chávez (✉ Av. Faucett s/n, El Callao ☎ 01/517–3100 ⊕ www.lap.com.pe/lap_portal/ingles).

Carriers LAN (☎ 01/213–8200 ⊕ www.lan.com). **Peruvian Airlines** (☎ 01/716–6000 ⊕ www.peruvianairlines.pe). **Star Peru** ☎ 01/705–9000 ⊕ www.starperu.com. **Taca** (☎ 01/511–8222 ⊕ www.taca.com).

BUS TRAVEL

Two types of buses—regular-size *micros* and the van-size *combis*—patrol the streets of Lima. Fares are cheap, usually S/1–2 for a ride, but the drivers are madmen and they resemble rolling sardine cans during rush hours, when there is a danger of pickpockets and bag slashers. A quicker and safer way to travel between Barranco, Miraflores, and El Centro is El Metropolitano, a modern bus that runs down the middle of the Paseo de la Republica to the underground Estación Central, in front of the Sheraton Lima Hotel. El Metropolitano runs from 6 AM to 9 PM and each trip costs S/1.50. The system uses rechargeable electronic cards that you can buy from a vending machine, or a person wearing a red vest at any station for S/5. Stations on Avenida Bolgnesia in Barranco and Avenida Benavides in Miraflores are walking distance from hotels, but the route is rather far from most San Isidro lodging.

Contacts **Metropolitano** (☎ *01/203–9000* ⊕ *www.metropolitano.com.pe*).

CAR TRAVEL

Lima is a difficult and confusing city to drive in, but most rental agencies also offer the services of a driver. In addition to offices downtown, Budget and Hertz have branches at Jorge Chávez International Airport that are open 24 hours.

Contacts **Budget** (☎ *01/444–4546*). **Hertz** (☎ *01/445–5716*). **National** (☎ *01/578–7878*).

TAXI TRAVEL

Taxis are the best way to get around Lima. Use only taxis painted with a company's logo and that have the driver's license prominently displayed. You need to negotiate the fare before you get in. A journey between two adjacent neighborhoods should cost between S/5 and S/8; longer trips should be about S/10 to S/15. If you hire one of the taxis parked in front of the tourist hotels, the price will be roughly double. Well-regarded companies include **Taxi Lima** (☎ *01/213–5030*), **Taxi Móvil** (☎ *01/422–6890*) and **Taxi Seguro** (☎ *01/241–9292*). If you're going to spend the day sightseeing, consider hiring a taxi for the day, which should cost about S/15 per hour.

HEALTH AND SAFETY

Drink only bottled water and order drinks *sin hielo* (without ice). Avoid lettuce and other raw vegetables. As for cebiche and *tiradito* (thinly-sliced, marinated fish), both made with raw seafood, the citric acid in the lime-juice marinade is as efficient at killing bacteria as cooking, but because they are often prepared to order, let yours stew in the lime juice for a bit before eating to ensure that you don't suffer after enjoying those delicacies.

El Centro is safe during the day, but the neighborhood grows dicey at night, when you should stick to the two main plazas and Jiron de la Union (the pedestrian mall that connects them). Residential neighborhoods like Miraflores, San Isidro, and Barranco have far less street crime, but you should be on your guard away from the main streets. Always be alert for pickpockets in crowded markets and on public transportation.

In case of trouble, contact the Tourist Police. The department is divided into the **northern zone** (☎ *01/423–3500*), which includes El Centro, and the **southern zone** (☎ *01/243–2190*), which includes Barranco, Miraflores, and San Isidro. English-speaking officers will help you negotiate the system. For emergencies, call the **police** (☎ *105*) and **fire** (☎ *116*) emergency numbers.

2

EMERGENCIES

Several clinics have English-speaking staff, including the Clinica Anglo-Americana and Clinica El Golf. Both are in San Isidro. There is a pharmacy on every other (or every third) block on Lima main streets.

Hospitals **Clinica Anglo-Americana** (⌧ *Av. Alfredo Salazar 350, San Isidro* ☎ *01/616–8900*). **Clinica El Golf** (⌧ *Av. Aurelio Miro Quesada 1030, San Isidro* ☎ *01/319–1500*).

Pharmacies **Farmacia Fasa** (⌧ *Los Eucaliptos 578, San Isidro* ☎ *01/619–0000* ⌧ *Av. Larco 129, Miraflores* ☎ *01/619–0000*). **InkaFarma** (⌧ *Av. Benavides 425, Miraflores* ☎ *01/314–2020*).

TOURS

Lima has many tour operators with experienced English-speaking guides for local and countrywide sightseeing. The most frequently recommended operator is Lima Vision, which offers various city tours. Lima Tours offers tours of the city and surrounding area and is one of the few companies that conducts tours for gay groups. The people at Caral Tours are the experts on Peru's oldest archaeological site, but they also offer trips to other areas. Condor Travel offers various city tours, including a gastronomic tour. Solmartour has an array of Lima tours and day trips to nearby sites. Ecocruceros offers half-day boat tours to the Islas Palomino—home to 4,000 sea lions—but it's a chilly trip from May to December. Turibus and Mirabus offer some of Lima's most affordable city tours in roofless, double-decker buses. Turibus departs from the Larco Mar and Mirabus departs from Parque Kennedy, both in Miraflores. Energetic travelers can pedal their way past Lima's sights on a guided tour with Bike Peru. Lima Gastronomic Tours can help you sample and understand the city's culinary cornucopia.

Operators **Bike Peru** (☎ *01/447–8888* ⊕ *www.thebikeperu.com*). **Caral Tours** (☎ *01/254–1748* ⊕ *www.caraltours.net*). **Condor Travel** (☎ *01/615–3000* ⊕ *www.condortravel.com*). **Ecocruceros** (☎ *01/226–8530* ⊕ *www.islaspalomino.com*). **Lima Gastronomic Tours** (☎ *01/447–7710* ⊕ *www.limagt.com*). **Lima Tours** (☎ *01/619–6900* ⊕ *www.limatours.com.pe*). **Lima Vision** (☎ *01/447–7710* ⊕ *www.limavision.com*). **Mirabus** (☎ *01/242–6699* ⊕ *www.mirabusperu.com*). **Solmartour** (☎ *01/444–1313* ⊕ *www.solmar.com.pe*). **TuriBus** (☎ *01/446–7575* ⊕ *www.turibusperu.com*).

VISITOR INFORMATION

Travelers can find information about the city and beyond at iPerú, which has English- and Spanish-language materials. The city runs the Oficina de Información Touristica, or Tourist Information Office, in the rear of the Municipalidad de Lima. It's a good place to pick up maps of the city, but the staff is not always that helpful.

Information **iPerú** (⌧ *Jorge Basadre 610, San Isidro* ☎ *01/421–1627* ⌧ *Malecón de la Reserva and Av. José Larco, Miraflores* ☎ *01/445–9400* ⊕ *www.peru.info*). **Oficina de Información Touristica** (⌧ *Pasaje de los Escribianos 145, El Centro* ☎ *01/315–1542*).

HISTORICAL WALK

Almost all Lima's most interesting historical sites are within walking distance of the **Plaza de Armas**. The fountain in the center can be used as a slightly off-center compass. The bronze angel's trumpet points due north, where you'll see the **Palacio de Gobierno**. To the west is the neocolonial **Municipalidad de Lima**, and to the east are the **Catedral** and the adjoining **Palacio Episcopal**. The cathedral, one of the most striking in South America, should be given a look inside. Head north on Jirón Carabaya, the street running beside the Palacio de Gobierno, until you reach the butter-yellow **Estación de Desamparados** (aka **Casa de la Literatura Peruana**), the former train station. Follow the street as it curves to the east. In a block you'll reach the **Iglesia de San Francisco**, the most spectacular of the city's colonial-era churches. Explore the eerie catacombs.

EXPLORING LIMA

Once a compact city surrounded by small towns, Lima is now a vast metropolitan area that is home to nearly nine million people. Most of it has little to offer travelers and some areas are dangerous, so you'll want to limit your exploration to the *distritos*, or neighborhoods, listed in this chapter. Most of the city's best hotels and restaurants are located in three adjacent neighborhoods—Barranco, Miraflores and San Isidro—to the south of the historic center, El Centro, but the bulk of its attractions are clustered in El Centro and nearby Pueblo Libre. You'll consequently need to take taxis between neighborhoods, though an express bus called the Metropolitano provides a quick connection between El Centro and the neighborhoods of Miraflores and Barranco. The airport is in a separate city called El Callao, about half an hour to the west of El Centro and an hour from most hotels. Trips between Barranco and Miraflores, or San Isidro should take 10 to 20 minutes, whereas the travel times between any of them and El Centro are 20 to 30 minutes. During the rush hours (7:30 to 9 AM and 5:30 to 7 PM), however, travel times double.

EL CENTRO

In the colonial era, Lima was the seat of power for the viceroyalty of Peru. It held sway over a swath of land that extended from Panama to Chile. With power came money, as is evident by the grand scale on which everything was built. The finely carved doorways of some mansions stand two stories high. At least half a dozen churches would be called cathedrals in any other city. And the Plaza de Armas, the sprawling main square, is spectacular.

But history has not always been kind to the neighborhood known as El Centro. Earthquakes struck in 1687 and 1746, leveling many of the buildings surrounding the Plaza de Armas. Landmarks, such as the

2

Iglesia de San Augustín, were nearly destroyed by artillery fire in skirmishes that have plagued the capital. But more buildings are simply the victims of neglect. It's heartbreaking to see the wall on a colonial-era building buckling, or an intricately carved balcony beyond repair. But the city government has made an effort to restore its historic center. After years of decline, things are steadily improving.

An unhurried visit to the historic district's main attractions takes a full day, with at least an hour devoted to each the Museo de Arte Nacional and the Museo de la Inquisición, though you can see a good bit of it all in half a day if you're rushed. ■TIP→ Even if you're short on time, don't bypass the guided tour of the underground catacombs of the Iglesia de San Francisco, and don't miss Plaza San Martin.

GETTING AROUND

Chances are you're staying in Miraflores or San Isidro, which are a quick taxi ride from El Centro. Since taxis usually take the expressway, you're downtown in 20 minutes. A slower but more interesting route is to have your driver take Avenida Arequipa and do a loop on Paseo Colón for a look at some lovely architecture. The journey takes a half hour, longer during rush hour. Once you're in El Centro, the best way to get around is by foot, since the historic area is rather compact.

TOP ATTRACTIONS

⑫ **Casa Riva-Agüero.** A pair of balconies with *celosías*—intricate wood screens through which ladies could watch passersby unobserved—grace the facade of this rambling mansion from 1760. A mildly interesting museum of folk art is on the second floor, but the real reason to come is for a glimpse into a colonial-era home. ⊠ *Jr. Camaná 459, El Centro* ☎ *01/626–6600* ⬜ *S/15* ⊗ *Mon.–Fri. 10–7, Sat. 11–5.*

⑧ **Catedral.** The first church on the site was completed in 1625. The layout for this immense structure was dictated by Francisco Pizarro, and his basic vision has survived complete rebuilding after earthquakes in 1746 and 1940. Inside are impressive baroque appointments, especially the intricately carved choir stalls. Because of changing tastes, the main altar was replaced around 1800 with one in a neoclassical style. At about the same time the towers that flank the entrance were added. Admission includes a 40-minute tour. Visit the chapel where Pizarro is entombed and the small museum of religious art and artifacts. ⊠ *East side of Plaza de Armas, El Centro* ☎ *01/427–9647* ⬜ *S/10* ⊗ *Mon.–Fri. 9–5, Sat. 10–1.*

④ **Correo Central.** Inaugurated in 1924 this regal structure looks more like a palace than a post office. You can buy a postcard or send a package, but most people come to admire the exuberance of an era when no one thought twice about placing bronze angels atop a civic building. At one time locals deposited letters in the mouth of the bronze lion by the front doors. The Museo Postal y Filatélico, a tiny museum of stamps, is next to the entrance on Jr. Camana. ⊠ *Jr. de la Unión 236, El Centro* ☎ *01/427–9370* ⬜ *Free* ⊗ *Mon.–Sat. 8–8, Sun. 9–1; Museum Mon.–Fri. 10–5.*

⑬ **Iglesia de la Merced.** Nothing about this colonial-era church could be called restrained. Take the unusual baroque facade. Instead of stately

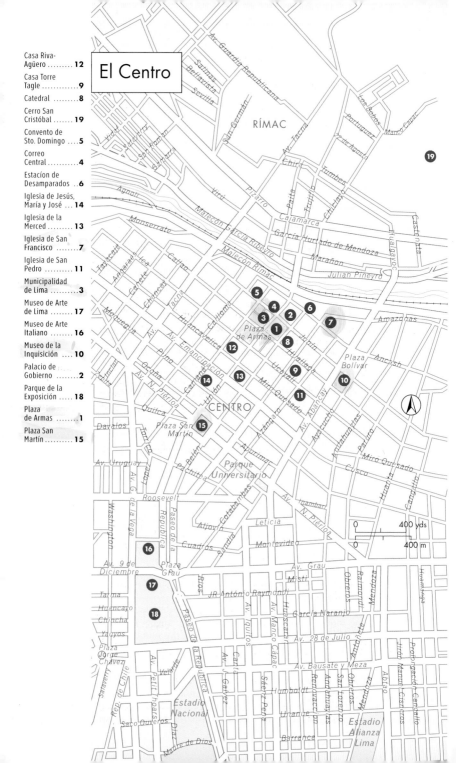

El Centro

Casa Riva-
Agüero **12**

Casa Torre
Tagle **9**

Catedral **8**

Cerro San
Cristóbal **19**

Convento de
Sto. Domingo **5**

Correo
Central **4**

Estación de
Desamparados .. **6**

Iglesia de Jesús,
María y José ... **14**

Iglesia de la
Merced **13**

Iglesia de San
Francisco **7**

Iglesia de San
Pedro **11**

Municipalidad
de Lima **3**

Museo de Arte
de Lima **17**

Museo de Arte
Italiano **16**

Museo de la
Inquisición **10**

Palacio de
Gobierno **2**

Parque de la
Exposición **18**

Plaza
de Armas **1**

Plaza San
Martín **15**

columns, the powers-that-be decided they should be wrapped with carefully carved grapevines. Inside are a series of retablos that gradually change from baroque to neoclassical styles. The intricately carved choir stalls, dating from the 18th century, have images of cherubic singers. The first house of worship to be built in Lima, Our Lady of Mercy was commissioned

> **STREET SMARTS**

Although El Centro is safe for daytime strolls, at night you'll want to take a taxi to your destination. If you find yourself on the street with few other people around in the late afternoon, it's probably time to hail a cab.

by Hernando Pizarro, brother of the city's founder. He chose the site because it was here that services were first held in the city. ⊠ *Jr. de la Unión at Jr. Miro Quesada, El Centro* ☎ *01/427–8199* ⊠ *Free* ⊗ *Tues.– Fri. 10:30–1 and 3–8, Sat. 8–1 and 2–5, Sun. 7–1 and 4–8.*

⑦ Iglesia de San Francisco. Bones—including thousands and thousands of human skulls—are piled in eerie geometric patterns in the crypt of this church. This was the city's first cemetery, and the underground tunnels contain the earthly remains of some 75,000 people, which you visit on a tour (available in English). The Church of Saint Francis is the most visited in Lima, mostly because of these catacombs. But it's also the best example of what is known as "Lima Baroque" style of architecture. The handsome carved portal would later influence those on other churches, including the Iglesia de la Merced. The central nave is known for its beautiful ceilings painted in a style called *mudejar* (a blend of Moorish and Spanish designs). On the tour you'll see the adjoining monastery's immense collection of antique texts, some dating back to the 17th century. ⊠ *Jr. Ancash 471, El Centro* ☎ *01/427–1381* ⊠ *S/5* ⊗ *Daily 9:30–5:45.*

Fodor's Choice ★

⑪ Iglesia de San Pedro. The Jesuits built three churches in rapid succession on this corner, the current one dating from 1638. It remains one of the finest examples of early-colonial religious architecture in Peru. The facade is remarkably restrained, but the interior shows all the extravagance of the era, including a series of baroque retablos thought to be the best in the city. Many have works by Italians like Bernardo Bitti, who arrived on these shores in 1575. His style influenced an entire generation of painters. In the sacristy is *The Coronation of the Virgin*, one of his most famous works. ■TIP→ Don't miss the side aisle, where gilded arches lead to chapels decorated with beautiful hand-painted tiles. ⊠ *Jr. Ucayali at Jr. Azángaro, El Centro* ☎ *01/428–3010* ⊠ *Free* ⊗ *Mon.–Sat. 7–12:30 and 5–8, Sun. 7–2 and 5–8.*

⑰ Museo de Arte de Lima. The Museum of Art is a gorgeous building that is lovingly cared for. Built in 1872 as the Palacio de la Expedición, this mammoth neoclassical structure was designed by Gustav Eiffel (who later built the famous Parisian tower). The ground floor holds temporary exhibitions, usually by international artists, whereas the second floor houses a permanent exhibition that contains a bit of everything, from pre-Columbian artifacts to colonial-era furniture. One of the highlights is the collection of 2,000-year-old weavings from Paracas. ■TIP→ Leave time to sip an espresso in the café near the entrance. ⊠ *Paseo*

Colón 125, El Centro ☎ *01/423–6332* ⊕ *museoarte.perucultural. org.pe* ☜ *S/12* ⏰ *Tues.–Fri. 10–8, Sat. and Sun. 10–5.*

🔟 **Museo de la Inquisición.** Visit the original dungeons and torture chambers of the Spanish Inquisition, where stomach-churning, life-size exhibits illustrate methods of extracting "information" from prisoners. This massive mansion later served as the temporary home of Congress, which found a permanent home in the neoclassical structure across the street. The guided tour, offered several times a day in English, lets you explore the beautiful building, especially the coffered ceilings dating from the 18th century. ⊠ *Jr. Junín 548, El Centro* ☎ *01/311–7777 Ext. 5160* ⊕ *www.congreso.gob.pe/museo.htm* ☜ *Free* ⏰ *Daily 9–5.*

CRAZY ABOUT FÚTBOL

Soccer—or *fútbol*—reigns supreme in Peru. When a highly contested match is televised, don't be surprised to see dozens of people in the street outside a bar or restaurant that happens to have a television. This is how most Peruvians watch matches, and it's the best way for newcomers to join in. Matches are usually played on weekends or weeknights, and the bars with the biggest TVs tend to get the best crowds. Grab a seat, pick a team, and join the fun.

❷ **Palacio de Gobierno.** The best time to visit the Governmental Palace is weekdays at noon, when you can watch soldiers in red-and-blue uniforms conduct an elaborate changing of the guard. (It's not Buckingham Palace, but it's impressive.) Built on the site where Francisco Pizarro was murdered in 1541, the Palacio de Gobierno was completed in 1938. The neobaroque palace is the official residence of the president. Tours were suspended years ago for security reasons. ⊠ *North side of Plaza de Armas, El Centro* ☎ *01/311–3908.*

❶ **Plaza de Armas.** This massive square has been the center of the city since 1535. Over the years it has served many functions, from an open-air theater for melodramas to an impromptu ring for bullfights. Huge fires once burned in the center for people sentenced to death by the Spanish Inquisition. Much has changed over the years, but one thing remaining is the bronze fountain unveiled in 1651. It was here that José de San Martín declared the country's independence from Spain in 1821. ⊠ *Jr. Junín and Jr. Carabaya, El Centro.*

Fodor's Choice ★

⓯ **Plaza San Martín.** This spectacular plaza is unlike any other in the city. It's surrounded on three sides by French-style buildings dating from the 1920s. Presiding over the western edge is the Gran Hotel Bolívar, a pleasant stop for afternoon tea, or a pisco sour. At the Plaza's center is a massive statue of José de San Martín, the Argentine general who led the independence of Argentina, Chile and Peru from Spain. ⊠ *Between Jr. de la Union and Jr. Carabaya, El Centro.*

WORTH NOTING

❾ **Casa Torre Tagle.** Considered one of the most magnificent structures in South America, this mansion sums up the graceful style of the early 18th century. Flanked by a pair of elegant balconies, the stone entrance is as expertly carved as that of any of the city's churches. It currently serves as the Foreign Ministry and is not open to the public, but you

RETABLOS EXPLAINED

You can tell a lot about colonial-era churches by their *retablos* (retables), the altarpieces that are almost always massive in scale and over-the-top in ornamentation. Most are made of elaborately carved wood and coated with layer after layer of gold leaf. Indigenous peoples often did the carving, so look for some atypical elements such as symbols of the sun and moon that figure prominently in the local religion. You may be surprised that Jesus is a minor player on many retablos,

and on others doesn't appear at all. That's because these retablos often depict the life of the saint for which the church is named. Many churches retain their original baroque retablos, but others saw theirs replaced by the much simpler neoclassical ones with simple columns and spare design. If you wander around the church, you're likely to find the original relegated to one of the side chapels.

can often get a peek inside through an open door. You might see the tiled ceilings, carved columns, and a 16th-century carriage. Across the street is **Casa Goyeneche,** which was built some 40 years later in 1771, and was clearly influenced by the rococo movement. ⊠ *Jr. Ucayali 363, El Centro.*

⑲ Cerro San Cristóbal. Rising over the northeastern edge of the city is this massive hill, recognizable from the cross at its peak—a replica of the one once placed there by Pizarro. If the air is clear—a rarity in Lima—you can see most of the city below. You'll want to hire a taxi to take you there and back, since the neighborhood that surrounds it is sketchy. ⊠ *Calle San Cristóbal, El Centro.*

❺ Convento de Santo Domingo. The 16th-century Convent of Saint Dominic is a great place to experience life in the cloister. This sprawling structure shows the different styles popular during the colonial era in Lima. The bell tower, for instance, has a baroque base built in 1632, but the upper parts rebuilt after an earthquake in 1746 are more rococo in style. The church is popular, as it holds the tombs of the first two Peruvian saints, Santa Rosa de Lima, and San Martín de Porres. The pair of cloisters in the convent are decorated with yellow-and-blue tiles imported from Spain in the early 17th century. Independent guides who wait by the entrance offer short tours for a negotiable fee. ⊠ *Conde de Superunda and Camaná, El Centro* 🕾 *01/427–6793* 🎫 *S/5* ☉ *Mon.– Sun. 9:30–6:30.*

❻ Estación de Desamparados (aka Casa de la Literatura Peruana). Inaugurated in 1912, Desamparados Station was the centerpiece for the continent's first railway. The building, using lots of glass for natural light, was based on styles popular in Europe. It has been turned into a museum called the Casa de la Literature Peruana (House of Peruvian Literature), which hosts literary exhibitions and activities. ⊠ *Jr. Ancash 207, El Centro* 🕾 *01/426–2573* 🎫 *Free* ☉ *Tue.–Sun. 10–8.*

⑭ Iglesia de Jesús, María y José. The 1659 Church of Jesus, Mary and Joseph may be smaller than some of El Centro's other churches, but inside is a

Country Club
Lima Hotel **1**

Huaca
Huallamarca **2**

Parque
El Olívar **3**

San Isidro

feast for the eyes. Baroque retablos representing various saints rise from the main altar and line both walls. ⊠ *Jr. Camaná and Jr. Moquegua, El Centro* ☎ *01/427–6809* ⊠ *Free* ⊗ *Mon.–Sat. 9–noon and 3–5.*

3 **Municipalidad de Lima.** Although it resembles the colonial-era buildings that abound in the area, City Hall was constructed in 1944. Step inside to see the stained-glass windows above the marble staircase. Alongside the building a lovely pedestrian walkway called the Paseo Los Escribanos, or Passage of the Scribes, is lined with inexpensive restaurants. On the south side is the tourist-information office. ⊠ *West side of Plaza de Armas, El Centro* ☎ *01/315–1542 tourist office* ⊗ *Tourist office Mon.–Sat. 9–6.*

16 **Museo de Arte Italiano.** Italian art in Peru? This small museum is one of the city's most delightful. Most of the art is about a century old, so it captures the exact moment when impressionism was melting into modernism, and the building itself is a work of art. Don't overlook the magnificent iron door, by Alessandro Mazzucotelli. ⊠ *Paseo de la República 250, El Centro* ☎ *01/423–9932* ⊠ *S/4* ⊗ *Tue.–Sun. 10–5.*

18 **Parque de la Exposición.** Eager to prove that it was a world-class capital, Lima hosted an international exposition in 1872. Several of the buildings constructed for the event still stand, including the neoclassical Palacio de la Exposición, which now serves as the Museo de Arte. Stroll through the grounds and you'll find the eye-popping Pabellón Morisco, or Moorish Pavillion. Painstakingly restored in 2005, this Gothic-style structure has spiral staircases leading to a stained-glass salon on the second floor. The nearby Pabellón Bizantino, or Byzantine Pavilion, is being slowly refurbished. Despite its name, it most closely resembles a turret from a Victorian-era mansion. ⊠ *Av. de la Vega and Av. Grau, El Centro* ☎ *01/423–4732* ⊙ *Daily 10–8.*

SAN ISIDRO

While strolling through the ancient olive trees of Parque El Olívar, you might be surprised by the light traffic. That's because this residential area of San Isidro lacks the fast pace of the rest of the city. But just a few blocks away, you'll find the busy boulevards of Camino Real, or Avenida Arequipa, which serve as reminders that San Isidro also holds the offices of the country's largest companies and banks, as well as most foreign embassies. It also has some of the city's best hotels and restaurants, so you are bound to spend some time. However, San Isidro's only real tourist attraction is the Huaca Huallamarca, where you can clamor around the ruins of a pre-Columbian temple.

Like nearby Miraflores, San Isidro is big on shopping, though more of its boutiques sell designer goods. Its bars serve up the latest cocktails, and its restaurants dish out cuisine from around the world, but it has a more subdued atmosphere than you'll find in the other neighborhoods.

GETTING AROUND

The best way to travel between San Isidro's widely dispersed attractions is by taxi. Walking through the neighborhood takes no more than a few hours. This is probably Lima's safest neighborhood.

TOP ATTRACTIONS

2 **Huaca Huallamarca.** The sight of this mud-brick pyramid catches many people off guard. The structure, painstakingly restored on the front side, seems out of place among the neighborhood's towering hotels and apartment buildings. The upper platform affords some nice views of the San Isidro. There's a small museum with displays of objects found at the site, including several mummies. This temple, thought to be a place of worship, predates the Incas. ⊠ *Av. Nicolás de Rivera and Av. El Rosario, San Isidro* ☎ *01/222–4124* ⊒ *S/5* ⊙ *Tues.–Sun 9–5.*

WORTH NOTING

1 **Country Club Lima Hotel.** Two magnificent palms stand guard at the entrance to this 1927 hotel, widely regarded as the most elegant hotel in the city. If you're here in the late afternoon, you might want to stop by for the English-style tea. ⊠ *Los Eucaliptos 590, San Isidro* ☎ *01/611–9000.*

3 **Parque El Olívar.** This pretty park was once an olive grove, so it's no surprise that you'll find an old olive press here. The gnarled old trees, some more than a century old, still bear fruit. Yellow and red irises line the walkways. ⊠ *East of Av. Conquistadores, San Isidro.*

Even the statues find love in the Parque del Amor, Miraflores.

MIRAFLORES

With flower-filled parks and wide swaths of green overlooking the ocean, it's no wonder travelers flock to this seaside suburb. Miraflores has Lima's best selection of hotels and restaurants, which is why most people stay here, but it is also the city's cultural hub. There are plenty of boutiques, galleries, and museums, as well as bars, cafés, and dance clubs. Some people who find themselves in Lima for a short time never leave this little haven.

At its center is Parque Miraflores, sitting like a slice of pie between Avenida José Larco and Avenida Diagonal. On the eastern side is the Iglesia de la Virgen Milagrosa, the neighborhood's largest church. The colonial-style building next door is the Palacio Municipal de Miraflores, where most governmental business takes place.

Where you go next depends on your areas of interest. If you're interested in ancient cultures, head to the towering temple of Pucllana. From the top you have a great view of the neighborhood. A tiny Museo Amano, six blocks to the west contains one of the city's best collections of ancient artifacts. If you want to shop, head for Avenida Petit Thouars just a few blocks north of the park, where a series of markets hold dozens of shops that offer some of the best deals in town. If you have romance on your mind, go south along Avenida Diagonal to Parque del Amor, a wonderful park with a splendid view of the coast and sea below. It attracts young lovers, paragliding enthusiasts, and just about everyone else on a sunny afternoon.

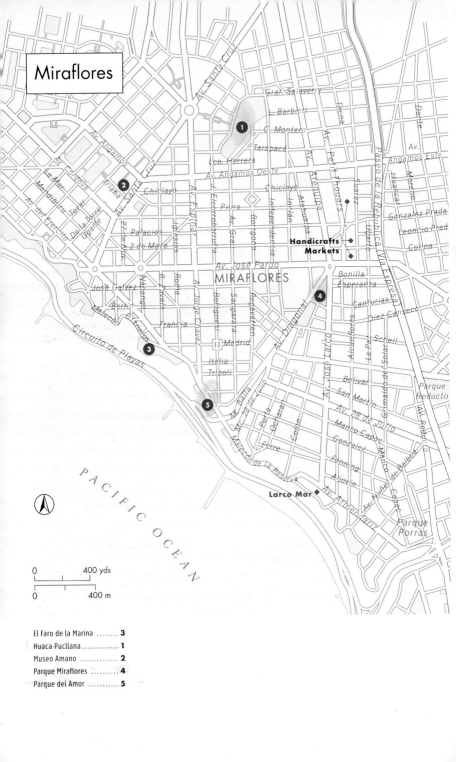

Miraflores

Av. Santa Cruz
Gral. Salavery
L. Barbieri
C. Montero
Tarapacá
Leo. Herrera
Av. Angamos Oeste
Chiclayo
Chiclayo
Piura
Palacios
2 de Mayo
Av. José Pardo
MIRAFLORES
José Galvez
Berlín
Francia
Madrid
Italia
Tripoli
Larco Mar

Handicrafts Markets

Av. Angamos
Trinita Santa
Av. Santa

La Mar
Medíoburu
Tovar
Av. del Ejército
Del la Torre
Ugarte
Bolognesi
Espinar
Av. Grau
Bellavista
Av. Larco
Independencia
Alcanfores
Atahualpa
Arequipa
Petit Thouars
Suárez
Av.
Reina
Paseo de la República (Vía Expreso)
Av. Angamos Este
Monte
Huaca
Duarte
Av.

Gonzalez Prada
Leoncio Prad
Colina

Bonilla
Esperanza
Canturias
Diez Canseco
Schell
La Paz
Bolívar
San Martín
Av. 28 de Julio
Manco Capac
Gonzalez
Fanning
Aljovin
Av. Armendáriz
Av. Nuñez de Balboa
Manco Cápac

Parque Reducto
Av. Reducto
Parque Porras

Circuito de Playas
Malecón Cisneros
Jorge Chavez
Sangara
Porta
Av. Diagonal
José Larco
Alcanfores

M. Balta
Mc. 28 de Julio
Porta
Ochoran
Colon
Ferre
Malecón de la Reserva

PACIFIC OCEAN

0			400 yds
0			400 m

El Faro de la Marina **3**
Huaca Pucllana **1**
Museo Amano **2**
Parque Miraflores **4**
Parque del Amor **5**

GETTING AROUND

A popular walk is the 20-minute stroll south from Parque Miraflores down busy Avenida José Larco to Larcomar, an open-air mall built into the side of a cliff, so that it has gorgeous views and ocean breezes to complement the shops, bars and restaurants. From there you can walk either east or west, since the top of the coast cliff is lined with a series of parks called Malecónes. Miraflores is about 20 minutes from El Centro by taxi or the Metropolitano bus.

TOP ATTRACTIONS

❶ Huaca Pucllana. Rising out of a nondescript residential neighborhood is this mud-brick pyramid. You'll be amazed at the scale—this pre-Inca *huaca*, or temple, covers several city blocks. The site, which dates back to at least the fourth century, has ongoing excavations, and new discoveries are often announced. ■TIP➔ Archaeologists working on the site are usually happy to share their discoveries about the people who lived in this area hundreds of years before the Inca. A tiny museum highlights some recent finds. Knowledgeable guides speak English and other languages. They will lead you around and over the pyramid to the area that is being excavated. This site is most beautiful at night, when partial tours can be arranged through the adjacent Huaca Pucllana restaurant if you dine there. ⊠ *General Borgoño cuadra 8 s/n (2 blocks north of Av. Angamos Oeste), Miraflores* ☎ *01/617–7367* ⊕ *pucllana.perucultural. org.pe* ✉ *S/10* ⊗ *Wed.–Mon. 9–4:30.*

❺ Parque del Amor. You might think you're in Barcelona when you stroll through this lovely park. Like Antonio Gaudí's Parque Güell, the park that provided the inspiration for this one, the benches are decorated with broken pieces of tile. Here, however, they spell out silly romantic sayings like *Amor es como luz* ("Love is like light"). The centerpiece is a massive statue of two lovers locked in a lewd embrace designed by the Peruvian sculptor Victor Delfin. ⊠ *Malecón Balta, Miraflores.*

❹ Parque Miraflores. What locals call Parque Miraflores is actually two parks. The smaller section, near the roundabout, is Parque 7 de Junio, whereas the rest of it is Parque Kennedy. To the east of Parque Kennedy stands Miraflores' stately Iglesia de la Virgen Milagrosa (Church of the Miraculous Virgin), built in the 1930s on the site of a colonial church. The equally young colonial-style building behind it is the Palacio Municipal de Miraflores (Town Hall). A tourist-information kiosk sits near the entrance to the church and several open-air cafés line Parque Kennedy's eastern edge. At night, a round cement structure in front of those cafés called La Rotonda fills up with handicraft vendors and the babbling sounds of shoppers fills the evening air. Nearby, street vendors sell popcorn and traditional Peruvian deserts such as *mazamora* (a pudding made with blue corn and prunes) and *arroz con leche* (rice pudding). ⊠ *Between Av. José Larco and Av. Diagonal, Miraflores.*

WORTH NOTING

❸ El Faro de la Marina. Constructed in 1900, this little lighthouse a short walk north from the Parque del Amor has steered ships away from the coast for more than a century. The classically designed tower is still in use today. On a sunny afternoon, the park that surrounds it is one of the most popular spots in Miraflores. ⊠ *Malecón Cisneros and Madrid, Miraflores.*

2 **Museo Amano.** Although only two rooms, this museum packs a lot into a small space. The private collection of pre-Columbian artifacts includes some of the city's best ceramics. Imaginative displays reveal how cultures in the northern part of the region focused on sculptural images, while those in the south used vivid colors. In between, around present-day Lima, the styles merged. A second room holds an impressive number of weavings, including examples from the Chancay people, who lived in the north between 1000 and 1500. Some of their work is so delicate that it resembles the finest lace. Call ahead: you need an appointment to join one of the two daily Spanish-language tours, which last an hour and start at 3 and 4. ⊠ *Retiro 160, Miraflores* ☏ *01/441–2909* ✉ *Free* ☉ *Weekdays 3–5 by appointment only.*

> ### PARAGLIDE, ANYONE?
>
> If you walk along the Malecón (a chain of parks with ocean views), you'll doubtless see a dozen or so brilliantly colored swaths of cloth in the sky above you. PerúFly (⊠ *Av. Jorge Chavez 658, Miraflores* ☏ *01/444–5004* ⊕ *www.perufly.com*) offers 15-minute tandem flights along the coast that take off from Parque del Amor and cost S/150.

BARRANCO

Barranco is a mix of bohemian, historic, and run-down, but the area along the coast is the most charming of Lima's neighborhoods. On weekend nights, it is a magnet for young people who come to carouse in its bars and dance clubs. Sleepy during the day, the neighborhood comes to life around sunset when artisans start hawking their wares on its central square and the bars begin filling up. Founded toward the end of the 19th century, Barranco was where wealthy Limeños built their summer residences. The streetcar line that once connected it to El Centro brought crowds of beach goers on weekends and holidays. The view proved so irresistible that some built huge mansions on the cliffs above the sea. Many of these have fallen into disrepair, but little by little they are being renovated.

GETTING AROUND

To get your bearings, head to Parque Municipal, one of the nicest of the city's plazas. To the south, the brick-red building with the tower is the Biblioteca Municipal, or Municipal Library. To the north is the parish church called La Santisima Cruz. To the west, steps lead down to Lima's own Bridge of Sighs, the Puente de los Suspiros. Directly below in the shade of ancient trees is the Bajada de Baños, lined with wonderful old houses and colorful bougainvillea. Head down this cobblestone street to the waves of Playa Barranquito by day, or to various bars and restaurants by night.

TOP ATTRACTIONS

4 **Museo Pedro de Osma.** Even if there were no art inside this museum,

Fodor's Choice
★

it would still be worth the trip to see the century-old mansion that houses it. The mansard-roofed structure—with inlaid wood floors,

Museo de la
Electricidad **3**

Museo Pedro de
Osma **4**

Parque
Municipal **2**

Puente de los
Suspiros **1**

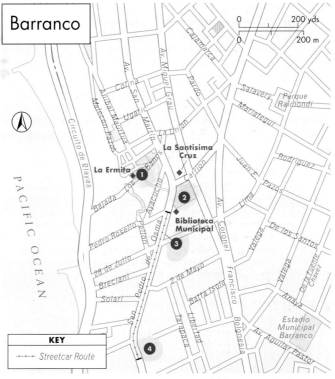

Barranco

KEY

⊢⊢⊢⊢ *Streetcar Route*

delicately painted ceilings, and breathtaking stained-glass windows in
every room—was the home of a wealthy collector of religious art. The
best of his collection is permanently on display. The finest of the paintings, the 18th-century *Virgen de Pomato*, represents the Earth, with her
mountain-shape cloak covered with garlands of corn. A more modern
wing contains some fine pieces of silver, including a lamb-shape incense
holder with shining ruby eyes. Make sure to explore the manicured
grounds. ⊠ *Av. Pedro de Osma 423, Barranco* ☎ *01/467–0141* 🎫 *S/10*
🕓 *Tues.–Sun. 10–6.*

2 **Parque Municipal.** Elegant swirls of colorful blooms and the surrounding colonial architecture make this park stand out from others in Lima.
Here you'll find locals relaxing on the benches, their children playing
nearby. ■ **TIP→** Around 6 every evening, artisans who live nearby show off
their works. ⊠ *Between Av. Pedro de Osma and Av. Grau, Barranco.*

1 **Puente de los Suspiros.** The romantically named Bridge of Sighs is a
wooden walkway shaded with flowering trees. Though the bridge itself
is nothing special, the view from it is priceless. It crosses over the Bajada
de Baños, a cobblestone walkway that descends to Playa Barranquito.
On the far side is La Ermita, a lovely little chapel painted a dazzling
shade of red. ⊠ *East of Parque Municipal, Barranco.*

WORTH NOTING

3 **Museo de la Electricidad.** In front of this tiny museum is a cherry-red *urbanito,* or streetcar, named Breda. From Tuesday to Sunday, for about 65 cents you can climb aboard and take a three-block trip down Avenida Pedro de Osma. Inside the museum are photos of other trolleys that once rumbled along Lima's streets. The captions are only in Spanish. ⊠ *Av. Pedro de Osma 105, Barranco* ☎ *01/477–6577* ⊕ *museoelectri. perucultural.org.pe* 🖂 *Free* ⊘ *Daily 9–5.*

NEED A BREAK?

Along a walkway leading past La Ermita is the gingerbread-covered La Flor de Canela (⊠ *Ermita 102, Barranco* ☎ *No phone*), a sweet little café with a porch overlooking much of Barranco. It's a great place for a cup of coffee or a pisco sour.

PUEBLO LIBRE

Instead of hurrying past, residents of Pueblo Libre often pause to chat with friends. There's a sense of calm here not found elsewhere in the capital. Plaza Bolívar, the park at the heart of Pueblo Libre, is surrounded by colonial-era buildings, many of which have shops and restaurants. On the south side, in the Municipalidad de Pueblo Libre, are governmental offices. A small gallery on the ground floor sometimes hosts painting and photography exhibitions.

Despite the pleasant surroundings, there would be little reason to venture this far if it weren't for the presence of two fine museums, the Museo Nacional de Antropología, Arqueología, e Historia del Perú, and the Museo Arqueológico Rafael Larco Herrera.

GETTING AROUND

The most convenient way to reach Pueblo Libre is a taxi ride, which should take 20–30 minutes.

TOP ATTRACTIONS

Fodor's Choice ★ **Museo Arqueológico Rafael Larco Herrera.** Fuchsia bougainvillea tumbles over the white walls surrounding the home of the world's largest private collection of pre-Columbian art. The oldest pieces are crude vessels dating back several thousand years. Most intriguing are the thousands of ceramic "portrait heads" crafted more than a millennium ago. Some owners commissioned more than one, allowing you to see how they changed over the course of their lives. The *sala erótica* reveals that these ancient artists were surprisingly uninhibited. Everyday objects are adorned with images that are frankly sexual and frequently humorous. This gallery is across the garden from the rest of the museum, so you can distance the kids from it. Guides are a good idea, and are just S/25 per group. ⊠ *Av. Bolívar 1515, Pueblo Libre* ☎ *01/461–1835* ⊕ *www. museolarco.org* 🖂 *S/30* ⊘ *Daily 9–6.*

WORTH NOTING

Museo Nacional de Antropología, Arqueología e Historia del Perú. The country's most extensive collection of pre-Columbian artifacts can be found at this sprawling museum. Beginning with 8,000-year-old stone tools, Peru's history is peeked at through the sleek granite obelisks of the

Chavín culture, the intricate weavings of Paraca peoples, and the colorful ceramics of the Moche, Chimú, and Inca civilizations. A fascinating pair of mummies from the Nazca region is thought to be more than 2,500 years old; they are so well preserved that you can still see the grim expressions on their faces. ■TIP➜ Not all the exhibits are labeled in English, but you can hire a guide for S/15. ✉ *Plaza Bolívar, Pueblo Libre* ☎ *01/463–5070* ⊕ *mnaah.perucultural.org.pe* ▣ *S/11* ☽ *Tues.–Sat. 9–5, Sun. 9–4.*

NEED A DRINK?

Saloon-style doors lead into the **Antigua Taberna Queirolo** (✉ *Jr. San Martín 1090, Pueblo Libre* ☎ *01/463–8777*), a charming little bar about a block west of Plaza Bolívar. Locals lean against round tables and sample the pisco bottled at the bodega next door.

ELSEWHERE AROUND LIMA

A few of Lima's most interesting museums are in outlying neighborhoods such as Monterrico and San Borja. The most convenient way to reach them is a quick taxi ride.

TOP ATTRACTIONS

Museo de Oro. When you see examples of how these societies manipulated gold—from a mantle made of postage-stamp-size pieces worn by a Lambayeque priest to an intricately designed sheet that once decorated an entire wall of the Chimú capital of Chán Chán—you begin to imagine the opulence of these ancient cities. The museum has other interesting items, including a child's poncho of yellow feathers and a skull with a full set of pink quartz teeth. Upstairs are military uniforms and weapons. None of the displays are particularly well marked, either in English or Spanish, so you might want to see the museum as part of an organized city tour; it's a pretty good deal, as you'll save the cost of a taxi. At any rate, be prepared to pay one of the steepest admissions of any of South America's museums. ✉ *Alonso de Molina 1100, Monterrico* ☎ *01/345–1271* ⊕ *www.museoroperu.com.pe* ▣ *S/33* ☽ *Daily 11:30–7.*

WORTH NOTING

Museo de la Nación. If you know little about the history of Peru, a visit to this fortresslike museum is likely to leave you overwhelmed. The number of cultures tracked over the centuries makes it easy to confuse the Chimú, the Chincha, and the Chachapoyas. The three floors of artifacts end up seeming repetitious. The museum is more manageable if you have a specific interest, say, if you're planning a trip north to Chiclayo and want to learn more about the Moche people. At this writing the museum was under renovation, which will hopefully result in improved exhibits. ✉ *Av. Javier Prado Este 2465, San Borja* ☎ *01/476–9873 Ext. 2484* ⊕ *inc.perucultural.org.pe* ▣ *S/6.50* ☽ *Tues.–Sun. 9–5.*

Pachacàmac. Dating back to the first century, this city of plazas, palaces, and pyramids, many of them painstakingly restored, was for centuries a stronghold of the Huari people. Here they worshipped Pachacámac, creator of the world. It was a pilgrimage site, and people from all over the region came to worship. In the 15th century the city was captured by the Inca, who added structures such as the *Acllahuasi*, the Palace of the Chosen Women. When the Spanish heard of the city, they dispatched troops to plunder its riches. In 1533, two years before the founding of Lima, they marched triumphantly into the city, only to find a few remaining objects in gold. Today you can visit the temples, including several that were built before the time of the Incas.

> ### SURFING
>
> With **Surf Express** (✉ 41001 N. Atlantic Ave. Ste A, Coco Beach, FL ☎ 321/779–2124 ⊕ www.surfex. com), run out of Florida in the U.S., surfers ride some of the best left-breaking waves in the world; Punta Rocas, south of Lima, is one of their destinations. You'll want to bring your wet suit, because the water is chilly.

The Incas built several more structures, including the impressive Templo del Inti, or Temple of the Sun. Here you'll find a grand staircase leading up to the colonnaded walkways surrounding the temple. The site has a small but excellent museum. Although it's a quick drive from the city, the easiest way to see Pachacámac is by a half-day guided tour offered by Lima Tours and several other agencies in Lima. ✉ *31 km (19 mi) south of Lima on Carretera Panamericana Sur* ☎ *01/430–0168* ⊕ *pachacamac.perucultural.org.pe* 🎟 *S/7* ☉ *Tues.–Sun. 9–4:30.*

OFF THE BEATEN PATH

Caral. Few people realize it, but the oldest urban site in the western hemisphere is just 220 km (120 mi) north of Lima. Caral was first settled around 5,000 BC, long before the rise of ancient Egypt, though Caral's squat Pirámide Mayor is slightly younger than Egypt's Great Pyramid of Giza. It may not be as spectacular as other Peruvian sites, but Caral has some interesting structures that evoke a well-developed people, who archaeologists have dubbed the Caral-Supe Culture. That culture influenced a series of increasingly developed cultures that culminated in the Incas. It takes nearly four hours to drive to Caral and it is not easy to find, so the best way to visit it is on a tour. As the name suggests, the people at Caral Tours are the experts; their 13-hour day trips take you to Caral and the nearby site of Chupacigarro. ✉ *200 km (124 mi) north of Lima via the Carretera Panamericana Norte* ☎ *01/205–2500, Ext. 517* ⊕ *www.caralperu.gob.pe* 🎟 *S/11* ☉ *Tues.–Sun. 9–5.*

WHERE TO EAT

Seafood, especially cebiche, is a Peruvian specialty, and the variety of the ingredients and recipes is impressive. Cebiche is traditionally only eaten at lunch, so most cebicherías (seafood restaurants) close in the late afternoon.

WHAT IT COSTS IN NUEVO SOLES					
	¢	$	$$	$$$	$$$$
RESTAURANTS	Under S/20	S/20–S/35	S/36–S/50	S/51–S/65	over S/65

Restaurant prices are per person for a main course.

Continued on page 76

FOOD IN PERU
by Mark Sullivan

When Peruvians talk about *comida criolla*, or typical food, they aren't talking about just one thing. This is a vast country, and dishes on the table in coastal Trujillo might be nowhere in mountainous Cusco. And all bets are off once you reach places like Iquitos, where the surrounding jungle yields exotic flavors.

REGIONAL CUISINE

THE CAPITAL
Lima cooks up the widest variety of Peruvian and international foods. One of the most influential immigrant communities is the Chinese, who serve traditional dishes in restaurants called *chifas.* One favorite, *lomo saltado*, strips of beef sautéed with onions, tomatoes, and friend potatoes, is now considered a local dish.

THE COAST
When you talk about the cuisine of the country's vast coastal region, you are talking about seafood. Peruvians are very particular about their fish, insisting that it should be pulled from the sea that morning. The most common dish is *ceviche,* raw fish "cooked" in lemon or lime juice. It comes in endless variations—all delicious.

THE ALTIPLANO
Hearty fare awaits in the altiplano. Because it keeps so well over the winter, the potato is the staple of many dishes, including the ubiquitous *cau cau,* or tripe simmered with potatoes and peppers. A special treat is *pachamanca*, a Peruvian-style barbecue where meat and potatoes are cooked in a hole in the ground lined with hot rocks. In Huancayo, the local specialty is *papa a la huancai'na,* boiled potato covered in yellow chili-cheese sauce.

THE AMAZON
Fish is a staple in the Amazon, and you'll know why once you taste paiche and other species unknown outside this area. One of the best ways to try local fish is *patarashca,* or fish wrapped in banana leaves and cooked over an open fire. Restaurants here are very simple, often just a few tables around an outdoor grill.

A woman preparing *anticuchos.*

Ceviche dish.

IT'S ALL ABOUT THE FISH

Peru's high-altitude lakes, including Lake Titicaca, and rivers spawn some very tastey *trucha* (trout).

In Peru, restaurants known as *cebicherías* serve more than the marinated fish called ceviche. The menu may intimidate those who can't tell *lenguado* (sole) from *langosta* (lobster). Don't worry—just order a series of dishes to share. Local families pass around huge platters of *pescado* until they are picked clean, then gesture to the server for the next course.

The fragrant *sopa de mariscos* is soup overflowing with *chorros* (mussels) still in their shells. *Tiradito* is similar to ceviche but leaves off the onions and adds a spicy yellow-pepper sauce. A platter of *chicharrones de calamar*, little ringlets of deep-fried squid, should be given a squeeze of lime. For a nice filet or whole fish, many restaurants suggest a dozen or more preparations. It's best grilled, or *a la plancha*.

ON THE SIDE

ELOTE
A pile of large-kernel corn.

Camote
Boiled sweet potatoes. The sweetness is a wonderful contrast to the citrus marinade.

Cancha
A basket full of fried corn that's usually roasted on the premises. Highly addictive.

Chifles
A northern coast specialty of thin slices of fried banana.

Zarandajas
A bean dish served in the northern coast.

A simple boiled potato
A dish you'll recognize.

SPUD COUNTRY

POTATO ON THE PLATE

The potato, or its cousin the yucca, is rarely absent from a Peruvian table. Any restaurant offering *comida criolla*, or traditional cuisine, will doubtless serve *cau cau* (tripe simmered with potatoes and peppers), *papa a la huancaina* (potatoes in a spicy cheese sauce), or *ocopa* (boiled potatoes in peanut sauce). Just about everywhere you can find a version of *lomo saltado*, made from strips of beef sautéed with tomatoes, onions, and fried potatoes. Some 600,000 Peruvian farmers, most with small lots in the highlands, grow more than 3,250,000 tons of potatoes a year.

GET YOUR PURPLE POTATOES HERE!

Peru's potatoes appear in all colors of the spectrum, including purple, red, pink, and blue. They also come in many strange shapes.

SCIENCE POTATO

The International Potato Center (Centro Internacional de la Papa), outside of Lima, conducts spud research to help farmers and open markets, particularly for the great variety of Andean potatoes. They recently sent 35 million potato seeds for safe-keeping to a genetic storage facility to Svaldbard, Norway, a large island of ice that is above the arctic circle—just so the Peruvian potato can outlive us all.

POTATO HISTORY

The potato comes from the Andes of Peru and Chile (not Idaho or Ireland), where it has been grown on the mountain terraces for thousands of years. There are endless varieties of this durable tuber: more than 7,000 of them, some of which are hardy enough to be cultivated at 15,000 feet. The Spanish introduced potatoes to Europe in the late 1500s.

(above) Preparing *pachamanca;* (left) Discovering the potato.

OTHER STAPLES

CORN: Almost as important as potatoes is corn. You might be surprised to find that the kernels are more than twice as large as their North American friends. Most corn dishes are very simple, such as the tamale-like *humitas*, but some are more complex, like the stew called *pepián de choclo*. A favorite in the humid lowlands is *inchi capi*, a chicken dish served with peanuts and toasted corn. A sweet purple corn is the basis for *chicha morada*, a thick beverage, and *mazamorra*, an even thicker jelly used in desserts. Even ancient Peruvians loved popcorn, kernels were found in tombs 1000 years old in eastern Peru. Also discovered were ceramic popcorn poppers from 3000 AD.

PEPPERS: Few Peruvian dishes don't include *ají*, the potent hot peppers grown all over the country. You'll find several everywhere—*amarillo* (yellow pepper), *rocoto* (a reddish variety), and *panca* (a lovely chocolate brown variety), but there are hundreds of regional favorites. Some, like ají *norteño*, are named for the region of origin, others, like the cherry-sized ají *cereza*, are named for what they resemble. Such is the case with the ají *pinguita de mono*, which, roughly translated, means "small monkey penis." It is one of the hottest that you'll find.

Hot pepper tip: Never rub your eyes after handling a hot pepper, and avoid contact with your skin.

FOR ADVENTUROUS EATERS

CUY: What was served at the Last Supper? According to baroque paintings hanging in the Iglesia de San Francisco in Lima and the Cathedral in Cusco, it was guinea pig. Both paintings show a platter in the middle of the table with a whole roasted guinea pig, including the head and feet.

This dish, called *cuy chactado* or simply *cuy*, has long been a staple of the antiplano. Cuy is a bit hard to swallow, mostly because it is served whole. The flavor is like pork, and can be sweet and tender if carefully cooked.

ANTOCUCHOS: When a street vendor fires up his grill, the savory scent of *anticuchos* will catch your attention. Beef hearts in the Andes are a delicacy. Marinated in herbs and spices, these strips of meat are incredibly tender. They have become popular in urban areas, and you're likely to run across restaurants called *anticucherías* in Lima and other cities.

ALPACA: Nearly every visitor to Cusco and the surrounding region will be offered a steak made of alpaca. It's not an especially tasty piece of meat, which may be why locals don't eat it very often. But go ahead—you can impress the folks back home.

(Top, right) *humita* (bottom) Peruvian eating guinea pig.

BARRANCO

In keeping with its reputation as a bohemian neighborhood, Barranco has a slew of bars and cozy cafés, but it also has very nice restaurants. The most picturesque of those eateries are around the Bajada a los Baños and the Puente de los Suspiros.

$ ✕**Antica Trattoria**. This Italian-style eatery is the place to head on a cool
ITALIAN night, since it offers a warm, cozy ambience and good food. Rough-wood tables are surrounded by old pots and pans hanging from the walls; the rafters hold wooden barrels. The extensive menu includes more than a dozen salads, various fresh pastas are served with your choice of a dozen sauces, and more than 50 different kinds of pizza are cooked in the wood-fired oven. You can't go wrong with dishes like risotto with *langostino* (shrimp), or ravioli stuffed with *granchio* (crab). ✉ *Av. San Martín and Av. Ugarte, Barranco* ☎ *01/247–3443* ⊕ *www. anticapizzeria.com.pe* ▭ *AE, MC, V.*

$$ ✕**Chala**. This small restaurant on the upper stretch of the Bajada a los
PERUVIAN Baños is a veritable Dr. Historic and Mr. Modernity. The exterior and
Fodor'sChoice wooden porch in front blend into the ancient surroundings, but step
★ through the door and you're back in the 21st century with a chic bar, lounge music, and wild art installation on the back wall. It befits an establishment that serves such Peruvian fusion dishes as *causa patri-otica* (a mashed potato appetizer filled with smoked trout, crab meat and cream cheese) and ravioli *italo-chalenos* (stuffed with *ají de gal-lina*—shredded chicken in a pepper cream sauce—and smothered in a shrimp cream sauce). ✉ *Bajada de Baños 343, Barranco* ☎ *01/252–8515* ⊕ *www.chala.com.pe* ▭ *AE, MC, V* ☉ *Closed 4–8 and Sun.*

$ ✕**Javier**. Javier has restaurants on both sides of the street leading down
PERUVIAN to the ocean, and what sets them apart from the competition are their views. Whether you choose the rooftop terrace of the restaurant on the left, or an intimate table on the ridge above the restaurant on the right, you'll overlook the historic architecture and crashing waves below. Start with cebiche, or *conchas a la parmesana* (clams with Parmesan cheese), then try the *chupe de camaron* (a creamy river-prawn soup), *corvina con salsa de alcachofa* (sea bass with an artichoke sauce) or the popular *jalea mixta* (deep-fried fish nuggets and seafood). A pisco sour—the first one is on the house—is a great way to start your meal. ✉ *Bajada de Baños 403, Barranco* ☎ *01/477–5339* ▭ *MC, V.*

$ ✕**Las Mesitas**. Filled with a dozen or so marble-topped tables, this
PERUVIAN small-but-charming, old-fashioned café is half a block north of Parque Municipal. The constant stream of Limeños informs you that the food is first-rate. Share a few *humitas,* steamed tamales that you season with pickled onions and bright yellow ají hot sauce, or try the local specialty *pescado a la chorrillana* (fish in a tomato, onion and hot pepper sauce) or *arroz con pato* (a rice and duck dish seasoned with beer). If the floor's pinwheel design doesn't put you off balance, then the spinning dessert display certainly will. Try the *manjar de lucuma,* a pudding made from a native fruit, or *mazamorra morada,* a sweet pudding with prunes and blue corn juice. ✉ *Grau 341, Barranco* ☎ *01/477–4199* ▭ *V.*

Restaurants ▼

Antica
Trattoria **1**

Chala **3**

Javier **5**

Las Mesitas **2**

Songoro
Cosongo **4**

Hotels ▼

La Quinta
de Allison **2**

Second Home
Peru **1**

Where to Eat and Stay in Barranco

KEY

❶ *Restaurants*

① *Hotels*

$ ✕ **Songoro Cosongo.** Eating here may by the closest you come to dining
PERUVIAN   with a Peruvian family short of doing a homestay, because this family-
run restaurant serves the kind of traditional dishes that most Limeño
families have eaten for generations. Located in a massive, red adobe
house at the top of the steps to the Puente de los Suspiros, the restaurant
has a high ceiling and walls decorated with a mix of historic photos,
Van Gogh prints and posters. A stage in the corner is sometimes used
for traditional *música criolla* concerts, and that genre is on the stereo
the rest of the time. The menu includes such Peruvian standards as *ají
de gallina* (shredded chicken in a pepper cream sauce), *lomo saltado*
(tenderloin slices sautéed with tomato, onions and ají peppers) and
sudado de pescado (fish filet in spicy broth), plus a selection of pisco
cocktails. For dessert, try *picarones* (sweet-potato donuts served with
molasses), or a *bruselina de lúcuma* (a crispy cake layered with cream
and a native fruit). ⊠ *Ayacucho 281, Barranco* ☎ *01/247–4730* ⊕ *www.
songorocosongo.com* ▭ *MC, V.*

EL CENTRO

El Centro has both quality cuisine and cheap, filling food. A highlight is
the Barrio Chino, packed with dozens of Chinese-Peruvian restaurants
called *chifas,* but the run-down neighborhood that surrounds it makes

Restaurants ▼

Estadio **5**

L'eau Vive **3**

Los Vitrales
de Gemma **2**

Tanta **1**

Wa Lok **4**

Hotels ▼

Gran Hotel
Bolívar **2**

Inka Path **3**

Kamana Hotel ... **1**

Sheraton Lima
Hotel & Casino ...**4**

it inadvisable to head there for dinner. Restaurants on the main plazas are better dinner options.

$ ✕ **Estadio.** If you want to watch the big game, you can't do better than

PERUVIAN Peru's original sports bar. Soccer paraphernalia covers nearly every square inch of the wood-paneled dining room. It's a more sedate place during the day, and you can order a lunch of typical dishes like ají de gallina and arroz con pato. ■TIP➔ On game days things can get out of hand; you'll want to head elsewhere for a quiet meal. ✉ *Av. Nicolás de Piérola 926, El Centro* ☎ *01/428–8866* ▭ *AE, MC, V.*

$ ✕ **L'eau Vive.** Calling to mind *The Sound of Music*, a group of nuns sings

FRENCH "Ave Maria" every night around 9. The holy sisters cook French food that, while not extraordinary, is satisfying. Trout baked in cognac and duck in orange sauce are two dishes that bring the locals back. In a beautifully restored mansion directly across from Palacio Torre Tagle, the restaurant is worth a visit just for a peek inside. The furnishings, especially the plastic chairs, don't do justice to the glorious architecture. ✉ *Ucayali 370, El Centro* ☎ *01/427–5612* ▭ *AE, MC, V* ☉ *Closed Sun.*

$ ✕ **Los Vitrales de Gemma.** Tucked into the courtyard of a beautiful colo-

CONTINENTAL nial-era building, this is one of the prettiest restaurants in the historic district. Tables covered with peach-color linens are set along a colonnade, under stained-glass windows or beneath a soaring dome. The food, creative takes on old recipes, is just as appealing. Start with a spinach salad tossed with bacon, walnuts, and slices of apples, then move on to *pescado en salsa langotinos* (fish in shrimp sauce) or fettuccine *con frutos del mar* (pasta with seafood). ⊠ *Jr. Ucayali 332, El Centro* ☎ *01/426–7796* ▭ *MC, V* ☺ *Closed Sun.*

$ ✕ **Tanta.** Nestled behind the Municipalidad and a hedge of potted plants, this popular Peruvian fusion restaurant offers an excellent mix of light fare, and irresistible desserts. There is an extensive salad selection, and the empanadas, with fillings such as ají de gallina and *lomo saltado* (beef sautéed with tomato and onion), are great. Share an order of *causushis* (cold mashed potato appetizers with various fillings), then try the ravioli *bachiche* (cheese ravioli in a spicy Huancaina cream sauce), or *arroz Tanta*, which is similar to paella. Save room for a *chocolúcuma* (cream of the native lúcuma fruit encased in dark chocolate), or a *maracuya* (passion fruit) torte. ⊠ *Pasaje Nicolás de Rivera 142, El Centro* ☎ *01/426–7796* ▭ *AE, DC, MC, V* ☺ *Closed Sun. dinner.*

PERUVIAN
Fodor's Choice
★

$ ✕ **Wa Lok.** Of the dozens of chifas in Chinatown, none comes close to Wa Lok. Attention to the smallest detail makes every meal memorable; *kun pou kay tien*—chicken stir-fried with asparagus and yellow peppers—arrives garnished with an impossibly elaborate hibiscus flower carved from a carrot. Vegetarians can choose from more than 30 dishes. Though they open for dinner, the surrounding neighborhood is dangerous, so head to the branch above the casino in Miraflores (⊠ *Av. Angamos Oeste 700, El Centro* ☎ *01/447–1329*) for dinner. ⊠ *Jr. Paruro 864, El Centro* ☎ *01/427–2750* ⊕ *www.walok.com.pe* ▭ *AE, DC, MC, V.*

CHINESE

MIRAFLORES

Although inexpensive eateries are clustered around Parque Miraflores, some of the more elegant ones are scattered further afield and some can only be reached by taxi. If you want to dine with an ocean view, Miraflores has more options than any other neighborhood.

$$$ ✕ **Astrid y Gaston.** The flagship of Peru's most celebrated and successful chefs (Gastón Acurio and his wife Astrid Gutsche), this popular restaurant serves inventive variations on traditional Peruvian cuisine. Acurio is a master of both flavor and presentation. You can't help but watch the kitchen door—each dish the waiters carry out is a work of art. Even a Peruvian standard such as *lomo saltado* (tenderloin slices sautéed with tomato, onions and ají peppers) gains a new personality here. The menu changes every six months, but is invariably original and delectable. ■TIP➜ **Take advantage of the wine list—it's one of the best in town.** The colonial-style building is lovely, with grey walls hung with modern artwork, but you'll spend most of your time ogling the food. ⊠ *Cantuarias 175, Miraflores* ☎ *01/242–4422* ⊕ *www.astridygaston. com* ⌂ *Reservations essential* ▭ *AE, MC, V* ☺ *Closed 3:30–7 and Sun.*

PERUVIAN
Fodor's Choice
★

$$ ✕ **Brujas de Cachiche.** Although the name conjures up a haunted house, Witches of Cachiche is a modern space with huge windows, soaring ceilings, and modern art. The magic is the cooking, which draws on Peru's traditional cuisines. The results include such delicacies as *corvina en salsa de camarones* (sea bass in a river prawn sauce) and *pato al ají* (a

PERUVIAN

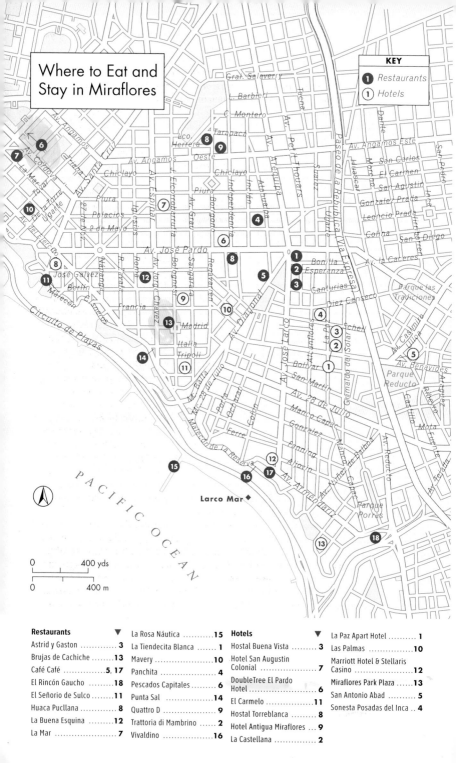

Where to Eat and Stay in Miraflores

Larco Mar ◆

PACIFIC OCEAN

0   400 yds

0   400 m

Restaurants ▼

Astrid y Gaston 3
Brujas de Cachiche 13
Café Café 5, 17
El Rincón Gaucho 18
El Señorio de Sulco 11
Huaca Pucllana 8
La Buena Esquina 12
La Mar 7

La Rosa Náutica 15
La Tiendecita Blanca 1
Mavery 10
Panchita 4
Pescados Capitales 6
Punta Sal 14
Quattro D 9
Trattoria di Mambrino 2
Vivaldino 16

Hotels ▼

Hostal Buena Vista 3
Hotel San Augustin
Colonial 7
DoubleTree El Pardo
Hotel 6
El Carmelo 11
Hostal Torreblanca 8
Hotel Antigua Miraflores ... 9
La Castellana 2

La Paz Apart Hotel 1
Las Palmas 10
Marriott Hotel & Stellaris
Casino 12
Miraflores Park Plaza 13
San Antonio Abad 5
Sonesta Posadas del Inca .. 4

2

spicy stewed duck). The Desgustación, a four-course meal with six items in each course, lets you sample an array of dishes. The wine list has several top South American vintages. ■TIP→ The cozy bar in back is a good spot for appetizers, or a light meal in the early evening, when most restaurants are closed. ⊠ *Bolognesi 460, Miraflores* ☎ *01/444–5310* ⊕ *www. brujasdecachiche.com.pe* ▭ *AE, DC, MC, V* ☉ *Closed Sun. night.*

$ ✕ **Café Café.** The drink of choice is the cappuccino calypso, combining a
CAFÉ jolt of joe with frangelica, Kahlua, and rum. Don't worry—you can still order your espresso straight up. Most people forgo the food, but that's a shame, as the roast-beef sandwich is a sizzling slab of meat atop a wedge of crusty bread. Even the BLT is decadent, served open-face with huge chunks of avocado. This is a see-and-be-seen kind of place. Tables on the sidewalk give you an unobstructed view of Parque Miraflores. ⊠ *Martir Olaya 250, Miraflores* ☎ *01/445–1165* ▭ *AE, DC, MC, V.*

$$$ ✕ **El Rincón Gaucho.** The cowhides and the paintings of gauchos on the
STEAK walls don't let you forget that this is a steak house. Even the menus are made of hand-tooled leather. But the abundant wine bottles are a reminder that man can't live on beef alone. The Argentine beef, always sliced to order, is displayed just inside the front door. If you want variety, try the *parrillada*, a mixed grill of steaks, kidneys, liver, pork chops, and blood pudding. The order for two will easily satisfy three people. You can't go wrong with a *bife de chorizo*, a thick sirloin cut. A handful of tables have views of the distant sea. ⊠ *Av. Armendariz 580, Miraflores* ☎ *01/447–4778* ▭ *AE, DC, MC, V* ☉ *No dinner Sun.*

$$ ✕ **El Señorío de Sulco.** It's no surprise that the food is so good when you
PERUVIAN learn that owner Isabel Alvarez has authored several cookbooks. The antique cooking vessels hanging on the walls reveal her passion for traditional Peruvian cuisine. Start with one of various cebiches, or *chupe de camarones* (a creamy river prawn soup) if in season, then move on to *arroz con pato* (rice and duck with a splash of dark beer), *congrio sudado* (a tender whitefish in a spicy broth), or *huatia sulcana* (a traditional beef stew). ■TIP→ Lunch buffets from Thursday to Sunday offer an excellent opportunity to sample a variety of Peruvian cuisine. ⊠ *Malecón Cisneros 1470, Miraflores* ☎ *01/441–0389* ⊕ *www.senoriodesulco.com* ▭ *AE, DC, MC, V* ☉ *No dinner Sun.*

$$ ✕ **Huaca Pucllana.** You feel like a part of history at this beautiful restau-
PERUVIAN rant, which faces the ruins of a 1,500-year-old pyramid. Rough-hewn
Fodor's Choice columns hold up the dining room's soaring ceiling, but the best tables
★ are outside, with a view of the Huaca, which is spectacularly lit at night. ■TIP→ A 20-minute, partial tour of those ruins is available to restaurant customers from 7:30–10:30, except on Tuesday. The *novo andino* cuisine served here improves on old recipes, such as *pastel de choclo* (a corn and beef casserole) and *chupe de corvina* (a creamy sea bass soup). It is one of the few places you can try *paiche*, an Amazon fish whose meat resembles swordfish, and the *cabrito al horno* (roasted kid) is simply a work of art. ⊠ *Av. General Borgoño cuadra 8 s/n, Miraflores* ☎ *01/445–4042* ⊕ *www.resthuacapucllana.com* ≜ *Reservations essential* ▭ *AE, DC, MC, V.*

¢ ✕ **La Buena Esquina.** If you're planning a picnic, stop by this little corner
CAFÉ bakery for tempting prepared sandwiches, such as the *tres jamones*,

piled high with three kinds of ham. If you're a do-it-yourselfer, buy a baguette and some cheese and you're all set. The Good Corner is also a nice spot for afternoon coffee and pastries. ⊠ *Av. José Galvez and Av. Jorge Chavez, Miraflores* ☎ *01/241–8603* ═ *MC, V* ⊘ *Closed Sun. after 2.*

$$
SEAFOOD
Fodor's Choice
★

✕ **La Mar.** Chef Gastón Acurio's reinvention of the traditional cebichería is not only one of Lima's most popular lunch spots, it is also the model for a franchise now found in six cities including San Francisco. The decor is minimalist with plenty of rock, bamboo, and palms along one wall, but the menu is kaleidoscopic. Start by sharing a *degustación de cebiche* (various types of fish or seafood marinated in lime juice), or a *bandeja de causas* (various mashed potato appetizers with seafood and mayonnaise fillings), then try the *saltado Pacífico* (sautéed seafood served over squash ravioli), *anticuchos de pulpo* (grilled octopus in a garlic, parsley sauce atop squashed potatoes), or the catch of the day. The servings tend to be large. ■ TIP➔ They don't take reservations, so arrive before 1, or you'll wait for a table. ⊠ *Av. La Mar 770, Miraflores* ☎ *01/421–3365* ⊕ *www.lamarcebicheria.com* ═ *AE, DC, MC, V* ⊘ *Lunch only.*

$$$
SEAFOOD

✕ **La Rosa Náutica.** One of the most recognizable landmarks in Miraflores, La Rosa Náutica is housed in a rambling Victorian-style building at the end of a prominent pier. The gazebo-like dining room has views of the surrounding sea, where surfers ride the breakers by day. Signature appetizers include grilled scallops topped with a chili sauce and tuna carpaccio. Sea bass is served various ways, such as sautéed in a pernod sauce with scallops and shrimp, or grilled with a leek fondue sauce. The meat dishes include chateaubriand, and you can't go wrong with the daily specials. For dessert, try the *crepes suchard* filled with ice cream and topped with hot fudge. ⊠ *Espigón 4, Miraflores* ☎ *01/447–0057* ⊕ *www.larosanautica.com* ═ *AE, DC, MC, V.*

$$
SWISS

✕ **La Tiendecita Blanca.** A shiny brass espresso machine is the only modern touch at this old-fashioned eatery that first flung open its doors in 1937. The fancifully painted woodwork on the doors and along the ceiling and the honey-color baby grand conjure up the Old Country. *Rösti* (grated potatoes with bacon and cheese) and five kinds of fondue, including a tasty version with ripe tomatoes, are among the traditional choices, but you may want to fast-forward to dessert, as the glass case is filled with eye-popping pies and pastries. You can also do as the locals do and sit outside on the terrace, the perfect people-watching spot. ⊠ *Av. José Larco 111, Miraflores* ☎ *01/445–9797* ═ *AE, DC, MC, V.*

$
ARGENTINE

✕ **Mavery.** This small restaurant on busy Avenida del Ejercito evokes a log cabin with its tables made from sliced tree trunks and rustic log walls. But this cabin belongs in the Pampa, since they specialize in that favorite Argentine snack: the empanada. They offer nine types of deep fried empanadas, from the traditional *carne* (ground beef) to *cangrejo y queso* (crab meat and cheese) and ají de gallina, as well as dozens of pizzas and several pasta dishes. Another option is *pastel de choclo* (corn casserole with beef, rasins, and olives). The food and prices make this a popular nightspot. ⊠ *Av. Del Ejercito 182, Miraflores* ☎ *01/441–3134* ═ *AE, DC, MC, V.*

\$\$ ✕ **Panchita.** Miraflores' premier steak house is more than that, since in
STEAK   addition to prime cuts of Brazilian and USDA beef, the menu features
such Peruvian specialties as *cochinillo* (roast suckling pig) with *tacu tacu* (mixed rice and beans) and grilled Chilean salmon. The U.S. beef is pricy, but the Brazilian beef is excellent. Try one of the Argentine malbecs on the wine list. The airy dining room has minimal decoration, but the colorful bar in the corner has a wild collection of statues and handblown glass. The service is also first-rate. It's no wonder the place is usually packed. ⊠ *Av. Dos de Mayo 298, Miraflores* ☎ *01/242–5957* ⊟ *AE, DC, MC, V* ☉ *No dinner Sun.*

\$\$ ✕ **Pescados Capitales.** If you can't get a table at La Mar, take a taxi six
SEAFOOD   blocks down the street to this vast, whitewashed restaurant with a beach ambience. The name is a play on the Spanish term for the seven deadly sins, but the only one they're promoting is gluttony, quite effectively at that. Consider such starters as *tequeños capitales* (shrimp egg-rolls), tuna cebiche, or grilled octopus. The entrée called Gluttony, grilled rockfish in a crispy garlic sauce, is a sin worth committing, but so are Envy (sole and prawns in a tomato sauce over rice), shrimp *picante* (in a spicy cream sauce), and *arroz con mariscos* (rice with seafood). So toss morality to the wind, and dig in! ■TIP→ This place is very close to San Isidro and it's the only cebichería that opens for dinner. ⊠ *Av. La Mar 1337, Miraflores* ☎ *01/421–8808* ⊕ *www.pescados-capitales.com* ⊟ *AE, DC, MC, V.*

\$ ✕ **Punta Sal.** On a sunny afternoon, the view of the sea and the para-
SEAFOOD   gliders from the upper floors of this restaurant is as good as the food.
Fodor's Choice   But the real excitement is on the platters streaming out of the kitchen,
★   such as the *tiradito criollo* (thin slices of marinated fish covered in a yellow pepper sauce), or *conchitas a la parmesana* (scallops in shells smothered in toasted cheese). *Piqueos*, platters with various dishes, are fun to share. This is also one of the few cebicherías that serves carpaccio. You can have your sole or sea bass cooked one of 10 different ways, including *al ajillo* (sautéed with garlic), *a la Chorrillana* (in a tomato, onion and chile sauce), or *en salsa de mariscos* (in a seafood sauce). ■TIP→ Arrive before 1 or call ahead to get a window table on the third floor; the view is what tips the scale and makes this a Fodor's Choice. ⊠ *Malecón Cisneros Cda. 3, esq. Av. Tripoli, Miraflores* ☎ *01/242–4524* ⊕ *www.puntasal.com* ⊟ *AE, DC, MC, V* ☉ *No dinner.*

\$ ✕ **Quattro D.** An emerald-green awning won't allow you to miss this
CAFÉ   café, a favorite among young couples on dates and harried parents with children in tow. They serve various pastas, sandwiches, and economical lunch specials, but most people come here for one thing: ice cream. They make and sell more than 50 varieties of gelato. Among the sassier tropical flavors are tamarindo, *coco* (coconut), and the local fruits chirimoya and lúcuma. ■TIP→ It's a good spot for a break if you walk to or from the nearby archaeological site of Pucllana. Grab a table by the window to choose from the daily specials. ⊠ *Av. Angamos Oeste 408, Miraflores* ☎ *01/445–4228* ⊟ *AE, MC, V.*

\$\$ ✕ **Trattoria di Mambrino.** After a quarter century in business, this trattoria
ITALIAN   remains one of Lima's best restaurants. You can watch cooks stuff the ravioli and drape the fettuccine on long wooden rods in the kitchen.

But the proof is on the plate: delicious dishes like artichoke ravioli and fettuccine magnifico (with a prosciutto, parmesan, and white truffle sauce) leave you satisfied but not stuffed. ■TIP→ Be sure to leave room for dessert. Co-owner Sandra Plevisanni is one of the country's best pastry chefs, so it would be a crime to leave without trying one of her creations. The only caveat is the service, which can be lackadaisical. ⊠ *Manuel Bonilla 106, Miraflores* ☎ *01/446–7002* ⊟ *AE, MC, V.*

$$ ✕**Vivaldino.** Wrought-iron tables covered with crisp white linens distin-
CONTINENTAL guish this classic eatery. Tall windows let you gaze down at the ocean; for an even better view, sit outside. The menu tends toward Mediterranean-style fare. Try the *solomillo caprese* (bits of steak with tomatoes and mozzarella cheese) or the *corvina princesa* (grilled sea bass and scallops with potato mousseline and fried artichoke hearts). If the dessert cart includes a mousse made with *lucuma*, a local fruit, snap one up immediately. ⊠ *Larcomar, Malecón de la Reserva and Av. José Larco, Miraflores* ☎ *01/446–3859* ⊕ *www.vivaldino.com* ⊟ *AE, MC, V.*

SAN ISIDRO

Most of San Isidro's restaurants are on or near Avenida Conquistadores, the neighborhood's main drag.

$ ✕**Chez Philippe.** Though French often connotes fancy, this laid-back
FRENCH restaurant is all about enjoying hearty food at comfortable prices. You enter through a small shop that sells fresh breads and homemade paté to a dining room that evokes a country home. The most popular seating is on a covered terrace in back, hemmed by greenery and stacked wood for the oven. The owner is from Alsace, so in addition to French standards such as duck in orange sauce and chicken cordon bleu, he offers *choucroute* (homemade sauerkraut with sausages and pork) and *knepfle* (sautéed pasta nuggets known as *spaetzle* in Germanic countries). Another house specialty is *trucha al horno* (baked trout). ■TIP→ They also serve some of the best pizza, and have the largest selection of European beers, in town. ⊠ *Av. Dos de Mayo 748, San Isidro* ☎ *01/222–4953* ⊕ *www.chez-philippe.net* ⊟ *MC, V* ⊘ *Closed Sun.*

$ ✕**Como Agua Para Chocolate.** You can't miss this cantina—the three-story
MEXICAN structure is an eye-catching yellow trimmed with royal blue. Once you duck in, you'll realize that the dining rooms are in equally vivid shades of red and green. Happily, the food doesn't pale in comparison. Among the house specialties are *barbacoa de cordero*, which is lamb steamed in avocado leaves, *pescado a la veracruzana*, fish in a slightly spicy tomato sauce, and *albóndagas al chipotle*, spicy meatballs served with yellow rice. They also offer meat or vegetarian tacos, burritos, and enchiladas. Whatever you choose, wash it down with the best margarita in town. If you want to take home some of the magic, there's a stand selling the namesake sweets. ⊠ *Pancho Fierro 108, San Isidro* ☎ *01/222–0174* ⊟ *AE, DC, MC, V* ⊘ *Closed Sun.*

$$ ✕**Lima 27.** There's no sign on this dark grey mansion, and at night,
PERUVIAN the somber edifice with a bright red foyer looks like Dracula's love shack. Step inside and veer right, and you enter one of Lima's hippest lounges with a colorful light display complemented by house music.

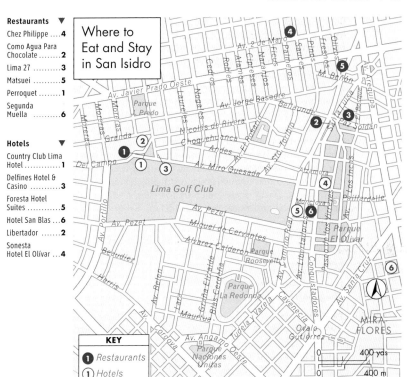

Restaurants ▼

Chez Philippe **4**

Como Agua Para
Chocolate **2**

Lima 27 ....**3**

Matsuei **5**

Perroquet **1**

Segunda
Muella **6**

Hotels ▼

Country Club Lima
Hotel **1**

Delfines Hotel &
Casino **3**

Foresta Hotel
Suites **5**

Hotel San Blas ...**6**

Libertador **2**

Sonesta
Hotel El Olívar ...**4**

**Where to
Eat and Stay
in San Isidro**

KEY

❶ *Restaurants*

① *Hotels*

The dining room, to the left, is more subdued, and the tables on the terrace, backed by a brick wall, are a lovely option when it isn't too cool. The food is Peruvian fusion: creative variations on Lima standards and local interpretations of Continental cuisine. The results include *risotto de camarones* (river prawn risotto), *cabrito lechón* (roast kid), *atún sellado* (seared tuna steak in a sesame and pepper crust), and *gnocchis crocantes* (crispy gnocchi smothered in a mushroom and artichoke heart ragout). The Count never had it so good. ⊠ *Santa Luisa 295, San Isidro* ☎ *01/422–8915* ▭ *AE, DC, MC, V* ⊗ *Closed 4–7, no dinner Sun.*

$$ ✕**Matsuei.** Chefs often shout out a greeting as you enter the teak-floored
JAPANESE dining room of this San Isidro standout. Widely considered the best Japanese restaurant in town, Matsuei specializes in sushi and sashimi. If raw is not your thing, they also offer plenty of hot food such as tempuras, teriyakis, and the house specialty *kushiyak*, a broiled filet with a ginger-flavored sauce. There's plenty for vegetarians, including *goma nasu,* Japanese eggplant grilled to perfection and served with a sweet sesame glaze. Sushi fans often sit at the bar, but there are tables on two floors and private rooms for groups. ⊠ *Manuel Bañón 260, San Isidro* ☎ *01/422–4323* ▭ *AE, DC, MC, V* ⊗ *Closed Sun.*

$$$ ✕**Perroquet.** There's not a more elegant dining room than Perroquet,
PERUVIAN tucked away in the Country Club Lima Hotel. You feel pampered in the main room, with its upholstered chairs and tables almost overloaded

with polished crystal and china. If it's a warm enough evening, you might prefer the terrace and its brass chandeliers. The atmosphere never feels stuffy, and neither does the menu. There are traditional dishes, but they have a modern flair. Try the lamb shank roasted for three hours in red wine and cilantro seeds, or the *corvina pintera asada* (sea bass sautéed in a lemon-orange butter). After dinner, retire to the English Bar for an aperitif. ⊠ *Country Club Hotel, Los Eucaliptos 50, San Isidro* ☎ *511/611–9000* ⚍ *Reservations essential* ⚍ *AE, D, DC, MC, V.*

$ **✕ Segundo Muelle.** Located in busy Avenida Conquistadores, this sleek
SEAFOOD seafood restaurant is one of Lima's most popular cebicherías. Choose from 10 different types of lip-smacking cebiche, or head straight for the *corvina a lo macho* (sea bass in a seafood sauce) or *chita al plato*, a whole fish grilled to perfection. They also have a selection of excellent rice and pasta dishes, such as *tortellines rellenos de cangrejo y ricotta* (cheese and crab tortellini). ⊠ *Av. Conquistadores 490, San Isidro* ☎ *01/421–1206* ⊕ *www.segundomuelle.com* ⚍ *AE, DC, MC, V* ☼ *No dinner.*

WHERE TO STAY

	Neighborhood Vibe	Pros	Cons
BARRANCO	Bohemian, historic atmosphere, appeals to younger people	Neighborhood vibe	Plenty of bars and restaurants, lovely architecture
EL CENTRO	Colonial-era splendor	Walking distance to the city's best-known sights	Clogged with traffic by day, deserted at night
MIRAFLORES	Bustling neighborhood filled with parks and galleries	Hundreds of dining options, seaside setting, pretty parks	Traffic noise permeates even the side streets
SAN ISIDRO	Mostly residential area with a few commercial strips	Peace and quiet, especially around Parque El Olivar	No major sights, a bit far from the action

THE SCENE
Lima isn't lacking for lodging—you can't go far before you see the flurry of flags above a doorway indicating that international travelers are welcome. If you have some money to spend, the capital has some astonishing accommodations. For something special, pass by the towers of glass and steel and head to such charmers as the Miraflores Park Plaza, the Country Club Lima Hotel, or the Gran Hotel Bolívar.

The area around the airport is a mix of factories and sketchy neighborhoods. The only decent lodging option here is the rather pricy Hotel Costa del Sol Ramada, which is next to the terminal. The next closest hotels are in El Centro, 20 to 40 minutes away, depending on traffic.

PLANNING
There are plenty of low-cost lodgings in Lima, many of them on quiet streets in the Miraflores and Barranco. These areas are safe, so you don't have to worry about taking a stroll during the day, and they're

quick cab rides to El Centro. The only decent hotel near the airport is in its parking lot, and is quite pricy, but it's just a 30-minute drive to the historic center, except during rush hour.

Although the historic center is safer than it once was, it has few decent hotels. If you decide to stay near the heart of the city, remember that you really can't go for a stroll at night. You'll also have far fewer options in terms of bars and restaurants than in other neighborhoods.

WHAT IT COSTS IN NUEVO SOLES					
	¢	$	$$	$$$	$$$$
HOTELS	under S/125	S/125–S/250	S/251–S/375	S/376–S/500	over S/500

Hotel prices are for a standard double room in high season, excluding tax.

AIRPORT

$$$$ ☎ **Hotel Costa del Sol Ramada.** Lima's only airport hotel is in the parking lot of the international airport. They make up for the view with a soothing, minimalist interior and an array of services. Sleek, carpeted rooms have long desks and picture windows with double glass to insulate you from the airport noise. Those on the terminal side of the hotel are quieter. The ground floor holds a hip little lounge, a restaurant that serves Peruvian fusion cuisine, and offers 24-hour room service, and a full spa with sauna, Jacuzzi, and dipping pool. ■TIP→ For $55, nonguests can get a 30-minute massage and use the spa for up to five hours. **Pros:** next to the airport; excellent rooms and facilities. **Cons:** expensive; some street noise. ⊠ *Aeropuerto Internacional Jorge Chávez, Av. Elmer Faucett s/n* ☎ *01/711–2000* ⊕ *www.costadelsolperu.com* ➦ *120 rooms, 10 suites* ⚷ *In-room: a/c, safe, refrigerator, DVD, Wi-Fi. In-hotel: restaurant, room service, bar, gym, spa, laundry service, Internet terminal, Wi-Fi hotspot, parking (paid)* ⊟ *AE, DC, MC, V* ⎮⊚⎮ *BP.*

BARRANCO

¢   ☎ **La Quinta de Allison.** On a busy side street in Barranco, this unassuming hotel is one of the cheapest places in the neighborhood. Rooms are on the small side, but are perfectly comfortable, considering the rates. A few of the more expensive rooms have whirlpool tubs. All of the neighborhood sights are within blocks. **Pros:** near dozens of restaurants; relatively clean and comfortable. **Cons:** basic rooms; busy street. ⊠ *Jr. 28 de Julio 281, Barranco* ☎ *01/247–1515* ➦ *20 rooms* ⚷ *In-room: no phone, no a/c, Wi-Fi. In-hotel: laundry service, Internet terminal* ⊟ *MC, V.*

$$ ☎ **Second Home Peru.** This 100-year-old, Tudor-style house on a cliff
Fodor'sChoice   overlooking the sea is Lima's most romantic lodging option. The home
★   and gallery of sculptor and painter Victor Delfin, it is a feast for the eyes, packed with art and backed by a sweeping view of the coast. Guest rooms are on the second floor with hardwood floors, high wooden ceilings and simple furnishings; rooms 2 and 3 have ocean views. The

gardens—decorated with massive sculptures and mosaic walls—and the surreal jaguar pool are idyllic spots to relax or sunbathe from January to May. Lilian Delfin can help with travel arrangements. **Pros:** gorgeous; quiet; near restaurants and bars. **Cons:** limited guest services; toilets, sinks, and shower facilities in rooms 3 and 4 are not a separate room. ⊠ *Ca. Domeyer 366, Barranco* ☎ *01/247–5522* ⊕ *www. secondhomeperu.com* ⤴ *5 rooms* ⌂ *In-room: no phone, no a/c, safe, DVD, Wi-Fi. In-hotel: laundry service, Wi-Fi hotspot, parking (free)* ⊟ *AE, MC, V.*

EL CENTRO

$ 🏨 **Gran Hotel Bolívar.** Tastes may have changed since 1924, but this grande dame retains the grandeur of the days when guests included Ernest Hemingway. As you enter the marble-columned rotunda, your eyes are drawn upward to the magnificent stained-glass dome. Off to one side is the wood-paneled bar, which remains as popular as ever. ■ TIP➔ The tables on the terrace are the perfect place to enjoy a pisco sour or a meal. A grand staircase sweeps you up to the rooms, which retain lovely touches like parquet floors, but have suffered years of neglect. They may lack some comforts and services, but for the price, it's a bargain. Pay the extra $10 for a suite, or get a standard room in front to enjoy an unforgettable view of Plaza San Martín. **Pros:** atmosphere to spare; convenient location; good value. **Cons:** furnishings are a bit threadbare; on a busy corner. ⊠ *Jr. de la Unión 958, El Centro* ☎ *01/619–7171* ⊕ *www.granhotelbolivar.com.pe* ⤴ *120 rooms, 5 suites* ⌂ *In-room: no a/c. In-hotel: 2 restaurants, room service, bar, laundry service, Internet terminal, Wi-Fi hotspot, parking (free)* ⊟ *AE, DC, MC, V* ⏏ *CP.*

¢ 🏨 **Inka Path.** The price is the main selling point of this downtown hotel. A double room for less than $40 makes this one of the city's best bargains. But you also get charm, as this second-floor lodging has rooms with double doors leading to balconies that overlook a colonial-era church. Rooms are scrupulously clean; get a suite, or room 214, 215, 216, or 217 if available. **Pros:** on a pedestrian street; near the major sites; welcoming staff. **Cons:** area unsafe after 10. ⊠ *Jirón de la Union 654, El Centro* ☎ *01/426–1919* ⊕ *hotelinkapath.com* ⤴ *18 rooms* ⌂ *In-room: no a/c, Wi-Fi. In-hotel: restaurant, room service, bar, laundry service, Internet terminal, Wi-Fi hotspot* ⊟ *MC, V* ⏏ *CP.*

$ 🏨 **Kamana Hotel.** Less than three blocks from the Plaza de Armas, this hotel puts you right in the middle of things. All the downtown sights are a short walk away. The best part is the price. Traditional textiles make each room a little different, and although rooms facing the street are sunnier, inside rooms get less traffic noise. The improbably named café, Mr. Koala, serves everything from Peruvian to Italian fare. **Pros:** close to the main square and dining options. **Cons:** a bit sterile; on a busy street; neighborhood dangerous late at night. ⊠ *Jr. Camaná 547, El Centro* ☎ *01/427–7106* ⊕ *www.hotelkamana.com* ⤴ *44 rooms* ⌂ *In-room: a/c, safe, Wi-Fi. In-hotel: room service, bar, laundry service, Internet terminal, Wi-Fi hotspot, parking (free)* ⊟ *AE, DC, MC, V* ⏏ *BP.*

2

$$$$ ⛆ **Sheraton Lima Hotel.** This massive hotel is a landmark, as its concrete facade is visible from far away. Perfectly serviceable rooms have subdued colors and surround a vast internal courtyard. There are two buffet restaurants in the lobby; La Cupula, a Brazilian-style rodizio, serves grilled meats at your table, whereas the less expense Las Palmeras has a folklore show on Friday nights. Popular with business travelers, as it has meeting rooms and a convention center, tourists appreciate its proximity to the city's historical district. The hotel is near the expressway, so it's also a short drive to San Isidro and Miraflores. **Pros:** plenty of amenities; central location. **Cons:** nothing Peruvian about the decor; neighborhood is dicey at night. ⊠ *Paseo de la República 170, El Centro* ☎ *01/315–5000* ⊕ *www.sheraton.com* ⇱ *410 rooms, 21 suites* ♻ *In-room: a/c, safe, Internet. In-hotel: 2 restaurants, room service, bar, tennis court, pool, gym, spa, laundry service, Internet terminal, Wi-Fi hotspot, parking (free)* ▭ *AE, DC, MC, V* �Ⓞ *BP.*

MIRAFLORES

$$$$ ⛆ **DoubleTree El Pardo Hotel.** This is one hotel where you won't want to go straight to your room. The open-air café on the ground floor is a great place for a cocktail, the rooftop pool and hot tub have a sweeping urban view, and the health club is among the city's best. This is a popular business hotel, so there is a well-stocked business center and half a dozen meeting rooms, but the restaurant offers a nightly folk dancing show that draws plenty of tourists. The casino next door does little for the look of the hotel, unfortunately. **Pros:** lots of services; near dining options; walking distance from Miraflores sights. **Cons:** impersonal feel. ⊠ *Jr. Independencia 141, Miraflores* ☎ *01/617–1000* ⊕ *www.doubletree.com* ⇱ *137 rooms, 18 suites* ♻ *In-room: a/c, safe, refrigerator, Wi-Fi. In-hotel: 2 restaurants, room service, bar, pool, gym, laundry service, Internet terminal, Wi-Fi hotspot, parking (free)* ▭ *AE, DC, MC, V* ⓄⒷ *BP.*

¢ ⛆ **El Carmelo.** A stone's throw from Parque del Amor, this little hotel is also just four blocks from Parque Miraflores. Simply furnished rooms with polished parquet floors are clean and comfortable. Some have interior windows; those facing the street are much brighter, though they get a lot of traffic noise. Guests mingle in a little bar in the lobby. **Pros:** a block from the oceanfront park; good value. **Cons:** basic rooms on a busy street. ⊠ *Bolognesi 749, Miraflores* ☎ *01/446–0575* ⊕ *www. hostalelcarmelo.com.pe* ⇱ *31 rooms* ♻ *In-room: no a/c, Wi-Fi. In-hotel: restaurant, room service, bar, laundry service, Internet terminal, Wi-Fi hotspot* ▭ *AE, MC, V.*

$ ⛆ **Hostal Buena Vista.** This colonial-style house furnished with antiques and hemmed by an exuberant garden is one of Lima's loveliest B&Bs. Rooms vary a lot, but those on the second floor have high, beamed ceilings and hardwood floors. Four rooms in exterior wings have terraces overlooking the garden, but they get a lot of street noise; downstairs interior rooms are the quietest. Complimentary breakfast is served on an interior patio with Spanish tiles on the walls and a parrot in an iron cage. **Pros:** charming house; near restaurants and bars; good value.

Cons: street noise, especially in rooms 13 and 14. ✉ *Grimaldo del Solar 202, Miraflores* 🕾 *01/447–3178* ⊕ *www.hostalbuenavista.com* ⇱ *16 rooms* ♿ *In-room: a/c, Internet (some), Wi-Fi (some). In-hotel: laundry service, Internet terminal, Wi-Fi hotspot* ⊟ *AE, D, DC, MC, V* ⵘ *BP.*

$ 🛏 **Hostal Torreblanca.** The name refers to the little white tower on the top floor of this rust-colored, colonial style building. It is an eclectic yet distinctive spot with a fireplace in the lobby and plenty of rounded walls decorated with framed, antique weavings. Although the hotel is a little far from the center of Miraflores, it's just a block from a park overlooking the ocean and is near several good restaurants. Locals frequent the hotel's restaurant, which has a huge grill for sizzling steaks. **Pros:** lots of atmosphere; near oceanfront park. **Cons:** on a busy traffic circle; long walk to center. ✉ *Av. José Pardo 1453, Miraflores* 🕾 *01/242–1876* ⊕ *www.torreblancaperu.com* ⇱ *30 rooms* ♿ *In-room: no a/c, refrigerator, Wi-Fi (some). In-hotel: restaurant, room service, bar, laundry service, Internet terminal, Wi-Fi hotspot* ⊟ *AE, DC, MC, V* ⵘ *BP.*

$$ 🛏 **Hotel Antigua Miraflores.** In a salmon-color mansion dating back nearly a century, this elegantly appointed hotel is one of the city's loveliest. Black-and-white marble floors and crystal chandeliers greet you as you stroll through the antique-filled lobby. Up the wooden staircase are guest rooms with hand-carved furniture. Those in front have more character, whereas the newer rooms in back surround a courtyard garden with a graceful fountain. Known for its friendly service, the hotel sees repeat business year after year. A small restaurant serves complimentary breakfasts and traditional Peruvian fare. **Pros:** gorgeous architecture; pleasant staff; short walk from restaurants. **Cons:** newer rooms have less charm. ✉ *Grau 350, Miraflores* 🕾 *01/241–6116* ⊕ *www.peru-hotels-inns.com* ⇱ *79 rooms* ♿ *In-room: a/c (some), safe, refrigerator (some), Wi-Fi. In-hotel: restaurant, room service, laundry service, Internet terminal, Wi-Fi hotspot, parking (free)* ⊟ *AE, DC, MC, V* ⵘ *BP.*

Fodor's Choice
★

$ 🛏 **Hotel San Agustín Colonial.** Elaborately carved wooden balconies accentuate the facade of this sky-blue colonial-style hotel, part of the small San Agustín chain. A huge fireplace dominates the lobby, where a graceful arch leads to the airy restaurant serving traditional fare. Religious relics such as heavy iron crosses decorate the common areas found on every floor. Rooms leading off the wrought-iron staircase have nice touches like wood wainscoting and beamed ceilings. One especially nice touch is the minuscule yet (or therefore?) charming bar, with a vault ceiling, padded wallpaper, and antique piano. **Pros:** atmosphere; value. **Cons:** on busy street; additions mar beauty of old house; off the beaten path. ✉ *Commandante Espinar 310, Miraflores* 🕾 *01/241–7471* ⊕ *www.hotelessanagustin.com.pe* ⇱ *34 rooms* ♿ *In-room: a/c, safe, refrigerator, Wi-Fi. In-hotel: restaurant, room service, bars, laundry service, Internet terminal* ⊟ *AE, DC, MC, V.*

$ 🛏 **La Castellana.** This exuberantly neoclassical structure resembles a small castle. The foyer and restaurant have wrought-iron lanterns and stained-glass windows. Rooms in the original house are lovely, especially No. 10, which overlooks the courtyard, and No. 15, which has a private balcony facing the street. Unfortunately, most rooms are in a newer annex and short on personality. Complimentary breakfast can be

Changing of the guard, Peru-style, in front of the Palacio de Gobierno (Government Palace), in El Centro.

taken in the lovely courtyard, and there is a cozy lounge/meeting room in back. This inn is quite popular and often fills up with tour groups, so make reservations well in advance. **Pros:** gorgeous colonial-style building; walking distance from restaurants. **Cons:** neighborhood can be noisy; newer section lacks charm. ⊠ *Grimaldo del Solar 222, Miraflores* ☎ *01/444–3530* ⊕ *www.castellanahotel.com* ☞ *42 rooms* ⌂ *In-room: no a/c, safe, refrigerator. In-hotel: restaurant, laundry service, Internet terminal, Wi-Fi hotspot* ▤ *AE, DC, MC, V* ⦿| *BP.*

$$ ☖ **La Paz Apart Hotel.** Each suite at this five-story hotel has a compact kitchenette and dining/living room in front and a bedroom in back, making it perfect for anyone staying for more than a few days. The decor is clean and simple, with modern furnishings and lots of big windows. It's an easy walk from dozens of shops, restaurants, and Parque Miraflores. **Pros:** near dozens of restaurants; friendly staff. **Cons:** lacks a Peruvian feel; street noise. ⊠ *Av. La Paz 679, Miraflores* ☎ *01/242–9350* ⊕ *www.lapazaparthotel.com* ☞ *22 suites* ⌂ *In-room: a/c, safe, kitchen, refrigerator, Wi-Fi. In-hotel: restaurant, room service, laundry service, Internet terminal, Wi-Fi hotspot* ▤ *AE, DC, MC, V* ⦿| *BP.*

$ ☖ **Las Palmas.** A block from Parque Miraflores, this apricot-color building puts you in the heart of a popular bar district. The paneled lobby and wood staircase call to mind an older European pension. Upstairs, things are more modern. Many of the simply furnished rooms are on the small side, so ask to see a few before you decide. **Pros:** inexpensive; near dozens of restaurants. **Cons:** basic rooms; near some noisy bars. ⊠ *Calle Bellavista 320, Miraflores* ☎ *01/444–6033* ⊕ *www.hotellaspalmas.com* ☞ *66 rooms, 3 suites* ⌂ *In-room: a/c (some), In-hotel: restaurant, room*

service, bar, laundry service, Internet terminal, Wi-Fi hotspot ⊟ *AE,
DC, MC, V* ⌷⍥⌷ *CP.*

$$$$ ⍟ **Marriott Hotel & Stellaris Casino.** This isn't a hotel—it's a small city. Just
about anything you long for, whether it's a chocolate-chip cookie or
diamond earrings, can be had in the shops downstairs. If not, there's the
Larcomar shopping center across the street. The views are spectacular
from this glass tower, which forever altered the skyline of Miraflores
when it opened. On clear days the entire coastline is visible. As if that
weren't reason enough to stay here, watercolors of traditional Andean
scenes grace the walls to remind you that you're in Peru. The Stellaris Casino is one of the city's most popular. **Pros:** impressive ocean
views; near many restaurants. **Cons:** expensive; on a busy intersection. ⊠ *Malecón de la Reserva 615, Miraflores* ☎ *01/217–7000* ⊕ *www.
marriotthotels.com* ⊅ *288 rooms, 12 suites* ⌂ *In-room: a/c, safe, refrigerator, Wi-Fi. In-hotel: 2 restaurants, room service, bar, tennis court,
pool, gym, spa, laundry service, Internet terminal, Wi-Fi hotspot, parking (free)* ⊟ *AE, DC, MC, V.*

$$$$ ⍟ **Miraflores Park Plaza.** From the moment you step into the elegant
Fodor's Choice   lobby with its gleaming marble floors and high columns, it is clear that
★   this is one of the city's best hotels. The ocean-view rooms are gorgeous,
and if you think the view from your room is breathtaking, just head
up to the rooftop pool overlooking the entire coastline. The city-view
rooms, on the other hand, overlook an uninspiring collection of apartment buildings. Rooms have sitting areas that make them seem like
suites, sumptuous beds and large marble bathrooms. For couples, suites
have hot tubs strategically close to the beds. The chic Mesa 18 restaurant serves excellent nouveau Peruvian cuisine, whereas the Dr. Jekyll
and Mr. Hyde bar resembles an English pub, with a snooker table in the
mezzanine. **Pros:** amazing ocean views; lots of atmosphere; on a lovely
park. **Cons:** very expensive; city-view rooms disappointing. ⊠ *Malecón
de la Reserva 1035, Miraflores* ☎ *01/610–4000* ⊕ *www.mirafloorespark.
com* ⊅ *64 rooms, 17 suites* ⌂ *In-room: a/c, safe, refrigerator, Wi-Fi. In-
hotel: 2 restaurants, room service, bar, pool, gym, spa, laundry service,
Internet terminal, Wi-Fi hotspot, parking (free)* ⊟ *AE, MC, V.*

$ ⍟ **San Antonio Abad.** This mansion in a residential neighborhood east
of the Via Express makes up for its slightly-off-the-beaten-path location with ambiance and service. The rambling old building has various
common areas with colonial-style furniture. A wood staircase leads up
to cozy rooms, many of which have wood floors and beamed ceilings.
Some have balconies that overlook the back patio. The hotel is a short
walk from several parks, including the lovely Parque Reducto, on the
other side of Av Benavides. The shops and restaurants of Miraflores are
a 10-minute walk away. They provide a free airport pickup. **Pros:** pretty
colonial-style building; friendly staff. **Cons:** long walk to restaurants;
on a fairly busy street; some dated furnishings. ⊠ *Ramón Ribeyro 301,
Miraflores* ☎ *01/447–6766* ⊕ *www.hotelsananantonioabad.com* ⊅ *24
rooms* ⌂ *In-room: a/c (some), safe. In-hotel: Internet terminal, Wi-Fi
hotspot* ⊟ *AE, MC, V* ⌷⍥⌷ *BP.*

$$ ⍟ **Sonesta Posada del Inca.** This narrow tower a few blocks from Parque
Miraflores has smaller versions of the rooms at the Sonesta El Olivar

with fewer services, but for a fraction of the price. Carpeted rooms are bright and tastefully decorated. ■**TIP**➔ Get a suite; you'll enjoy twice the room for a little more money. Ask for one with a balcony. There are dozens of restaurants, bars and shops within blocks. **Pros:** good value; convenient location. **Cons:** smallish rooms; some street noise. ⊠ *Alcanfores 329, Miraflores* ☎ *01/241–7688* ⊕ *www.sonestaperu.com* ⤳ *28 rooms* ⌂ *In-room: a/c, safe, refrigerator, Wi-Fi. In-hotel: restaurant, room service, bar, laundry service, Internet terminal, Wi-Fi hotspot, parking (free)* ⊟ *AE, DC, MC, V* ❘⦿❘ *BP.*

SAN ISIDRO

$$$$ ⚏ **Country Club Lima Hotel.** Priceless paintings from the Museo Pedro de
Fodor'sChoice   Osma hang in each room in this luxurious lodging. The colonial-style
★   hotel, dating from 1927, is itself a work of art. Just step into the lobby, where hand-painted tiles reflect the yellows and greens of the stained-glass ceiling. The air of refinement continues in the rooms, with their high ceilings, marble-topped desks and beds draped with fine fabrics. Some have private balconies that overlook the small, oval-shaped pool or the grounds of the adjacent Club Real. Locals frequently come by for high tea from 5 to 8 in the stained-glass atrium bar, or traditional fare in the elegant Perroquet restaurant. **Pros:** architectural gem; doting service; one of the city's best restaurants. **Cons:** a bit removed from the action; newer sections are less charming. ⊠ *Los Eucaliptos 590, San Isidro* ☎ *01/611–9000* ⊕ *www.hotelcountry.com* ⤳ *75 rooms, 7 suites* ⌂ *In-room: a/c, safe, refrigerator, Wi-Fi. In-hotel: restaurant, room service, bar, pool, gym, laundry service, Internet terminal, Wi-Fi hotspot* ⊟ *AE, DC, MC, V* ❘⦿❘ *BP.*

$$$$ ⚏ **Delfines Hotel & Casino.** It's not every day that a pair of dolphins greets you near the entrance of your hotel. Yaku and Wayra do just that in the lobby of this high-rise in San Isidro. Kids love to help feed them as their parents look on from the adjacent café, where crisscrossing ribbons of steel hold aloft the glass roof. Although they're on the small side, the rooms are bright and comfortably furnished, and many have sweeping views of the adjacent Club Lima Golf. **Pros:** good location for business travelers; nice views. **Cons:** expensive for what you get. ⊠ *Los Eucaliptos 555, San Isidro* ☎ *01/215–7000* ⊕ *www.losdelfineshotel. com* ⤳ *173 rooms, 24 suites* ⌂ *In-room: a/c, safe, refrigerator, Wi-Fi. In-hotel: restaurant, room service, bar, pool, gym, spa, laundry service, Internet terminal, Wi-Fi hotspot* ⊟ *AE, DC, MC, V* ❘⦿❘ *BP.*

$$$$ ⚏ **Foresta Hotel & Suites.** With dozens of bars and restaurants within walking distance, this hotel puts you in the middle of the action. It has all the amenities—except a pool—of its neighbors, but the price tag is considerably less. Rooms, decorated in brown and orange, are spacious and have large desks. Sun streams through the windows, double-paned to keep out the noise from the street. Relax with a pisco sour in Aguaymanto, the café in the corner of the lobby. Wheelchair ramps allow free movement for those who can't manage steps. **Pros:** quiet; central location; good value. **Cons:** chain-hotel feel. ⊠ *Av. Libertadores 490, San Isidro* ☎ *01/630–0000* ⊕ *www.libertador.com.pe* ⤳ *45 rooms, 5 suites* ⌂ *In-room: a/c, safe, refrigerator, Wi-Fi. In-hotel: restaurant,* *room service, bar, laundry service, Internet terminal, Wi-Fi hotspot* ⊟ *AE, DC, MC, V* ⏀❘*BP.*

$ ⊞ **Hotel San Blas.** The best deal in San Isidro, this little gem has a budget price tag, but the amenities of a big, expensive hotel. The rooms are big and modern with double-glass picture windows. Economical suites have Jacuzzis that turn the baths into spas. A well-equipped meeting room on the ground floor opens out into a sunny patio. The café in the lobby serves three meals a day. The hotel is a short walk through El Olivar Park to San Isidro restaurants, and a quick taxi or bus ride to Parque Miraflores. **Pros:** spacious rooms; central location; generous breakfast buffet. **Cons:** street noise from a busy boulevard. ⊠ *Av. Arequipa 3940, San Isidro* ☎ *01/222–2601* ⊕ *www.sanblashotel.com* ↪ *38 rooms* ⟁ *In-room: a/c, refrigerator, Wi-Fi. In-hotel: room service, laundry service, Internet terminal, Wi-Fi hotspot* ⊟ *AE, DC, MC, V* ⏀❘*BP.*

$$$$ ⊞ **Libertador San Isidro Golf.** Because this hotel is in the heart of San Isidro's business district, but costs considerably less than nearby properties, it is popular with business travelers who want a good address but are watching their budget. The small lobby is attractive, but lacks any indication that you're in Peru. Rooms are surprisingly quiet and those on upper floors have views of the nearby golf course. They're decorated in bright fabrics and original artwork, which belie the fact that it's a chain resort. **Pros:** nice views; elegant feel. **Cons:** far from most dining options; too formal for families with kids. ⊠ *Los Eucaliptos 550, San Isidro* ☎ *01/518–6300* ⊕ *www.libertador.com.pe* ↪ *53 rooms* ⟁ *In-room: a/c, safe, Wi-Fi. In-hotel: 2 restaurants, room service, bar, gym, laundry service, Internet terminal, Wi-Fi hotspot* ⊟ *AE, DC, MC, V* ⏀❘*BP.*

$$$$ ⊞ **Sonesta Hotel El Olívar.** Standing at the edge of an old olive grove, this
Fodor's Choice luminous hotel has one of the most relaxed settings in San Isidro. This
★ is especially true if you avail yourself of the sundeck and pool on the top floor. Rooms are tastefully decorated; standards are a bit small, but executive rooms are amply proportioned and suites have private balconies overflowing with greenery. The clientele is mostly business travelers, but this is an excellent option for tourists since it faces a vast park, is walking distance from plenty of restaurants, and lies a short drive from most sights. Italian cuisine is served with a view of the park at El Olivar, whereas Ichi Ban, downstairs, offers an array of sushi and sashimi. **Pros:** lovely location; top-notch dining; near shops and restaurants. **Cons:** chain-hotel feel. ⊠ *Pancho Fierro 194, San Isidro* ☎ *01/712–6000* ⊕ *www.sonestaperu.com* ↪ *134 rooms, 11 suites* ⟁ *In-room: a/c, safe, refrigerator, Internet. In-hotel: 2 restaurants, room service, bar, pool, gym, laundry service, Internet terminal, Wi-Fi hotspot, parking (free)* ⊟ *AE, DC, MC, V* ⏀❘*BP.*

NIGHTLIFE AND THE ARTS

Lima may not be the city that doesn't sleep, but it certainly can't be getting enough rest. Limeños love to go out, as you'll notice on any Friday or Saturday night. Early in the evening they're clustered around movie theaters and concert halls, while late at night they are piling into taxis headed to the bars and clubs of Miraflores and Barranco. Ask at your hotel for a free copy of *Peru Guide,* an English-language monthly full of information on bars and clubs as well as galleries and performances.

THE ARTS

GALLERIES

Miraflores is full of art galleries that show the works of Peruvian and occasionally foreign artists.

The gallery in the lower floor of the **Instituto Cultural Peruano Norteamericano** (⌧ *Av. Angamos Oeste and Av. Arequipa, Miraflores* ☎ *01/706–7000*) exhibits both contemporary art and traditional handicrafts. In the rear of the Municipalidad de Miraflores, the **Sala Luis Miró Quesada** (⌧ *Av. Larco Herrera and Calle Diez Canseco, Miraflores* ☎ *01/617–7271*) sponsors exhibits of sculpture, painting, and photography. **Trapecio** (⌧ *Av. Larco Herrera 743, Miraflores* ☎ *01/444–0842*) shows works by contemporary Peruvian artists.

In San Isidro **Artco** (⌧ *Ca. Rouad and Paz Soldán, San Isidro* ☎ *01/221–3579*) sponsors cutting-edge art, sometimes involving different mediums such as painting and video. **Praxis** (⌧ *Av. San Martín 689, at Diez Canseco, Barranco* ☎ *01/477–2822*) has constantly rotating exhibits of international artists experimenting with different forms.

MUSIC

The Orquestra Sinfónica Nacional, ranked one of the best in Latin America, performs at the Museo de la Nación's **Auditoria Sinfónica** (⌧ *Av. Javier Prado Este 2465, San Borja* ☎ *01/476–9933*). In the heart of Barranco, the **Centro Cultural Juan Parra del Riego** (⌧ *Av. Pedro de Osma 135, Barranco* ☎ *01/247–8643*) sponsors performances by Latin American musicians, as well as plays.

The theater in the **Centro Cultural Ricardo Palma** (⌧ *Av. Larco Herrera 770, Miraflores* ☎ *01/617–7263*) hosts frequent concerts, as well as films, theater, dance and poetry readings. The **Instituto Cultural Peruano Norteamericano** (⌧ *Av. Angamos Oeste and Av. Arequipa, Miraflores* ☎ *01/706–7000*) offers frequent concerts ranging from jazz to classical to folk, as well as dance and theater.

NIGHTLIFE

BARS

When you're in Barranco, a pleasant place to start off the evening is **La Posada del Mirador** (⌧ *Ermita 104, Barranco* ☎ *01/256–1796*), at the end of the path behind La Ermita. The bar has a second-story balcony that looks out to sea, making this a great place to watch the sunset. **Picas** (⌧ *Bajada de Baños 340, Barranco* ☎ *01/247–1225*), in a remodeled old building next to the Puente de los Suspiros, is the hippest bar on the Bajada de Baños. It also has an excellent kitchen, making it a good option for a late-night snack.

The refurbished 19th-century mansion that houses **Ayahuasca** (⌧ *Av. Prolongación San Martín 130, Barranco* ☎ *01/9810–44745*) would

The courtyard of the mansion-museum, Casa Riva-Agüero, in El Centro.

be worth visiting even if it wasn't Barranco's most chic bar. The wild decor—it is named for a hallucinogen used by Amazonian Indians—and tasty tapas only add to the allure. **Bar Huaringas** (⊠ *Ovalo Bolognesi, Miraflores* ☏ *01/444–5310*), on the second floor of a lovely old house next to the restaurant Brujas de Cachiche, is a pleasant place for a drink, though it can get packed on weekends.

Chocolate Bar (⊠ *Pancho Fierro 108, San Isidro* ☏ *01/222–0174*), above the restaurant Como Agua Para Chocolate, not only has an excellent selection of European beers, they also offer 40 brands of tequila and a damned good margarita.

DANCE CLUBS

In Barranco, the most popular dance club is the second-floor **Déjà Vu** (⊠ *Av. Grau 294, Barranco* ☏ *01/247–3742*). A triangular wood staircase leads up to a collection of odd-shape rooms where little tables are pushed together to accommodate big groups. The dance floor, off to one side, is something of an afterthought. There are plenty of places to dance in Miraflores, but a Cuban-owned bar on the Calle de las Pizzas, **Son de Cuba** (⊠ *San Ramón 277, Miraflores* ☏ *445–1444*) is the most entertaining. On weekends, they offer salsa classes from 7 to 9, and a live band plays Cuban salsa from 11:30 to 2:30. They also have short concerts around midnight on Wednesday and Thursday, and the DJ spins Latin dance music the rest of the time.

GAY AND LESBIAN CLUBS

After 10 PM you'll definitely want to stop for a drink at **La Sede** (⊠ *Av. 28 de Julio 441, Miraflores* ☏ *01/242–2462* ⊕ *www.publasede.com*), one of the city's more sophisticated bars. **BoBo Bar** (⊠ *Manuel Bonilla*

CLOSE UP | Peña Party

Popular weekend destinations are *peñas*, bars that offer *música criolla*, a breathless combination of Spanish and African influences. Peñas that cater to tourists, however, offer a more varied show that includes folk music and dancing from the country's coastal and Andean regions. Peñas that cater to locals start their show at 10:30 and continue until the wee hours, whereas the tourist peñas start at around 8.

La Dama Juana (⊠ *Larco Mar local 301, Miraflores* ☎ *01/447–3686* ⊕ *ladamajuana.com.pe*), in the Larco Mar shopping complex, is the most tourist-friendly peña, with dinner shows starting at 8:30 every night but Sunday. Tickets can be purchased with or without a traditional Peruvian buffet, which opens at 7:30.

Vying for both the local and tourist markets, **La Candelaria** (⊠ *Av.* *Bolognesi 292, Barranco* ☎ *01/247–1314* ⊕ *www.lacandelariaperu.com*) is located in a lovely old building in Barranco. Shows combining the folklore of the coast, mountains, and jungle start at 9 on Thursday, Friday, and Saturday nights.

The facade may be dull, but the attitude is anything but at **De Rompe y Raja** (⊠ *Jr. Manuel Segura 127, Barranco* ☎ *01/247–3271*). In a slightly sketchy neighborhood, this peña attracts mostly locals with *música negra*, a variant of música criolla.

Junius (⊠ *Av. Independencia 125, Miraflores* ☎ *01/617–1000* ⊕ *www. junius.com.pe*), in the Doubletree Hotel, has dinner shows featuring traditional music and dances of the coast and sierra and a dinner buffet. It's geared mostly to tourists, with two-hour shows from Tuesday to Sunday starting at 7:30.

109, Miraflores ☎ 01/243–2139 ⊕ www.bobobar.us) is a chic club a few blocks east of Parque Miraflores that draws a mix of gay, lesbian, bisexual, and straight people who are in the mood to party. After midnight head to the most popular disco, **Downtown Todo Vale** (⊠ Pasaje Los Pinos 160, Miraflores ☎ 01/242–6875 ⊕ www.valetododowntown. com/miraflores). A balcony filled with comfy couches overlooks the cavernous dance floor. Psychotic drag queens dressed as hula dancers or space mutants shout epithets from the stage at the appreciative crowd of men and women. There's a more laid-back scene at **Punto 80** (⊠ Manuel Bonilla, Miraflores ☎ 01/446–7567), a neighborhood hangout.

LIVE MUSIC

Clubs with live music are scattered around Miraflores and Barranco. **Posada del Ángel** (⊠ Av. Pedro de Osma 164, Barranco ☎ 01/247–0341 ⊠ Av. Pedro de Osma 222, Barranco ☎ 01/251–3778 ⊠ Prolongación San Martín 157, Barranco ☎ 01/247–5544) offers Latin guitar music at three locations, each of which is decorated with a wild collection of antiques and art, including statues of angels. They are some of the few bars in Barranco where you can actually hold a conversation, and the singer/guitarists who perform Latin American classics from 10 PM to 2 AM, are usually quite good. **El Tayta** (⊠ Av. José Larco 421, Miraflores ☎ 01/242–4958), in the second floor of an old building across Avenida

Larco from Parque Kennedy, has live guitar music most nights and opens up an adjacent dance club on weekends. It draws a young crowd.

La Noche (⊠ *Bolognesi 307, Barranco* ☎ *01/477–4154*) is in a funky old house at the far end of a pedestrian street called Bulevar Sánchez Carrión. The local rock bands booked here may not be your cup of tea, but it's a fun place for a drink before the shows start.

It's easy to miss the **Jazz Zone** (⊠ *Av. La Paz 656, Miraflores* ☎ *01/241–8139*), hidden in a colonial-style shopping complex call El Suche. You head up a bright red stairway to the dimly lit second-story lounge. Peru has some excellent Latin jazz groups that improvise on local rhythms. **Cocodrilo Verde** (⊠ *Francisco de Paula Camino 226, Miraflores* ☎ *01/242–7583* ⊕ *www.cocodriloverde.com*), two blocks west of Parque Kennedy, features some of Peru's best musicians and visiting acts that play everything from música criollo to jazz to salsa to bossa nova. Check their website to see who is booked.

> **PISCO STOP**
>
> Founded in 1880, Santiago Queirolo (⊠ *Av. San Martín 1062, Pueblo Libre* ☎ *01/463-1008*) has had years to perfect their pisco, and even won the prize for the country's best pisco back in 2002. Besides four types of pisco, they bottle nine types of wine, none of which are especially good. The lunch specials, on the other hand, are usually worth stopping for.

SHOPPING

Hundreds of stores around Lima offer traditional crafts of the highest quality. The same goes for silver and gold jewelry. Wander down Avenida La Paz in Miraflores and you'll be astounded at the number of shops selling one-of-a-kind pieces of jewelry; the street also yields clothing and antiques at reasonable prices. Miraflores is also full of crafts shops, many of them along Avenida Petit Thouars. For upscale merchandise, many people now turn to the boutiques of San Isidro. For original works of art, the bohemian neighborhood of Barranco has some excellent small galleries.

MALLS

Limeños love to shop, as you'll discover when you walk through any of the city's massive malls. With more than 200 shops, **Jockey Plaza** (⊠ *Av. Javier Prado 4200, Surco* ☎ *01/716–2000*) is by far the largest in Lima. The only trouble is that it's a long drive from most hotels. Right in the heart of things is **Larcomar** (⊠ *Malecón de la Reserva and Av. José Larco, Miraflores* ☎ *01/620–6000*), a surprisingly appealing, open-air shopping center in Miraflores. It's built into the cliff at the end of Avenida José Larco, so it's almost invisible from the street. Its dozens of shops, bars, and restaurants are terraced and have impressive views of the coast and ocean.

MARKETS

On the northern edge of Miraflores, Avenida Petit Thouars has at least half a dozen markets crammed with vendors. They all carry pretty much the same merchandise.To get a rough idea of what an alpaca sweater or woven wallet should cost, head to **Artesanías Miraflores** (✉ *Av. Petit Thouars 5541, Miraflores* ☎ *No phone*). It's small but has a little of everything. Better-quality goods can be found at **La Portada del Sol** (✉ *Av. Petit Thouars 5411, Miraflores* ☎ *No phone*). In this miniature mall the vendors show off their wares in glass cases lighted with halogen lamps. Some even accept credit cards. Ask a local about the best place for handicrafts and you'll probably be told to go to **Mercado Indios** (✉ *Av. Petit Thouars 5245, Miraflores* ☎ *No phone*). The selection ranges from mass-produced souvenirs to one-of-a-kind pieces, and since most vendors will bargain, you can often get a very good deal.

SPECIALTY SHOPS

ANTIQUES

Dozens of shops selling *antigüedades* line Avenida La Paz, making this street in Miraflores a favorite destination for shoppers. It may be small, but **El Detalle** (✉ *Av. La Paz 668, Miraflores* ☎ *01/242–4698*) holds an incredible variety of antiques, including many smaller items. **Antigüedades Siglo XVIII** (✉ *Av. La Paz 661, Miraflores* ☎ *01/445–8915*) specializes in silver. The selection includes ornate picture frames and *milagros*, or miracles—heart-shape charms that are placed at the feet of a staint's statue as the physical representation of prayers. Brooding saints dominate the walls of **El Frailero** (✉ *Av. La Paz 551, Miraflores* ☎ *01/447–2823*). These small statues and paintings, most of which were made for private homes, date back to the colonial period.

CLOTHING

Fodor's Choice ★ Lots of stores stock clothing made of alpaca, but one of the few to offer articles made from vicuña is **Alpaca 111** (✉ *Av. Larco 671, Miraflores* ☎ *01/447–1623* ✉ *Larcomar Malecón de la Reserva and Av. José Larco, Miraflores* ☎ *01/241–3484* ✉ *Av. Jorge Bassadre, San Isidro* ☎ *01/440–2320*). This cousin of the llama produces the world's finest wool. It's fashioned into scarves, sweaters, and even knee-length coats.

There are several other shops specializing in alpaca in Miraflores and San Isidro. **All Alpaca** (✉ *Av. Schell 375, Miraflores* ☎ *01/446–0565* ✉ *Av. Emilio Cavenecia 209, San Isidro*) sells sweaters and other pieces of clothing in sophisticated styles. Bright colors reign at **La Casa de la Alpaca** (✉ *Av. La Paz 665, Miraflores* ☎ *01/447–6271*). The patterns are updated takes on Andean designs.

FABRIC

Lanifico (✉ *Av. Alberto del Campo 285, San Isidro* ☎ *01/264–3186* ✉ *Larcomar, Level 1, Tienda 153, Miraflores* ☎ *01/447–7126*) offers fine fabrics made from baby alpaca—wool from animals no older than two years—as well as designer clothes made from alpaca, wool, and cotton.

HANDICRAFTS

For beautiful pottery, head to **Antisuyo** (⊠ *Tacna 460, Miraflores* ☎ *01/447–2557*), a cooperatively owned shop that sells indigenous pottery and other handicrafts from around the country. The tiny but charming **La Floristeria** (⊠ *Av. La Paz 444, Miraflores* ☎ *01/444–2288*), in the front the El Suche complex, is packed with quality handicrafts: retablos, jewelry, weavings, candles. Tiny *retablos* (boxes filled with scenes of village life) are among the eye-catching objects at **Raices Peru** (⊠ *Av. La Paz 588, Miraflores* ☎ *01/447–7457*).

Fodor's Choice Housed in a restored mansion where Barranco's stately Avenida Sáenz
★ Peña meets the Malecón, **Dédalo** (⊠ *Av. Sáenz Peña 295, Barranco* ☎ *01/652–5400*) is worth a visit even if you don't want to shop. It is packed with the colorful works of dozens of independent artists and artisans and the little café in the back garden is a pleasant place to take a break from exploring Barranco.

Anonima (⊠ *Av. Libertadores 256, San Isidro* ☎ *01/222–2382*) is known for its handmade glass bowls, vases, and other objects in wonderfully wacky color combinations. On a quiet street in San Isidro, **Indigo** (⊠ *Av. El Bosque 260, San Isidro* ☎ *01/440–3099*) lets you wander through at least half a dozen different rooms filled with unique items. There's a selection of whimsical ceramics inspired by traditional designs, as well as modern pieces. In the center of it all is an open-air café. Walking through the gates of **Kolke** (⊠ *Av. Conquistadores 325, San Isidro* ☎ *01/421–0688* ⊕ *www.kolkeperu.com*) puts you inside a walled courtyard overflowing with tropical plants. You'll love the handmade items, including picture frames, bowls and boxes made of Peruvian hardwoods.

JEWELRY

It's unlikely you'll find gold jewelry elsewhere in designs as distinct as those at **H. Stern** (⊠ *Museo de Oro, Alonso de Molina 1100, Monterrico* ☎ *01/345–1350*). The well-regarded South American chain knows that people head to Peru for a taste of the culture. Many of their designs are influenced by pre-Colombian art. Look for branches in top hotels, including the Marriott and the Miraflores Park Hotel. For one-of-a-kind gifts, try **Migue** (⊠ *Av. La Paz 311, Miraflores* ☎ *01/444–0333*), where you'll find jewelers fashioning original pieces in gold and other precious metals.

For sterling you can't beat the classic designs at **Camusso** (⊠ *Av. Oscar Benavides 679, El Centro* ☎ *01/425–0260* ⊠ *Av. Rivera Navarrete 788, San Isidro* ☎ *01/442–0340*), a local *platería*, or silver shop, that opened its doors in 1933. Call ahead for a free guided tour of the factory, which is a few blocks west of El Centro. Chic designs fashioned in silver are the trademark of **Ilaria** (⊠ *Av. Dos de Mayo 308, San Isidro* ☎ *01/221–8575* ⊠ *Los Eucaliptos 578, San Isidro* ☎ *01/440–4875*). They also have a shop in the airport.

The Southern Coast

WORD OF MOUTH

"Nazca Lines are amazing and well worth the trip. If you get at all air sick take something beforehand, because you don't want to spoil a pretty short flight by feeling bad . . . and don't try taking photos out of the window."

—Mincepie

WELCOME TO THE SOUTHERN COAST

TOP REASONS TO GO

★ **Mysteries in the Desert.** Marvel over the mysterious Nazca Lines, giant figures etched into the desert floor by an enigmatic ancient civilization, from the sky.

★ **Island Life.** Boats cruise around the Islas Ballestas for viewing sea lions, condors, flamingoes, and millions of guano-producing sea birds in the Paracas National Reserve.

★ **Fun with Grapes.** Go wine tasting in the grape-growing valleys of Lunahuaná and Ica and sample Peru's most famous drink, pisco, in the best *bodegas* (traditional wineries).

★ **Staying Seaside.** Tranquil beaches and fishing villages dot the coast just south of Lima. Top-notch surfing awaits at Punta Hermosa and Punta Rocas, and Pucusana is a charming, cliffside resort town.

★ **Sandboarding.** Test your nerve and skill sandboarding down the giant dunes at the oasis town of Huacachina, then nurse your injuries in the lagoon's magical healing waters.

1 North of Pisco. Deserted beaches beloved by surfers and charming fishing villages where you can relax and chow down on great seafood await in one of Peru's favorite and most accessible holiday regions. Forget the noise and chaos of Lima and head to gorgeous Pucusana or tiny Cerro Azul to enjoy the quiet life, or grab your board and hop a bus to Punta Hermosa where the surf's always up.

TO LIMA, PUNTA HERMOSA & PUNTA ROCAS
Pucusana
Puerto Viejo
Mala
Asia
Quilmana
Punta Corriene — Lunahuaná Valley
Cerro Azul — Lunahuaná
San Vicente de Cañete — Imperial
1
Cinco Cruces
Palca
Chincha
Tambo Colorado
ISLAS DE CHINCHA — Bahía Paracas — San Clemente
ISLAS BALLESTAS — Pisco — Humay
Puerto San Martín
ISLAS SAGAYÁI — **2** — Pozo Sante
Peninsula de Paracas
Paracas National Reserve
Laguna Grande
Punta Carreta
Bahía Independencia — Carhua
ISLA INDEPENDENCIA
Punta Grande
TABLASA DE ICA
Punta de Asma
Faro del Infiernillo
PACIFIC OCEAN

Sandboarding

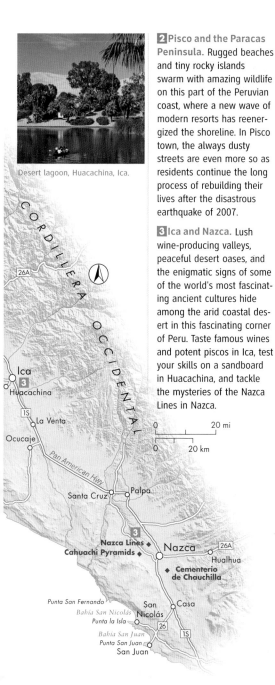

Desert lagoon, Huacachina, Ica.

2 **Pisco and the Paracas Peninsula.** Rugged beaches and tiny rocky islands swarm with amazing wildlife on this part of the Peruvian coast, where a new wave of modern resorts has reenergized the shoreline. In Pisco town, the always dusty streets are even more so as residents continue the long process of rebuilding their lives after the disastrous earthquake of 2007.

3 **Ica and Nazca.** Lush wine-producing valleys, peaceful desert oases, and the enigmatic signs of some of the world's most fascinating ancient cultures hide among the arid coastal desert in this fascinating corner of Peru. Taste famous wines and potent piscos in Ica, test your skills on a sandboard in Huacachina, and tackle the mysteries of the Nazca Lines in Nazca.

GETTING ORIENTED

3

Southern Peru is connected to Lima by the Pan-American Highway, which runs down the coast to Pisco and the Paracas Peninsula before cutting inland to Ica and Nazca. Between Lima and Pisco are a variety of small coastal towns all located just off the Panamericana. Towns are laid out in the usual Spanish colonial fashion around a central Plaza de Armas. This is usually a good place to look for services such as banks, lodgings, and transport.

Man showing off Peruvian grapes.

Updated by
Nicholas
Gill and Katy
Morrison

From vineyards to arid coastal desert, surf beaches to rolling sand dunes, the area south of Lima is wild, contradictory, and fascinating. Jump a bus on the Pan-American Highway, which cuts a black ribbon of concrete south all the way to Chile, and you'll see mile after mile of nothing but sand, cactus, and wind-torn brush clinging to the stark, rocky earth.

It seems arid and inhospitable, yet keep traveling and you'll begin to discover the reasons why this region has been home to some of the world's most amazing ancient civilizations. Lush desert oases hide among the sweeping dunes, fertile river valleys tuck swatches of green into the gray folds of the mountains, and amazing wildlife lounges offshore on rocky islands.

This region was home to the Nazca, a pre-Colombian civilization that created the enigmatic Nazca Lines. ■TIP➔ Hundreds of giant diagrams depicting animals, humans, and perfectly drawn geometric shapes are etched into the desert floor over areas so vast that they can only be seen properly from the air. The mystery of how, why, and who they were created for is unexplained, although theories range from irrigation systems to launch pads for alien spacecraft.

This is also where the Paracas culture arrived as early as 1300 BC and over the next thousand years established a line of fishing villages that exist today. The Paracas are long gone, and the Inca Empire conquered the region in the 16th century, yet the Paracas left behind some of Peru's most advanced weavings, ceramics, stone carvings, metal jewelry, and thousands of eerie cemeteries in the desert.

Yet it's not all ancient civilizations, pottery, and mysterious drawings. With a sunny climate, great wines, and charming fishing villages, this region has been a favorite holiday destination for generations of Limeños anxious to escape the big city. It's also been a commercial hub. For years during the mid-19th century the region was the center of Peru's riches, which took the rather odorous form of guano—bird droppings (found in vast quantities on the islands off the coast of Paracas) that are a rich source of natural fertilizer. Shipped to America and Europe from the deep-water port of Pisco, the trade proved so lucrative that there was even a war over it—the Guano War of 1865–66 in which Spain battled Peru for possession of the nearby Chincha Islands.

Today the region capitalizes on its natural beauty, abundant wildlife and enigmatic archaeological sites to draw tourists from all parts of the world. When the earthquake struck the coast of Pisco on August 15, 2007, it was a double calamity for the region. Settled above the Nazca and South American tectonic plates, southern Peru is no stranger to earthquakes and Pisco town has been destroyed several times over the course of its history. Tsunamis, some 7 meters (23 feet) high, often accompany the quakes and can splash in as much as 1 km (½ mi) from the coast. The 2007 quake that leveled much of Pisco and left the fishing industry in tatters due to boat damage also severely affected the region's tourism. As people struggled in the aftermath to rebuild houses, churches, hospitals, and roads, reduced tourist numbers have further strained the precarious economy.

With wines and piscos to taste in Ica, dunes to board down in Huacachina, mysterious Lines to puzzle over in Nazca, idyllic coastal resorts in Paracas, and tranquil fishing villages to relax in in Pucusana and Cerro Azul, this part of Peru will seduce and charm you. Forget the whistle-stop tour and hire a car or take a bus along the Panamericana, stopping whenever and wherever you feel the urge. From Lima the road leads to the towns of Pisco and Paracas, where you can choose side trips southwest to Paracas National Reserve, the Islas Ballestas, or east to Ayacucho. Continuing south, you'll pass through the desert towns of Ica and Nazca, the take-off point for flights over the Nazca Lines as well as trips east to Cusco and Machu Picchu. Farther south is the lovely colonial town of Arequipa, the largest settlement in the region, as well as the gateway to some of the world's deepest canyons and Lake Titicaca. From Arequipa, it's a long, parched desert drive to Tacna at the Chilean border. The "gringo trail" it may be, but just because the path is well-beaten doesn't mean there's not always something new to discover.

PLANNING

WHEN TO GO

Although the weather in southern Peru is fairly even and arid throughout the year, the best time to visit is in summer and autumn, November through April, when the rivers are ripe for rafting and kayaking and harvest festivals spice up the small towns. Around Christmas, Carnival, the grape harvest, Easter, the mid-June religious festivals, and Peru's independence day in July, hotels are often booked to capacity.

GETTING HERE AND AROUND

With the Panamericana following the coastline all the way to Chile, Southern Peru is prime territory to explore by road. Bus travel is easy and inexpensive. Larger companies such as Peru Bus serve all major towns. Minivans called combis, and share taxis, shuttle between smaller towns and usually depart from the Plaza de Armas.

AIR TRAVEL

While there is talk of building an international airport near Pisco, right now there are only landing strips in Nazca and Paracas that do not accept commercial traffic. The nearest airport to this region is in Lima, where ground transportation can be arranged via bus or tour operator.

BUS TRAVEL

Numerous companies work the route from Lima to Arequipa. Always take the best service you can afford—aside from the comfort issue, cheaper carriers have less stringent safety standards and the section of highway between Pisco and Tacna is notorious for robbery, especially on overnight services. Cruz del Sur and Ormeño provide the most reliable service and have the most departures from Ica, while the quality of vehicles and onboard service is notoriously patchy with other operators.

CAR TRAVEL

The Pan-American Highway runs the length of southern Peru, some of it along the coast, some through desert, and some over plateaus and mountains. It's paved and in good condition, but have fully equipped first-aid and repair kits packed. Besides breakdowns, hazards include potholes, rock slides, sandstorms, and heat. You'll find many service stations along this route, most of which have clean bathrooms and convenience stores. Off the highway conditions are less predictable. Roads may be poor in the eastern highlands and around the Paracas Reserve. Four-wheel-drive vehicles are recommended for all driving except on the main highway and within major cities.

Your only real options to rent a car are in Lima or Arequipa.

HEALTH AND SAFETY

The main health advice for the rest of Peru also applies to this region: Don't drink the water (or use ice), and don't eat raw or undercooked food.

Theft can be a problem in crowded tourist areas, such as beaches, or on economy-class transport. Police are helpful to most foreign travelers, but procedures can be slow, so take care with your valuables. If you lose something important, like your passport, report it to the police and to your embassy.

RESTAURANTS

Casual dress is the order of the day. Reservations are seldom necessary. If you're on a budget, look for the excellent value set menus during lunchtime, where a three-course meal can be as little as S/5. Throughout the south seafood is king, and your chef might blend local farm goods and the catch of the day with international seasonings. In Ica, try *tejas*, candies made of *manjar blanco*, a sweet, pudding-like milk spread. A treat available only during harvest festivals is *cachina*, a partially fermented wine.

HOTELS

Accommodations in southern Peru range from luxury resorts to spartan *hostals* that run less than S/15 per night. Hotels rated $$$$ usually have more than standard amenities, which might include such on-site extras as a spa, sports facilities, and business and travel services, and such room amenities as minibars, safes, faxes, or data ports. Hotels rated $$$ and $$ might have only some of the extras. Accommodations rated ¢–$ are basic and may have shared baths or be outside the central tourist area. If you're arriving without a reservation, most towns have accommodations around the Plaza de Armas or transport stations.

3

WHAT IT COSTS IN NUEVO SOLES					
	¢	$	$$	$$$	$$$$
RESTAURANTS	under S/20	S/20–S/35	S/36–S/50	S/51–S/65	over S/65
HOTELS	under S/125	S/125–S/250	S/251–S/375	S/376–S/500	over S/500

Restaurant prices are per person for a main course. Hotel prices are for a standard double room, excluding tax.

NORTH OF PISCO

Tired of the noise, smog, and traffic chaos of Lima? A couple of hours' drive south is all that's required to leave behind any trace of the big city. Glistening beaches, tranquil fishing villages, and great surf spots are on this easily accessible section of the Peruvian coast. This is the favored weekend getaway for wealthy Limeños whose grand summer residences lie side-by-side with local fishermen's houses. Follow their lead and head south to enjoy the sun, sand, and the freshest seafood you'll ever eat.

GETTING HERE AND AROUND

Traveling from town to town is easy in this part of Peru—distances are short and no town is more than an hour or so from the last. ■TIP→ Car rental is a convenient way to get around, although you'll have to organize this in Lima as there are no rental services between Lima and Arequipa. If you don't have a rental car, hotels and travel agencies in Ica and Paracas offer four-hour tours of Tambo Colorado for around S/75.

Minibuses (called combis) shuttle between most towns and are the cheapest, although not the most comfortable, way of getting around. Look on the side of the combi for the painted signs displaying its route. If you choose to travel by taxi, agree on a price before setting off.

From Cerro Azul, combis depart to Cañete from the Plaza de Armas for S/1. To get to Luanahuaná, take a combi from Canete to Imperial for S/0.70, then another combi to Luanahuaná for S/3. Perubus and Flores both offer a bus service between Cañete and Pisco for S/3.

PUCUSANA

67 km (42 mi) south of Lima on the Carretera Panamerica Sur.

Welcome to the Riviera, Peru-style. Colorful fishing boats jostle for space in the crowded harbor, fantastic cebicherias dish up the day's catch on the waterfront, and expensive holiday houses for Lima's wealthy occupy the hillsides. Pucusana is a gem well-known to locals but undiscovered by many foreign tourists. Arrive in the Peruvian summer (December to March) and you'll find this harbor town packed with vacationing Limeños who flock here for its beautiful setting, tranquil atmosphere, and the freshest seafood around. During the rest of the year you may have the town to yourself. The tiny brown-sand beaches of Las Ninfas and Pucusana Playa lie around the harbor and are good for a dip if you don't mind the boats—the more adventurous can swim (or take a boat ride) to La Isla—the island on the other side of the harbor with another small beach. For a better swimming spot take a five-minute walk around the point to get to the beach of Naplo.

If the chilly waters don't tempt you, stroll through the fish market to see the day's catch and stop for cebiche at one of the tiny stalls on the beach. Afterward walk away from the harbor toward the cliff to watch the waves crash through the **Boquerón del Diablo**. Balancing things out in the biblical stakes is the Rostro de Cristo, a rock formation on the side of the hill containing the Boquerón said to resemble the profile of Christ. It's a little hard to make out so you may need a local to point it out.

GETTING HERE AND AROUND

Any bus, such as Perubus or Flores, heading to Mala, Chincha, Ica, and points south will pass Pucusana (S/8-S/12 depending on the bus) on the Pan-American Highway, from where you can catch a combi for S/1 or mototaxi S/6 to the center. Just be sure to tell the bus driver to let you off at the turnoff into town.

WHERE TO STAY

¢ 🍽 **El Mirador.** Don't be put off by the steep climb up to this family-run guesthouse. Perched high on the hillside overlooking the harbor this charming spot wins the prize for the best views in town. Blue-and-white decor and glittering ocean views lend a ramshackle Mediterranean air while the warm welcome from hostess Elizabeth and her grandchildren is truly Peruvian. Rooms are basic but comfortable and let's face it, with views this good who wants to stay indoors? Grab a chair or a hammock on the wide veranda and enjoy the sunset, or, if you're here during the summer months (December—February) when the restaurant is functioning, let Elizabeth cook you up a home-style Peruvian meal. If you visit during the peak periods of Christmas and New Year, book ahead. **Pros:** spectacular views over the harbor; welcoming reception; veranda for lounging on. **Cons:** hard climb up some steep stairs to hotel; no vehicle access; no off-season restaurant. ⊠ *Prolg. Miguel Grau Mz. 54 Lote 1* ☏ *01/430–9228* ⊕ *www.elmiradordepucusana.com* ⤢ *6 rooms* ⌂ *In-room: no a/c, no phone. In-hotel: restaurant, laundry service, parking (free)* ▭ *No credit cards.*

Surfing

South of Lima you'll find a string of sandy beaches, most of them backed by massive sand dunes. The water is cold and rough, the waves are big, and lifeguards are nonexistent.

Sound appealing? Then pick up your board and head south to see why Peru is becoming one of South America's hottest surfing destinations.

For a sure bet, head to **Punta Hermosa**, a town near Km 44 on the Pan-American Highway (about an hour's drive south of Lima), which, with its numerous reefs and coves, has the highest concentration of quality surf spots and breaks all year round.

Fancy yourself a pro? The largest waves in South America, some 7 meters (20 feet) high, roll into nearby **Pico Alto**, with nearly 20 good breaks around the Pico Alto Surf Camp. Paddle out from Punta Hermosa via Playa Norte to reach the reef, although be warned—these waves are for the very experienced and crazy only!

Excellent surfing is also much closer to shore at the town of **Cerro Azul**, at Km 132 of the Panamericana. Long tubular waves break right in front of the town, so be prepared for an audience. A pleasant fishing village, Cerro Azul is a popular weekend and holiday destination and the beach gets crowded during peak times. Go mid-week if you want the place to yourself.

Peru doesn't have a huge surfing tradition, but to see where a small slice of local history was made, head to **Punta Rocas**, 42 km south of Lima, where in 1965 Peruvian surfer Felipe Pomar converted himself into something of a national hero when he won

Costa Verde

the World Surfing Championships. The reef-break here provides a classic wave for beginners and advanced surfers alike.

There's even some decent surfing in the middle of Lima. Just off the coast of Miraflores, on the **Costa Verde** beach road you can find four surfable beaches, all within a 15-minute walk of each other. Right near the Rosa Nautica restaurant, Redondo, Makaha, La Pampilla, and Waikiki are breaks for beginners but with their proximity to the city the water can be more than a little polluted. Think you've just paddled past a jellyfish? It's more likely a plastic bag.

Surfing in Peru is best from March to December, with May probably being ideal. While the climate is dry year-round, in winter the Pacific Ocean can get very chilly (although it's never particularly warm and wetsuits are advisable year-round), and coastal fog can leave you with little to look at.

—Katy Morrison

CERRO AZUL

71 km (45 mi) south of Pucusana; 15 km (9 mi) north of Cañete.

"Aqui esta tranquilo" say the locals, and tranquil it certainly is in this small fishing town, made famous by the Beach Boys' song "Surfin' Safari," between Cañete and Pucusana. The hustle and bustle of the old days, when the town made its living as a port for the exportation of guano and pisco, is gone and now the only industry you'll see is the fishermen repairing their nets down by the waterfront.

Limeños trickle in on the weekends, arriving as much for the town's charmingly off-beat character as for the peace and quiet. On the weekend the local brass band parades through the streets before and after the church services. The local church, instead of ringing its bell, sets off fireworks in the Plaza de Armas as an unconventional call to prayer.

Walk along the waterfront where fish restaurants dish up deliciously fresh cebiche, then, if you're not too full, scramble over the dunes behind the pink and green former customs house to find what remains of the ancient Inca sea-fort of Huarco. In the evenings head to the Plaza, where several tiny restaurants serve up soups and chifa for a little over S/4.

GETTING HERE AND AROUND

Any bus heading south from Lima will pass by Cerro Azul (S/10–S/15 depending on the bus) on the Pan-American Highway, from where you can catch a combi for S/1 or mototaxi S/6 to the center.

WHERE TO STAY

¢ ⊡ **Cerro Azul Hostal.** In a town short on accommodation this little hostel is one of the most reliable options and fills up quickly on weekends and holidays. Relaxed and low-key, what this place lacks in character it makes up for by being a step away from the beach. Single travelers and couples may find the standard rooms rather small and dark. Groups are more fortunate—spacious apartments sleeping up to eight are a good deal and come with their own private terraces for lounging on and taking in the sea views. Between December and February the small cafeteria on the premises functions as a restaurant, serving up Peruvian and fish dishes. **Pros:** close to the beach; good lodgings for groups; pricing packages for longer stays. **Cons:** small rooms; no restaurant during the off-season; off-season repairs leave the place looking a little chaotic. ⊠ *Puerto Viejo* ☎ *01/284–6052* ⊕ *www.cerroazulhostal.com* ↵ *12 rooms, 4 apartments* ⚴ *In-room: no a/c, no phone, refrigerator (some), no TV (some). In-hotel: restaurant, laundry service, parking (free)* ⊟ *AE, DC, MC, V.*

$ ⊡ **Las Palmeras.** Although worn around the edges these days, this long-running hotel still merits a mention for its prime beach-front location. With their old-fashioned furnishings the rooms may not be very stylish, but many have excellent sea views and tiny balconies. During the summer months the pool and terrace overlooking the beach are pleasant spots to kick back with a pisco sour. Be warned—bring your own party if you want to stay here during the off-season—with only a skeleton service (no pool, no restaurant, and practically no staff) it may feel a little lonesome. **Pros:** beachfront location; sea views from most rooms; pool during summer months. **Cons:** worn-looking rooms; highly scaled-back service during off-season. ⊠ *Puerto Viejo* ☎ *01/284–6005* ⊷ *16 rooms* ⛭ *In-room: a/c, no phone. In-hotel: restaurant, bar, pool, laundry service, parking (free)* ⊟ *AE, DC, MC, V.*

LUNAHUANÁ

14 km (8 mi) east of Cerro Azul; 150 km (93 mi) south of Lima; 85 km (54 mi) north of Pisco.

Flanked by arid mountains, the beautiful valley of the Río Cañete cuts a swathe of green inland from Cañete to reach the tiny but charming town of Lunahuaná, nestled against the river. It's the center for some of Peru's best white-water rafting. The season is from December to March when the water is at its highest, creating rapids that can reach up to class IV. Most of the year, however, the river is suitable for beginners. Rafting companies offering trips line Calle Grau in town.

If you're more interested in whetting your palate, Lunahuaná is a great spot to enjoy the products of the region—wines and piscos from the surrounding wineries and freshwater prawns straight from the river. ■TIP➜ In March you can celebrate the opening of the grape pressing season at the Fiesta de la Vendimia. The rest of the year, join the locals and while away the afternoon trying the variety of cocktails from the pisco stands dotted around the flower-filled main plaza—the *maracuya* (passion fruit) sour is a winner. If the cocktails, sun, and lazy atmosphere don't get the better of you, just down the road from Lunahuaná lies the **Incahuasi** ruins—an Inca site said to have been the military headquarters of Túpac Yupanqui. There's not a great deal to see, although Inca enthusiasts may find it interesting.

GETTING HERE AND AROUND

To reach Lunahuaná, take a bus to Km 143 on the Pan-American Highway to the turnoff to San Vicente de Cañete and Imperial. There you can catch a combi for the hour-long ride to Luanahuaná for S /7.50.

ESSENTIALS

Tour Operators Hemiriver Adventures (☎ *01/534-2339* ⊕ *www.hemiriver.com*). **Warko Adventures** (☎ *01/403–6285* ⊕ *www.warkoadventures.com*).

WHERE TO STAY

$ ☖ **Río Alto Hotel.** Just ½ km from Lunahuana, this hacienda-style hotel has a family vibe and is popular with visitors from Lima. Cozy public spaces with bamboo decor, a flower-filled courtyard,

GRAPE HARVEST

If you happen to be in the San Vicente de Cañete region in March, drop by Cañete, which holds one of Peru's most exciting *Fiestas de la Vendimia* (grape-harvest festivals) on the first weekend of that month. The event stems from the town's proximity to the Valle Cañete, best known for its fertile vineyards that produce some of Peru's greatest wines. During the rest of the year there's little in Cañete to hold your interest, and most people head straight to the far nicer town of Cerro Azul, 30 minutes to the north.

and the sounds of the river create a restful atmosphere. The restaurant's terrace is a great spot to enjoy pisco sours or river prawns while keeping an eye on the kids in the nearby pool. Rooms are small, although they have broad windows, slightly worn but comfortable furnishings, private bathrooms, and TVs. For groups, there are two fully equipped bungalows; one sleeps five (S/243), the other sleeps seven (S/340). **Pros:** riverside location; pool; flower-filled terrace to kick back in. **Cons:** small rooms; out of town location; no travel services. ⊠ *Cañete–Lunahuana Hwy., Km 39.5* ☎ *01/284–1125* ⊕ *www. rioaltohotel.com* ⤳ *23 rooms, 2 bungalows* ♿ *In-room: no a/c, kitchen (some), refrigerator (some). In-hotel: restaurant, bar, pool, parking (free)* ▭ *AE, DC, MC, V.*

> **AFRO-PERUVIAN BEAT**
>
> A sprawling town midway between Cañete and Pisco, Chincha is famous for its riotous Afro-Peruvian music. If you're nearby during late February, head here to celebrate the Fiesta de Verano Negro when Chincha's neighborhood of El Carmen shakes its booty day and night in the peñas and music clubs. A highlight is El Alcatraz, a dance in which a hip-swiveling male dancer tries to set his partner's cloth tail on fire with a candle. Outside of festival time, there are several good pisco bodegas to tour and a couple of excellent criollo restaurants, but not much else.

$ ⊞ **Villasol Hotel.** Listen to the sounds of the Rio Cañete from your room or enjoy the river views while floating lazily in the swimming pool at this large hotel that makes the most of its spectacular riverside location. The pool area, with its terraced lawns, access to the riverbank, and two saunas, is a winner, as is the cavernous on-site restaurant with its menu designed by renowned Peruvian chef Michel Vasquez Rebaza. Ignore the terrible plastic floor tiles in the otherwise comfortably furnished rooms and head straight for the windows for the spectacular views over the Rio Cañete. A few extra dollars gets you a room with a private balcony and river views. **Pros:** riverside location; spectacular pool area; river views from some rooms. **Cons:** some rooms only have views to the lawn; unimaginative room furnishings; parking on the front lawns. ⊠ *Cañete–Lunahuana Hwy., Km 37.5* ☎ *01/344–4611* ⊕ *www.hotelvillasolperu.com* ⤳ *55 rooms* ♿ *In-room: no a/c, refrigerator (some). In-hotel: restaurant, room service, bar, pool, parking (free)* ▭ *AE, DC, MC, V.*

TAMBO COLORADO

132 km (84 mi) southeast of Lunahuaná; 48 km (30 mi) southeast of Pisco.

Fodor's Choice   Tambo Colorado is one of Peru's most underrated archaeological sites.
★   This centuries-old burial site, extremely well-preserved in this bone-dry setting, was discovered beneath the sand dunes by Peruvian archaeologist Julio Tello in 1925. Dating back to the 15th century, Tambo Colorado or Pucahuasi in Quechua (*Huasi* means "resting place," and *puca* means "red," after the color of the stone it was built from), is

thought to have been an important Inca administrative center for passing traffic on the road to Cusco. It was also where Inca runners waited to relay messages. With runners waiting at similar stations every 7 or so kilometers, messages could be passed from one end of the country to the other in just 24 hours.

The site comprises several sections laid out around a large central plaza. ■TIP➔ Notice that the plaza's distinctive trapezoid shape is reflected throughout the site—look for trapezoid windows and other openings—and thought to have been an earthquake-proofing measure, necessary in this extremely volatile region. The site has withstood the test of time, but that hasn't stopped generations of visitors from etching personalized graffiti into its walls. A small museum is on-site, which has some of Julio Tello's original finds, including funeral *fards* (burial cocoons), dating from 1300 BC to AD 200 and wrapped in bright cotton and wool textiles embroidered with detailed patterns. Some skulls showed evidence of trepanation, a sophisticated medical procedure involving the insertion of metal plates to replace sections of bone broken in battles where rocks were used as weapons. Samples from Tello's original dig are also on display at the Museo Julio Tello near Paracas. ⊠ *Paracas Bay* ☎ *No phone* ⬚ *S/7.50* ⊙ *Daily 9–5.*

GETTING HERE AND AROUND

There is no public transportation to Tambo Colorado. Most hotels and travel agencies in Ica and Paracas offer four-hour tours of the archeological site for around S/75.

EXPLORING

Huaytara. Catch your breath and drive up to this beautiful modern Catholic church built on the foundation of an Inca temple 2,800 meters (9,200 feet) above sea level.

Puente Colgante. If you have time, drive up the road past Tambo Colorado to this suspension bridge. The original wooden bridge built in the early-20th century and a newer one installed in 2004 span the river side by side. If you're brave, cross the older version.

PISCO AND THE PARACAS PENINSULA

With spectacular natural surroundings and diverse wildlife, Pisco and neighboring Paracas have long been featured as a stop on Peru's well-beaten tourist trail. At less than half a day's drive from the capital, for many years Pisco was a favorite holiday destination for Limeños anxious to escape the big smoke. Sadly, the earthquake that struck in August 2007 left little of the colonial town standing and both the city and country reeling with the scale of the destruction. Life continues, however, and as Pisco has struggled to rebuild, the town of Paracas is booming and several major new resorts opened in 2009 with more on the way. The rugged coastline of the Paracas Peninsula and spectacular rocky Ballestas Islands draw visitors keen to experience the area's wild scenery and to see flamingos, penguins, sea lions, and every imaginable type of guano-producing sea bird.

PISCO

30 km (19 mi) south of Chincha.

Lending its name to the clear brandy that is Peru's favorite tipple and a source of fierce national pride, the coastal town of Pisco and its surroundings hold a special place in the national psyche. It's the point where the Argentinean hero, General San Martín, landed with his troops to fight for Peru's freedom from Spanish rule. It's the city from which *pisco,* the clear grape alcohol that is the country's national drink, was first exported, and it's also an important sea port that had its heyday during the 1920s, when guano (bird droppings used as fertilizer) from the nearby Islas Ballestas were worth nearly as much as gold.

Modern-day Pisco shows little evidence of its celebrated past. Instead, what you'll find is a city struggling to get back on its feet after the disaster of August 2007, when a magnitude 8 earthquake shook the town for three minutes. Disregard for planning permission, illegal building extensions, and the use of adobe (mud brick) as the main building material had left a vast number of Pisco's buildings unable to withstand the quake, and hundreds of lives were lost as homes, churches, and hospitals collapsed during the tremor.

Undoubtedly a town that's had more than its fair share of hardship and natural disaster, 2007 was not the first time Pisco has suffered from earthquake damage. The city stands where it does today because an earthquake in 1687, and pirate attacks in its aftermath, destroyed so many structures that viceroy Count de la Monclova decided to give up on the old location and start afresh where the city lies today.

Modern-day Pisco is a shadow of its former self and most travelers instead base themselves in Paracas, just a few kilometers down the coast. But National Pisco Day, the third Saturday in September, draws thousands to the city. For travelers wishing to assist Pisco's recovery, there are numerous opportunities to volunteer. While organizations active in the area vary over time, a good place to start looking for current opportunities is *www.idealist.org.* Even those without the time to volunteer should know that every Nuevo Sol spent in local businesses is contributing to rebuilding the region's economy.

GETTING HERE AND AROUND

Transport within Pisco is generally not necessary: the central area is easily covered on foot, although those venturing out at night should take a taxi. If you arrive by bus you may find yourself dropped off at the Pisco turn-off on the Panamericana rather than in town itself—ask for a direct service. If you do end up disembarking on the highway there are taxis waiting, which make the run into town for around S/5. Drivers who work this route have a bad reputation for taking travelers only to hotels from which they receive a commission—always insist on being taken to the destination of your choice and ignore anyone who tells you that the hotel has closed, moved, or changed its name.

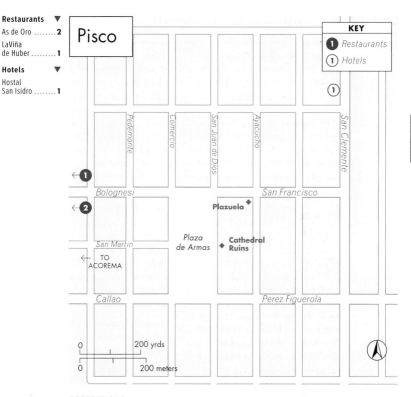

Restaurants ▼
As de Oro **2**
LaViña
de Huber **1**

Hotels ▼
Hostal
San Isidro **1**

KEY
1 Restaurants
1 Hotels

ESSENTIALS

Bus Contacts Empresa José de San Martín (✉ *2 de Mayo y San Martín* ☎ *034/543–167*). **Ormeño** (✉ *Av. San Francisco* ☎ *056/532–764*). **Paracas Express** (✉ *Pan-American Hwy., Km 447* ☎ *056/533–623*). **San Martín** (✉ *San Martín 199* ☎ *056/522–743 or 051/363–631*).

Currency Banco de Crédito (✉ *Plaza de Armas*). **Banco de la Nación** (✉ *Calle San Fransisco, primera cuadra*).

Medical San Juan de Dios (Hospital) (✉ *Calle San Juan de Dios, tercera cuadra* ☎ *056/532-332*).

Police Comisaría Sectorial (✉ *Calle San Fransisco, primera cuadra* ☎ *056/532–884*).

WHERE TO EAT AND STAY

The 2007 earthquake destroyed many accommodations in Pisco and most have closed up shop or moved to nearby Paracas, which has become the base for most travelers here. It's recommended to stay in Paracas, but if you must stay in Pisco the option listed is structurally sound and has been repaired after the quake. If you decide to stay elsewhere, stay away from hotels housed in precarious-looking multistory adobe constructions.

CLOSE UP

Pisco Country

El Pisco es Peruano! and don't try to tell the locals any different. This clear brandy that takes its name from the port town of Pisco is Peru's favorite tipple and a source of fierce national pride. It would take a brave and foolish man to raise the suggestion that pisco was invented in Spain, or worse still, in neighboring Chile. Yes, when in Peru, the only thing you need to know is that el pisco es 100% Peruano.

Fiery and potent, Pisco is hands-down the most popular liquor in Peru, and is drunk on just about every social occasion. Invited to someone's house for dinner? Chances are you'll be welcomed with a Pisco Sour, a tart cocktail made from pisco, lime juice, egg white, sugar, and bitters. Heading to a party? You're sure to see at least a couple of people drinking Peru Libres—a Peruvian take on the classic cuba libre, using pisco instead of rum and mixed with Coca-Cola. Of course, the real way to drink pisco is *a lo macho*—strong and straight up. It will certainly put hair on your chest.

Pisco is derived from grapes, like wine, but is technically an *aguardiente*, or brandy. Through a special distillation process involving a serpentine copper pipe, the fermented grapes are vaporized and then chilled to produce a clear liquor. In Peru there are four main variations of Pisco: the one grape *pisco puro*; a blend of grapes such as quebranta mixed with torontel and muscatel produce *pisco acholado*; straight muscatel grapes make *pisco aromatico*; and *pisco mosto verde*, in which the green musts are distilled during the fermentation process.

Legend has it that pisco got its name from sailors who tired of asking for "aguardiente de Pisco" and shortened the term to pisco. (The name meant "place of many birds" in the language of the indigenous people, and it still refers to the port city as well as a nearby river.)

Today Peru produces more than 7.5 million liters annually, 40% of which is exported to the United States. In 1988 the liquor was designated a national patrimony, and each year Peruvians celebrate an annual Pisco Festival in March as well as the National Day of the Pisco Sour every February 8.

Bottoms up!

—Brian Kluepfel & Katy Morrison

$　✕ **As de Oro.** It may look a little like a gas station cafeteria but what
PERUVIAN　this restaurant lacks in style it makes up for with terrific local cuisine, especially fresh seafood. Try the tangy cebiche or one of the seafood stews; if you like heartier fare, sample roast chicken and grilled meats. If you want to nosh between meals, there are plenty of salads, soups, coffees, and desserts. ✉ *Av. San Martín 472* ☎ *056/532–010* ⊟ *AE, DC, MC, V* ☾ *Closed Mon.*

$　✕ **LaViña de Huber.** Locals recommend this restaurant on the outskirts of
PERUVIAN　town as the best around, and judging from the lunchtime crowds, they can't be too far wrong. Run by three brothers who take turns in the kitchen, this friendly spot cooks up hip modern Peruvian cuisine with enticing dishes such as sole fillets rolled with bacon and served with passion fruit dipping sauce, or fish stuffed with spinach and sautéed in

a pisco and pecan broth. Everything is delicious and the portions are enormous so order a few dishes to share. ✉ *Prolg. Cerro Azul, next to Parque Zonal* ☎ *056/533–199* ═ *No credit cards.*

¢ ⊞ **Hostal San Isidro.** A relaxing oasis away from the dust of the Pisco streets, this friendly, family-run guesthouse is a top place to drop your bags and rest your weary bones. The cozy rooms have bright Peruvian motifs and there's a sunny patio and swimming pool to hang out in. Complimentary coffee in the morning and a free laundry service ensure that you'll leave feeling and looking rejuvenated and ready for the next adventure. The hostel is near the cemetery; take a taxi if arriving at night. **Pros:** very welcoming hosts; great pool; free laundry service. **Cons:** near the cemetery; expensive dorm rooms; high walls somewhat fortresslike. ✉ *San Clemente 103* ☎ *056/536–471* ⊕ *www. sanisidrohostal.com* ⥱ *18 rooms* ♻ *In-room: no phone, Wi-Fi. In-hotel: pool, laundry service, Internet, Wi-Fi* ═ *No credit cards.*

PARACAS

15 km (10 mi) south of Pisco.

After the 2007 quake, Paracas quickly leapfrogged Pisco as the most important tourist hub on the south coast. Several major coastal resorts from big name chains like Doubletree and Libertador opened in 2009 and several more are on the way in the coming years. The small town feel and cluster of small inns and restaurants around a central fishing pier are still there, though for the passing tourist the options of things to do have quadrupled. Apart from being the launching point for trips in the Paracas National Reserve and Islas Ballestas, you can base yourself here to go pisco tasting or dune buggy riding near Ica or for trips to the Nazca Lines.

GETTING AROUND

A taxi from Pisco to Paracas runs about S/15, or you can take a half-hour Chaco–Paracas–Museo *combi* to El Chaco for S/2. From Paracas, you can catch a slow motorboat to the reserve and islands.

To visit Islas Ballestas, you must be on a registered tour, which usually means an hour or two cruising around the islands among sea lions and birds. Motorboat tours usually leave from the El Chaco jetty at 8 and 10 AM. For the calmest seas, take the early tour. ■TIP→ You'll be in the open wind, sun, and waves during boat trips, so dress appropriately, and prepare your camera for the mists in July and August. It takes about an hour to reach the park from the jetty; you're close when you can see the Candelabra etched in the coastal hills. A two-hour tour costs around S/80. Some tours continue on to visit the Paracas Peninsula during the afternoon for around S/30 extra.

ESSENTIALS

Tour Operators **Ballestas Expeditions** (☎ *056/532–373*).

BEACHES

Most beaches at Paracas are rugged and scenic, top-notch for walking but dangerous for swimming due to rip tides and undertow. Beware in the shallows, too—there are often stingrays and giant jellyfish. Calmer stretches include La Catedral, La Mina, and Mendieta, as well as

Seals observe congregation of floating humans at Isla Ballestas.

Atenas, a prime windsurfing section. Dirt roads lead farther to Playa Mendieta and Playa Carhaus. Small, open restaurant shacks line the more popular beaches.

EXPLORING

Fodors Choice
★

Islas Ballestas. Spectacular rocks pummeled by waves and wind into *ball-estas* (arched bows) along the cliffs mark this haven of jagged outcrops and rugged beaches that shelter thousands of marine birds and sea lions. You're not allowed to walk on shore, but you wouldn't want to—the land is calf-deep in *guano* (bird droppings). ■ TIP→ **Bring a hat, as tourists are moving targets for multitudes of guano-dropping seabirds. Also, be prepared for the smell—between the sea lions and the birds the odor can drop you to your knees.** A boat provides the best views of the abundant wildlife: sea lions laze on the rocks surrounded by penguins, pelicans, seals, boobies, cormorants, and even condors, which make celebrity appearances for the appreciative crowds in February and March. On route to the islands is Punta Pejerrey, the northernmost point of the isthmus and the best spot for viewing the enormous, cactus-shape **Candelabra** carved in the cliffs. It's variously said to represent a symbol of the power of the northern Chavín culture, a Masonic symbol placed on the hillside by General Jose San Martín, leader of the liberation movement, or a pre-Inca religious figure.

Fodors Choice
★

Reserva Nacional de Paracas. If a two-hour jaunt around the Islas Ballestas doesn't satisfy your thirst for guano, sea lions, and sea birds, then a land trip to this 280,000-hectare (700,000-plus-acre) park just might. The stunning coastal reserve, on a peninsula south of Pisco, teems with wildlife. Pelicans, condors, and red-and-white flamingos congregate

CLOSE UP

Area Tours

In Ica, Costa Linda and Pelican Travel Service offer tours of the city and can arrange trips to Paracas National Park and the Nazca Lines. One fellow you can't miss in Ica is Roberto Penny Cabrera, a direct descendent of Ica's founding family with a home right on the Plaza de Armas. After a long career in mining, Roberto started his company, Ica Desert Trip Peru, and began offering tours of the nearby desert in his fully equipped four-wheel-drive Jeep. He's fascinated with the fossils of gigantic sharks and whales he's come across and has a collection of huge incisors that would make Peter Benchley jump.

Guided tours of Paracas National Park and the Ballestas Islands are offered by Zarcillo Connections in Paracas. Ballestas Travel Service represents several travel agencies who sell park packages. Just about every hotel in Pisco and Paracas will assist booking tours, and most include transport to and from the dock at Paracas. Make sure your boat has life jackets.

Most hotels can arrange tours of the Nazca Lines, but several travel companies also specialize in local explorations. The going rate for a flight over the lines ranges US$40–US$60, depending on the season. Book ahead, because the flights are often sold out. The inexpensive and often recommended Alegría Tours includes stops at several archaeological sites, maps, guides, and options for hiking the area. Nasca Trails arranges flights over the Nazca Lines, trips to the Pampas Galeras vicuña reserve, and tours of the Cementerio Chauchills in Spanish, Italian, French, German, and English.

Make sure the guide or agency is licensed and experienced. Professional guides must be approved by the Ministry of Tourism, so ask for identification before you hire.

ICA
Ica Desert Trip Peru (Roberto Penny Cabrera) (✉ *Bolivar 178, Ica* ☎ *056/231–933*). **Huacachina Tours** (✉ *Perotti s/n, Balneario de Huacachina Ica* ☎ *051/113–252* ⊕ *www. huacachina.com*).

NAZCA LINES
Alegría Tours (✉ *Calle Lima 168, Nazca* ☎ *056/522–444 or 056/506–722*). **Nasca Trails** (✉ *Ignacio Morsequi, Nazca* ☎ *056/522–858*).

PARACAS AND ISLAS BALLESTAS
Ballestas Travel Service (✉ *San Francisco 249, Pisco* ☎ *034/533–095*). **Costa Linda** (✉ *Prolongación Ayabaca 509, Ica* ☎ *056/234–251*). **Pelican Travel Service** (✉ *Independencia 156, Galerías Siesta, Ica 051/456–7802*). **Peru Kite** (✉ *Paracas L-10, Paracas* ☎ *056/225–211* ⊕ *www. perukite.com*). **Tikary** (☎ *056/58-1333* ⊕ *www.tikary.com.pe*). **Zarcillo Connection** (✉ *Paracas* ☎ *056/536–543* ⊕ *www.carcilloconnections.com*).

3

and breed here; the latter are said to have inspired the red-and-white independence flag General San Martín designed when he liberated Peru. On shore you can't miss the sound (or the smell) of the hundreds of sea lions, while in the water you might spot penguins, sea turtles, dolphins, manta rays, and even hammerhead sharks.

Named for the blustering *paracas* (sandstorms) that buffet the west coast each winter, the Reserva Nacional de Paracas is Peru's first park for marine conservation. Organized tours take you along the thin dirt tracks that crisscross the peninsula, passing by sheltered lagoons, rugged cliffs full of caves, and small fishing villages. This is prime walking territory, where you can stroll from the bay to the **Julio Tello Museum,** and on to the fishing village of **Lagunilla** 5 km (3 mi) farther across the neck of the peninsula. Adjacent to the museum are colonies of flamingos, best seen June through July (and absent January through March, when they fly to Sierra). Hike another 6 km (4 mi) to reach **Mirador de Lobos** (Sea-Lion Lookout) at Punta El Arquillo. Carved into the highest point in the cliffs above Paracas Bay, 14 km (9 mi) from the museum is the **Candelabra.** Note that you must hire a guide to explore the land trails. Minibus tours of the entire park can be arranged through local hotels and travel agencies for about S/35 for five hours.

WHERE TO EAT AND STAY

Sleepy Paracas really only comes alive during the Peruvian summer (December to March), when city dwellers arrive to set up residence in their shore-front holiday homes. If visiting out of season, be warned—many hotels close during the low season, or take the opportunity to scale back their service and concentrate on repairs.

$ ✕ **El Chorito.** Spacious, light-filled, and with minimalistic white decor
SEAFOOD and polished wood, this eatery would not look out of place in a much larger and more cosmopolitan city. The emphasis is on seafood, dished up in delicious creations such as *conchitas à la parmesana* (baked mussels with Parmesan cheese). The dish to try is the cebiche *asesino,* or "killer cebiche," which packs a spicy punch. ⊠ *Av. Paracas s/n, in front of Plazuela Abelarolo Quiñorez* ☎ *056/545–045* 🖃 *AE, MC, V.*

$$$$ 🛏 **Hotel Paracas Libertador.** The best of the new resorts to have opened
Fodor'sChoice in Paracas in recent years, the ultra-chic Libertador hotel was created
★ from the rubble of the once famous Hotel Paracas, destroyed in the 2007 earthquake. World-renowned designer Bernardo Fort-Brescia used more than $2 million USD in bamboo in the two trendy restaurants and lounge, and the world-class spa ups the resort's coolness factor significantly. The two sparkling pools are lined with daybeds and the hotel has its own pier for trips to the Islas Ballestas, as well as a private jet that does flyover trips of the Nazca Lines. The spacious rooms are done in earthy tones and add every modern amenity imaginable. All feature a private terrace. **Pros:** Beachfront location; sea views; one of Peru's most luxurious hotels. **Cons:** Wind can pick up at times near the pool. ⊠ *Av. Paracas 173* ☎ *056/581–333* ⊕ *www.libertador.com* ⤵ *120 rooms* ☺ *In-room: a/c, Internet, Wi-Fi, safe. In-hotel: two restaurants, spa, room service, bar, pools, laundry service, parking (free).* 🖃 *AE, DC, MC, V.*

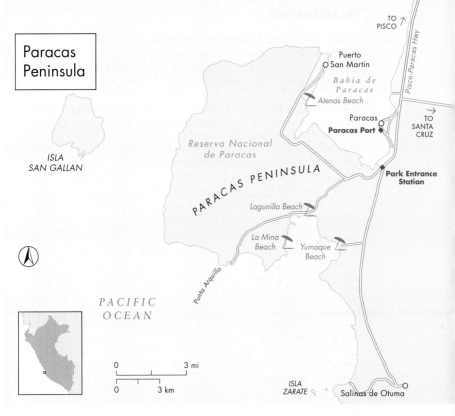

Paracas
Peninsula

TO
PISCO

Pisco-Paracas Hwy

Puerto
San Martin

*Bahia de
Paracas*
Atenas Beach

Paracas
Paracas Port ◆

TO
SANTA
CRUZ

*Reserva Nacional
de Paracas*

ISLA
SAN GALLAN

PARACAS PENINSULA

**Park Entrance
Station**

Lagunilla Beach

La Mina
Beach
Yumaque
Beach

Punto Arquillo

*PACIFIC
OCEAN*

0   3 mi

0   3 km

ISLA
ZARATE
Salinas de Otuma

$$$ ☼ **La Haceinda Bahia Paracas.** Open since mid-2009, the La Hacienda may not be as flashy as the nearby Libertador or Doubletree, but it's nearly as nice. Part of the massive pool area butts right up against several of the rooms so you can swim right off your porch. The rooms feature clay tile floors and textiles modeled after the Paracas culture designs, many of the same electronics of the pricier hotels, and a private patio. **Pros:** less expensive than other nearby resorts; amazing pool. **Cons:** slow during the week; only one restaurant. ⊠ *Santo Domingo Lote 25* ☎ *056/213–1000* ⊕ *www.hoteleslahacienda.com* ⇥ *68 rooms* ☐ *In-room: a/c, Internet, Wi-Fi, safe. In-hotel: restaurant, spa, room service, bar, pool, laundry service, parking (free)* ☐ *AE, DC, MC, V* ❖❙ *CP.*

¢ ☼ **Refugio del Pirata.** Friendly and terrifically located for those heading out to early-morning boat tours, this ramshackle guesthouse is popular with backpackers and tour groups alike. The slightly worn-looking rooms may be nothing to write home about, but the breakfast terrace with views over the port is the best spot in town to catch up on post-card writing or enjoy a pisco sour. Try to get a room with sea views; those that face the internal corridor are small and dark. **Pros:** central location in town; terrific terrace with port views; easy to organize tours via the affiliated travel agency on the ground floor. **Cons:** no restaurant; rooms lack style. ⊠ *Av. Paracas Lote 6* ☎ *056/545–054* ⇥ *14 rooms*

♿ *In-room: no a/c, no phone. In-hotel: bar, laundry service, Internet terminal, parking (free)* ⊟ *No credit cards.*

ICA AND NAZCA

South of Pisco, the thin black highway cuts through desert vast and pale as cracked parchment, and there's nothing but sand and sky as far as the eye can see. As you gaze out the bus window at mile upon endless mile of arid coastal desert, you'd be forgiven for thinking that there's little to hold your attention in this part of Peru.

You couldn't be more wrong. With good wines, year-round sunshine, spectacular desert landscapes, and giant desert drawings left by one of the world's most mysterious and enigmatic ancient cultures, there's definitely more to this region than meets the eye.

Head to Nazca to puzzle over the mystery of the world-famous Nazca Lines—giant drawings of animals, geometric shapes, and perfectly straight lines that stretch for miles across the desert floor. Who created them and why? Theories range from ancient irrigation systems to alien spaceship landing sites. Hop on a light aircraft for a dizzying overflight and try and cook up your own theory.

Or try tackling the easier problem of discerning which of Ica's numerous bodegas produces the best pisco, and if you're around in March, have a go at stamping the grapes during the pressing season.

Adrenaline seekers will find their mecca in Huacachina, where the dazzling dunes can be explored in a hair-raising dune buggy ride or slid down on a sandboard. The oasis town just outside Ica also draws the health-conscious, who come to enjoy the lagoon's reputedly magical healing qualities.

ICA

56 km (35 mi) southeast of Paracas.

A bustling commercial city with chaotic traffic and horn-happy drivers, Ica challenges you to find its attractive side. Step outside the city center, however, and you'll see why this town was the Nazca capital between AD 300 and 800, and why the Nasca people couldn't have picked a better place to center their desert civilization. Set in a patch of verdant fields and abutted by snow-covered mountains, Ica is serene, relaxing, and cheerful, with helpful residents—likely due as much to the nearly never-ending sunshine as to the vast selection of high-quality wines and piscos produced by dozens of local bodegas. This is a town of laughter and festivals, most notably the Fiesta de Vendimia, the wine-harvest celebration that takes place each year in early March. Ica is also famous for its pecans and its high-stepping horses called *caballos de paso*.

The city's colonial look comes from its European heritage. Ica was founded by the Spanish in 1536, making it one of the oldest towns in southern Peru. The city suffered badly in the August 2007 earthquake, however, and sadly many of the colonial-era buildings, including most of the famous churches, were damaged.

Today Peru's richest wine-growing region is a source of national pride, and its fine bodegas are a major attraction. Most are open all year, but the best time to visit is February to April, during the grape harvest. The Tacama and Ocucaje bodegas are generally considered to have the best-quality wines and the Quebranta and Italia grape varietals are well regarded. ■TIP→ The Peruvian autumn is the season for Ica's Fiesta de la Vendimia, where you can enjoy parades, sports competitions, local music, and dancing, and even catch beauty queens stamping grapes. It's also a great time to be introduced to the vast selection of local wines and piscos, as well as an opportunity to try homemade concoctions not yet on the market.

The city's excitement also heightens for such festivals as February's Carnival, Semana Santa in March or April, and the all-night pilgrimages of El Señor de Luren in March and October. Other fun times to visit are during Ica Week, around June 17, which celebrates the city's founding, and the annual Ica Tourist Festival in late September.

GETTING AROUND

Surrounded as it is by vineyards, tourism in Ica is all about wineries. Most are close to the city and are easily accessed by road. ■TIP→ If you don't have your own car (or you don't want to be designated driver on a winery trip), pick the wineries you'd like to see and ask a taxi driver to give you a price. Or hop on one of the prearranged tours offered by most hotels. The going rate for a four-hour taxi ride taking in three wineries close to the city is around S/50; if you go on a formal tour you'll pay up to S/40 per person.

Taxis in Ica include the noisy but distinctive three-wheeled "moto-taxis." A taxi ride between Ica and Huacachina costs S/3–S/4.

The bus company Ormeños has the most departures from Ica, although the quality of their vehicles and onboard service is notoriously patchy. Buses usually depart from the park at the western end of Salaverry and go to Lima (5 hours, S/16), Pisco (1 hour, S/4), and Nazca (3 hours, S/7). Taxis *colectivos* to Lima (3 ½ hours, S/42) and Nazca (2 hours, S/7) leave from the southwest corner of Municipalidad and Lambayeque when full.

ESSENTIALS

Bus Contacts Ormeño (✉ *Lambayeque 180* ☎ *056/215–600*).

Currency Banco de Crédito (✉ *Av. Grau 105* ☎ *056/235–959*).

Internet Cetelica (✉ *Huánico* ☎ *056/221–534*).

Mail Post Office (✉ *Lima y Moquegua* ☎ *056/221–958*). **DHL** (✉ *Av. San Martín 398* ☎ *056/234–549*).

Visitor Info Inrena (✉ *Petirrojos 355* ☎ *01/441–0425*). **Tourist Office** (✉ *Caja-marca 179*).

EXPLORING

❺ **Iglesia San Francisco.** Soaring ceilings, ornate stained-glass windows, and the fact that it's the only one of Ica's colonial era churches left standing after the 2007 earthquake make this the city's grandest religious building. Yet even this colossal monument didn't escape the quake unscathed.

■TIP➔ If you look on the floor toward the front of the church you can see the gouges left in the marble blocks by falling pieces of the church altar. It's said that the statues of the saints stood serenely throughout the quake and didn't move an inch. ⊠ *At Avs. Municipalidad y San Martín* ☎ *No phone* 🎫 *Free* ☉ *Mon.–Sat. 6:30–9:30 and 4:30–7:30.*

❻ Museo Cabrera. Curious to find the *real* meaning of the Nazca Lines? Head to this small, unmarked building on the Plaza de Armas, which contains a collection of more than 10,000 intricately carved stones and boulders depicting varied pre-Colombian themes ranging from ancient surgical techniques to dinosaurs. The charismatic and eccentric owner, Dr. Javier Cabrera, has studied the stones for many years and is more than happy to explain to you how they prove the existence of an advanced pre-Colombian society who created the Nazca Lines as a magnetic landing strip for their spacecraft (he even has the diagram to prove it!). ⊠ *Bolívar 170* ☎ *056/231–933 or 056/213–026* 🎫 *S/10 with guided tour* ☉ *Weekdays 9:30–1 and 4:30–7, weekends by appointment only.*

❼ Museo Histórico Regional. It may be a little out of the way, but don't

Fodor'sChoice let that stop you from visiting this fantastic museum with a vast and
★ well-preserved collection on regional history—particularly from the Inca, Nazca, and Paracas cultures. Note the quipas, mysterious knotted, colored threads thought to have been used to count commodities and quantities of food. ■TIP➔ Fans of the macabre will love the mummy display, where you can see everything from human mummies to a mummified bird. The squeamish can head out back to view a scale model of the Nazca Lines from an observation tower. You can also buy maps (S/0.50) and paintings of Nazca motifs (S/4). The museum is about 1½ km (1 mi) from town. It's not advisable to walk, so take the opportunity to jump into one of the distinctive three-wheeled *mototaxis* that will make the trip for around S/2. ⊠ *Ayabaca s/n* ☎ *056/234–383* 🎫 *S/11, plus S/4 camera fee* ☉ *Weekdays 8–7, Sat. 9–6, Sun. 9–1, or by appointment.*

WINERIES

If you can't imagine anything better than sampling different varieties of wine and pisco at nine in the morning, then these winery tours are most definitely for you. Most wineries in the Ica region make their living from tourism and as a way of boosting sales devote a good portion of the winery tour to the tasting room. Tours are free although the guides do appreciate tips.

■TIP➔ Peruvians like their wines sweet and their pisco strong. If you're unused to drinking spirits straight up, follow this tried and true Peruvian technique for a smoother drop—after swirling the pisco around the glass, inhale the vapors. Before exhaling, take the pisco into your mouth and taste the flavor for four seconds. As you swallow, exhale!

❷ Bodega El Carmen. Look for this small winery on the right side of the road when you're driving south into Ica; it makes a good stop for sampling fine pisco. Look for the ancient grape press, which was made from an enormous tree trunk. ⊠ *3 km (2 mi) north of Ica, Guadalupe* ☎ *056/233–495* 🎫 *Free* ☉ *Mon.–Sat. 10–4.*

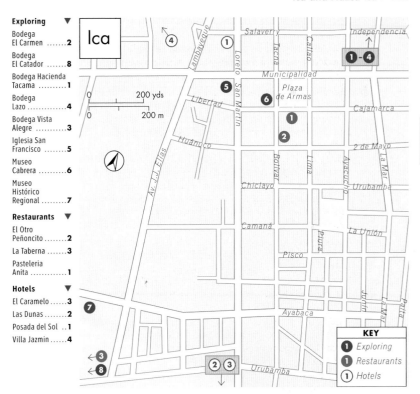

Exploring ▼

Bodega
El Carmen **2**

Bodega
El Catador **8**

Bodega Hacienda
Tacama **1**

Bodega
Lazo **4**

Bodega Vista
Alegre **3**

Iglesia San
Francisco **5**

Museo
Cabrera **6**

Museo
Histórico
Regional **7**

Restaurants ▼

El Otro
Peñoncito **2**

La Taberna **3**

Pasteleria
Anita **1**

Hotels ▼

El Caramelo **3**

Las Dunas **2**

Posada del Sol ..**1**

Villa Jazmin **4**

8 Bodega El Catador. A favorite stop on the tour circuit, this family-run winery produces wines and some of the region's finest pisco. If you're here in March, watch out for the annual Fiesta de Uva where the year's festival queen tours the vineyard and gets her feet wet in the opening of the grape-pressing season. If you miss the festival, check out the photos in the small museum near the restaurant. The excellent Taberna restaurant and bar is open for lunch after a hard morning's wine tasting. If you don't want to drive, take a taxi or wait at the second block of Moquegua for Bus 6 (S/1), which passes by about every half hour. ✉ *Pan-American Hwy. S, Km 294, Fondo Tres Equinas 102* ☎ *056/403– 295* 💲 *Free* ☉ *Daily 8–6.*

1 Bodega Hacienda Tacama. After suffering earthquake damage in 2007, this 16th-century farm hacienda has taken the opportunity to overhaul its now very modern operation. Internationally renowned, it produces some of Peru's best labels, particularly the Blanco de Blancos. Stroll through the rolling vineyards—still watered by the Achirana irrigation canal built by the Inca—before sampling the end result. The estate is about 11 km (7 mi) north from town. ✉ *Camina a la Tinguiña s/n* ☎ *056/228–395* 🌐 *www.tacama.com* 💲 *Free* ☉ *Weekdays 9–2.*

4 Bodega Lazo. One of the more fun alcohol-making operations to visit is owned by Elar Bolivar, who claims to be a direct descendent of the

Bodega
El Catador **1**

Bodega Hacienda
Tacama **3**

Bodega
Lazo **2**

Bodega Vista
a Alegre **4**

Ocucaje **5**

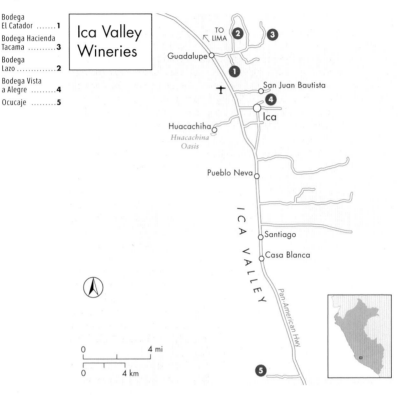

Ica Valley
Wineries

Libertador Simón Bolívar himself (some locals shrug their shoulders at this boast). Regardless, Elar's small artisanal operation includes a creepy collection of shrunken heads (Dutch tourists, he says, who didn't pay their drink tab), ancient cash registers, fencing equipment, and copies of some of the paintings in Ica's regional museum. The question is, who really has the originals—Elar or the museum? As part of your visit, you can taste the bodega's recently made pisco, straight from the clay vessel. Some organized tours include this bodega as part of a tour. It's not a safe walk from town, so take a cab if you come on your own. ✉ *Camino de Reyes s/n, San Juan Bautista* ☎ *056/403–430* ✉ *Free.*

❸ **Bodega Vista Alegre.** A sunny brick archway welcomes you to this large, pleasant winery, which has been producing fine wines, pisco, and sangria since it was founded by the Picasso brothers in 1857. The largest winery in the valley, this former monastery is a popular tour bus stop so come early to avoid the groups. Tours in English or Spanish take you through the vast pisco and wine-making facilities at this industrial winery before depositing you in the tasting room. Take a taxi or city bus 8 or 13 to get there. *Don't walk from downtown Ica,* as robberies have been reported along this route. ✉ *Camina a la Tinguiña, Km 205* ☎ *056/238–735* ✉ *Free* ⊙ *Weekdays 9–2.*

WHERE TO EAT AND STAY

$
PERUVIAN

✕ **El Otro Peñoncito.** Three generations have had a hand in this family business, one of the oldest and most respected restaurants in Ica. Dishing up traditional Peruvian cuisine and the self-proclaimed best pisco sours around, this classic spot is a welcome change from the usual fried chicken and rice joints on every other corner. Local specialties include the *pollo a la Iqueña* (chicken in a rich pecan, pisco, and spinach sauce) and the traditional *papas a la huancaina* (potatoes with cheese sauce). Owner Hary Hernandez says he won't accept credit cards, although precious stones, gold, and silver are fine. Art by Iqueño artists adorns the walls. ⊠ *Bolívar 255* ☎ *056/233–921* ▭ *No credit cards.*

$$
PERUVIAN

✕ **La Taberna.** After a hard morning's wine tasting, stop in this cheerful open-air restaurant in Bodega El Catador to take in some carbohydrates and soak up the pisco. Like an outdoor rural dining room, this pleasant spot dishes up local specialties such as *carapulcra con sopa seca*, a stew of dried potatoes and dried meat, washed down with one of El Catador's excellent wines. If you want to keep up the pace, Catador's bar with its extensive range of piscos is within arm's reach. ⊠ *José Carrasco González, Km 296* ☎ *056/403–295* ▭ *AE, MC, V.*

$
CAFÉ

✕ **Pasteleria Anita.** High ceilings lend an openness to this popular spot on the Plaza de Armas, which makes it perfect for people-watching. Everything from cappuccino to shrimp cocktail is available, and although it's not the cheapest venue in town, the range of delicious pastries and locally famous *tejas* (manjar blanco or chocolate-coated pecans) make it a top pick for sweet tooths. ⊠ *Jr. Libertad 133, Plaza de Armas* ☎ *056/218–582* ▭ *AE, DC, MC, V.*

$
☉

🏨 **El Carmelo Hotel & Hacienda.** Hotel or bodega-related theme park? It's hard to tell at the oddball spot on the road between Ica and Huacachina, where rooms are built around a central courtyard complete with ancient grape press and working pisco distillery. It's strange but it works, giving the place a unique and charming air. There's something for everyone—an adventure playground for the kids, a small zoo, and of course, the bodega. Rooms are simple but comfortable with pastel furnishings and wood fittings. In March, you're invited to use your feet in the annual grape pressing. **Pros:** wicker-filled open-air sitting room; chance to see the pisco-making process up close; zoo to entertain the kids. **Cons:** out of town location; rooms are on the small side; eccentric design. ⊠ *Pan-American Hwy., Km 301.2* ☎ *056/232–191* ⊕ *www.elcarmelohotelhacienda.com* ⤶ *58 rooms* ☉ *In-room: a/c, Wi-Fi. In-hotel: restaurant, bar, pool, laundry service, Internet, Wi-Fi, parking (free)* ▭ *AE, MC, V.*

$$$
☉

🏨 **Hotel Las Dunas.** For a taste of the good life, Peruvian style, head to this top-end resort on the road between Ica and Huacachina. A cluster of whitewashed buildings at the foot of the dunes, this colonial-style holiday resort is a favorite getaway for Peruvian families. Llamas roam freely in the grounds. The ponds and canals that run between the buildings are full of fish. Spacious rooms have balconies overlooking lush lawns, and suites have sunny courtyards and whirlpools. You can dine poolside or in a breezy gazebo at the restaurant and enjoy such dishes as flounder with seafood sauce and spicy *lomo saltado*, an enormous pile of stir-fried beef, tomatoes, chips, and rice. Rent sandboards, play golf on the dunes, ride horseback, or fly over the Nazca Lines (S/350) from the hotel's airstrip. Book weekdays to save 20%. **Pros:** beautiful grounds; activities for children; top restaurant. **Cons:** out of town; resort aesthetic; rooms look a little frumpy for the price. ⊠ *La Angostura 400* ☎ *056/213-5000* ⊕ *www.lasdunashotel.com* ⤵ *130 rooms, 3 suites* ⚑ *In-room: a/c, safe, refrigerator, Internet, Wi-Fi (some). In-hotel: restaurant, bars, golf course, tennis court, pools, gym, bicycles, laundry service, Internet terminal, parking (free)* ═ *AE, DC, MC, V.*

¢ ⌅ **Posada del Sol.** Surly staff and a noisy street frontage take the shine off this small hotel in central Ica, yet given the dearth of decent lodgings it remains one of the best options in town. The rooms are clean but characterless, and some only have internal windows. The corner suites are far nicer with lots of natural light and space but are only for heavy sleepers on account of the horn-happy drivers on the road below. **Pros:** central location near the Plaza de Armas; secure; comfortable beds. **Cons:** noisy street frontage; standard rooms only have internal windows; unhelpful staff. ⊠ *Esquina Loreto y Salvaverry 193* ☎ *056/238–446* ⤵ *50 rooms* ⚑ *In-room: no a/c, no TV. In-hotel: laundry service, Internet terminal, parking (free)* ═ *No credit cards.*

$$ ⌅ **Villa Jazmin.** Open since 2008, this rival to Las Dunas has been garnishing rave reviews from every visitor that passes through its doors. It's considerably smaller and the personable owner will be there to welcome you with a pisco sour; the charming dune setting and small but inviting pool make this a good place to chill out for a few days while exploring the area. Rooms are modern, clean, and feature bright cheery colors that help make up for the lack of natural light. **Pros:** new, clean, and less crowded than other Ica resorts. **Cons:** rooms can be dark; the pool is more for lounging than swimming. ⊠ *Los Girasoles MZ C-1, La Angostura* ☎ *056/258-179* ⊕ *www.villajazmin.net* ⤵ *20 rooms* ⚑ *In-room: Wi-Fi. In-hotel: restaurant, bar, pools, laundry service, Internet terminal, parking (free)* ═ *AE, DC, MC, V.*

SHOPPING

Ica is an excellent place to pick up Peruvian handicrafts with regional styles and motifs. Tapestries and textiles woven in naturally colored llama and alpaca wool often have images of the Nazca Lines and historical figures. In particular, look for *alfombras* (rugs), *colchas* (blankets), and *tapices* (hangings).

HUACACHINA

5 km (3 mi) southwest of Ica.

Drive 10 minutes through the pale, mountainous sand dunes southwest of Ica and you'll suddenly see a gathering of attractive, pastel-color buildings surrounding a patch of green. It's not an oasis on the horizon, but rather the lakeside resort of Laguna de Huacachina, a palm-fringed lagoon of jade-color waters whose sulfurous properties are reputed to have healing powers. The view is breathtaking: a collection of attractive, colonial-style hotels in front of a golden beach and with a backdrop of snow-covered peaks against the distant sky. In the 1920s Peru's elite traveled here for the ultimate holiday, and today the spacious resorts still beckon. The lake is also a pilgrimage site for those with health and skin problems, sandboarders who want to tackle the 100-meter (325-foot) dunes, and budget travelers who pitch tents in the sand or sleep under the stars.

GETTING HERE AND AROUND

Huacachina sits on the opposite side of the highway from the center of Ica. Take any bus to Ica and hire a mototaxi to the oasis for about S/8.

EN ROUTE

About 40 km (27 mi) southeast of Huacachina is **Bodega Ocucaje**, a famous winery in an old Spanish mansion, whose vintages—including the famous Vino Fond de Cave—are considered among Peru's best. Because of the isolation, the bodega gets few visitors so be sure to call ahead in advance. Also on the property is the Ocucaje Sun & Wine Resort, though it was heavily damaged in the 2007 earthquake and has yet to reopen. ⊠ *Av. Principal s/n* ☎ *056/836–101* ⊕ *www.ocucaje.com* ✉ *S/15* ☽ *Weekdays 9–noon and 2–5, Sat. 9–noon.*

WHERE TO EAT AND STAY

PERUVIAN

¢ ✕**Arturo's Restaurant Taberna.** In a town severely lacking dining options, this new restaurant holds some promise. With plastic furniture and a concrete floor, it's not winning any style prizes, but the hearty Peruvian cooking hits the spot and with most meals going for around S/7 to S/10 it's by far the best deal on food in town. Owner Arturo has grand plans to turn it into a more upmarket eatery, so expect changes. There's a good selection of wines from the local bodegas, and prices are almost as cheap as buying direct from the winery. ⊠ *Av. Perotti, lote 3* ☎ *No phone* ⊟ *No credit cards.*

¢ ⛺**Carola del Sur.** This place is party central—just follow the sounds of Bob Marley drifting on the night air and you'll be sure to end up here. Rooms are basic, but then again people don't come here to hang out in their rooms. Instead, they spend their time lounging by the pool, playing with (and rescuing their belongings from) Marvin, the resident spider monkey, and chowing down on great Peruvian and international food in the central bar and restaurant. Carola del Sur is affiliated with Casa de Arena just up the road, and together they run an extensive and professional dune buggy service. **Pros:** good restaurant and bar; pool has views of the dunes; Huacachina's largest and longest running dune buggy service. **Cons:** terrible fluorescent lighting in the rooms; small windows; loud music makes getting an early night impossible. ⊠ *Av Perotti s/n, Balneario de Huacachina* ☎ *056/215–439* ⤳ *50 rooms* ⚑ *In-room: no phone, no TV, no a/c. In-hotel: restaurant, bar, pool, laundry service, parking (free)* ⊟ *No credit cards.*

¢ ⛺**El Hauchachinero.** Hands-down Huacachina's best budget lodging, this is a beautiful bargain in the oasis of Peru. Clean, safe, and with its own little bar featuring a mural of Ica's now-disappeared camel herd, this place is very popular, so call ahead or risk missing out. Thoughtful design touches are everywhere, from the Peruvian art and artesanía adorning the walls to the gorgeous bamboo fittings and wooden balconies and walkways. If you want to relax, the pool area with its hammocks for lounging in is super inviting. If you're feeling more adventurous, head out on a dune buggy and sandboarding tour. The

Fodor's Choice
★

collection of raucous parrots will ensure that you're up in time for breakfast. **Pros:** fantastic pool area with hammocks for lounging; dune-buggy service and sandboard rental; attractively furnished rooms and common areas. **Cons:** often full; noisy parrots. ⊠ *Av. Perotti, Balnea-ria de Huacachina* ☎ *056/271–435* ⊕ *www.elhuacachinero.com* ⬐ *21 private rooms, 3 shared rooms* ⚒ *In-room: no phone, no TV, no a/c. In-hotel: bar, pool, laundry facilities, parking (free)* ▭ *No credit cards* ⦿ *CP.*

¢ ☷ **Hosteria Suiza.** It may not be the most jumping joint in town, but this guesthouse is a good spot for enjoying the beauty of the desert landscape and lush oasis without having to deal with the constant party that exists in some other hotels. The gorgeous manicured garden with pool and outdoor *parrilla* (barbecue) looks right onto the dunes, and some rooms have balconies overlooking the oasis. **Pros:** peaceful atmosphere; lovely garden; great pool. **Cons:** restaurant only serves breakfast; furnishings are a little old-fashioned. ⊠ *Balneario de Huacachina* ☎ *056/238–762* ⬐ *17 rooms* ⚒ *In-rooms: no a/c, no TV. In-hotel: restaurant, bar, pool, parking (free)* ▭ *V* ⦿ *CP.*

$$ ☷ **Hotel Mossone.** Imagine life as it was in Huacachina's heyday in the oasis's original hotel. With a picture-postcard location fronting onto the lagoon and gorgeous Spanish colonial–style architecture, this dilapidated spot has lost the sparkle that made it so popular when it opened in the 1920s. An internal courtyard lined with tall ficus trees is the focal point of this century-old mansion. Watch out for Jennifer, the (male) tortoise who likes to stroll here during the day. Rooms look out onto gardens overflowing with flowers and the elegant bar and restaurant have splendid lake views. The hotel provides free bicycles and sandboards for guests, but if you're staying elsewhere you can still stop in for excellent *comida criolla* (cuisine rich in peppers, onions and other spices), especially *papas a la huancaina*, a potato dish served with a creamy mustard sauce. **Pros:** fantastic location in front of the lagoon; great pool; the elegant lounge bar is the best spot in town from which to watch the sun set over the dunes. **Cons:** rooms look a little tired; hotel is often full with tour groups. ⊠ *Balneario de Huacachina s/n* ☎ *056/213–630; 01/261–9605 in Lima* ⬐ *41 rooms* ⚒ *In-room: safe, refrigerator, a/c. In-hotel: restaurant, bar, pool, bicycles, laundry service, Internet terminal, parking (free)* ▭ *AE, DC, MC, V.*

NAZCA

Fodor's Choice   *120 km (75 mi) southeast of Ica.*

★   What do a giant hummingbird, a monkey, and an astronaut have in common? Well, apart from the fact that they're all etched into the floor of the desert near Nazca, no one really seems to know. Welcome to one of the world's greatest mysteries—the enigmatic Nazca Lines. A mirage of green in the desert, lined with cotton fields and orchards and bordered by crisp mountain peaks, Nazca was a quiet colonial town unnoticed by the rest of the world until 1901, when Peruvian archaeologist Max Uhle excavated sites around Nazca and discovered the remains of a unique pre-Colombian culture. Set 598 meters (1,961 feet) above sea

SANDBOARDING

Ever fancied having a go at snow-boarding but chickened out at the thought of all those painful next-day bruises? Welcome to the new adventure sport of sandboarding, a softer and warmer way to hit the slopes. Surrounded by dunes, Huacachina is the sandboarding capital of the world: every year European sports fans arrive here in droves to practice for the international sand-surfing competitions on Cerro Blanco, the massive dune 14 km (8 mi) north of Nazca.

With no rope tows or chairlifts to get you up the dunes, the easiest way to have a go at sandboarding is to go on a dune buggy tour, offered by just about every hotel in town. In these converted vehicles you'll be driven (quickly) to the top of the dunes, upon which you can board, slide, or slither down to be picked up again at the bottom. Drivers push their vehicles hard, so be prepared for some heart-stopping moments. Carola del Sur guesthouse has the biggest fleet of dune buggies and runs two tours daily at 10 AM and 4 PM. The tours last around two hours and cost S/45.

level, the town has a dry climate—scorching by day, nippy by night—that was instrumental in preserving centuries-old relics from Inca and pre-Columbian tribes. ■TIP→ **The area has more than 100 cemeteries, where the humidity-free climate has helped preserve priceless jewelry, textiles, pottery, and mummies.** Overlooking the parched scene is the 2,078-meter (6,815-foot) Cerro Blanco, the highest sand dune in the world.

GETTING AROUND

Be prepared: Nazca is all about tours and it may seem like everyone in town is trying to sell you one at once. The minute you poke your nose outside the bus door you'll be swamped with offers for flights over the Lines, hotels, and trips to the Chauchilla cemetery. Be wise about any offers made to you by touts at the bus station—if it's cheap, there's probably a good reason why. That said, a tour with a reputable agency is a great way to catch all of Nazca's major sites. Recommended agencies include Alegria Tours and Nasca Trails.

All buses arrive and depart from the *óvalo* (roundabout). To see the lines from ground level, taxis will make the 30-minute run out to the mirador for around S/40, or do it the local way and catch any northbound bus along the Panamericana for just S/3. ■TIP→ **Flights over the Lines are best in early morning before the sun gets too high and winds make flying uncomfortable.** Standard flights last around 30 minutes and cost between $70 USD and $1,000 USD, depending on the season. You'll also have to pay an airport tax of S/10 (watch out for cheeky operators who will try and tell you that the tax is $10 USD, it's not!). You can buy flight tickets from travel agencies and many hotels in town, or directly from the airline offices near the airport. Buying tickets in advance will save you time. Tickets are available on the spot at the airport but as planes won't take off until all seats are filled you may spend most of your morning hanging around the dusty Panamerica Sur watching while others take off and land.

Nazca Lines flights depart from the small Aeropuerto Nazca, cost S/191 for a 40-minute flight plus lunch, a tour of Nazca's archaeological museum, and a trip to the *mirador*. Note that these flights are often overbooked year-round; arrive early to check-in for your flight, as many are full and there's a chance you'll get bumped if you're late. Aero Ica and upstarts Aero Palpa, Aeroparacas, Aero Palcazu, TAE, Travel Air, and Taxi Aereo all offer services. As these latter lines are small operations with varying office hours, check at the airport for schedules. Most sightseeing flights depart from Nazca, although Aero Paracas also originates in Lima and Pisco.

Safety records for many of the airlines are spotty at best. In February 2010, seven tourists were killed when their Nazca Airlines flight crashed into the desert. Airlines change owners and names frequently, so it's hard to know exactly who you are flying with. Check with PromPeru in Lima before booking a flight.

ESSENTIALS

Air Carriers Aero Ica (☎ *01/440–2140* ⊕ *www.aeroica.net*). **Aero Palcazu** (☎ *061/990–0247*). **Aero Paracas** (☎ *01/265–8073 or 01/265–8173* ⊕ *www.aeroparacas.com*).

Bus Contacts Cruz del Sur (☎ *034/522–484* ⊕ *www.cruzdelsur.com.pe*). **Wari Tours** (☎ *056/534–967*).

Currency Banco de Crédito (✉ *Lima y Grau*).

Internet Speed Service (✉ *Bolognesi 299* ☎ *056/522–176*).

Medical Hospital de Apoyo (✉ *Calle Callao s/n* ☎ *056/522–486*). **Es Salud** (✉ *Juan Matta 613* ☎ *056/522–446*).

Mail Post Office (✉ *Jr. F. de Castillo 379* ☎ *056/522–947*).

Police Comisaría Sectorial (✉ *Av. Los Incas* ☎ *056/522–2084*).

EXPLORING

Cahuachi Pyramids. Within a walled, 4,050-square-yard courtyard west of the Nazca Lines is an ancient ceremonial and pilgrimage site. Six adobe pyramids, the highest of which is about 21 meters (70 feet), stand above a network of rooms and connecting corridors. Grain and water silos are also inside, and several large cemeteries lie outside the walls. Used by the early Nazca culture, the site is estimated to have existed for about two centuries before being abandoned about AD 200. Cahuachi takes its name from the word *qahuachi* (meddlesome). El Estaquería, with its mummification pillars, is nearby. Tours from Nazca visit both sites for around S/60 and take four hours. ✉ *34 km (21 mi) west of Nazca* ☎ *No phone* ☲ *Free* ☉ *Daily 8–5.*

Casa-Museo Maria Reiche. To see where a lifelong obsession with the Nazca lines can lead you, head to the former home of the German anthropologist who devoted her life to studying the mystery of the lines. There's little explanatory material among the pottery, textiles, mummies, and skeletons from the Paracas, Nazca, Wari, Chincha, and Inca cultures, so don't expect any of the area's mysteries to be solved here, but the museum does a great job of showing the environment in

Continued on page 141

by Ruth Anne Phillips

NAZCA LINES

On the surface of the southern Peruvian coastal desert or "Pampa" between the Nazca and Ingenio River valleys are the Nazca Lines. The Nazca Lines are enormous figures, geometric designs and straight lines etched into the desert's surface called geoglyphs. There are more than 1,000 enormous figures, geometric shapes and straight lines, some arranged as ray centers. While the most famous of the lines appear on the Pampa de San José near Nazca as well as on the hillsides of the valleys of the Río Grande de Nazca, the geoglyphs are throughout a larger area that comprises 400 square miles.

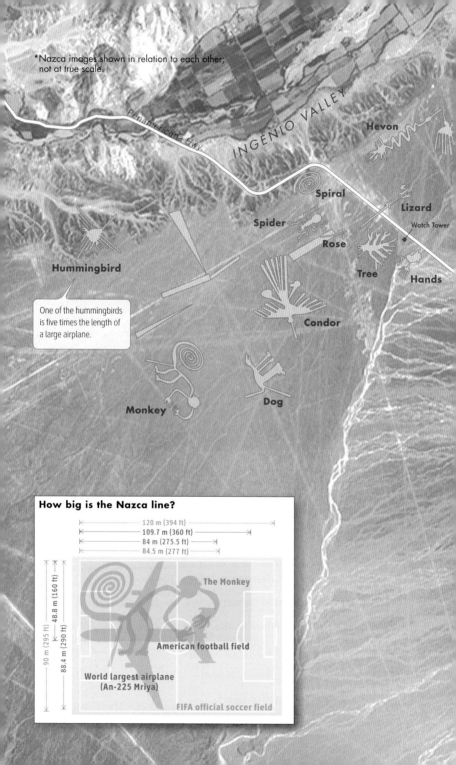

THINGS TO LOOK FOR

The biomorphic designs include monkeys, birds, a spider, plants, and a number of fantastical combinations and somewhat abstracted humanoid creatures. One of the monkeys is 180 feet long while a hummingbird is five times the length of a large airplane. At least 227 spirals, zigzags, triangles, quadrangles, and trapezoids make up the geometric designs, with one trapezoid measuring over 2,700 feet by 300

A trapezoid.

feet. The straight lines represent the greatest proportion of the geoglyphs: 800 single or parallel lines stretch on for miles, ranging in width from less than two feet to hundreds of feet.

Many of the lines haphazardly overlap each other, which indicates that as a group they were not pre-planned.

CONSTRUCTION
Modern archaeologists have recreated surprisingly simple construction methods for the geoglyphs using basic surveying techniques. Sight poles guided the construction of straight lines and strings tied to posts helped create circular designs. Wooden posts that may have been used as guides or end markers and an abundance of fancy potsherds, possibly used in rituals, have been found along many of the lines.

AGE
The extremely dry climatic conditions of the Pampa have helped preserve the lines; most date from c. 500 AD, during the florescence of the Nazca culture (c. 1–700 AD). A small number, however, may date to after the Nazca period to as late as 1000 AD.

Shell

Parrot

(78 miles from Nazca to Ingenio Valley)

Panamericana Hwy.

3

IN FOCUS NAZCA LINES

TO NAZCA

Astronaut

HISTORY AND MYSTERY

An archaeologist examines the lines.

Though the Nazca Lines are difficult to see from the ground due to their enormous size, some can be seen from nearby hillsides. It's widely believed that the lines were first properly seen from an airplane, but they were "discovered" by archaeologists working near Cahuachi in the mid-1920s. American archaeologist, Alfred L. Kroeber was the first to describe them in 1926, but it was Peruvian archaeologist Toribio Mejía Xesspe who conducted the first extensive studies of the Nazca Lines around the same time.

By the late 1920s, commercial planes began flying over the Pampa and many reported seeing the Nazca Lines from the air. It was not until American geographer and historian, Paul Kosok and his second wife Rose, flew over the Nazca drainage area in 1941, however, that the Nazca Lines became a widely known phenomenon in the United States and Europe.

THE CREATIVE PROCESS

The dry desert plain acts as a giant scratchpad as the darker oxidized surface can be swept away to reveal the lighter, pale pink subsurface. Many of the shapes are made with one continuous line that has piles of dark rocks lining the edges creating a dark border.

Stylistic comparisons between the figural Nazca Lines and images that appear on Nazca ceramics have helped establish their age.

THEORIES ABOUND

The Nazca Lines have incited various scholarly and popular theories for their construction and significance. Kroeber and Xesspe, observing the lines from the ground, believed that they served as sacred pathways. Kosok, seeing the lines from the air, observed the sun setting over the end of one line on the day of the winter solstice and thought they must have marked important astronomical events. German mathematician Maria Reiche, who studied the lines and lived near them for decades, expanded upon Kosok's astronomical theories. Modern scholars, however, have demonstrated that the lines' alignment to celestial events occurred at a frequency no greater than chance. Other theories posit that they were made for earth, mountain, or sky deities. After Cahuachi was determined in the 1980s to have been a large pilgrimage center, the idea that the lines acted as a sacred pathway has gained new momentum. Another plausible theory suggests that the Nazca Lines marked underground water sources.

IT'S THE ALIENS, OF COURSE
Popular theories have promoted the "mystery" of the Nazca Lines. One influential author, Erich von Däniken, suggested in his 1968 best-selling book *Chariots of the Gods* (reprinted several times and made into a film) that these giant geoglyphs were created as landing

Spaceman figure, San Jose Pampa

markers for extraterrestrials. Archaeologists and other scientists have dismissed these theories. The aliens deny them as well.

VISITING THE NAZCA LINES

The "Candelabra of the Andes" or the "Paracas Candelabra" on the Peninsula de Paracas.

The best way to view the Nazca Lines is by air in small, low-flying aircraft. Local companies offer flights usually in the early morning, when viewing conditions are best. You can fly over several birds, a few fish, a monkey, a spider, a flower, a condor, and/or several unidentified figures. While seeing the amazing Nazca Lines is a great experience, the sometimes questionable-looking airplanes with their strong fumes and pilots who seem to enjoy making nausea-inducing turns and twists can be worrisome. Because of poor safety records, planes are often grounded. Check with your tour operator before booking a trip with any local airline.

Nazca

KEY
- 🔵 Exploring
- 🔴 Restaurants
- ① Hotels

Exploring ▼	Restaurants ▼	Hotels ▼
Tallera de Artesania de Andre Calle Flores **1**	Cevicheria El Limon **1**	Casa Andina **5**
	Chifa Nam Kug **4**	Hotel Alegría **3**
	Restaurant Don Carlos **3**	Hotel Maison Suisse **1**
	Via la Encantada **2**	Hotel Majoro **2**
		Hotel Nazca Lines **4**

which Maria Reiche lived and worked, and her vast collection of tools, notes, and sketches is impressive. A scale model of the lines is behind the house. Take a bus from the Ormeño terminal to the Km 416 marker to reach the museum, which is 1 km (½ mi) from town. ⊠ *Pan-American Hwy., Km 416, San Pablo* ☎ *034/255734* 🖃 *S/3.50* ⊗ *Daily 9–4.*

Cementerio de Chauchilla. In the midst of the pale, scorched desert, the ancient cemetery is scattered with sun-bleached skulls and shards of pottery. *Huaqueros* (grave robbers) have ransacked the site over the years, and while up until a couple of years ago the mummies unearthed by their looting erupted from the earth in a jumble of bones and thread-bare weavings, they are now housed neatly inside a dozen or so covered tombs. It's nevertheless an eerie sight, as the mummies still have hair attached, as well as mottled, brown-rose skin stretched around empty eye sockets and gaping mouths with missing teeth. Some are wrapped in tattered burial sacks, though the jewelry and ceramics with which they were laid to rest are long gone. Tours from town take about three hours and cost around S/30. Visits to the cemetery are also packaged with Nazca Lines flights. ⊠ *30 km (19 mi) from Nazca, the last 12 km (7 mi) of which is unpaved* ☎ *No phone* 🖃 *S/5* ⊗ *Daily 8–6.*

El Estaquería. The wooden pillars here, carved of *huarango* wood and placed on mud-brick platforms, were once thought to have been an astronomical observatory. More recent theories, however, lean toward their use in mummification rituals, perhaps to dry bodies of deceased tribal members. You can take a private tour of the site for about S/25 with a three-person minimum. ⊠ *34 km (21 mi) west of Nazca* ☎ *No phone* 🖃 *Free* ⊗ *Daily 8–4.*

Museo Antonini. For an overview of the Nazca culture and the various archaeological sites in the region, this Italian-run museum is the best in town. The displays, made up of materials excavated from the surrounding archaeological digs, are heavy on scientific information and light on entertainment, although the display of Nazcan trophy skulls will appeal to the morbid among us and textiles fans will appreciate the display of painted fabrics from the ancient adobe city of Cahuachi. All the signage is in Spanish, so ask for the translation book at the front desk (there's only one copy, however). Don't miss the still-working Nascan aqueduct in the back garden. ⊠ *Av. de la Cultura 600* ☎ *056/265–421* 🖃 *S/15, S/20 with a camera* ⊗ *Daily 9–7.*

Fodor's Choice ★   **Nazca Lines.** Even with the knowledge of the Nazca culture obtained from the archeological discoveries, it was not until 1929 that the Nazca Lines were discovered, when American scientist Paul Kosok looked out of his plane window as he flew over them. Almost invisible from ground level, the Lines were made by removing the surface stones and piling them beside the lighter soil underneath. More than 300 geometrical and biomorphic figures, some measuring up to 300 meters (1,000 feet) across, are etched into the desert floor, including a hummingbird, a monkey, a spider, a pelican, a condor, a whale, and an "astronaut," so named because of his goldfish-bowl-shape head. Theories abound as to their purpose, and some have devoted their lives to the study of the Lines. Probably the most famous person to investigate the origin of the

Nazca Lines was Kosok's translator, German scientist Dr. Maria Reiche, who studied the Lines from 1940 until her death in 1998. ⊠ *Pampas de San José, 20 km (12 mi) north of Nazca town.*

Tallera de Artesania de Andres Calle Flores. Everyone comes to Nazca for the Lines, but it's worth visiting Mr. Flores, a 91-year-old wonder who years ago discovered old pottery remnants and started making new pottery based on old designs and forms. Andres's son, Tobi, hosts a funny and informative talk in the kiln and workshop, and afterward you can purchase some beautiful pottery for S/30 to S/60. It's a quick walk across the bridge from downtown Nazca; at night, take a cab. ⊠ *Pje. Torrico 240, off Av. San Carlos* ☎ *056/522–319* 🎟 *Free* ⊙ *By appointment only.*

WHERE TO EAT

$ ✕ **Cevicheria "El Limón".** It may not look like much, but this small restau-
PERUVIAN   rant next door to Hotel Alegría serves a variety of delicious Peruvian dishes. The cebiche is the best in town and has made this restaurant a favorite with locals and travelers. Friendly and attentive service round out the experience, although the music (which at the time we visited seemed to be Greatest Hits of the '90s played on Andean pan-flute) leaves something to be desired. Top off your meal with the best pisco sour in town for a truly Peruvian experience. ⊠ *Calle Lima 168* ☎ *056/523–877* 🍴 *V.*

¢ ✕ **Chifa Nam Kug.** Enduringly popular, this landmark chifa near the
CHINESE   Plaza de Armas continues to satisfy the crowds with cheap Chinese fare. There's not much that sets this chifa apart from any other in Peru, but the food is delicious and a two-course lunch is just S/5. Fried rice dominates the menu, but the garlic beef and fried prawns entrées are excellent. ⊠ *Bolognesi 448* ☎ *056/522–151* 🍴 *No credit cards.*

¢ ✕ **Restaurant Don Carlos.** For a truly local experience, follow the crowds
PERUVIAN   to this tiny restaurant, which dishes up tasty Peruvian meals in huge portions. The restaurant won't dazzle you with its design, but what it lacks in style it more than makes up for with home-style Peruvian cuisine just like your grandmother used to make (or your grandmother's Peruvian cousin). The set-lunch—a soup, a main course, and a drink—is a steal at only S/4.50 and you may need to fight to get a table. The menu changes daily but specialties include *aji de gallina*, chicken in creamy hollandaise sauce served with boiled rice and a sliced egg. There's no street sign; look for RESTAURANT painted over the door. ⊠ *Calle Fermín del Castillo 375* ☎ *056/524–087* 🍴 *No credit cards.*

$ ✕ **Via La Encantada.** This stylish eatery on restaurant row adds some
PERUVIAN   class to the Nazca dining scene. ■ TIP➔ With food that is as modern as
Fodor'sChoice   the decor, this is the best spot in town to try Peruvian-fusion cuisine. The
★   *pollo a lo Oporto*, chicken in a port wine sauce, is a stand-out, as is the cocktail list, including tri-color Macchu Pichu pisco. Head upstairs for a spot on the balcony overlooking the street, and while there, sneak a peek through the back window and you can see the parrilla chef working over the restaurant's giant barbecue. ⊠ *Calle Bolognesi 282* ☎ *056/524–216 or 056/964–3426* 🍴 *V.*

WHERE TO STAY

$ ⌂ **Casa Andina.** A relative newcomer, this hotel, part of a national chain,

Fodor's Choice offers the best value for the money of any of Nazca's top-end lodgings.

★ Catering to business travelers and tourists, the smartly furnished rooms come fully equipped with safes and Wi-Fi Internet access, and a small business center has computer access and endless coffee and tea. Those interested strictly in pleasure can instead spend their time relaxing by the hotel's small pool. **Pros:** Wi-Fi Internet access in rooms; welcoming service. **Cons:** small pool. ⌧ *Bolognesi 367* ☎ *056/523–563* ⊕ *www. casa-andina.com* ↙ *60 rooms* ⌂ *In-room: safe, Wi-Fi. In-hotel: restaurant, bar, pool, laundry service, Internet, Wi-Fi, parking (free)* ▭ *AE, DC, MC, V* ⍾ *CP.*

$ ⌂ **Hotel Alegría.** Long a favorite with travelers, this classic Nazca hotel has recently had a facelift and is now better than ever. Clean, comfortable rooms are set around a sunny courtyard with swimming pool— a perfect spot to relax after a dusty morning flight over the Lines. The reception is extremely welcoming, and knowledgeable staff can help book flights and tours. Across from the bus station, the hotel is often full. Call ahead or risk missing out. **Pros:** friendly staff; good pool; book exchange. **Cons:** smallish rooms; no Internet access; often full. ⌧ *Calle Lima 166* ☎ *056/522–702* ⊕ *www.hotelalegria.net* ↙ *42 rooms, 3 bungalows* ⌂ *In-hotel: restaurant, pool, laundry service, parking (free), Internet* ▭ *No credit cards* ⍾ *BP.*

$ ⌂ **Hotel Maison Suisse.** Although a bit worn-looking these days, this long-running hotel across from the airport provides a peaceful green refuge from the Nazca dust. Kids splashing in the small pool and the school-canteen–like decor in the dining area give the hotel an atmosphere of a summer holiday camp, with bungalow-style accommodation dotted among the palm trees and green lawns. The underground bar is definitely the coolest room in the hotel. The hotel also runs Aero Ica, so arranging flights over the Lines is a breeze. **Pros:** peaceful; convenient for the airport; lovely garden. **Cons:** out of town; small pool; characterless rooms. ⌧ *Km 445, Pan-American Hwy. S* ☎ *056/522–434* ↙ *39 rooms, 6 suites* ⌂ *In-room: a/c, Wi-fi. In-hotel: restaurant, bar, pool, laundry service, parking (free)* ▭ *AE, V.*

$$ ⌂ **Hotel Majoro.** In fragrant gardens surrounded by cotton fields, this quiet, 80-year-old hacienda and former Augustine convent 1½ km (1 mi) from the airport offers a taste of life on a coastal farm. Set in 15 acres of gorgeous gardens, the hotel offers simple but charming rooms set around courtyards and overlooking colorful blossoms. Having been given a facelift in the last couple of years, the hotel feels reinvigorated, and you'll appreciate the Nazca-theme decorative touches. The excellent restaurant serves local specialties, and the English-speaking staff can organize horseback rides, mountain-bike trips, or four-wheel-drive excursions. **Pros:** peaceful atmosphere; charming gardens; good travel services. **Cons:** out of town; popular with tour groups; some airplane noise. ⌧ *Pan-American Hwy. S, Km 452* ☎ *056/522–750; 01/451–3897 in Lima* ⊕ *www.hotelmajoro.com* ↙ *62 rooms* ⌂ *In-room: Wi-Fi. In-hotel: restaurant, room service, bar, pools, bicycles, laundry service, parking (free), Internet terminal* ▭ *DC, MC, V* ⍾ *BP.*

$$ Hotel Nazca Lines. Mixing colonial elegance with all the mod-cons,
Fodor'sChoice   this top-end hotel is a Nazca landmark. Formerly the home of Maria
★   Reiche, this historic hacienda has long drawn international tourists
and adventurers seeking to solve the mysteries of the Lines. Stylish
colonial rooms with private terraces and piped-in music deliver a touch
of the good life, and the enormous central courtyard with its invit-
ing pool make it hard to drag yourself away to explore the Lines.
With nightly planetarium shows and lectures about the Lines, you can
attempt to solve the mystery without leaving poolside. Delicious meals
served on a tiled walkway beside the courtyard are worth the expense,
and nonguests can have lunch and use the pool for S/16. The hotel is
extremely charming; the staff, perhaps overwhelmed by the tour groups
that march nightly through the doors, not so much. **Pros:** magnificent
pool; nightly lectures; colonial charm. **Cons:** busy staff; tour groups;
expensive. ⊠ *Jr. Bolognesi S/N* ☎ *056/522–293; 01/261–9605 in Lima*
⤵ *78 rooms* ⬧ *In-room: safe, refrigerator. In-hotel: restaurant, bar,
pool, laundry service, Internet, Wi-Fi, parking (free)* ▭ *AE, DC, MC, V.*

The Southern Andes and Lake Titicaca

WORD OF MOUTH

"We loved Arequipa. We were there at the time of a major festival competition. Santa Catalina is not to be missed. I was not aware that the place opened late on some nights—that really would be atmospheric lit up in the evening—probably worth two trips!"

—crellston

WELCOME TO THE SOUTHERN ANDES AND LAKE TITICACA

TOP REASONS TO GO

★ **Wild Rivers:** Fantastic rapids and gorges make Colca Canyon and Cotahuasi Canyon the region's best-known kayaking and rafting spots.

★ **Folk Fiestas:** Whether it's the La Virgen del Candelaria festival in Puno, Arequipa's annual Anniversary, or Semana Santa in Chivay, Peru's culture is celebrated with more than 300 festive folkloric dances and brightly colored costumes.

★ **Wildlife:** Llamas, vicuñas, and alpaca roam the Reserva Nacional Salinas y Aguada Blanca, giant Andean condor soar above Colca Canyon, and rare bird species nest at Lake Titicaca and in the coastal lagoons of Meija.

★ **Shopping:** Along with Arequipa's alpaca stores, this region is also a mine of yarn, leather products, guitars, and antiques.

★ **Floating Islands:** On Lake Titicaca, made from the lake's totora reeds, the series of Uros islands float, providing residence to more than 3,000 Aymara and Quechua inhabitants.

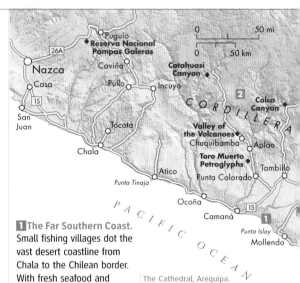

1 **The Far Southern Coast.** Small fishing villages dot the vast desert coastline from Chala to the Chilean border. With fresh seafood and plenty of sun, coastal towns like Chala, Camana, and Mollendo buzz with people from December to March. Outside this time, the flat beaches, dramatic cliffs, and icy waters seem almost alone.

2 **Canyon Country.** Dusty and dry, this is a place of striking geology, wildlife, and history. It's also a playground for adventure sports lovers. Five hours northeast of Arequipa is Colca Canyon, the second deepest gorge in the world. It's home to the intense Río Colca, 14 tiny villages, the giant Andean condor, and great hiking. Nine hours away is Colca's sister gorge, the world's deepest canyon, Cotahuasi Canyon.

The Cathedral, Arequipa.

3 **Arequipa.** Arequipa is known as *La Cuidad Blanca*, or the white city, for its dazzling *sillar*—a white volcanic rock, from which nearly all the Spanish-colonial buildings are constructed. The most Spanish city in all of Peru, it's also the most romantic one. Its home to Juanita the ice mummy, the Santa Catalina Monastery, and scores of museums.

GETTING ORIENTED

A good jumping-off point is Arequipa. Acclimatize while taking in the sights, then head to the Colca Canyon Valley. The five-hour drive travels over the Patapampa pass for views of the Valley of the Volcanoes, and through the Reserva Nacional Salinas y Aguada Blanca, where herds of wild vicuñas, llamas, and alpaca graze. At the Canyon, you can go on a multiday hike or relax at a resort, but nearly everyone comes to spy condors at Cruz del Condor. After, head back to Arequipa and on to Puno and Lake Titicaca where you can book an overnight island homestay and visit the floating islands and the Sillustani ruins. From Puno some head to Bolivia (⇨ *see Chapter 10*) while others go to Cusco by train, bus, or plane. Similarly, you can travel to Puno from Cusco and begin your exploration in the opposite direction.

4 Puno and Lake Titicaca.
Known as the folkloric capital of Peru, Puno's annual festivals shine with elaborate costumes, music, and dancing in the streets. Puno has quality hotels and good restaurants, and it's the jumping-off point to Lake Titicaca, the world's highest navigable lake and the reason travelers come here. Outdoor adventures and unique island cultures can be found throughout the lake's 62 islands.

Children in traditional costume

Updated by
Nicholas Gill
and Marlise
Kast

In no other part of Peru does the scenery change so rapidly and dramatically. Peru's off-the-beaten-path far southern desert coast is a vast plain against the Pacific Ocean. Unpopulated and underdeveloped, life is about fishing. Little villages are full of hole-in-the-wall *cebicherías* (seafood restaurants) and miles of beach.

Arequipa, Peru's second largest city, is a Spanish-colonial maze, with volcanic white sillar buildings, well-groomed plazas, and wonderful food, museums, and designer alpaca products. Arequipa is close to Colca Canyon, where many head to see the famed gorge for its stunning beauty, depth, and Andean condors. Several hours farther out is the very remote Cotahuasi Canyon, the world's deepest gorge.

Second in tourism to Machu Picchu, Lake Titicaca is home to the floating islands. The Los Uros islands are nearly 40 man-made islands—constructed from the lake's tortora reeds—and are literally floating. The natives are the Quechua and Aymara peoples, who still speak their respective languages.

Puno, an agricultural city on the shores of Titicaca, is the jumping-off point for exploring the lake, and is Peru's folkloric capital. A dusty-brown city most of the time, Puno is a colorful whirlwind during festivals. The region's many fiestas feature elaborate costumes, story-telling dances, music, and lots of merrymaking. Each November and February, Puno puts on two spectacular shows for local holidays.

PLANNING

WHEN TO GO
Southern coastal Peru is always warm and arid. In the mountains and high plains, from May through early November the blistering sun keeps you warm, but nights get cold. Rainy season is from mid-November until April, when it's cooler and cloudy, but rain isn't a guarantee. Use sunscreen, even if it's cloudy.

GETTING HERE AND AROUND

AIR TRAVEL

Flights take between 30 minutes and an hour to fly anywhere in southern Peru, and a one-way ticket costs $50 to $150 USD. LAN (⊕ *www.lan.com*) has daily flights between Lima and Rodríguez Ballón Airport, 7 km (4½ mi) from Arequipa. Peruvian Airlines (⊕ *www.peruvianairlines.com.pe*) and Star Peru (⊕ *www.starperu.com*) also have daily flights. Only LAN offers daily flights to Aeropuerto Manco Cápac in Juliaca, the closest airport to Puno and Lake Titicaca. It takes 45 minutes to drive from Juliaca to downtown Puno.

BUS TRAVEL

The road between Arequipa and Puno has been paved, so instead of 20 hours, now it only takes about six. Service is also good between Puno and Cusco, and so is the road between Puno and Copacabana in Bolivia. Cruz del Sur (⊕ *www.cruzdelsur.com.pe*), CIVA, Tour Peru, Inka Express, Flores and Ormeño (⊕ *www.grupo-ormeno.com.pe*) have offices in Puno and Arequipa. For your comfort and safety, take the best service you can afford. There has been crime on night buses from Arequipa to Nazca and Puno to Cusco. Several bus companies sell tickets that go direct, so buy one of those. Bus stations in Peru are known for crime, mostly theft of your belongings, so always hold on to your bags.

CAR TRAVEL

Car rental services are in Arequipa center and at the airport. Keep your car travel to daylight hours: night driving poses a number of risks—blockades, crime on tourists, and steep roads. A 4x4 is needed for the canyons. While the road from Arequipa to Chivay has improved, the last hour of the journey is rough and has steep cliffs. Use even more caution if traveling into Cotahuasi Canyon: only a quarter of the 12-hour ride is paved.

TAXI TRAVEL

Ask any Arequipeño and they'll tell you Arequipa has three major concerns: earthquakes, the looming threat of volcanoes, and taxis.

Arequipa has the most taxis per capita of any city in Peru. Pint-size yellow cars, namely miniature Daewoo Ticos, clog the streets. Pollution is high, accidents aplenty, and rush-hour traffic rivals that of Los Angeles.

About 40 years ago, driving taxis became the hot job to have, especially for young people looking to make a quick sole. As the industry grew, immigrants from Bolivia, Chile, and elsewhere came swarming in, creating stiff competition. Soon paying off government agents for valid taxi licenses became commonplace. Officially, this practice no longer occurs, but there remains an overload of little yellow hotwheels. In fact, a 2006 United Nations study on air pollution in Arequipa said on average 50 cars per minute cross the Plaza de Armas. The study also said that since 1992 the number of taxis in Arequipa has increased by more than 250%.

TRAIN TRAVEL

Train travel on PeruRail (⊕ *www.perurail.com*) is slow but scenic and more relaxing than a bus playing reggaeton. A Pullman train ticket means more comfort, not to mention a meal and increased security. The train only goes from Cusco to Puno. It's a popular way to take in the dramatic change of scenery as you ride over La Raya pass at 4,315 meters (14,156 feet). The trip takes about nine hours and includes a stop at the highest point. For a full listing of PeruRail trips, check out ⊕ *www.perurail.com.* It's now possible to book online.

HEALTH AND SAFETY

Mountain towns and Lake Titicaca are home to *soroche* (altitude sickness). Temporary cures include *mate de coca* (coca tea) or *chancaca* (crystallized pure cane sugar). Drink lots of bottled water and forgo alcohol and coffee.

Colca Canyon is generally safe, as are Arequipa and Puno. However, don't walk alone at night, know where your money is, and educate yourself on the good and bad parts of town. Police presence has increased in Arequipa. Use only recommended taxi companies or have someone call you one. But walking around the Plaza, even at night, is safe in Arequipa. Hiking El Misti alone is not recommended. Puno is generally safe in the tourist areas, but at night the port and the area in the hills are not safe.

RESTAURANTS

If you can't wait to try *cuy* (guinea pig) or if you prefer wood-fired pizza, Arequipa and Puno have some excellent restaurants, ranging from gourmet Novo Andino cuisine to traditional fare and international grub. Food in Arequipa is known for strong, fresh flavors, from herbs and spices to vegetables served with native Andean foods like grilled alpaca steaks. If you're headed to the coast, hold out for the freshest fish around, as cheap, delicious seafood and shellfish are the specialty. In the mountains, the cool, thin Andean air calls for hearty, savory soups and heaps and heaps of carbs in the form of the potato. Whether they're fried, boiled, baked, with cheese, in soup, or alone, potatoes you will be eating. In Puno fresh fish from the lake is served in almost every restaurant. Puno also has a special affection for adobe oven, wood-fired pizza.

HOTELS

Arequipa and Puno are overloaded with hotels. This is good for you, the traveler, considering you reap the benefit of great service for a low price. Puno lives and breathes for tourists. While a growing number of resorts and chain hotels are set along the lakeside, most of the properties within the city are small boutique hotels with local owners pining to get in on the tourist boom in this otherwise agricultural town. As a commercial business center, Arequipa has more high-end hotels that cater to the business traveler, and given its fame for being the romance city, it also has lots of small inns.

WHAT IT COSTS IN NUEVO SOLES					
	¢	$	$$	$$$	$$$$
RESTAURANTS	under S/20	S/20–S/35	S/36–S/50	S/51–S/65	over S/65
HOTELS	under S/125	S/125–S/250	S/251–S/375	S/376–S/500	over S/500

Restaurant prices are per person for a main course. Hotel prices are for a standard double room, excluding tax.

THE FAR SOUTHERN COAST

The southern coast is a vast rugged desert, with jutting cliffs and a handful of green valleys. Not nearly as populated as the north coast, the southern shore is slower paced. It's perfect for light hiking, bird-watching, fishing, sampling fresh seafood, and sunbathing. Unfortunately, swimming is not advised, thanks to the strong Humboldt Current, which makes this section of the Pacific icy cold and creates a strong undertow. There isn't much happening here, but the fresh ocean breeze and nearly 600 km (372 mi) of beachfront make it a good place to get off the gringo trail and relax. The Mejía Lagoons large bird sanctuary, the beaches of Mollendo, and the pre-Inca ruins of Puerto Inca are the most interesting places to visit. Summer season is from December to March when towns along the coast swell with southern Peruvians on vacation. Outside this time, they're like ghost towns.

The economy along the coast revolves around catching fish, and cooking it. From Chala to Chile, endless cebicherías dish up cebiche and lobster-size prawns, *camarones,* another local specialty.

GETTING AROUND

In this region the Pan-American Highway parallels an ancient 240-km (149-mi) Inca footpath to Cusco, which was once used for transporting goods and for communication between the Sacred Valley and Puerto Inca, an Inca shipping port that was rediscovered in the 1950s. Unless you're driving the length of the Pan-American Highway, you'll likely be coming here from Arequipa, which is the only city with regular bus service to the region and where many Arequipeños have summer homes. Taxis and *combis* (van buses) will link each town to the next, but service tends to be limited to the daylight hours and is cut back drastically outside of the summer season.

CHALA

173 km (107 mi) southwest of Nazca.

If you're driving along the coast, Chala, with nearby Puerto Inca, is a good place for an afternoon stretch. The coastal village is surrounded by quiet beaches. The shore is lined with hole-in-the-wall restaurants, which lack names but serve enormous plates of fresh-cooked fish. There isn't much here, but after grabbing a bite you can walk along the beach, Playa Grande, or visit the ruins of Puerto Inca.

Informally, the village is now split into two, Chala Norte and Chala Sur. The town isn't large enough to warrant such separation, but the north (Chala Norte) is an older, dodgy part of town, and the south (Chala Sur) is the newer section of town.

GETTING HERE AND AROUND

From Arequipa's Terminal Terrestre, several small bus companies head to Chala (1.5 hours, 15 soles) every few hours from about 6 AM to 6 PM. The center is walkable, though you'll need to catch a taxi to hit Puerto Inca.

EXPLORING

Playa Grande. A gorgeous stretch of soft sand is cradled by dark rocky coves that jut out into the Pacific. If you enjoy seafood, watching the fishermen bring home loads of fresh jumbo shellfish and fish is a sight not to miss. The action can be seen from the main pier (more like a small dock) and it's also perfect for casting a line (bring your own).

Puerto Inca. Ten km (6 mi) north of Chala is the old Inca port at the base of an ancient 240-km (149-mi) Inca footpath to Cusco. This path was once used for transporting goods and messages between the Sacred Valley and the coast. ■TIP➔ Nearly every 7 km (4 mi) along the path you'll see a post where Inca runners relayed notes and changed messengers so that news could be passed from the coast to the mountains within 24 hours. Still in excellent condition, the road exemplifies how important the ocean resources were to the Inca Empire and how resourceful the Incas were. You can hike in for a few miles on the trail or walk around the ruins in Puerto Inca where you'll find a cemetery temple and many tools used by the coastal Incas. Watch your step: large holes in the ground mark where drying and storage buildings once stood. To get to Puerto Inca, you can walk from Chala in two hours, or get dropped off at Km 603 and hike 3 km (2 mi). If you take a *colectivo* (shared taxi), you will be packed in like a sardine, but it only costs about S/3. A taxi from Chala runs about S/17.

WHERE TO STAY

$ ⛺ **Hotel Puerto Inka.** This economical resort is in a small, quiet bay. Depending on the day you might encounter archaeologists or ecologists, honeymooners, tour groups, and backpackers. The rooms are large and hot water is always available. Camping on the beach is also an option for S/15. The on-site restaurant cooks great breakfasts and good fish plates for dinner but their day long à la carte menu is hit or miss. The bilingual staff is helpful and since Chala has little to offer, the hotel provides lots to keep you entertained: two private beaches, kayak and wave-running rentals, hiking trails, evening bonfires, endless games of volleyball, a good outdoor bar, and proximity to the ruins. If you rent a room, you also have access to the swimming pool, but campers don't. **Pros:** lots of activities; large, clean rooms; near the ruins. **Cons:** restaurant is inconsistent; hotel is sometimes too crowded. ⊠ *Pan-American Km 610* ☎ *054/778–458* ⊕ *www.puertoinka.com.pe* ⟳ *24 rooms* ⌂ *In-room: a/c, safe (some). In-hotel: restaurant, bar, pool, beachfront, water sports, laundry service, Internet terminal, Wi-Fi hotspot, parking (free)* ⊟ *AE, MC, V* ⟊ *CP.*

CAMANÁ

222 km (138 mi) south of Chala.

Known for its beaches, Camaná is a magnet for Arequipeños in the summer months (December–March). Outside this time, this small fishing village, like all the other coastal villages, is nearly empty.

Camaná, the capital of the province with the same name, played an important role during colonial times when supplies were unloaded here before being transferred to Arequipa and the silver mines in Posotí,

Bolivia. It was also once home to the Waris, Collaguas, and Incas. But perhaps the most significant history was more recent—and devastating. In 2001 Camaná was on the brink of becoming the coast's next big tourist destination, but a tsunami, resulting from a 8.4 earthquake, leveled hotels, homes, and restaurants. Eight-meter-high (26 feet) waves wiped out most beach resorts along the popular beach La Punta. Camaná is slowly becoming a beachgoers' haven again.

GETTING HERE AND AROUND

From Arequipa's Terminal Terrestre, several small bus companies head to Camaná (2.5 hours, S/20), first stopping in Chala, several times a day from about 6 AM to 6 PM. Combis ply the route from Chala to Camaná every hour or so during the summer and just a few times per day during the rest of the year.

RESERVA NACÍONAL PAMPAS GALERAS

Take the paved road (Hwy. 26) east from Nazca for two hours and you'll reach this nature reserve with herds of the rare, slender brown vicuña. Established in 1967, the 6,500-hectare park is composed of flat, windy grasslands where Andean condors and guanaco can also be spotted. A military base is on the site, and a park guard records all entrances and exits. Admission is S/7; the park is open daily 8–6.

ESSENTIALS

Currency Banco de Crédito BCP (⊠ *Av. 9 de Noviembre 139*). Banco Continental BBVA (⊠ *28 de Julio 405*).

EXPLORING

La Miel. Just outside of town this rocky inlet has calm waters. It's a popular place for camping and watching sunsets.

La Punta. Camaná's most popular beach is a stretch of brown granular sand 5 km (3 mi) from town. While the waves are small and not much swimming goes on here, there's lots of sunbathing, beer-sipping, and volleyball. Discos and bars stand edge to edge, among little hotels and cafés, which provide an alternative to bronzing and bikini-watching. ■TIP→ At the very south of La Punta is an area called the caves, a small rocky inlet that's good for wading.

WHERE TO EAT AND STAY

¢
PERUVIAN
✕**Cevicheria Rosa Nautica.** Not to be confused with the famous Lima institution, this Rosa Nautica isn't nearly as fancy, pricey, or good, but it makes an effort. A hole-in-the-wall, family-style restaurant serves heaping plates of mostly cebiche. If you want to share it's possible to order it *para compartir.* Try the *cebiche mixto.* ⊠ *La Punta* ☎ *No phone* 🚫 *No credit cards.*

$
☾
🏨 **Hotel de Turistas.** Beautiful colonial architecture makes this hacienda an attractive inn that has lured travelers since the 1960s. Spacious accommodations have high ceilings, arched doorways, and long windows overlooking lush gardens. The indoor sauna and hot tub are nice, and children can play in the outdoor pool, which has water slides. The restaurant serves a good breakfast and dishes out local delicacies and desserts all day. **Pros:** hot water; sauna; friendly atmosphere. **Cons:** furniture doesn't match; sells out quickly in summer. ⊠ *Av. Lima 138*

☎ *054/571–113* ⊕ *www.hoteldeturistas.net* ✒ *21 rooms* ⚹ *In-room: a/c, safe (some). In-hotel: restaurant, room service, spa, bar, pool, laundry service, parking (free)* ⊟ *AE, DC, MC, V* ⊺⃒ *BP.*

¢ 🔭 **Sun Valley.** Go to this resort near the beach for water sports and sand
☉ boarding. After a day of play you can relax in a modern, if blandly decorated, clean room with a hot bath. The restaurant serves Peruvian comfort food. **Pros:** clean; modern; near the beach. **Cons:** small rooms; 15 minutes from town. ⊠ *Cerrillos 2, Km 843* ☎ *054/283–056 or 054/969–4235* ⊕ *www.sunvalleycamana.shutterfly.com* ✒ *42 rooms* ⚹ *In-room: no a/c, safe (some). In-hotel: restaurant, bar, pool, gym, water sports, laundry service, parking (free)* ⊟ *AE, DC, MC, V* ⊺⃒ *BP.*

MOLLENDO

113 km (70 mi) southwest of Arequipa.

Mollendo is a cheerful, Spanish-influenced port town with colorful, colonial architecture and 35 km (21 mi) of clean, sandy beach. The brightly painted colonial homes and groomed plazas appear as if they were plucked from the Costa del Sol in Spain. A great place to view these homes is around Plaza Bolognesi and Plaza Grau. Castle Forga, a bright yellow colonial-style castle, perches over a cliff above the sea. While Castle Forga is vacant and not technically a museum, visitors are allowed to look around, though the hours are inconsistent. Mollendo is the most attractive beach community in the Southern coast. The water is still not desirable for a swim but the waves are fairly subdued. A strong recycling program keeps the beaches clean. You'll also find many of the freshest cebicherías in the south.

GETTING HERE AND AROUND

Two bus companies make the two-hour trip from Arequipa to Mollendo (S/10) three or four times each day. Combis and taxis make trips every 20 minutes or so to nearby Meijia.

EXPLORING

Santuario Nacional Lagunas de Mejía. Three miles down the coast from Mollendo are the **Mejía Lagoons**. The reserve protects wetlands, including swamps, salt marshes, and totora reeds. More than 200 bird species have been sighted here, including the rare red-fronted coot and the Chilean flamingo. ■**TIP**➔ While the most pleasant season is October to May, the best sightings are from January to April at the crack of dawn. The reserve is open from sunrise to sunset and the cost of admission is S/5 or a three-day pass for S/10. From Mollendo it takes about 15 minutes to reach the lagoons. Colectivos run frequently between the two and cost S/5. ⊠ *Km 32, Carretera Mollendo, Valle Tambo* ☎ *054/800–004.*

BEACHES

Five primary beaches are along the coast of Mollendo, which start in the northern part of town and progressively get nicer as they continue south.

Albatros is a large beach with rental umbrellas. **Catarindo**, which is not technically one of Mollendo's beaches, is only 2 km (1.2 mi) north of Mollendo on the Pan-American highway. A small inlet, it has almost no waves and is the place to swim, or to put in a kayak. **Las Rocas**, "The Rocks," is wider and cleaner and has permanent tents and umbrellas set up, and a sea of wealthy Peruvian sunbathers. **Playa Tercera** has tents and umbrellas for rent and it's a sea of red and blue awnings. Along the beach are lifeguards and a few outdoor seafood restaurants. **Primera Playa** is a small stretch of sand complete with a beach club ambience including lifeguards, a bathhouse (with toilets and showers), a parking area, snack shop, a swimming pool, and tennis courts. There's a S/7 fee for use of the pool and facilities. **Segunda Playa** is your standard beach with sun, sand, and waves.

> ## PETROGLYPHS
>
> **Toro Muerto** is the world's largest petroglyph field, where hundreds of volcanic rocks are thought to have been painted more than 1,000 years ago by the Huari (or Wari) culture. There are sketches of pumas, llamas, guanacos, and condors, as well as warriors and dancers. Head higher for expansive views of the desert. It's hot and windy, so bring water, a hat, and sunglasses. Toro Muerto is 164 km (102 mi) northwest of Arequipa.

WHERE TO EAT AND STAY

¢ ✕ **Restaurant Marco Antonio.** This charming hole-in-the-wall is a family
SEAFOOD operation—your fish is cooked upstairs and brought down a winding stairway to the spartan but comfortable dining area. The catch of the day varies with the season, but it's always fresh and delicious. Ask for the criolla-style mixto. ⊠ *Comercio 254–258, Parque Bolognesi* ☏ *No phone* ⊟ *V.*

¢ ☱ **Hostal Cabaña.** We wouldn't recommend this place for your honeymoon—there are no frills and the old lodge feels camp-like—but it's clean and has what you'll need to get a good night's rest after a day at the beach. **Pros:** large rooms; private bath; hot water. **Cons:** a little loud on the weekends; restaurant is breakfast only. ⊠ *Comercio 240* ☏ *054/534–57* ⅏ *In-room: no a/c. In-hotel: restaurant, laundry service, parking (free)* ⊟ *No credit cards* ⑁ *CP.*

CANYON COUNTRY

Colca and Cotahuasi Canyons, the two deepest canyons on earth, are two of Peru's greatest natural wonders. Colca is the far more visited, more accessible, and recently has a seen a boom in five-star resorts and laid-back family inns. Cotahuasi, a little more than 150 meters (500 feet) deeper than Colca, is much more remote and only reached by the most rugged adventurers, though if you can withstand long, bumpy hours in a car or bus, you'll find an unspoiled terrain rarely visited by outsiders.

COTAHUASI VILLAGE AND VICINITY

379 km (236 mi) north of Arequipa.

Cotahuasi is the largest town in canyon country and the first you'll stumble upon. In the hills at 2,680 meters (8,620 feet), whitewashed colonial-style homes line slim, straight lanes before a backdrop of Cerro

CLOSE UP

On The Menu

With the altitude and cool weather, southern Peru is famous for its hearty and savory soups. Quinoa and potatoes typically provide the base, and with the emergence of Novo Andino cuisine, the addition of meats, vegetables, and spices make these soups meals unto themselves. Cheese, potatoes, cuy, and quinoa make up the diets in traditional villages around Lake Titicaca and the canyons.

SEAFOOD

In coastal towns you'll dine in cebicherías and more upscale *marisquerías* (seafood restaurants). The best are along the coast and in Puno.

cebiche: Fish or shellfish (marinated in lime juice, cilantro, onions, tomatoes, and chilies), served raw as a salad or cocktail and usually accompanied by *canchas,* toasted corn kernels sprinkled with salt. *Cebiche mixto* is a mix of shellfish and fish and is best along the coast.

escabeche: Raw fish and prawns with chilies, cheese chunks, sliced eggs, olives, and onions, found in Arequipa.

MEATS

cuy chactado: roasted guinea pig.

filet de cuy: A Novo Andino style of cuy cut in filets instead of whole; found in Arequipa.

lomo a la huancaina: beef strips with egg and cheese sauce.

rocoto relleno: baked spicy red peppers stuffed with ground beef, olives, and queso fresco.

SOUPS AND STEWS

chupe de camarones: spicy shrimp stew; found on the coast.

chupe verde: potatoes, cheese, eggs, and herbs; found in Arequipa and Canyonlands.

créma de quinoa: creamed soup made of quinoa. Found in mountainous areas like Lake Titicaca and the Canyonlands.

hualpa chupe: chicken, chilies, and spices; found in Arequipa.

Mollejitas: chicken innards are a specialty in Arequipa.

sopa a la criolla: onions, peppers, and potatoes; found in Arequipa.

BAKED GOODS AND DESSERTS

alfajores: shortbread.

churros: fried dough sprinkled with sugar.

cocadas al horno: macaroons.

ganja blanco: boiled evaporated milk and sugar mixed with pineapple or peanuts.

mazamorra morada: purple maize, cinnamon, milk, and sugar—a specialty from small street stands in Arequipa.

pan integral: grain bread.

panaderías: are places to find fresh-baked rolls.

queso helado: The signature ice cream of Arequipa. Creamy coconut ice cream with cinnamon.

REFRESHMENTS

The Mountain Dew–like Inka Cola is the local soda brand. Regional beers includes Cusqueña and Arequipeña. *Chicha* (a fermented corn drink) is the national beverage for fiestas and celebrations, not to be confused with *chicha morada* (a nonalcoholic drink from purple corn). *Vino Calliente* is hot-mulled red wine served across the country but especially in the highlands and in Puno.

Hiunao. Most visitors kick off their stay in this Quechua-speaking community of 3,500 residents, where there are a few basic hostels, restaurants, a small *tienda* (grocery store), a bell tower, and Plaza de Armas. It's also where most hiking trails begin or end. Many families rent *burros* (mules) to tourists to help carry their load, especially kayakers who walk eight hours down to the gorge with their boats.

Three hours farther south along a thin track against the canyon wall—which climbs to 400 meters (1,312 feet) above the river—you'll reach Chaupo, a settlement surrounded by groves of fruit trees. You can camp here and hike through Velinga to ruins at Huña before reaching Quechualla where you can see the ancient farming terraces of Maucullachta, an old Wari city across the gorge.

In Cotahuasi Village the route forks, leading northeast along the Río Cotahuasi or due north. Either way is possible by 4x4, colectivo, or on foot. Heading northeast, about 10 km out of town, you'll discover the village of Tomepampa. After that is the small town of Alca, near the hot springs of Luicho. Even further east is Puica at 3,700 meters (8,440 feet). Traveling northwest from Cotahuasi village will lead you to Pampamarca, a town known for weaving exquisite rugs. Two hours by car, Pampamarca is three hours from the hot springs of Josla and Uskuni.

CROSSING INTO CHILE

The border with Chile, about 40 km (25 mi) from Tacna or 440 km (272 miles) from Arequipa, is open daily and very easy to cross. All you need is your passport. From Tacna there are scores of colectivos that will give you a ride to the other side for S/20, or you can take a bus from Tacna, which is headed to Arica and departs hourly. You can also take the train, which leaves several times a day.

Typically drivers will help with border formalities, even the colectivos. The road journey takes about an hour. Any train aficionado will enjoy the slow, somewhat bumpy, but beautiful train ride from Tacna to Arica, which takes more than an hour and costs S/6.

GETTING HERE AND AROUND

Cotahuasi Canyon is a travel destination in the making, but outside of expert extreme sports enthusiasts, few people venture here. Unless you're taking a bus or coming with a tour operator, driving anything but a 4x4 is asking for trouble. The jagged, rocky dirt roads are full of cliffs and narrow corners. Dry for most of the year, the roads get muddy from December to April (rainy season), a time when you're also likely to encounter random streams flowing across the road.

Hire a guide, regardless of season and not just for safety: Since this region is so remote, you're likely to see a lot more with a guide. All buses travel through the night. Three bus companies go from Arequipa to Cotahuasi daily; each leaves around 5 PM, arriving in Cotahuasi village in time for sunrise: Transportes Cromotex (☎ *054/421–555*), Transportes Reyna (☎ *054/430–612*), and Alex Bus (☎ *054/424–605*).

■ **TIP→** If you're driving, know that gas stations are few between the long stretch from Corire (near Toro Muerto) to the village of Cotahuasi.

EXPLORING

Cataratas de Sipia. Below the village of Cotahuasi is the valley of Piro, the gateway to the canyon, which is close to this 150-meter (462-foot), 10-meter-wide waterfall. ■**TIP➜** Sipia Falls is the most visited attraction in the entire canyon.

Cotahuasi Canyon. Colca Canyon may be the region's most famous natural attraction, but at 3,354 meters (11,001 feet), Cotahuasi is the world's deepest gorge, beating Colca Canyon by 163 meters (534 feet). It's nearly twice as deep as the Grand Canyon. The canyon has been carved by the Río Cotahuasi, which changes into the Río Ocuña before connecting to the Pacific. Its deepest point is at Ninochaco, below the quaint administrative capital of Quechualla, and accessible only by kayak. Kayak explorations first documented the area in the mid-1990s and measured its depth. Since then, paddling the Cotahuasi river's Class V rapids is to kayakers what scaling Mount Everest is to mountaineers.

The ride from Arequipa to the Cotahuasi Canyon ranks with the great scenic roads of the world. As you pass Corire and Toro Muerto, the road rides the western side of snow-capped Nevado Coropuno (6,424 meters, 21,079 feet), Peru's third-highest volcano, for spectacular views as you descend into the valley of Cotahuasi. ■**TIP➜** Logistically speaking, it's a bumpy 11- to 13-hour bus ride or 10 hours by four-wheel drive from Arequipa. The pavement ends in Chuquibamba. Some of the road from Chuquibamba to Cotahuasi, the longest stretch of the ride, is in the process of being graded. There's no fee to enter the canyon.

SPORTS AND THE OUTDOORS

Many operators in Arequipa and Cusco offer multiday excursions. Most tours are at least four days, five nights and some last up to 17 nights. A few local hikers provide custom tours for visitors as well.

HIKING

Cotahuasi Canyon is an awesome place to explore by foot. The backdrop of snowcapped Volcano Coropuna and Solimana is fantastic, the high desert plains offer a rest from the steep upward rocky canyon terrain, and the untouched villages provide a cultural aspect. Hikes can go between 1,830 meters (6,000 feet) and 6,400 meters (21,000 feet) in height so prepare for the altitude. Temperatures remain about 65–70°F during the day, dipping below 45°F on any given night. Ancient Inca paths wind throughout the canyon and its terraces. ■**TIP➜** Beware, many of these ancient trails are narrow, rocky, and hang over the side of the canyon. Newer trails parallel some of the ancient ones, and are generally safer.

Sipia Falls is a solid three- to four-hour trek from Cotahuasi Village and it's a hard-on-your-knees hike down that includes two bridge crossings, but the first taste of being in the canyon is a surreal experience. It's also possible to reach the falls by hailing a colectivo or in your own 4x4

ADVANCE PREP

Cotahuasi is not traveler-savvy yet so it's not possible to show up in a town, buy a map, hire a guide, and get on your way. You'll want to buy a map of the canyon at the Instituto Geográfico Militar in Lima or at the South American Explorers clubhouse in Lima or Cusco.

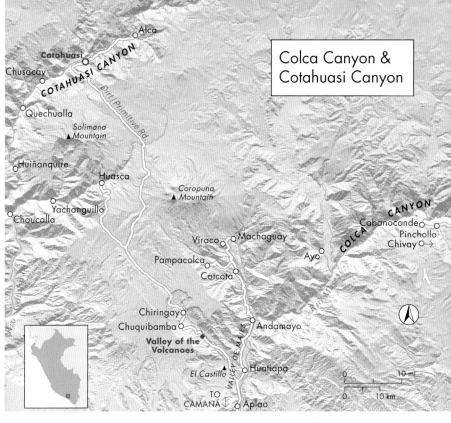

Colca Canyon &
Cotahuasi Canyon

from the Cotahuasi road to the Sipia Bridge where the road ends. From here it's a 45-minute hike to the falls.

If you're going on a multiday excursion, continue on the trail from Cotahuasi to Sipia to the Chaupo Valley and the citrus tree village of Velinga, a good place to camp. From Velinga it's on to Quechualla where you'll pass through the 1,000-year-old old Wari ruins, rock forests, and cactus forests. One of the last major points along this route is Huachuy where you can again camp. Beyond this point things get trickier as you'll have to cross the Rió Cotahuasi. Many guides use a cable system to reach Yachau Oasis, Chaucalla Valley, and eventually Iquipi Valley.

WHITE-WATER RAFTING

Kayakers and white-water rafters can challenge the rapids anywhere from the upper Cotahuasi, near the village, almost to the Pacific. The river is divided into four sections: the Headwaters, beginning upstream from Cotahuasi village, Aimaña gorge, Flatwater Canyon, and the Lower Canyon.

SETTING UP CAMP

With no official campgrounds, setting up a tent most anywhere is customary. You'll likely encounter very few people, if any, on your trek.

The Lower Canyon is a mix of Class III and V rapids, without much portage. Most rafting tour operators put in at the village of Velinga and use this part of the river for tours. These tours are done fairly frequently by operators from Arequipa. Depending upon skill level, adventure-craving kayakers tend to put in upriver and have to portage on several occasions.

Kayakers put in at Headwaters in the village of Chuela. Here the rapids ring in at a Class III, but by the time the Aimaña gorge starts in the waters tug at Class V. White-water season is June through November when the rapids are Class III to V. But the best time to go is mid-May to mid-June. The water is snowmelt, so wet suits are necessary.

CHIVAY

136 km (85 mi) north of Arequipa.

The largest town in the Colca Canyon region is Chivay, a small, battered-looking village with a population of 3,000. Most tourist facilities are here, which are not many, but include restaurants, hotels, a medical clinic, and a tourist information center. As you approach Chivay, you'll pass through a stone archway signifying the town entrance, where AUTOCOLCA, the government authority over Colca Canyon, stops cars to ask if they are headed to see the condors. If you're headed to Cruz del Condor or any of the churches in the 14 villages you must purchase a S/35 entry ticket, which will be asked for again at the entrance of the Mirador. Nearly all agency tours do not include this entry fee in their all price.

Chivay marks the eastern end of the canyon's rim; the other end is Cabonconde, a developing village where most multiday hikes into the canyon begin and end. As you come into Chivay the road splits off into two: one, less traveled because of its rocky rutted surface, goes along the canyon's northern edge to the villages of Coporaque, Ichupampa, and Lari; the other follows the southern rim and although it's a bumpy dirt road, it's better for travel and leads to Cruz del Condor, and the small towns of Yanque, Maca, and Cabanaconde.

GETTING HERE AND AROUND

By hiring a private guide, renting a four-wheel-drive vehicle, joining a tour from Arequipa, or going by bus you can explore the area. A standard two-wheel drive car won't do. Arequipa is the jumping-off point for nearly everyone headed to Colca Canyon and most will either come on a tour or take a bus that

VALLEY OF THE VOLCANOES

This spectacular, 65-km (40-mi) crevasse north of Colca Canyon includes a line of 80 extinct craters and cinder cones. Looming over the scene is active Volcán Coropuna, the third highest peak in Peru. Andagua, at the head of the valley, has the best tourist facilities in the area. The valley is about five hours by a rocky, half-paved, half-dirt road from Colca Canyon. There are several multiday hikes from Colca Canyon that must be arranged in Arequipa. If you're going to Cotahuasi or Colca Canyon, you're bound to pass through this high-altitude valley.

Llamas take the high road in Colca Canyon.

stops direct at either Chivay, the first town you come to that takes about five hours to reach from Arequipa, or Cabanaconde, about another hour farther. Sporadic combi service links each town in the middle.

Chivay is a five-hour drive from Arequipa. The road takes you through the Reserva Nacional Aguada Blanca y Salinas and over the Patapampa Pass where at 4,825 meters (15,830 feet) you can view nearly the entire Valley of Volcanoes. The road is only paved about half of the way; going toward the Patapampa Pass is dirt, but has been graded and smoothed out. The last quarter of the ride is rocky. Most everyone going to Colca Canyon will experience altitude problems along the way, so bring plenty of water. Some of the nicer hotels will have oxygen tanks.

Taxis are a good way to go from town to town if long hikes or mountain biking isn't your thing. Taxis line up around the Plaza de Armas in Chivay. Most rides will cost S/20–S/25.

EXPLORING
Colca Canyon. Flying overhead, you can't miss the green, fertile trough as it cuts through the barren terrain, but it's all an illusion; only scrub brush and cactus cling to the canyon's sheer basalt sides and miles of ancient terraces. ■TIP→ The canyon is named for the stone warehouses (colcas) used to store grain by an ancient society living along the walls of the gorge.

Carved into the foothills of the snow-covered Andes and sliced by the silvery Río Colca, Colca Canyon drops 3,182 meters (10,607 feet) down. The more adventurous can embark on a multiday hike into the canyon—typically a two-, three-, or five-day excursion. Bird lovers (and anyone with an eye for amazement) can visit the Cruz del

Canyon Life

Quechua farmers once irrigated narrow, stacked terraces of volcanic earth along the canyon rim to make this a productive farming area. These ancient fields are still used for quinoa and kiwicha grains, and barley grown here is used to brew Arequipeña beer.

Most of those who live along the rim today are Collagua Indians, whose settlements date back more than 2,000 years. Their traditions persevered through the centuries. In these unspoiled Andean villages you'll still see Collaguas and Cabana people wearing traditional clothing and embroidered hats. Spanish influence is evident in Achoma, Maca, Pinchollo, and Yanque, with their gleaming white sillar (volcanic-stone) churches.

Steeped in colorful folklore tradition, locals like a good fiesta. Some of the larger festivals include La Virgen del Candelaria, a two-day fiesta in Chivay on February 2 and 3; later in the month Carnivál is celebrated throughout the valley. Semana Santa (holy week) in April is heavily observed, but for a more colorful party don't miss Chivay's annual anniversary fiesta on June 21. From July 14 to 17 the Virgen del Carmen, one of the larger celebrations kicks off with parades on both ends of the canyon: Cabanaconde and Chivay. All Saints Day is well-honored on November 1 and 2 as is La Virgen Imaculada on December 8.

Condor. Culture seekers can spend a night with a native family. Light hikers and archaeology aficionados can observe points along the rim, or those seeking pure relaxation can hit one of the all-inclusive lodges with horseback riding and thermal baths.

Cruz del Condor is a haunt for the giant birds, particularly at dawn, when they soar on the winds rising from the deep valley. At 1,200 meters (4,000 feet), the "condor cross" precipice between the villages Pinchollo and Cabanaconder is the best place to spot them. ■ TIP→ From June to August, you're likely to spot close to 20 or more condors during a morning visit. By October and November many of the female birds are nesting, so your chances of eyeing flocks are slim, but you'll likely spot a few birds.

SPORTS AND THE OUTDOORS

Most organized adventure sport activities should be arranged from Arequipa, especially kayaking, rafting, and multiday treks into the canyon. Many upper-tier hotels and resorts offer packages, have their own tour guides, and have activities like horseback riding and mountain bike rentals. So check with your hotel before booking anything else. There's only one official tour operator in Chivay and it specializes in mountain bike rentals. However, local guides for hiking can be hired by asking around; the most experienced guides are in Cabanaconde and Chivay. The average price is S/60 or $25 USD a day for a local guide.

HIKING

Bring lots of water (the valley has water, but it's grossly expensive, as it's "imported" from Arequipa), sunscreen, a hat, good hiking shoes, high-energy snacks, sugar or coca leaves to alleviate the altitude sickness, and layer your clothes. One minute the wind may be fierce and the next you may be sweltering in the strong sun.

SCARY BRIDGES

A hallmark of Cotahausi Canyon is its bridges, which are all hanging (and swinging) across the Río Cotahuasi. They're cool to look at, nerve-racking to consider, but there's only one way over.

Along the canyon: Along the south side of the canyon it's possible to do an easy hike from the observation points between Cruz del Condor and Pinchollo. Paths are along the canyon rim most of the way; however, in some places, you have to walk along the road. The closer to Cruz del Condor you are, the better the paths and lookouts get.

Another short hike, but more uphill, is on the north rim starting in Coporaque. At the Plaza de Armas, to the left of the church in the corner of the Plaza, you'll see an archway. Go through the archway and take a right uphill and you'll be on the trail, which goes from wide to narrow, but is defined. ■ TIP→ Following it up about an hour, you'll come to ancient burial tombs (look down) with actual skeletons. The trail climbs up a cliff, which overlooks the valley. It's about a two-hour hike to the top and in some spots is very steep and rocks are crumbly. After the tombs the path becomes confusing and splits in many directions.

Into the canyon: Trails into the canyon are many as well as rough and unmarked, so venture down with a guide. Several adventure tour operators provide governmental certified hiking guides; local guides are also easily found. Packages range from two- to eight-day treks. The Cabanaconde area is the entry point for most of these.

The most popular multiday hike is the three-day/two-night trek. Starting about 20 minutes (by foot) east of Cabanaconde at Pampa San Miguel, the trail to San Juan Chuccho (one of the larger villages along the river) begins. The steep slope has loose gravel and takes about four hours. In San Juan Chuccho sleeping options are family-run hostels or a campsite. Day two consists of hiking on fairly even terrain through the small villages of Tapay, Cosnirhua, and Malata before crossing the river and into the lush green village of Sangalle, or as locals call it, Oasis, a mini-paradise along the Río Colca, with hot springs and waterfalls. On day three, you'll hike four to five hours uphill to the rim and arrive in Cabanaconde by lunch.

We do not recommend hiking alone here. So many paths are in this area that it can be overwhelming to even the most experienced trekkers.

WHITE-WATER RAFTING

The Río Colca is a finicky river. Highly skilled paddlers long to run this Class IV–V river. Depending upon the season, the water level and the seismic activity of the local volcanoes, the rapids change frequently. In some areas it's more than a Class V and in other areas it's slow enough that it could be considered a Class II–III. Below Colca Canyon

Llamas, Vicunas and Alpacas

Alpaca

Llamas, vicuñas, guanacos, and alpacas roam the highlands of Peru, but unfortunately not in the great herds of pre-Inca times. However, there are always a few around, especially the domesticated llama and alpaca. The sly vicuña, like the guanaco, refuses domestication. Here's a primer on how to tell them apart.

The alpaca is the cute and cuddly one, especially while still a baby. It grows a luxurious, long wool coat that comes in as many as 20 colors and its wool is used in knitting sweaters and weaving rugs and wall hangings. Its finest wool is from the first shearing and is called "baby alpaca." When full-grown it's close to 1½ meters (4.9 feet) tall and weighs about 7 kg (15 pounds). Its size and the shortness of its neck distinguish it from the llama. There are two types of alpaca: the common huancayo with short thick legs; and the less-predominant suri, which is a bit taller, and also nicknamed the Bob Marley for its shaggy curly dreadlocks that grow around its face and chest.

The guanaco, a cousin of the delicate vicuña, is a thin-legged wild endangered camelid, with a coarse reddish-brown coat and a soft white underbelly. Its hair is challenging to weave on its own, so often it's mixed with other fibers, like alpaca. The guanaco weighs about 200 pounds and can be up to 5 feet long and 3–4 feet high. Eighty percent of Guanacos live in Patagonia, but the other 20% are scattered through the altiplano of southern Peru, Chile, and Bolivia. It's the only camelid that can live at sea level and in the high-altitude Andes.

The llama is the pack animal with a course coat in as many as 50 colors, though one that's unsuitable for weavings or fine wearing apparel. It can reach almost 2 meters (6 feet) from its hoofs to the top of its elongated neck and long, curved ears. It can carry 40–60 kilograms (88–132 pounds), depending on the length of the trip. It can also have some nasty habits, like spitting in your eye or kicking you if you get too close to its hind legs.

The vicuña has a more delicate appearance. It will hold still (with help) for shearing, and its wool is the most desirable. It's protected by the Peruvian government, as it was almost killed off by unrestricted hunting. It's the smallest of the Andean camelids, at 1.3 meters (4 feet) and weighs about 40 kg (88 pounds) at maturity. It's found mostly at altitudes over 3,600 meters (12,000 feet).

—By Joan Gonzalez

conditions on the Río Majes (the large downstream section of the Río Colca) are reliable with superb white-water rafting. Skilled rafters start in Huambo by renting mules for S/20 and for the next eight hours descend to the river. The waters at this point rank in at Class III, but when the Río Mamacocha dumps in it's Class IV and V rapids.

> **HIGH SUN**
>
> Don't forget sunblock! At high altitudes the rays can be fierce, even with clouds. Often the brisk mountain temperatures trick you into thinking it's too cool for a burn.

Paddlers who have tried to run the entire river through the canyon have had more casualties than successes. There are a few well-known operators to consider, which is important given the river's intensity.

4

CANYON TOUR OPERATORS IN AREQUIPA

For the standard one- or two-day tours of Colca Canyon most agencies pool their customers, so quality varies little. For about S/140 per day you can hire **Carlos Zárate Aventuras** (⊠ *Santa Catalina 204* ☎ *054/263–107* ⊕ *www.zarateadventures.com*) and his hiking and mountain guides, who conduct tours in Spanish, English, and French.Other travelers interested in multiday trekking trips of Colca Canyon, Misti, and Chachani use **Land Adventures** (⊠ *Santa Catalina 118-B* ☎ *054/204–872* ⊕ *www.landadventures.net*).

Colca Trek (⊠ *Jerusalén 401-B* ☎ *054/206–217*)is a specialist in longer trekking tours and comes highly recommended. Upscale travelers go with **Condor Travel** (⊠ *Santa Catalina 210 in la Casona de Santa Catalina shopping center* ☎ *054/237–821 Santa Catalina 117* ⊕ *www. condortravel.com*). Slightly less expensive, but still good, is **Giardino** (⊠ *Jerusalén 604-A* ☎ *054/221–345* ⊕ *www.giardinotours.com*).

The king of all kayaking and rafting operators around the world, **Bio Bio Expeditions** (⊠ *Jerusalén 408-A, Arequipa* ☎ *800/246–7238* ⊕ *www. bbxrafting.com*) puts on multiday runs down the Colca and Cotahuasi rivers. All guides are trained in first aid and swiftwater rescue. Class IV, V, and VI rafting adventures through the Colca Canyon are operated May through September by **Apumayo Expediciones** (⊠ *Garcilaso 316-A, Cusco* ☎ *084/246–018* ⊕ *www.apumayo.com*).

WHERE TO EAT AND STAY

Chivay is tiny, but has plenty of small budget hotels and a few restaurants. You'll come into town on 22 de Agosto, which leads to the Plaza de Armas, where you'll find **Lobo's Pizzeria, McElroy's Pub** (a gringo magnet owned by a true Irishman), and **El Balcón de Don Zacarias**, which serves very good traditional food. An organic Novo Andino restaurant, **Kantua**, on Calle Garcilazo 510, is worthy of a visit.

If you're planning on staying one night in Colca Canyon it makes sense to stay in Chivay. If you'll be in the area for longer, we recommend one of the lodges in the valley, which are more inclusive and offer activities like hiking, biking, horseback riding, and have a restaurant on-site.

$ 🏠 **Casa Andina.** This hotel from the national chain of the same name ☯ seems like a Swiss ski lodge, with bungalow cabins made of locally quarried rock. Medium-size rooms with rustic furnishings have private baths with hot water. The restaurant serves excellent Peruvian fare. **Pros:** planetarium and observatory; good breakfast; cozy lounge and fireplace. **Cons:** no easy access to the outdoors; small bathrooms. ✉ *Calle Huayna Capac s/n, Chivay* ☎ *054/53–1020* ⊕ *www.casa-andina.com* ⤶ *52 rooms* ⌂ *In-room: a/c, safe, refrigerator (some), Wi-Fi (some). In-hotel: restaurant, bar, laundry service, Internet terminal, Wi-Fi hotspot, parking (free)* ▭ *AE, DC, MC, V* ⏀ *BP.*

> **BRING CASH!**
>
> There are no ATMs in the Colca Canyon or valley area, nor is it possible for credit cards to be processed. Soles and U.S. dollars (no bills larger than $10 USD) are accepted.

$$$ 🏨 **Colca Lodge.** The hotel's understated look, with adobe and clay walls ☾ and thatched roof, compliment the terrain. The location between Yanque and Ichupampa offers plenty to do, including canyon hikes, horseback rides, biking, and trout fishing. It's family-friendly and kids will love the nonstop activities. Rooms are simple, perhaps too much so, but the heat works thanks to the solar panel system. Above all, this hotel has the best hot springs around. Next to the river, they're made of stone, and have a spectacular view. **Pros:** lots of activities; hot springs; solar heating. **Cons:** hot springs are closed in February and March; rooms are plain. ✉ *Fundo Puye s/n, Caylloma, Yanque* ☎ *054/202–587* 🖶 *054/220–407* ⊕ *www.colca-lodge.com* ⤶ *25 rooms* ⌂ *In-room: a/c, safe (some). In-hotel: restaurant, room service, bar, pool, bicycles, laundry service, parking (free)* ▭ *AE, MC, V* ⏀ *BP.*

$ 🏨 **La Casa de Mama Yacchi.** Perhaps the best food around, and the best pillows, too. Owned by the same folks of Casa de Mi Abuela in Arequipa, this rustic thatched-roof hotel is a great economical choice. Its main lodge is cozy, the restaurant specializes in local fare, such as the alpaca barbecue, and there's a good bar. The rooms are simple bungalows with standard beds and excellent bedding. On the north rim, in Coporaque, it's very peaceful. Horseback riding and hikes can be arranged daily. **Pros:** delicious food; good water pressure and pillows. **Cons:** gets cold; far from Cruz del Condor. ✉ *Calle Jerusalén 606, Coporaque* ☎ *054/241–206* ⊕ *www.lacasademamayacchi.com* ⤶ *50 rooms* ⌂ *In-room: no phone, no a/c, safe. In-hotel: restaurant, bar, laundry service, parking (free)* ▭ *No credit cards* ⏀ *BP.*

$$$$ 🏨 **Las Casitas del Colca.** It doesn't get better than this, at least not in
Fodor's Choice Colca. One of the region's newest hotels is also the most luxurious,
★ and by far the most expensive. It's an all-inclusive resort with cooking and painting classes, fly-fishing, horseback riding, hiking tours, and a full-service spa. Thatch-roof bungalows with terraces have spectacular views over the silvery Río Colca. ■**TIP➡** All outdoor terraces also have small private hot springs tubs, an open-fire pit, and couches. Rooms are bright with comfortable furnishings, including wrought-iron beds piled with heaps of elegant bedding and leather armchairs. The smooth stone floors are heated and the deep bathtubs have glass ceilings so at night you can also soak in the amazing stars above. An on-site Novo Andino restaurant serves creative fare made using vegetables from the garden.

All meals are offered à la carte. **Pros:** all-inclusive; heated floors; private hot springs. **Cons:** pricey. ⊠ *Parque Curiña Yanque* ☎ *051/610–8300* ⊕ *www.lascasitasdelcolca.com* ⤸ *19 rooms, 1 suite* ⌂ *In-room: no a/c, safe, refrigerator, no TV, Wi-Fi. In-hotel: restaurant, room service, bar, pools, spa, bicycles, laundry service, Internet terminal, Wi-Fi hotspot, parking (free)* ⊟ *AE, MC, V* ⊺◎⫶ *AI.*

$ ⌷ **Pozo del Cielo.** Across the river on top of a hill on the outskirts of Chivay sits one of the most quaint lodges in the valley. A series of chalets are made of adobe, wood, and stone. Simple rooms have beds piled with warm blankets and include a modern bathroom. The dark-wood window shades and low wooden doorways seem out of a fairy tale. All rooms lead to the main lodge by narrow, outdoor cobbled stone pathways. In the lodge the restaurant is composed of endless windows and an adobe fireplace. ■**TIP➜** The views over Chivay, the valley, and volcanoes are stunning. Good Novo Andino food is served and there's always hot tea. **Pros:** hot-water bottles at bedtime for extra warmth; on the outskirts of Chivay; good views. **Cons:** must walk outside to get to breakfast; no bureaus or closets. ⊠ *Calle Huáscar B-3 Sacsayhuaman* ☎ *054/531–041* ⊕ *www.pozodelcielo.com.pe* ⤸ *20 rooms* ⌂ *In-room: no phone, a/c, safe (some), no TV (some). In-hotel: restaurant, room service, bar, laundry service, parking (free)* ⊟ *AE, MC, V* ⊺◎⫶ *BP.*

HOMESTAYS In the small settlements of Cabanaconde, Coporaque, Ichupampa, Madrigal, and Yanque you can experience local life by staying with families. In addition to exploring ruins and historic sites with family guides, you'll help out with daily chores and participate in seasonal festivities. This option is difficult to arrange in advance and from afar, but possible. Colonial Tours in Arequipa can make advance arrangements but details will be limited. These types of trips should only cost about $20 USD, including private transportation to the canyon from Arequipa.

If you don't mind uncertainty, it's quite simple to come to Chivay or Cabanaconde and ask around about staying with a family. Locals are friendly and know families in the canyon who want visitors. Arriving as early as possible is essential. It takes a few hours to network, find a family, and travel to their village.

AREQUIPA

150 km (93 mi) south of Colca Canyon; 200 km (124 mi) south of Cotahuasi Canyon.

Cradled by three steep, gargantuan, snow-covered volcanoes, the jaw-dropping white-stoned Arequipa, one of the most visually stunning city's in Peru, shines under the striking sun at 2,350 meters (7,709 feet). This settlement of 1 million residents grew from a collection of Spanish-colonial churches and homes constructed from white sillar (volcanic stone) gathered from the surrounding terrain. The result is nothing less than a work of art—short gleaming white buildings contrast with the charcoal-color mountain backdrop of El Misti, a perfectly shaped cone volcano.

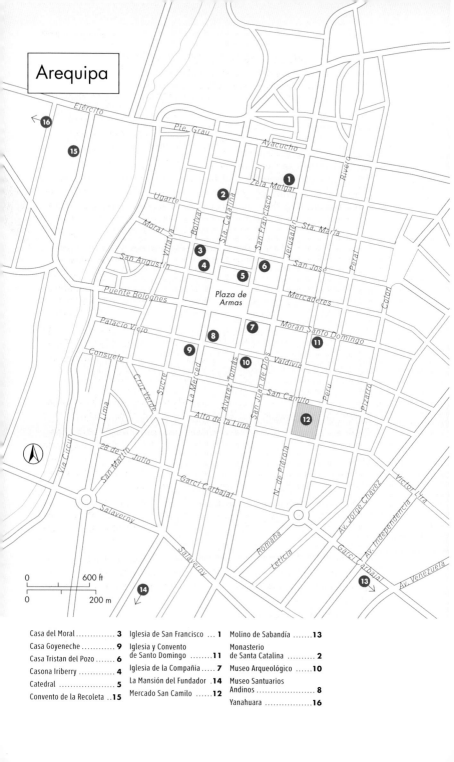

Arequipa

Casa del Moral **3**

Casa Goyeneche **9**

Casa Tristan del Pozo **6**

Casona Iriberry **4**

Catedral **5**

Convento de la Recoleta ..**15**

Iglesia de San Francisco ... **1**

Iglesia y Convento
de Santo Domingo **11**

Iglesia de la Compañia **7**

La Mansión del Fundador .**14**

Mercado San Camilo **12**

Molino de Sabandía **13**

Monasterio
de Santa Catalina **2**

Museo Arqueológico **10**

Museo Santuarios
Andinos **8**

Yanahuara **16**

The town was a gathering of Aymara Indians and Inca when Garci Manuel de Carbajal and nearly 100 more Spaniards founded the city on August 15, 1540. After the Spanish arrived, the town grew into the region's most profitable center for farming and cattle-raising—businesses that continue to be important in Arequipa's economy.

> ### TIPPING THE GUARD
>
> In colonial mansions, museums, or landmarks that are free, guards are happy to show you around, but they typically work for tips. Anything from 5 to 10 soles is appropriate.

The settlement was also on the silver route linking the coast to the Bolivian mines. By the 1800s Arequipa had more Spanish settlers than any town in the south.

Arequipeños call their home Cuidad Blanca, "White City," and the "Independent Republic of Arequipa"—they have made several attempts to secede from Peru and even designed the city's own passport and flag. Today the town is abuzz with adventure outfitters leading tours in the surrounding canyons, bars and cafés in 500-year-old sillar buildings, and the finest alpaca threads anywhere in the country. ■ TIP➔ On August 15, parades, fireworks, bullfights, and dancing celebrate the city's founding.

Arequipa enjoys fresh, crisp air, and warm days averaging 23°C (73°F) and comfortable nights at 14°C (57°F). To make up for the lack of rain, the Río Chili waters the surrounding foothills, which were once farmed by the Inca and now stretch into rows of alfalfa and onions.

GETTING HERE AND AROUND

Arequipa's airport is large and it's easy to hail a taxi to your hotel. Many hotels also offer pickup and drop-off. The cost is about S/15.

Walking is the best option around the city center. Most sights, shops, and restaurants are near the Plaza de Armas. For a quick, cheap tour, spend S/3 and catch a Vallecito bus for a 1 1/2-hour circuit around Calles Jerusalén and San Juan de Díos. Taxis are everywhere and cost about S/3 to get around the center or to Vallecito.

Arequipa has two bus terminals side by side on Avenida Ibañez and Avenida Andrés Avelino Cáceres. Most people leave out of the older Terminal Terreste, where most bus companies have offices, while the newer terminal Terrapuerto sees less traffic.

TIMING

Most sites are open morning and afternoon, but close for a couple of hours midday. Churches usually open 7 to 9 AM and 6 to 8 PM, before and after services.

SAFETY AND PRECAUTIONS

Wear comfortable walking shoes, and bring a hat, sunscreen, a Spanish dictionary, some small change, and a good map of town. Be street-smart in the Arequipa market area—access your cash discreetly and keep your valuables close. At 2,300 meters (7,500 feet) Arequipa is quite high. If you're coming directly from Lima or from the coast, carve out a day or two for acclimatization.

ESSENTIALS

Currency Banco Continental BBVA (⊠ San Francisco 108). Banco de Tra-bajo (⊠ Calle Moral 201). Banco de Crédito BCP (⊠ San Juan de Dios 123 ☎ 054/283–741). Caja Municipal Arequipa (⊠ La Merced 106). Scotiabank (⊠ Mercaderes 410).

Internet C@tedral Internet (⊠ Pasaje Catedral 101 ☎ 054/282–074). Cyber-market (⊠ Santa Catalina 115 ☎ 054/284–306).

Mail Serpost Arequipa (⊠ Calle Moral 118 ☎ 054/215–247 ⊕ www. serpost.com.pe ☉ Mon.–Sat. 8–8, Sun. 9–2). DHL (⊠ Santa Catalina 115 ☎ 054/234–288).

Medical Clínica Arequipa SA (⊠ Puente Grau y Av. Bolognesi ☎ 054/253–416 or 054/253–424). Hospital Goyeneche (⊠ Av. Goyeneche s/n, Cerado ☎ 054/231–313). Honorio Delgado Espinoza Regional Hospital (⊠ Av. A. Carrión s/n ☎ 054/231–818, 054/219–702, or 054/233–812).

Police Police (⊠ Av. Emmel 106, Yanahuara ☎ 054/254–020). Policía de Tour-ismo (⊠ Jerusalén 315 ☎ 054/201–258).

Rental Car Akal Rent A Car (⊠ Av. Bolognesi 903 Cayma ⊕ www.akalrentacar. com). Avis Arequipa (⊠ Ugarte 216 ⊕ www.avisperu.com). Exodo (⊠ Manuél Belgrado F-1, Urb. Alvarez Thomas ☎ 054/423–756). Hertz (⊠ Palacio Viejo 214 ☎ 054/282–519 ⊕ www.hertz.com ⊠ Rodriguez Ballón Airport ☎ 054/443–576).

Taxi Taxi Turismo Arequipa (☎ 054/458–888 or 054/459–090 ⊕ www. taxiturismo.com.pe). 454545 (☎ 054/454–545).

Visitor Info Iperu Oficina de Información Turística (⊠ Portal de la Munici-palidad 110, Plaza de Armas ☎ 054/223–265 ⊠ Santa Catalina 210, Casona Santa Catalina ☎ 054/221–227 ⊠ Rodríguez Ballón Airport, 1st fl., Main Hall ☎ 054/444–564). Touring and Automobile Club of Peru (⊠ Goyeneche 313 ☎ 054/603–131 or 054/603–333).

EXPLORING

TOP ATTRACTIONS

❸ Casa del Moral. One of the oldest architectural landmarks from the Areq-uipa Baroque period was named for the ancient *mora* tree (mulberry tree) growing in the center of the main patio. One of the town's most unusual buildings, it now houses the Banco Sur, but it's open to the pub-lic. Over the front door, carved into a white sillar portal, is the Spanish coat of arms as well as a baroque-mestizo design that combines puma heads with darting snakes from their mouths—motifs found on Nazca textiles and pottery. The interior of the house is like a small museum with alpaca rugs and soaring ceilings, polished period furniture, and a gallery of colonial period Cusco School paintings. Originally a lovely old colonial home, it was bought in the 1940s by the British consul and renovated to its former elegance in the early 1990s. ⊠ Moral 318 and Bolívar ☎ 054/285–371 ⊠ S/6 ☉ Mon.–Sat. 9–5, holidays 9–1.

❺ Catedral. You can't miss the imposing twin bell towers of this 1612
Fodor's Choice cathedral, whose facade guards the entire eastern flank of the Plaza de
★ Armas. ■TIP→ As the sun sets the imperial reflection gives the Cathedral

Courtyard in Monasterio de Santa Catalina, Arequipa.

an amber hue. The inside has high-vaulted ceilings above a beautiful Belgian organ. The ornate wooden pulpit, carved by French artist Rigot in 1879, was transported here in the early 1900s. In the back, look for the Virgin of the Sighs statue in her white wedding dress, and the figure of Beata Ana de Los Angeles, a nun from the Santa Catalina monastery who was beatified by Pope John Paul II when he stayed in Arequipa in 1990. A fire in 1844 destroyed much of the cathedral, as did an 1868 earthquake, so parts have a neoclassical look. In 2001 another earthquake damaged one of the bell towers, which was repaired to match its sister tower. ⊠ *Plaza de Armas, between Santa Catalina and San Francisco* ☎ *054/23–2635* ☜ *S/7* ⊙ *Daily 7–11 and 4–7.*

⑦ Iglesia de la Compañía. Representative of 17th-century religious architecture, the complex was built by the Jesuits in 1573. ■TIP➔ A series of bone-white buildings incorporate many decorative styles and touches. The detail carved into the sillar arcades is spectacular. The side portal, built in 1654, and main facade, built in 1698, show examples of Andean mestizo style with carved flowers, spirals, birds—and angels with Indian faces—along gently curving archways and spiral pillars. Inside, **Capilla St. Ignatius** (St. Ignatius Chapel) has a polychrome cupola and 66 canvases from the Cusco School, including original 17th-century oil paintings by Bernardo Bitti. Hike up to the steeple at sunset for sweeping views of Arequipa. The former monastery houses some of the most upscale stores in the city and contains two cloisters, which can be entered from General Morán or Palacio Viejo. The main building is on the southeast corner of the Plaza de Armas. ⊠ *General Morán* *at Álvarez Tomás* ☎ *054/21–2141* ⬙ *Chapel S/6* ⊙ *Church weekdays 9–12:30 and 3–6:30, Sat. 3–4:30, Sun. 5–6 PM.*

❷ Monasterio de Santa Catalina. A city unto itself, this 5-acre complex of
Fodor's Choice mud-brick, Iberian-style buildings surrounded by vibrant fortress-like
★ walls and separated by neat, open plazas and colorful gardens, is a
ⓒ working convent and one of Peru's most famed cultural treasures.
■TIP→ Founded in 1579 and closed to the public for the first 400 years,
Santa Catalina was an exclusive retreat for the daughters of Arequipa's
wealthiest colonial patrons. Visitors can catch a peek at life in this historic monastery. Narrow streets run past the Courtyard of Silence,
where teenage nuns lived during their first year, and the Cloister of
Oranges, where nuns decorated their rooms with lace sheets, silk cur-
tains, and antique furnishings. Though about 400 nuns once lived here,
fewer than 30 do today. Admission includes a one-hour guided tour (tip
S/10–S/20) in English. Afterward, head to the cafeteria for the nuns'
famous *torta de naranja* (orange cake), pastries, and tea. There are
night tours on Tuesday and Thursday, but check the times before you
go, as they sometimes change. ⊠ *Santa Catalina 301* ☎ *054/229–798*
⬙ *S/30* ⊙ *Mon., Wed., Fri.–Sun. 8–5; Tues. and Thurs. 8–8. Last entry
1 hr before closing.*

❽ Museo Santuarios Andinos. Referred to as the Juanita Museum, this fas-
Fodor's Choice cinating little museum at the Universidad Católica Santa Maria holds
★ the frozen bodies of four young girls who were apparently sacrificed
more than 500 years ago by the Inca to appease the gods. The "Juanita"
mummy, said to be frozen around the age of 13, was the first mummy
found in 1995 near the summit of Mt. Ampato by local climber Miguel
Zarate and anthropologist Johan Reinhard. ■TIP→ When neighboring
Volcán Sabancaya erupted, the ice that held Juanita in her sacrificial tomb
melted and she rolled partway down the mountain and into a crater. English-speaking guides will show you around the museum, and you can
watch a video detailing the expedition. ⊠ *La Merced 110* ☎ *054/215–
013* ⬙ *S/11* ⊙ *Mon.–Sat. 9–6, Sun. 9–3.*

WORTH NOTING

❾ Casa Goyeneche. This attractive Spanish-colonial home was built in
1888. Ask the guard for a tour, and you'll enter through a pretty courtyard and an ornate set of wooden doors to view rooms decorated in
period-style antiques and Cusco School paintings. ⊠ *La Merced 201
y Palacio Viejo* ☎ *054/352–674* ⬙ *Free, but if you get a tour a small
donation is expected* ⊙ *Weekdays 9:15–3.*

❻ Casa Tristan del Pozo. This small museum and art gallery was built in
1738 and is now the Banco Continental. Look for the elaborate puma
heads spouting water. Inside you'll find colonial paintings, ornate Peruvian costumes, and furniture. ⊠ *San Francisco 108* ☎ *054/21–1101*
⬙ *Free* ⊙ *Weekdays 9:15–6:30, Sat. 9:30–12:30.*

❹ Casona Iriberry. Unlike the other mansions, Casona Iriberry has religious
overtones. Small scriptures are etched into its structure, exemplifying
Arequipa's catholic roots. The back of the house is now the Centro Cultural Cháves la Rosa, which houses some of the city's most important
contemporary arts venues, including photography exhibits, concerts,

and films. The front of the compound is filled with colonial-period furniture, paintings, and decor. ⊠ *Plaza de Armas, San Augustin y Santa Catalina* 🕾 *054/20–4482* 🖃 *Free to look around, admission price for certain events* ⊘ *Mon.–Sat. 9–1 and 4–8.*

⑮ **Convento de la Recoleta.** One of Peru's most extensive and valuable libraries is in this 1648 Franciscan monastery. With several cloisters and museums on-site, it's a wonderful place to research regional history and culture. Start in the massive, wood-paneled, wood-floored library, where monks in brown robes quietly browse 20,000 ancient books and maps, the most valuable of which were printed before 1500 and are kept in glass cases. Pre-Columbian artifacts and objects collected by missionaries to the Amazon are on display, as is a selection of elegant colonial and religious artwork. Guides are available, just remember to tip. To reach the monastery, cross the Río Chili by Puente Grau. It's a 10- to 15-minute walk from the Plaza de Armas. ⊠ *Recoleta 117* 🕾 *054/27–0966* 🖃 *S/2* ⊘ *Mon.–Sat. 9–noon and 3–5.*

❶ **Iglesia de San Francisco.** This 16th-century church has survived numerous natural disasters, including several earthquakes that cracked its cupola. Inside, near the polished silver altar, is the little chapel of the Sorrowful Virgin, where the all-important Virgin Mary statue is stored. ■**TIP➔** On December 8, during Arequipa's Feast of the Immaculate Conception, the Virgin is paraded around the city all night atop an ornate carriage and surrounded by images of saints and angels. A throng of pilgrims carry flowers and candles. Visit the adjoining convent (S/5) to see Arequipa's largest painting and a museum of 17th-century religious furniture and paintings. ⊠ *Zela 103* 🕾 *054/223–048* 🖃 *Free* ⊘ *Church: Weekdays 7–10 AM and 4–8; Sat 4–8; Sun. 7–12:45 and 6–8. Convent: Mon.–Sat. 9–12 and 3–5. Closed Sun.*

⑪ **Iglesia y Convento de Santo Domingo.** With hints of Islam in its elegant brick arches and stone domes, this cathedral carries an aura of elegance. Step inside to view simple furnishings and sunlight streaming through stained-glass windows as small silver candles flicker along the back wall near the altar. A working Dominican monastery is in back. ⊠ *Santo Domingo y Piérola* 🕾 *054/213–511* 🖃 *Free* ⊘ *Weekdays 7–noon and 3:30–7:45, Sat. 6:45–9 AM and 3–7:45, Sun. 5:30 AM–1.*

⑭ **La Mansión del Fundador.** First owned by the founder of Arequipa Don Garcí Manuel de Carbajal, La Mansión del Fundador is a restored colonial home and church. Alongside the Río Sabandía, the sillar-made home perches over a cliff and is about 20 minutes from the center of town. Said to have been built for Carbajal's son, it became a Jesuit retreat in the 16th century and in the 1800s was remodeled by Juan Crisostomo de Goyeneche y Aguerreverre. While intimate, the chapel is small and simple, but the home is noted for its vaulted arch ceilings and spacious patio. There's also a cafeteria with a bar on-site. To reach the home, go past Tingo along Avenida Huasacanche. ⊠ *Av. Paisajesta s/n, about 6.5 km outside of Arequipa, Socobaya* 🕾 *054/442–460* 🖃 *S/9* ⊘ *Daily 9–5.*

⑫ **Mercado San Camilo.** This jam-packed collection of shops sells everything from snacks and local produce to clothing and household goods. It's

Short Trips from Arequipa

CLOSE UP

Reserva Nacional Salinas y Aguada Blanca. Herds of beige-and-white vicuñas, llamas, and alpacas graze together on the sparse plant life in the midst of the open fields that encompass this vast nature reserve of desert, grass, and flamingo-filled lakes. Wear good walking shoes for the uneven terrain and bring binoculars. Also bring a hat, sunscreen, and a warm jacket, as the park sits at a crisp 3,900 meters (12,800 feet). The reserve is 35 km (22 mi) north of Arequipa, just beyond El Misti. If you're headed to Colca Canyon or Puno from Arequipa, you have to pass through the reserve to get there.

Yura. About a half-hour drive from Arequipa, this serene little town is settled in the western foothills of the Volcán Chachani. Take the road 27 km (17 mi) farther to reach the famous thermal baths where you can take a dip in naturally heated water that ranges from 70 to 82°F. You can soak in any weather and enjoy a picnic along the river in summertime. If you don't bring your own food, you can lunch at the Hotel Libertador. Admission to the hot springs is S/10, and they're open daily from sunrise until 3 PM. From San Juan de Dios, you can catch buses to Yura for S/3.

4

an excellent place to spot rare types of potatoes, sample queso helado, or eat *chicharrones* (deep fried pork). You can find it around Perú, San Camilo, Piérola, and Alto de la Luna. ⊠ *San Camilo 352* ☎ *No phone* 💰 *Free* ☉ *Daily 7–5.*

⑬ **Molino de Sabandía.** There's a colorful story behind the area's first stone *molina* (mill), 7 km (4 mi) southeast of Arequipa. Built in 1621 in the gorgeous Paucarpata countryside, the mill fell into ruin over the next century. Famous architect Luis Felipe Calle was restoring the Arequipa mansion that now houses the Central Reserve Bank in 1966 when he was asked to work on the mill project. By 1973 the restoration of the volcanic-stone structure was complete—and Calle liked the new version so much that he bought it, got it working again, and opened it for visitors to tour. Bring your swimsuit and walking shoes in good weather; there's a pool and trails around the lovely countryside. Adjoining the site is Yumina, which has numerous Inca agricultural terraces. If you're not driving, flag a taxi for S/16 or take a colectivo from Socabaya in Arequipa to about 2 km (1 mi) past Paucarpata. ⊠ *8 km (5 mi) south of Arequipa, Sabandia* ☎ *No phone* 💰 *S/7* ☉ *Daily 9–5.*

⑩ **Museo Arqueológico.** With a solid collection of native pottery and textiles, human-sacrificed bones, along with gold and silver offerings from Inca times, this archaeology museum at the Universidad de San Augustín provides a background on local archaeology and ruins. Apply to the director for an appointment to visit; once you're approved, you'll have an expert guide to tell all the stories behind the displays. ⊠ *Av. Independencia, between La Salle y Santa Rosa* ☎ *054/288–881* 💰 *S/3* ☉ *Weekdays 9–4.*

⑯ **Yanahuara.** The eclectic little suburb of Yanahuara, northwest of the city, is perfect for lunch or a late afternoon stroll. The neighborhood is above Arequipa and has amazing views over the city at the lookout constructed of sillar stone arches. On a clear day views of volcanos El Misti, Chachani, and Picchu can be had. Stop in at the 1783, mestizo-style Iglesia Yanahuara. The interior has wrought-iron chandeliers and gilt sanctuaries surrounding the nave. Ask to see the glass coffin that holds a statue of Christ used in parades on holy days. To reach Yana-huara, head across the Avenida Grau bridge, then continue on Avenida Ejército to Avenida Lima, and from here, it's five blocks to the Plaza. It's a 15-minute walk or an eight-minute cab ride from the city center.

WHERE TO EAT

Comida Arequipa (Arequipan cuisine) is a special version of *comida criolla*. Perhaps the most famous dish is *rocoto relleno*, a large, spicy red pepper stuffed with meat, onions, and cheese. Other specialties to try are *cuy chactado* (roasted guinea pig), and *adobo* (pork stew), a local cure for hangovers. *Picanterías* are where locals head for good, basic Peruvian meals and cold Arequipeña beer served with *cancha* (fried, salted corn).

The west side of the Plaza de Armas has dozens of restaurants along the balcony above the Portal San Augustín. The first blocks of Calle San Francisco and Calle Santa Catalina north of the Plaza de Armas are lined with cafés, restaurants, and bars.

¢ ✕ **Café Peña Anuschka.** European expats and travelers craving the sour
GERMAN flavorings of German cuisine frequent this busy, dinner-only restaurant. You can also drop in after supper for a fruity cocktail or coffee and a freshly baked German pastry. The café, open 7–9 PM, transforms into a peña with live music Friday and Saturday nights. ⌧ *Santa Catalina 204* ☏ *054/213–221* ▭ *No credit cards* ☽ *Closed Sun. No lunch.*

$ **Chi Cha.** Celebu-chef Gastón Acurio's stylish Peruvian bistro serves up
PERUVIAN a wide range of contemporary Peruvian fare ranging from regional
Fodor's Choice specialties to national plates in what feels like a trendy extension of
★ the Santa Catalina monastery, right across the street. Start your meal with a pisco-based cocktail that uses Peruvian fruits like tumbo or camu camu, and then make your way around the menu sampling traditional Arequipeñan dishes such as adobo or rocoto relleno, or more creative plates like the chupe de camarones pizza or alpaca ossobuco. ⌧ *Santa Catalina 210* ☏ *054/28–7360* ▭ *AE, MC, V.*

¢ ✕ **Crepisimo.** This artistic, Euro-styled restaurant offers more than 100
FRENCH crêpes, filled with a variety of sauces, as entrées and desserts. Little sister to the Zig Zag restaurant on Calle Zela, look for such crêpe specialties as the Cubana, filled with banana slices, sugar, and rum. Exotic fruit juices like the *boa–boa* (tropical fruit punch) can be had, as can a glass of *vino* (wine) or high-grade espresso drinks. Check out the terrace for great views of the Monastery de Santa Catalina and volcanoes. Look for the restaurant in the Alianza Francesa compound. Open until 11:30. ⌧ *Santa Catalina 208* ☏ *054/206–620* ▭ *AE, D, MC, V.*

¢ ✕ **Cusco Coffee Company.** If you're missing home, this Starbucks-esque
CAFE coffee shop, owned by a Peruvian and American couple, will fix any caffeine craving. You can order-up fresh ground coffee drinks, or if tea

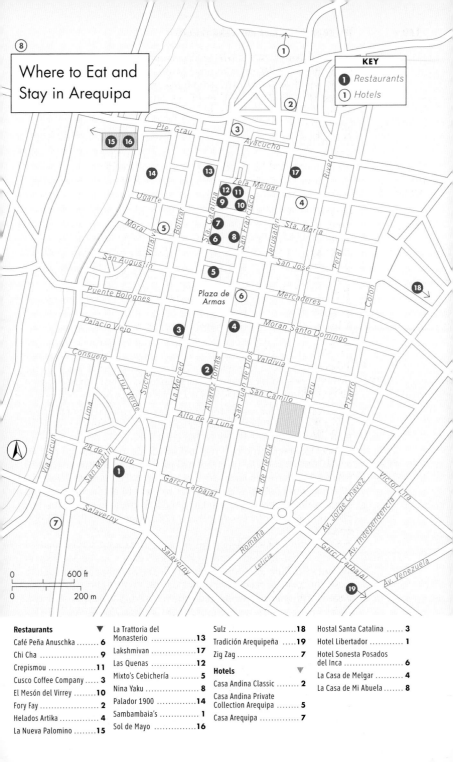

Where to Eat and Stay in Arequipa

KEY

1 Restaurants
1 Hotels

Plaza de Armas

Restaurants ▼

Café Peña Anuschka **6**
Chi Cha **9**
Crepismou **11**
Cusco Coffee Company **3**
El Mesón del Virrey **10**
Fory Fay **2**
Helados Artika **4**
La Nueva Palomino **15**

La Trattoria del
Monasterio **13**
Lakshmivan **17**
Las Quenas **12**
Mixto's Cebichería **5**
Nina Yaku **8**
Palador 1900 ....**14**
Sambambaia's **1**
Sol de Mayo **16**

Sulz **18**
Tradición Arequipeña **19**
Zig Zag **7**

Hotels ▼

Casa Andina Classic **2**
Casa Andina Private
Collection Arequipa **5**
Casa Arequipa **7**

Sulz **18**
Tradición Arequipeña **19**
Zig Zag **7**

Hostal Santa Catalina **3**
Hotel Libertador **1**
Hotel Sonesta Posados
del Inca **6**
La Casa de Melgar **4**
La Casa de Mi Abuela **8**

is your thing, go for a maté (try the eucalyptus), and there's a small selection of desserts. Comfortable leather couches make this a great place to plan your day or read the *International Herald Tribune*. ⊠ *La Merced 135* ☎ *054/281–152* ⊟ *AE, D, MC, V.*

$ ✕**El Mesón del Virrey.** This spacious upscale restaurant is donned in
PERUVIAN antiqued Spanish-colonial motif. The meat-heavy menu is infused with Italian and coastal influences. ■TIP➜ Quinoa con camarones (quinoa with shrimp) is one of the best dishes in Arequipa. Much like a risotto, the quinoa is cooked in a creamy tomato sauce with vegetables and a large fresh jumbo-size shrimp that looks more like a lobster. Lamb, beef, alpaca, and ostrich can also be enjoyed. The pisco sour is one of the best around. Hear live music nightly from 8 to 10. ⊠ *San Francisco 305* ☎ *054/202–080* ⊟ *AE, D, MC, V.*

$ ✕**Fory Fay Cevicheria.** Ask any Arequipeño to name their favorite fish
SEAFOOD joint and Fory Fay tops the list. For more than 22 years they've served
Fodor'sChoice some of the freshest cebiche around. Its owner, the personable Alex
★ Aller, grew up in the coastal port of Mollendo and travels there daily to check on the catch. Fishing bric-a-brac and photos of New York, where Aller once lived, line the walls. ⊠ *Alvarez Thomas 221* ☎ *054/242–400* ⊟ *AE, MC, V.*

¢ ✕**Helados Artika.** The small, retro-style *helados* (ice-cream) café next
CAFÉ to La Compañía is the perfect stop after shopping around town. We recommend the famous Arequipeño *queso helado*, or cheese ice cream— it's sweet milk with cinnamon and a dash of coconut. If you're in for a fruitier treat go for a scoop of the guanabana. Open from 8 AM until 10 PM. ⊠ *Morán 120* ☎ *054/284–915* ⊟ *No credit cards.*

$ ✕**La Nueva Palomino.** Chef Monica Huertas, who uses many of the same
PERUVIAN classic recipes her mother and her grandmother used that date back
Fodor'sChoice more than a century, is one of the great promoters of Arequipeñan
★ cuisine. Her preparations of regional standards such as rocoto relleno, adobo, *lechón al horno* (oven roasted pork), chupe de camarones, and queso helado have become the definitive recipes. This *picanteria* (simple, traditional restaurant) is a great place to come to on the weekend and spend the entire day eating, drinking, and listening to live music on their pleasant patio. ⊠ *Psje Leoncio Prado 122, Yanahuara* ☎ *054/253–500* ⊟ *AE, DC, MC, V.*

$ ✕**La Trattoria del Monasterio.** This intimate restaurant serves some of
ITALIAN the best Italian food in southern Peru. Its location in the Monasterio de Santa Catalina (the entrance is outside the compound) is enough to make this place special. Homemade pastas, ravioli, gnocchi, risottos, paired with seafood, meats and creative, savory sauces are offered. There's an extensive wine list. ⊠ *Santa Catalina 309* ☎ *054/204–062* ⊟ *AE, V.*

¢ ✕**Lakshmivan.** A herbivore's paradise, this tasty vegetarian restaurant
VEGETARIAN will delight any traveler in search of leafy greens. Inexpensive and mostly organic, it's been an Arequipa staple for more than 25 years. Specializing in soups and salads (16 different kinds), all meals fuse healthy ingredients with Peruvian flavors. You can sit outside in the courtyard among the colorful blossoms and birds, or inside, amid dazzling water-

SOUNDS OF NIGHT

Peñas start the party early, around 8 or 9 PM, and many of the traditional restaurants sponsor a show on Friday and Saturday nights. A quiet restaurant can quickly turn into a Broadway-like show and you could very well become the star.

Most of the after-dark entertainment revolves around a number of cafés and bars near the city center along Calle San Francisco. Close by on

Calle Zela, near the Catedral de San Francisco, bars seem to change daily, and on Calle Santa Catalina you'll find small cafés that suit the more artsy, avant-garde folk. In a seedier section across town, teenagers and twentysomething Arequipeños head to discos and Salsatecas on Avenida Dolores.

color portraits by local artists. ✉ *Jerusalén 408* ☎ *054/228–768* ▭ *No credit cards.*

$ ✗ **Las Quenas.** This rustic restaurant, filled with antiques and musical
PERUVIAN instruments, offers complete immersion into Arequipeñan life and traditions. Lunch and tea are served daily, but set dinners are the specialty, served nightly except Sunday to the accompaniment of a live folkloric performance. Dinners start at 8, and there's an extra S/5 charge if you stay for the music, which lasts until after midnight. ✉ *Santa Catalina 302* ☎ *054/281–115* ▭ *AE, DC, MC, V* ☼ *Closed Sun.*

$ ✗ **Mixto's Cebichería.** Above the Catedral, this ultraromantic spot serves
SEAFOOD up some great seafood dishes. Cebiche is the focus, but you'll also find shellfish empanadas and mixed stews. They also serve pastas, salads, and grilled meats. It's not the culinary gem it once was, but the food remains good and it's a beautiful spot. On the terrace above the Catedral entrance, the views of the city and El Misti are stunning. ✉ *Pasaje Catedral 115* ☎ *054/205–343* ▭ *AE, MC, V.*

$ ✗ **Nina Yaku.** This exclusive Novo Andino restaurant creates innovative
PERUVIAN Peruvian-style pastas, meats, and vegetarian dishes, all presented artfully. Drizzled in flavorful sauces, from sweet and tangy to savory and rich, the alpaca and beef are especially appetizing. It's a relaxing spot for after-dinner cocktails; ask for the *vino caliente*, mulled hot red wine. Reservations accepted. ✉ *San Francisco 211* ☎ *054/281–432* ▭ *AE, D, MC, V* ☼ *Closed Sun.*

$ **Paladar 1900.** The latest eatery from the restauranteur known as El
PERUVIAN Turko is by far his best yet and easily one of Arequipa's top restau-
Fodor's Choice rants. The contemporary digs, stylishly designed using sillar stone and
★ floor-to-ceiling glass windows that can slide open on nice days, are the place where Arequipa's sophisticated elite come to wine and dine. The lengthy menu is adventurous and travels to the Mediterranean, Middle East, Southeast Asia, Switzerland, and of course, Peru. Start with the Escribano fusion, a typical Arequipeñan salad that adds octopus, and then move on to one of the heartier entrées like the Bardo Immortal (corn cake stuffed with shrimp tails) or a 350-gram cut of Argentinian Bife Ancho. Finish your evening with a lucuma version of the classic Peruvian sweet, *suspiro a la limeña*, or a shot of pisco. Note: Paladar's

pisco and wine selections are tops in the city. ⊠ *Villaba 307* ☎ *054/226–295* ⊕ *www.paladar.com.pe* ⊟ *AE, MC, V.*

\$ ✕ **Sambambaia's.** Specializing in classic Andean meat and fish dishes, try
PERUVIAN the chef's favorite, a tender, juicy lomo al vino tinto, but if you're craving more familiar fare, order a wood-oven pizza or the grilled chicken. Live Latin jazz plays on Friday nights; if you're not eating dinner, you can pay S/5 for the performance, which begins at 8. In the quiet residential neighborhood of Vallecito, it's a 10-minute walk from the Plaza de Armas. ⊠ *Luna Pizarro 304, Vallecito* ☎ *054/223–657* ⊟ *AE, DC, MC, V.*

\$ ✕ **Sol de Mayo.** This charming garden restaurant in the colonial Yana-
PERUVIAN huara neighborhood is worth the expense to taste true Arequipan cooking. Specialties include *ocopa arequipeña* (boiled potato slices in spicy sauce and melted cheese), and *rocoto relleno* (spicy peppers stuffed with cheese, meat, and raisins). Only open for lunch. ⊠ *Jerusalén 207, Yanahuara* ☎ *054/254–148* ⊟ *AE, D, MC, V.*

\$ ✕ **Sulz.** Come hungry to this spacious, elegant restaurant that serves
PERUVIAN Arequipan food at its best. Enormous rooms packed with tables accommodate the flood of local families and tourists. If you can't decide what to order from the extensive menu, choose the Triple, which includes *rocoto* (a large red chili pepper), *chicharran* (pork rind), and *patitas de carnero* (mutton in sauce). There's a S/25 fee for patrons on weekend and holiday nights, when the live orchestra plays to those on the dance floor. ⊠ *Progreso 202A* ☎ *054/449–787* ⊟ *No credit cards.*

\$ ✕ **Tradición Arequipeña.** It may be a S/8 taxi ride to this restaurant in the
PERUVIAN Paucarpata district, but locals come in droves for the fantastic Arequipan food. The decor is Peruvian country, but the flavors lean toward Creole. Get ready for *cuy chactado* (deep-fried guina pig) and *ocopa arequipeña* (potato-based dish with garlic, olives, onion, and fresh cheese). If you crave seafood, try the *chupe de camarones* (a creamy shrimp chowder). Open from noon to 7, it's primarily a lunch-only venue Sunday through Thursday, but on Friday and Saturday it doesn't close until 10 (sometimes later) when live music can be heard, including an orchestra on Saturday nights. Reservations recommended. ⊠ *Dolores 111, Paucarpata* ☎ *054/426–467* ⊟ *AE, D, MC, V.*

\$ ✕ **Zig Zag Restaurant.** Everything at Zig Zag—from its grand iron spiral
FRENCH staircase to its Novo Andino cuisine, extensive wine list and decadent desserts—is done with exquisite detail and attention. Using a fusion of gourmet techniques from the Alps and Andes, the menu is a harmonious mix of fresh local foods. Try the quinoa potato gnocchi, the meat fondue, or the notable Trios, a prime cut of three meats: alpaca, ostrich, and beef, slow-cooked and served on a hot stone with three dipping sauces. Call ahead and reserve one of the romantic balcony nooks. Top it all off with a chocolate mousse. ⊠ *Zela 210* ☎ *054/206–020* ⊕ *www.zigzagrestaurant.com* ⊟ *AE, D, MC, V.*

WHERE TO STAY

Arequipa has one of the highest-quality collections of inns and hotels anywhere in Peru. While the larger resorts and chain hotels tend to cater to tour groups and business travelers, there are dozens of charming, small, independently run bed-and-breakfasts within a few blocks of the Plaza de Armas.

$ ⌂ **Casa Andina Classic.** The Peruvian equivalent to a Holiday Inn, the cookie-cutter rooms, nicely decorated with Andean textiles, are comfortable but basic. Bathrooms are clean, breakfast is good, and the bilingual staff is helpful. The hotel is one of the oldest in the Casa Andina chain, though apart from a few worn carpets it's still a decent property. **Pros:** good location; good breakfast; clean. **Cons:** tour-group heavy; flat pillows; bad ventilation. ⊠ *Calle Jerusalén 603* ☎ *054/202–070* ⊕ *www. casa-andina.com* ↝ *103 rooms, 1 suite* ⌂ *In-room: a/c, safe, refrigerator (some), DVD (some), Wi-Fi. In-hotel: restaurant, bar, laundry service, Internet terminal, Wi-Fi hotspot, parking (paid)* ¶⊙¶ *BP.*

$$$ ⌂ **Casa Andina Private Collection Arequipa.** As upscale as it gets, this is the
Fodor's Choice place to go for top-of-the-line amenities. Housed in the city's former
★ coin mint and national historical monument, this midsize hotel opened in February 2008 after an extensive renovation to a building that sat decrepit for decades. Colonial suites are as atmospheric as those you would find at the much more expensive Hotel Monasterio in Cusco. The arched-stone-walled rooms are massive in size and are decorated with oil paintings and period furnishings, and modern amenities barely alter the vibe. The modern section of the hotel has rooms and suites featuring Andean weaves, newfangled furniture, plush modern bedding, and elegant fixtures. Many rooms have romantic views of the city. Two colonial courtyards beg for a night walk. The gourmet restaurant serves creative novo cuisine in its hip dining area and there's a coin museum in honor of the building's history. **Pros:** historic building; comfortable bedding; large bathrooms. **Cons:** modern rooms do not match the colonial ones. ⊠ *Ugarte 403* ☎ *054/226–907* ⊕ *www.casa-andina. com* ↝ *41 rooms, 7 suites* ⌂ *In-room: a/c, safe, refrigerator (some), DVD (some), Wi-Fi. In-hotel: restaurant, bar, laundry service, Internet terminal, Wi-Fi hotspot, parking (paid)* ¶⊙¶ *BP.*

$ ⌂ **Casa Arequipa.** With seven individually designed rooms, all donned
Fodor's Choice in luxuriously high-quality motif and bedding, every last detail has
★ been thought of—and applied. It's so personalized it's like you're visiting your best friends. This neocolonial boutique hotel books up fast and has won several awards. Filled with antique furnishings typical of the region, the hand-carved beds are piled high with alpaca blankets and 400-thread-count sheets to counter the cool Andean air. The extra charm comes from those who run it, the hospitable staff (they'll retrieve your luggage from the airport if it's delayed, iron your clothes, and throw you a party for your birthday). A lavish breakfast buffet includes an assortment of coffee, tea, breads, fruits, and eggs, served in the dining room. In an upscale, residential neighborhood, it's a 10- to 15-minute walk from the center of town. **Pros:** impeccable service; new and comfortable bedding; quiet neighborhood. **Cons:** not near any stores; need a taxi at night. ⊠ *Av. Lima 409, Vallecito* ☎ *054/284–219;*

4

202/518–9672 from U.S. ⊕ *www.arequipacasa.com* ⟟ *7 rooms* ⬩ *In-room: no a/c, safe, DVD (some), Wi-Fi. In-hotel: restaurant, room service, bar, laundry service, Internet terminal, Wi-Fi hotspot, parking (free)* ▭ *AE, DC, MC, V* ⦿ *BP.*

$ 👕**Hostal Santa Catalina.** This bright-yellow hostel (and it's very much like a youth hostel, minus the youth part) offers shared and private quarters. The clean rooms, friendly owners, dependable hot water, and laundry facilities attract repeat customers—mostly European—year-round, so call ahead for reservations. Check out the stunning views on the roof terrace, or kick back in the central courtyard and read your guidebook while your clothes hang to dry in the sunshine. **Pros:** great place to meet other travelers; central location; friendly staff. **Cons:** old furniture and bedding; a bit noisy; some communal bathrooms. ⊠ *Santa Catalina 500* 🕾 *054/243–705 or 054/221–766* ⊕ *www.hostalsantacatalinaperu. com* ⟟ *8 rooms, 3 dorms* ⬩ *In-room: no phone, no a/c, safe (some). In-hotel: restaurant, laundry facilities, Internet terminal, parking (free)* ▭ *No credit cards* ⦿ *EP.*

4

$$ 👕**Hotel Libertador.** Amid sprawling gardens, this 1940 Spanish-colonial villa creates an oasis of old Arequipa. The grand hotel in a leafy suburb outside of the town center had long been Arequipa's best property until the Casa Andina Private Collection sprung up. Sillar arches, wrought-iron window screens, and Peruvian details give this luxury hotel the intimate feel of an old family home. Have breakfast on the terrace, then dip in the pool overlooking Volcán Misti and the Andean panorama. Nonguests can stop in the pub-style bar or splurge on the Continental delights at Restaurant Los Robles. In 2010 rooms were being renovated one by one, which should put this stylish property back on top. **Pros:** well-kept; helpful staff; Jacuzzi and sauna. **Cons:** older rooms are a little bit outdated; far from town. ⊠ *Plaza Bolívar, Selva Alegre* 🕾 *054/215–110* ⊕ *www.libertador.com.pe* ⟟ *80 rooms, 8 suites* ⬩ *In-room: a/c, safe, refrigerator, DVD (some), Wi-Fi. In-hotel: restaurant, room service, bar, pool, gym, laundry service, Internet terminal, Wi-Fi hotspot, parking (free)* ▭ *AE, DC, MC, V* ⦿ *BP.*

$$ 👕**Hotel Sonesta Posadas del Inca.** On the Plaza de Armas, this upscale hotel has top-rate modern facilities and services and the location is superb. Ask for a room overlooking the square to view the constant stream of activities. Hit up the Inkafe Café & Bar for a light dinner while overlooking the Plaza, followed by a dip in the rooftop pool. **Pros:** great location; bilingual staff; late check-out. **Cons:** can be a little noisy on the plaza side; little colonial feel. ⊠ *Portal de Flores 116* 🕾 *054/215–530* ⊕ *www.sonesta.com* ⟟ *57 rooms, 1 suite* ⬩ *In-room: a/c, safe, refrigerator (some), DVD (some), Wi-Fi* ▭ *AE, DC, MC, V* ⦿ *BP.*

$ 👕**La Casa de Melgar.** In a beautiful tiled courtyard surrounded by fragrant blossoms and dotted with trees is this 18th-century home, believed to have been the one-time temporary residence of Mariano Melgar, Peru's most romantic 19th-century poet. This bright blue-and-adobe-color Spanish colonial has double rooms that have towering, vaulted brick ceilings, as well as private baths with hot water. The single suite has an original cookstove from its early days. A small on-site café, Flor de Café, serves breakfast. **Pros:** high on the charm scale; garden is great for relaxing; quiet; close to shops and restaurants. **Cons:** rooms can get cold in rainy season; some have thin walls; front desk staff can be curt. ✉ *Melgar 108* ☎ *054/222–459* ⊕ *www.lacasademelgar.com* ⤳ *30 rooms, 1 suite* ⚓ *In-room: no a/c, safe. In-hotel: restaurant, laundry service, parking (free)* ═ *V, MC* ⓘⓞⓘ *CP.*

$ 🍴 **La Casa de Mi Abuela.** An old stone wall circles this famous budget-
☾ traveler haunt. Extensive gardens, with 2,000 square meters of green space grace this compound-like resort, but the English-speaking owners show their sense of humor in its centerpiece: a rusted Fiat van. The basic, wood-paneled standard rooms with well-worn furniture and tiny bathrooms do the job, but for only $10 USD more, the junior garden suites—with contemporary furnishings and amenities—are much nicer. Regardless of the room, the elaborate breakfast buffet in the garden terrace is hard to top. ■**TIP**➔ At night you can clean up, read a book in a hammock, listen to the live piano music at the bar or take a dip in the pool. It's a five- to seven-minute walk to the Plaza de Armas. **Pros:** best breakfast buffet in town; free airport pickup; large grounds; security gate. **Cons:** standard room bathrooms are old and small; lots of tour groups. ✉ *Calle Jerusalén 606* ☎ *054/241–206* ⊕ *www.lacasademiabuela.com* ⤳ *57 rooms* ⚓ *In-room: no a/c, safe (some), kitchen (some), refrigerator (some), Wi-Fi. In-hotel: restaurant, bar, pool, laundry service, Internet terminal, Wi-Fi hotspot, parking (paid)* ═ *AE, DC, MC, V* ⓘⓞⓘ *BP.*

NIGHTLIFE

BARS

Ad Libitum (✉ *San Francisco 233* ☎ *054/993–1034*) is a relaxed artistic heaven for thirsty locals in need of cheap cocktails and music. **Café Bar Istanbul** (✉ *San Francisco 231-A* ☎ *54/203–862*) is a tiny eclectic bar, great for martinis and small sillar bites to eat. Enter a large sillar building called **Casona Forum** (✉ *San Francisco 317* ☎ *054/204–294* ⊕ *www. casonaforum.com*) and chill in one of four bars: Retro, Forum, Terrasse, and Club Zero. At Retro you can enjoy live concerts and dance to hits from the 1970s and 1980s. Over at Zero, belly up to the pub-styled bar, grab a beer, and shoot some pool. While you can dine at Forum among tropical furnishings or dance the night away, at Terrasse you can eat among great views and sharpen your karaoke skills. **Déja Vu** (✉ *San Francisco 319B* ☎ *054/221–904*), open 9 AM to 4 AM, is a popular place to have a light meal. The two-floor venue has live Latin pop music and/or a DJ spinning every night with a dance club downstairs. Eurocentric **Mistica** (✉ *San Francisco 213* ☎ *054/224–436*) is a flashback to the 1980s with white fixtures and cherry-red leather couches accompanied by candlelight. A restaurant, Mistica turns into a relaxed lounge come evening.

GAY BARS

Although not as gay-friendly as Lima, there's a small progressive gay and lesbian scene. **SKP** (✉ *Calle Villalba 205* ☎ *054/934–7169 or 054/934–2108*), a gay and lesbian disco, opens at 8 PM, no cover charge before 11 PM. Closed Monday and Tuesday. **Open Night** (✉ *Corner of Salaverry and Jorge Chavez* ☎ *054/960–0981*) is a gay and lesbian bar/disco with live concerts on weekends.

LIVE MUSIC

The **Instituto Cultural Peruano Norteamericano** (✉ *Melgar 109* ☎ *054/243–201* ⊕ *www.cultural.edu.pe*) hosts evening concerts of traditional and classical music. **Kibosh** (✉ *Zela 205* ☎ *054/203–837*) has a lively night scene, good pizza and beer, and is a popular dance bar. **La Troica** (✉ *Calle Jerusalén 522-A* ☎ *054/225–690*), open Monday through Saturday from 7 PM, specializes in Afro-Peruvian music, but also has groups from all over South America and sometimes a folkloric show on Saturday. For other good peña shows we recommend **Las Quenas** and **Tradicion Arequipeña** (⇨ *see restaurants*).

SHOPPING

4

Arequipa has the widest selection of Peruvian crafts in the south. Alpaca and llama wool is woven into brightly patterned sweaters, ponchos, hats, scarves, and gloves, as well as wall hangings, blankets, and carpets. Look for *chullos* (woolen knitted caps with ear flaps and ties), transported from the Lake Titicaca region. Ceramic *toros* (bulls) are a local favorite to hold flowers or money, and you can even see them sitting in the rafters of homes to bring good luck.

At the Plaza San Francisco, the cathedral steps are the site of a daily flea market that has delicate handmade jewelry. Across the street at the Fundo el Fierro, crafts vendors tout bargains on clothing, ceramics, jewelry, and knickknacks in a cobblestone courtyard; deals can be had until about 8 PM. Arequipa is also an excellent place to purchase inexpensive but well-constructed handmade guitars. Avenida Bolognesi has lines of such workshops. Behind the cathedral on the narrow Pasaje Catedral, boutiques sell jewelry and knickknacks made of Arequipa agate and along Santa Catalina there are many clothing stores.

In recent years several new upscale shopping centers have popped up. **Casona de Santa Catalina** (✉ *Santa Catalina 210* ☎ *054/281–334*) features a number of upscale shops like Kuna and Tienda del Ekeko. **Patio del Ekeko** (✉ *Mercaderes 141* ☎ *054/215–861*) is a good shopping complex to scout quality souvenirs.

If you're looking for baby alpaca yarn **Alpa Wool** (✉ *Santa Catalina 120-B* ☎ *054/220–992*) carries a small selection of high-quality and cheap baby alpaca yarn. **Camping Equipment** (✉ *Jerusalén 307* ☎ *054/331–248*) carries everything for a last-minute outdoor adventure. For high-quality, reasonably priced jewelry, stop at **L. Paulet** (✉ *Claustros de la Compañia, General Morán 118* ☎ *054/287–786*). **Ranticuy Baby Alpaca** (✉ *Claustros de la Compañia, General Morán 118* ☎ *054/232–801*) has intricately designed sweaters and accessories made with lots of bright colors.

Arequipa is a great place to pick up colonial-era antiques, high-quality copies of Pre-Colombian ceramics, and even authentic Inca archeological pieces. Most shops are found on Santa Catalina facing the monastery. **Curiosidades** (✉ *Zela 207* ☎ *054/232–703*) is a five-and-dime type of curiosity shop carrying everything from furniture and weapons to postcards and silver.

Antiquedades y Objectos de Arte (⊠ *Santa Catalina 406* ☎ *054/229–103*) has large furniture pieces and vintage tapestries. Cash only. **El Anticuario** (⊠ *Santa Catalina 300* ☎ *054/234–474*) is a mom-and-pop shop that resells treasures from tables to teapots. All credit cards accepted. Will assist in shipping.

PUNO AND LAKE TITICACA

Lake Titicaca is one of the most breathtaking parts of Peru, though that may have something to do with the altitude. The azure blue waters of the lake paired with an even bluer sky are a sight to behold indeed. The region is one of the most culturally significant places in Peru. There are not only more festivals here than anywhere else, but Quechua and Aymara people who inhabit isolated islands like Taquile and Amantani have preserved their customs over centuries with little change. The Islas de Uros, made of floating tortora islands, are a magical display of color and originality. This is where the Incas were born and ancient ruins, such as those at Sullustani, are scattered all over the area. For many travelers, a visit to Lake Titicaca is the highlight of their trip.

PUNO

975 km (609 mi) southeast of Lima.

Puno doesn't win any beauty pageants—brown unfinished cement homes, old paved roads, and a dusty desert has been the landscape for years. It's a sharp contrast to Puno's immediate neighbor, Lake Titicaca. Some people arrive in town, and scram to find a trip on the lake. Don't let the dreary look of Puno stop you from exploring its shores; it's considered Peru's folklore capital.

Puno retains traits of the Aymará, Quechua, and Spanish cultures that settled on the northwestern shores of the lake. Their influence is in the art, music, dance, and dress of today's inhabitants, who call themselves "Children of the Sacred Lake." Much of the city's character comes from the continuation of ancient traditions—at least once a month a parade or a festival celebrates some recent or historic event.

GETTING HERE AND AROUND

While Puno does not have an airport, you can fly into Juliaca's Aeropuerto Manco Capac, about one hour away. The airport is only served by LAN airlines (⊕ *www.lan.com*) for flights between Juliaca and Lima, sometimes stopping in Arequipa, once per day. Most hotels in Puno will pick you up on arrival; otherwise you can take one of the waiting tourists buses (S/15). The bus Terminal Terreste is at 1 de Mayo 703 and Bolivar and many companies also have offices here. Puno is a connection point for trips between Arequipa, Cuzco, and La Paz, Bolivia, so there are frequent buses throughout the day for each destination.

The train station for PeruRail for the daily trip to/from Cusco, Estación Huanchaq (☎ *084/238–722*), is at the end of Avenida Sol on Avenida La Torre just outside of the center of town.

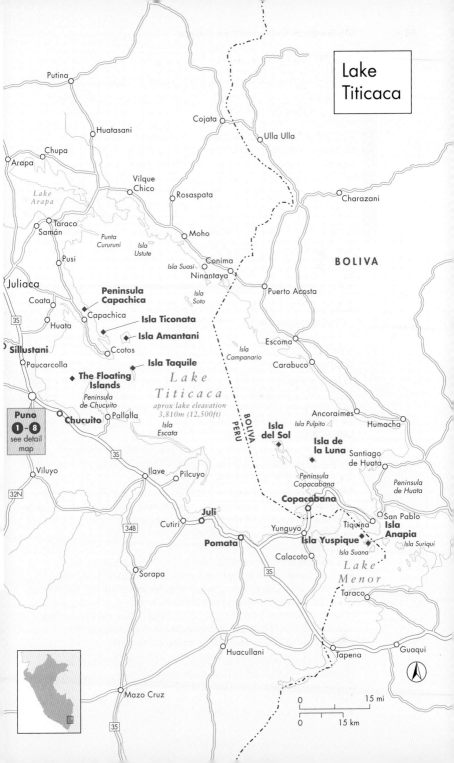

Lake
Titicaca

Putina

Huatasani

Chupa

Arapa

*Lake
Arapa*

Taraco
Samán

Pusi

Juliaca

Coata

Huata

Sillustani

Paucarcolla

Vilque
Chico

Rosaspata

Moho

*Punta
Cururuni*

*Isla
Ustute*

Isla Suasi

Conima

Ninantaya

*Isla
Soto*

**Peninsula
Capachica**

Capachica

Isla Ticonata

Ccotos

Isla Amantani

Isla Taquile

**The Floating
Islands**

*Peninsula
de Chucuito*

Chucuito

Pallalla

*Isla
Escata*

**Puno
1 - 8
see detail
map**

Viluyo

Ilave

Pilcuyo

32N

Cutiri

Juli

Pomata

Sorapa

Cojata

Ulla Ulla

Charazani

BOLIVA

Puerto Acosta

Escoma

*Isla
Campanario*

Carabuco

*Lake
Titicaca*
*aprox lake eleavation
3,810m (12,500ft)*

**BOLIVA
PERU**

Ancoraimes

Isla Pulpito

Humacha

**Isla
del Sol**

**Isla de
la Luna**

Santiago
de Huata

*Peninsula
Copacabana*

*Peninsula
de Huata*

Copacabana

Yunguyo

Tiquina

San Pablo

**Isla
Anapia**

Isla Yuspique

Isla Suana

Isla Suriqui

Calacoto

*Lake
Menor*

Taraco

Huacullani

Tapena

Guaqui

Mazo Cruz

35

0   15 mi

0   15 km

Festival Time!

While any time of year is suitable for traveling to Puno and Lake Titicaca, visiting during a festival of dance, song, and parades is ideal. The streets are flooded with people; the folklore experience is passionate and very fun. Preserving the choreography of more than 140 typical dances, Puno's most memorable celebration is the *Festival of the Virgin de la Candelaria* (candle), held on February 2 and during carnival. A cast of several hundred elaborately costumed Andean singers, dancers, and bands from neighboring communities parades through the streets carrying the rosy-white complexioned statue of the Virgin. During the rest of the year, the statue rests on the altar of the San Juan Bautista Church. Puno week, as it's informally known, occurs the first week of November and is equally fun. When Puno isn't having a celebration, it reverts to its true character, that of a small, poor Andean agriculture town. On the lake, Isla Taquile celebrates a vivid festival the last week of July.

Restaurants, shops, Internet services, banks, and drugstores line the four-block pedestrian-only street Jirón Lima, between Pino Park (sometimes called Parque San Juan after the San Juan Bautista Church nearby) and the Plaza de Armas.

Puno has tricycle taxis, which resemble Asian tuk-tuks, and are driven by bicycle peddlers with a supped-up carriage and costs S/1 to go nearly anywhere in the city. However, if you're heading to a mirador high up on the hill, and you don't want the peddler to keel over, take an auto taxi, which costs S/3.

SAFETY AND PRECAUTIONS

At 3,827 meters (12,553 feet) above sea level Puno challenges your system, so eat lightly, skip the alcohol (trust us!), forgo your morning jog, and take it easy your first two or three days.

■ TIP→ Walking around the port after dark is not smart. When the sun goes down, the port gets desolate and unsuspecting tourists become targets for crime. So if you're at the handicraft market or are getting back from an outing on the lake, and suddenly it's dusk, catch a cab.

ESSENTIALS

Bus Cruz del Sur (⊠ *Terminal Terrestre C-10* ☎ *051/368–524* ⊕ *www. cruzdelsur.com.pe*). **CIVA** (⊠ *Terminal Terrestre C-35* ☎ *051/365–882*). **Inka Express** (⊠ *Jr. Melgar N 226* ☎ *051/365–654*). **Flores** (⊠ *Terminal Terrestre C-5, 6, 7, 8* ☎ *051/366–734*). **Julsa** (⊠ *Terminal Terrestre C-10* ☎ *051/364-080*). **Ormeño** (⊠ *Terminal Terrestre C-11* ☎ *051/368–176*). **Tour Peru** (⊠ *Terminal Terrestre C-10* ☎ *051/621–112* ⊕ *www.tourperu.com.pe*). **Turismo Mer** (⊠ *Terminal Terrestre C-10* ☎ *051/367–223* ⊕ *www.turismomer.com*).

Currency Banco de Crédito BCP (⊠ *Jr. Lima 510* ☎ *051/352–119*). **Banco Continental BBVA** (⊠ *400 Jr. Lima*). **Scotiabank** (⊠ *Plaza de Armas, corner of Duestra and Jr. Lima*).

Exploring ▼

Catedral **2**

Conde de Lemos
Balcony **1**

Cerrito de
Huajsapata **7**

El Yavari **8**

Iglesia San Juan
Bautista **5**

La Casa del
Corregidor **3**

Museo de la Coca
& Costumbres ...**6**

Museo Carlos
Dreyer **4**

Restaurants ▼

CECOVASA **6**

Chifa Shanghai ..**7**

Coca K'into **4**

Don Piero **5**

La Plaza **1**

Mojsa **2**

Restaurant Museo
la Casona **3**

Hotels ▼

Colon Inn **4**

Hotel La
Hacienda **3**

Hotel Italia **5**

Intiqa Hotel **1**

Qelqatani **2**

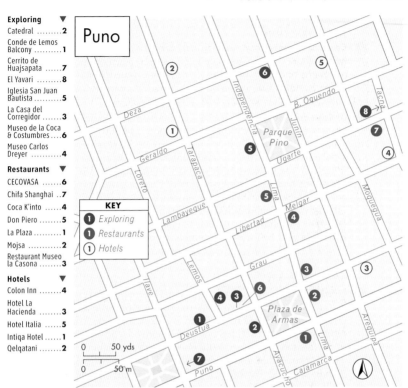

Internet Choz@Net (✉ *Jr. Lima 339, 2nd Floor* ☏ *051/367–195*). **La Casa del Corregidor** (✉ *Deustua 576* ☏ *051/351–921* ☉ *Tues.–Sat. 10–10*). **Top Net** (✉ *208 Duestra*).

Mail Serpost Puno (✉ *Av. Moquegua 269* ☏ *051/351–141* ☉ *Mon.–Sat. 8–8*).

Medical Carlos Monge Medrano Hospital (✉ *Kil. 2 of Huancane Hwy., sector San Ramon, Juliaca* ☉ *Daily 24 hrs* ☏ *051/321–901, 051/321–750, 051/321–131, or 051/321–370*). **Manuel Nuñez Butron National Hospital** (✉ *Av. El Sol 1022* ☉ *Daily 24 hours* ☏ *051/351–021, 051/369-286, or 051/369-696*).

Police Police (✉ *Jr. Deustua 530* ☏ *051/366–271 or 051/353–988*). **Policía de Tourismo** (✉ *Jr. Deustua 538* ☏ *051/354–764, 051/354–774, or 051/353–3988*).

Taxis Radio Taxi Milenium (☏ *051/353–134*). **Servitaxi Turistico** (☏ *051/369–000*). **Tonocar Titikaka** (☏ *051/368–000*).

Trains PeruRail (✉ *Estacion Puno, La Torre 224* ☏ *084/238–722* ⊕ *www.perurail.com* ☉ *Weekdays 7–5, weekends 7–noon*).

Visitor Info Iperu Oficina Información Turística (✉ *Corner of Jr. Deustua and Jr. Lima, Plaza de Armas* ☏ *051/365–088*).

EXPLORING

TOP ATTRACTIONS

1 Conde de Lemos Balcony. An intricately carved wooden balcony marks the home where viceroy Conde de Lemos stayed when he arrived in Puno to counter rebellion around 1668. Behind the Catedral, it is today home of the National Culture Institute of Puno. ⊠ *Corner of Calles Deustua and Conde de Lemos* ☞ *Free* ⊙ *Weekdays 8:30–4.*

3 La Casa del Corregidor. Reconstructed more than five times, this 17th-century colonial, once a chaplaincy, is now a brightly colored cultural center. It was originally home to Silvestre de Valdés, a Catholic priest who served as a *corregidor* (a Spanish official who acts as governor, judge, and tax collector) and oversaw construction of the nearby Catedral. The house had a long history of changing owners until its present owner, Sra. Ana Maria Piño Jordán, bought it at public auction. Now a vibrant cultural locale, with an arts cooperative, it houses a fair-trade café and a few upscale handicraft stores. The exhibition hall displays works by local artists and hosts music events. ⊠ *Deustua 576* ☎ *051/351–921* ⊕ *www.casadelcorregidor.pe* ⊙ *Wed.–Fri. 10–10, Sat 10–2:30 and 5–10.*

Fodor's Choice ★

WORTH NOTING

2 Catedral. Etchings of flowers, fruits, and mermaids playing an Andean guitar called the *charango* grace the entrance of the Spanish baroque-style church. Sculpted by Peruvian architect Simon de Asto, the 17th-century stone cathedral has one of the more eclectically carved facades of any church in the area. Plain on the inside, its main decorations are a silver-plated altar and paintings from the Cusco School. ⊠ *Plaza de Armas* ☞ *Free* ⊙ *Weekdays 7–noon and 3–6, Sat. 7–noon and 3–7.*

7 Cerrito de Huajsapata. A statue honoring Manco Cápac, the first Inca and founder of the Inca empire, sits on this hill overlooking Puno. Legend has it that there are caves and subterranean paths in the monument, which connect Puno with the Koricancha Temple in Cusco. It's technically a 10-minute walk from town, but it's all uphill and a bit off the beaten path where a few robberies have been reported, so stick with a group or take a taxi. ⊠ *4 blocks southwest of Plaza de Armas.*

8 El Yavari. The restored Victorian iron ship was built in Birmingham, England, in 1861. It was subcontracted by the Peruvian Navy to patrol the waters of Titicaca, so it was dismantled and its 2,766 pieces and two crankshafts were loaded onto a freighter and shipped to the Peruvian Port of Arica on the Pacific coast, which today belongs to Chile. Mules and porters carried the pieces 290 mi through the Andes Mountains to Puno. The journey took six years and it was Christmas Day 1870 before it was reassembled and launched on Lake Titicaca. Now a museum, it's docked at the end of a pier by the Sonesta Posada del Inca Hotel. After remaining idle for 40 years, the vessel took a trial run in 1999 after volunteers rebuilt its engine. ⊠ *Avenida Sesquicentenario 610, Sector Huaje, pier behind Sonesta Posada del Inca Hotel* ☎ *051/369–329* ⊕ *www.yavari.org* ☞ *Donation* ⊙ *Daily 8:30–6.*

5 Iglesia San Juan Bautista. This 18th-century church has been entrusted with the care of the Virgin of the Candlemas, the focus of Puno's most important yearly celebration in February, the Festival de la Virgen de la Candelaria. The statue rests on the main altar. ⊠ *Jr. Lima and Parque Pino.*

❹ **Museo Carlos Dreyer.** An exhibit of 501 gold pieces called the "Great Treasure of Sillustani" has classified the intimate museum as one of the most important regional archaeological museums in southern Peru. The museum is named for famed Puno painter and antiques collector Carlos Dreyer Spohr. You can view the oil canvasses by Dreyer and explore exhibits of pre-Hispanic and colonial art, weavings, silver, copper works, delicate Aymará pottery, pre-Inca stone sculptures, and historical Spanish documents on the founding of Puno. ⊠ *Conde de Lemos 289* ☜ *S/15* ☽ *Mon.–Sat. 9:30–7:30, Sun, 2–7:30.*

❻ **Museo de la Coca y Costumbres.** A hidden gem, this museum pays tribute to the infamous coca leaf and Peruvian folklore. The quaint museum, tucked away on a second-floor building, is sliced into rooms, one that houses the folklore exhibit and the other displays everything you'd ever want to know about the coca leaf. Presented in English and Spanish, displays are well constructed with educational videos and photographs. The mission is not to promote coca, but merely to share the plant's history and culture. You can enlist the help of a bilingual guide if you wish or mosey on your own. The folklore exhibit displays elaborately constructed costumes worn during festivals and shares the history behind the dances. ⊠ *Jr. Deza 301* ☏ *051/977–0360* ⊕ *www.museodelacoca. com* ☜ *S/5* ☽ *Daily 9–1 and 3–8.*

WHERE TO EAT

Many small restaurants line Jirón Lima, and include a mix of Novo Andino and classic regional foods. On the menu you'll find fresh fish from the lake, an abundance of quinoa dishes, along with typical Peruvian fare like *lechón al horno o cancacho* (highly spiced baked suckling pig); *pesque o queso de quinua* (resembling ground-up barley), prepared with cheese and served with fish fillet in tomato sauce; *chairo* (lamb and tripe broth cooked with vegetables, and frozen-dried potato known as *chuño*). Particularly good are *trucha* (trout) and *pejerrey* (Kingfish mackerel) from the lake.

¢ **✕ CECOVASA.** In La Casa del Corregidor, this charming and poetic café is run by a union of eight cooperatives and coffee producers who grow
CAFÉ and sell organic fair-trade coffee from Puno's eastern regions that was recently named among the world's best. Eight java varieties are available to taste, along with a collection of teas, cocktails, smoothies, and healthy café foods including salads, soups, sandwiches, along with more sweet treats like cakes and pies. A book exchange and sun-filled patio make this a great relaxation station. ⊠ *Deustua 576, La Casa del Corregidor* ☏ *051/351–921* ⊟ *No credit cards.*

¢ **✕ Chifa Shanghai.** Among the half dozen *chifas*—the Peruvian name for
CHINESE Chinese restaurants—around the central market, Chifa Shanghai is the best. This is where the locals go and at night the place gets crowded. Though you wouldn't know it by the grungy interior, Shanghai is among a chain of chifas scattered around Peru. The menu is varied and includes chifa classics, and set menus for less than S/.10 pair wonton soup with

dishes such as Aeropuerto (fried rice and noodles) or Chi Jau Kay (breaded pork). ⊠ *Arbulu 169* ☏ *051/167–171* ▭ *V.*

$ **╳ Coco K'intu.** While Novo Andino cuisine is all the rage around Peru, it had yet to really hit Puno until this restaurant opened. It's not nearly as creative as restaurants in Cusco or Arequipa, but several traditional dishes make creative, sophisticated, down-right delicious entrées. The food bursts with flavor, especially the *sopa incasica*, a thick, creamy quinoa soup with peppers and onions, and a kick of spice. Slow-cooked alpaca entrées include the alpaca *con salsa de maracuya*, a tender alpaca steak cooked in a passion-fruit sauce. Open for breakfast, lunch, and dinner. ⊠ *Jr. Lima 401* ☏ *051/365–566* ▭ *V, MC.*

PERUVIAN
Fodor's Choice
★

¢ **╳ Don Piero.** Colorful paintings of Quecha people partaking in various rituals hang above you as you enjoy such typical dishes as barbecued chicken, fresh fish (pejerrey and trucha) fried in oil and garnished with potatoes and toasted chili peppers. Local musicians entertain on most nights. It's open for breakfast, lunch, and dinner. ⊠ *Lima 364* ☏ *051/365–943* ▭ No *credit cards.*

PERUVIAN

¢ **╳ La Plaza.** A grand colonial dining room with hand-carved fixtures gives this restaurant a sense of old-world Europe. Prices are inversely proportional to the large portions, so try a hearty regional dish like *chairo puneño* (soup with dehydrated potatoes and beef), cuy, or trucha. A separate location named La Hosteria, two blocks away on Avenida Lima, has a similar menu. ⊠ *Jr. Puno 425, Plaza de Armas* ☏ *051/366–871* ▭ *AE, DC, MC, V.*

PERUVIAN

¢ **╳ Mojsa.** The window seats overlooking the Plaza de Armas are for a romantic dinner or a cup of fresh local coffee. Mojsa, which mean "delicious" in Armaya language, serves reasonably priced Novo Andino cuisine, fused with fresh traditional and criollo flavors. Tender, juicy cuts of grilled beef and alpaca for less than S/20 are favorties, but creative pastas and crispy brick-oven pizza are also good. Open for breakfast, lunch, and dinner. ⊠ *Lima 635, Plaza de Armas* ☏ *051/363–182.*

PERUVIAN

¢ **╳ Restaurant Museo La Casona.** Museum-like, this quaint 17-year-old institution is filled with wrought-iron antiques and artwork including a display of antique irons and sewing machines. Divided into four intimate rooms, the polished hardwood floors, lace tablecloths, and burning candles make it feel like having dinner at great-grandma's. Luckily there are no old home odors here, only savory aromas of hearty soups and grilled meats and fish. Try local fare, such as *lomo de* alpaca (alpaca steak) or one of their thick soups (the cream of quinoa is amazing) made with vegetables and meat or fish. Ask for the Menu Turistico and have a great set meal for S/25, and a pisco sour for less than S/6. ⊠ *Av. Lima 517* ☏ *051/351–108 or 051/967–9207* ▭ *AE, MC, V.*

PERUVIAN

WHERE TO STAY

Puno can be cold so bring warm clothes. Not even the fanciest hotels have internal heating systems, but most have portable electric heaters. Air conditioning is unheard of here; you won't miss it. Always ask about heat when you book and ask for extra blankets. As Puno has few notable attractions, there is less of a need to stay in town as in other Peruvian cities. A surge of new hotel development has occurred on the lakeshore outside of town, particularly at the higher end, which aims to give a more authentic Titicaca experience.

$$ ☒ **Casa Andina Private Collection.** Out of the three Casa Andina properties in Puno (the other two are less expensive Casa Andina Classic properties), this lakeside hotel is the best. Just outside of town, the two-floor building has large stone and slate walls, and a fireplace in the lobby. Clean rooms and baths share a similar style and are basic, full of natural light, and have all modern amenities, even cribs for babies if needed. A restaurant serves up good Novo Andino food and the bar is probably too well-stocked. The only real downside: even with space heaters, it tends to get cold. **Pros:** good atmosphere; oxygen tank; great terrace. **Cons:** gets cold; rooms are small. ☒ *Av. Sesquicentenario 1970-1972, Sector Huaje* ☎ *051/363–992* ⊕ *www.casa-andina.com* ☜ *45 rooms, 1 suite* ⸹ *In-room: safe, refrigerator (some), DVD (some), Wi-Fi. In-hotel: restaurant, room service, bar, laundry service, Internet terminal, Wi-Fi hotspot, parking (free)* ▱ *AE, DC, MC, V* ⎅ *BP.*

$$$$

Fodor's Choice

★

☺

☒ **Casa Andina Private Collection Suasi.** An ecological paradise for those who can afford it, at this exclusive hotel on Isla Suasi on Lake Titicaca you can hike among wild llamas, canoe, study astronomy, learn Andean spirituality, marvel at flower-filled terraces, discuss ecosystems, or just relax with a massage. Rooms are comfortable and most have balconies. All meals are provided in the gourmet restaurant (or barbecue pit) and for an extra special treat, a private cottage comes with your own butler. It's three hours from Puno. **Pros:** cultural activities; child-friendly. **Cons:** charges extra for transportation. ☒ *Isla Suasi Lago Titicaca* ☎ *051/950–4235* ⊕ *www.casa-andina.com* ☜ *24 rooms, 2 suites* ⸹ *In-room: no phone, safe (some), kitchen (some), Wi-Fi. In-hotel: restaurant, room service, bar, spa, beachfront, water sports, laundry service, Internet terminal, Wi-Fi hotspot* ▱ *AE, DC, MC, V* ⎅ *AI, FAP.*

$ ☒ **Colon Inn.** With an air of old Europe, this Belgian-owned 19th-century republican-era inn is draped in dark mahogany wood and colonial furnishings. But at the center of this three-story hotel is a sky-lighted atrium with overflowing greenery and several tables. Rooms are clean and comfortable with outdated flowery comforters. All room sizes vary, from tiny to extra large, so ask to see your options. On the top floor a bar carries an impressive selection of European wines. The small restaurant prepares a quality breakfast buffet. Both venues prepare meals throughout the day. **Pros:** a hospitable staff speaks English; free coca tea is always on hand; great water pressure. **Cons:** dark decor; small bathrooms. ☒ *Calle Tacna 290* ☎ *051/351–432* ⊕ *www.coloninn.com* ☜ *22 rooms, 1 suite* ⸹ *In-room: safe, Wi-Fi. In-hotel: restaurant, bar, laundry service, Internet terminal, Wi-Fi hotspot* ▱ *DC, MC, V* ⎅ *BP.*

¢ ☒ **Hotel Italia.** A lovely, flower-filled courtyard, rooftop terrace, and scrumptious restaurant are all pluses at this hotel a block from Parque Pino. Rooms are simple but comfortable, with parquet floors and wood furniture; those on the fourth floor have lake views. As the former "it" hotel, no major renovations have occurred in several years to keep up with the more modern hotels. **Pros:** friendly Peruvian–Italian owner is always around to help; excellent soups; active communal lounge. **Cons:** furniture is old and bathrooms are small. ☒ *Theodoro Valcarcel 122*

4

🖷 *051/367–706* ⊕ *www.hotelitaliaperu.com* ⤳ *33 rooms* ♿ *In-room: safe (some). In-hotel: restaurant, bar, laundry service, Internet terminal, parking (free)* ▭ *MC, V* †◯| *CP.*

$ 🛏 **Hotel La Hacienda.** Panoramic views of Lake Titicaca and its surroundings can be viewed from the endless window-filled restaurant atop of this Spanish-colonial hotel, two blocks from Plaza de Armas. All rooms are spacious, bright, and clean. The bedding, especially the pillows, is plush. Most rooms have big bay windows for a view of the city or lake. A grand spiral staircase extends through all six floors. **Pros:** free Internet; large bathrooms; complimentary pisco sour upon arrival. **Cons:** can be noisy along Avenida Deustua. ⊠ *Deustua 297* 🖷 *051/365–134* ⊕ *www.lahaciendapuno.com* ⤳ *58 rooms* ♿ *In-room: safe, Wi-Fi. In-hotel: restaurant, room service, bar, laundry service, Internet terminal, Wi-Fi hotspot* ▭ *DC, MC, V* †◯| *BP.*

$ 🛏 **Intiqa Hotel.** Looking as if it were lifted out of Miraflores, all the rooms are spacious, sleek, and modern, and have lots of natural light, flat-screen TVs with DIRECTV, plush brown bedding, and polished hardwood floors. Indigenous art hangs on the walls. Stained-glass windows, which permeate light from the hotel's large atrium, line the hallways. A service-oriented staff is helpful and can help plan local trips. **Pros:** big bathrooms; spacious rooms; new. **Cons:** breakfast café doesn't have enough seating. ⊠ *Tarapacá 272* 🖷 *051/366–900* ⊕ *www.intiqahotel. com* ⤳ *17 rooms* ♿ *In-room: safe, Wi-Fi. In-hotel: restaurant, laundry service, Wi-Fi hotspot, parking (free)* ▭ *AE, MC, V* †◯| *CP.*

$$$ 🛏 **Libertador Hotel Isla Esteves.** The Libertador, a gleaming white, futuristic-looking, low-rise hotel, which functions more like a resort, is 5 km (3 mi) from Puno. The Libertador chain is spending tons of money to refurbish this classic property, but even so it is still one of the area's most luxurious lodgings. It's on Isla Esteves, an island in Lake Titicaca, but which is connected to the mainland by a causeway. Rooms and bathrooms are all comfortable, large, clean, and modern, with stunning views of the lake. While taxis are the only way to get into town, after a long day if you're too beat to head into town, you're in luck because there's an upscale international restaurant, Los Uros, a coffee shop, and cozy bar that has beautiful night views, good pisco sours, and a fireplace. **Pros:** knowledgeable staff; on the lake; heating; Jacuzzi and sauna. **Cons:** five minutes from town; rooms lack charm. ⊠ *Isla Esteves* 🖷 *051/367–780* ⊕ *www.libertador.com.pe* ⤳ *111 rooms, 12 suites* ♿ *In-room: safe, refrigerator (some), DVD (some), Wi-Fi. In-hotel: 2 restaurants, room service, bar, gym, beachfront, laundry service, Internet terminal, Wi-Fi hotspot, parking (free)* ▭ *AE, DC, MC, V* †◯| *BP.*

$ 🛏 **Qelqatani.** This small hotel owned by tour operator Arcobaleno on a quiet street about a five-minute walk from Jirón Lima is an affordable and cozy place to lay your head after a day on the lake. Rooms and private baths are large, beds are new, and all rooms have individual space heaters. This hotel has been around for more than two decades, though continual upgrades have kept it among the best spots in the center of Puno. In the morning a large breakfast spread is served and at night a lengthy cocktail menu can double your fun. **Pros:** excellent staff; quiet; good place to meet other travelers. **Cons:** dark interior; older building.

✉ *Tarapacá 355* ☎ *051/366–172* ⊕ *www.qelqatani.com* ⤵ *39 rooms, 3 suites* ⚐ *In-room: safe, Wi-Fi. In-hotel: restaurant, bar, laundry service, Internet terminal, Wi-Fi hotspot, parking (free)* ▭ *AE, MC, V* ⚑ *BP.*

$$ 🛏 **Sonesta Posadas del Inca.** Weavings, polished wood, and native art give character to this thoroughly modern Sonesta hotel on the shores of Lake Titicaca. It's 4 km (2 mi) from the center of town and has its own dock that extends out into the lake with *El Yavari,* the world's oldest motorized iron ship, anchored at the end. Rooms are clean and decorated with Pucara bulls and Andean textiles and feature top-notch electronics. Eating in the hotel's restaurant, Inkafé, is a pleasure, as large picture windows offer a panoramic view of the lake. It's one of few hotels in town that has accessible rooms for people with disabilities. **Pros:** on the lake; good heating; comfortable beds; near El Yavari. **Cons:** five minutes from town. ✉ *Sesquicentenario 610, Sector Huaje* ☎ *051/364–111* ⊕ *www.sonesta.com* ⤵ *62 rooms* ⚐ *In-room: safe, refrigerator (some), DVD (some), Wi-Fi (some). In-hotel: restaurant, room service, laundry service, Internet terminal, Wi-Fi hotspot, parking (free)* ▭ *AE, DC, MC, V* ⚑ *BP.*

$$$$ 🛏 **Titilaka.** The best hotel on the lake, period. The newish ecotourism resort with contemporary flair is all-inclusive and offers an off-the-beaten-path location, overlooking the lake next to the Chucuito Peninsula, on Peninsula Titilaka, about a 30-minute boat ride from Puno. The brick exterior resembles more of a lake house than a boutique hotel, but the interior—classic euro-contemporary with hints of Peruvian color—make this all-inclusive resort truly unique. Paper mache cows adorn the sleek lobby where guests' oxygen levels are tested upon arrival. All rooms at this hotel have nice furnishings, high-quality linens, plasma TVs, heated floors, and lake views. Titilaka offers excursions to the islands, gourmet cuisine, massage services, and a heated outdoor pool. **Pros:** all inclusive; heated floors. **Cons:** secluded; far from Puno; slow Internet connection. ✉ *Huenccalla, Centro Poblado Menor de Titilaka, District of Plateria, Peninsula Titilaka* ☎ *800/422–5042 from USA, 511/610–0400 in Peru* ⊕ *www.titilaka.com* ⤵ *18 suites* ⚐ *In-room: safe, refrigerator, Wi-Fi. In-hotel: restaurant, room service, bar, spa, beachfront, water sports, laundry service, Wi-Fi hotspot, parking (free)* ▭ *AE, MC, V* ⚑ *AI.*

Fodor's Choice
★

$ 🛏 **Yavari B&B.** The old iron ship that has long been docked in front of the Hotel Sonesta has been turned into one of Puno's most unique bed-and-breakfasts. The historic iron ship has just simple facilities: a few small bunks, a sitting room with a TV, and a basic breakfast is served. If you're a history buff with a yearning to get intimate with the Yavari, this is your chance. **Pros:** unique experience. **Cons:** you'll live like a sailor. ✉ *Muelle de Hotel Sonesta Posadas el Inca* ☎ *051/369–329* ⤵ *2 rooms* ▭ *No credit cards.*

NIGHTLIFE

There are dozens of small bars and lounges packed inside of Jiron Lima, often one flight up from the street. **Clan Destinos** (✉ *Lima 345* ☎ *051/368–252*) lures in young travelers off the street with two-for-one happy hour specials that seem to go on all night. For a more posh experience the **Colors Lounge** (✉ *Lima 342* ☎ *051/369–254*) is the most

Manhattan-styled bar in Puno and attracts an older crowd. After dinner the restaurant **IncaBar** (⊠ *Jr. Lima 348* ☏ *051/368–031*) turns into a low-key lounge where you'll find a 30s-and-over crowd. For live rock and pizza check out **Kamizaraky Rock Pub** (⊠ *Pasaje Grau 148*). One of the best pubs in town, **Positive** (⊠ *Jr. Lima 378, 1st fl.* ⊕ *www.positive-bar. com*) is a cozy watering hole that plays reggae and rock while serving up an eclectic cocktail menu, which includes drinks like the Amanti Island for a pricey S/12. **Pub Ekeko's** (⊠ *Lima 365* ☏ *051/365–986*) is a town staple for soccer. When there are no games on, there's music and dancing. The quiet downstairs venue serves wood-fired pizza.

SHOPPING

For fine alpaca clothing head to the Peruvian retail chain **Kuna** (⊠ *Jr. Lima 343* ☏ *051/366–050*). **Casa del Artesano** (⊠ *Lima 549* ☏ *No phone*) sells a modest selection of locally made alpaca items, including sweaters, scarves, and ponchos. Also look for Puno's signature pottery, the Torito de Pucara (Little Bull from Pucará). The pot is a receptacle used to hold a mixture of the bull's blood with chicha in a cattle-branding ceremony. If you don't find what you want here, just walk on down Calle Lima, as there are more artisans' shops along the way. **La Casona Parodi** (⊠ *Jr. Lima 316*) is a collection of small high-end shops selling alpaca sweaters, jewelry, and handicrafts.

Model reed boats, small stone carvings, and alpaca-wool articles are among the local crafts sold near the Port at Puno's **Mercado Artesanal** (⊠ *Av. Simon Bolivar and Jr. El Puerto* ☏ *No phone*). If you find you aren't dressed for Puno's chilly evenings, it's the place to buy a good woolen poncho for less than $10 USD. Open 8–6. Make sure you know where your wallet or purse is while you're snapping a photo of the colorful market. ■TIP➔ Never walk to the docks after the sun has set; robberies are frequent at night.

Q'ori Ch'aska (⊠ *Jr. Lima 435* ☏ *051/364–148*) is a small store where you'll find ceramics and jewelry.

LAKE TITICACA

Forms Puno's eastern shoreline.

Stunning, unpredictable, and enormous, Lake Titicaca is a world of unique flora, fauna, cultures, and geology. Lago Titicaca, which means lake of the grey (*titi*) puma (*caca*) in Quechua, borders Peru and Bolivia, with Peru's largest portion to the northwest. While Peru boasts the largest port in Puno (57% of the lake is in Peru), Bolivia's side has Isla del Sol and Isla de la Luna, two beautiful islands with great views and Inca ruins (⇨ *For coverage of Bolivia's side of Lake Titicaca, see Chapter 10*). The lake itself is larger than Puerto Rico, with an average depth of 7.5 meters (25 feet) and a minimum temperature of 38° F. Lake Titicaca gains 5 feet of water in summer (rainy season) and loses 5 feet in winter (dry season).

The Bahía de Puno, separated from the lake proper by the two jutting peninsulas of Capaschica and Chucuito, is home to the descendents of the Uro people, who are now mixed with the Aymará and Quechua. The

Continued on page 203

THE ISLANDS
of Lake Titicaca

According to legend, under orders from their father, the Sun God, the first Inca—Manco Cápac—and his sister—Mama Ocllo rose from the deep blue waters of Lake Titicaca and founded the Inca empire. Watching the mysterious play of light on the water and the shadows on the mountains, you may become a believer of the Inca myth.

Reed Boat Head, Uros

This is the altiplano—the high plains of Peru, where the earth has been raised so close to the sky that the area takes on a luminous quality. Lake Titicaca's sharp, sparkling blue waters may make you think of some place far from the altiplano, perhaps someplace warm. Then its chill will slap you back to reality and you realize that you're at the world's highest navigable lake, 12,500 feet above sea level. The lake's surface covers 8,562 sq km (3340 sq mi) and drops down 282 meters (925 ft) at its deepest.

Most of Lake Titicaca is a National Reserve dedicated to conserving the region's plant and animal life while promoting sustainable use of its resources. The reserve extends from the Bay of Puno to the peninsula of Capachica. It's divided into two sectors: one surrounds the Bay of Puno and protects the resources of the Uros-Chuluni communities; the other, in the Huancané area, preserves the totora-reed water fields and protects the nesting area of more than 60 bird species, including the Titicaca grebe.

DID YOU KNOW?

The floating islands likely
date from before the Inca
empire. But since the reeds
are constantly replenished,
they've found a way to
remain forever young.

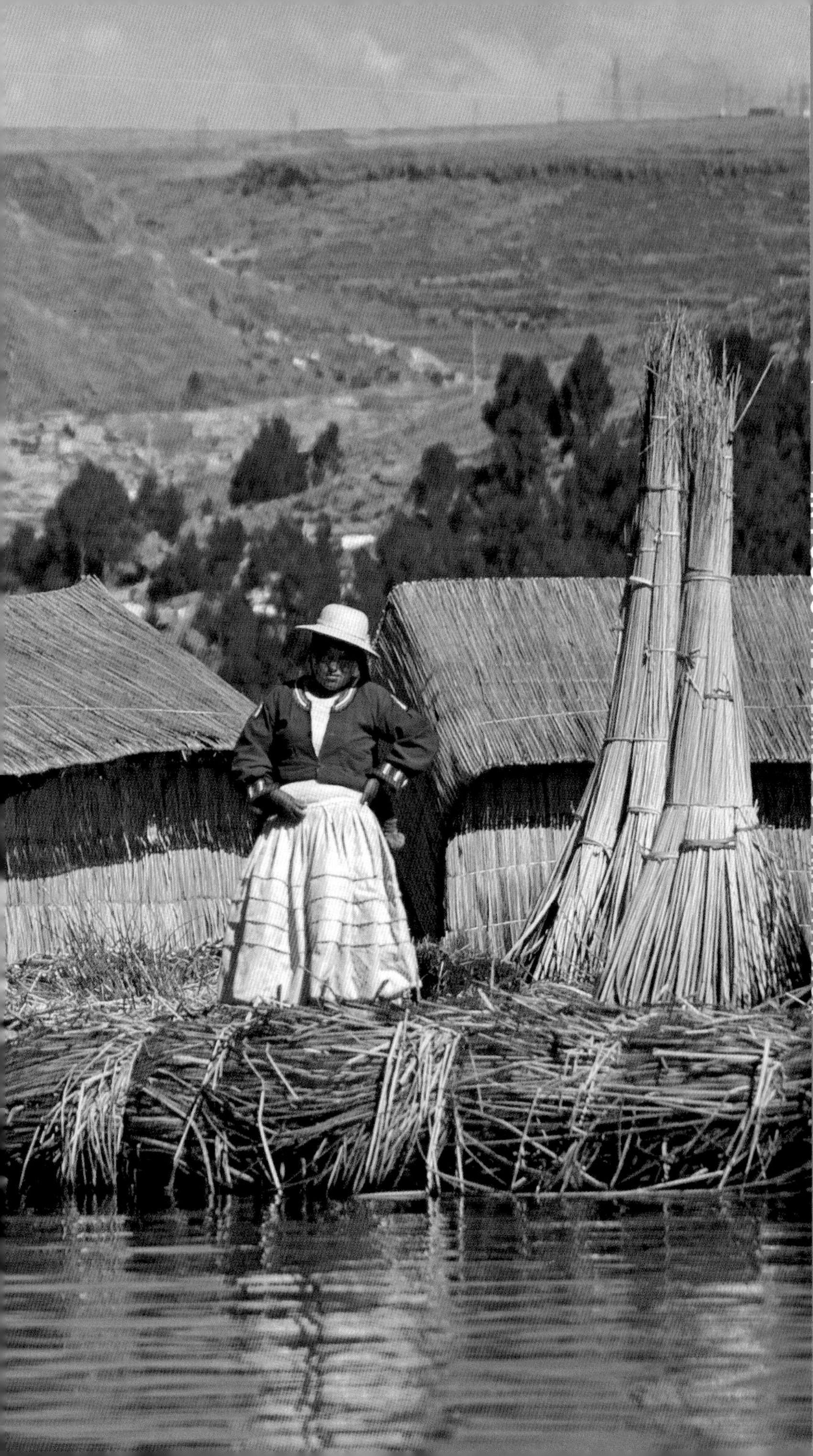

THE FLOATING ISLANDS

Uru indian woman and totora reeds boat.

ISLAS LOS UROS

Islas Los Uros, known as the Floating Islands, are man-made islands woven together with tótora reeds that grow in the lake shallows. Replenished often with layers because the underbelly reeds rot, these tiny islands resemble floating bails of hay. Walking on them feels like walking on a big waterlogged sponge, but they are sturdy.

VISITING

Trips to the Los Uros typically take 30 minutes and can be arranged from the port in the Puno Bay or with a guide through one of the many agencies in town. While some travelers marvel at these 62-plus islands, some call them floating souvenir stands. Yes, locals sell trinkets, but visiting the floating islands is a glimpse into one of the region's oldest cultures, the Uros. Now mixed with Aymara culture it's a form of human habitation that evolved over centuries. The closest group of "floating museums" is 7 km (4.35 mi) from Puno.

ISLAND LIFE

The islanders make their living by fishing, trapping birds, and selling visitors well-made miniature reed boats, weavings, and collages depicting island life. You can hire an islander to take you for a ride in a reed boat. Although there's no running water, progress has come to some of the islands in the form of solar-powered energy and telephone stations. Seventh Day Adventists converted the inhabitants of one island and built a church and school.

HOMESTAY TIP

It's tradition for most families not to have visitors help in the kitchen, and on several islands families will not eat with visitors. It's also customary to bring a gift—usually essentials like fruit, dried grains, matches, and candles.

TAQUILE & AMANTANI ISLANDS

Folk dances on Taquile island.

TAQUILE ISLAND

35 km (22 mi) east of Puno in the high altitude sunshine, Taquile's brown dusty landscape contrasts with green terraces, bright flowers, and the surrounding blue waters. Snow-capped Bolivian mountains loom in the distance.

Taquile folk are known for weaving some of Peru's loveliest textiles, and men create textiles as much as the women. Islanders still wear traditional dress and have successfully maintained the cooperative lifestyle of their ancestors. The annual Taquile festival the third week of July is a great time to visit.

Taquile is on a steep hill with curvy long trails, which lead to the main square. There are many ways to reach the top of Taquile where there are Inca and Tiahuanaco ruins—the most common, you can climb up the 533 stone steps, or take a longer path.

AMANTANI ISLAND

The island of Amantani is 45 km (28 mi) from Puno and almost three hours away by boat from Taquile. Amantani has pre-Inca ruins, and a larger, mainly agrarian society, whose traditional way of life has been less exposed to the outside world until recently. Not as pretty as Taquile, Amantani is dusty and brown.

Locals were losing population to the mainland before a community-based project helped them dive into the tourist industry and organize homestays. Although the project has been a success, make sure you will be your host's only guests for a more intimate experience.

Most of the younger generations speak Spanish and even a smidgen of English, but the older generation speaks only Quechua. Amantani has a population of 3,500 Quechua. Sacred rituals are held in its two pre-Inca temples, dedicated to the earth's fertility.

Amantani woman spinning yarn from wool.

ISLA DEL SOL, BOLIVIA

Adventurous travelers, with a couple days to spare, will want to journey on to Bolivia. After crossing the border, and getting to the pleasant lakeside town of Copacabana (visit the striking Moorish-style cathedral), go on by boat to the Isla del Sol, Lake Titicaca's largest island, where there are tremendous views, Inca ruins, and hotels.

Isla del Sol is the best place to visit and to stay on the lake and is the mythological birthplace of the pre-Inca and Inca. The views of the Cordillera Real mountains are amazing, especially at dawn and dusk, and the island has beautiful white sandy beaches and an extraordinary terraced landscape. Ruins include the Inca palace of Pilkokaina and a strange rock formation said to be the birthplace of the sun and moon, and an excellent Inca trail across the island. Alternatively, you can just laze around and soak up the cosmic energy.

En route to Isla del Sol, boats sometimes stop at **Isla de la Luna**, where the ruins of Iñacuy date back to the Inca conquest. You'll find an ancient con-

vent called Ajlla Wasi (House of the Chosen Women). Stone steps lead up to the unrestored ruins of the convent.

The legends that rise out of Lake Titicaca are no more mysterious than discoveries made in its depths. In 2000 an international diving expedition bumped into what is believed to be a 1,000-year-old pre-Inca temple. The stone structure is 660 feet long and 160 feet wide, with a wall 2,699 feet long. The discovery was made between Copacabana and the Sun and Moon islands.

(pictured top and bottom) Isla del Sol, the Island of the Sun, on Lake Titicaca, Bolivia.

Tours of Lake Titicaca

Excursions to the floating islands of the Uros as well as to any of the islands on Lake Titicaca can be arranged through tour agencies in Puno. Most tours depart between 7:30 and 9 AM, as the lake can become choppy in the afternoon. You also can take the local boat at the Puno dock for about the same price as a tour, although boats don't usually depart without at least 10 passengers.

All Ways Travel (✉ *Jr. Tacna 285* ☎ *051/355-552* ⊕ *www.titicacaperu. com*). **The Andean Experience** (✉ *Saenz Pena 129, Lima 4* ☎ *051/1700-5170* ⊕ *www.andean-experience.com*). **Condor Travel** (✉ *Tarapacá* ☎ *051/364-763* ⊕ *www. condortravel.com*). **Edgar Adventures** (✉ *Jr. Lima 328* ☎ *051/353-444* ⊕ *www.edgaradventures.com*). **Kingdom Travel** (✉ *Jr. Lima 369* ☎ *051/364-318*). **Kontiki Tours** (✉ *Jr. Melgar 188* ☎ *051/353-473* ⊕ *www. kontikiperu.com*). **Solmartour** (✉ *Jr. Libertad 229-231* ☎ *051/352-901* ⊕ *www.solmar.com.pe*). **Titikayak Kayak Tours** (✉ *Jr. Bolognesi 334* ☎ *051/367-747* ⊕ *www.titikayak. com*). **Traficoperu** (✉ *Av. Pardo 620 oficina 506, Lima 18* ☎ *051/447-1676* ⊕ *www.traficoperu.com*). **Turpuno** (✉ *Jr. Lima 208 Ofic. 5 Segundo Piso* ☎ *051/352-001*).

4

lakeshores are lush with totora reeds—valuable as building material, cattle fodder, and, in times of famine, food for humans.

Although it's generally cold, the beaming sun keeps you warm and, if you don't watch it, burned.

GETTING HERE AND AROUND

A boat is necessary for traveling the lake. Most people go to the islands with a tour, but colectivo boats in Puno Bay will transport you for S/20–S/40. Most boats are super slow, super old, and they won't leave port unless at least 10 people are smooshed aboard. A four-hour trip will take only an hour in one of the newer speedboats that the higher-end tour companies now use.

EXPLORING

Anapia and Yuspique Island. In the Winaymarka section of Lake Titicaca, near the Bolivian border are the Aymara-speaking islands of Anapia and Yuspique. This off-the-beaten-path two-day trip can be done with a tour operator or on your own. With 280 families living on the islands, very few people speak English or even Spanish, but rather traditional Aymara.

The trip usually begins in Puno, where you board a bus for two hours to the village of Yunguyo near Punta Hermosa, where you catch a 1.5-hour sailboat ride to the flat but fertile Anapia. On arrival hosts will meet visitors and guide them back to their family's home for an overnight stay. The day is then spent farming, tending to the animals, or playing with the children, and also includes a hiking trip to nearby Yuspique Island, where lunch is cooked by the women on the beach. Typically, *huatia,* potatoes cooked in a natural clay oven and buried in hot soil with lots of herbs, is served along with fresh fish. Yuspique is not very populated, but is home to more than 100 wild vincuñas.

After returning to Anapia you'll follow an evening's activities of traditional family life, such as music or dance. All Ways Travel and Edgar Adventures run tours. Proceeds go to the families. You can do this trip on your own for about $50 USD by following the itinerary and taking a water colectivo from Punta Hermosa to Anapia. Public transportation to the islands only runs on Thursday and Sunday.

Llachon Peninsula. One of the peninsulas that form the bay of Puno, Llachon juts out on the lake near Amantani and Taquile. ■TIP➜ The land is dry and barren with rows of pre-Inca terraces, and original ancient paths and trails, which are great for exploring. Locals are more than willing to guide visitors on a light trek to Cerro Auki Carus. Here a circular temple remains the sacred place for villagers to honor the Pachamama (Mother Earth). As the highest point on the peninsula, Cerro Auki Carus serves as an excellent viewpoint to admire the splendor of Lake Titicaca. You can venture out yourself from the port in Puno via water colectivo and then arrange a homestay once in Llachon, or for slightly more money, you can have a tour operator arrange the accommodations for you. By land back from Puno it's about 2–3 hours. Llachon is also a great place to kayak. Kayaking operator Titikayak has lots of trips around here.

Ticonata Island. A hidden island in a corner of Lake Titicaca, Ticonata is one of the greener islands on the lake. It has a warm microclimate that allows lush green grass to grow, crops to bloom, and many birds to be spied. In 2004 the Quechua-speaking natives of this island were nearly gone—only two families remained on the island. But a community-based project began to teach locals how to use their resources for travel tourism. Today more than a dozen families have returned and ancient island practices are being taught to younger generations. Only a small number of visitors are allowed at a time and the focus of a trip is to help families farm and fish while learning the ancient traditions of the Ticonatas.

It's typically a two-day trip that starts by visiting the floating islands, then the Capachica Peninsula and Llachon, where you can hike through an original pre-Inca path or kayak in the lake. Following a picnic lunch, you head to Ticonata eco-village where you overnight in thatched-roof homes. ■TIP➜ After helping families farm or fish, you help prepare dinner, followed by a bonfire and native dances. In the morning you'll head two hours to Amantani Island by rustic sailboats and then back to Puno by late afternoon. Most visits need to be arranged by Edgar Adventures. A group tour is easier to book, but a private tour is an option as is volunteering on the island for several days.

SILLUSTANI

30 km (19 mi) northwest of Puno.

High on a hauntingly beautiful peninsula in Lake Umayo is the necropolis of Sillustani. Twenty-eight stone burial towers represent a city of the dead that both predated and coincided with the Inca empire. ■TIP➜ The proper name for a tower is ayawasi (home of the dead), but they're generally referred to as chullpas, which are actually the shrouds used to cover the mummies inside. This was the land of the Aymará-speaking Colla people, and the precision of their masonry rivals that of the Inca. Sillustani's mystique is heightened by the view it provides over Lake Umayo and its mesa-shape island, El Sombrero, as well as by the utter silence that prevails, broken only by the wind over the water and the cries of lake birds.

Most of the chullpas date from the 14th and 15th centuries, but some were erected as early as AD 900. The tallest, known as the Lizard because of a carving on one of its massive stones, has a circumference of 28 feet. An unusual architectural aspect of the chullpas is that the circumference is smaller at the bottom than the top. To fully appreciate Sillustani, it's necessary to make the long climb to the top; fortunately, the steps are wide and it's an easy climb. Some schoolchildren will put on dances; if you take photos of mothers and children, and pet alpacas, a donation of a couple of soles will be appreciated.

> **TOTORA REEDS**
>
> The totora reeds of Islas los Uros are 70% chloride and 30% iodine and calcium. Once the reed is pulled from its root, the white base known as *chullo* is often eaten for its iodine or wrapped around wounds to relieve pain or cure hangovers. It can also serve as a natural "cooling pack" by splitting it open and placing it on the forehead. Uros commonly use it to brew reed flower tea, and in desperate times it can be eaten as food.

CHUCUITO

20 km (12 mi) southeast of Puno.

Chucuito (in Aymará: Choque-Huito, Mountain of Gold) is the first of several small towns that dot the lake as you travel from Puno into Bolivia. If you aren't interested in architecture, colonial churches, or don't care to see another undeveloped Peruvian town, then chances are you won't enjoy these little towns. Having said that, Chucuito, surrounded by hillsides crisscrossed with agricultural terraces, has one novelty you won't find elsewhere—its Temple of Fertility, or Templo de Inca Uyu.

The temple is the most interesting thing to see in Chucuito. Almost a ghost town, the main plaza has a large stone Inca sundial as its centerpiece. There are two Renaissance-style 16th-century churches, **La Ascunción** alongside the plaza and the **Santo Domingo** on the east side of town. Neither one has been maintained, but both are open for services.

Templo de Inca Uyu. This "temple" doesn't quite meet the dictionary's description of a temple as a stately edifice, but that's what it's called. ■ TIP➔ It's an outdoor area surrounded by a pre-Inca and Inca-made stone walls that block the view of a "garden" of anatomically correct phallic stone sculptures. Each 3-foot-tall penis statue points toward the sky at the Inca sun god, or toward the ground to the Pachamana, the mother earth. It's better known as the Temple of the Phallus. In ancient times it was—and is still today—visited by females who sit for hours on the little statues believing it will increase their fertility. 🎫 *S/5.*

WHERE TO STAY

$ 🛏 **Taypikala Hotel & Spa**. Owned by an Aymara shaman and healer, the design of this building, a stone's throw from the Templo de Fertilidad, is as unusual as you will find in Peru. Pumas, condors, and other sacred altiplano wildife are incorporated into the whimsical, Disneyesque design of the building's rocky facade. Rooms tend to be less adventurous, with a sort of worn, basic decor. This hotel is especially useful if you want to prolong the journey along the lake before heading into Bolivia. **Pros:** creative. **Cons:** far from Puno. ✉ *Chucuito, Calle Sandia* ☎ *051/792–252* ⊕ *www.taypikala.com* ⤵ *39 rooms, 2 suites* ♨ *In-room: safe. In-hotel: restaurant, room service, bar, spa, Internet terminal, Wi-Fi hotspot* ▭ *AE, MC, V.*

JULI

On Lake Titicaca, 84 km (52 mi) southeast of Puno.

At one time this village may have been an important Aymará religious center, and it has served as a Jesuit training center for missionaries from Paraguay and Bolivia. Juli has been called "Little Roma" because of its disproportionate number of churches. Four interesting churches in various stages of restoration are **San Pedro Mártir, Santa Cruz de Jerusalén, Asunción,** and **San Juan de Letrán.** The latter has 80 paintings from the Cusco School and huge windows worked in stone. Juli has a Saturday morning bartering market in the main square. It's not a handicraft market, but a produce and animal market where the barter system is in full effect and the trade of animals is interesting to watch. It starts at 9 AM and is done by noon. The drive from Puno to Juli takes about 1½ hours.

POMATA

108 km (67 mi) southeast of Puno.

The main attraction in the small lakeside town of Pomata is the church of **Santiago Apóstol de Nuestra Señora del Rosario.** It was built of pink granite in the 18th century and has paintings from the Cusco School and the Flemish School. Its mestizo baroque carvings and translucent alabaster windows are spectacular. Its altars are covered in gold leaf. Pomata is also famous for its fine pottery, especially for its Toritos de Pucará (bull figures).

BOLIVIA SOJOURN

⇨ *For full Bolivia coverage, see Chapter 10.*

You'll hear lots of talk about crossing Lake Titicaca from Peru to Bolivia via hydrofoil or catamaran. At this time you cannot go completely across without stopping at the border and walking from Peru into Bolivia or vice versa. ■TIP→ You can still use hydrofoils (only through Crillion Tours) and catamarans in your journey to Bolivia's side of the lake

A boat sails across Lake Titicaca, located on the border between Bolivia and Peru.

from Copacabana on the Bolivian side, then on to the Sun and Moon islands for an overnight or two on Sun Island.

CROSSING THE BORDER

Bolivia now requires U.S. citizens to obtain a visa to travel in the country. For a price tag of $150 USD, the visa is good for up to 90 days in a calendar year. The application can be done by mail or in person at any Bolivian Consulate, not by the Internet. Additionally a yellow fever vaccination certificate (approximately $150 USD, valid for 10 years) is necessary for Americans to show upon entry. The vaccine must be taken at least 10 days before exposure. At this writing, you were allowed to pay a $150 USD fine for not having a visa to get into the country. How long this will last is anyone's guess, but you could always give it a try.

If you're taking a bus from Puno, three hours into the ride the bus will stop just after Yunguyo for border-crossing procedures. Most higher-end bus services hand you immigration forms on the bus. As you leave Peru you'll get off to get an exit stamp from the Peruvian immigration, and then walk through to the small Bolivian immigration building, where you get an entrance stamp and will have to show your visa. From there you catch up with your bus, which will be waiting for you. Keep all immigration documents, your passport and visa safe; you may need these when leaving Bolivia. The border closes at 6 PM daily.

Those entering from Peru generally overnight in Copacabana, a pleasant, if touristy, town that provides easy access to the lake and the surrounding countryside. Buses from Puno to Copacabana are available through Tour Peru. They cost S/20 and depart from the Puno Bus Terminal at 7:30 AM daily.

GETTING AROUND

The border-crossing tours have packages from $150 USD to $400 USD. Reputable agencies include Crillón Tours and Transturin Ltd; based in Bolivia, tours go from Puno to La Paz and vice versa. Both include a pickup from your hotel in Puno, and transfer by first-class bus to the border in Yunguyo (a three-hour drive). After crossing the border you take a bus to Copacabana, a funky beach town (30 minutes). The most expensive—and comfortable way—to get to Isla del Sol and Isla de la Luna is by Crillón Tours hydrofoil from the **Inca Utama Hotel** but cheaper boats leave from Copacabana at 8:30 and 1:30 daily. The journey takes about two hours and costs (Bs)20. Once you are on the island, it's walking all the way, unless a mule has been organized through your hotel ahead of time. The tourist office, located on the northern side of Isla del Sol, offers private guides for (Bs)90, or (Bs)10 per person when booking groups of 10.

ESSENTIALS

Tour Operators **Crillón Tours** (☎ 591/233-7533; 305/358-5853 in U.S. ⊕ www.titicaca.com). **Edgar Adventures** (☎ 051/353-444 ⊕ www.edgaradventures.com). **Transturin** (☎ 02/242-2222 ⊕ www.transturin.com).

Boat Transportation **Andes Amazonia** (☎ 02/862-2616).

Bus Transportation **Tour Peru** (☎ 51-676600).

Cusco and The Sacred Valley

WORD OF MOUTH

"I have to admit that when it comes to natural beauty [Cusco] ranks number one among the places of the world I have visited. The people, the food, the mysticism of this ancient culture are beyond what I ever thought to find."

—crownmaria

WELCOME TO CUSCO AND THE SACRED VALLEY

Santo Domingo Church in Cuzco

TOP REASONS TO GO

★ **Alpaca Clothing:** Nothing says "Cusco" quite like a sweater, shawl, poncho, or scarf woven from the hair of the alpaca.

★ **Andean Cuisine:** Where else in the world will you find roasted *cuy* (guinea pig) and alpaca steaks rubbing shoulders on fine-dining menus?

★ **Inca Architecture:** How did the Inca construct stone walls so precisely using 15th-century technology? How could they position a temple so it would be illuminated best at the exact moment of the solstice?

★ **Layered Religion:** Take a closer look at the walls— every Catholic church was built on the site, and often the foundation, of an Inca *huaca*, or sacred place.

★ **Hotels with History:** Cusco's hostelries brim with history. Many are former convents, monasteries, dwellings of sacred women, or palaces of Spanish conquerors.

★ **Sacred Playground:** The Sacred Valley is brimming with history, but it's also an adventurer's playground for hiking, biking, and rafting.

1 Cusco. You'll be missing out if you skip Cusco on your way to Machu Picchu or the Sacred Valley. This city is a mix of new and old: ancient Inca walls holding up baroque colonial buildings, inside of which lie some of the city's most contemporary restaurants and shops. Colonial churches and cultural museums dot the plaza, while funky modern cafés sit side by side with traditional galleries of Cusqueñan art in San Blas. Inca gems are everywhere, even along the traffic heavy business district of Avenida El Sol, home of Cusco's star attraction, the Qorikancha Sun Temple.

2 Side Trips—The Southeastern Urubamba Valley. What really made the Inca civilization so successful? Their appreciation of a good view! Gorgeous Andean landscapes characterize almost every important Inca site in the area surrounding Cusco. For a bird's-eye perspective on the city, head uphill to the second most famous Inca site of them all—the "sexy woman" herself, Sacsayhuamán.

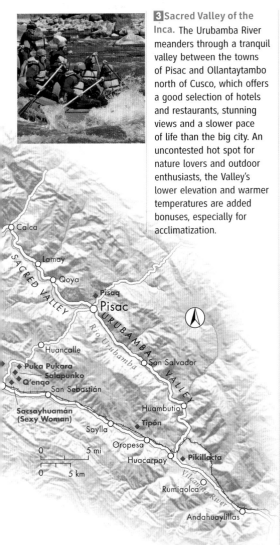

3 Sacred Valley of the Inca. The Urubamba River meanders through a tranquil valley between the towns of Pisac and Ollantaytambo north of Cusco, which offers a good selection of hotels and restaurants, stunning views and a slower pace of life than the big city. An uncontested hot spot for nature lovers and outdoor enthusiasts, the Valley's lower elevation and warmer temperatures are added bonuses, especially for acclimatization.

GETTING ORIENTED

At the center of Cusco is the colonial Plaza de Armas, slightly sloped, with streets heading downhill, most prominently the Avenida El Sol, leading to the more modern sections of the city. Heading uphill takes you to the city's older neighborhoods, notably the artisan quarter of San Blas and its web of pedestrian-only walkways. If you look up and to the left, you'll see that towering over the lot is the archaeological site of Sacsayhuamán, which sits just to the left of the Christo Blanco. This white Christ statue is most clearly seen at night when it's lighted by floodlights. The Urubamba mountain range on the north side and Cusco and environs on the south side watch over the river basin known as the Sacred Valley. Transportation to the Sacred Valley is straightforward, with roads fanning out from the Urubamba, the valley's small hub city, and back to Cusco.

5

Updated by Michelle Hopey and Katie Tibbetts

"Bienvenidos a la ciudad imperial del Cusco," announces the flight attendant when your plane touches down at a lofty 3,300 meters above sea level. "Welcome to the imperial city of Cusco." This royal greeting hints at what you're in for in Cusco, one of the world's great travel destinations.

The city has stood for nine centuries, a wellspring of culture and tradition soaring above the fertile Andean Valley. The area's rich history springs forth from the Inca tale that describes how Manco Capac and his sister-consort Mama Ocllo were sent by the Sun and Moon to enlighten the people of Peru. Setting off from Lake Titicaca with the directive to settle only where their golden staff could be plunged fully into the soil, they traveled far across the altiplano until reaching the fertile soils surrounding present-day Cusco. They envisioned Qosqo (Cusco) in the shape of a puma, the animal representation of the Earth in the indigenous cosmos, which is evident today if someone traces the animal outline for you on a city map. But not all was Inca in southern Peru. Not far from Cusco sits Pikillacta, a pre-Inca city constructed by the Wari culture that thrived between AD 600 and 1000. It's an indication that this territory, like most of Peru, was the site of sophisticated civilizations long before the Inca appeared.

By the time Francisco Pizarro and the Spanish conquistadors arrived in 1532, the Inca Empire had spread from modern-day Ecuador in the north down through Peru and Bolivia to Chile. Sadly, the city's grandeur could do little to save an Empire weakened by internal strife and civil war. Stocked with guns and horses, which the Inca had never seen, and carrying new diseases, against which they had no immunity, the Spanish arrived with the upper hand, despite lower numbers. In 1532, the Spanish seized Atahualpa, the recently instated Inca ruler, while he was in Cajamarca to subdue rebellious forces. The Inca's crumbling house of cards came tumbling down, though pockets of resistance remained for years in places like Ollantaytambo.

After sacking the Inca Empire, Spanish colonists instated new political and religious systems, superimposing their beliefs onto the old society and its structures. They looted gold, silver, and stone and built their own churches, monasteries, convents, and palaces directly onto the foundations of the Inca sites. This is one of the most striking aspects of the city today. The Santo Domingo church was built on top of the Qorikancha, the Temple of the Sun. And it's downright ironic to think of the cloistered convent of Santa Catalina occupying the same site as the equally cloistered Acllawasi, the home of the Inca chosen women, who were selected to serve the sun in the Qorikancha temple. The cultural combination appears in countless other ways: witness the pumas carved into the cathedral doors. The city also gave its name to the Cusqueña school of art, in which New World artists combined Andean motifs with European-style painting, usually on religious themes. You'll chance on paintings that could be by Van Dyck but for the Inca robes on New Testament figures, and last supper diners digging into an Andean feast of guinea pig and fermented corn.

Throughout the Cusco region, you'll witness this odd juxtaposition of imperial and colonial, indigenous and Spanish. Traditionally-clad Quechua-speaking women sell their wares in front of a part-Inca, part-colonial structure as a business executive of European heritage walks by carrying on a cell-phone conversation. The two cultures coexist, but have not entirely embraced each other even five centuries after the conquest.

The Río Urubamba flows, at its closest, about 30 km (18 mi) north of Cusco and passes through a valley about 300 meters (980 feet) lower in elevation than Cusco. The northwestern part of this river basin, romantically labeled the Sacred Valley of the Inca, contains some of the region's most appealing towns and fascinating pre-Columbian ruins. A growing number of visitors are heading here directly upon arrival in Cusco to acclimatize. The valley's altitude is slightly lower and its temperatures slightly higher, and make for a physically easier introduction to this part of Peru.

PLANNING

WHEN TO GO

Cusco's high season is June through early September (winter) and the days around the Christmas and Easter holidays. Winter means drier weather and easier traveling, but higher lodging prices and larger crowds. Prices and visitor numbers drop dramatically during the November through March summer rainy season, except around the holidays.

GETTING HERE AND AROUND
AIR TRAVEL

LAN Peru (⊕ *www.lan.com*) connects Cusco with Lima, Arequipa, Juilaca, and Puerto Maldonado. Peruvian Airlines (⊕ *www. peruvianairlines.pe*) offers connecting service from Lima to Cusco, Arequipa, Tacna, and Iquitos. Star Perú (⊕ *www.starperu.com*) and TACA Peru (⊕ *www.taca.com*) fly from Cusco to Lima.

ACCLIMATIZING THE COCA WAY

Take it easy! Cusco is a breathless 3,300 meters (10,825 feet) above sea level—a fact you'll very soon appreciate as you huff and puff your way up its steep cobbled streets. With 30% less oxygen in the atmosphere, the best way to avoid altitude sickness is to take it easy on your first few days. There's no point in dashing off on that Inca hike if you're not acclimatized—altitude sickness is uncomfortable at best and can be very dangerous.

Locals swear by *mate de coca,* an herbal tea brewed from coca leaves that helps with altitude acclimatization. Indigenous peoples have chewed the leaves of the coca plant for centuries to cope with Andean elevations. But the brewing of the leaves in an herbal tea is considered a more refined and completely legal way to ingest the substance, in Andean nations at least. Most restaurants and many hotels have a pot steeping constantly.

BUS TRAVEL

Cusco's bus terminal is at the Terminal Terrestre on Pachacútec, not far from the airport. The best company running from Cusco is Cruz del Sur (⊕ *www.cruzdelsur.com.pe*). Bus travel between Cusco and the Sacred Valley is cheap, frequent . . . and sometimes accident-prone.

CAR TRAVEL

For exploring the Sacred Valley, a car is the best option. The vehicular tourist route ends at Ollantaytambo. Cusco is the only place to rent a vehicle. However, you won't need or want to drive inside the city; heavy traffic, lack of parking, and narrow streets, many of them pedestrian only, make a car a burden.

TAXI TRAVEL

Cusco's licensed taxis bear a black-and-gold checkered rectangle on each side, and a light-color official taxi sticker on the windshield. Fares are S/2.50 within the central city and S/4 after 10 PM. Have your hotel or restaurant call a taxi for you at night.

Honda Motokar taxis—semi-open, three-wheeled motorized vehicles with room for two passengers—ply the streets of Sacred Valley towns. Touring the Sacred Valley from Cusco with one of the city's taxis costs about $60–70 USD.

TRAIN TRAVEL

PeruRail is the most established operator in Peru; its *Andean Explorer* train departs from Cusco (at Wanchaq Station on Pachacutec) Monday, Wednesday, and Saturday at 8 AM for Puno, with a stop in Juliaca. The scenic journey takes 10 hours. Three classes of daily service to Machu Picchu depart from Cusco's Poroy station. Trains depart super early in the morning—except the luxury Hiram Bingham service, which departs from Poroy at 9 AM. Purchase tickets in advance from the PeruRail sales office in the Plaza de Armas, online (⊕ *www.perurail.com*), or from a travel agency. ⇨ *see The Train to Machu Picchu, Chapter 6.*

HEALTH AND SAFETY

Altitude Sickness Known as *soroche,* you'll likely encounter altitude sickness at Cusco's 3,500-meter (11,500-foot) elevation. Drink lots of fluids but eliminate or minimize alcohol and caffeine consumption. Many hotels have an oxygen supply for their guests' use. The prescription drug acetazolamide can help. Check with your physician about this, and about traveling here if you have a heart condition or high blood pressure, or are pregnant.

Warning: Sorojchi pills are a Bolivian-made altitude-sickness remedy whose advertising pictures a tourist vomiting at Machu Picchu. Its safety has not been documented, and we don't recommend trying it.

Water Tap water is not safe to drink here. Stick with the bottled variety, *con gas* (carbonated) or *sin gas* (plain).

Safety Security has improved dramatically in Cusco. A huge police presence is on the streets, especially around tourist centers such as the Plaza de Armas. Nonetheless, petty crime, such as pickpocketing, is not uncommon: use extra vigilance in crowded markets or when getting on and off buses and trains. Robbers have also targeted late-night, early-morning revelers stumbling back to their hotels.

VISITOR INFORMATION

Offering access to 16 of Cusco's best-known tourist attractions, the *Boleto Turístico* (tourist ticket) is the all-in-one answer to your tourism needs. Most agree that the ticket represents good value. There are four different passes you can purchase. For S/130 you can get a 10-day pass that let's you visit all 16 sites in the city and around the Sacred Valley. Alternatively, you can opt for one of three amended circuits outlined in the Boleto Parcial, each S/70. Be aware the scheme isn't set in stone and participating sites have a propensity to change. Certain big name attractions (such as the Catedral) have withdrawn from the Boleto Turístico in order to levy their own fees. Regardless, if you want to see sites like Sacsayhuamán and Pisac, you have to buy the ticket, which can be purchased at the **Comite de Servicios Integrados Turisticos Culturales del Cusco** (*COSITUC ⊠ Av. El Sol 103* ☎ *084/261–465 Ext. 203* ⊕ *www. cosituc.gob.pe*), open Monday through Saturday 8–5 and Sunday 8–2.

The **South American Explorers** (⊠ *Atoqsaycuchi 670* ☎ *084/245–484* ⊕ *www.saexplorers.org* ⊗ *Mon.–Fri. 9:30–5, Sat. 9:30–1*) is a membership organization. Its $60 USD annual dues get you a wealth of information at its clubhouse in Cusco, as well as in Lima and other South American cities.

CUSCO

If you arrive in Cusco with the intention of hopping on the train to Machu Picchu the next morning, you'll probably only have time to take a stroll through the Plaza de Armas and visit Qorikancha (Temple of the Sun) and the Catedral. However, the city merits exploration, either at the start or end of your trip. We recommend spending at least two days in Cusco, giving you time to acclimate to the altitude and get to know this city of terra-cotta roofs and cobblestone streets. The churches and some restaurants close for a few hours in the middle of the day. Most of the city's museums close on Sunday.

Cusco takes its newest role as tourist favorite in stride, and absorbs thousands of travelers with an ample supply of lodgings, restaurants, and services. That a polished infrastructure exists in such a remote, high-elevation locale is a pleasant surprise.

GETTING AROUND

Cusco's Aeropuerto Internacional Teniente Alejandro Velasco Astete (CUZ) is about 15 minutes from the center of town. An army of taxis waits at the exit from baggage claim, and charge S/10 to take you to the city center.

Cusco's center city is most enjoyably explored on foot. Many of the streets open to vehicular traffic are so narrow that it's simply faster to walk. ■TIP→ Cusco streets have a habit of changing names every few blocks, or even every block. Many streets bear a common Spanish name that everyone uses, but have newly designated street signs with an old Quechua name in order to highlight the city's Inca heritage: the Plaza de Armas is Haukaypata, the Plaza Regocijo is Kusipata, Triunfo is Sunturwasi, Loreto is Intikijlli, Arequipa is Q'aphchijk'ijllu, and intermittent blocks of Avenida El Sol are labeled Mut'uchaka. And so on.

SAFETY

Report any problems with tour companies, hotels, restaurants, etc. to INDECOPI, a tourist-focused government agency.

ESSENTIALS

AIRPORT   **Aeropuerto Internacional Teniente Alejandro Velasco Astete** (⊠ *Av. Velasco Astete s/n* ☎ *084/222–611*).

BUS   **Cruz del Sur** (⊠ *Pachacutec 510* ☎ *084/221–909*). **Ormeño** (⊠ *San Juan de Dios 657* ☎ *084/227–501*).

CURRENCY   **Banco de Crédito** (⊠ *Av. El Sol 189* ☎ *084/235–255*). **Banco Wiese Sudameris** (⊠ *Maruri 315* ☎ *084/264–300*). **Diners Club** (⊠ *Av. El Sol 615* ☎ *084/234–051*). **Western Union** (⊠ *Av. El Sol 627A* ☎ *084/248–028*).

MAIL   **SERPOST** (⊠ *Av. El Sol 800* ☎ *084/224–212*). **DHL** (⊠ *Av. El Sol 608* ☎ *084/244–167*). **Scharff International/FedEx** (⊠ *Tacna 208-Wanchaq* ☎ *084/264–141*).

MEDICAL   **Clínica Pardo** (⊠ *Av. de la Cultura 710, Plaza Tupac Amaru* ☎ *084/240–387*). **Hospital Regional** (⊠ *Av. de la Cultura s/n-Wanchaq* ☎ *084/227–661*).

POLICE   **Policia Nacional** (☎ *084/249–654*). **Tourism Police** (*POLTUR*⊠ *Plaza Tupac Amaru s/n* ☎ *084/235–123*). **INDECOPI** (⊠ *Manco Inca 209-Wanchaq* ☎ *084/252–987*).

RENTAL CAR   **Avis** (⊠ *Garcilaso 210 office 125* ☎ *084/241–824* ⊕ *www.avisperusur.com*). **Hertz** (⊠ *Av. El Sol 808* ☎ *084/248–800* ⊕ *www.gygrentacar.com*). **Explores Transportes** (⊠ *Plateros 356* ☎ *084/261–640*). **OSDI Rent-a-Car** (⊠ *Urb. Mateo Pumacahua B-10* ☎ *084/251–616*).

TAXI   **Alo Cusco** (☎ *084/222–222*). **Llama Taxi** (☎ *084/222–000*). **Taxi Turismo Cusco** (☎ *084/245–000*).

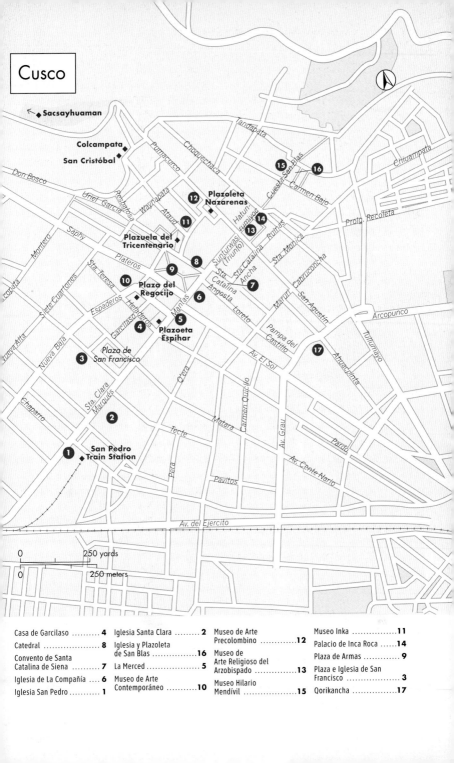

Cusco

← ◆ **Sacsayhuaman**

◆ **Colcampata**
◆ **San Cristóbal**

Casa de Garcilaso **4**	Iglesia Santa Clara **2**	Museo de Arte Precolombino **12**	Museo Inka **11**
Catedral **8**	Iglesia y Plazoleta de San Blas **16**	Museo de Arte Religioso del Arzobispado **13**	Palacio de Inca Roca **14**
Convento de Santa Catalina de Siena **7**	La Merced **5**		Plaza de Armas **9**
Iglesia de La Compañía **6**	Museo de Arte Contemporáneo **10**	Museo Hilario Mendívil **15**	Plaza e Iglesia de San Francisco **3**
Iglesia San Pedro **1**			Qorikancha **17**

TRAIN **PeruRail** (✉ *Portal de Carnes 214 Plaza de Armas Cusco* ☎ *084/581–414*
or *084/233–551* ⊕ *www.perurail.com).* **Inca Rail** (✉ *Av. El Sol, 611 Cusco*
☎ *084/233–030* ⊕ *www.incarail.com).* **Andean Railways** (✉ *Av. El Sol 576*
Cusco ☎ *084/221–199* ⊕ *www.machupicchutrain.com).*

VISITOR INFO **Dirección Regional de Industria y Turismo** (✉ *Plaza Tupac Amaru*
☎ *084/222–032* ◷ *Weekdays 9–1 and 4–7).* **iPerú** (✉ *Av. El Sol 103*
☎ *084/252–974; 24 hour service 01/574–8000* ◷ *Daily 8:30–7:30).*

EXPLORING

PLAZA DE ARMAS

For thousands of years the heart of Cusco, formerly called Haukaypata and now known as the **Plaza de Armas,** has served as the pulse of
the city. Yet where you once would have found Inca ceremonies and
parades in front of the many palaces that stood here, today you'll find a
more modern procession of postcard sellers, shoe-shiners, and photog-
raphers angling for your attention. It's no surprise that they congregate
here—with the stupendous **Catedral** dominating the northeastern side
of the Plaza, the ornate **Iglesia de La Compañía** sitting to the southeast,
and gorgeous Spanish-colonial arcades forming the other two sides, the
Plaza is one of the most spectacular areas of Cusco.

TOP ATTRACTIONS

❽ **Catedral.** Dominating the Plaza de Armas, the monumental cathedral
Fodor'sChoice is one of Cusco's grandest buildings. Built in 1550 on the site of the
★ palace of the Inca Wirachocha and using stones looted from the nearby
Inca fortress of Sacsayhuamán, the cathedral is a perfect example of
the imposition of the Catholic faith on the indigenous population. The
grander the building, went the theory, the more impressive (and seduc-
tive) the faith. With soaring ceilings, baroque carvings, enormous oil
paintings, and glittering gold-and-silver altars, the cathedral certainly
seemed to achieve its aim.

Today Cusco's Catedral is one of the town's star attractions, noted
mainly for its amazing collection of colonial art that mixes Christian
and non-Christian imagery. Entering the Catedral from the Sagrada
Familia chapel, head to your right to the first nave where you'll find
the famous oil painting (reputed to be the oldest in Cusco) depicting
the earthquake that rocked the town in 1650. Among the depictions of
burning houses and people fleeing, you'll see a procession in the Plaza.
Legend has it that during the earthquake, the citizens took out from
the Catedral a statue of Jesus on the cross and paraded it around the
Plaza—halting the quake in its tracks. This statue, now known as the
Señor de los Temblores, or Lord of the Earthquakes, is Cusco's patron,
and you'll find him depicted in many Cusqueñan paintings—you'll recognize him by his frilly white skirt.

To see the famous statue, head across the Catedral to the other side,
where in the nave and to the right of the passage connecting the Catedral to the adjoining Iglesia del Triumfo, you'll find el Señor himself.
The dark color of his skin is often claimed to be a representation of
the indigenous people of Cusco; the scientific explanation is that it's

natural discoloration due to the statue's age.

Those interested in the crossover between indigenous and Catholic iconography will find lots to look at. Figures of pumas, the Inca representation of the earth, are carved on the enormous main doors, and in the adjoining Iglesia del Triumfo you'll see an Andean Christ in one of the altars flanking the exit. ■TIP➡ No one should miss the spectacular Last Supper, painted by the indigenous artist Marcos Zapata, where you'll see the diners tucking into a delicious feast of cuy (guinea pig) and chicha (corn beverage)!

> ### UNA FOTO AMIGO?
>
> Cusco is one of the most colorful cities in the world, and you can't be here for more than five minutes without noticing all the women and young girls walking the streets in full traditional costume, most towing a llama or endearingly cuddling a lamb or puppy. They are more than happy to pose for photos. In fact, that's how they make their money, so make sure you pay up when asked. The going rate for a photo is S/1.

The cathedral's centerpieces are its massive, solid-silver altar, and the enormous 1659 María Angola bell, the largest in South America, which hangs in one of the towers and can be heard from miles away. Behind the main altar is the original wooden *altar primitivo* dedicated to St. Paul. The 64-seat cedar choir has rows of carved saints, popes, and bishops, all in stunning detail down to their delicately articulated hands.

Labels in Spanish and English are slowly being added to the more famous attractions in the Catedral. ■TIP➡ If you're interested in a more in-depth look, enlist the services of a guide—they're easy to spot by their tracksuit-jacket uniforms. Agree on a price before you start. An audioguide system is currently in the works; these should be included in your ticket price when they are up and running. ⊠ *Plaza de Armas* ☎ *084/254–285* ⌂ *S/16* ⊗ *Daily 9–5.*

❾ **Plaza de Armas.** With park benches, green lawns, and splendid views of the Catedral, Cusco's gorgeous colonial Plaza de Armas invites you to stay awhile. Pull up one of those park benches and the world will come to you—without moving an inch you'll be able to purchase postcards, paintings, and snacks, organize a trip to Machu Pichu, get your photograph taken, and get those dirty boots polished. ■TIP➡ What you see today is a direct descendant of imperial Cusco's central square, which the Inca called the Haukaypata (the only name indicated on today's street signs) and it extended as far as the Plaza del Regocijo. According to belief, this was the exact center of the Inca empire, Tawantinsuyo, the Four Corners of the Earth. Today, continuing the tradition, it's the tourism epicenter. From the Plaza you'll see the Catedral and Iglesia de la Compañía on two sides, and the graceful archways of the colonial *portales,* or covered arcades, lining the other sides. Soft lighting bathes the plaza each evening and creates one of Cusco's iconic views. On Sunday mornings a military parade marches on the cathedral side of the plaza, drawing hundreds of spectators and a few protesters. Enjoy the views of colonial Cusco but remember that any attempt to sit on one of those inviting green lawns will prompt furious whistle-blowing from the guards.

WORTH NOTING

🕖 **Convento de Santa Catalina de Siena.** An extensive collection of Cusqueñan religious art is the draw at this still-working Dominican convent, which incorporates a 1610 church

with high and low choirs and baroque friezes. Although there's not much to show of it these days, the convent represents another example of the pasting of Catholic religion over indigenous faiths—it was built on the site of the Acllawasi, the house of some 3,000 Inca chosen women dedicated to teaching, weaving Inca ceremonial robes, and worship of Inti, the Inca sun god. The entire complex was given a face-lift in 2010. ⊠ *Santa Catalina Angosta 401* ☏ *084/223–245* 💰 *S/8 or S/15 for ticket that also includes Qorikancha* ☺ *Mon.–Sat. 8:30–5:30, Sun. 2–5.*

🕕 **Iglesia de La Compañía.** With its ornately carved facade, this Jesuit church on the Plaza gives the Catedral a run for its money in the beauty stakes. The Compañía, constructed by the Jesuits in the 17th century, was intended to be the most splendid church in Cusco, which didn't sit too well with the archbishop. The beauty contest between the churches grew so heated that the pope was forced to intervene. He ruled in favor of the Catedral, but by that time the Iglesia was nearly finished, complete with baroque facade to rival the Catedral's grandeur. The interior is not nearly so splendid, however, although it's worth seeing the paintings on either side of the entrance depicting the intercultural marriage between a Spanish conquistador and an Inca princess. If you don't have a Boleto Turístico, the church is open several times a day for mass and tourists are admitted under the condition that they participate in the mass—start wandering around and taking photos and you'll be shown the door. ⊠ *Plaza de Armas* ☏ *No phone* 💰 *S/10* ☺ *Mon.–Sat. 9–11:45 and 1–5:30, Sun. 9–10:45 and 1–5:30; Masses: Mon.–Sat. noon and 6 PM, Sun. 11:30 AM, and 6 and 7 PM.*

SAN BLAS

Huff and puff your way up the narrow cobbled streets north of the Plaza de Armas about four steep blocks to the trendy artisan district of San Blas. This is *the* spot in Cusco to pick up treasures such as ornate *Escuela Cusqueña*–style paintings and carved traditional masks. The streets are steep but you'll have plenty of opportunity to catch your breath admiring the spectacular views along the way.

TOP ATTRACTIONS

San Blas. For spectacular views over Cusco's terra-cotta rooftops, head to San Blas. This is where the Incas brought the choicest artists and artisans, culled from recent conquests, to bolster their own knowledge base. The district has maintained its Bohemian roots for centuries and remains one of the city's most picturesque districts. Recently restored, its whitewashed adobe homes with bright-blue doors shine anew. ■TIP→ The area is possibly one of the trendiest parts of Cusco, with many of the city's choicest restaurants and bars opening their doors here. The Cuesta de San Blas (San Blas Hill), one of the main entrances into the area, is sprinkled with galleries that sell paintings in the Cusqueña-school style of the 16th through 18th centuries. Many of the stone streets are built as stairs or slopes (not for cars) and have religious motifs carved into them.

WORTH NOTING

⑯ Iglesia y Plazoleta de San Blas. The little square in San Blas has a simple adobe church with one of the jewels of colonial art in the Americas—the pulpit of San Blas, an intricately carved 17th-century cedar pulpit, argu-ably Latin America's most ornate. Tradition holds that the work was hewn from a single tree trunk, but experts now believe it was assembled from 1,200 individually carved pieces. Figures of Martin Luther, John Calvin, and Henry VIII—all opponents of Catholicism—as well as those representing the seven deadly sins are condemned for eternity to hold up the pulpit's base. The work is dominated by the triumphant figure of Christ. At his feet rests a human skull, not carved, but the real thing. It's thought to belong to Juan Tomás Tuyrutupac, the creator of the pulpit. ☎ *084/254–285* 💲 *S/15* ☉ *Church Mon.–Sat. 8–6, Sun. 10–6.*

⑮ Museo Hilario Mendívil. As San Blas's most famous son, the former home of 20th-century Peruvian religious artist Hilario Mendívil (1929–77) makes a good stop if you have an interest in Cusqeñan art and iconog-raphy. Legend has it that Mendívil saw llamas parading in the Corpus Christi procession as a child and later infused this image into his reli-gious art, depicting all his figures with long, llama-like necks. ■ TIP➡ In the small gallery are the maguey-wood and rice-plaster sculptures of the Virgin with the elongated necks that were the artist's trademark. There's also a shop selling Mendívil-style work. ✉ *Plazoleta San Blas 634* ☎ *084/240–527* ⊕ *www.artemendivil.com* 💲 *Free* ☉ *Mon.–Sat. 9–1 and 2–6.*

NORTH OF THE PLAZA DE ARMAS

Directly north of the Plaza de Armas, behind La Catedral, and to the east and west for about three blocks is a section of the city that boasts scores of upscale shops, fine restaurants and some of the city's newest cultural museums, Museo Inka and Museo de Arte Precolombino. Walk 15 minutes to the Northwest to Colcampata, said to be the palace of the first Inca ruler, Manco Cápac. The charming Plazoleta Nazarenas, is the perfect place to stroll around, and is far quieter than the bustling Plaza de Armas. Many travelers often mistake this section for the artist's neighborhood of San Blas, but San Blas requires a bit more of a hike, about two steep blocks further, uphill.

TOP ATTRACTIONS

⑪ Museo Inka. Everyone comes to "ooh" and "eeww" over this archaeo-logical museum's collection of eight Inca mummies but the entire facil-ity serves as a comprehensive introduction to pre-Columbian Andean culture. Jam-packed with textiles, ceramics, and dioramas, there's a lot to see but the displays look dated and there's not much in the way of English-language labeling. So brush up on your Spanish or hire a guide. One room is dedicated to the story of Mamakuka ("Mother Coca")

Tours of Cusco, the Sacred Valley & Machu Picchu

The typical tour of the Cusco region combines the city with the Sacred Valley and Machu Picchu in three whirlwind days, including the full Boleto Turístico. We recommend devoting five days to get the most out of your visit—including one day to get acclimated to the high altitude.

Many excellent tour operators and travel agents are in Cusco, and some have offices in Lima. Several companies specialize in adventure tours, others in rafting excursions, still others in llama-assisted treks.

Several outfitters offer rafting trips on the Río Urubamba, close enough to Cusco to be done as a day excursion from the city. The river is navigable year-round, with rains turning it into a Class V from November–May, but a more manageable Class III the rest of the year. All also do multiday trips to the Río Apurimac, outside the Sacred Valley south of Cusco, during its May–December rafting season.

SELECTING A TRAVEL AGENCY

"Holaaaa—trip to Machu Picchu?" With so many touts in Cusco's streets hawking tours to Peru's most famous sight, it's tempting to just buy one in order to make them stop asking. Anyone who offers an Inca Trail trek departing tomorrow should be taken with more than a grain of salt—Inca Trail walks need to be booked months in advance. Don't make arrangements or give money to someone claiming to be a travel agent if they approach you on the street or at the airport in Cusco or Lima. Instead choose an agency that has a physical address. Better yet, select one that is listed in this book or on ⊕ *www.peru.info*. Below are several reputable travel agencies.

Amazonas Explorer has 20 years of experience organizing top-quality alternative adventure and cultural tours. All guides are safety certified and equipment is top-shelf. One percent of profits are donated to sustainable tourism and native tree planting. ☎ *084/252-846* ⊕ *www.amazonas-explorer.com.*

Amazing Peru organizes group and individual guided luxury tours. Transportation services and accommodations are top-notch, and the guides are flexible and extremely helpful. ☎ *800/704-2915* ⊕ *www.amazingperu.com.*

Andina Travel specializes in trekking and alternatives to the Inca Trail, and offers standard Sacred Valley and Machu Picchu tours. ☎ *084/251-892* ⊕ *www.andinatravel.com.*

Another Planet specializes in custom-built hiking, biking, rafting and city tours, as well as healing retreats. The foreign-owned and family operated company has more than 15 years of guiding experience, and also runs the popular Casa de la Gringa Hostal and Andean Wings Boutique Hotel. ☎ *084/243-166* ⊕ *www.andeanwingshotel.com.*

Apumayo Expediciones offers a full gamut of adventure tours and nonconventional treks, including trips geared toward the disabled. ☎ *084/246-018* ⊕ *www.apumayo.com.*

The Cusco Adventure Team targets outdoor enthusiasts eager to tear it up on the back roads and wild rapids of Cusco's surroundings—without skimping out on service and style. Guides and gear are five-star (and safety certified). ☎ *084/228-032.*

Cusco Top Travel & Treks, run by the wildly talented and witty David Choque, specializes in a range of packaged and comfort-class custom-built tours. ☎ 084/251-864 ⊕ www.cuscotoptravelperu.com.

El Chalan organizes single and multiday horseback riding treks for all levels (beginner to professional) throughout the Sacred Valley. Riders and horses alike are carefully tended to and looked after. ☎ 084/201-541 ⊕ www.ranchoelchalan.com.

Enigma specializes in small, customized adventure trips. Enjoy trekking, rafting, mountain climbing, mountain biking, or horseback riding led by professional guides. ☎ 084/222-155 ⊕ www.enigmaperu.com.

Explorandes is a large and long-running company that organizes customized guided trips and expeditions through the Andes in Peru and Ecuador, including rafting and trekking trips around Cusco. ☎ 084/238-380 ⊕ www.explorandes.com.

Inkaterra is a top-end agency specializing in nature-and-culture orientated trips. A 30-year veteran of sustainable tourism, the company customizes tours around Cusco and the Sacred Valley with however much guide accompaniment you desire. ☎ 800/442-5042 ⊕ www.inkaterra.com.

Kuoda Travel packages top-tier personalized tours, including an eight-day journey from the Amazon to Cusco and the Sacred Valley. ☎ 084/221-773 ⊕ www.kuodatravel.com.

Overseas Adventure Travel offers fully escorted 11-day tours of Cusco and the surrounding region with groups no larger than 16 people. A popular OAT add-on is a trip to Ecuador's Galápagos Islands. ☎ 800/493-6824 ⊕ www.oattravel.com.

River Explorers takes you on one- to six-day rafting and kayaking excursions on the Urubamba and Apurimac rivers, and offers the standard trekking tours. ☎ 084/233-680 ⊕ www.riverexplorers.com.

Cusco-based **SAS Travel** has made a name for itself in trekking circles, but can also customize tours and accommodations. ☎ 084/249-194 ⊕ www.sastravelperu.com.

TopTurPeru is an internationally recognized, local company run by Raul Castelo and family. An archaeoastronomy expert, Raul has been sought out by National Geographic and other documentary-filmmaking entities worldwide. ☎ 084/243-234 ⊕ www.topturperu.com.

Wayki Trek is a unique, indigenously managed operator specializing in Inka Trail and alternative trekking. ☎ 084/224-092 ⊕ www.waykitrek.net.

For a tame adventurer, **Wilderness Travel** has a Peru Llama Trek that follows an off-Inca trail route to Machu Picchu where llamas carry your gear and you have the trail to yourself until near the end. ☎ 510/558-2488; 800/368-2794 in U.S. ⊕ www.wildernesstravel.com.

X-treme Tourbulencia leads mountain climbing, biking, trekking, and multisport trips. ☎ 084/224-362 ⊕ www.x-tremetourbulencia.com.

5

and documents indigenous people's use of the coca leaf for religious and medicinal purposes. The building was once the palace of Admiral Francisco Aldrete Maldonado, the reason for its common designation as the Palacio del Almirante (Admiral's Palace). ⊠ *Ataúd at Córdoba del Tucumán* ☎ *084/237–380* 🌐 *S/10* 🕙 *Weekdays 8–6, Sat. 9–4.*

WORTH NOTING

OFF THE
BEATEN
PATH

Colcampata. To behold colonial Cusco in all its beauty, take the 15-minute walk up to Colcampata. Following Procuradores from the Plaza de Armas to Waynapata and then Resbalosa, you'll come to a steep cobblestone staircase with a wonderful view of La Compañía. Continuing to climb, you'll find the church of San Cristóbal, which is of little intrinsic interest but affords another magnificent panorama of the city. The church stands atop Colcampata, believed to have been the palace of the first Inca ruler, Manco Cápac. The Inca wall to the right of the church has 11 niches in which soldiers may once have stood guard. Farther up the road, the lane on the left leads to a post-conquest Inca gateway beside a magnificent Spanish mansion.

WATCHFUL

To protect historical artifacts from light, guards in Cusco's museums and churches are notoriously watchful about prohibiting all types of photography, flash or not, still or video, within their confines. The exception is the Qorikancha, which allows limited photography, but not of the fragile Cusqueña-school paintings on its walls.

12 Museo de Arte Precolombino. For a different perspective on pre-Colombian ceramics head to this spectacular new museum, known as MAP, where art and pre-Colombian culture merge seamlessly. Twelve rooms in the 1580 Casa Cabrera, which was used as the convent of Santa Clara until the 17th century, showcase an astounding collection of pre-Columbian art from the 13th to 16th centuries, mostly in the form of carvings, ceramics, and jewelry. The art and artifacts were made by the Huari and Nasca, as well as the Inca, cultures. The stylish displays have excellent labels in Spanish and English that place the artifacts in their artistic and historical context. On the walls is commentary from European artists on South American art. Swiss artist Paul Klee wrote: "I wish I was newly born, and totally ignorant of Europe, innocent of facts and fashions, to be almost primitive." Most Cusco museums close at dark but MAP remains open every evening. For a break after a walk around, find your way to the on-site café. ⊠ *Plazoleta Nazarenas 231* ☎ *084/233–210* 🌐 *S/20* 🕙 *Daily 8 AM–10 PM.*

13 Museo de Arte Religioso del Arzobispado. The building may be on the dark and musty side, but this San Blas museum has a remarkable collection of religious art. Originally the site of the Inca Roca's Hatun Rumiyoq palace, then the juxtaposed Moorish-style palace of the Marqués de Buenavista, the building reverted to the archdiocese of Cusco and served as the archbishop's residence. The primary repository of religious art in the city, many of the paintings in the collection are anonymous but you'll notice some by the renowned indigenous artist Marcos Zapata. A highlight is a series of 17th-century paintings that depict the city's Corpus Christi procession. Many of the works in the museum's 12 rooms are not labeled so you may want the services of a guide. ✉ *Hatun Rumi-yoq and Herejes* ☎ *084/222–781* 🎫 *S/15* 🕐 *Mon.–Sat. 8–6, Sun. 10–6.*

⑭ Palacio de Inca Roca. Inca Roca lived in the 13th or 14th century. Halfway along the palace's side wall, nestled amid other stones, is the famous 12-angled stone, an example of masterly Inca masonry. There's nothing sacred about the 12 angles: Inca masons were famous for incorporating stones with many more sides than 12 into their buildings. If you can't spot the famous stone from the crowds taking photos, ask one of the shopkeepers or one of the elaborately dressed Inca figures hanging out along the street to point it out. Around the corner is a series of stones on the wall that form the shapes of a puma and a serpent. Kids hang out there and trace the forms for a small tip. ✉ *Hatun Rumiyoc and Palacio.*

SOUTH OF THE PLAZA DE ARMAS
After the colonial charm of central Cusco and San Blas, head south of the Plaza for a timely reminder that you're still in Peru. Traffic, smog, and horn-happy drivers welcome you to the noisy and unattractive Avenida El Sol, where the colonial charm of the city is hidden but for one glaring exception: Cusco's if-you-have-time-for-only-one-thing tourist attraction, the Qorikancha, or temple of the sun. Don't miss it. ■TIP➜ Plaza Regocijo, while still south of the plaza, has re-created itself in the last five years from a once low-level tourist area to a clean, upscale plaza (catering to Cusqueños and travelers alike) with gourmet restaurants and high-end shopping.

TOP ATTRACTIONS

⑰ Qorikancha. If the Spanish came to the new world looking for El Dorado, the lost city of gold, they must have thought they'd found it when they laid eyes on Qorikancha. Built during the reign of the Inca Pachacutec to honor the Sun, Tawantinsuyos' most important divinity, Qorikancha translates as "Court of Gold." Conquistadors' jaws must have dropped when they saw the gold-plated walls of the temple glinting in the sunlight. Then their fingers must have started working because all that remains today is the masterful stonework.

Fodor's Choice
★

If Cusco was constructed to represent a puma, then Qorikancha was positioned as the animal's loins, the center from which all creation emanated; 4,000 priests and attendants are thought to have lived within its confines. Walls and altars were plated with gold, and in the center of the complex sat a giant gold disc, positioned to reflect the sun and bathe the temple in light. At the summer solstice, sunlight reflected into a niche in the wall where only the Inca were permitted to sit. Terraces that face it were once filled with life-size gold-and-silver statues of plants and animals. ■TIP➜ Much of the wealth was removed to pay ransom for the captive Inca ruler Atahualpa during the Spanish conquest, blood money paid in vain since Atahualpa was later murdered. Eventually, Francisco Pizarro awarded the site to his brother Juan. Upon Juan's death, the structure passed to the Dominicans, who began to construct the church of Santo Domingo, using stones from the temple and creating perhaps Cusco's most jarring imperial–colonial architectural juxtaposition.

An ingenious restoration to recover both buildings after the 1953 earthquake lets you see how the church was built on and around the walls and chambers of the temple. In the Inca parts of the structure left exposed, estimated to be about 40% of the original temple, you can admire the mortarless masonry, earthquake-proof trapezoidal doorways, curved retaining wall, and exquisite carvings that exemplify the artistic and engineering skills of the Inca. Bilingual guides lead tours every day except Sunday; the service is included in your admission price. A small museum down the hill with an entrance on Avenida El Sol contains a few artifacts from the site but doesn't warrant a huge amount of your time. ■TIP→Only entrance to the museum is covered in the Boleto Turístico. A separate fee is applied to enter the ruins and the church. For S/15 you can buy a ticket that grants you entrance to the Convento Santa Catalina, and Qorikancha's ruins and church. ⊠ *Pampa del Castillo at Plazoleta Santo Domingo* ☎ *No phone* 🖭 *Ruins and church, S/10; museum, Boleto Turístico* ⊙ *Ruins and church: Mon.–Sat. 8:30–6:30, Sun. 2–5; museum: Mon.–Sat. 9–6, Sun. 8–1.*

WORTH NOTING

❹ Casa de Garcilaso (Museum of Regional History). You'll find a bit of everything in this spot, which may leave you feeling like you've seen it all before. Colonial building? Check. Cusqueña-school paintings? Check. Ancient pottery? Check. Inca mummy? Check. This is the colonial childhood home of Inca Garcilaso de la Vega, the famous chronicler of the Spanish conquest and illegitimate son of one of Pizarro's captains and an Inca princess. Inside the mansion, with its cobblestone courtyard, is the Museo de Historia Regional, with Cusqueña-school paintings and pre-Inca mummies—one from Nazca has a 1½-meter (5-foot) braid—and ceramics, metal objects, and other artifacts. ⊠ *Heladeros at Garcilaso* ☎ *084/223–245* 🖭 *Boleto Turístico* ⊙ *Daily 8–5.*

❶ Iglesia San Pedro. Stones from Inca ruins were used to construct this church. Though spartan inside, San Pedro is known for its ornately carved pulpit. The vendors you see on the front steps are a spillover from the nearby central market. Though colorful, this neighborhood shopping area is not the safest for tourists—leave important belongings in your hotel room. ⊠ *Santa Clara at Chaparro* ☎ *No phone* 🖭 *Free* ⊙ *Mon.–Sat. 7–11:30 and 6–7:30.*

❷ Iglesia Santa Clara. Austere from the outside, this incredible 1588 church takes the prize for most eccentric interior decoration. ■TIP→Thousands of mirrors cover the interior, competing with the gold-laminated altar for glittery prominence. Legend has it that the mirrors were placed inside in order to tempt locals into church. Built in old Inca style, using stone looted from Inca ruins, this is a great example of the lengths that the Spanish went to in order to attract indigenous converts to the Catholic faith. ⊠ *Santa Clara* ☎ *No phone* 🖭 *Free* ⊙ *Daily 9–noon and 3–5.*

❺ La Merced. The church may be overshadowed by the more famous Cathedral and Iglesia de la Compañía, but La Merced contains one of the city's most priceless treasures—the Custodia, a solid gold container for communion wafers more than a meter high and encrusted with thousands of precious stones. ■TIP→Two of the city's most famous conquistadors are buried here—Diego de Almagro and Gonzalo Pizarro. Rebuilt in the 17th century, this monastery, with two stories of portals and a colonial

fountain, gardens, and benches, has a spectacular series of murals that depict the life of the founder of the Mercedarian order, St. Peter of Nolasco. ⊠ *Mantas 121* ☏ *084/231–831* ⌁ *S/3* ⊘ *Church: Mon.–Sun. 8 AM–12 PM and 2–5 PM; museum: Mon.–Sat. 8–12:30 and 2–5:30.*

⑩ Museo de Arte Contemporáneo. Take a refreshing turn back toward the present in this city of history. Yet even the modern-art museum, in the Cusco municipal hall, focuses on the past. Twentieth-century artists have put a modern-art spin on imperial and colonial themes. ⊠ *Kusipata s/n (Plaza Regocijo)* ☏ *084/240–006* ⌁ *Boleto Turístico* ⊘ *Mon.-Fri. 8 AM–6 PM.*

❸ Plaza e Iglesia de San Francisco. Close to the Plaza de Armas, this plaza is a local hangout. There's not a lot to see, apart from an intriguing garden of native plants. More interesting, if you've wandered this way, is the church with its macabre sepulchers with arrangements of bones and skulls, some pinned to the wall to spell out morbid sayings. A small museum of religious art with paintings by Cusqueña-school artists Marcos Zapata and Diego Quispe Tito is in the church sacristy. ⊠ *3 blocks south of Plaza de Armas* ☏ *084/221–361* ⌁ *S/1* ⊘ *Weekdays 9–noon and 3–5.*

WHERE TO EAT

Cusco's dining scene is surprisingly vast. You'll encounter everything from Andean grills to Middle Eastern kebab shops. Restaurant employees on Cusco's Plaza de Armas and Plateros and Procuradores streets—any of these could be renamed "Restaurant Row"—stand in their doorways, touting their establishments, menus in hand, to entice you. Browsing any menu you're sure to come across the Andean specialties of cuy and alpaca. The former you'll know as guinea pig and is usually served roasted (sometimes with peppers stuffed charmingly in its mouth). The latter is the cute furry llama-like creature you'll see wandering the Cusco streets with its indigenous owner for photo ops.

PLANNING

Lunch is served between 1 and 3. Dinner begins around 7, with prime rush around 8:30, and most restaurants start winding down service at about 9:30. Most places do stay open continually throughout the afternoon.

WHAT IT COSTS IN NUEVO SOLES					
	¢	$	$$	$$$	$$$$
RESTAURANTS	under S/20	S/20–S/35	S/36–S/50	S/51–S/65	over S/65
HOTELS	Under S/125	S/125–S/250	S/251–S/375	S/376–S/500	over S/500

Restaurant prices are based on the median main course price at dinner. Hotel prices are for two people in a standard double room in high season.

PLAZA DE ARMAS

$
PERUVIAN
Fodor's Choice
★

✕**Greens.** A new addition to town, Greens' reputation for top-quality, locally produced organic food already extends past the cobblestone streets of Cusco—travelers as far away as the Sacred Valley boast of its home-made wheat pasta dishes and overstuffed sandwiches. The only problem you'll have here is figuring out which culinary creation to try. We recommend at least starting with a fresh fruit juice or tea infusion and finishing with a triple-layered latte or full-on dessert. ⊠ *Santa Catalina Angosta 135, 2nd Floor, Plaza de Armas* ☎ *084/243–379* ⊕ *www.cuscorestaurants.com* ▭ *AE, MC, V.*

$$
MEDITERRANEAN

✕**Incanto.** Stylish contemporary design in an Andean setting has made this large upmarket restaurant near the Plaza a hit with those looking for a classy night out. Dishing up Mediterranean-Andean fusion cuisine as well as more traditional dishes such as delicious thin-crust pizza, this has got to be the only place in the world where you'll find ravioli *aji de gallina*, a traditional creamy chicken sauce usually served with rice, on the menu. Wander down the back to the open kitchen, and don't forget to have a look at the original Inca wall on the way. ⊠ *Catalina Angosta 135, Plaza de Armas* ☎ *084/254–753* ⊕ *www.cuscorestaurants.com* ▭ *AE, DC, MC, V.*

$$
PERUVIAN
☾

✕**Inka Grill.** Centrally located in the Plaza de Armas, this popular restaurant offers a wide variety of Peruvian and international fare. From fresh quinoa-battered shrimp salad to homemade ravioli in Andean herb sauce, the extensive menu is sure to please even the pickiest of palettes. Cozy and chic, order up a glass of red and listen to the live nightly music. ⊠ *Portal de Panes 115, Plaza de Armas* ☎ *084/262–992* ⊕ *www.inkagrillcusco.com* ▭ *AE, MC, V.*

$–$$
PERUVIAN

✕**La Retama.** One of the better offerings on the Plaza, this tourist-oriented second-floor eatery wins points for its view over the Catedral and Iglesia de la Compañía. Pull up a stool on the balcony to drink in the vista while you tuck into an Andean river trout in garlic sauce or trout cebiche. A cozy fireplace, Andean tapestries, and a nightly folk-music show complete the experience. ⊠ *Portal de Panes 123, Plaza de Armas* ☎ *084/242–620* ⊕ *www.laretama.info* ▭ *MC, V.*

$$
PERUVIAN

✕**Paititi.** On the Plaza de Armas, this quiet, tourist-oriented restaurant that encompasses part of the original Inca wall has good fish, especially the grilled or fried trout. It's also a fine place to introduce yourself to alpaca: Paititi's specialty is this peculiarly Andean delicacy basted in a *sauco* (cranberry-like Peruvian fruit) sauce. Additional lures are live folk-music shows nightly and a free pisco sour for all diners. ⊠ *Portal de Carrizos 270, Plaza de Armas* ☎ *084/252–686* ▭ *AE, DC, MC, V.*

$$$$
PERUVIAN

✕**Tunupa.** With subdued lighting and thoughtful touches like Andean textiles on the walls, Tunupa effectively plays down its barn-like size. An endless buffet combines traditional Andean delicacies with more familiar Thai and Japanese offerings, and there's platter after platter of desserts, and free pisco sours. A nightly show makes this upstairs venue on the Plaza de Armas hugely popular with tour groups. More intimate seating is on the balcony (glassed-in for those chilly Andean nights), but bookings are advisable regardless of your group size. Try the carpaccio *de lomo* (beef marinated in herbs, olive oil, and Parmesan cheese)

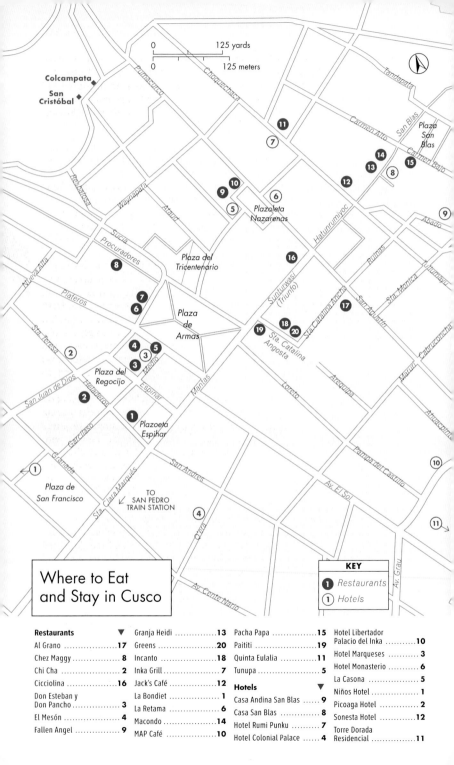

Where to Eat and Stay in Cusco

KEY

❶ Restaurants
① Hotels

Restaurants ▼

Al Grano **17**
Chez Maggy **8**
Chi Cha **2**
Cicciolina **16**
Don Esteban y
Don Pancho **3**
El Mesón **4**
Fallen Angel **9**

Granja Heidi **13**
Greens **20**
Incanto **18**
Inka Grill **7**
Jack's Café **12**
La Bondiet **1**
La Retama **6**
Macondo **14**
MAP Café **10**

Pacha Papa **15**
Paititi **19**
Quinta Eulalia **11**
Tunupa **5**

Hotels ▼

Casa Andina San Blas ... **9**
Casa San Blas **8**
Hotel Rumi Punku **7**
Hotel Colonial Palace ... **4**

Hotel Libertador
Palacio del Inka **10**
Hotel Marqueses **3**
Hotel Monasterio **6**
La Casona **5**
Niños Hotel **1**
Picoaga Hotel **2**
Sonesta Hotel **12**
Torre Dorada
Residencial **11**

and finish with a rich *suspiro a la limeña*, a sweet Peruvian mousse. If you make it to this Tunupa in Cusco, there's one in Urubamba, too; it offers the same enticing menu, and is located inside an old garden-filled hacienda by the river. ⊠ *Portal de Confituría 233, Plaza de Armas* ☎ *084/252–936 Cusco; 084/201–471 Urubamba* ⊕ *www. tunuparestaurant.com* ⊟ *AE, DC, MC, V.*

SAN BLAS

$ ✕ **Granja Heidi.** Don't be mistaken: Heidi is not the owner, but rather the
GERMAN   mule who resides on the nearby farm where the owners get much of the produce for this San Blas restaurant. Yep, it's all about the farm here, especially the farm-fresh yogurt—we recommend you give it try. Service can be tough going, but lunch with rich yogurts and curds accompanying crepes and fruits is quite satisfying. Dinner means meat and vegetarian dishes, soups, and stir-fries. ⊠ *Cuesta San Blas 525* ☎ *084/238–383* ⊟ *No credit cards* ⊘ *Closed Sun.*

$ ✕ **Jack's Cafe.** Scrumptious breakfasts can be had all day at this bright
CAFÉ   and busy Aussie- and Irish-owned café in San Blas. Order up granola and yogurt, large fluffy pancakes, or a grand "brekkie" (breakfast) with bacon and eggs. Also adorning the menu are gourmet sandwiches, fresh salads, and a variety of other satifying dishes. Jack's is a stand-out hit. Come during peak season and you may have to line up to get a table. Everything is prepared in-house, including the delicious breads, and the coffee and hot chocolate are to die for. This jumping spot stays open well into the night. ⊠ *Choquechaca 509* ☎ *084/254–606* ⊟ *No credit cards.*

$ ✕ **Macondo.** Part art gallery, part café, and entirely hip, the Macondo
LATIN AMERICAN   takes its name from the land of magical realism in Gabriel García Márquez's *One Hundred Years of Solitude.* Like the novel's invented land, this eatery dishes up what they like to call "invented food" with mouthwatering Nuevo-Peruvian dishes such as "euphoria chicken" served in a mango and orange sauce or alpaca mignon with white wine and mushrooms. Bring your old books to swap at the book exchange, or kick back and play a board game. ⊠ *Cuesta San Blas 571* ☎ *084/229–415* ⊟ *V* ⊘ *No lunch Sun.*

$$ ✕ **Pacha Papa.** If you've been putting off trying the famous Andean
PERUVIAN   dishes of guinea pig or alpaca, then wait no longer. This fabulous restau-
Fodor's Choice   rant is hands-down the best place in town for Peruvian food. Modeled
★   after a typical Peruvian open-air *quinta*, wooden tables are scattered around a large patio. The menu takes influences from all over Peru and the waiters are happy to explain what makes each dish special. Try the delicious *anticuchas de* alpaca, skewers of tender alpaca meat with local spices, and don't miss the sensational *adobo de chancho*, a tangy pork stew with meat that melts in your mouth. For a special treat go for the underground-oven baked *pachamanca*, a stew where different types of meats are slow roasted together with potatoes and aromatic herbs (*pacha* is Quechua for ground, *manca* means pot). This dish has to be ordered 24 hours in advance, so plan ahead. ⊠ *Plazoleta San Blas 120* ☎ *084/241–318* ⊟ *AE, DC, MC, V.*

$ ✕ **Quinta Eulalia.** A *quinta* is a típico semi-open-air Peruvian restaurant,
PERUVIAN   and Eulalia's is the oldest such place in the city, cooking up hearty, filling

5

portions of down-home food since 1941. Only open for lunch, specialties include *chicharrones* (fried pork and cabbage), *trucha al horno* (oven-baked trout), and *cuy chactado* (guinea pig with potatoes). ⊠ *Choquechaca N. 384* ☎ *084/234–495* ▤ *No credit cards* ⊘ *No dinner.*

NORTH OF PLAZA DE ARMAS

$

ASIAN

✕ **Al Grano.** Don't let the Andean tapestries fool you: this small restaurant off the Plaza de Armas specializes in Asian rice plates. It offers a fantastic selection of affordable dishes from India, Thailand, Malaysia, Sri Lanka, Vietnam, Myanmar, and Indonesia. The rich dessert cakes and brownies *are* Peruvian rather than Asian, however, and we suggest you don't miss them. ⊠ *Santa Catalina Ancha 398* ☎ *084/228–032* ▤ *No credit cards* ⊘ *Closed Sun.*

$

PIZZA

✕ **Chez Maggy.** If the mountain air is a little chilly, warm up in front of the open brick ovens that produce the café's great pizzas and calzones. (Peruvian food is on the menu, but everyone comes for the pizza.) Four branches in Cusco are within a block of each other. The tables are smaller and more intimate at the main location on Plateros, but you're sure to trade tales with other travelers around the corner at Procuradores 344, as seating is at very long wooden tables. You'll also find Maggy and her pizza at Procuradores 365 and 374. ⊠ *Plateros 348* ☎ *084/234–861* ⊕ *www.pizzeriachezmaggy.com* ▤ *MC, V.*

$$

MEDITERRANEAN

Fodor's Choice

★

✕ **Cicciolina.** Everyone seems to know everyone and greet each other with a peck on the cheek at this second-floor eatery, part lively tapas bar, part sit-down, candlelit restaurant. The bar wraps around the kitchen area where a small army of cooks prepare your food. You'll strain to see as they set out each new platter of tapas—perhaps some bruschetta or prawns and sweet potato in wasabi sauce—and be tempted to say, "I want one of those." The restaurant half of Cicciolina is much more subdued, with a complete selection of homemade pastas with Mediterranean sauces on the menu. You can order off the restaurant menu in the tapas bar, but not the other way around. Note that, while not required, reservations are very strongly encouraged and available only through the Web site. ⊠ *Sunturwasi 393, 2nd fl., Triunfo* ☎ *084/239–510* ⊕ *www.cicciolinacuzco.com* ▤ *AE, DC, MC, V.*

$$

CONTINENTAL

Fodor's Choice

★

✕ **Fallen Angel.** Suppress your gasps as you walk in and are greeted by images of heaven, hell, earth, limbo, purgatory, and variations on those themes. ■ TIP➔ This was one of Francisco Pizarro's houses, and it's doubtful that he envisioned anything so avant-garde. You'll dine off bathtubs that double as fish tanks, watched over all the while by baroque angels. The steak-driven menu, just like the decoration, is absolutely fabulous, darling. ⊠ *Plazoleta Nazarenas 221* ☎ *084/258–184* ⊕ *www. fallenangelincusco.com* ▤ *MC, V.*

$$$$

PERUVIAN

✕ **MAP Café.** Museum eateries don't routinely warrant separate guidebook listings, but this small, elegant café inside the glass-enclosed courtyard of the Museo de Arte Precolombino is actually one of the city's top restaurants—and top prices to boot, but we think it's worth it. Dishing up novel and exciting twists on traditional Peruvian cuisine, try tuna with an Andean chili chutney or baked cuy, served with an accompaniment of pureed Andean potatoes. The menu is prix-fixe after 6 PM.

✉ *Plazoleta Nazarenas 231* ☎ *084/242–476* ✎ *Reservations essential* ▱ *AE, DC, MC, V.*

SOUTH OF PLAZA DE ARMAS

$$
PERUVIAN
✕ **Chi Cha.** Inspired by Gastón Acurio—renowned chef and godfather of the Novo-Andino culinary craze—this hip and hopping restaurant dishes up regional Cusqueña cuisine with a modern twist. If you haven't tried cuy yet, this trendy, open-kitchen restaurant may inspire you to pull the trigger. Those who are intrigued but not

ready for the guinea pig plunge can still experience the thrill of trying traditional recipes peppered with innovative additions: consider *kapchi de habas* (fava bean casserole), *anticuchos* (Peruvian kebabs), or *Sancochado Chicha* (served in three mouthwatering parts: slow-cooked meats, sauces, and vegetables with broth). Standbys like pizza and pasta are top-notch if that's more your speed, and we think the cocktails aren't too shabby either. ✉ *Plaza Regocijo 261, 2nd fl.* ☎ *084/240–520* ⊕ *chicha.com.pe* ▱ *AE, MC, V.*

$
PERUVIAN
✕ **Don Esteban y Don Pancho.** At this contemporary Andean restaurant, starched white tablecloths and impeccable service lend a polished air, while design touches such as a cobbled floor and natural fibers are reminders that you're in the Andes. The menu is as well-crafted as the service, with traditional Peruvian Criolle dishes. The *carapulcra,* dried potato with pork ribs, and the traditional bean dish *tacu tacu* are standouts. Even if you don't eat, drop in for cocktails—the Chicha Tu May, which puts a twist on the pisco sour by adding a dash of ruby-red chicha, is a happiness inducer. ✉ *Portal Espinar 144, Plaza Regociga* ☎ *084/244–664* ⊕ *www.donestebanydonpancho.com* ▱ *AE, DC, MC, V.*

$$$$
PERUVIAN
✕ **El Mesón de Espaderos.** You'll drink in the city's history as you dine on a rustic second-floor terrace with stucco walls and high-beamed ceilings above the Plaza de Armas. ■TIP➔ The parrilladas (barbecued meats) are the best in Cusco. The platter for one person is more than enough for two, and the *Parrilla Inca,* with its mix of Andean meats, provides a good opportunity to try that cuy that you've been putting off. Vegetarians may want to pass, or resign themselves to dining from the salad bar. ✉ *Espaderos 105* ☎ *084/235–307* ▱ *AE, DC, MC, V.*

¢
CAFÉ
✕ **La Bondiet.** Although we all know that you come to Peru to experience Peru, sometimes you need a break. This is a great spot to regroup and recaffeinate after a hard morning's sightseeing. The coffee is of a high standard, there's a huge range of mouthwatering cakes and slices to dig into, and the unusual "Inca Punch" (a milk punch with a shot of pisco) awaits those who need something a little stronger. ✉ *Heladeros 118* ☎ *084/246–823* ▱ *V.*

WHERE TO STAY

No matter what your travel budget, you won't be priced out of the market staying in Cusco: luxury hotels, backpackers' digs, and everything in between await. Most lodgings discount rates during the unofficial off-season of September through May. With a few exceptions, absent are the international hotel chains. In their place are smaller, top-end, independently run lodgings offering impeccable service, even if they lack swimming pools and concierges. Lodgings in all price ranges, whether housed in a former 17th-century convent or newly built, mimic the old Spanish-colonial style of construction arranged around a central courtyard or patio.

You may have to adjust your internal thermostat in moderate or budget lodgings at this altitude, but all provide extra blankets. Most places provide hot water around the clock, but if you're wondering just ask if there's *agua caliente*. Many accommodations keep an oxygen supply on hand for those having trouble adjusting to the thin air.

PLANNING

Lodgings in Cusco keep shockingly early checkout times. (Flights to Cusco arrive early in the morning.) ■ TIP→ Expect to have to vacate your room by 9 or 10 am, though this is less strictly enforced in the off-season. Nearly all lodgings will hold your luggage if you're not leaving town until later in the day. Breakfast, at least a Continental one (and usually something more ample), is included in most lodging rates.

SAN BLAS

$$$

Fodor's Choice

★

🍴 **Casa Andina San Blas.** Taking its lead from the Spaniards, Casa Andina is slowly colonizing Cusco all over again with five branches now existing in various locales throughout the city, including one of its premier luxury hotels, Casa Andina Private Collection. Part of a national chain, all of the Casa Andina hotels exude professionalism and are great value for money. Fortunately for them, this is where the resemblance ends, as each hotel differs in style. The San Blas branch, in a colonial house perched up on the hillside offers great views over the city's terra-cotta rooftops. The modern and comfortable rooms are tastefully furnished with Andean touches. **Pros:** good value for top-end lodgings; excellent location with spectacular views over Cusco; professional atmosphere and pleasant service. **Cons:** can be a hard walk uphill to get here; some rooms have subpar views over the neighboring houses. ⊠ *Chihuampata 278* ☎ *084/263–694* ⊕ *www.casa-andina.com* ⤳ *38 rooms* ⚠ *In-room: a/c, safe. In-hotel: restaurant, bar, laundry service, Internet terminal, Wi-Fi hotspot* ☰ *AE, MC, V.*

$$

🍴 **Casa San Blas.** This small hotel with a large staff—there's a 2-to-1 staff-to-guest ratio—prides itself on exceptional service. Regular rooms are quite comfortable, with colonial-style furniture and hardwood floors, but with more modern amenities than this restored 250-year-old house would imply. The top-floor suites and one apartment (perfect for a family of four or five) are similar in style, but larger, with wood-beamed ceilings and great views over the city. The spacious apartment is a great option for those considering a longer stay, and has a fully equipped kitchen. All rooms are decorated with handmade textiles (each with a design reflecting the room's name), which can be purchased if you want a keepsake. ■TIP➜ The hotel sits a block off the Cuesta San Blas, the "staircase" street leading up from the Plaza de Armas, and could not be more central for sightseeing. **Pros:** fabulous views; warm welcome from staff; fantastic location. **Cons:** furnishings are fairly plain in regular rooms; it's a steep uphill walk to get here. ⊠ *Tocuyeros 566, San Blas* ☎ *084/237–900; 888/569–1769 toll-free in North America* ⊕ *www. casasanblas.com* ➧ *12 rooms, 4 suites, 1 apartment* ◌ *In-room: a/c, safe, Wi-Fi. In-hotel: restaurant, bar, laundry service, Internet terminal, Wi-Fi hotspot* ⊟ *AE, DC, MC, V* ⫶○⫶ *BP.*

$ ⌖ **Hotel Rumi Punku.** A massive stone door—that's what Rumi Punku means in Quechua—opens onto a rambling complex of balconies, patios, gardens, courtyards, terraces, fireplace, and bits of Inca wall scattered here and there. It all links a series of pleasantly furnished rooms with hardwood floors and comfy beds covered with plush blankets. The top-level sauna and gym has stupendous views of the city. The recently added Rumi Punku Superior section offers slightly larger, more lavish rooms, but everyone can enjoy lounging in the cafeteria and courtyards. **Pros:** great views from the upstairs sauna ($10 USD extra); good hot water 24 hours a day; charming rambling layout. **Cons:** located a huff and puff up the hill. ⊠ *Choquechaca 339* ☎ *084/221–102* ⊕ *www.rumipunku.com* ➧ *40 rooms* ◌ *In-room: no a/c, safe, Wi-Fi. In-hotel: room service, bar, laundry service, Internet terminal, Wi-Fi hotspot* ⊟ *AE, DC, MC, V* ⫶○⫶ *CP.*

NORTH OF PLAZA DE ARMAS

$$$$ ⌖ **Hotel Monasterio.** One of Cusco's top hotels, this beautifully restored
Fodor's Choice 1592 monastery of San Antonio Abad is a national historic monument.
★ Planners managed to retain the austere beauty of the complex—the lodging even counts the original chapel with its ornate gold altar and collection of Cusqueño art—yet updated the compact rooms with stylish colonial furnishings and all the mod-cons such as remote-operated window blinds and TVs that pop out of cabinet tops. The public spaces such as the elegant lounge bar and serene cloisters will take your breath away. Renovations to the adjacent convent are underway and are sure to enhance its already palatial personality. ■TIP➜ For those having trouble adjusting to the altitude the hotel offers an in-room oxygen enrichment service, the only such hotel system in the world. For S/130 per night you can elect to have your room pressurized with a flow of enriched oxygen, much like in an airplane cabin, duplicating conditions of those 1,000 meters (3,300 feet) lower than Cusco. **Pros:** stylish rooms with all the conveniences; stunning public spaces; attentive service. **Cons:** rooms are small for the price tag; *everything* (including Internet access) is charged. ⊠ *Palacio 136, Plazoleta Nazarenas* ☎ *084/604–000; 01/610–8300* ⊕ *www.monasteriohotel.com* ➧ *120 rooms, 6 suites* ◌ *In-room: a/c, safe, refrigerator, Wi-Fi. In-hotel: 2 restaurants, bar, spa, laundry service, Internet terminal, Wi-Fi hotspot* ⊟ *AE, DC, MC, V* ⫶○⫶ *BP.*

$$$$ ⌖ **La Casona.** Colonial with a touch of class, this 11-room boutique
Fodor's Choice casa (they are adamant that it not be called a hotel) comes complete
★ with a manicured interior courtyard, stately sitting and dining areas, and rooms with heated floors, antique-looking but modern bathtubs,

and marbled Spanish-showers. Every detail inspires appreciation, from the chic furnishings to the intricately carved wooden doors, soaring stone archways and smiling staff. The hotel captures all the charm of a 16th century mansion while offering all the amenities of a modern world-class retreat. After a day of tromping about town, you may find yourself cozying up and settling in, but be sure to pull yourself away from your private nook long enough to enjoy afternoon tea and biscuits. **Pros:** serenely situated and spoil-yourself stylish. **Cons:** tucked away from the Plaza de Armas. ⊠ *Plaza Nazarenas 113* ☎ *084/245–314* ⊕ *www.inkaterra.com* ↳ *11 rooms* ⌂ *In-room: a/c, safe, refrigerator, DVD, Wi-Fi. In-hotel: restaurant, room service, laundry service, Wi-Fi hotspot* ⊟ *AE, D, DC, MC, V* ⊺◎⊺ *BP.*

SOUTH OF PLAZA DE ARMAS

$ ⊡ **Hotel Colonial Palace.** Built inside the 17th-century Convent of Santa Teresa, this hotel has simply furnished rooms on two floors laid out around two lovely courtyards. The former convent forms the older wing. Its rooms have character, if occasional leaky faucets. You'll find more modern furnishings in the newer wing in front of the old convent, though it's still constructed in the colonial style. The staff is exceptionally friendly and eager to please. **Pros:** central location; colonial charm; how often do you get to sleep in a convent? **Cons:** not much is "palatial" about the simple rooms; breakfasts on the patio can make for a chilly early morning. ⊠ *Quera 270* ☎ *084/232–151* ⊕ *www.colonialpalace.net* ↳ *40 rooms* ⌂ *In-room: no a/c. In-hotel: laundry service* ⊟ *AE, MC, V* ⊺◎⊺ *CP.*

$$$$ ⊡ **Hotel Libertador Palacio del Inka.** Close enough, but still removed from the hubbub of the Plaza de Armas, this hotel on the tiny Plazoleta Santo Domingo was the last home of Francisco Pizarro, the first governor of Peru. The glass-covered lobby may look like an airport, but it gives you a good idea of the sleek contemporary design that is the signature of this hotel chain. The modern rooms have colonial touches, some with original furniture, and all have central heating to keep out the chill. The plush bar makes a mean pisco sour. **Pros:** contemporary rooms with all the conveniences; some rooms have views to the Sun Temple; close to the action but not in the thick of it. **Cons:** near the unattractive Avenida El Sol; modern rooms lack the character of other lodgings; customer service is reportedly uneven. ⊠ *Plazoleta Santo Domingo 259* ☎ *084/231–961; 01/518-6500 (reservations)* ⊕ *www.libertador.com.pe* ↳ *254 rooms, 14 suites* ⌂ *In-room: a/c, safe, Wi-Fi. In-hotel: restaurant, room service, bar, gym, laundry service, Internet terminal, Wi-Fi hotspot* ⊟ *AE, DC, MC, V* ⊺◎⊺ *BP.*

$ ⊡ **Hotel Marqueses.** Historic architecture enthusiasts may forgive the shabby carpets and days-gone-by appearance once they lay eyes on the spectacularly carved wooden doors, intricately paved courtyard, and Catedral views of this restored 16th-century building near the Plaza. Rooms congregate around an arcaded courtyard with grand old staircases and are furnished in full colonial style with tapestry bed covers and period details. Shell out a few extra soles to get a two-level suite, with balconies from which you can see the Catedral, colonial paintings on the walls, and wonderful carved wood throughout. **Pros:** wonderful period details; views of the Catedral from some rooms; good value suites. **Cons:** in the heart of the tourist action; standard rooms are a decided cut below the quality of the suites. ⊠ *Garcilaso 256* ☎ *084/264–249* ⊕ *www.hotelmarqueses.com* ↝ *32 rooms* △ *In-room: no a/c, safe, Wi-Fi. In-hotel: bar, laundry service* ▤ *AE, DC, MC, V* ⏍ *BP.*

$ ⊞ **Niños Hotel.** If you prefer lodging with a social conscience—and even if you don't—this is a great budget find; proceeds from your stay at the "Children's Hotel" provide medical and dental care, food, and recreation for 250 disadvantaged Cusqueño children who attend day care on the premises and cheerfully greet you as you pass through the courtyard. Rooms tend toward the spartan side with painted hardwood floors, but mattresses are firm and comfy and there's an endless supply of hot water. For longer stays, a few other rooms as well as four apartments with shared bath are down the street on Calle Fiero. The catch? The place is immensely popular. Make reservations weeks in advance. **Pros:** wonderfully welcoming staff; charming colonial building; you can sleep soundly with the knowledge that your money is going to a good cause. **Cons:** slightly out of the way; some rooms are small and very basic. ⊠ *Meloq 442* ☎ *084/231–424* ⊕ *www.ninoshotel.com* ↝ *20 rooms, 13 with bath* △ *In-room: no a/c, no phone, no TV. In-hotel: laundry service* ▤ *No credit cards* ⏍ *EP.*

$$$ ⊞ **Picoaga Hotel.** An upscale option at a fraction of the price of some Cusco lodgings, this hotel mixes the best of the new and old Cusco. The front half drips with colonial charm—rooms are set around an attractive arcaded courtyard in the 17th-century former home of the Marquis of Picoaga. Behind is a modern wing with a restaurant that overlooks the Plaza de Armas. Rooms in the front colonial section are charming, although for style and comfort, the minimalist modern rooms with their truly enormous beds can't be beat. The bar, with its open wood fire, huge leather couches and cozy atmosphere, is the best spot in Cusco on a cold Andean night. **Pros:** good value for top-end lodgings; mix of modern and colonial room options; great view from the restaurant. **Cons:** can be either overrun with tour groups or eerily empty; among the favorite stomping ground of Cusco's street sellers. ⊠ *Calle Santa Teresa 344* ☎ *084/252–330* ⊕ *www.picoagahotel.com* ↝ *72 rooms* △ *In-room: a/c, safe, Wi-Fi. In-hotel: restaurant, room service, bar, laundry service, Internet terminal, Wi-Fi hotspot* ▤ *AE, DC, MC, V* ⏍ *BP.*

$$ ⊞ **Sonesta Hotel.** Renamed (this was previously the Savoy) and revamped, Sonesta Hotel offers a modern and quiet place to duck away from the hubbub of the Plaza de Armas. The sleek yet comfortable lobby introduces you to this hotel's conservative yet friendly style; this hotel is popular with business travelers and tourists alike. Beyond the sparkling bathrooms and plush new comforters, the excellent staff helps with many things including travel plans and restaurant reservations. **Pros:** newly renovated and clean; comfortable lobby; friendly staff; in-room safes hold laptops. **Cons:** the inconvenient location means a 10-minute stroll to get into town. ⊠ *Av. El Sol 954* ☎ *084/223–031* ⊕ *www.sonesta.com/cusco* ↝ *121 rooms, 6 suites* △ *In-room: a/c, safe, refrigerator, Wi-Fi. In-hotel: restaurant, room service, bar, laundry service, Wi-Fi hotspot* ▤ *AE, DC, MC, V* ⏍ *BP.*

5

$ ⊞ **Torre Dorada Residencial.** What this hotel lacks in location, it more than makes up for with its cheerful staff and clean, comfortable rooms. Sitting on a quiet patch of suburban Cusco and run by the ever-endearing Peggy, Torre Dorada makes a great place to regroup after a long flight or strenuous tour. Each floor boasts its own common area with comfy couches and ample tea supply, great for kicking back and relaxing with a book or chatting with fellow travelers. Oxygen is also available upon request. Some rooms feature stunning views, and all are encouraged to enjoy the rooftop terrace. A free shuttle service is available to anyone wishing to spend the day or evening in town. Guests are also introduced to Cusco and surroundings with a free map and brief run-down with Peggy. **Pros:** quiet and comfortable with a noteworthy staff and variety of other travelers. **Cons:** a bit far from the center of town. ⊠ *Calle los Cipreses N-5* ☎ *084/241–698* ⊕ *www.torredorada.com.pe* 🛏 *18 rooms* 🛎 *In-room: no a/c, safe, no TV, Wi-Fi. In-hotel: room service, laundry service, Internet terminal, Wi-Fi hotspot.* ═ *V* ⏐◎⏐ *BP.*

NIGHTLIFE AND THE ARTS

Cusco is full of bars and discos with live music and DJs playing everything from U.S. rock to Andean folk. Though dance clubs levy a cover charge, there's usually someone out front handing out free passes to tourists. Many clubs cater to an under-thirty crowd. Bars, especially around the Plaza de Armas, frequently position someone in front to entice you in with a coupon for a free drink, but that drink is sometimes made with the cheapest, gut-rottingest alcohol the bar has available. On the brighter side, in recent years as Cusco's culinary scene has moved in, so have more upscale, less clubby lounges that are popular with the over-thirty crowd.

BARS AND PUBS

For a cold beer and English soccer broadcast via satellite, try **The Cross Keys** (⊠ *Triunfo 350 2nd fl., Plaza de Armas* ☎ *084/229–227* ⊕ *www.cross-keys-pub-cusco-peru.com*), a classy pub that will make London expats homesick. Challenge the regulars to a game of darts at your own risk. For more upscale drinks, check out the pisco bar at **Limo** (⊠ *Portal de Carnes 236, 2nd fl., Plaza de Armas* ☎ *084/240–668* ⊕ *www.cuscorestaurants.com*). While also functioning as a high-end restaurant, the bar here mixes some of the tastiest pisco drinks—in any variation or flavor—around. Not cheap, but if you like pisco sours, don't miss it. The second-floor, dark-wood **Paddy Flaherty's** (⊠ *Triunfo 124, Plaza de Armas* ☎ *084/247–719*) mixes pints of Guinness and old-fashioned Irish pub grub with Philly steaks, pita sandwiches, and chicken baguettes. The second-floor **Norton Rat's Tavern** (⊠ *Santa Catalina Angosta N. 116, Plaza de Armas* ☎ *084/246–204* ⊕ *www.nortonrats.com*) is Cusco's answer to a U.S.-style sports bar, with billiards, good burgers, darts, and a big-screen satellite TV showing U.S. sports. It also has a great outdoor balcony over the Plaza de Armas. In San Blas, the intimate **7 Angelitos Cafe** (⊠ *Siete Angelitos 638, San Blas* ☎ *084/806–070*) often highlights live local eclectic, but mostly rock, bands. While you're in San Blas you should check out the comfy **Muse Too** (⊠ *Tandapata 917, San*

Blas ☎ *084/762–602*), a small, sleek euro-styled café that serves drinks and live music nightly.

DANCE CLUBS

Step into the Plaza at night and you'll be fighting off offers of free entry passes and free drinks from touts eager to get you into their sticky-carpeted venue. The drinks may be rotten and the music may be reggaeton, but they're good fun if you want to boogie. **El Muki** (✉ *Santa Catalina Angosta 114* ☎ *084/227–797*), resembling a little cave, is a pop music playground that's popular with the younger crowd. Reputed to be Cusco's first disco, dating all the way back to 1985, **Kamikase** (✉ *Kusipata 274, Plaza Regocijo* ☎ *084/233–865*) is a favorite gringo bar, though plenty of locals visit, too, and has a mix of salsa, rock, and folk music. **Mama Africa** (✉ *Portal de Panes 109, 2nd fl., Plaza de Armas*), Cusco's hottest reggae and hip-hop dance venue, has a small cyber café. Dance the night away at **Ukukus** (✉ *Plateros 316, 2nd fl.* ☎ *084/254–911* ⊕ *www.ukukusbar.com*), a hugely popular pub and disco that hops with a young crowd most mornings until 5 AM.

FOLKLORE

If you don't fancy the show at the Qosqo Centro de Arte Nativo many of the restaurants around the Plaza de Armas (like Paititi) offer you a similar package. Starting at around 8 PM you'll be treated to an Andean folkloric show while you're dining, the cost of which is usually included in the meal price.

A fun addition to the Boleto Turístico scheme is the **Qosqo Centro de Arte Nativo** (✉ *Av. El Sol 604* ☎ *084/227–901*). The cultural center holds hour-long folkloric dance performances in its auditorium each night at 6:30 and 8, with introductions in Spanish and English. You may be one of the lucky audience members called up to participate in the final number.

Tunupa (✉ *Portal de Confiturías 233, Plaza de Armas* ☎ *084/252–936*) has a nightly folklore show along with fine dining. At **La Retama** (✉ *Portal de Panes 123, Plaza de Armas* ☎ *084/242–620* ⊕ *www.laretama. info*) you'll enjoy Andean music during dinner each evening. **Paititi** (✉ *Portal de Carrizos 270, Plaza de Armas* ☎ *084/252–686*) presents a folklore show during dinner most nights. **Bagdad Café** (✉ *Portal de Carnes 216, Plaza de Armas* ☎ *084/239–949*) has live music during dinner many nights of the week, but with no fixed schedule.

GAY AND LESBIAN

Rainbow flags fly everywhere in Cusco and you might think the city is just really gay-friendly. But you're actually seeing the flag of Cusco, based on the banner of Tawantinsuyo, the Inca empire. The gay scene is actually pretty limited. **Fallen Angel** (✉ *Plazoleta Nazarenas 221* ☎ *084/258–184* ⊕ *www.fallenangelincusco.com*) sponsors occasional gay and lesbian events, such as cabaret nights, holiday celebrations, and parties. Check out the Web site for dates and more information.

LECTURES AND MUSEUMS

Most museums close their doors before dark, but the **Museo de Arte Precolombino** (✉ *Plazoleta Nazarenas 231* ☎ *084/233–210*) stays open until 10 each evening year-round, if your nightlife tends toward the artsy pre-Columbian kind. Top off an evening of intellect with a late-night bite at the museum's snazzy, glassed-in **MAP Café** (☎ *084/242–476*).

If you're up for an intellectual, but fun, evening, **South American Explorers** (✉ *Atoqsaycuchi 670, San Blas* ☎ *084/245–484* ⊕ *www.saexplorers. org*) holds talks on themes of tourist or cultural interest almost every week. The subject might be a mini-Quechua lesson, Peruvian food and drink, a shamanic ceremony, or the screening of a Latin American film. The cost and schedule varies; check the Web site for monthly activities and prices. The gatherings are a great way to meet other travelers.

THEATER

Fodor's Choice
★
☪

Kusikay (✉ *Teatro Kusikay, Calle Unión 117* ☎ *084/255–414* ⊕ *www. kusikay.com*) should not be missed. Devoted to presenting Andean history and mythology, Kusikay is a theater-dance-acrobatics spectacular, with some of the best costumes this side of Cirque du Soleil. It's a surprisingly modern setup, with moving sets and a huge cast of more than 30 actors. Each show runs for around a year; all take local history and mythology as their subject. ■TIP➜This is a great opportunity to hear Quechua spoken, as the performances mix Spanish and Quechua dialogue. Brochures in English explain the plot, and kids will be entranced by the colorful spectacle and acrobatics.

SHOPPING

Cusco is full of traditional crafts, artwork, and clothing made of alpaca, llama, or sheep wool. Beware of acrylic fakes. For the best quality products, shop in the higher end stores. The export of artifacts would require a government permit, so banish any thoughts of waltzing off with the Inca ruler Pachacutec's cape for a song.

Vendors, usually children, will approach you relentlessly on the Plaza de Armas. They sell postcards, finger puppets, drawings, and CDs of Andean music. A simple "no, gracias" is usually enough to indicate you're not interested; if that doesn't work, just keep walking and say it again. Going to art school is a popular thing for students, so you are likely to find some nice paintings in the mix. Several enclosed crafts markets are good bets for bargains. Even the upscale shops are sometimes amenable to offering a discount if these three conditions are met: 1) it's the September–May off-season; 2) you came into the store on your own, without a guide who will expect a commission from the shop; and 3) you pay in cash. General rule of thumb: the more items you buy, the more of a discount you'll get.

ART REPLICAS

Apacheta (✉ *Calle San Juan de Dios 250* ☎ *084/238–210* ⊕ *www. apachetaperu.com*) deals in replicas of pre-Columbian art, mostly ceramics, and contemporary designs. The shop works directly with its artisan suppliers, giving fair prices to them and to you, and a high degree of attentive service. **Ilaria** is an internationally recognized shop based in Lima, with multiple shops in Cusco. This is Cusco's finest jewelry, with an ample selection of replicas of colonial-era pieces. We list the address of the main shop in Cusco, but both the Monasterio and Libertador Hotels have an Ilaria as well. (⊠ *Portal de Carrizos 258, Plaza de Armas* ☎ *084/246– 253* ⊕ *www.ilariainternational.com*)

CERAMICS

In San Blas, the **Galería Mérida** (⊠ *Carmen Alto 133* ☎ *084/221–714*) sells the much-imitated ceramics of Edilberto Mérida. **Seminario** (⊠ *Portal de Carnes, Haukaypata, Plaza de Armas* ☎ *084/201–002* ⊕ *www. ceramicaseminario.com*) is the Cusco shop of famed ceramics maker Pablo Seminario. Prices are lower at the source in the Sacred Valley town of Urubamba.

CRAFTS AND GIFTS

Galería Latina (⊠ *Calle Mantas 118* ☎ *084/228–931* ⊕ *www.galerialatina-quito.com*) is a reasonably priced crafts shop with many original pieces, tapestries, ceramics, and alpaca clothing among them. Religious art, including elaborately costumed statues of the Virgin Mary, is sold at the shop at the **Galería Mendívil** (⊠ *Plazoleta San Blas* ☎ *084/240–527, 084/274–6622* ⊕ *www.artemendivil.com*). The popular Museo Hilario Mendívil is located across the Plaza.

Triunfo is lined with crafts shops as far as San Blas. One of the best, **Muñecas Maxi** (⊠ *Sunturwasi [Triunfo] 393* ☎ *084/225–492*), sells dolls in historical and local costumes. You can even have one custom-made. Also on display are *retablos* (wooden boxes) that show Cusco's most popular sites and alpaca jackets decorated with local weavings. If you're looking for modern twists on folkloric crafts, check out **Arte y Canela** (⊠ *Portal de Panes 143, Plaza de Armas* ☎ *084/221–519* ⊕ *www. arteycanela.com*), which sells a variety of high-end silver jewelry and household goods, all with a regional artistic flair.

TEXTILES

Long-established and über-modern **Kuna** (⊠ *Plaza Regicijo 202* ☎ *084/243–233*) has alpaca garments, and is one of the only authorized distributors of high-quality vicuña scarves and sweaters. Run by Peruvian design company Alpaca 111, they have shops at the Libertador and Monasterio hotels as well as at the airport. **Perú Étnico** (⊠ *Portal Mantas 114* ☎ *084/232–775* ⊠ *Portal de Carnes 232, Haukaypata, Plaza de Armas* ☎ *084/238–620* ⊠ *Santa Catalina* ☎ *084/229–184*) has three downtown locations with fine alpaca coats, sweaters, scarves, and shawls. With several stores in Cusco, **Alpaca's Best** (⊠ *Portal Confiturias 221, Haukaypata, Plaza de Armas* ☎ *084/249–406*) sells quality knits, but also has a good selection of jewelry. If you knit or know of someone back home who does, check out **Hilados de Alpaca** (⊠ *Av. Diagonal/ Ramon Zavaleta N. 110 Wanchaq* ☎ *084/601–434*) in the commercial

CLOSE UP

Alpaca Or Acrylic?

Vendors and hole-in-the-wall shop-keepers will beckon you in to look at their wares: "One of a kind," they proudly proclaim. "Baby alpaca, hand woven by my grandmother on her deathbed. It's yours for S/70."

Price should be the first giveaway. A real baby-alpaca sweater would sell for more than S/200. So maintain your skepticism even if the label boldly states 100% BABY ALPACA. False labels are common on acrylic-blend clothing throughout the Cusco area. Which brings us to our next clue: A good-quality label should show the maker's or seller's name and address. You're more likely to find quality goods at an upscale shop, of which there are several around town. Such a business is just not going to gamble its reputation on inferior products.

Texture is the classic piece of evidence. Baby-alpaca products use hairs, 16–18 microns in diameter, taken from the animal's first clipping. Subsequent shearings from a more mature alpaca yield hairs with a 20-micron diameter, still quite soft, but never matching the legendary tenderness of baby alpaca. (For that reason, women tend toward baby-alpaca products; men navigate toward regular alpaca.) A blend with llama or sheep's wool is slightly rougher to the touch and, for some people, itchier to the skin. And if the garment is too silky, it's likely a synthetic blend. (The occasional 100% polyester product is passed off as alpaca to unsuspecting buyers.)

While "one of a kind" denotes unique-ness—and, again, be aware that much of what is claimed to be handmade here really comes from a factory—the experts say there is nothing wrong with factory-made alpaca products. A garment really woven by someone's grandmother lacks a certain degree of quality control, and you may find later that the dyes run or the seams come undone.

—by Jeffrey Van Fleet

district. This is luxury clothier and the Michell Group's alpaca yarn outlet; choices include much sought after baby alpaca. While it may be several soles and lots of traffic lights to get there, it's worth it—you can't get 12 spools of pure baby alpaca yarn for S/60 any place else.

Alpaca gets the camelid's share of attention for use in making fine garments, but **La Casa de la Llama** (⊠ *Palacio 121* ☎ *084/240–813*) sells a fine selection of expensive clothing made from the softer hairs sheared from its namesake animal's chest and neck. It's difficult to tell the difference in texture between llama and adult alpaca, at least in this shop.

Several artisan markets and cooperatives populate the city. The **Center for Traditional Textiles of Cusco** (⊠ *Av. El Sol 603* ☎ *084/228–117*) is a nonprofit organization dedicated to the survival of traditional textile weaving. Weavers from local villages work in the shop, and the on-site museum has informative exhibits about weaving techniques and the customs behind traditional costume. Sweaters, ponchos, scarves, and wall hangings are sold at fair-trade prices. The municipal government operates the **Centro Artesanal Cusco** (⊠ *Tullumayo and El Sol* ☎ *No phone*), containing 340 stands of artisan vendors.

The **Feria Inca** (⊠ *At San Andrés and Quera*) is a small and informal crafts market, but bargains can be found. Forget to pack your winter jacket for the Inca Trail? No problem: check out **RKF** (⊠ *Portal Carrizos 252, Plaza de Armas* ☏ *084/254–895*), where you'll find a variety of quality (mostly imported) outdoor goods like North Face jackets and Merrill boots. If you are looking for technical trekking gear you'll likely find it at **Tatoo** (⊠ *Medio 130, Plaza de Armas* ☏ *084/247–277*).

SIDE TRIPS FROM CUSCO

Cusco may be enchantingly beautiful, but with the constant hassle to *buy buy buy,* it's not the most relaxing place on earth. Yet just outside the city lies one of Peru's most spectacular and serene regions, filled with Andean mountains, tiny hamlets, and ancient Inca ruins. In a half-day trip you can visit some of Peru's greatest historical areas and monuments, just beyond Cusco's city limits, such as Sacsayhuamán, perched high on a hill overlooking the city, or the spectacular sights of Qenko, Puka Pukara, and Tambomachay.

The Urubamba Valley, located northwest of Cusco and functioning as the gateway to the Sacred Valley of the Inca, which extends further northwest, attracts the puma's share of visitors going to Machu Picchu, especially those looking to catch their breath—and some R & R—in the region's idyllic setting. Additionally, the Valle del Sur, a stretch of highway running southeast of Cusco to Sicuani, boasts lesser-known, but equally impressive, Inca and pre-Inca sites.

GETTING HERE AND AROUND

The sites immediately north of Cusco (Sacsayhuamán, Qenko, Puka Pukara, and Tambomachay) are best and most easily taken in via an organized tour. Although both the Urubamba Valley and Valle del Sur are readily accessible by public transportation, most travelers prefer the convenience of a tour to bouncing between buses—the entire site-seeing circuit is about 170 km (105 mi).

Tours are easily organized from one of the many kiosks in Cusco ($15–$30 USD), or if you prefer a more intimate, less tourist-driven trip you can hire a taxi ($60–$70 USD) and a guide ($60 USD). Both PeruRail and Inca Rail offer train service from Cusco to Ollantaytambo. ⇨ *see By Train at the start of this chapter.*

SACSAYHUAMÁN

Fodor'sChoice   *2 km (1 mi) north of Cusco.*
★
Towering high above Cusco, the ruins of Sacsayhuamán are a constant reminder of the city's Inca roots. You may have to stretch your imagination to visualize how it was during Inca times—much of the site was used as a convenient source of building material by the conquering Spanish, but plenty remains to be marveled at. Huge stone blocks beg the question of how they were carved and maneuvered into position, and the masterful masonry is awe-inspiring. If you're not moved by stonework, the spectacular views over the city are just as eye-catching.

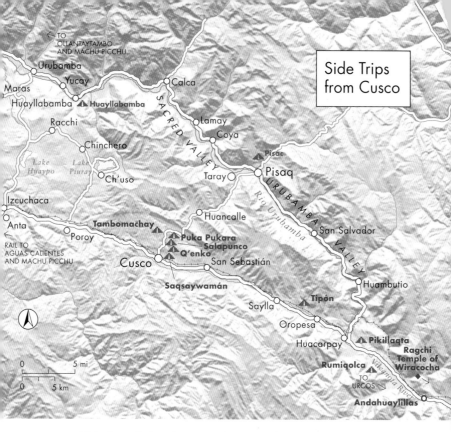

If the Incas designed Cusco in the shape of a puma, then Sacsayhuamán represents its ferocious head. ■TIP➔ Perhaps the most important Inca monument after Machu Picchu, Sacsayhuamán is thought to have been a military complex during Inca times. From its strategic position high above Cusco, it was excellently placed to defend the city, and its zigzag walls and cross-fire parapets allowed defenders to rain destruction on attackers from two sides.

Construction of the site began in the 1440s, during the reign of the Inca Pachacutec. It's thought that 20,000 workers were needed for Sacsayhuamán's construction, cutting the astonishingly massive limestone, diorite, and andesite blocks—the largest is 361 tons—rolling them to the site, and assembling them in traditional Inca style to achieve a perfect fit without mortar. The probable translation of Sacsayhuamán, "city of stone," seems apt. The Inca Manco Cápac II, installed as puppet ruler after the conquest, retook the fortress and led a mutiny against Juan Pizarro and the Spanish in 1536. Fighting raged for 10 months in a valiant but unsuccessful bid by the Inca to reclaim their empire. History records that thousands of corpses from both sides littered the grounds and were devoured by condors at the end of the battle.

Today only the outer walls remain of the original fortress city, which the Spanish tore down after the rebellion and then ransacked for years as a source of construction materials for their new city down the hill, a practice that continued until the mid-20th century. One-fifth of the original complex is left; nonetheless, the site is impressive. Sacsayhuamán's three original towers, used for provisions, no longer stand, though the foundations of two are still visible. The so-called Inca's Throne, the Suchuna, remains, presumed used by the emperor for reviewing troops. Today those parade grounds, the Explanada, are the ending point for the June 24 Inti Raymi festival of the sun, commemorating the winter solstice and Cusco's most famous celebration.

> ### ACCLIMATIZING IN THE SACRED VALLEY
>
> An increasingly popular option for acclimatizing is to touch down in Cusco and head directly to the Sacred Valley. The patchwork of pastures roll loosely alongside rocky red cliffs, and life sways lazily to the sibilant croon of the Urubamba river; a balmy and breath-catching 2,000 meters (6,562 feet) below the clamoring cobblestone streets of Cusco. Most Sacred Valley hotels will provide transportation to and from the airport in Cusco upon request.

These closest Inca ruins to Cusco make a straightforward half-day trip from the city, and provide a great view over Cusco's orange rooftops. If you don't have a car, take a taxi, or if you want to test yourself, the ruins are a steep 25-minute walk up from the Plaza de Armas. ■TIP→ A large map at both entrances shows the layout of Sacsayhuamán, but once you enter, signage and explanations are minimal. Self-appointed guides populate the entrances and can give you a two-hour tour for S/40. Most are competent and knowledgeable, but depending on their perspective you'll get a strictly historic, strictly mystical, strictly architectural, or all-of-the-above type tour. (But all work the standard joke into their spiel that the name of the site is pronounced "sexy woman.")

It's theoretically possible to sneak into Sacsayhuamán after hours, but lighting is poor, surfaces are uneven, and robberies have occurred at night.

GETTING HERE AND AROUND

Sacsayhuamán sits a stone's throw from Cusco and is easily visited in a half-day organized tour (the tour will likely also visit Puka Pukara, Salapunco, and Tambomachay, and possibly other destinations). If your lungs and legs are up to it, the self-guided 40-minute ascent to Sacsayhuamán offers an eye-catching introduction to colonial Cusco. The walk starts from the Plaza de Armas and winds uphill along the pedestrian-only Resbalosa Street. Make your way past San Cristóbal Church, hang a left at the outstretched arms of the white statue of Christ, and you're almost there. ⊠ *Km 2, Hwy. to Pisac* 🕾 *No phone* 🎟️ *Boleto Turístico* ⊙ *Daily 7–6.*

QENKO

4 km (2½ mi) north of Cusco.

It may be a fairly serene location these days, but Qenko, which means "zigzag," was once the site of one of the Incas' most intriguing and potentially macabre rituals. Named after the zigzagging channels carved into the surface, Qenko is a large rock thought to have been the site of an annual pre-planting ritual in which priests standing on the top poured *chicha*, or llama blood, into a ceremonial pipe, allowing it to make its way down the channel. If the blood flowed left, it boded poor fertility for the coming season. If the liquid continued the full length of the pipe, it spelled a bountiful harvest. ■ TIP➔ Today you won't see any blood, but the carved channels still exist and you can climb to the top to see how they zigzag their way down. Other symbolic carvings mix it up on the rock face, too—the eagle-eyed might spot a puma, condor, and a llama. ⊠ *Km 4, Hwy. to Pisac* ☎ *No phone* ⬚ *Boleto Turístico* ⊗ *Daily 7–6.*

SALAPUNCO

5 km (3 mi) northeast of Cusco.

In a culture that worshipped the sun, dark and cavernous Salapunco denotes an intriguing change. A collection of small caves that once held Inca mummies, Salapunco is thought to have been devoted to the worship of the moon. Inside each of the caves were altars and walls decorated with puma and snake motifs, the Inca symbols for earth and the underworld, respectively. The largest cavern saw elaborate full-moon ceremonies in Inca times. The position of the entrance allows the interior to be bathed once a month by the light of the moon. Unfortunately all the mummies are long gone. ⊠ *Km 5, Hwy. to Pisac* ☎ *No phone* ⬚ *Free* ⊗ *Daily 7–5:30.*

PUKA PUKARA

10 km (6 mi) north of Cusco.

Little is known of the archaeological ruins of Puka Pukara, a pink-stone site guarding the road to the Sacred Valley. Some archaeologists believe the complex was a fort—its name means "red fort"—but others claim it served as a hunting lodge and storage place used by the Inca nobility. Current theory holds that this center, likely built during the reign of the Inca Pachacutec, served all those functions. Whatever it was, it was put in the right place. Near Tambomachay, this enigmatic spot provides spectacular views over the Sacred Valley. Pull up a rock and ponder the mystery yourself. ⊠ *Km 10, Hwy. to Pisac* ☎ *No phone* ⬚ *Boleto Turístico* ⊗ *Daily 7–6.*

TAMBOMACHAY

11 km (6½ mi) north of Cusco.

Ancient fountains preside over this tranquil and secluded spot, which is commonly known as "El Baño del Inca," or, Inca's Bath. The name actually means "cavern lodge" and the site is a three-tiered *huaca* built of elaborate stonework over a natural spring, which is thought to have been used for ritual showers. Interpretations differ, but the site was likely a place where water, considered a source of life, was worshipped (or perhaps just a nice place to take a bath). The huaca is almost certain to have been the scene of sacred ablutions and purifying ceremonies for Inca rulers and royal women. ⊠ *Km 11, Hwy. to Pisac* 🕾 *No phone* 📧 *Boleto Turístico* ⊘ *Daily 7–6.*

VALLE DEL SUR

The Río Urubamba runs northwest and southeast from Cusco. The northwest sector of the river basin is the romantically named "Sacred Valley of the Inca," but along the highway that runs southeast of Cusco to Sicuani is an as-interesting region locals call the Valle del Sur. The area abounds with opportunities for off the beaten path exploration. Detour to the tiny town of Oropesa and get to know this self-proclaimed capital of brick-oven bread making; a tradition that's sustained local families for more than 90 years. Or you can side-trip to more pre-Inca and Inca sites. ■TIP➜ You may have these magnificent ruins all to yourself, as they are off the traditional tourist circuit. Only admission to Tipón and Pikillacta is included in the Boleto Turístico. ⇨ *see Buying a Boleto Turístico, above.*

TIPÓN

26 km (15½ mi) southeast of Cusco.

Everyone has heard that the Incas were good engineers, but for a real look at just how good they were at land and water management, head to Tipón. Twenty kilometers (12 miles) or so south of Cusco, Tipón is a series of terraces, hidden from the valley below, crisscrossed by stone aqueducts and carved irrigation channels that edge up a narrow pass in the mountains. A spring fed the site and continually replenished a 900-cubic-meter reservoir that supplied water to crops growing on the terraces. ■TIP➜ So superb was the technology that several of the terraces are still in use today, and still supplied by the same watering system developed centuries ago. The ruins of a stone temple of undetermined function guard the system, and higher up the mountain are terraces yet to be completely excavated. The rough dirt track that leads to the complex is not in the best of shape and requires some effort to navigate. If you visit, either walk up (about two hours each way) or go in a four-wheel-drive vehicle (about 45 minutes to the site and 30 minutes back). ⊠ *4 km (2½ mi) north of Km 23, Hwy. to Urcos* 🕾 *No phone* 📧 *Boleto Turístico* ⊘ *Daily 7–6.*

PIKILLACTA

6 km (3½ mi) east of Tipón; 7 km (4 mi) south of Oropesa.

For a reminder that civilizations existed in this region before the Incas, head to Pikillacta, a vast city of 700 buildings from the pre-Inca Wari culture, which flourished between AD 600 and 1000. Over a 2-km site you'll see what remains of what was once a vast walled city with enclosing walls reaching up to 7 meters (23 feet) in height and many two-story buildings, which were entered via ladders to doorways on the second floor. Little is known about the Wari culture, whose empire once stretched from near Cajamarca to the border of the Tiahuanaco near Lake Titicaca. It's clear, however, that they had a genius for farming in a harsh environment and like the Incas built sophisticated urban

Peruvian women lead furry animals by the Inca site of Sacsayhuamán.

centers such as Pikillacta (which means the "place of the flea"). At the thatch-roofed excavation sites, uncovered walls show the city's stones were once covered with plaster and whitewashed. A small museum at the entrance houses a scattering of artifacts collected during site excavation, along with a complete dinosaur skeleton. Across the road lies a beautiful lagoon, Lago de Lucre. ⊠ *Km 32, Hwy. to Urcos* ☎ *No phone* ✉ *Boleto Turístico* ☉ *Daily 7–6.*

RUMICOLCA
3 km (2 mi) east of San Pedro de Cacha.

An enormous 12-meter- (39-foot-) high gate stands at Rumicolca, sitting a healthy walk uphill from the highway. It served as the border checkpoint and customs post at the southern entrance to the Wari empire. The Inca enhanced the original construction of their predecessors, fortifying it with andesite stone and using the gate for the same purpose. ⊠ *Km 32, Hwy. to Urcos* ☎ *No phone* ✉ *Free* ☉ *Daily 24 hrs.*

ANDAHUAYLILLAS
40 km (32 mi) southeast of Cusco.

The main attraction of the small town of Andahuaylillas, 8 km (5 mi) southeast of Pikillacta, is a small 17th-century adobe-towered **church** built by the Jesuits on the central plaza over the remains of an Inca temple. The contrast between the simple exterior and the rich, expressive, colonial baroque art inside is notable: fine examples of the Cusqueña school of art decorate the upper interior walls. ■ **TIP→** Traces of gilt that once covered the church walls are still visible. The town's name is a corruption of *Antawaylla,* Quechua for "copper prairie." ⊠ *Km 40,*

Hwy. to Urcos ☎ *No phone* 🖥 *S/5* 🕐 *Daily 7:30–5:30. Masses: Tues. andThurs. 8 am, Sat. 6 pm, Sun. 10:30 am.*

RAQCHI (TEMPLE OF WIRACOCHA)
4 km (2½ mi) east of San Pedro de Cacha.

The ruins of this large temple in the ancient town of Raqchi give little indication of their original purpose, but if size counts, then they are truly impressive. ■TIP→ Huge external walls up to 12 meters (39 feet) high still tower overhead. You'll be forgiven for thinking that the place was once an Inca version of the Colossium, or a football stadium. Legend has it that the Temple of Raqchi was built in homage to the god Viracocha, to ask his intercession in keeping the nearby Quimsa Chata volcano in check. The ploy worked only some of the time. The site, with its huge adobe walls atop a limestone foundation, performed multiple duties as temple, fortress, barracks, and storage facility. ✉ *Km 80, Urcos–Puno Hwy.* ☎ *No phone* 🖥 *S/5* 🕐 *Daily 9–5:30.*

SACRED VALLEY OF THE INCA

A pleasant climate, fertile soil, and proximity to Cusco made the Urubamba River valley a favorite with Inca nobles, many of whom are believed to have had private country homes here. Inca remains, ruins, and agricultural terraces lie throughout the length of this so-called Sacred Valley of the Inca. Cusco is hardly the proverbial urban jungle, but in comparison the Sacred Valley is positively captivating with its lower elevation, fresher air, warmer temperatures, and rural charm. You may find yourself joining the growing ranks of visitors who base themselves out here and make Cusco their day trip, rather than the other way around.

WHEN TO GO
The valley has increasingly taken on a dual personality, depending on the time of day, day of the week, and month of the year. Blame it on Pisac and its famous three-times-weekly market. Every Cusco travel agency offers a day tour of the Sacred Valley each Tuesday, Thursday, and Sunday to coincide with the town's market days, and they all seem to follow the same schedule: morning shopping in Pisac, buffet lunch in Urubamba, afternoon browsing in Ollantaytambo. You can almost always sign up for one of these tours at the last minute—even early on the morning of the tour—especially if you're here in the September-to-May off-season. On nonmarket days and during the off-season, however, Pisac and the rest of the Sacred Valley is relatively quiet. In any case, the valley deserves more than a rushed day tour if you have the time.

> ### BOLETO TURÍSTICO
>
> Four Sacred Valley sites (Pisac, Chinchero, Moray, and Ollantaytambo) fall under Cusco's Boleto Turístico scheme. ⇨ *see Buying a Boleto Turístico at the start of this chapter.* The ticket's 10-day validity lets you take in these four attractions as well, and is the only way to gain admission. An abbreviated S/70 ticket, valid for two days, also gains you admission to the four sites in the valley.

GETTING AROUND

Highways are good and traffic is relatively light in the Sacred Valley, but any trip entails a series of twisting, turning roads as you head out of the mountains near Cusco and descend into the valley. Most people get here by way of an organized tour. However, you can grab one of PeruRail's trains from Cusco to Ollantaytambo and then hire a taxi or collectivo to take you around the Valley. Alternatively, you can hire a taxi from Cusco ($60–70 USD), or take a bus ($2–$3.50 USD). Buses depart daily from Av. Grau 525 in Cusco. ■TIP➔ Watch for the rompe-muelle signs warning you of the series of speed bumps as you pass through populated areas. The road to Machu Picchu ends in Ollantaytambo; beyond that point, it's rail only.

TARAY

23 km (14 mi) north of Cusco.

The road from Cusco leads directly to the town of Taray. The Pisac market beckons a few kilometers down the road, but Taray makes a worthwhile pre-Pisac shopping stop. Devastating flooding in March 2010 destroyed nearly 80% of the town's homes. At this writing rebuilding is still underway, with some residents residing in makeshift tents. However, a herculean effort has been made to get the town's main infrastructure up and running at full steam again.

Awana Kancha, whose Quechua name loosely translates as "palace of weaving," provides an opportunity to see products made from South America's four camelids (alpaca, llama, vicuña, and guanaco) from start to finish: the animal, the shearing, the textile weaving and dyeing, and the finished products, which you can purchase in the show room. ✉ *Km 23, Carretera a Pisac* ☎ *084/203–287* ⊕ *www.awanakancha. com* ✉ *Free* ⊗ *Daily 8–5.*

PISAC

9 km (5 mi) north of Taray.

The colorful colonial town of Pisac, replete with Quechua-language masses in a simple stone church, a well-known market, and fortress ruins, comes into view as you wind your way down the highway from Cusco. (You're dropping about 600 meters (1,970 feet) in elevation when you come out here from the big city.) Pisac, home to about 4,000 people, anchors the eastern end of the Sacred Valley and, like much of the region, has experienced a surge of growth in recent years, with new hotels and restaurants popping up in and around town. An orderly grid of streets forms the center of town, most hemmed in by a hodge-podge of colonial and modern stucco or adobe buildings, and just wide enough for one car at a time. (Walking is easier and far more enjoyable.) The level of congestion (and fun) increases dramatically each Tuesday, Thursday, and especially Sunday when one of Peru's most celebrated markets comes into its own, but much more spectacular are the ruins above. Admission to the ruins is included in both the Boleto Turístico and Boleto Parcial.

WHERE TO EAT AND STAY

$ **✕ Mullu Café.** Rustic but stylish, Mullu Café has a cosmopolitan flair
PERUVIAN and specializes in Andean fusion fare. The food and drinks, along with
the upbeat atmosphere, can't be topped. Grab a table for dinner overlooking the Plaza de Armas and you might think you were in Cusco
for the night. If you're looking for a lunch spot, come early as the place
tends to fill up. ⊠ *Plaza de Armas 352, Pisac* ☎ *084/203–073* ⊟ *MC, V.*

¢ **✕ Panadería.** The unnamed bakery just off the Plaza Constitución is
VEGETARIAN a Pisac institution. Vegetarian empanadas and homemade breads are
delivered from the clay oven and into your hands. The lines are long
on Tuesday, Thursday, and Sunday market days but it's worth the wait.
⊠ *Mariscal Castilla 372* ☎ *No phone* ⊟ *No credit cards* ⊙ *No dinner.*

$ **✕ Ulrike's Café.** German transplant Ulrike Simic and company dish up
CAFÉ food all day long, the perfect refueling stop during a day of market
shopping. Breakfast gets underway, before the market does, at 7:30
AM. ■**TIP→** Stop by for the S/20 prix-fixe lunch, with a lot of vegetarian
options on the menu, a real rarity in this part of Peru. They've got good à
la carte soups and pizzas, too. Yummy brownies, muffins, cheesecake,
and chocolate-chip cookies are the draw all day long between rounds of
shopping. ⊠ *Plaza Constitución 828* ☎ *084/203–061* ⊟ *No credit cards.*

$ **⊞ Hotel Royal Inka Pisac.** Just outside of town is the newest branch of
Peru's Royal Inka hotel chain, and the closest lodging to the Pisac ruins.
Bright carpeted rooms congregate around acres of wooded and flowered
grounds, and have print spreads and drapes and white walls. All third-
level rooms have a fireplace. With all the activities and facilities here,
you really never have to leave the grounds. **Pros:** lots of activities; clean
and comfortable. **Cons:** outside of town. ⊠ *Km 1½, Carretera a Pisac
Ruinas* ☎ *084/203–064; 866/554–6028 in North America* ⊕ *www.
royalinkahotel.com* ↝ *80 rooms* ⟁ *In-room: safe, Wi-Fi. In-hotel: 2
restaurants, room service, bar, tennis court, pool, bicycles* ⊟ *AE, DC,
MC, V* ⊺⊙⊦ *BP.*

$ **⊞ Paz y Luz.** Bright airy rooms, sky-lighted bathrooms, and mountain
☽ views characterize this growing hotel just outside of town. The entire
complex conjures feelings implied in its name: peace and light. Besides
relaxation, Paz y Luz also offers organized tours and healing ceremonies. Families looking to stay a bit longer can settle into one of the
four on-site suites, complete with a kitchen. The hotel doesn't have a
street address, but it's easily found by following the signs around town.
Pros: excellent for families and big groups, especially conference cadres.
Cons: not the most centrally-located. ⊠ *1 km (1/2 mi) past the bridge,
one the right* ☎ *084/203–204* ⊕ *www.pazyluzperu.com* ↝ *24 rooms*
⟁ *In-room: safe. In-hotel: restaurant, room service, laundry service,
Wi-Fi hotspot* ⊟ *No credit cards.* ⊺⊙⊦ *BP.*

$ **⊞ Pisac Inn.** Renovated in 2010, this already homey place now boasts
☽ an even brighter face, and it's on the main square. Common areas have
murals crafted by the Peruvian-American owners; Andean tapestries
hang in the rooms. Breakfasts feature delicious homemade bread from
on-site Cuchara de Palo restaurant. **Pros:** convenient location; serene
space. **Cons:** basic room amenities. ⊠ *Plaza de Armas* ☎ *084/203–
062* ⊕ *www.pisacinn.com* ↝ *12 rooms* ⟁ *In-room: no phone, no TV.*

Restaurants ▼

Mullu Café **3**

Panaderia **1**

Ulrike's Cafe **2**

Hotels ▼

Hotel Royal
Inka Pisac **2**

PazyLuz **3**

Pisac Inn **1**

In-hotel: room service, bicycles, laundry service, Internet terminal ▭ *MC, V* ⧉ *BP.*

YUCAY

46 km (28 mi) northwest of Pisac.

The explosive growth of nearby Urubamba has practically engulfed the tiny village of Yucay, to the point of barely being able to tell where one ends and the other begins. Yucay proper is only a few streets wide, with a collection of attractive colonial-era adobe and stucco buildings, and a pair of good-choice lodgings on opposite sides of a grassy plaza in the center of town.

WHERE TO STAY

$$ ⛪ **La Casona de Yucay.** The 1810 home of Manuel de Orihuela hosted South American liberator Simón Bolívar, and you can stay in Room 136 where he slept during his 1825 visit. Spacious rooms contain colonial-style furnishings and are arranged in blocks around four courtyards, lush with flowered gardens. **Pros:** historic setting. **Cons:** some people think history is boring. ⊠ *Plaza Manco II 104* ☎ *084/201–116* ⊕ *www. hotelcasonayucay.com* ⤳ *53 rooms* ⚬ *In-room: safe, no TV. In-hotel:*

restaurant, room service, bar, spa, laundry service, Internet terminal ⊟ *AE, DC, MC, V.*

$$$ ⚏ **Sonesta Posada del Inca Valle Sagrado.** In the heart of the Sacred Val-
★ ley is this 300-year-old former convent (monastery). The cobblestone
walkways are the perfect complement to the well-preserved colonial-
era church on the grounds. The rooms, with tile floors, wood ceilings,
and hand-carved headboards, have balconies that overlook the gardens
or the terraced hillsides. A few rooms have access for people with dis-
abilities, a rarity in this part of the country, but they must be reserved
in advance. The restaurant has excellent regional fare and a popular
Sunday lunch buffet. **Pros:** good restaurant; historic setting. **Cons:** some
people prefer modern. ⊠ *Plaza Manco II 123* ☏ *084/201–107; 01/712–
6060 in Lima; 800/766–3782 in North America* ⊕ *www.sonestaperu.
com* ⤳ *84 rooms* ⚐ *In-room: safe. In-hotel: restaurant, bar, spa, laun-
dry service, Wi-Fi hotspot* ⊟ *AE, MC, V.*

URUBAMBA

2 km (1 mi) west of Yucay; 29 km (17 mi) northwest of Chinchero.

Spanish naturalist Antonio de León Pinedo rhapsodized that Urubamba
must have been the biblical Garden of Eden, but you'll be forgiven if
your first glance at the place causes you to doubt that lofty claim: the
highway leading into and bypassing the city, the Sacred Valley's admin-
istrative, economic, and geographic center, shows you miles of gas sta-
tions and convenience stores. But get off the highway and get lost in
the town's tidy streets, awash in flowers and pisonay trees, and enjoy
the spectacular views of the nearby mountains. You might agree with
León Pinedo after all. Urubamba holds little of historic interest but the
scenery, a growing selection of top-notch hotels and restaurants, and
easy access to Machu Picchu rail service make the town an appealing
place in which to base yourself.

ESSENTIALS

CURRENCY   Banco de la Nación (⊠ *Mariscal Castilla s/n* ☏ *084/201–291*).

MAIL   SERPOST (⊠ *Jr. Comercio 407, Urubamba*).

WHERE TO EAT AND STAY

$ ✕ **Inka's House.** Urubamba has become buffet-lunch central—it's the
PERUVIAN midday stopping point for the organized Sacred Valley day tours—but
this second-floor restaurant on the main road in the center of town is
the best of the bunch. Whether you come in a group or on your own,
the friendly staff greets you with a complimentary pisco sour before
you get up from your table to get in line for a more than ample sup-
ply of food. (You can order from the à-la-carte menu, too.) It's all to
the accompaniment of live Andean folk music. ⊠ *Av. Ferrocarril s/n*
☏ *084/434–616* ⊟ *AE, DC, V.*

¢ ⚏ **Hospedaje Los Jardines.** Some remodeling coupled with the carefully
tended and colorful grounds continues to sustain this longtime favor-
ite in the center of town. Eleven rooms populate a rambling house
behind a wall on a quiet street. All have hardwood floors, tile baths, and
attractive Venetian blinds. Lovely wood headboards and dressers and

Continued on page 263

Valley in the vicinity of Ollantaytambo near Cusco, Peru.

TOURING THE SACRED VALLEY

by Jeffery Van Fleet

You've come to Cusco to see Machu Picchu, but you'll spend at least one day touring the Sacred Valley. Not only is it chock-full of major archaeological sights, but its small towns and easy-living pace invite you to slow down. If the Inca emperors favored the warm, fertile valley as a place for cultivation and recreation, so should you.

The Sacred Valley follows the Urubamba River from the town of Pisac, about 30 km (18 mi) northeast of Cusco, and ends 60 km (36 mi) northwest of Cusco at Ollantaytambo. Beyond that point, the cliffs flanking the river grow closer together, and the agriculturally rich floodplain thins to a gorge as the Urubamba begins its abrupt descent toward the Amazon basin.

What makes the valley "sacred"? The Inca named rivers by sector and called this stretch of the Urubamba Wilcamayu, "the sacred river." Spanish explorers applied the concept to the entire valley, calling it the Valle Sagrado. The tourist industry likes the appealing, evocative name, too.

The entire area, though very rural, is served by good roads and public transportation except to the Moray and Salineras sites. The best options are to rent a car or join a tour.

SACRED VALLEY

2,460m
(8,072ft)
Machu
Picchu

Aguas Calientes
2,082m (6,833ft)

Inti Punku
Wiñay Wayna
Huyupatamarka
Sayacmarca
Yancachimpa
Runkurakay
Wayllabamba
Llactapata

The Inca Trail

CORDILLERA

URUBAMBA

SACRED VALLEY

Río Urubamba

Ollantaytambo
One of the region's loveliest towns, with its namesake ruins high above, marks the beginning of the Inca Trail and has a rail connection to Machu Picchu.

Yucay & Urubamba
Two pleasant towns with some good hotels and restaurants are alternatives to staying in the "big city" of Cusco.

Ollantaytambo
2,800m
(9,186ft)

Salineras
Moray
Maras

Urubamba

Yucay

Huayllabamba

Anta
Iscuchaca
Racchi
Chinchero

Huayllabamba

Calca

Chuso

Lamay

Poroy

Coya

Sacsayhuamán
Tambomachay
Puka
Pukara
Huancalle
Qenko
Salapunco
Taray

3,310m
(10,860ft)

Cusco

Paro Parc
Pisac

Pisac

3,444m
(11,300ft)

San Sebastián

San Salvador

Saylla

Tipón

Salineras
These centuries-old terraced Inca salt pans are still used today.

Moray
This site is an ancestor of the modern experimental agricultural station. The Inca created varying environmental zones with their enormous circular terraces.

0   5 mi

0   5 km

Pisac Market
Travelers throng to Pisac's famous twice-weekly market; this is one of Peru's most touristy things to do. On Sunday, catch the colorful mass.

Pisac Ruins
A masterpiece of Inca engineering, centuries later the site is in remarkable condition, with masonry more precise than Machu Picchu's.

PISAC

Pisac market vendor

PISAC MARKET

Pisac's famous market—held each Tuesday, Thursday, and Sunday—draws locals and tourists alike. Fruits, vegetables, and grains share the stage with ceramics, jewelry, and woolens on the central plaza and spill over into the side streets. Sellers set up shop about 9 AM on market days and start packing up at about 5 PM. The market is not so different from many others you'll see around Peru, only larger. Go on Sunday if your schedule permits; you'll have a chance to take in the 11 AM Quechua Mass at the Iglesia San Pedro Apóstolo and watch the elaborate costumed procession led by the mayor, who carries his *varayoc*, a ceremonial staff, out of the church afterward. Sunday afternoon sees bands and beer tents—this is small-town Peru at its best. ☉ Sun., Tues., and Thurs. 9 to 5.

PISAC RUINS

From the market area, drive or take a taxi S/15–S/20 one-way up the winding road to the Inca ruins of Pisac. Visiting on market day is your best bet for finding easy transportation up; the alternative is a steep two-hour walk from town. It's most crowded on Sunday; the rest of the week there will be few other people.

Archaeologists originally thought the ruins were a fortress to defend against fierce Antis (jungle peoples), though there's little evidence that battles were fought here. Now it seems that Pisac was a bit of everything: citadel, religious site, observatory, and residence, and may have served as a refuge in times of siege. The complex also has a temple to the sun and an astronomical observatory, from which priests calculated the growing season each year. Narrow trails wind tortuously between and through solid rock. You may find yourself practically alone on the series of paths in the mountains that lead you among the ruins, through caves, and past the largest known Inca cemetery (the Inca buried their dead in tombs high on the cliffs). Just as spectacular *as* the site are the views *from* it.

Farther above are more ruins and burial grounds, still in the process of being excavated. ▨ Boleto Turístico ☉ Daily 7–6.

Inca Pisac ruins on a high bluff.

OLLANTAYTAMBO

Women in Ollantaytambo, Peru.

The town is pronounced "oy-yahn-tie-tahm-bo" but everyone calls it "Ollanta" for short. It was named for Ollantay, the Inca general who expanded the frontiers of Tawantinsuyo as far north as Colombia and as far south as Argentina during the reign of the Inca Pachacutec. The general asked for the hand of the emperor's daughter, a request Pachacutec refused. Accomplished though Ollantay was, he was still a commoner. The general rebelled against the ruler and was imprisoned. Ollantay's love may have met a bad end, but yours will not when you glimpse the stone streets and houses, mountain scenery, some of the most lush territory in the valley, and great ruins.

Inca ruins, Ollantaytambo.

FORTRESS OF OLLANTAYTAMBO

Walk above the town to a formidable stone structure where massive terraces climb to the peak. It was the valley's main defense against the Antis tribes from the neighboring rain forests. Construction began during the reign of Pachacutec but was never completed. The rose-color granite used was not mined in this part of the valley. The elaborate walled complex contained a temple to the sun, used for astronomical observation, as well as the Baños de la Ñusta (ceremonial princess baths), leading archaeologists to believe that Ollantaytambo existed for more than defensive purposes.

The fortress was the site of the greatest Inca victory over the Spanish during the wars of conquest. The Manco Inca fled here in 1537 with a contingent of troops after the disastrous loss at Sacsayhuamán and routed Spanish forces under Hernando Pizarro. The victory was short-lived: Pizarro regrouped and took the fortress. ⊠ Plaza Mañay Raquy 🎫 Boleto Turístico ⊙ Daily 7–6.

OLLANTAYTAMBO HERITAGE TRAIL

This self-guided trail allows you to tour the original layout of the town, following a series of blue plaques that outline important sites. Attribute the town's distinctive appearance to Inca organization. They based their communities on the unit of the cancha, a walled city block, each with one entrance leading to an interior courtyard, surrounded by a collection of houses. The system is most obvious in the center of town around the main plaza. You'll find the most welcoming of these self-contained communities at Calle del Medio.

armoires fill each room in this entirely no-smoking property. Breakfast is served in an antique-filled dining room. **Pros:** cozy setting; good value. **Cons:** service is very hands-off, so not for people seeking instant attention when needed. ⊠ *Jr. Convencíon 459* ☎ *084/201–331* ⊕ *www.los-jardines-urubamba.com* ⤵ *11 rooms* ⚬ *In-room: no TV (some)* ⊟ *AE, MC, V.*

$$ ⊞ **Hotel Libertador Tambo del Inka.** Renovated in 2008, the sprawling complex sits on the edge of Urubamba's curving river. All 128 state-of-the-art rooms have hardwood floors, two beds, and great mountain views. The sophisticated restaurant specializes in a variety of Peruvian and international dishes, and the über-trendy bar features an entirely onyx-clad wall. With plenty of room to spare, the hotel also offers an on-site spa and fitness center. Access to the Machu Picchu trains doesn't get any better: the hotel sits right across from Urubamba's rail station. **Pros:** secluded with riverfront views. **Cons:** huge modern resort; not for those seeking intimate atmosphere. ⊠ *Av. Ferrocarril s/n* ☎ *511/518-6500; 084/581–777* ⊕ *www.libertador.com.pe* ⤵ *128 rooms* ⚬ *In room: safe, Wi-Fi. In-hotel: restaurant, bar, pools, gym, spa, laundry service* ⊟ *AE, DC, MC, V* �|◎| *BP.*

$$$$ ⊞ **Hotel San Agustín (Monasterio de la Recoleta).** The San Agustín, part of a Peruvian hotel chain, is the quintessential two-in-one lodging. On the main road is a modern hacienda-style hotel with gleaming rooms, modern services, and all the comforts you could desire. Up the hill is the scaled-up Recoleta, a 16th-century Franciscan monastery with a cavernous dining room; guest rooms with hardwood floors, white walls, and Cusqueña paintings, and a bell tower with great views of the valley. There are fewer services at the monastery, though most guests don't mind. All have access to the facilities down the hill. **Pros:** historical setting. **Cons:** slightly outside of town. ⊠ *Km 69, Carretera Pisac–Ollantaytambo* ☎ *084/201–443 or 084/201–666* ⊕ *www.hotelessanagustin.com.pe* ⤵ *30 rooms* ⚬ *In room: safe, Wi-Fi. In hotel: restaurant, room service* ⊟ *AE, DC, MC, V* �|◎| *BP.*

$$$$ ⊞ **Rio Sagrado.** Drop your bags at Rio Sagrado and you'll quickly check stress at the door. Sprawled across 2.5 hectares of greenery, and situated alongside the Urubamba River, this retreat gives tranquility a run for its money. Each room comes with riverfront views, outshined only by the cheery alpaca blankets and embroidered throw pillows—both of which, along with shampoos and soaps, are locally made. The only thing better than the views and the rooms is the sanguine staff and first-rate service. Even if you came to see the valley, don't be afraid to spend a couple days idling about the property; horseback riding and adventure tours can be arranged at reception, and cooking classes are available on request. The Friday night barbeque on the terrace is another must-do. Rio Sagrado's charm isn't surprising: the hotel is an offshoot of Orient Express (owners of Cusco's Monasterio) and PeruRail. **Pros:** self-sufficient, serene, and personalized service. **Cons:** a bit outside of town. ⊠ *Km 75.8 Carratera Cusco-Urubamba* ☎ *084/201–631, 511/610–8300* ⊕ *www.riosagrado.com* ⤵ *24 rooms* ⚬ *In-room: no phone (some), safe, Wi-Fi. In-hotel: restaurant, room service, bar, spa, laundry service, Wi-Fi hotspot* ⊟ *AE, D, DC, MC, V* �|◎| *BP.*

5

☎ **Sol y Luna Lodge & Spa.** A lovely addition to the Sacred Valley of the Inca, this hotel has bungalows surrounded by flower gardens. Nearby are the Perol Chico stables, where you can book trips through this beautiful valley on the stable's famous Peruvian *caballos de paso*. The Viento-Sur Adventure Club at the hotel also offers paragliding, biking, and walking tours. **Pros:** tranquil setting; many activities. **Cons:** a few miles outside of town. ⊠ *Fundo Huincho, 2 km west of Urubamba* ☎ *084/201–620* ⊕ *www.hotelsolyluna.com* ☞ *24 bungalows* ♿ *In-room: safe, DVD (some), Wi-Fi. In-hotel: restaurant, room service, bar, pool, spa, laundry service* ⊟ *AE, DC, MC, V* ⦾⦿ *BP.*

SHOPPING

Cusco transplants and husband-and-wife team Pablo Seminario and Marilú Bejar and their German shepherds run the **Cerámica Seminario** in the center of town. They take the valley's distinctive red clay and turn it into ceramic works using modern adaptations of ancient indigenous techniques and designs. ⊠ *Berriozabal 111* ☎ *084/201–002* ⊕ *www. ceramicaseminario.com* ☉ *Daily 8–7.*

CHINCHERO

28 km (17 mi) northwest of Cusco.

Indigenous lore says that Chinchero, one of the valley's major Inca cities, was the birthplace of the rainbow. Frequent sightings during the rainy season might convince you of the legend's truth. Chinchero is one of the few sites in the Sacred Valley that's higher (3,800 meters or 12,500 feet) than Cusco.

Today, tourists and locals frequent the colorful Sunday artisan market on the central plaza, an affair that gets rave reviews as being more authentic and less touristed than the larger market day in neighboring Pisac. A corresponding Chinchero produce market for locals takes place at the entrance to town.

Amble about the collection of winding streets and adobe houses, but be sure to eventually make your way towards one of the weaving cooperatives, where a gaggle of local women will entertain you into understanding the art of making those lovely alpaca sweaters you eyed in the market.

EXPLORING

A 1607 colonial **church** in the central plaza was built on top of the limestone remains of an Inca palace, thought to be the country estate of the Inca Tupac Yupanqui, the son of Pachacutec. ⊠ *Plaza de Armas* ☎ *No phone* ☒ *Boleto Turístico* ☉ *Tues.–Sun. 8–5.*

Centro de Producción Artesanías Andina. This is one of the more organized places to learn about Chinchero's weaving tradition and techniques. Guests are welcomed with a cup of coca tea and then whisked through a series of hands-on explanations of the washing, dyeing, and weaving processes. There is also a good selection of hand-woven sweaters and tapestries for sale. ⊠ *Calle Albergue 5* ☎ *084/876–246* ⊟ *MC, V* ☉ *Daily 10–6.*

Trails Other Than The Inca Trail

Trekking to this Inca site of Choquequirao is a serious trek of at least four days.

The popularity of the Inca Trail and the scarcity of available spots have led to the opening of several alternative hikes of varying length and difficulty.

The two- to seven-day **Salcantay** trek is named for the 6,270-meter (20,500-foot) peak of the same name. It begins at Mollepata, four hours by road from Cusco, and is a strenuous hike that goes through a 4,800-meter (15,700-foot) pass. The Salcantay excursion joins the Inca Trail at Huayllabamba.

The **Ausangate** trek takes its name from the Nevado Ausangate, 6,372 meters (20,900 feet) in elevation, and requires a day of travel each way from Cusco in addition to the standard five to six days on the trail. Nearly the entire excursion takes you on terrain over 4,000 meters (13,100 feet).

Multiday hikes through the **Lares Valley**, north of Urubamba and Ollantaytambo, offer a little bit of everything for anyone who enjoys the outdoors; a series of ancient trails once used by the Inca wind their way through native forests and past lakes fed by runoff from the snowcapped mountains nearby. Excursions also offer a cultural dimension, with stops at several traditional Quechua villages along the way. The Lares trek compares in difficulty to the Inca Trail.

The lesser-known but remarkably rewarding trek to **Choquequirao** (Cradle of Gold) takes in stunning Andean scenery as you make your way to ruins that have been heralded as Machu Picchu's "Sacred Sister." The site, another long-lost Inca city still under excavation and not yet engulfed by mass tourism, sits at 3,100 meters (10,180 feet). The 4- to 11- day treks entail a series of steep ascents and descents.

The **Chinchero–Huayllabamba** trek has two selling points: it can be accomplished in one day—about six hours—and is downhill much of the way, although portions get steep. The hike begins in Chinchero, north of Cusco, and follows an Inca trail that offers splendid views as you descend into the Sacred Valley towards the small village of Huayllabamba.

WHERE TO STAY

¢ ⊞ **La Casa de Barro.** This "house of adobe," with its ochre walls and eucalyptus-wood roof, is the main lodging option here, and its just fine if you're looking for a cute hotel and don't mind not being right in town. Rooms have wood floors, bright spreads, drapes, throw rugs, and big windows with views of the valley. Some come with their own small balconies. **Pros:** cozy setting; good value. **Cons:** isolated location. ⊠ *Miraflores 147* ☎ *084/306–031* ⊕ *www.lacasadebarro.com* ⟲ *11 rooms* ⌂ *In-room: no phone, no TV. In-hotel: restaurant, bar, laundry service* ⊟ *No credit cards* ◎ *BP.*

MORAY AND SALINERAS

48 km (29 mi) northwest of Cusco.

Scientists still marvel at the agricultural technology the Inca used at Moray. Taking advantage of four natural depressions in the ground and angles of sunlight, indigenous engineers fashioned concentric circular irrigation terraces, 150 meters (500 feet) from top to bottom, and could create a difference of 15°C (60°F) from top to bottom. The result was a series of engineered mini-climates perfect for adapting, experimenting, mixing, matching, and cultivating foods, especially varieties of maize, the staple of the Inca empire, normally impossible to grow at this altitude. Though the technology is attributed to the Inca, the lower portions of the complex are thought to date from the pre–Inca Wari culture. Entrance to Moray is included in the Boleto Turístico.

The famed terraced Inca salt pans of Salineras are still in use and also take advantage of a natural phenomenon: the Inca dug shallow pools into a sloped hillside. The pools filled with water, and upon evaporation salt crystallized and could be harvested.

S/5 per person, but well-worth it. They're difficult to reach without a tour, and almost impossible during the rainy season. No public transportation serves Moray or Salineras. A taxi can be hired from Maras, the closest village, or from Cusco. Alternatively, it's a two-hour hike from Maras to either site.

OLLANTAYTAMBO

19 km (11 mi) west of Urubamba.

Poll visitors for their favorite Sacred Valley community and the answer will likely be Ollantaytambo—endearingly nicknamed Olly—which lies at the valley's northwestern entrance. Ollantaytambo's traditional air has not been stifled by the invasion of tourists. Ask around for the local *mercado*, situated just off the Plaza de Armas, close to the pick up point for collectivos and taxis. This busy marketplace quietly evades tourism's grasp and offers a behind-the-scenes peak at life beyond the ruins. The juice stations on the second floor, towards the back, might just be the town's best kept secret.

■ **TIP →** Ollantaytambo makes a superb base for exploring the Sacred Valley and has convenient rail connections to Machu Picchu.

Ollantaytambo is also the kickoff point for the Inca Trail. You'll start here at nearby Km 82 if you wish to hike to the Lost City. Walk up to discover the **fortress of Ollantaytambo,** one of the most fantastic ruins in the Sacred Valley.

BCP ATM, on Ventidero 248 inside the entrance to Hostal Sauce, is the most reliable ATM in town. There is one in the Plaza de Armas, but we don't recommend using that one.

> **WIFI IN OLLY**
>
> Wi-Fi is nearly everywhere in town. Many hotels offer computer terminals and a place to check your email or to look up tour information. There are also several cafés along the Plaza de Armas.

ESSENTIALS

ATMs **BCP ATM** (✉ *Ventidero 248, inside the entrance to Hostal Sauce*).

EXPLORING

Awamaki. If you've made it to the Sacred Valley, you've likely seen your share of woven garments. But it's worth swinging by this fair trade shop just down the road from the Plaza de Armas. All goods are produced as part of the Awamaki weaving project, which supports a cooperative of Quechua women from the Patacancha Valley. At this writing, several of the programs normally run through Museo CATCCO (Spanish abbreviation for "Andean Center for Technology and Culture of Ollantaytambo"), are temporarily closed. ✉ *Pilcohausi s/n* ☎ *084/204–149* ⊕ *www.awamaki.org* ☉ *Daily 10–6.*

WHERE TO EAT

¢ ✕ **Café Mayu.** We recommend hunkering down for at least a day or two
CAFÉ in Ollantaytambo, but if you've only got time for a pit stop, Café Mayu is the place to lunch. Located right in front of the train station, this tiny spot serves up big-city-style coffee and a variety of yummy treats. The chocolate chip cookies are as good as they smell, but you can't go wrong with the other treats here, either. ✉ *Train Station* ☎ *084/204–014* ▭ *No credit cards.*

¢ ✕ **Hearts Café.** Occupying a small corner of the Plaza de Armas, Hearts
CAFÉ Café packs a puma's punch worth of tasty, down-home soups, sandwiches, baked goods, and fresh juices. This is the place to come if you're craving comfort food (did we mention the pancakes, French toast, chicken burgers, or birthday cakes made to order?). Besides the food, this place dishes up a hearty serving of humanitarian aid, doubling as both eatery and NGO. Seventy-six-year-old British transplant Sonia Newhouse set up the café-slash-foundation in 2007. She makes it clear, however, that Living Heart is not a handout organization; profits feed into a variety of educational support programs for local women and children. ✉ *Plaza de Armas* ☎ *084/204–078* ⊕ *www.heartscafe.org, www.livingheartperu.org* ▭ *No credit cards.*

$ ✕ **Mayupata.** Spacious and airy, furnished with large wooden tables and
PERUVIAN chairs, this restaurant has the unmistakable air of a tourist-friendly Andean establishment. The menu ranges from traditional Peruvian grilled meats and fish to slightly edgier dishes like Andean ravioli (filled with alpaca). For an all-around good meal, try their specialty—mayupata trucha—with a miracuya-sour cocktail. You'll also find

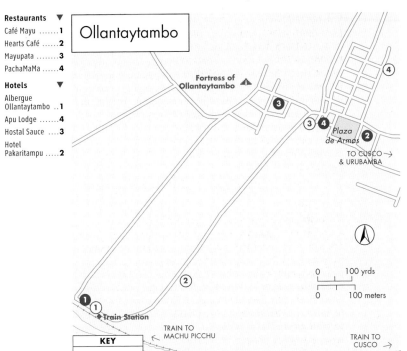

Restaurants ▼
Café Mayu **1**
Hearts Café **2**
Mayupata **3**
PachaMaMa **4**

Hotels ▼
Albergue
Ollantaytambo ..**1**
Apu Lodge **4**
Hostal Sauce **3**
Hotel
Pakaritampu **2**

Ollantaytambo

Fortress of
Ollantaytambo

Plaza
de Armas

TO CUSCO →
& URUBAMBA

5

0   100 yrds
0   100 meters

②

① ①
◆ Train Station

TRAIN TO
← MACHU PICCHU

TRAIN TO
CUSCO →

Rio Urubamba

KEY
❶ *Restaurants*
① *Hotels*

foreigner-friendly staples like wood-oven pizza and Thai fusion plates. ✉ *Av. Concepcion* ☎ *084/204–009* ▭ *MC, V.*

$ ✕**Pachamama.** White linen tablecloths, carefully folded napkins, and
PIZZA   cruets of olive oil and balsamic vinegar give this pizzeria-restaurant the mark of a sophisticated European eatery. A rustic timbered interior adds to the intimate atmosphere and makes an ideal spot to sit back and sip some wine. Get here before dark and watch the ruins turn a kaleidoscope of colors with the descending sun. ✉ *Calle Ventiderio s/n* ☎ *084/204–168* ▭ *AE, DC, MC, V.*

WHERE TO STAY

$ 🛏 **Albergue Ollantaytambo.** Everyone in town knows the Albergue, the town's first hotel. Located right at the train station, it is owned by exuberant longtime American resident and artist Wendy Weeks. Dark-wood rooms here are rustic and spacious, with historic black-and-white photos of the region. The lodging has homey touches like a wood-fired sauna, huge breakfasts, and a cozy sitting room. If you're lucky, you'll arrive just when the chocolate chip cookies emerge from the oven and the whole place smells like Grandma's kitchen. Reserve in advance: the place is popular with groups about to embark on, or just returning from, the nearby Inca Trail. **Pros:** convenient to rail station; relaxing sauna. **Cons:** it's no secret. ✉ *Estación de Ferrocarril* ☎ *084/204–014*

⊕ *www.elalbergue.com* ↵ *16 rooms* ⚘ *In-room: safe, Wi-Fi. In-hotel: restaurant, room service, bar, bicycles, laundry facilities* ⊟ *V* ‖○‖ *BP.*

$ ⊡ **Apu Lodge.** Surrounded by flowers and maturing gardens, Apu Lodge
ↂ   commands a delightful view of the Ollantaytambo ruins from its private grassy perch and is well worth the five-minute meander up cobbled Inca streets from the center of town. Taking its name from the spirit of the mountains, the Lodge offers guests clean, bright, and artfully furnished rooms, complete with celestially comfortable beds. Besides her cheery disposition, owner Louise Norton also offers an endless supply of tea and advice on touring the area. Breakfast commences early in the morning over a communal table and is a great spot to pick other people's brains on things to see and do. **Pros:** gorgeous location and lovely rooms. **Cons:** a few blocks from the center of town. ⊠ *Lari Calle* ☎ *084/797–162* ⊕ *www.apulodge.com* ↵ *11 rooms* ⚘ *In-room: safe, Wi-Fi. In-hotel: Wi-Fi hotspot* ⊟ *No credit cards* ‖○‖ *BP.*

$$ ⊡ **Hostal Sauce.** This cozy, 10-year-old hotel is named for a type of tree found in the Sacred Valley and has nothing to do with gastronomy. Thanks to the hotel's hillside location, half of the vaulted-ceiling rooms have a superb view of the Ollantaytambo ruins. The quaint lobby fireplace is usually stoked with a fire on brisk evenings, which here happens often. **Pros:** clean and modern furnishings; new bedding; good value; great views; has the only reliable ATM in town. **Cons:** no elevator; lots of stairs. ⊠ *Ventiderio 248* ☎ *084/204–044* ⊕ *www.hostalsauce.com. pe* ↵ *8 rooms* ⚘ *In-room: no TV. In-hotel: laundry service, Internet terminal, Wi-Fi hotspot* ⊟ *V* ‖○‖ *BP.*

$$ ⊡ **Hotel Pakaritampu.** Ollantaytambo's best lodging has a Quechua name
Fodor's Choice   that translates as "house of dawn." Reading rooms with fireplaces and
★   Cusqueño art invite you to settle in with a good book and a hot cup of coffee on a chilly evening. Rooms with modern furnishings, plush blue comforters, and green-tile bathrooms extend through two buildings. The on-site orchard supplies the fruit that ends up on your breakfast plate, and in the Peruvian cuisine served in the restaurant. **Pros:** tranquil setting; good restaurant. **Cons:** not for the party types. ⊠ *Av. Ferrocarril s/n* ☎ *084/204–020; 01/242–6278 in Lima* ⊕ *www.pakaritampu.com* ↵ *32 rooms, 1 suite* ⚘ *In-room: no TV. In-hotel: restaurant, bar, laundry service, Internet terminal* ⊟ *AE, MC, DC, V* ‖○‖ *BP.*

Machu Picchu and the Inca Trail

WORD OF MOUTH

"The ride up is amazing as you are getting closer to the mountains. We arrive and there it is in all of its magical splendor. The sun just coming up—I was quite emotional for several hours. A culmination of a life's dream. Hubby just let me blubber. I never dreamed I would be so lucky to see it in person."

—parrmt

WELCOME TO MACHU PICCHU AND THE INCA TRAIL

TOP REASONS TO GO

★ **Discover Ancient Kingdoms:** Hiram Bingham "discovered" Machu Picchu in 1911. Your first glimpse of the fabled city from the Guardhouse will be your own discovery, and every bit as exciting.

★ **The Trail:** The four-day hike of the Inca Trail from near Ollantaytambo to Machu Picchu is Peru's best-known outdoor expedition. Spaces fill up quickly, but never fear: tour operators have opened up some alternative treks.

★ **Ye Olde Technology:** It was the 15th century, yet the Inca made the stones fit perfectly without mortar. The sun illuminates the windows perfectly at the solstice, and the crops grow in an inhospitable climate. And they did it all without bulldozers, tractors, or Google Earth.

★ **Mystery:** Mystics, shamans, spiritualists, astrologers, and UFO spotters, professionals and wannabes, flock to this serene region. Even the most no-nonsense curmudgeons find themselves contemplating history's secrets.

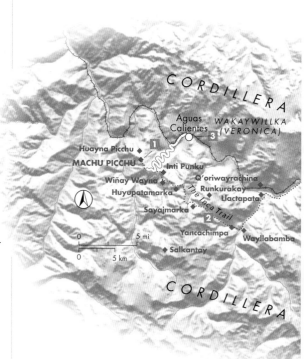

1 Machu Picchu. The two words that are synonymous with Peru evoke images of centuries-old Inca emperors and rituals. Yet no one knows for certain what purpose this mountaintop citadel served or why it was abandoned. Machu Picchu is an easy day trip from Cusco, but an overnight in Aguas Calientes or Ollantaytambo gives you more time to explore and devise your own theories.

2 The Inca Trail. A 50-km (31-mi) sector of the original Inca supply route between Cusco and Machu Picchu has become one of the world's signature treks. No question: you need to be in good shape, and the four-day excursion can be rough going at times, but it's guaranteed to generate bragging rights and immense satisfaction upon completion.

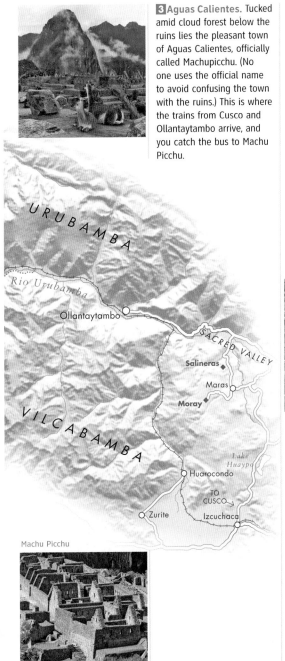

3 **Aguas Calientes.** Tucked amid cloud forest below the ruins lies the pleasant town of Aguas Calientes, officially called Machupicchu. (No one uses the official name to avoid confusing the town with the ruins.) This is where the trains from Cusco and Ollantaytambo arrive, and you catch the bus to Machu Picchu.

GETTING ORIENTED

The famed ruins of Machu Picchu, accessible only via rail or foot, lie farther down the Río Urubamba, among the cloud forests on the Andean slopes above the jungle. Cusco, the region's largest city, is about 112 kilometers (70 miles) southeast.

6

Inca Drawbridge, Machu Picchu.

URUBAMBA

Río Urubamba

Ollantaytambo

SACRED VALLEY

Salineras

Maras

Moray

VILCABAMBA

Lake Huaypo

Huarocondo

TO CUSCO

Zurite

Izcuchaca

Machu Picchu

PLANNING

WHEN TO GO

All the high-season/low-season trade-offs are here. Winter (June through August) means drier weather and easier traveling, but it's prime vacation time for those in the northern hemisphere. Don't forget that three major observances—Inti Raymi (June 24), Peru's Independence Day (July 28), and Santa Rosa de Lima (August 30)—fall during this time, and translate into exceptionally heavy crowds of Peruvian travelers. (Also consider that Sundays are free for Cusqueños.) The result is higher lodging prices and larger crowds. Prices and visitor numbers drop dramatically during the summer rainy season (October through April). Note that January is the height of rainy season and the Inca Trail is closed in February. For near-ideal weather and manageable crowds, consider a spring or fall trip.

On a high-season weekend, Machu Picchu might host in excess of 3,000 visitors a day. By September, daily totals fall to 1,500 visitors, and a typical February day, in the lowest of the low season, sees a relatively paltry 1,000 people pass through the entry turnstiles.

While many travelers day trip to Machu Picchu, an overnight in Aguas Calientes (the town below the site) lets you experience the ruins long after the day-trippers have left, and before the first train and tour groups arrive in the morning.

GETTING HERE AND AROUND

Unless you're hiking the Inca Trail, you must first catch a train to Aguas Calientes. From here, there is an official Consettur tourist bus that takes you to the famed ruins. The 20-minute ride offers hair-raising turns and stunning views of the Vilcanota Valley below. You cannot drive yourself here. ⇨ *For information about seeing the region with a tour operator, also see Chapter 5 "Tours of Cusco, the Sacred Valley, and Machu Picchu."*

BUS TRAVEL

Unless you plan on walking up to Machu Picchu (about an hour up the road from Aguas Calientes) you will have to catch a bus, easily identifiable by the Consettur name on the front. Consettur buses depart from the intersection of Imperio de los Incas Ave and the Aguas Calientes River. Tickets cost $7 USD each way, and can be purchased in advance from the small kiosk across the street from the departure point. Buses leave every 10 minutes starting at 5:30 AM. During peak season, lines for the first bus can get long, so it's recommended that you arrive by 5 AM or earlier.

TRAIN TRAVEL

It's an easy train ride from Cusco or Ollantaytambo to Machu Picchu. Most visitors board the train in Cusco. PeruRail is the longest-standing operator, and offers services from Cusco, Ollantaytambo, and Aguas Calientes. The *Vistadome*, the luxury *Hiram Bingham* and the new *Expedition* (formerly known as the Backpacker) trains leave from Cusco's Poroy station, a 15-minute taxi ride from the Plaza de Armas. Newly operating Inca Rail and Andean Railways offer services only between Ollantaytambo and Aguas Calientes; both rails are expected to increase services by the end of 2011. ⇨ *For a full review of options see the Train to Machu Picchu box in this chapter.*

HEALTH AND SAFETY

Machu Picchu and the Inca Trail are a breath-catching 300–700 meters (980–2,300 feet) *lower* than Cusco. But to be on the safe side about altitude effects, locally known as *soroche*, get an ample intake of fluids and eliminate or minimize alcohol and caffeine consumption. (Both can cause dehydration, already a problem at high altitudes.) Smoking aggravates the problem. Some hotels have an oxygen supply for their guests' use. The prescription drug acetazolamide can help offset the alkalosis caused by low oxygen at high elevations.

Tap water is generally not safe to drink. Stick with the bottled variety, *con gas* (carbonated) or *sin gas* (plain). The San Luis brand is for sale everywhere.

Aguas Calientes employs a cadre of tourist police, whom you'll find stationed throughout the streets. Mudslides are an occasional problem from October–April. Severe flooding in January 2010 destroyed areas along the river, stopping railway service and leaving some tourists stranded. Despite damage to the tracks, rail services resumed in early April 2010, and at the time of this writing it's business as usual in the valley.

RESTAURANTS

The town of Aguas Calientes near Machu Picchu has numerous restaurants, each offering its own take on traveler-tested and approved plates like pizza, Mexican, Chinese, and typical Andean food. Recently Andean fusion, a gourmet play on traditional Peruvian high mountain fare, has also found its way to this once gastronomically boring town. Lunch is served between 1 and 3, the busiest time for restaurants here. Dinner begins around 7, and most restaurants start winding down service at about 9. Most places do stay open in the afternoon if you wish to dine outside these hours.

HOTEL

There is only one hotel at Machu Picchu itself and that is the Machu Picchu Sanctuary Lodge. It will cost you to stay there no doubt, as it's an exclusive property owned by Orient-Express, the same company that operates PeruRail, but it's also the only place you can sit in a

Jacuzzi and look at the Inca city long after the crowds have left. In Aguas Calientes you'll find many hostels and cheaper hotels lining the railroad tracks—that's not as down-at-the-heels as it first sounds: many rooms have great waterfront views. Aguas Calientes' budget lodgings are utilitarian places to lay your head, with a bed, a table, a bathroom, and little else. A handful of hotels offer surprising luxury for such an isolated location. Their rates can be shockingly luxurious, too.

The Big Four lodgings here (Sanctuary Lodge, Inkaterra, Sumaq, and Hatuchay Tower) meet their guests on the rail platforms—look for their signs when you get off the train—and deliver your luggage right to your hotel room. Some of the main roads in this town are quite steep, making such a service especially nice. (They deliver your luggage from hotel to train for your departure, too, but reconfirm this; the train might pull out with you, minus your bags.) Smaller hotels usually meet guests with advance reservations just outside the train station.

Lodgings keep surprisingly early checkout times. (Hotels free up the rooms for mid-morning Cusco–Ollantaytambo–Machu Picchu trains.) Expect to vacate by 9 AM, though this is less strictly enforced in the off-season. Most hotels will hold your luggage if you're not leaving town until later in the day.

Many hotels keep the same official rates year-round but unofficially discount rates during the off-season of mid-September through May.

WHAT IT COSTS IN NUEVO SOLES					
	¢	$	$$	$$$	$$$$
RESTAURANTS	under S/20	S/20–S/35	S/36–S/50	S/51–S/65	over S/65
HOTELS	under S/125	S/125–S/250	S/251–S/375	S/376–S/500	over S/500

Restaurant prices are per person for a main course. Hotel prices are for a standard double room, excluding tax.

AGUAS CALIENTES

But for the grace of Machu Picchu discoverer Hiram Bingham, Aguas Calientes would be just another remote, forgotten crossroads. But 1911, and the tourist boom decades later, forever changed the community. At just 2,040 meters (6,700 feet) above sea level, Aguas Calientes will seem downright balmy if you've just arrived from Cusco. There are but two major streets—Avenida Pachacutec leads uphill from the Plaza de Armas, and Avenida Imperio de los Incas isn't a street at all, but the rail-road tracks; there's no vehicular traffic on the former except the buses that ferry tourists to the ruins. You'll have little sense of Aguas Calientes if you do the standard day trip from Cusco. But the cloud-forest town pulses to a very lively tourist beat with hotels, restaurants, hot springs, and a surprising amount of activity, even after the last afternoon train has returned to Cusco. At this writing, construction was underway for a new sports stadium and theater complex, to be completed in fall 2011.

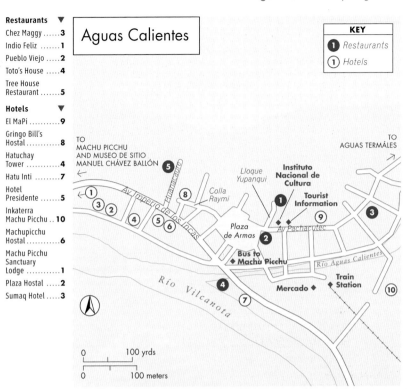

Restaurants ▼

Chez Maggy **3**
Indio Feliz **1**
Pueblo Viejo **2**
Toto's House **4**
Tree House Restaurant **5**

Hotels ▼

El MaPi **9**
Gringo Bill's Hostal **8**
Hatuchay Tower **4**
Hatu Inti **7**
Hotel Presidente **5**
Inkaterra Machu Picchu .. **10**
Machupicchu Hostal **6**
Machu Picchu Sanctuary Lodge **1**
Plaza Hostal **2**
Sumaq Hotel **3**

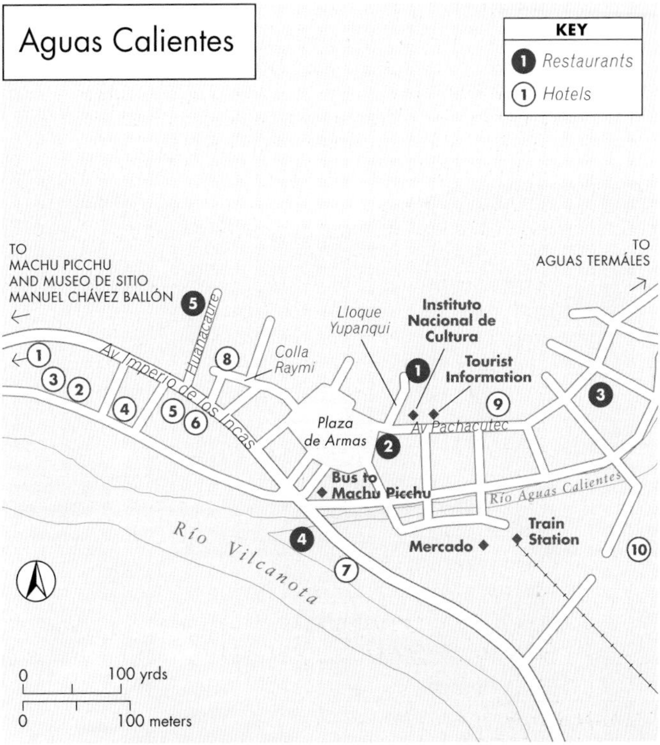
Aguas Calientes
KEY
1 Restaurants
1 Hotels
TO MACHU PICCHU AND MUSEO DE SITIO MANUEL CHÁVEZ BALLÓN
TO AGUAS TERMÁLES
Huanacaure
Av. Imperio de los Incas
Colla Raymi
Lloque Yupanqui
Instituto Nacional de Cultura
Tourist Information
Av Pachacutec
Plaza de Armas
Bus to Machu Picchu
Río Aguas Calientes
Train Station
Mercado
Río Vilcanota
0
100 yrds
0
100 meters

GETTING HERE AND AROUND

Trains to Aguas Calientes depart daily from Cusco's Poroy Station, as well as Ollantaytambo, and Urubamba. In spite of its steep side streets, the city is small and easily explored by ambling about on foot.

ESSENTIALS

Currency **Banco de Crédito** (✉ *Av. Imperio de los Incas s/n* ☎ *084/211–342*).

Mail **SERPOST** (✉ *Collaraymy 13*).

EXPLORING

Aguas Termales. Aguas Calientes (literally "hot waters") takes its name from these thermal springs that sit above town. Don't expect Baden Baden, but if you aren't too fussy, this can be a refreshing dip at the end of a hot day. ✉ *Top of Av. Pachacutec* ☎ *No phone* 🎫 *S/10* 🕒 *Daily 6 AM–8 PM.*

Mercado Artesanal (Craft market). A warren of vendors' stalls lines the couple of blocks between the rail station and the bus stop for shuttle transport up to the ruins. Most newly arrived passengers fresh off the train are anxious to get to the bus and up to Machu Picchu, but you'll likely find yourself with more time to spend in the afternoon before your train leaves. Don't expect anything *too* out of the ordinary; it's

Continued on page 295

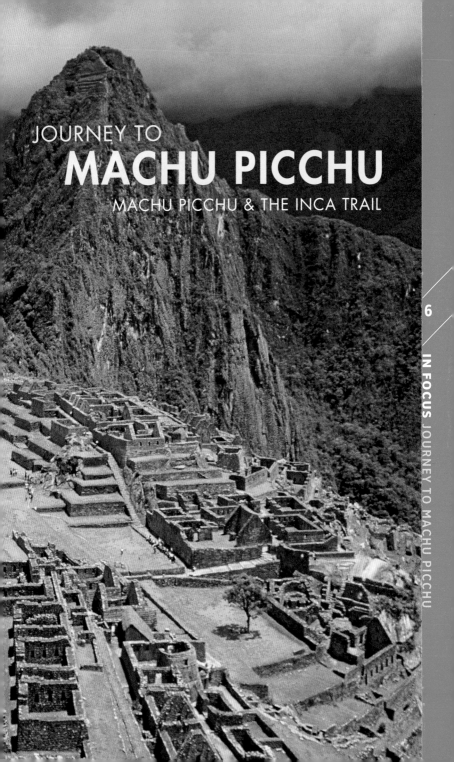

JOURNEY TO
MACHU PICCHU
MACHU PICCHU & THE INCA TRAIL

MACHU PICCHU & THE INCA TRAIL

Guardhouse

The exquisite architecture of the massive Inca stone structures, the formidable backdrop of steep sugarloaf hills, and the Urubamba River winding far below have made Machu Picchu the iconic symbol of Peru. It's a mystical city, the most famous archaeological site in South America, and one of the world's must-see destinations.

The world did not become aware of Machu Picchu's existence until 1911 when Yale University historian Hiram Bingham (1875–1956) announced that he had "discovered" the site. "Rediscovery" is a more accurate term; area residents knew of Machu Picchu's existence all along. This "Lost City of the Inca" was missed by the ravaging conquistadors and survived untouched until the beginning of the 20th century.

You'll be acutely aware that the world has since discovered Machu Picchu if you visit during the June–mid–September high season. Machu Picchu absorbs the huge numbers of visitors, though, and even in the highest of the high season, its beauty is so spectacular that it rarely disappoints.

DISCOVERY

American explorer and historian Hiram Bingham, with the aid of local guides, came across the Lost City in 1911. Though the name appeared on maps as early as 1860, previous attempts to find the site failed. Bingham erred in recognizing what he had uncovered. The historian assumed he had stumbled upon Vilcabamba, the last real stronghold of the Inca. (The actual ruins of Vilcabamba lie deep in the rain forest, and were uncovered in the 1960s.)

Bingham, who later served as governor of and senator from Connecticut, transported—some say stole—many of Machu Picchu's artifacts to Yale in 1912. They are still on display at the Peabody Museum. The museum is in no hurry to give them back, but negotiations, often contentious, are under way to return some of the treasures to Peru.

In 1915, Bingham announced his discovery of the Inca Trail. As with Machu Picchu, his "discovery" was a little disingenuous. Locals knew about the trail, and that it had served as a supply route between Cusco and Machu Picchu during Inca times. Parts of it were used during the colonial and early republican eras as well.

Though archaeological adventuring is viewed differently now, Bingham's slog to find Machu Picchu and the Inca Trail was no easy feat. Look up from Aguas Calientes, and you still won't know it's there.

HISTORY
Ever since Bingham came across Machu Picchu, its history has been debated. It was likely a small city of some 200 homes and 1,000 residents, with agricultural terraces to supply the population's needs and a strategic position that overlooked—but could not be seen from—the valley floor.

New theories suggest that the city was a transit station for products, such as coca and hearts of palm that were grown in the lowlands and sent to Cusco. Exactly when Machu Picchu was built is not known, but one theory suggests that it was a country estate of an Inca ruler named Pachacuti, which means its golden age was in the mid-15th century.

Historians have discredited the romantic theory of Machu Picchu as a refuge of the chosen Inca women after the Spanish conquest; analysis shows a 50/50 split of male and female remains.

The site's belated discovery may indicate that the Inca deserted Machu Picchu before the Spanish conquest. The reason for the city's presumed abandonment is as mysterious as its original function. Some archaeologists suggest that the water supply simply ran out. Some guess that disease ravaged the city. Others surmise it was the death of Pachacutec, after which his estate was no longer needed.

"INDIANA" BINGHAM

Hiram Bingham at Machu Picchu, 1912.

A globe-trotting archaeological explorer, which was an especially romantic figure in early 20th century America, Hiram Bingham was a model for the Indiana Jones character in the film *Raiders of the Lost Ark*.

Storage Houses

Guardhouse

EXPLORING THE RUINS

Everyone must go through the main entrance to have their ticket stamped. Those arriving from the Inca Trail enter the park via a path leading past the Guardhouse, away from the main entrance but they must exit the park, then enter again through the ticket booth. From there you work your way up through the agricultural areas and to the urban sectors.

There are almost no signs inside to explain what you're seeing; booklets and maps are for sale at the entrance. Restrooms are outside the front gate, but not inside the ruins. You can exit and re-enter as many times as you'd like as long as you show your ticket.

The English-language names to the structures within the city were assigned by Bingham. Call it inertia, but those labels have stuck, even though the late Yale historian's nomenclature was mostly offbase.

The Storage Houses are is the first structures you encounter after coming through the main entrance. The Inca carved terraces into the hillsides to grow produce and minimize erosion. Corn was the likely crop cultivated. The semitropical climate meant ample rain for most of the year.

The Guardhouse and Funeral Rock are a 20-minute walk up to the left of the entrance, and provide the quintessential Machu Picchu vista. You've seen the photos, yet nothing beats the view in person, especially with a misty sunrise. Bodies of nobles likely lay in state here, where they would have been eviscerated, dried, and prepared for mummification.

The Temple of the Sun is a marvel of perfect Inca stone assembly. On June 22 (winter solstice in the southern hemisphere), sunlight shines through a small, trapezoid-shape window and onto the middle of a large, flat granite stone presumed to be an Inca calendar. Looking out the window, astronomers saw the constellation Pleiades, revered as a symbol of crop fertility. Bingham dubbed the small cave below the Royal Tomb, though no human remains were found here.

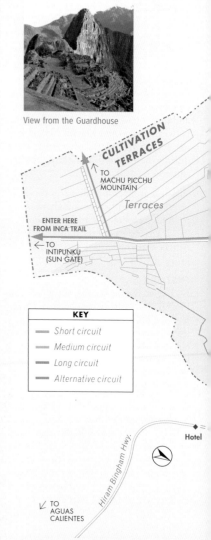

View from the Guardhouse

KEY
▬▬ *Short circuit*
▬▬ *Medium circuit*
▬▬ *Long circuit*
▬▬ *Alternative circuit*

CULTIVATION TERRACES

TO MACHU PICCHU MOUNTAIN

Terraces

ENTER HERE FROM INCA TRAIL

← TO INTIPUNKU (SUN GATE)

Hotel

Hiram Bingham Hwy.

↙ TO AGUAS CALIENTES

Main Gate

Temple of the Sun

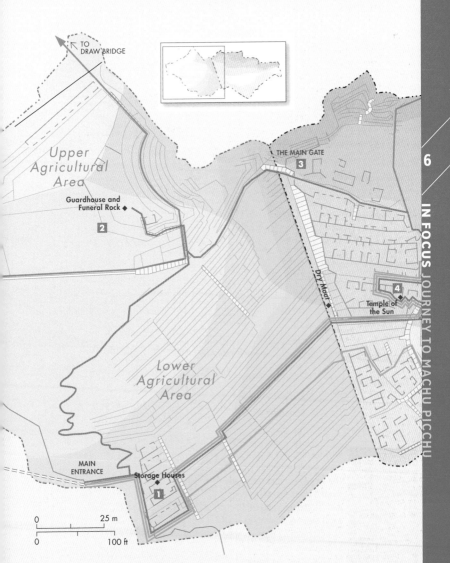

TO
DRAW BRIDGE

Upper
Agricultural
Area

THE MAIN GATE

3

Guardhouse and
Funeral Rock ♦

2

Dry Moat ♦

4

Temple of
the Sun

Lower
Agricultural
Area

MAIN
ENTRANCE

Storage Houses ♦

1

0   25 m

0   100 ft

Principal Temple

Three Windows

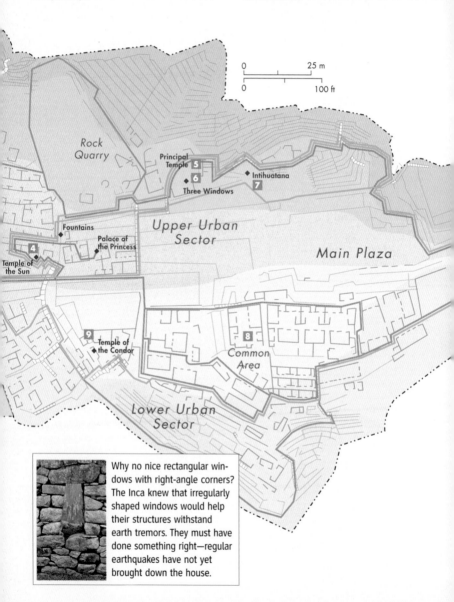

0   25 m

0   100 ft

Rock
Quarry

Principal
Temple **5**

6
Three Windows

Intihuatana
7

Fountains

Palace of
the Princess

4

Temple of
the Sun

Upper Urban
Sector

Main Plaza

9 Temple of
the Condor

8

Common
Area

Lower Urban
Sector

Why no nice rectangular windows with right-angle corners? The Inca knew that irregularly shaped windows would help their structures withstand earth tremors. They must have done something right—regular earthquakes have not yet brought down the house.

7

8

Intihuatana

Common Area

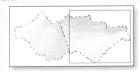

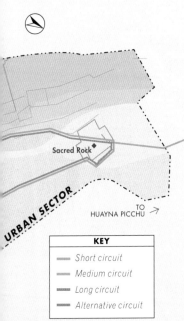

Sacred Rock

URBAN SECTOR

TO
HUAYNA PICCHU →

KEY
Short circuit
Medium circuit
Long circuit
Alternative circuit

Temple of the Condor.

9

Fountains. A series of 16 small fountains are linked to the Inca worship of water.

Palace of the Princess, a likely misnomer, is a two-story building that adjoins the temple.

The Principal Temple is so dubbed because its masonry is among Machu Picchu's best. The three-walled structure is a masterpiece of mortarless stone construction.

Three Windows. A stone staircase leads to the three-walled structure. The entire east wall is hewn from a single rock with trapezoidal windows cut into it.

Intihuatana. A hillock leads to the "Hitching Post of the Sun." Every important Inca center had one of these vertical stone columns (called gnomons), but their function is unknown. The Spanish destroyed most of them, seeing the posts as objects of pagan worship. Machu Picchu's is one of the few to survive—partially at least. Its top was accidentally knocked off in 2001 during the filming of a Cusqueña beer commercial.

The Sacred Rock takes the shape in miniature of the mountain range visible behind it.

The Common Area covers a large grassy plaza with less elaborately constructed buildings and huts.

Temple of the Condor is so named because the positioning of the stones resembles a giant condor, the symbol of heaven in the Inca cosmos. The structure's many small chambers led Bingham to dub it a "prison," a concept that did not likely exist in Inca society.

DID YOU KNOW?

The step terraces you see here were used to grow crops but their main purpose was to minimize erosion.

THE SKINNY ON MACHU PICCHU

DAY TRIPPING VS. OVERNIGHT

You can visit Machu Picchu on a day trip, but we recommend staying overnight at the hotel near the entrance or in Aguas Calientes. A day trip allows you about four hours at Machu Picchu. If you stay overnight you can wander the ruins after most tourists have gone or in the morning before they arrive.

BUYING A TICKET

If you arrive without an admission ticket, you must purchase one in Aguas Calientes at the **Instituto Nacional de Cultura** (⊠ *Avenida Pachacutec s/n,* ☎ *084/211–196* ⚌ *S/126* ⊗ *Daily 5 AM–10 PM* ⊟ *No credit cards*). There is no ticket booth at the ruins' entrance. If you are with a tour, the tickets are most likely taken care of for you. Buy your ticket the night before if you want to get in the park right away; bus service begins at 5:30 AM. From the time you purchase the ticket, you have three days to enter the Inca city, however, once you enter the citadel, the ticket is only valid for that day. So if you arrive in the afternoon and visit the ruins, then stay the night and want to return the next morning, you'll have to buy two tickets.

CATCHING THE BUS

If you're a day-tripper, follow the crowd out of the rail station about two blocks to the **Consettur Machupicchu** shuttle buses, which ferry you up a series of switchbacks to the ruins, a journey of 20 minutes. Buy your $14 round-trip ($7 for children) ticket at a booth across from the line of buses before boarding. Bus tickets can be purchased in US dollars or soles. If you're staying overnight, check in to your lodging first, and then come back to buy a bus ticket.

Buses leave Aguas Calientes for the ruins beginning at 5:30 AM and continue more or less every 10 minutes, with a big push in mid-morning as the trains arrive, until the historic site closes around 5:30 PM. If you're heading back to Cusco, take the bus back down at least an hour before your train departs. It's also possible to walk to and from the ruins to Aguas Calientes but this hike will take you a good hour and a half either way.

BEING PREPARED

Being high above the valley floor makes you forget that Machu Picchu sits 2,490 meters (8,170 ft) above sea level, a much lower altitude than Cusco. It gets warm, and the ruins have little shade. Sunscreen, a hat, and water are musts. Officially, no food or drinks are permitted, but you can get away with a bottle of water. Large packs must be left at the entrance. ■TIP➔ If you want to get your passport stamped, stop by the office inside the gate to the left as you enter.

PRACTICALITIES

A snack bar is a few feet from where the buses deposit you at the gate to the ruins, and the **Machu Picchu Sanctuary Lodge** has a S/100 lunch buffet open to the public. Bathrooms cost S/1, and toilet paper is provided. There are no bathrooms inside the ruins but you may exit and re-enter to use them.

THE INCA TRAIL, ABRIDGED

Some Cusco tour operators market a two-day, one-night Inca Trail excursion as the **Sacred Inca Trail** or **Royal Inca Trail**. It's easier to procure reservations for these trips, but advance reservations with a licensed operator are still essential. The excursion begins at **Km 104**, a stop on the Cusco–Machu Picchu trains. All of the hiking happens on the first dy, and you spend the night at a hotel in Aguas Calientes. The second day is not a trail hike, but a visit to the ruins.

Who needs gardeners? Llamas roam Machu Picchu and keep the grass nice and short.

EXPLORING BEYOND THE LOST CITY

Huiñay Huayna

Several trails lead from the site to surrounding ruins.

If you come by train, you can take a 45-minute walk on a gentle arc leading uphill to the southeast of the main complex. **Intipunku**, the Sun Gate, is a small ruin in a nearby pass. This small ancient checkpoint is where you'll find that classic view that Inca Trail hikers emerge upon. The walk along the way yields some interesting and slightly different angles as well. Some minor ancient outbuildings along the path occasionally host grazing llamas. Intipunku is also the gateway to the **Inca Trail**. A two- or three-hour hike beyond the Intipunku along the Inca Trail brings you to the ruins of **Huiñay Huayna**, a terrace complex that climbs a steep mountain slope and includes a set of ritual baths.

Built rock by rock up a hair-raising stone escarpment, The **Inca Bridge** is yet another example of Inca engineering ingenuity. From the cemetery at Machu Picchu, it's a 30-minute walk along a narrow path.

The **Huayna Picchu** trail, which follows an ancient Inca path, leads up the sugarloaf hill in front of Machu Picchu for an exhilarating trek. Climbers must register at the entrance to the path behind La Roca Sagrada (the Sacred Rock). Limited to 400 visitors daily, no one is permitted entry after 1 PM—the limit is reached long before 1 PM in the high season—and all must be out by 4 PM. The walk up and back takes at least two hours and is only for the sure-footed. Bring insect repellent; the gnats can be ferocious. An alternate route back down takes you to the Temple of the Moon (about 1.5 hours down and back over to Machu Picchu). The map at the entrance to the Huayna Picchu trail designates it as Gran Caverno (Great Cave).

Looking down onto Inca ruins at base of Huayna Picchu.

Aguas
Calientes

Huayna
Picchu

Km 112

The Sacred Rock
Inca Bridge
Temple of the Sun
Entrance Station   MACHU PICCHU
Parking   COMPLEX

Intipunku

Inca Trail

Choquesuysuy

Huiñay
Huayna

Walking the Inca trail through the Sacred Valley.

Inca Trail

Patallaqta

Train to Machu Picchu

INCA TRAIL

The Inca Trail (*Camino Inca* in Spanish), a 50-km (31-mi) sector of the stone path that once extended from Cusco to Machu Picchu, is one of the world's signature outdoor excursions. Nothing matches the sensation of walking over the ridge that leads to the Lost City of the Inca just as the sun casts its first yellow glow over the ancient stone buildings.

Though the journey by train is the easiest way to get to Machu Picchu, most travelers who arrive via the Inca Trail wouldn't have done it any other way. There are limits on the number of trail users, but you'll still see a lot of fellow trekkers along the way. The four-day trek takes you past ruins and through stunning scenery, starting in the thin air of the highlands and ending in cloud forests. The orchids, hummingbirds, Andean condors, and spectacular mountains aren't bad either.

The impressive Puyupatamarca ruins.

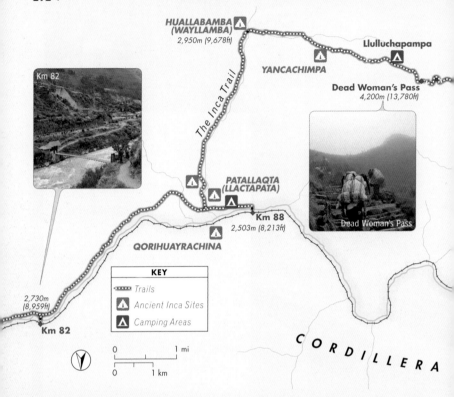

Km 82

**HUALLABAMBA
(WAYLLAMBA)**
2,950m (9,678ft)

YANCACHIMPA

Lllulluchapampa

Dead Woman's Pass
4,200m (13,780ft)

The Inca Trail

**PATALLAQTA
(LLACTAPATA)**

Km 88
2,503m (8,213ft)

Dead Woman's Pass

QORIHUAYRACHINA

2,730m
(8,959ft)

Km 82

KEY	
〜〜	*Trails*
⛺	*Ancient Inca Sites*
⛺	*Camping Areas*

0   1 mi

0   1 km

C O R D I L L E R A

INCA TRAIL DAY BY DAY

The majority of agencies begin the traditional Inca Trail trek at **Km 82** after a two-to-three-hour bus ride from Cusco.

DAY 1

Compared to what lies ahead, the first day's hike is a reasonably easy 12 km (7½ mi). You'll encounter fantastic ruins almost immediately. An easy ascent takes you to the first of those, **Patallaqta** (also called Llactapata). The name means "town on a hillside" in Quechua, and the ruins are thought to have been a village in Inca times. Bingham and company camped here on their first excursion to Machu Picchu. As at most Inca

sites, you'll see three levels of architecture representing the three spiritual worlds of the Inca—the world above (a guard tower), the world we live in (the main complex), and the world below (the river and hidden aqueducts).

At the end of the day, you arrive at **Huayllabamba** (also called as Wayllamba), the only inhabited village on the trail and your first overnight

DAY 2

It's another 12-km (7½-mi) hike, but with a gain of 1,200 m (3,940 ft) in elevation. The day is most memorable for the spectacular views and muscular

aches after ascending **Dead Woman's Pass** (also known as Warmiwañuscca) at 4,200 m (13,780 ft). The pass is named for the silhouette created by its mountain ridges—they resemble a woman's head, nose, chin, and chest.

A tricky descent takes you to **Pacaymayu,** the second night's campsite, and you can pat yourself on the back for completing the hardest section of the Inca Trail.

DAY 3

Downhill! You'll cover the most ground today (16-km, 9.9 m) but descending down 1,500 meters

View of the Inca Trail

Km. 82 · Patallaqta · Huallabamba · Warmi Wañusca Pass · Runkuranqay Pass · Sayacmarca · Puyupatamarca Pass · Huiñay Huayna · Machu Picchu

MODERATE · CHALLENGE · UNFORGETTABLE · UNIQUE

SAYACMARCA

3,350m (10,991ft)

RUNKURAQAY   **Runkuranqay Pass** 3,850m (12,631ft)

The Inca Trail

Runkuraqay

PUYUPATAMARCA (PHUYUPATAMARCA) 3,650m (11,975ft)

HUIÑAY HUAYNA (WIÑAYWAYNA)   2,587m (8,490ft)

CHOQUESUYSUY

Sun Gate

CHACHABAMBA   **Km 101**

Rio Urubamba

2,730m (8,957ft)   2,460m (8,072ft)

INTIPUNKU   **MACHU PICCHU**

2,046m (6,715ft)   **Km 112**   **HUAYNA PICCHU**

U R U B A M B A

2,082m (6,833ft)

Aguas Calientes

to the subtropical cloud forest where the Amazon basin begins. There's some of the most stunning mountain scenery you'll see during the four days. The ruins of **Runkuraqay** were a circular Inca storage depot for products transported between Machu Picchu and Cusco.

You also pass by **Sayacmarca**, possibly a way station for priests traversing the trail.

Most excursions arrive by mid-afternoon at **Huiñay Huayna** (also known as Wiñaywayna), the third-night's stopping point, at what may now seem a low and balmy

2,712 m (8,900 ft). The first possibility of a hot shower and a cold beer are here.

There is time to see the ruins of **Puyupatamarca** (also known as Phuyupatamarca) a beautifully restored site with ceremonial baths, and perhaps the best ruins on the hike. At this point you catch your first glimpse of Machu Picchu peak, but from the back side.

DAY 4

This is it. Day 4 means the grand finale, arrival at **Machu Picchu**, the reason for the trail in the first place. You'll

be roused from your sleeping bag well before dawn to hike your last 6-km (3.7 m) to arrive at the ruins in time to catch the sunrise. You'll be amazed at the number of fellow travelers who forget about their aching muscles and sprint this last stretch.

The trail takes you past the **Intipunku**, the Sun Gate. Bask in your first sight of the ruins and your accomplishment, but you'll need to circle around and enter Machu Picchu officially through the entrance gate.

PREPPING FOR THE INCA TRAIL

YOU MUST GO WITH A GUIDE

The days of setting off on the Inca Trail on your own, along with free-for-all rowdiness and litter, ended years ago. You must use a licensed tour operator, one accredited by the Unidad de Gestión Santuario Histórico de Machu Picchu, the organization that oversees the trail and limits the number of hikers to 400 per day, including guides and porters. There are some 30 such licensed operators in Cusco.

WHEN TO GO

May through September is the best time to make the four-day trek; rain is more likely in April and October and a certainty the rest of the year. The trail fills up during the dry high season. Make reservations months in advance if you want to hike then—weeks in advance the rest of the year. The trek is doable during the rainy season, but can become slippery and muddy by December. The trail closes for maintenance each February.

GETTING READY

Tour operators in Cusco will tell you the Inca Trail is of "moderate" difficulty, but it can be rough going, especially the first couple of days. You must be in decent shape, even if your agency supplies porters to carry your pack—current regulations limit your load to 20 kg (44 lb). The trail is often narrow and hair-raising.

As the mountains sometimes rise to over 13,775 feet, be wary of altitude sickness. (Give yourself two or three days in Cusco or the Sacred Valley to acclimatize.)

Your gear should include sturdy hiking boots, a sleeping bag (some outfitters rent them); clothing for cold, rainy weather, a hat, and a towel. Also bring plenty of sunblock and mosquito repellent. Toilet paper is essential; walking sticks can be helpful.

There are seven well-spaced, designated campsites along the trail.

WHILE YOU'RE HIKING

Food: All operators have their own chefs that run ahead of you with the porters, set-up camp, and create culinary feasts for breakfast, lunch, and dinner. This will probably be some of the best camp food you'll ever have and maybe some of the best food while in Peru. We're talking quinoa porridge with blueberries, chicken soup, and gourmet pasta dishes.

Coca Leaves: Although after Day 2 it is a gradual descent into Machu Picchu, you're still high enough to feel the thin air. You'll notice porters chewing coca throughout the trek. It's like drinking a cup of coffee. Coca leaves are a mild stimulant as well as an appetite, pain, and hunger suppressant. You'll only need about one bag of your own (about S/1) for the trail. To properly enjoy the leaves, take about 15 of them and pick the stems off. Stack them on top of each other and roll into a tight little bundle. Place the bundle between your gum and cheek on one side, allowing the leaves to soften up for about two minutes. Eventually start chewing to let the juice out. It's quite a bitter taste, but you'll feel better. All tour operators will also serve tea during coca breaks.

Bathrooms: Toilets could be a lot worse. You won't be able to sit down, but most porcelain-lined holes in the ground do flush. Bathrooms usually have working sinks, too. You must bring your own toilet paper wherever you go. Camp sites all have toilets, but the trail itself does not.

Luggage: Check with your tour operator before you go, and pack as lightly as possible. If you hire porters, they're probably going to be carrying a lot more than just your things on their backs. An American-style backwoods backpack may not be the right piece of luggage—it weighs a lot on its own and is an awkward shape for the porters to incorporate into their massive bundles. A simple duffle bag is often best.

standard, decent souvenir fare, mainly T-shirts, wood carvings, and weavings. ☉ *Daily 8–6.*

Museo de Sitio Manuel Chávez Ballón. The museum, dedicated to the history, culture, and rediscovery of Machu Picchu, sits on the way up to the ruins about 2 km (1 mi) from the edge of town at the entrance to the national park. The buses that ferry visitors up to Machu Picchu normally do not stop along the way, but the museum's in-town office, next to the Insituto Nacional de Cultura just off the main plaza, can arrange transportation for a small fee. Hoofing it is the best way to get here. Plan on about a 30-minute walk. The museum provides valuable bilingual insight into South America's premier tourist attraction, which you don't get at the ruins themselves. ⊠ *Puente de Ruinas, 2 km (1 mi) from Aguas Calientes* ☏ *No phone* 💲 *S/22* ☉ *Daily 9–4.*

WHERE TO EAT

Pizza once took Aguas Calientes by storm, and while you can still order up a cheesy pie cooked in the traditional Peruvian wood-burning clay ovens, the luxury hotel chefs have raised the bar, creating noteworthy Andean fusion, or as sometimes it's referred to, Novo Andino fare, a twist on traditionally bland Peruvian food of the high Andes. The result is creative, gourmet dishes—sometimes influenced by Asian flavors and other times marked by typical California cuisine or European delicacies.

$ ✕ **Chez Maggy.** A branch of the well-known Maggy's in Cusco is the
PIZZA best of the ubiquitous pizzerias in Aguas Calientes, and they serve the cheesy pie fresh out of the clay oven. ⊠ *Pachacutec 156* ☏ *084/211–006* 🖃 *MC, V.*

$ ✕ **Indio Feliz.** An engaging French-Peruvian couple manage the best res-
FRENCH taurant in Aguas Calientes. Quiche lorraine, ginger chicken, and spicy
Fodor'sChoice *trucha macho* (trout in hot pepper and wine sauce) are favorites here,
★ and are usually part of the reasonably priced (S/49) prix-fixe menu, all to the accompaniment of homemade bread. Top it off with a fine coffee and apple pie or flan for dessert. The French-European hand-painted decor keeps the atmosphere elegant and intimate, even on the outdoor terrace upstairs. ⊠ *Lloque Yupanqui 4-12* ☏ *084/211–090* 🖃 *AE, MC, V.*

$$ ✕ **Pueblo Viejo.** Hearty food comes easy for this 12-year-old restaurant.
PERUVIAN Everyone gathers around an open-fire grill in the middle of the restaurant where cuts of beef, alpaca, lamb, and trout are prepared and served with the typical fries, rice, or potato. Off to the side is the clay oven where pizzas are baked. If you're seeking veggies, the salad bar (already pre-boiled) is one of the best we've seen. Live Andean music and a good wine menu keep this place hopping long after the last tour bus has left. ⊠ *Pachacutec s/n* ☏ *084/211–193* 🖃 *AE, DC, MC, V.*

$ ✕ **Toto's House.** The sister restaurant to Pueblo Viejo has long tables set up
PERUVIAN in the center of its cavernous dining room to accommodate tour groups who come for the huge buffet lunch (S/60). Grab one of the smaller tables with a river view by the window or out on the shaded front patio for some good people watching. Evenings are more sedate—that's the case with the dining scene in all the restaurants here—with such dishes

6

as *trucha andina* (Andean trout) and cebiche set to the entertainment of a folklore music show. ⊠ *Av. Imperio de los Incas* ☎ 084/211–020 ═ AE, DC, MC, V.

$$ **✕ Tree House Restaurant.** Perched
PERUVIAN high above the streets of Aguas Caliente sits this small, rustic, yet classy restaurant that serves up some of the best Novo Andino cuisine, adding a twist of Italian, Thai, and coastal flavors to this town's gourmet palate. Fresh, locally grown produce is the backbone for the creatively tossed dishes like *quinotto* (similar to risotto but made with quinoa), homemade ravioli, along with fine cuts of beef, fish, and alpaca. With ample candlelight as your ambiance, you'll probably want to add a fine bottle of red, and a slice of passion fruit pie to top your culinary adventure off. Boxed–lunches are available to take on your tour of Machu Picchu. ⊠ *Calle Huanacaure 180* ☎ *084/211–101, 084/791–929* ⊕ *www. rupawasitreehouse.net* ═ *MC, V.*

INDIGENOUS TERMINOLOGY

Stick to the term "indigenous" (*indígena*) to describe Peru's Inca-descended peoples. Avoid "Indian" (*indio*), which is considered pejorative here, that is, unless you're describing an Indian restaurant. Likewise, among people in Peru, "native" (*nativo*) and "tribe" (*tribú*) conjure up images best left to old Tarzan movies.

WHERE TO STAY

$$$$ ☖ **El MaPi.** Designed to save travelers some dollars and cents without skimping on comfort and class, El MaPi delivers what it promises: simple but stylish rooms, top-tier service, and the same amenities you might expect from one of the more luxurious joints in town. Besides the traditional pisco-sour welcome drink, served at the modish bar on-site, the hotel also extends the offer of organizing tickets and travel arrangements to the nearby hillside thriller, Machu Picchu. Just ask at reception when you check in. Its informal-with-flair atmosphere and sleek interior design should come as no surprise: the establishment is managed by Inkaterra, the same guys who run the decadent Inkaterra Machu Picchu Pueblo Hotel up the road. **Pros:** great service; good value. **Cons:** not for those seeking a boutique hotel. ⊠ *Av. Pachachutec 109, Aguas Calientes* ☎ *084/211–011* ⊕ *www.elmapihotel.com* ↵ *48 rooms* ⌂ *In-room: no a/c, safe, refrigerator (some), Wi-Fi. In-hotel: restaurant, room service, bar, laundry service, Internet terminal, Wi-Fi hotspot* ═ *AE, DC, MC, V* ⦿� *BP.*

$$ ☖ **Gringo Bill's Hostal.** Bill has hosted Machu Picchu travelers since 1979, and his was one of the first lodgings in town. This house, just off the Plaza de Armas, has some of the finest stonework and lush gardens around. Once a budget option, competition has forced Bill to take his rooms—and rates—up a notch. The result is fresh paint, new bedding, and updated furniture. Despite the renovations, we still think the rates are a bit steep, but Bill's architect son, Lawrence, now a co-manager, has plans to spiff the place up even more. At the time of this writing he was building new suites, a rooftop wine bar, and new lounge on the first floor. **Pros:** cozy setting; good place to meet other travelers; friendly

The pros of spending a night at the Sanctuary Lodge.

staff. **Cons:** price not quite justified; outdoor hot tub doesn't always work; lots of stairs. ⊠ *Colla Raymi 104, Aguas Calientes* ☎ *084/211–046* ⊕ *www.gringobills.com* ⟿ *29 rooms* ⚷ *In-room: no a/c. In-hotel: restaurant, bar, laundry service, Wi-Fi hot spot* ⊟*AE, V* ⭦*BP.*

$$$$ 🏨 **Hatuchay Tower.** One of the larger, more standard hotels in town, Hatuchay Tower stands above the river at the edge of town on the road heading to the ruins. Clean, large, carpeted rooms are comfortable with modern furnishings and amenities, but the interior design is nothing fancy. If you prefer a Marriot to a boutique hotel, this is a good bet. If you can swing it, go for a suite. **Pros:** good location; quiet; breakfast and dinner included. **Cons:** not exceptional. ⊠ *Av. Hermanos Ayar 401* ☎ *084/211–201, 01/447–8170 in Lima* ⊕ *www.hatuchaytower. com* ⟿ *37 rooms, 5 suites* ⚷ *In-room: a/c, safe, refrigerator. In-hotel: restaurant, room service, bar, laundry service, Wi-Fi hotspot* ⊟*AE, MC, V* ⭦*MAP.*

$ 🏨 **Hotel Presidente.** Orange and open, the Presidente is one of the more moderately priced hotels in Aguas Calientes. About half of the carpeted rooms here have big windows and balconies that overlook the Río Vilcanota, but none of the rooms have phones, safes, or public Wi-Fi. These folks manage three *hostales*— the Machupicchu, the Plaza, and Los Andinos. **Pros:** good value; prime location; nice views. **Cons:** nothing fancy; bathrooms and rooms a bit outdated. ⊠ *Av. Imperio de los Incas 135, Aguas Calientes* ☎ *084/211–034* ⟿ *28 rooms* ⚷ *In-room: no a/c. In-hotel: restaurant, laundry service* ⊟*MC, V* ⭦*BP.*

$$$$ 🏨 **Hatun Inti.** Polished wood floors, white walls, and tasteful furnishings give this hotel an elegantly rustic and homey feel. As if the large modern bathroom and central fireplace were not appealing enough,

Train To Machu Picchu

PeruRail held a near monopoly over train travel from Cusco and Ollyantaytambo to Machu Picchu for more than 10 years, but now two additional companies have entered the picture: Inca Rail and Andean Railways. The new trains allow for more frequent and easier travel from the Sacred Valley, specifically from Ollantaytambo and Urubamba to Aguas Calientes.

PeruRail is still the only way to get from Cusco to Ollyantaytambo. As of this writing, it is still not possible to go directly from Cusco to Urubamba or Ollyantaytambo and back; you must still go through Aguas Calientes.

Most tour packages include rail tickets as well as bus transport to and from Aguas Calientes and Machu Picchu and admission to the ruins and lodging if you plan to stay overnight. Tourists are not permitted to ride the Tren Local, the less expensive, but slower train intended for local residents only.

PERURAIL

At least two PeruRail trains depart from Cusco's Poroy station daily for Aguas Calientes, near Machu Picchu. The *Vistadome* leaves at 6:50 AM and arrives in Aguas Calientes at 10:40. It returns from Aguas Calientes at 4 PM, arriving in Cusco at 7:45. The round-trip fare is S/412. Snacks and beverages are included in the price, and the cars have sky domes for great views. The return trip includes a fashion show and folklore dancing.

PeruRail also offers a new economic coach, the *Expedition* to replace their old budget trains. The new cars have comfortable seats and tables, with sky windows for a full peek of the Sacred Valley. As PeruRail's cheapest option, the *Expedition* departs from Poroy Station at 7:40 AM and arrives in Aguas Calientes at 11:50 AM. The return train departs Aguas Calientes at 5 PM, arriving in Cusco at 9 PM. The round-trip fare is S/285. Conditions are comparable to second-class trains in Western Europe and are plenty comfortable. A second *Vistadome* or *Expedition* train may be added during the June–August high season, depending on demand.

PeruRail's luxury *Hiram Bingham* train provides a class of service unto itself (with prices to match). The train departs at 9:10 AM, arriving in Aguas Calientes at 1:10 PM. It leaves Aguas Calientes at 6:05 PM and arrives back in Cusco at 10 PM. Trains consist of two dining cars, a bar car, and a kitchen car, and evoke the glamour of the old Orient Express rail service, no surprise, since Orient Express the parent company of PeruRail. The round-trip price tag includes brunch on the trip to Machu Picchu, bus transport from Aguas Calientes up to the ruins and back in vehicles exclusively reserved for *Hiram Bingham* clients, admission to the ruins, guide services while there, and an afternoon buffet tea at the Machu Picchu Sanctuary Lodge. The trip back entails cocktails, live entertainment, and a four-course dinner. This luxury comes at a price tag of S/852 one-way.

Trains stop at Ollantaytambo, Km 88 (the start of the Inca Trail), and Km 104 (the launch point of an abbreviated two-day Inca Trail). Arrival is in Aguas Calientes, where you catch the buses up to the ruins.

If you're using the Sacred Valley as your base, PeruRail operates a daily *Vistadome* train departing from Ollantaytambo at 6:59, 7:45, and 10:30 AM, and 1:50 and 4:15 PM. A daily *Expedition* train departs Ollantaytambo at 9:10 AM, arriving at Aguas Calientes at 11:18 AM. PeruRail began running a new train called the Auto Wagon from Urubamba to Aguas Calientes in November 2010. With only one departure a day, the train leaves the new Urubamba station at 7 AM daily, arriving in Aguas Calientes at 10 AM. The train departs Aguas Calientes at 3:20 PM arriving back in Urubamba at 6:40 PM. A one-way ticket runs S/174.

A full train schedule is available on PeruRail's website and timetable fliers can be picked up from almost any tourist agency, including the iPeru kiosk when you arrive at the airport.

PeruRail's service is generally punctual. Schedules and rates are always subject to change, and there may be fewer trains per day to choose from during the December to March low season.

In theory, same-day tickets can be purchased, but waiting that late is risky. Procure tickets in advance from PeruRail's sales office in the Plaza de Armas in Cusco (✉ *Portal de Carnes 214, Plaza de Armas*) weekdays from 10 AM to 10 PM and weekends and Peruvian holidays from 2 PM to 11 PM. You can purchase tickets online at ⊕ *www.perurail.com*, or by phone at ☎ *084/581–414*.

INCA RAIL

Inca Rail runs trains from Ollantaytambo to Aguas Calientes and vice versa three times daily. Trains leaves Ollantaytambo at 6:30 and 11:25 AM and 4:45 PM. Trains depart Aguas Calientes for Ollantaytambo at 8:50 AM, 2:12, and 7:38 PM.

There are two types of tickets offered on Inca Rail: Executive class, which will cost you S/300 for an adult and S/150 for a child age 12 or under, and First Class, costing S/450 per adult and S/225 per child. To purchase tickets you can go to the kiosk at the train station in Aguas Calientes or to the office just outside the rail stop in Ollantaytambo. In Cusco you can also buy tickets at the office (✉ *Av. El Sol 611*) or by phone at ☎ *084/233–030*. It is also possible to purchase at ⊕ *www.inkarail.com* but that could get cumbersome since it requires a bank and wire transfer.

ANDEAN RAILWAYS

Andean Railways began service in late 2010 from Ollantaytambo to Aguas Calientes. The scheduled twice-daily service was not running consistently at the time of this printing, although the price was S/165 each way. They are also expected to expand service going from Urubamba to Aguas Calientes in the coming year; that date is unknown. Check their website for more information (⊕ *www.machupicchutrain.com*).

Information Asociación de Agencias de Turismo de Cusco (✉ *Nueva Baja 424, Cusco* ☎ *084/222–580*). **Andean Railways** ✉ *Av. El Sol 576, Cusco* ☎ *084/221–199* ⊕ *www.machupicchutrain.com*. **Inca Rail** (✉ *Av. El Sol, 611, Cusco* ☎ *084/233–030* ⊕ *www.incarail.com*). **PeruRail** (✉ *Portal de Carnes 214, Plaza de Armas, Cusco* ☎ *084/581–414, 084/233–551* ⊕ *www.perurail.com*).

6

most rooms also come with a lovely riverfront view. Warm and inviting, this is an ideal spot to rest up before or after a day at the famed ruins. The owners manage two other hotels, Inti Inn and Inti Orquideas, which offer slightly less luxurious rooms at lower prices. **Pros:** prime location; clean; modern. **Cons:** not the cheapest beds in town. ⊠ *Av. Imperio de los Incas s/n* ☎ *084/211–365* ⊕ *www.grupointi.com* ⤴ *14 rooms* ⚲ *In-room: a/c, safe, refrigerator, Wi-Fi. In-hotel: room service, laundry service* ⊟ *AE, D, DC, MC, V.*

$$$$ ⛲ **Inkaterra Machu Picchu Pueblo Hotel.** A five-minute walk from the center
Fodor's Choice   of town takes you to this stunning eco-lodge in its own private tropical
★   cloud forest, complete with 372 varieties of orchids and 18 species of hummingbirds. The stone bungalows, none with the same design, have a rustic elegance, with exposed beams and cathedral ceilings. Suites include their own private hot tubs for guests to sit and soak in the tranquil surroundings. Activities, packaged together as part of your room cost, include a one-day Inca Trail trek, bird-watching excursions, and orchid tours, as well as a twilight nature walk. You can also schedule a visit to the small on-site tea and coffee plantation where you can learn how to make those brews you enjoyed at breakfast. And if you're feeling weary at the end of an action-packed day, schedule a massage at the lodge's UNU Spa. The restaurant overlooking the surrounding hills is first-rate—try the delicious *crema de choclo* (corn chowder). **Pros:** natural setting; many activities. **Cons:** expensive. ⊠ *Av. Imperio de los Incas s/n, Aguas Calientes* ☎ *084/211–032; 51/610–0400 in Lima; 800/442–5042 in North America* ⊕ *www.inkaterra.com* ⤴ *83 rooms, 2 suites* ⚲ *In-room: a/c, safe, refrigerator, DVD, Internet, Wi-Fi. In-hotel: restaurant, room service, bar, pool, spa, laundry service* ⊟ *AE, DC, MC, V* ⵙ⦿*MAP.*

$ ⛲ **Machupicchu Hostal.** Probably one of the best hostal deals in town, the rooms here have all been redone with modern furnishings and renovated bathrooms. Still an economic hostal, the rooms are fairly simple and line motel-style the length of a small courtyard, blooming with a lush flower garden and home to the owner's pet parrot. You'll find three huge double rooms at the back facing the river. An ample breakfast is included in the rates and served at the Hotel Presidente next door. **Pros:** good value; river-facing rooms; good location. **Cons:** pretty basic. ⊠ *Av. Imperio de los Incas 135* ☎ *084/211–034* ⤴ *12 rooms* ⚲ *In-room: a/c, no TV. In hotel: laundry service* ⊟ *MC, V* ⵙ⦿*BP.*

$$$$ ⛲ **Machu Picchu Sanctuary Lodge.** This upscale hotel at the entrance to Machu Picchu puts you closest to the ruins, a position for which you do pay dearly. But nowhere else can you sit in a hot tub, sip pisco sours or tea, and watch the sunset over the famed ruins after the last of the tourists depart each afternoon. At night, any astronomer or novice stargazer will appreciate the big Andean sky. In the morning, not only will you have the thrill of watching the sun rise over the crumbling stone walls but you'll be the first ones through the ruins' gate. For the past 10 years, Orient-Express, owners of PeruRail have run the elegant hotel and made the once-government-owned hotel a vacation in itself considering all 31 rooms come with top-of-the-line amenities. While expensive, the all-inclusive rates include meals from the restaurant and

Machu Picchu and Inca Trail Tour Operators

The following Cusco-based operators run either four-day or two-day treks to Machu Picchu, along the famed Inca Trail. Most companies also provide alternative multiday Inca Trail treks including the Lares Valley, Salkantay, and Choquequirao. These treks often are cheaper in cost and just as magnificent, if not more challenging. The average cost of a four-day Inca Trail excursion runs about $500 USD. Most companies listed can also organize one-day tours to Machu Picchu from Cusco.

PERU-BASED GUIDES

Another Planet. Specializes in custom-built multiday Inca Trail treks. The foreign-owned and family operated company has more than 15 years of guiding experience. ☎ 084/243–166 ⊕ www.andeanwingshotel.com.

CuscoTopTravel&Treks. Run by the wildly talented and witty David Choque, who specializes in a range of packaged and comfort-class custom-built multiday treks along the Inca Trail and the Sacred Valley. Also offers one-day tours to Machu Picchu. ☎ 084/251–864 ⊕ www.cuscotoptravelperu.com.

SAS. One of the longest-running operators in the region. Just about any hiking tour from the four-day Inca Trail trek to a variety of alternative treks are offered. ☎ 084/241–920 ⊕ www.sastravelperu.com.

Sun Gate Tours. Specializes in one- and two-day trips to Machu Picchu and Aguas Calliente. ☎ 084/237–197 ⊕ www.sungatetours.com.

TopTurPeru. An internationally recognized, local company run by Raul Castelo and family has been guiding hiking groups along the Inca Trail for many years. Raul has been sought out by National Geographic and other documentary-filmmaking entities worldwide. ☎ 084/252–846 ⊕ www.topturperu.com.

United Mice. One of the more popular Inca Trail operators. Offering a variety of alternative Inca trail treks from across the Sacred Valley, they've been guiding adventurers on multiday hikes since 1990. They only offer Inca Trail hikes one to two times a week. Book in advance. ☎ 084/221–139 ⊕ www.unitedmice.com.

U.S. AND CANADA-BASED GUIDES

Backroads. This active travel company provides luxury all-inclusive trips in Peru for families and individuals. Packages include several Inca trail trekking trips, lodge-to-lodge hiking throughout the Sacred Valley, and combination biking and hiking trips to Machu Picchu. ☎ 510/527–1555 ⊕ www.backroads.com.

GAP Adventures. Eco-conscious, Canadian-run tour company that provides multiple levels of trips based on comfort and activity styles. Offers traditional Inca trail treks and alternative Inca trail multiday hikes. Many can be combined with other GAP tours of Peru. Check out last-minute deals on the Web site. ☎ 888/800-4100 ⊕ www.gapadventures.com.

Wilderness Travel. Specializes in small group, family, and private journeys, with an emphasis on education. ☎ 510/558–2488 ⊕ www.wildernesstravel.com.

6

bar exclusive to hotel guests. There is an additional restaurant that has an excellent international menu and serves a popular S/100 buffet lunch open to the public. **Pros:** prime location at ruins' entrance; great astronomy; personalized service. **Cons:** expensive. ⊠ *Machu Picchu* ☎ *084/211–094; 01/610–8300 in Lima; 800/237–1236 in North America* ⊕ *www.machupicchu.orient-express.com* ⌁ *29 rooms, 2 suites* ⚒ *In-room: a/c, safe, refrigerator. In-hotel: 3 restaurants, room service, bar, laundry service* ═ *AE, DC, MC, V* ¦⊙¦ *FAP.*

$ 🏨 **Plaza Hostal.** This small, quiet hotel faces the river on the road heading out of town up to the ruins. Rooms are bright and simply furnished. If you're looking for more than a place to lay your head, you'll want to go elsewhere, but for a quick night stopover, this is a good deal. Breakfast is included in the rates and served at the Hotel Presidente around the corner. **Pros:** good location; well priced; quiet. **Cons:** some rooms better than others; simple. ⊠ *Av. Hermanos Ayar L-3* ☎ *084/211–192* ⌁ *7 rooms* ⚒ *In-room: no phone, no a/c, no TV. In-hotel: laundry service* ═ *MC, V* ¦⊙¦ *BP.*

$$$$
Fodor's Choice
★

🏨 **Sumaq Hotel.** This large hotel sits at the edge of town along the highway heading up toward the ruins. Upscale and comfortable, the list of nice touches and amenities is great: grand staircases, elegant restaurant with a terrific cross selection of Peruvian cuisine, huge rooms, some with fireplace, all with wood-beam ceilings, flat-screen TVs, box spring mattresses, and porcelain basin sinks. ■**TIP**➜ Sumaq means "beautiful" in Quechua and the name is apt. Rates include a breakfast buffet and lunch or dinner. **Pros:** many amenities; great restaurant, cooking class and tea time included. **Cons:** luxury costs; simply decorated rooms. ⊠ *Av. Hermanos Ayar Mz.1 L-3, Aguas Calientes* ☎ *084/211–059; 01/447–0579 in Lima* ⊕ *www.sumaqhotelperu.com* ⌁ *60 rooms* ⚒ *In-room: a/c, safe, refrigerator, DVD, Wi-Fi. In-hotel: restaurant, room service, bar, spa, laundry service, Internet terminal* ═ *AE, DC, MC, V* ¦⊙¦ *MAP.*

The Amazon Basin

WORD OF MOUTH

"Beautiful rainforests for walks. Fragrant flowers. Fishing. Visited a school and played soccer with the kids. Herbal treatments from the Amazon ladies. Fresh foods. Wonderful hammocks for relaxing in the afternoon rains. Loved it. But about three days without electricity and running water was enough."

—kywood1955

WELCOME TO THE AMAZON BASIN

TOP REASONS TO GO

★ **The River:** The Amazon is a natural choice for adventures, but sign up with a tour operator, who will know the safest places to explore.

★ **Wild Things:** Peru's Amazon basin has more than 50,000 plant, 1,700 bird, 400 mammal, and 300 reptile species. Bring binoculars.

★ **Bass Fishing:** Anglers test their skills versus the peacock bass, one of the world's strongest freshwater fighters.

★ **River Lodges:** Staying at a lodge on the Amazon, or one of its tributaries, is almost a prerequisite to visiting the Amazon Basin, where river and jungle life surround you.

★ **Bird World:** The incredible array of fantastical-looking birds will make an avian fanatic out of you. Boat cruise by the Allpahuayo Mishana National Reserve, Tamshiyacu Tahuayo Reserve, or Pacaya Samiria National Reserve.

1 **Madre de Dios.** The national parks, reserves, and other undeveloped areas of the southern department of Madre de Dios are among the most biologically diverse in the world. Puerto Maldonado is an ugly frontier town that is mostly used by travelers as a place to fly into, board a boat, and go to the jungle lodge.

2 **Iquitos and Environs.** The jungle-locked city of Iquitos has a party-going, city-on-the-edge attitude with more than 400,000 cooped-up residents. Nature lodges with private reserves offer bird-watching, wildlife observation, and rain forest exploration. The region's three top eco-destinations can only be accessed by boat—Allpahuayo Mishana Nacional Reserve, Tamshiyacu Tahuayo Reserve, and Pacaya Samiria National Reserve.

Iquitos.

ECUADOR

GETTING ORIENTED

The logistics of travel and isolation make it unlikely that you could visit both the northern and southern Amazon regions—separated by 600 km (370 mi) at their nearest point— during one trip to Peru. The city of Iquitos is the jumping-off point for the northern Amazon; Puerto Maldonado, for the south. Some 1,200 km (740 mi) and connecting flights back in Lima separate the two cities. Neither will disappoint, and both are dotted with the region's famed jungle lodges.

COLOMBIA

CONAPAC Biological Reserve

Amazon

Iquitos Caballococha

Tamshiyacu Tahuayo Reserve

Nauta

BRAZIL

0   100 mi

0   100 km

Tree frog in Amazon rain forest.

Atalaya

Park Nacional Alto Purus

Iñapari

Iberia

Manu Biosphere Reserve

Boca Manu

Madre de Dios River

Puerto Maldonado

Itahuania

Shintuya

26 B

Machu Picchu

CORDILLERA

Urubamba Pisac

Cusco

3 S

Parque Nacional Bahuaja-Sonene

URUBAMBA

BOLIVIA

Black berries.

7

Updated by David Dudenhoefer

Peru's least-known region occupies some two-thirds of the country, an area the size of California. The *selva* (jungle) of the Amazon Basin is drained by the world's second longest river and its countless tributaries. What eastern Peru lacks in human population it makes up for in sheer plant and animal numbers, more than you knew could exist, for the viewing. There are lodges, cruise boats, and guides for the growing number of people who arrive to see the spectacle.

The northern Amazon is anchored by the port city of Iquitos—the Amazon Basin's second biggest city after Manaus, Brazil, and the gateway to the rain forest. From Iquitos you can head out on an Amazon cruise, or to any of a dozen jungle lodges to experience the region's diverse flora and fauna.

Though the area has been inhabited by small indigenous groups for more than 5,000 years, it wasn't "civilized" until Jesuit missionaries arrived in the 1500s. The Spanish conquistador Francisco de Orellana was the first white man to see the Amazon. He came upon the great river, which the indigenous people called Tunguragua (King of Waters), on his trip down the Río Napo in search of El Dorado. He dubbed it Amazonas after he met with extreme opposition from female warriors along the banks of the river.

The area was slow to convert to modern ways, and remained basically wild until the 1880s, when there was a great rubber boom. The boom changed the town of Iquitos overnight; rubber barons installed themselves in lavish homes, and the city's population exploded. Local people were put to work, often under slave-like conditions as rubber tappers who headed into the jungle each day to collect the sap from rubber trees scattered through the forest. The boom went bust in the first part of the 20th century, when a British entrepreneur transported some seeds out of Brazil and established plantations on the Malay Peninsula. The invention of synthetic rubber in the mid–20th century only made things worse. You can still see remnants of the boom in the somewhat dilapidated palaces in Iquitos.

Most of the indigenous tribes—many small tribes are found in the region, the Boras, Yaguas, and Orejones being the most prevalent—have given up their traditional hunter-gatherer existence and now live in small communities along the backwaters of the great river. You will not see the remote tribes unless you travel far from Iquitos and deep into the jungle, a harrowing and dangerous undertaking. What you will see are people who have adopted western dress and other amenities, but who still live in relative harmony with nature and preserve traditions that date back thousands of years. A common sight might be a fisherman paddling calmly up the Amazon in his dugout canoe, angling to reel in one of its many edible fish.

The lesser-known southern Amazon region is traversed by one of the big river's tributaries—the Rio Madre de Dios. Few travelers spend much time in Puerto Maldonado, the capital of Madre de Dios department, using the city instead as a jumping-off point to the Manu, or Tambopata reserves. Manu is the less accessible but more pristine of the two, but Tambopata will not disappoint, and much of the jungle outside those protected areas still holds remarkable flora and fauna.

Be prepared to spend some extra soles to get here. Roads, when they exist, are rough-and-tumble, and often impassible during the November through April rainy, and flooding season. A dry-season visit is recommended, but of course dry is a euphemism in the rain forest. You'll most likely jet into Iquitos or Puerto Maldonado, respectively the northern and southern gateways to the Amazon, and climb into a boat to reach the region's famed nature lodges.

7

PLANNING

WHEN TO GO

As you might expect, it rains plenty in the Amazon Basin, though that precipitation is somewhat seasonal. Although there's no true dry season in the Iquitos area, it rains less from June to October in Madre de Dios. For Amazon cruises out of Iquitos, high water season is best (December–June); tributaries become too shallow during the dry months.

The southern Amazon basin has a pronounced dry season between May and October; the lodges are open year-round, though rivers may overflow and mosquitoes can be voracious between December and April. Tambopata sees a well-defined wet season/dry season; Manu's rainfall is more evenly dispersed throughout the year. Plan well in advance for trips in July and August, the peak tourist season, when some jungle lodges often take in large groups and cruise boats can be full. During the dry season, especially July and August, sudden *friajes* (cold fronts) bring rain and cold weather to Madre de Dios, so be prepared for the worst. Temperatures can drop from 32°C (90°F) to 10°C (50°F) overnight. No matter when you travel, bring a rain jacket or poncho and perhaps rain pants.

GETTING HERE AND AROUND

AIR TRAVEL

LAN flies to Iquitos several times daily from Lima. Peruvian Airlines and Star Peru fly to Iquitos less frequently, but usually cost considerably less than LAN. Iquitos's Aeropuerto Internacional Francisco Secada Vignetta is 8 km (5 mi) from the city center. A taxi to the airport should cost around S/10. LAN has two daily flights from both Lima and Cusco to Aeropuerto Padre Aldámiz, 5 km (3 mi) from Puerto Maldonado. Star Peru also has two Lima–Puerto Maldonado flights daily, at least one of which stops in Cusco, and are usually the best deal.

BOAT TRAVEL

Boats are the most common form of transportation in the Amazon Basin and most of the nature lodges, with the exception of those in the cloud forests of Manu. If you stay at one of those lodges, you will be met at the airport in Puerto Maldonado or Iquitos and transported to a riverbank spot where you board a boat that takes you to your lodge. Once there, most excursions will also be by boat. If you opt for an Amazon cruise, you'll spend most of your time in this region on the water.

BUS TRAVEL

The only areas that can be reached by road are Puerto Maldonado and the buffer zone of Manu National Park. The windy road to Puerto Maldonado from Cusco is a 20-hour bus ride that only a backpacker on a very tight budget would take. Several tour companies offer slower, but incredible, overland trips from Cusco to Manu, including 12 hours over rugged terrain via Paucartambo. The road plunges spectacularly from the *páramo* (highlands) into the cloud forests at Atalaya, near which travelers spend a night in a cloud forest. Here or at Shintuya, farther down the river, you take a boat along the Alto Madre de Dios River.

HEALTH AND SAFETY

Traveler's stomach Avoiding an upset stomach and diarrhea can be difficult. Drink only bottled water, and use it even to brush your teeth. Peel fruits and vegetables before you eat them. Fasting while maintaining a strict regimen of hydration (bottled water, or a hydration fluid sold at pharmacies such as "Frutiflex") is the quickest way to cure traveler's stomach.

Malaria There is no vaccine but prescription drugs help minimize your likelihood of contracting this mosquito-borne illness. Strains of malaria are resistant to the traditional regimen of chloroquine. There are three recommended alternatives: a weekly dose of mefloquine; a daily dose of doxycycline; or a daily dose of Malarone (*atovaquone/proguanil*). Any regimen must start before arrival and continue beyond departure. Ask your physician. Wear long sleeves and pants if you're out in the evening, and use a mosquito repellent containing DEET whenever you enter the jungle.

Yellow fever The Peruvian Embassy recommends getting a yellow-fever vaccine at least 10 days before visiting the Amazon. Though recent cases of yellow fever have occurred only near Iquitos, southern Amazon lodges in Manu and Tambopata tend to be sticklers about seeing your yellow-fever vaccination certificate. Carry it with you.

EMERGENCIES

The **Policía Nacional** (☎ *082/803–504 or 082/573–605*), Peru's national police force, handles emergencies. At jungle lodges minor emergencies are handled by the staff. For serious emergencies, the lodge must contact medical services in Puerto Maldonado, Cusco, or Iquitos.

RESTAURANTS

You can dine out at restaurants only in Iquitos and Puerto Maldonado, the Amazon basin's two main cities, and even they have limited choices. Your sole dining option is your lodge if you stay in the jungle. Meals are often served family-style at fixed times with everyone seated around a big table, and you can swap stories with your fellow lodgers about what you saw on your day's excursion. The food, usually made of local ingredients, can be quite tasty.

HOTELS

Puerto Maldonado and Iquitos have typical, albeit small, hotels. Iquitos also has a few hotels geared to business travelers. Beyond those urban centers lie the region's jungle lodges. They are reachable only by boat and vary in degree of rusticity and remoteness. They range from camping sites a cut above the norm to upscale eco-lodges with swimming pools and Wi-Fi. Most have limited electricity, however, and few offer air-conditioning. Showers are usually refreshingly cool.

All nature lodges offer some variation on a fully escorted tour, with packages from one to several nights including guided wildlife-viewing excursions. They all provide mosquito nets and all meals are included. Most lodges quote rates per person, double occupancy, that include meals and transportation and some tours, and many take so long to reach that it's simply not realistic to stay for just one night. The price ranges given for lodges in this chapter reflect the cost of one night's stay for two people, meals included. All lodges accept soles, and most accept U.S. dollars for drinks and souvenirs.

WHAT IT COSTS IN NUEVO SOLES					
	¢	$	$$	$$$	$$$$
RESTAURANTS	under S/20	S/20–S/35	S/36–S/50	S/51–S/65	over S/65
HOTELS	under S/125	S/125–S/250	S/251–S/375	S/376–S/500	over S/500

Restaurant prices are per person for a main course. Hotel prices are for a standard double room, excluding tax.

MADRE DE DIOS

Do the math: 20,000 plant, 1,200 butterfly, 1,000 bird, 200 mammal, and 100 reptile species (and many more yet to be identified). The southern sector of Peru's Amazon basin, most readily approached via Cusco, is famous among birders, whose eyes glaze over in amazement at the dawn spectacle of macaws and parrots gathered at one of the region's famed *collpas* (clay licks). Ornithologists speculate that the birds ingest clay periodically to neutralize toxins in the seeds and fruit they eat. Madre de Dios also offers a rare chance to see large mammals, such as coatis (raccoon cousins), capybaras (dog-sized rodents), and anteaters. If the zoological gods smile upon you, you may even encounter a tapir, or a jaguar. Animal and plant life abound, but this is the least populated of Peru's departments: a scant 76,000 people reside in an area slightly smaller than South Carolina, and almost two-thirds of them are in Puerto Maldonado.

The southern Amazon saw little incursion at the time of the Spanish conquest. The discovery in the late 19th century of the *shiringa*, known in the English-speaking world as the rubber tree, changed all of that. Madre de Dios saw outside migration for the first time with the arrival of the *caucheros* (rubber men) and their minions staking out claims. The discovery of gold in the 1970s drew new waves of fortune seekers to the region, and you are bound to encounter mining barges on the river.

> **RIBEREÑOS**
>
> Peruvians in the Amazon region are a mix of native and Spanish ancestry. Ribereños (river people) live simple lives close to the land and water, much like their native ancestors. They depend on fish and crops for their survival. Not far from Iquitos are numerous small communities of the Amazon's original peoples. They include the Yagua, Bora, Huitoto, Ticuna, and Cocama, whose people generally speak very little Spanish. If you do visit a native village, be sure to take small bills (soles or dollars) to buy artisan items.

Tourism and conservation have triggered the newest generation of explorers in the species-rich southern Amazon. Two areas of Madre de Dios are of special interest. One is around the city of Puerto Maldonado, including the Tambopata National Reserve and the adjoining Bahuaja-Sonene National Park; easily accessible, they offer lodges amid primary rain forest and excellent birding. Tambopata also exists for sustainable agriculture purposes: some 1,500 families in the department collect Brazil nuts from the reserve, an economic incentive to keep the forest intact, rather than cut it down for its lumber. The Manu Biosphere Reserve, directly north of Cusco, though more difficult to reach, provides unparalleled opportunity for observing wildlife in one of the largest virgin rain forests in the New World.

PUERTO MALDONADO

500 km (310 mi) east of Cusco.

The inland port city of Puerto Maldonado lies at the confluence of the Madre de Dios and Tambopata rivers. The capital of the department of Madre de Dios, it is a rough-and-tumble town with 50,000 people and nary a four-wheeled vehicle in sight, but with hundreds of motorized two- and three-wheeled motorbikes jockeying for position on its few paved streets.

The city is named for two explorers who ventured into the region 300 years apart: Spanish conquistador Juan Álvarez de Maldonado passed through in 1566; Peruvian explorer Faustino Maldonado explored the

CLOSE UP

Amazon Tours

MADRE DE DIOS

One of the most experienced guide services, **Manu Expeditions** offers five- to nine-day trips to the Manu Wildlife Center. ☎ 084/225–990 ⊕ www.manuexpeditions.com.

Manu Nature Tours operates tours with the only full-service lodge within the Manu Biosphere Reserve, a cloud-forest lodge. The Manu Lodge is often used by scientists who are studying the reserve's ecology. ☎ 084/252–721⊕ www.manuperu.com.

InkaNatura Travel manages lodges in Manu and the Tambopata National Reserve. ☎ 014/203–5000; 877/827–8350 in U.S.⊕ www.inkanatura.com.

Inkaterra Nature Travel runs tours to Reserva Amazónica, a private reserve 45 minutes downriver from Puerto Maldonado that has a canopy walkway, a network of trails and a small collpa. ☎ 01/610–0400; 800/442–5042 in U.S. ⊕ www. inkaterra.com.

Pantiacolla organizes five-, seven- and nine-day ecotours in Manu that include nights at various rustic nature lodges on the Alto Madre de Dios river. ☎ 084/238–323 ⊕ www. pantiacolla.com.

Peruvian Safaris offers customized trips to the Tambopata Reserve, and trips to a jungle lodge near Iquitos. ☎ 01/447–8888 ⊕ www. peruviansafaris.com.

Rainforest Expeditions runs three- to seven-day tours including nights at the company's three nature lodges: the Tambopata Research Center, Refugio Amazonas and Posada Amazonas. ☎ 01/719–6422 in Miraflores; 9847–05266 in Cusco; 082/571–056

in Puerto Maldonado; 877/870–0578 in U.S. ⊕ www.perunature.com.

IQUITOS AREA

Aqua Expeditions runs high-end nature cruises up the Amazon from Iquitos to the Pacaya Samiria Reserve, where tributaries and lakes are explored in small boats. Cruises last for three, four, or seven days. ☎ 01/368–3868, or 65/601–053 ⊕ www.aquaexpeditions.com.

Delfin offers three-, four-, and seven-day eco-cruises on the Amazon on two boats, the Delfin I and the slightly nicer Delfin II. Passengers board smaller boats each day for trips into the Pacaya Samiria Reserve. ☎ 01/719–0998 ⊕ www. delfinamazoncruises.com.

Explorama Tours offers three- to seven-day boating and hiking trips along the Amazon River with stays at the Explorama, Ceiba Tops, and ExplorNapo lodges. ☎ 065/252–530; 800/707–5275 in U.S. ⊕ www. explorama.com.

International Expeditions offers 10-day nature cruises to the Pacaya Samira Reserve and other areas departing from Iquitos. Cruises can be booked only from the company's offices in the United States. ☎ 800/234–9620 ⊕ www.ietravel.com.

Paseos Amazonicos runs a variety of trips to its three lodges in the Iquitos area, one of which is on the edge of Pacaya Samiria. ☎ 065/231–1618 ⊕ www.paseosamazonicos.com.

7

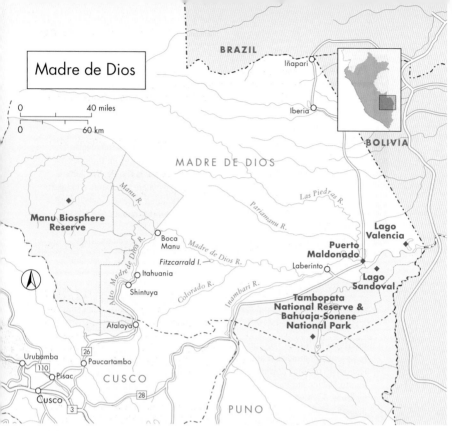

still-wild area in the 1860s, never completing his expedition, drowning in the nearby Madeira River. Rubber barons founded this youngster of Peruvian cities in 1912, and its history has been a boom-or-bust roller-coaster ride ever since. The collapse of the rubber industry in the 1930s gave way to decades of dormancy ended by the discovery of gold in the 1970s and the opening of an airport 10 years later. High prices for gold and steady improvements to the road there—part of a "highway" connecting Peru with Brazil—have brought an influx of settlers in recent years, which has been a scourge for the region's forests and indigenous peoples.

Nevertheless, Puerto Maldonado bills itself as the "Biodiversity Capital of the World," since it is the jumping-off point for visiting the Tambopata National Reserve and surrounding rain forest. ■ TIP→ Few travelers spend any time in the city, heading from the airport directly to the municipal docks, where they board boats to their respective jungle lodges. Still, Puerto Maldonado has a handful of decent hotels that can be used as a base for day trips. And this is the only place to use an ATM machine, or cash a traveler's check.

GETTING HERE AND AROUND

It's fun to get around town in Puerto Maldonado's fleet of mototaxis, semi-open three-wheeled motorized vehicles with room for two passengers in the back seat. They patrol the main streets from dawn to well past dusk.

ESSENTIALS

Airport Aeropuerto Internacional Padre José Aldamiz (✉ *Ca. Faucett km. 7* ☎ *082/571–531*).

Currency Banco de Crédito (✉ *Jr. Daniel A. Carrion 201* ☎ *082/571–193*).

Mail SERPOST (✉ *Av. León Velarde 675* ☎ *082/571–088*).

Medical Hospital de Apoyo Santa Rosa (✉ *Jr. Cajamarca 171* ☎ *082/571–019*).

Visitor Info Dirección Regional de Industria y Turismo (✉ *Jr. San Martin Urb. Fonavi F20* ☎ *082/571–164*).

EXPLORING

Obelisco. The southern Amazon has a skyscraper! The 35-meter (115-foot) strangely designed building, shaped like a prison-guard post but colored like it belongs on a different planet, is a few blocks north of Puerto Maldonado's downtown. Bas-relief scenes from the history of Madre de Dios decorate the lookout tower's base, and the top has a vista of the nearby rain forest and the city. ✉ *Fitzcarrald and Madre de Dios* ☎ *082/572–993* 🎫 *S/1* ⊗ *Daily 8–8.*

WHERE TO EAT AND STAY

$ 🏨 **Hotel Cabaña Quinta.** The rambling chestnut-wood Victorian-style house, the tropical veranda, the arched doorways, the latticework, and the red-and-green *sangapilla* plants in the garden could have come right out of a Graham Greene novel. The rooms are a little less evocative but pleasantly furnished with wood paneling, print spreads, and drapes. The restaurant is one of Puerto Maldonado's best and serves a small menu of fish, meats, and soups, with plenty of yucca (cassava) chips on the side. **Pros:** good restaurant; pleasant staff. **Cons:** basic rooms. ✉ *Cusco 535* ☎ *082/571–045* ⊕ *www.hotelcabanaquinta.com.pe* ➟ *51 rooms, 3 suites* ♻ *In-room: a/c, refrigerator, Wi-Fi. In-hotel: restaurant, room service, pool, laundry service, Internet terminal, Wi-Fi hotspot* ▭ *V* ⦿ *BP.*

$ 🏨 **Hotel Don Carlos.** By the Tambopata River, the Don Carlos is more rustic than the other hotels in this small Peruvian chain but it is still one of the best lodges in town. Unexciting rooms with high ceilings and tile floors enclose a pleasant garden and a much-appreciated pool—the largest one around. **Pros:** pool; quiet. **Cons:** rooms are boring. ✉ *León Velarde 1271* ☎ *082/571–029* ⊕ *www.hotelesdoncarlos.com* ➟ *31 rooms* ♻ *In-room: a/c, refrigerator. In-hotel: restaurant, room service, pool, laundry service, Internet terminal* ▭ *MC, V* ⦿ *BP.*

$ 🏨 **Wasaí Maldonado Lodge.** The Wasaí gives you that jungle-lodge feel right in town, a block from the Plaza de Armas. Bungalows on stilts are scattered amidst lush foliage on a hillside leading down from the lobby toward the pool and riverbank. The shady grounds overlook the Madre de Dios River and the massive bridge that spans it; the thatched-roof, tornillo-wood bungalows make for a surprisingly cool place in an otherwise sweltering town. You can book any of various day trips, such as to Sandoval Lake, or head to their lodge on the Tambopata River for a couple of nights. **Pros:** convenient; jungle setting. **Cons:** you're still in Puerto Maldonado. ⊠ *Bellinghurst s/n* ☎ *082/572–290 or 01/436–8792* ⊕ *www.wasai.com* ⊃ *17 cabins* ⌂ *In-room: no phone, a/c (some), refrigerator. In-hotel: restaurant, room service, bar, pool, laundry service, Wi-Fi hotspot* ⊟ *AE, MC, V* ⊺⊙⊺ *CP.*

TAMBOPATA NATIONAL RESERVE AND BAHUAJA-SONENE NATIONAL PARK

5 km (3 mi) south of Puerto Maldonado.

From Puerto Maldonado, the Madre de Dios River flows east to the Bolivian border. The river defines the northern boundary of the Tambopata National Reserve and passes some nearby, easy-to-reach jungle lodges. The Tambopata River flows out of the reserve and into the Madre de Dios at Puerto Maldonado, and a boat trip up that waterway can take you deep into that protected area: a 3.8-million-acre rain-forest reserve about the size of Connecticut. Officially separate from the reserve, but usually grouped for convenience under the "Tambopata" heading, is the Bahuaja-Sonene National Park, created in 1996 and taking its moniker from the names in the local indigenous Ese'eja language for the Tambopata and Heath rivers, respectively. (The Río Heath forms Peru's southeastern boundary with neighboring Bolivia.) The former Pampas de Río Heath Reserve along the border itself is now incorporated into Bahuaja-Sonene, and encompasses a looks-out-of-place secondary forest more resembling the African savanna than the lush tropical Amazon.

Peru works closely on joint conservation projects with Bolivia, whose adjoining Madidi National Park forms a grand cross-border 7.2-million-acre reserve area. Only environmentally friendly activities are permitted in Tambopata. The area functions partially as a managed tropical-forest reserve; local communities collect *castañas*, or Brazil nuts, from the forest floor.

Elevations here range from 500 meters (1,640 feet) to a lofty 3,000 meters (9,840 feet), providing fertile homes for an astounding number of animals and plants. The area holds a world record in the number of butterfly species (1,234) recorded by scientists. Within the reserve, the Explorer's Inn holds the world-record bird-species sighting for a single lodge: 600 have been recorded on its grounds, 331 of those sighted within a single day. ■TIP➔ Tambopata holds the most famous and largest of Madre de Dios's collpas, visited by approximately 15 species of parrots and macaws who congregate at dawn to collect a beakful of mineral-rich clay, an important but mysterious part of their diet.

GETTING HERE AND AROUND

The Tambopata jungle lodges are easier to reach—and less expensive—than those in the Manu Biosphere Reserve, Madre de Dios's more famous ecotourism area. And Tambopata is no poor man's Manu either—its numbers and diversity of wildlife are very impressive. A

Continued on page 319

THE JUNGLE LIFE

by Doug Wechsler

Green-winged Macaw (Ara chloroptera) foraging high in rain forest canopy.

An observant naturalist living in the Peruvian Amazon can expect to see something new and exciting every day in his or her life. To the casual traveler much of this life remains hidden at first but reveals itself with careful observation.

Western Amazonia may be the most biologically diverse region on earth. The areas around Puerto Maldonado and Iquitos are two of the best locales to observe this riot of life.

On the Tambopata Reserve, for example, 620 species of birds and more than 1,200 species of butterflies have been sighted within a few miles of Explorer's Inn. To put that into perspective, only about 700 species of birds and 700 species of butterflies breed in all of North America. Within the huge Manu National Park, which includes part of the eastern slope of the Andes, about $\frac{1}{10}$ of the world's bird species can be

sighted. A single tree can harbor the same number of ant species as found in the entire British Isles. A single hectare (2.4 acres) of forest might hold nearly 300 species of trees.

This huge diversity owes itself to ideal temperatures and constant moisture for growth of plants and animals and to a mixture of stability and change over the past several million years. The complex structure of the forest leads to many microhabitats for plants and animals. The diversity of plants and animals is overwhelming and the opportunity for new observations is limitless.

STARS OF THE AMAZON

Pink River Dolphin: The long-snouted pink river dolphin enters shallow waters, flooded forest, and even large lakes. Unlike the gray dolphin of river channels, this species rarely jumps out of the water.
Eats: Fish. **Weighs:** 350 lbs. **Myth:** Often blamed for pregnancies when father is unknown.

Red-and-Green Macaw: The loud, raucous shrieks first call attention to red-and-green macaws, the largest members of the parrot family in the Amazon. Clay licks near a number of jungle lodges in Madre de Dios are great places to observe these spectacular birds.
Eats: Seeds of trees and vines. **Weighs:** 3 lbs.
Length: 3 ft. **Odd habit:** Consumes clay from steep banks.

Hoatzin: The clumsy-flying, chicken-sized Hoatzin sports a long frizzled crest and bare blue skin around the eye, suggesting something out of the Jurassic. Its digestive system features a fermentation chamber and is more bovine than avian.
Eats: Leaves, especially arum. **Weighs:** 1.8 lbs.
Unusual feature: Nestlings can climb with claws on their wings. **Favorite Hangout:** Trees and shrubs in swampy vegetation near lakes.

Squirrel Monkey: The small, active squirrel monkeys live in groups of 20 to 100 or more. These common monkeys can be distinguished by a black muzzle and white mask.
Eats: Large insects and fruit. **Weighs:** 2 lbs.
Favorite Hangout: Lower and mid-levels of vine-tangled forest especially near rivers and lakes. **Associates:** Brown capuchin monkeys often hang out with the troop.

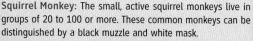

Red Howler Monkey: A loud, long, deep, roaring chorus from these large, sedentary, red-haired monkeys announces the coming of dawn, an airplane, or a rainstorm. The swollen throat houses an incredible vocal apparatus.
Eats: Leaves and fruits. **Weighs:** 8 to 23 lbs.
Favorite Hangout: Tree tops and mid-levels of forest.
Unfortunate trait: They will urinate and defecate on you if you walk beneath them.

Three-toed Sloth: This slow-moving, upside down ball of fur is easiest to spot in tree crowns with open growth like cecropias. The dark mask and three large claws on the hands distinguish it from the larger two-toed sloth.

Eats: Leaves. **Weighs:** 5 to 11 lbs. **Favorite Hangout:** Tree tops and mid-levels of forest. **Unusual habit:** Sloths climb to the ground once a week to move their bowels.

Cecropia Tree: The huge, multi-lobed leaves, open growth form, and thin light-colored trunks make cecropias among the most distinctive Amazonian trees. Cecropias are the first trees to shoot up when a forest is cut or a new river island is formed. Their long finger-like fruits are irresistible to birds.

Height: Up to 50 ft. or more. **Bark:** Has bamboo-like rings. **Attracts:** Toucans, tanagers, bats, monkeys, sloths. **Relationships:** The hollow stems house stinging ants that protect the tree—beware.

Horned Screamer: A bare, white quill arches from the crown of this ungainly, dark, turkey-sized bird. Its long toes enable it to walk on floating vegetation. Occasionally it soars among vultures.

Eats: Water plants. **Weighs:** up to 7 lbs.
Favorite Hangout: Shores of lagoons and lakes.
Relatives: Screamers are related to ducks and geese—who would have guessed?

Russet-backed Oropendola: What the yellow tailed, crow-sized, oropendola lacks in beauty, it makes up for in its liquid voice. The remarkable three-foot long woven nests dangle in groups from an isolated tree—protection from monkeys.

Eats: Insects and fruit. **Favorite Hangout:** Forest near clearings and rivers. **Look for:** Flocks of hundreds going to and from roosting islands in the river at dusk and dawn.

Giant Amazon Water Lily: This water lily has leaves up to 7 ft. across and 6–12 inch white or pink flowers that bloom at night. The edges of the leaves bend upward. Leaf stems grow with the rising flood.

Length: Stems up to 20 ft. **Eaten by:** Fish eat the seeds.
Favorite Hangout: River backwaters, oxbow lakes.
Sex changes: Female parts flower the first night, then the flower turns pink and the male parts open.

TIPS:

Don't expect all those species to come out and say hello! The Amazon's great biodiversity is made possible by the jungle's sheltering, almost secretive nature. Here are tips to help train your eye to see through nature's camouflage.

1. Listen for movement. Crashing branches are the first clue of monkeys, and rustling leaves betray secretive lizards and snakes.

2. Going upstream on the river means your boat will stay steady close to shore—where all the wildlife is.

3. Look for birds in large mixed-species flocks; stay with the flock while the many birds slowly reveal themselves.

4. Concentrate your observation in the early morning and late afternoon, and take a midday siesta to save energy for night-time exploration.

5. Wear cloths that blend in with the environment. Exception: hummingbird lovers should wear shirts with bright red floral prints.

6. Train your eye to pick out anomalies—what might, at first, seem like an out-of place ball of debris in the tree could be a sloth.

7. At night, use a bright headlamp or hold a flashlight next to your head to spot eye-shine from mammals, nocturnal birds, frogs, boas, moths, and spiders.

8. Crush leaves and use your nose when getting to know tropical plants.

Hanging bridge over the Tambopata rainforest.

half-hour flight from Cusco takes you to Puerto Maldonado, the Tambopata jumping-off point. The easiest lodges to reach are less than an hour-long boat trip down the Madre de Dios River, on or near Lake Sandoval. Lodges up the Tambopato River take anywhere from a few hours to two days to reach, but they lie near areas of impressive biodiversity. Some of the lodges offer two-day/one-night packages that amount to little more than 24 hours, but three days is really the least you should spend in this area, and if you really want to go deep into Tambopata, you'll need five days.

EXPLORING

Lago Sandoval. Changes in the course of the Río Madre de Dios have created many so-called oxbow lakes, which were formed when riverbeds shifted and the former beds filled with water. Lago Sandoval, east of Puerto Maldonado in the Tambopata National Reserve, is the most famous of these. It brims with parrots and macaws, but also plenty of waterfowl, most notably herons and kingfishers. A family of elusive and endangered giant otters also lives in Lake Sandoval. The lake is a 30-minute boat ride from Puerto Maldonado; once you disembark there's an easy 2-km (1-mi) hike to the actual lake. ⊠ *9 km (5½ mi) east of Puerto Maldonado.*

Lago Valencia. Two hours northeast of Puerto Maldonado, just outside the boundaries of Tambopata, is Lago Valencia. The Wasaí Maldonado Lodge offers day trips that visit Lagos Sandoval and Valencia, which can also be visited from the Sandoval Lake Lodge. ■TIP➔ Expect to see abundant wildlife, avian (herons, cormorants, and kingfishers) and otherwise. Turtles abound, and your best chance of glimpsing caimans (like a small alligator) is around sunset. A community of the indigenous Ese'eja is nearby. This section of the river is a favorite lucky site for Madre de Dios's gold panners. Carry your passport on the trip to Valencia; you'll be a mere 5 km (3 mi) from the Bolivian border, and Peruvian authorities may inspect documentation of those who float this close. ⊠ *23 km (14 mi) east of Puerto Maldonado.*

WHERE TO STAY

The listings below are for lodges consisting of wooden huts raised on stilts. They range from rustic to the jungle luxury of the Reserva Amazónica. Rates for all lodges include river transportation from Puerto Maldonado, bilingual nature guides, three meals per day, and varied excursions. The Reserva Amazónica and Sandoval Lake Lodge are the region's most accessible lodges, less than an hour down the Madre de Dios River from Puerto Maldonado. The next closest is Posada Amazonas, which is less than 90 minutes up the Tambopata River, whereas the rest require at least a three-hour boat trip. Whichever lodge you choose, you will be met at the Puerto Maldonado Airport and transported to and from the lodge by bus and boat.

$$$ 🛏 **Explorer's Inn.** No place in the world tops this one for the number of bird species (600) sighted at a single lodge, though you'll need to stay more than a few days to match that number. The lodge, managed by Peruvian Safaris, was one of the country's ecotourism pioneers, and consequently has a reference library and knowledgeable guides.

CLOSE UP

Jungle Days

The knock at the door comes early. "*¡Buenos días!* Good morning!" It's 5 AM and your guide is rousing you for the dawn excursion to the nearby *collpa de guacamayos*. He doesn't want him to miss the riotous, colorful spectacle of hundreds of parrots and macaws descending to the vertical clay lick to ingest a beakful of mineral-rich earth. Roll over and go back to sleep? Blasphemy! You're in the Amazon.

A stay at any of the remote Iquitos or Madre de Dios lodges is not for the faint of heart. You'll need to gear up for a different type of vacation experience. Relaxing and luxuriating it will not be, although some facilities are quite comfortable. Your days will be packed with activities: bird- and wildlife-watching, boat trips, rain-forest hikes, visits to indigenous communities, mountain biking, and on. You'll be with guides from the minute you're picked up in Iquitos, Puerto Maldonado, or Cusco. Most lodges hire top-notch guides who know their areas well, and you'll be forever amazed at their ability to spot that camouflaged howler monkey from a hundred paces.

The lodge should provide mosquito netting and sheets or blankets, and some type of lantern for your room. (Don't expect electricity.) But check the lodge's Web site, or with your tour operator, for a list of what to bring and what the lodge provides. Your required inventory will vary proportionally by just how much you have to rough it. Pack sunscreen, sunglasses, insect repellent, a hat, hiking boots, sandals, light shoes, a waterproof bag, and a flashlight. Also, a light, loose-fitting, long-sleeve shirt and equally loose-fitting long trousers and socks are musts for the evening when the mosquitoes come out. Carry your yellow-fever vaccination certificate and prescription for malaria prevention and an extra supply of any medicine you might be taking. Bring along antidiarrheal medication, too. You'll need a small day pack for the numerous guided hikes, and bring plastic bags to protect your belongings from the rain and humidity. Also bring binoculars, and your camera. Everything is usually included in the package price, though soft drinks, beer, wine and cocktails carry a hefty markup.

Few things are more enjoyable at a jungle lodge than dinner at the end of the day. You'll dine family style around a common table, discussing the day's sightings, comparing notes well into the evening, knowing full well there will be another 5 AM knock in the morning.

—By Jeffrey Van Fleet

It accommodates tourists and visiting scientists alike in its thatched-roof bungalows. All can be seen exploring the lodge's 30 km (18½ mi) of trails. There's no electricity in the rooms. The minimum stay is three days/two nights. **Pros:** knowledgeable guides; in the Tambopata Reserve; responsible tourism. **Cons:** rustic; basic meals; noise from neighboring rooms. ⊠ *Tambopata River, 58 km (36 mi) southwest of Puerto Maldonado* ☎ *01/447–8888* ⊕ *www.explorersinn.com* ↝ *30 rooms* ⅙ *In-room: no phone, no a/c, no TV. In-hotel: restaurant, Internet terminal, Wi-Fi hotspot* ⓘ|*AI.*

\$\$\$\$ ⊡ **Posada Amazonas.** This attractive lodge is owned jointly by Rainforest
Fodor'sChoice Expeditions and the Ese'eja Native Community of Infierno, and some
★ of the guides and staff are locals. Rooms are in long buildings with
high, thatched roofs, mosquito nets over the beds, and wide, screenless
windows to welcome cooling breezes; however, cane walls that don't
reach the roof mean limited privacy. Kerosene lanterns provide light at
night, but electricity is available in common areas for several hours to
recharge batteries. Activities include kayaking, bird watching, guided
hikes through the lodge's 6,000-hectare (14,820-acre) nature reserve, a
boat tour of a nearby lake, and a medicinal plant tour led by an Ese'eja
herbalist. Packages include all transportation—first in a thatched truck
then in a boat—lodging, buffet meals, and naturalist guides. The lodge is
a one-hour drive, one-hour boat ride, and 15-minute walk from Puerto
Maldonado, and the minimum stay is three days/two nights. **Pros:** lot's
of wildlife; good range of guided excursions; lodge benefits local people
and nature. **Cons:** no electricity in rooms; you hear everything in neighboring rooms. ⊠ *Tambopata River, 40 km (25 mi) southwest of Puerto
Maldonado* ☎ *01/719–6422 or 9935–12265; 877/870–0578 in U.S.*
⊕ *www.perunature.com* ↝ *30 rooms* ⌂ *In-room: no phone, no a/c, safe,
no TV. In-hotel: restaurant, bar, Wi-Fi hotspot* ═ *AE, MC, V* ⦿ *FAP.*

\$\$\$\$ ⊡ **Refugio Amazonas.** Since it lies halfway between Puerto Maldonado
☾ and the Tambopata Research Center, most travelers spend a night here
on the way to and from the Center. The Refugio sits at the edge of
a Brazil nut concession—a vast tract of wilderness managed sustain-
ably by local people—that is contiguous with the Tambopata National
Reserve. It lies near a parrot and a mammal collpa, so it is a good place
to see wildlife. ■**TIP**➡ A canopy tower provides a great view of the rain
forest. The lodge caters to families, with special environmental education activities for children. Rooms are rustic but comfortable, comparable to those of the Refugio Amazonas. The lodge is a one-hour drive,
three-hour boat ride, and 15-minute walk from Puerto Maldonado.
Pros: surrounded by rain forest; children's program; responsible company. **Cons:** no electricity in rooms; you hear everything in neighboring rooms. ⊠ *Tambopata River, 80 km (50 mi) southwest of Puerto
Maldonado* ☎ *01/719–6422, or 9935–12265; 877/870–0578 in U.S.*
⊕ *www.perunature.com* ↝ *32 rooms* ⌂ *In-room: no phone, no a/c, no
TV. In-hotel: restaurant, bar, Wi-Fi hotspot, children's programs (ages
6–12)* ═ *AE, MC, V* ⦿ *FAP.*

\$\$\$\$ ⊡ **Reserva Amazónica.** A 45-minute boat ride downriver from Puerto
☾ Maldonado on the Madre de Dios River, this is the area's most accessible and comfortable jungle lodge. Private bungalows, set amid trees
near the river, define "jungle chic" with their solar-heated showers,
solar-powered fans and lights, and porch hammocks. They even have a
tree-house bungalow. The lodge is on a 42,000-acre, private ecological
reserve that is traversed by trails and a canopy walkway, with suspension bridges strung between treetops. The reserve is home to jungle
rodents called agoutis, various kinds of monkeys and an array of birds;
a small collpa on the riverbank attracts flocks of parakeets at dawn. For
more wildlife viewing, consider a day trip to nearby Lago Sandoval. The
lodge runs an environmental-education program for children. Dinners

complete the jungle experience with dishes such as *pacamoto* (fish or chicken cooked inside bamboo over coals). **Pros:** easy to get to; good excursions; children's programs; environmentally friendly. **Cons:** bungalows are close enough to hear neighbors; expensive. ⊠ *Km 15, Madre de Dios River, Puerto Maldonado* ☎ *084/245–314* ⊕ *www.inkaterra.com* ⤳ *33 rooms, 2 suites* ⚒ *In-room: no phone, no a/c, no TV. In-hotel: restaurant, bar, spa, Internet terminal, children's programs (ages 6–12)* ⊟ *AE, MC, V* ⦿| *FAP.*

$$$$
Fodor's Choice
★

⊞ Sandoval Lake Lodge. Despite its proximity to Puerto Maldonado, this lodge owned by InkaNatura Travel puts you in the midst of Amazonian nature. The lodge overlooks Lago Sandoval, an oxbow lake surrounded by palms in the Tambopata Reserve. The palm fruit attracts macaws and parrots, whereas the lake is home to rare giant otters. A stay includes excursions on the lake and into the surrounding forest with bilingual naturalist guides. Comfortable rooms have private baths, hot water showers, fans, and electricity during certain hours. To get here, you take a 30-minute boat ride from Puerto Maldonado on the Madre de Díos River, hike down a forest trail for about 1 mi, then get into a canoe for a 30-minute paddle to the lodge. The minimum stay is two nights. **Pros:** beautiful location; good excursions; lots of wildlife. **Cons:** small rooms; the boat-hike-boat access isn't for everyone. ⊠ *10 km (6 mi) east of Puerto Maldonado* ☎ *01/440–2022, or 203–5000* ⊕ *www. inkanatura.com* ⤳ *25 rooms* ⚒ *In-room: no phone, no a/c, safe, no TV. In-hotel: restaurant, bar* ⦿| *FAP.*

$$$$

⊞ Tambopata Ecolodge. This lodge, about four hours south of Puerto Maldonado on the Tambopata River, has some of the region's most comfortable accommodations. Standard rooms in thatched duplexes lack electricity, though they have solar-powered hot water. Free-standing bungalow suites have electricity and offer more privacy. All rooms have screened windows, mosquito nets, and porches with comfy hammocks in which to curl up at the end of a day of sightseeing on the lodge's 25 km (15½ mi) of trails. The minimum stay is three days/two nights, with meals and guides included. **Pros:** nice rooms; good programs; sustainable tourism. **Cons:** you can hear your neighbors; less wildlife than other lodges. ⊠ *Tambopata River, 70 km (44 mi) southwest of Puerto Maldonado* ☎ *082/571–397* ⊕ *www.tambopatalodge. com* ⤳ *28 rooms, 6 suites* ⚒ *In-room: no phone, no a/c, safe, no TV. In-hotel: restaurant, bar* ⊟ *AE, MC, V* ⦿| *FAP.*

$$$$
Fodor's Choice
★

⊞ Tambopata Research Center. A four-hour upriver boat journey from the Refugio Amazonas lodge brings you to this rustic lodge in the heart of the Tambopata National Reserve. It is one of the best places in Peru, if not the Amazon Basin, to see wildlife; you may see several kinds of monkeys and, if you're lucky, rain-forest wildlife such as peccaries (wild pigs), jaguars, and anteaters. Hundreds of parrots and dozens of macaws visit the nearby clay lick each day at dawn. The rooms are small and lack private baths; a separate building has four showers and another, four toilets. Because of the distance, stays here are combined with overnights at the Refugio Amazonas on tours with a five-day/four-night minimum. **Pros:** deep in the wilderness; lots of macaws and other wildlife. **Cons:** thin walls and shared bath mean little privacy.

✉ *Tambopata River, 150 km (93 mi) southwest of Puerto Maldonado* ☎ *01/421–8347 or 9935–12265; 877/870–0578 in U.S.* ⊕ *www.perunature.com* ⇘ *18 rooms with shared bath* ♨ *In-room: no phone, no a/c, no TV. In-hotel: bar* ▭ *MC, V* ⦿*FAP.*

$$$$ ⛺ **Wasaí Tambopata Lodge.** This attractive lodge, set deep in the wilderness (a three-and-a-half-hour boat ride up the Tambopata River from Puerto Maldonado), has comfortable rooms, good guides, and lots of wildlife. It is surrounded by a 4,000-hectare (9,884-acre) private rain forest reserve that can be explored on 15 km (9 mi) of trails. They also have a canopy tower, kayaks and canoes, and offer tours to a large macaw collpa. Lodging is in bungalows with screened windows, electricity, hot water, and porches; the dining area and lounge are also quite pleasant. Be sure to request a private bungalow. **Pros:** comfortable rooms; privacy; owner managed; good excursions; sustainable tourism. **Cons:** a three-and-half-hour boat trip to reach. ✉ *Tambopata River, 100 km (62 mi) southwest of Puerto Maldonado* ☎*01/436-8792* ⊕ *www.wasai.com* ⇘ *19 cabins* ♨ *In-room: no phone, no a/c. In-hotel: restaurant, bar, Wi-Fi hotspot* ▭ *AE, MC, V* ⦿*FAP.*

Fodor's Choice
★

MANU BIOSPHERE RESERVE

Fodor's Choice
★

90 km (55 mi) north of Cusco.

Readers of the British children's series *A Bear Called Paddington* know that the title character "came from darkest Peru." The stereotype is quite outdated, of course, but the Manu Biosphere Reserve, which has been called "the most biodiverse park on earth," will conjure up the jungliest Tarzan-movie images you can imagine. And the reserve really does count the Andean spectacled bear, South America's only ursid, and the animal on which Paddington was based, among its 200 mammals.

This reserve is Peru's largest protected area and straddles the boundary of the Madre de Dios and Cusco departments. Manu encompasses more than 4½ million acres of pristine primary tropical-forest wilderness, ranging in altitude from 3,450 meters (12,000 feet) down through cloud forests and into seemingly endless lowland tropical rain forests at 300 meters (less than 1,000 feet). This geographical variety shelters a stunning biodiversity. A near total absence of humans and hunting has made the animal life less skittish and more open to observation. ■**TIP→ The reserve's 13 monkey species scrutinize visitors with the same curiosity they elicit.** White caimans sun themselves lazily on sandy riverbanks, whereas the larger black ones lurk in the oxbow lakes. With luck, you'll see tapirs at the world's largest tapir collpa. Giant river otters and elusive big cats such as jaguars and ocelots sometimes make fleeting appearances. But it's the avian life that has made Manu world famous. The area counts more than 1,000 bird species, fully one-ninth of those known. Some 500 species have been spotted at the Pantiacolla Lodge alone. Birds include macaws, toucans, roseate spoonbills, and 1½-meter- (5-foot-) tall wood storks.

Manu, a UNESCO World Heritage Site, is divided into three distinct zones. The smallest is the so-called "cultural zone" (Zone C), with several indigenous groups and the majority of the jungle lodges. Access is

7

permitted to all, even to independent travelers in theory, though vast distances make this unrealistic for all but the most intrepid. About three times the size of the cultural zone, Manu's "reserve zone" (Zone B) is uninhabited but contains the Manu Lodge. Access is by permit only, and you must be accompanied by a guide from one of the 10 agencies authorized to take people into the area. The western 80% of Manu is designated a national park (Zone A). Authorized researchers and indigenous peoples who reside there are permitted in this zone; visitors may not enter.

GETTING HERE AND AROUND

A Manu excursion is no quick trip. Overland travel from Cusco, the usual embarkation point, takes two days with an overnight in the cloud forest. A charter flight in a twin-engine plane to the small airstrip at Boca Manu shaves that time down to 45 minutes and adds a few hundred dollars onto your package price, and there have been accidents. From Boca Manu you'll still have several hours of boat travel to reach your lodge. The logistics of travel to this remote part of the Amazon mean you should allow at least five days for your excursion.

WHERE TO STAY

$$$$ ⬚ **Cock of the Rock Lodge.** Higher elevation means fewer mosquitoes, and this lodge is nestled in the cloud forest of the Kosñipata River Valley, in Manu's cultural zone. Owned by the respected InkaNatura Travel, the lodge takes its name from Peru's red-and-black national bird, which frequents the grounds. It is one of hundreds of avian species found in the lodge's vast nature reserve, among them 35 types of hummingbird and more than 40 tanager species. The lodge's bungalows are a notch above the competition's, with balconies, decent beds, and an ample supply of hot water, but only half have private bathrooms and none have electricity. The minimum stay is three days/two nights, with transportation and guided excursions included. It can also be combined with the Manu Wildlife Center on a one-week trip. **Pros:** great bird watching; gorgeous setting; pleasant climate. **Cons:** not cheap; a long drive from Cusco. ✉ *177 km (110 mi or a 7-hr drive) northeast of Cusco* ☎ *01/440–2022, 203–5000, 084/255–255* ⊕ *www.inkanatura. com* ⟿ *12 rooms, 6 with bath* ⌂ *In-room: no phone, no a/c, no TV. In-hotel: restaurant, bar* ▯⊙▯ *FAP.*

$$$$ ⬚ **Manu Cloud Forest Lodge.** High in the cloud forest of Manu's cultural zone, this lodge overlooking the rushing Río Unión in a forest blooming with orchids and busy with hummingbirds. Rooms are rustic with basic beds and tables, but all have a private bath and plenty of hot water (no electricity). The Lodge also has a sauna and there is electricity in the main building at night. The lodge is owned by the highly respected Manu Nature Tours, whose naturalist guides can help you spot the local birdlife. The minimum stay is three days/two nights, which is often combined with a stay at the Manu Lodge. Guide and ground transportation are included. White-water rafting is an optional add-on. **Pros:** great scenery, birds, and guides; only 12 rooms. **Cons:** basic rooms; a long drive to reach. ✉ *About 178 km (110 mi, or a 7-hr drive) north of Cusco* ☎ *084/252–721* ⊕ *www.manuperu.com* ⟿ *8 rooms, 4 cab-*

ins ☆ *In-room: no phone, no a/c, no TV. In-hotel: bar, bicycles* ⊟ *AE, MC, V* ⊙ *FAP.*

$$$$ ⊞ **Manu Lodge.** Built by Manu Nature Tours from mahogany salvaged from the banks of the Manu River, this is the only lodge inside the national park's reserved zone. It stands at the edge of a 2-km- (1-mi-) long oxbow lake called Cocha Juárez. ■ **TIP→** **Frequently seen in the lake are giant river otters and black and white caimans.** The rustic-but-comfortable, screened-in lodge has a two-story dining area, and you have access to three habitats: the lakes, the river, and a trail network spanning 10 square km (4 square mi) of rain forest. The lodge has tree-climbing equipment to lift visitors onto canopy platforms for viewing denizens of the treetops. The minimum stay is five days/four nights (with a stay en route at Manu Cloud Forest Lodge), and includes bilingual guides, ground transportation, and meals. Rooms have solar-heated showers and the main building has electricity for several hours each night. **Pros:** knowledgeable guides; prime location for wildlife watching. **Cons:** not for the urban minded; a long trip to reach. ✉ *30 min by air and two hours by boat from Cusco* ☎ *084/252–721* ⊕ *www.manuperu. com* ↗ *12 rooms* ☆ *In-room: no phone, no a/c, no TV. In-hotel: restaurant, bar* ⊟ *AE, MC, V* ⊙ *FAP.*

$$$$ ⊞ **Manu Wildlife Center.** As the name suggests, this is a great place for wildlife viewing, as it sits close to macaw and tapir collpas and has 48 km (30 mi) of trails through a forest adjacent to Manu National Park. The MWC, as it's known, is jointly owned by InkaNatura Travel and Manu Expeditions, and services are top-notch. Raised thatched-roof bungalows have screens and wooden latticework walls as well as tiled hot-water baths. Electricity is available in the main building for a few hours each night. InkaNatura also offers the option of spending nights at a tent camp inside Manu National Park. Rates include round-trip charter flight from Cusco. **Pros:** wildlife central; knowledgeable guides. **Cons:** rustic, remote, but not cheap. ✉ *30 min by air and 90 min by boat from Cusco* ☎ *084/255–255; 877/827–8350 in U.S.* ⊕ *www. inkanatura.com* ↗ *22 cabins* ☆ *In-room: no phone, no a/c, no TV. In-hotel: bar* ⊟ *AE, MC, V* ⊙ *FAP.*

$$$ ⊞ **Pantiacolla Lodge.** Named for the mountain range that towers over it, the Pantiacolla Lodge sits in a 900-hectare (2,223-acre) nature reserve in Manu's cultural zone. The reserve is home to about 600 bird species as well as an array of mammals that ranges from troops of fluffy titi monkeys to herds of wild pigs called peccaries. It is higher, and thus slightly cooler, than the lowland lodges, and has fewer mosquitoes. Rooms lack electricity and are very basic, with beds, mosquito netting, tables, and wooden floors. In addition to wildlife that includes eight monkey species and some very rare birds, the lodge offers presentations by people from a nearby Harakmbut indigenous community. Tours here include overnights at the company's cloud forest lodge, and can be combined with a few days at their lodge in Manu's reserved zone. **Pros:** relatively inexpensive; great bird watching; excellent guides. **Cons:** basic rooms; you can hear your neighbors; remote. ✉ *290 km (180 mi) northeast of Cusco* ☎ *084/238–323* ⊕ *www.pantiacolla.com* ↗ *11 rooms, 8 with shared bath* ☆ *In-room: no a/c, no phone, no TV* ⊟ *AE, MC, V* ⊙ *FAP.*

IQUITOS AND ENVIRONS

Founded by Jesuit priests in the 1500s, Iquitos was once called the "Pearl of the Amazon." It isn't quite that lustrous today, but it's still a pleasant, friendly town that provides access to the Amazon River, rainforest wildlife, and various indigenous cultures. Although most travelers fly here specifically for an excursion into the surrounding rain forest, Iquitos has comparable sites nearby that can be visited in a few hours, or a day, and deserves at least a night. The city itself may grow on you as you become accustomed to the humid climate and relaxed, easy ways of its citizens. A revamped Malecón (riverwalk) is the popular place for an evening stroll, and you can enjoy a meal of river fish, or another rain-forest delicacy, while floating on that waterway.

GETTING AROUND

The best way to travel around the Iquitos area is by boat, and hundreds of vessels come and go each day, from seagoing ships that travel all the way through Brazil to the Atlantic Ocean to tiny dugout canoes bound for jungle enclaves.

Various companies run cruises out of Iquitos, or the nearby town of Nauta, that provide comfortable access to the province's protected areas and indigenous villages. Nature lodges transport guests in swift launches with outboard engines and canvas tops to protect you from the sun and rain. If you have plenty of time, and are up for an adventure, you could take a local boat to one of the region's other towns or cities, though you'll need to bring a hammock, food, water, and lots of bug spray. Passage to Pucallpa, for example, takes four to eight days and costs around $40 USD.

BORDER CROSSINGS Various companies offer speedboat service to the border with Brazil and Colombia. It's an 8- to 10-hour boat ride to the border town of Santa Rosa, across the river from Leticia, Colombia and Tabatinga, Brazil; the one-way trip costs only $70 USD. Each company runs twice a week, so boats depart every day; all the ticket offices are on the 300 block of Calle Raymondi, a few blocks from the Plaza de Armas, so you simply go there and buy a ticket from the company that departs the day you want to travel.

American citizens don't need a visa to enter Colombia, but they do need one for Brazil; you can try to pick one up at the **Brazilian Consulate** (⊠ *Sgto. Lores 363, Iquitos*), but you're best off getting it before leaving home.

IQUITOS

1,150 km (713 mi) northeast of Lima.

A sultry port town on the Río Amazonas, Iquitos is quite probably the world's largest city that cannot be reached by road. The city has nearly 500,000 inhabitants and is the capital of the vast Loreto department. The area around Iquitos was first inhabited by small, independent Amazonian tribes. In the 1500s Jesuit missionaries began adventuring in the area, trying to Christianize the local population, but the city wasn't officially founded until 1757.

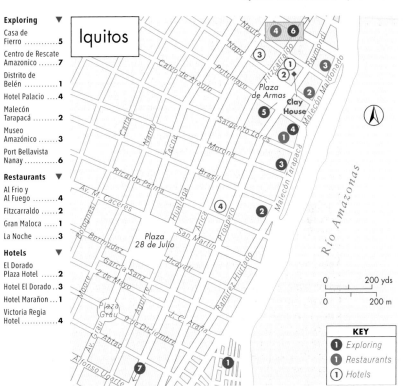

Exploring ▼

Casa de
Fierro **5**

Centro de Rescate
Amazonico **7**

Distrito de
Belén **1**

Hotel Palacio **4**

Malecón
Tarapacá **2**

Museo
Amazónico **3**

Port Bellavista
Nanay **6**

Restaurants ▼

Al Frio y
Al Fuego **4**

Fitzcarraldo **2**

Gran Maloca **1**

La Noche **3**

Hotels ▼

El Dorado
Plaza Hotel **2**

Hotel El Dorado ..**3**

Hotel Marañon ...**1**

Victoria Regia
Hotel **4**

Iquitos saw unprecedented growth and opulence during the rubber boom, but became an Amazonian backwater overnight when the boom went bust. The economy slouched along, barely sustaining itself with logging, exotic-animal exports, and Brazil-nut harvesting. In the early 1970s, petroleum was discovered. The black gold, along with ecotourism and logging, have since become the backbone of the region's economy, though drug running also provides significant income.

The city's historic center stretches along a lagoon formed by the Río Itaya, near the confluence of the Río Nanay and the Río Amazonas. Most of its historic buildings, hotels, restaurants, and banks are within blocks of the Plaza de Armas, the main square, and the nearby Malecón Maldonado riverwalk. It is a bustling town where motor scooters outnumber cars and the typical family transportation is a three-wheeler with a canvas top.

GETTING AROUND

The most common mode of transportation in Iquitos is the mototaxi, a three-wheeled motorcycle with a canvas top. Service in town costs around S/1.50, whereas a trip to the outskirts costs around S/10 an hour. Always negotiate the price beforehand. It should cost S/3 to Port Bellavista Nanay, where you can hire a boat to the butterfly farm, serpentarium and a Yagua, or Bora Indian village, though those places are best visited with a guide.

SAFETY AND PRECAUTIONS

Though violent crime is not common in Iquitos, pickpockets are. And remember your mosquito repellent.

ESSENTIALS

Currency **BBVA Banco Continental** (✉ *Jr. Putumayo 253* ☎ *065/231–038*). **Banco de Crédito** (✉ *Av. Putumayo at Jr. Prospero* ☎ *065/233–838*). **Scociabank** (✉ *Av. Próspero 278* ☎ *065/232–350*).

Mail **Serpost Iquitos** (✉ *Av. Arica 402* ☎ *065/231–915*).

Medical **Clinica Adventista Ana Stahl** (✉ *Av. de la Marina 285* ☎ *065/252–528*). **Hospital Regional de Iquitos** (✉ *Av. 28 de Julio, Cuadra 15* ☎ *065/251–882*).

Taxi **Grupo Franchini** (✉ *Yurimaguas s/n* ☎ *065/264–458*).

Tour Operators **Grupo Dorado Tours** (✉ *El Dorado Plaza HotelNapo252* ☎ *065/222–555* ⊕ *www.grupo-dorado.com*). **Iquitos Tours** (✉ *Malecón Maldonado s/n* ☎ *065/620–107* ⊕ *www.iquitostravel.com*).

Visitor Info **iPerú** (✉ *Airport* ☎ *065/260–251*). **Tourist Information Office** (✉ *Napo 226* ☎ *065/236–144*).

EXPLORING

⑤ Casa de Fierro. The most interesting structure on the Plaza de Armas is this *iron house*, designed by Gustave Eiffel (of Eiffel Tower fame) and forged in Belgium. A wealthy rubber baron bought the house at the Parisian International Exposition of 1889 and had it shipped to Iquitos, where it was reassembled. The building now houses a pharmacy and the Amazon Café on the second floor. ✉ *Putumayo at Jr. Prospero* ☎ *No phone* ☒ *Free* ⊙ *Daily 8 AM–midnight.*

⑦ Centro de Rescate Amazónico. This animal rescue center is a short trip south of town where you can get a close look at one of the region's rarest, and most threatened species: the manatee. Despite being protected by Peruvian law, manatees continue to be hunted for their meat. The Centro, a collaboration of the Dallas World Aquarium and two Peruvian institutions, raises orphaned manatees and nurses injured ones back to health for eventual release in the wild. It also serves as an environmental education center to raise awareness of the gentle creature's plight. ✉ *Km, 4.6 Carretera Iqiutos-Nauta* ☎ *965–834–684* ⊕ *www.acobia-dwazoo.org/in_index.php* ☒ *S/15* ⊙ *Tues.–Sun. 9–12:30, 2–5.*

① Distrito de Belén *(Belén District).* Iquitos's most fascinating neighborhood is along the Itaya River. The market sells goods from the area's jungle villages; you'll find sundry items from love potions to fresh *suri* (palm-tree worms). It's not the cleanest or sweetest-smelling market but it's worth the visit. Near the center of the market is a port where you can head out in a dugout through the floating Belén District. ■TIP→ This slummy area is often called the Venice of the Amazon (a diplomatic euphemism), but navigating between its floating homes is really a kick. The houses are built on balsa rafts. Most of the year they float placidly on

the Amazon, though during the low-water season (June–November) they sit in the mud and can attract disease-carrying mosquitoes. The area should be avoided then. During high-water season (December–May), you can hire a boat for one- to two-hour trip for S/40 from Iquitos Travel, which usually has a stand on the Malecón Maldonado. Do not explore Belén on your own—muggings have been reported and it should be avoided at night. Be wary of pickpockets and bag slashers in and around the market. Stay alert, access your cash discreetly when you need it, and keep your valuables close.

❹ **Hotel Palacio.** Iquitos enjoyed its heyday as a port during the rubber boom a century ago. Some of the wealth of that time can still be detected in the *azulejos* (imported tiles) that cover many buildings along the riverbank, notably the former Hotel Palacio. The hotel was the city's best when it opened for business in 1908; it has since been converted into an army barracks and is looking a little worn around the edges. ✉ *Putumayo and Malecón Tarapacá* ☎ *No phone* ⊙ *Daily.*

❷ **Malecón Tarapacá (aka Malecón Maldonado).** A good place for an evening stroll is this pleasant waterfront walk between Brasil and Pevas. You'll find good bars and restaurants here, as well as some lovely rubber-boom-era architecture.

❸ **Museo Amazónico.** This museum is dedicated to the region's rich indigenous culture, with "bronzed" fiberglass statues of local tribespeople made by plastering real people and a few faded paintings. One room is dedicated to exhibits by local artists. The building itself, a former town hall constructed in 1863, would be worth visiting even if it wasn't a museum given its ornately carved hardwoods and courtyard gardens. ✉ *Malecón Tarapacá 386* ☎ *065/234–031* 🖥 *Free* ⊙ *Mon–Sat 9–1, 2–5.*

NEED A BREAK?
The equatorial heat provides ample motivation to pop into **Helados Giornata** (✉ *Jr. Prospero 139* ☎ *No phone*), an ice cream parlor on the Plaza de Armas that specializes in sherbets made from rain-forest fruits. Try the refreshing *camu camu, tangy arazá, ungurahui,* or *guanabana.*

❻ **Port Bellavista Nanay.** About 3 km (1½ mi) north of downtown Iquitos at the end of Avenida La Marina is a muddy beehive of activity with boats of all shapes and sizes, floating restaurants and open-air shops. You can hire a boat to take you to a village of either the Bora or Yagua Indians or the Pilpintuwasi Butterfly Farm. Bringing a donation of school supplies (pencils, crayons, and notebooks) is a kind gesture that will be appreciated by the Boras and Yaguas, who live in small communities near the pueblo San Andrés. A 20-minute boat ride from the port will bring you to **Pilpintuwasi Butterfly Farm**, which raises some 42 butterfly species and also serves as home for wild animals that have been confiscated from hunters and wildlife traffickers. It thus has macaws, monkeys, a jaguar, a tapir and other animals. During the dry season you'll need to walk along a forest path for 15 minutes to get there. It's best to go with a guide. ✉ *Near village of Padre Cocha on Nanay River, 5 km (3 mi) from downtown Iquitos* ☎ *063/232–665* ⊕ *www.amazonanimalorphanage.org* 🖥 *S/15 without transportation* ⊙ *Tues.–Sun. 9–4.*

WHERE TO EAT

$$ ✕**Al Frío y al Fuego.** Even if you just
PERUVIAN go for a drink and an appetizer,
Fodor's Choice a visit to this floating restaurant
★ on the Río Itaya is highly recom-
mended. Step through the unas-
suming doorway on Avenida La
Marina, descend the long thatched
stairway to the dock, and a boat

will ferry you there. At first glance, the rustic, thatched structure on a
balsa-log raft belies the service and gourmet Peruvian fusion cuisine that
await you. The menu offers innovations on traditional dishes using local
ingredients, from such Lima standards as *cebiche* to jungle favorites
such as *patarashca*, fish in a garlic cream cooked in a *bijao* leaf, and *pes-
cado a la Loretana*, a tender *doncella* filet in a sweet chili cream served
with *chonta* (shredded palm heart) and *tacacho* (fried plantain-and-
pork dumplings). The ravioli *Loretanos*, stuffed with *cecina* (smoked
pork) and sweet chili and topped with a leek cream sauce and a piece of
doncella (a river fish) is decadently rich. If fish isn't your thing, try the
steak with cassava gnocchi and onion marmalade. ∎TIP➔ The restau-
rant's floating swimming pool is a great place to spend an afternoon (bring a
bathing suit and towel), whereas the view of the city lights at night is lovely.
✉ *Av. La Marina 134-B, next to "Embarcadero El Huecito", Iquitos*
☎ *965/607–474* ⊕ *www.alfrioyalfuego.com* ⌂ *Reservations essential*
☐ *AE, DC, MC, V* ☉ *No dinner Sun.*

$ ✕**Fitzcarraldo.** On the Malecón Maldonado, this attractive restaurant
PERUVIAN overlooking the river specializes in Amazon fish and other local dishes.
Try the *dorado en salsa de camu camu*, a tender whitefish with a jungle
fruit sauce, or the *cecina charapito*: a smoked pork steak with chonta
(shredded palm heart) salad and fried yuca (cassava). Top off the meal
with a frothy *caipirinha* (a Brazilian drink with lime, sugar, and the sug-
arcane liquor *cachaça*). You can eat in an air-conditioned room, under
ceiling fans in the main dining room, or on the sidewalk. ✉ *Napo and
Malecón Maldonado* ☎ *065/236–536* ☐ *AE, DC, MC, V.*

$$ ✕**Gran Maloca.** The city's most elegant restaurant is in a lovely building
PERUVIAN encrusted with colorful azulejos. ∎TIP➔ The nicest seating is in front of
the bar, surrounded by photos of Sophia Lauren and other icons. They serve
both local specialties and international fare. If you feel adventurous,
try the *suri al ajo* (palm-tree grubs cooked in wine and garlic sauce) for
an appetizer. Other jungle treats include *chicharrón de lagarto* (fried
caiman nuggets) and Amazon fish dishes such as *paiche* in a *carambola*
(starfruit) sauce and the traditional dorado *a la loretana*, a sautéed filet
with fried yuca and chonta salad. Gran Maloca has an extensive wine
list and locally-made fruit liqueurs. ✉ *Sargento Lores 170* ☎ *065/233–
126* ☐ *AE, DC, MC, V.*

$ ✕**La Noche.** Big windows smile onto the Itaya River from this bistro.
PERUVIAN The menu has de rigueur international standards and local favorites
such as *tacacho con cecina* (smoked pork steak and pork dumpling),
and *patarashca* (fish cooked in a bijao leaf) with *patacones* (fried plantain chips). This is a good night spot, with music and tasty pisco sours.

7

The restaurant sits right on the Malecón Maldonado riverwalk and has tables on the sidewalk and a second-floor balcony. ⊠ *Malecón Maldonado 177* ☎ *065/222–373* ▬ *V.*

WHERE TO STAY

$$$$

Fodor's Choice

★

🏨 **El Dorado Plaza Hotel.** This contemporary hotel is in the heart of the city, on the Plaza de Armas. The spacious lobby has a large fountain and a glass elevator. Behind it is a pool with a bridge leading to an elevated Jacuzzi. Carpeted rooms have all the modern conveniences and are equipped with double glass to protect you from the incessant cacophony of downtown Iquitos. Those in front overlook the plaza, whereas rooms in back glimpse the river over rusty metal roofs. The small restaurant is quite good, and the in-house tour agency is excellent. **Pros:** best in town; friendly staff; airport shuttle. **Cons:** expensive; a few stains on walls and carpets. ⊠ *Napo 252* ☎ *065/222–555* ⊕ *www.grupo-dorado.com* ⥽ *56 rooms, 9 suites* ⌂ *In-room: a/c, safe, refrigerator, Wi-Fi. In-hotel: restaurant, room service, bar, pool, gym, laundry service, Internet terminal, Wi-Fi hotspot, parking (free)* ▬ *AE, DC, MC, V* ⸰⃝ *BP.*

$$

🏨 **Hotel El Dorado Isabel.** A small, grotto-like pool and the adjacent patio are among the few redeeming characteristics of this hotel half a block off the main square. The rooms are on the small side, dark, and slightly dank from nonstop air-conditioning. They have varnished wood ceilings and furniture, but there are nicks here and there, and stains on the carpet. The hotel's restaurant, Bambu, is decent. **Pros:** good location; decent restaurant. **Cons:** rooms are a little dingy. ⊠ *Napo 362* ☎ *065/231–742* ⊕ *www.grupo-dorado.com* ⥽ *53 rooms, 3 suites* ⌂ *In-room: a/c, refrigerator, Wi-Fi. In-hotel: restaurant, room service, bar, pool, laundry service, Internet terminal, Wi-Fi hotspot* ▬ *AE, DC, MC, V* ⸰⃝ *BP.*

$

🏨 **Hotel Marañon.** There's a slightly institutional feel to this ultra-clean, relatively inexpensive hotel, thanks mostly to the tile floors, high ceilings, and unadorned walls. The front of the hotel faces a busy street; rooms in the back are quieter. The pool and small terrace in the back are a nice addition. It's a block from the Plaza de Armas. **Pros:** good value; central location. **Cons:** not the character choice. ⊠ *Nauta 289, at Fitzcarrald* ☎ *065/242–673* ⊕ *www.hotelmaranon.com* ⥽ *38 rooms* ⌂ *In-room: a/c, refrigerator, Wi-Fi. In-hotel: restaurant, room service, pool, laundry service, Internet terminal, Wi-Fi hotspot* ▬ *DC, MC, V* ⸰⃝ *CP.*

$$

🏨 **Victoria Regia Hotel.** This modern lodging has the second-best rooms in town, dressed in bright colors and most of them surrounding a courtyard with a small swimming pool. Rooms in the back are quieter, but darker, and the double glass on the front rooms keeps most of the noise out. Colorful paintings by local artists, blond-wood furniture, and large,

---

RAFT RACE

The self-proclaimed "longest raft race in the world," the Great River Amazon Raft Race is not for the nervous. The race lasts three days down 132 miles of the Amazon to Iquitos and starts the third week of September every year. Teams of four build their rafts out of balsawood (provided) and then get to paddling. Anyone can enter, but not everyone should enter.

CLOSE UP

Crocodile Nuggets, Anyone?

Amazonian cuisine, with its jungle game meats and off-color local dishes, is truly far-out. *Chicharron de lagarto* (caiman nuggets) *venado a la Loretana* (Loreto-style venison), and *sopa de motelo* (turtle soup served in the shell) are on many a menu. Unfortunately, hunting to supply Iquitos' restaurants and households poses a serious threat to the region's wildlife. The more venison that is eaten in Iquitos, the less likely it becomes that you'll encounter a deer in the woods, so please don't order it.

Luckily, there are plenty of local dishes that aren't a threat to wildlife. The best bets are the tasty fish caught in the region's rivers, or *cochas* (oxbow lakes). *Doncella,* a tender white fish, and the comparable, though slightly fatty dorado are the most popular fish. *Paiche,* a giant lake fish, is another favorite, though it is slightly tough—a cross between swordfish and pork—and it is not

always available. Try one of these fish in *patarashca* (cooked in bijao leaves), *timbuche* (a tasty fish soup), or *a la Loretana:* a seasoned filet served with fried plantains, cassava, and chonta salad.

Other local favorites are *tacacho,* a grilled ball of plantain and pork bits, and *juanes* (chicken and rice wrapped in a banana leaf). Brazil nuts, locally called *castañas,* make a tasty snack, and by purchasing them you'll be supporting a sustainable use of the rain forest. For a thirst quencher, try fresco de *camu camu* made from a sweet jungle fruit, or c*hapo,* a banana-milk-and-sugar drink. *Masato* is an indigenous beverage prepared by mashing cassava in water and then fermenting it, though in the Indian villages, they chew the cassava and spit it into bowls. You're safer ordering a *caiparinha,* a refreshing Brazilian cocktail made with lime juice and the rum-like *cachaça.*

comfy beds add to the attractiveness. It's also a short walk from the Plaza de Armas and Malecón Tarapacá. It is named after the giant lily pads found in the region's lakes. **Pros:** attractive rooms; good beds; convenient location. **Cons:** rooms on the small side; those in back a bit dark. ⊠ *Ricardo Palma 252* ☎ *065/231–983* ⊕ *www.victoriaregiahotel. com* 🛏 *56 rooms, 6 suites* ♻ *In-room: a/c, safe, refrigerator, Wi-Fi. In-hotel: restaurant, room service, pool, laundry service, Internet terminal, Wi-Fi hotspot, parking (free)* ═ *AE, DC, MC, V* ⋈ *BP.*

NIGHTLIFE AND THE ARTS

Maybe it's the proximity to the jungle and its innate, inexplicable sensuality. Whatever the reason, Iquitos heats up after dark, and the dancing and bar scene is spectacular. You should begin your night at one of the many bars along the Malecón Maldonado. **Arandú Bar** (⊠ *Malecón Maldonado 113* ☎ *065/243–434*) is one of the riverwalk's best bars, with good music, river views and wild interior murals. **La Noche** (⊠ *Malecón Maldonado 177* ☎ *065/222–373*) is another popular spot on the riverwalk. The funky **Café Teatro Amauta** (⊠ *Nauta 250* ☎ *065/233–109*) has live music and performances most nights and serves local concoctions such as *siete raizes* and *chuchuwasa.* **Discotec Noa** (⊠ *Fitzcarraldo 298* ☎ *065/222–993*) is the biggest, liveliest dance club in town.

SHOPPING

Street vendors display their wares at night on the Malecón Maldonado and the Plaza de Armas. Look for pottery, hand-painted cloth from Pucallpa, and jungle items such as preserved piranhas, seed necklaces, fish and animal teeth, blowguns, spears, and balsa-wood parrots. The **Mercado Belén** is a riot of colors and smells where they sell everything from love potions to souvenirs made from snake and caiman skins and toucan beaks, which you should definitely not buy. Beware of pickpockets in that close-quartered market. T-shirts emblazoned with images of the region's wildlife and native peoples, painted by local artists, are on sale near the Malecón Maldonado at **Boa Arts** (✉ *Putumayo 124* ☎ *065/611–155*). Handicrafts from several of the province's indigenous cultures can be found in the souvenir stands at the **Casa del Artesano Amazónico** (✉ *Malecón Maldonado 113* ☎ *No phone*).

THE PERUVIAN AMAZON

The Amazon basin is the world's most diverse ecosystem. The numbers of cataloged plant and animal species are astronomical, and scientists are discovering new species all the time. More than 25,000 classified species of plants are in the Peruvian Amazon (and 80,000 in the entire Amazon basin), including the 2-meter-wide (6-foot-wide) Victoria Regia water lilies. Scientists have cataloged more than 4,000 species of butterfly and more than 2,000 species of fish—a more diverse aquatic life than that of the Atlantic Ocean. Scientists estimate that the world's tropical forests, while comprising only 6% of the Earth's landmass, may hold up to 75% of the planet's plant and animal species. This land is also the largest natural pharmacy in the world: one-fourth of all modern medicines have botanical origins in tropical forests.

Most mammals are nocturnal and difficult to spot, and hunting has made them wary of humans. ■TIP➔ You're likely to see an array of birds, butterflies and monkeys, and if you're lucky, you'll spot bufeos (pink freshwater dolphins), or caimans along the Amazon tributaries.

It's interesting and worthwhile to visit the small villages of indigenous people. When the boat stops at these settlements, you'll usually find half the village waiting to sell you handicrafts, or trade them for whatever you have with you; items perpetually in demand include umbrellas, hammers, fishing hooks, flashlights, sewing supplies, lipstick, clothing, and school supplies.

The best way to visit the jungle is with a prearranged tour with one of the many jungle lodges, or cruise boats. All the lodges and cruise boats have highly trained naturalist guides. Among the activities offered are nature walks, birding tours, nighttime canoe outings, fishing, and trips to indigenous villages. Some lodges have canopy towers, or walkways that take you into the seldom-explored rain-forest canopy.

GETTING HERE AND AROUND

With the exception of Reserva Nacional Allpahuayo Mishana, which is a one-hour drive from town, you'll reach the Amazon's sites by water. You basically have two options: travel to a nature lodge in one of that company's boats or take a cruise. The cruises are more expensive, but

Hotels ▼

Amazon
Rainforest
Lodge **7**

Amazon Yarapa
River Lodge **2**

Ceiba Tops **3**

Explorama
Lodge **5**

ExplorNapo **6**

Heliconia Amazon
River Lodge **4**

Muyuna Lodge ...**1**

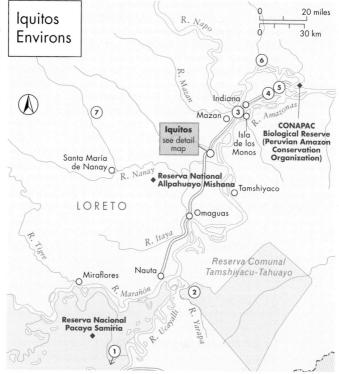

quite comfortable, and they allow you to explore different protected areas on daily excursions in small boats. Otherwise, you can book a stay at a nature lodge, in which case a guide will meet you at the airport, take you to the port, and accompany you to the lodge in a small, fast boat.

ESSENTIALS

Tour Operators Aqua Expeditions (☎ *01/368–3868, or 65/601–053* ⊕ *www. aquaexpeditions.com*). **Delfin** (☎ *01/719–0998* ⊕ *www. delfinamazoncruises. com*). **Explorama Tours** (☎ *065/252–530; 800/707–5275 in U.S.* ⊕ *www. explorama.com*).

EXPLORING

☺ **Isla de los Monos.** An easy reserve to visit, and a popular spot for explorers of all ages, Isla de los Monos is Peru's "Monkey Island." The 250-hectare (618-acre) island is a private reserve where monkeys that were once held in captivity, or were confiscated from animal traffickers, now live in a natural environment. The island is home to eight monkey species, as well as sloths, parrots, macaws and other wildlife. Since most of the animals are former pets, you can get very close to them; maybe closer than you want. It is near the Ceiba Tops hotel. ⊠ *40 km (25 mi) south of Iquitos* ☎ *065/233–801* ⊕ *www.monkeyislandperu. com* 🎟 *S/20* ⊙ *Daily 6–6.*

Reserva Nacional Allpahuayo Mishana. Around Iquitos there are large tracts of virgin rain forest and several reserves worth visiting. Allpahuayo Mishana is the easiest protected area to get to, just 15 miles (25 km) southwest of Iquitos by road. One of the country's smallest and newest reserves, it is not a great place to see large animals, but it is an excellent destination for bird watchers. Scientists have identified 475 bird species in the reserve, including such avian rarities as the pompadour cotinga and Zimmer's antbird. It is also home to several endangered monkey species. Allpahuayo Mishana is best visited on a guided tour, which can be arranged through the Hotel Dorado. ⊠ *Km 25 Carretera Iquitos-Nauta* 🖀 *No phone* 💲 *Free* ☉ *Daily 6–6.*

Reserva Nacional Pacaya Samiria. This hard-to-reach park sits at the confluence of the Marañón and Ucayali rivers. The reserve is Peru's second largest and encompasses more than 20,000 square km (7,722 square mi) of land, about the size of El Salvador. It comprises seasonally flooded forests, oxbow lakes, and vast expanses of lowland rain forest and is home to pink river dolphins, caimans, turtles, various kinds of monkeys, and hundreds of bird species. As with many reserves in South America, there are a number of people living in Pacaya Samiria, around 30,000 according to recent estimates. Park rangers try to balance the needs of these local communities with efforts to protect the environment, and occasionally request a minimal S/120 for seven days entrance fee. It takes several hours by boat to reach the park and at least five days to visit it. ⊠ *Confluence of Marañón and Ucayali rivers* 🖀 *No phone* ☉ *Daily.*

Sucusuri Biological Reserve (CONAPAC). This smaller private rain-forest reserve is northeast of Iquitos, near the confluence of the Napo and Amazon rivers. CONAPAC (the Peruvian Amazon Conservation Organization) manages this 1,000-square-km (386-square-mi) multiuse reserve, known as the Sucusuri Biological Reserve, which can be explored from the ExploNapo lodge. ⊠ *Near confluence of Napo and Amazon rivers, 70 km (43 mi) downriver from Iquitos* 🖀 *065/252–530 Explorama Tours; 800/707–5275 in U.S.* ⊕ *www.explorama.com* 💲 *Free* ☉ *Daily.*

WHERE TO STAY

Rates for the rain-forest lodges near Iquitos include transportation, meals, and guided excursions. Transportation to the lodges is either by *palmcaris* (large wooden boats with thatched roofs) or speedboats. Three lodges—Ceiba Tops, Explorama Lodge, and ExplorNapo—are owned and operated by Explorama Tours.

$$$$ ⊡ **Amazon Rainforest Lodge.** An hour by speedboat from Iquitos, this network of thatched-roof bungalows sits on the Momon River and offers a family-friendly Amazon experience. The attractive structures, upgraded in 2007, have twin beds and private baths, and are lighted by gas lanterns. Activities include guided walks, piranha fishing, canoeing, and visits to Yagua villages. They cater to a much younger crowd than most of the jungle lodges in the area. **Pros:** only an hour trip from Iquitos; visits to local tribe; swimming pool. **Cons:** not a nature lodge. *40 km (25 mi) northwest of Iquitos* 🖀 *065/233–100 or 01/226–3388*

⊕ *www.amazon-lodge.com* ↰ *26 bungalows* ⚬ *In-room: no phone, a/c (some). In-hotel: restaurant, bar, pool, spa, water sports, laundry service, Wi-Fi hotspot* ▭ *MC, V* ⏀ *FAP.*

$$$$ ⚏ **Amazon Yarapa River Lodge.** This lodge is at the forefront of sustain-
Fodor's Choice able tourism with solar power, composting, native wood structures
★ built by local Indians, even a biology lab used by Cornell University.
■TIP➔ Jungle cruises and rain-forest hikes are led by some of the best
informed guides of all the lodges. The lodge also has some great communal spaces, and the rooms—some with private bath (cold water only),
others with shared—are rustic, but comfortable. It's a 3–4 hour boat
journey upriver from Iquitos and can only be visited on four- or seven-
day tours. Rooms with private bath are better all around. **Pros:** great
guides; good food. **Cons:** rustic. *125 km (78 mi) southwest of Iquitos* ☎ *065/223–320 or 965/931–172; 315/952–6760 in U.S.* ⊕ *www.
yarapa.com* ↰ *16 rooms with shared bath, 8 rooms with private bath*
⚬ *In-room: no phone, no a/c, no TV. In-hotel: restaurant, bar* ▭ *AE,
MC, V* ⏀ *FAP.*

$$$$ ⚏ **Ceiba Tops.** The most comfortable accommodations of any Amazon
Fodor's Choice eco-lodge are just 45 minutes downriver from Iquitos. After a jungle
★ trek, you can plunge into the pool, take a nap in your air-conditioned
room, or relax with a book in a hammock. You can even take a hot
shower before dinner. The rooms are several notches above the other
lodges, with tile floors, colorful bedspreads and paintings, and picture
windows with views of tropical nature. The private rain-forest reserve
behind the hotel holds a massive ceiba tree. Excursions include a trip
to a cocha with giant lily pads, nearby Monkey Island, or a full-day
trip to ExplorNapo and the canopy walkway. Three buffet meals per
day are served in a massive, thatched dining hall. **Pros:** amenities on
the Amazon; easy to reach; good excursions. **Cons:** may be a little too
Florida-resort-like; less wildlife than other lodges. ⊠ *40 km (25 mi) east
of Iquitos* ☎ *065/253–301; 800/707–5275 in U.S.* ⊕ *www.explorama.
com* ↰ *72 rooms, 3 suites* ⚬ *In-room: no phone, a/c, no TV, refrigerator
(some). In-hotel: restaurant, bar, pool, Internet terminal, Wi-Fi hotspot*
▭ *AE, MC, V* ⏀ *FAP.*

$$$$ ⚏ **Explorama Lodge.** One of the area's original nature lodges, this place
was built in 1964. It offers rustic accommodations and access to a large
rain-forest reserve. Rooms are in palm-thatched long houses divided
by walls that end well below the roof. Kerosene lamps light the rooms,
covered walkways and the dining room where buffet meals are served.
Various guided walks and boat trips into the reserve are offered, as well
as a visit to a nearby Yagua Indian village. The rooms are extremely
simple: tiled bathrooms have cold-water showers and the requisite mosquito nets, which ensure a night's sleep relatively free from bites. It's
80 km (50 mi) from Iquitos and the minimum stay is two nights, but a
three-night stay that includes a day trip to the canopy walkway in the
Sucusuri Biological Reserve is recommended. **Pros:** you're definitely
in the jungle; good guides. **Cons:** very rustic rooms with thin walls.
⊠ *80 km (50 mi) east of Iquitos* ☎ *065/253–301; 800/707–5275 in
U.S.* ⊕ *www.explorama.com* ↰ *55 rooms* ⚬ *In-room: no phone, no*

7

a/c, no TV. In-hotel: restaurant, bar, Internet terminal, Wi-Fi hotspot ⊟ *AE, MC, V* ○ *FAP.*

$$$$ ⊤ **ExplorNapo Lodge.** The remote ExplorNapo Lodge is at the edge of the CONAPAC Sucusari Biological Reserve, a vast protected forest on the Napo River, 160 km (100 mi) east of Iquitos and 1½ hours by boat from Explorama Lodge. There's a 1,500-foot-long, 120-foot-high canopy walkway at the nearby Amazon Conservatory of Tropical Studies (ACTS) center for exploring the seldom-seen upper-reaches of the rain forest, as well as an informative medicinal plant garden. ■TIP➜This is a prime place for spotting wildlife on guided walks, canoe trips, or from the lodge itself. Facilities at ExplorNapo are very rustic, with kerosene lighting, one building with cold-water showers, and another with out-house latrines. There's a screened dining room and bar where the staff members often perform music at night. You can substitute a night or two with a stay at the nearby ACTS lodge, which is closer to the canopy walkway, or the remote ExplorTambos Camp, a three-hour hike into the rain forest, where you sleep on a mattress on a platform under a mosquito net. Most people spend a night at the Explorama Lodge en route to ExplorNapo, whereas many end their trip at Ceiba Tops. **Pros:** great wildlife; deep in the jungle experience. **Cons:** far from Kansas; very rustic. ⊠ *160 km (100 mi) east of Iquitos on Napo River* ☎ *065/253–301; 800/707–5275 in U.S.* ⊕ *www.explorama.com* ⊸ *30 rooms with shared bath* ⌂ *In-room: no phone, no a/c, no TV. In-hotel: restaurant, bar, Internet terminal, Wi-Fi hotspot* ⊟ *AE, MC, V* ○ *FAP.*

$$$$ ⊤ **Heliconia Amazon River Lodge.** An hour downriver from Iquitos, the Heliconia has some of the nicest rooms on the river. The lodge has a big thatched-roof dining hall, a conical bar building, and a blue-tiled pool. Rooms have screened windows, firm beds, and private bathrooms with hot-water showers; they have electric power for a few hours before dawn and after dusk. Guided tours include a hike through the lodge's private reserve, piranha fishing, and a night boat ride. **Pros:** comfortable rooms; pool; river views. **Cons:** less exposure to wildlife than other lodges. ⊠ *80 km (50 mi) east of Iquitos, Yanamono* ☎ *065/231–959 or 01/421–9195* ⊕ *www.amazonriverexpeditions.com* ⊸ *21 rooms* ⌂ *In-room: no phone, no a/c, safe, no TV. In-hotel: restaurant, bar* ⊟ *AE, MC, V* ○ *FAP.*

$$$$ ⊤ **Muyuna Lodge.** You go 140 km (84 mi) up the Amazon and the Rio Yanayacu to reach this remote eco-lodge sequestered in a primary rain forest. Guests are guaranteed to see wildlife, and the guides are very good. Seventeen thatch-roof cabins are on stilts to keep from drowning when the water rises. They have screened windows, private baths with cold-water showers and porches with hammocks. Kerosene lanterns provide light at night. Activities include jungle hikes and boat trips to see giant lily pads, pink dolphins, and an array of rare birds. **Pros:** great activities and guides; wildlife. **Cons:** accommodations are fairly basic. ⊠ *140 km (87 mi) southeast of Iquitos* ☎ *065/242–858* ⊕ *www. muyuna.com* ⊸ *17 cabins* ⌂ *In-room: no phone, no a/c, no TV. In-hotel: restaurant* ⊟ *AE, DC, MC, V* ○ *FAP.*

The Central Highlands

WORD OF MOUTH

"In Huancayo I taught the children in Peru Luz de Esperanza's after school program. Volunteers help construct classrooms, some did house visits and provided basic knowledge on nutrition and health, others helped mothers make scarves or bake bread for self-income."

—SmileyKrn

WELCOME TO
THE CENTRAL HIGHLANDS

TOP REASONS
TO GO

★ **Handicrafts:** Ayacucho has *retablos*—three-dimensional scenes of religious and historical events. Quinua has ceramic workshops. The Mantaro Valley has *Mates Burilados,* silver filigree, and alpaca textiles.

★ **Warm Mugs:** Street vendors sell *calientitos,* a pisco-spiked herbal tea, and *ponche,* a sweet, frothy blend of milk, sesame, cloves, cinnamon, and walnuts.

★ **Market Day:** Villagers trek in with their goods ready to hawk and trade for whatever they can. Head to the Mantaro Valley and there's a market every day.

★ **Ethnotourism:** Design silver jewelry, learn to weave, cook papas a la huancaína, or help orphaned children. Huancayo has excellent interactive tourism opportunities.

★ **World's Second-Highest Train:** It's no longer number one, but you can still chug your way from Lima to 4,782 meters (15,685 feet) before dropping down to the valleys surrounding Huancayo.

1 Huánuco. Increased mining activity has increased attention to this small Andean hamlet only a few hours from the Amazon. Don't miss the Temple of the Crossed Hands of Kotosh a few kilometers from the main plaza, one of the earliest settlements in the Americas.

2 Huánuco South to Tarma. The road ascends to more than 5,000 meters (16,400 feet) over a barren, windswept landscape and past herds of wild alpacas and llamas. Spelunk in the deepest cave in South America, soak in a hot spring, or spot flamingos on Peru's largest lake after Titicaca.

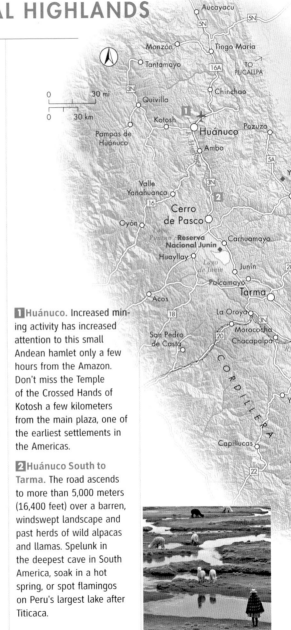

3 **Tarma South to Ayacucho.** Some of the country's worst roads have kept outside influences away and maintained the traditional Andean values in places such as Huancavelica. These small villages, lost on high altitude and barren plains, are the preferred hangouts of soroche, or altitude sickness, so taking it slow and drinking coca tea is the way of life here.

4 **Huancayo.** Among the most tourist-friendly towns in Peru, craft capital Huancayo is within a few minutes of vibrant Andean festivals and markets occurring every day. Many come for a weekend on the world's second-highest train, but then stay to study Spanish or take a cultural course from area craftspeople.

5 **Ayacucho.** Terrorism once cut Ayacucho off from the rest of the country but with stability, improved roads, and regular flights from Lima, the church-filled town is firmly on the tourist trail. This is particularly true during the weeklong celebration of Semana Santa, when a passionate and deeply religious fervor blankets the town.

GETTING ORIENTED

A mere hour east of Lima puts you in the foothills of the Andes, a windy, barren landscape where llamas and alpacas wander upon vast, puddle-filled fields. Roads and rails twist around the peaks and pass by ramshackle mountain towns before gradually sliding down from the highlands into muggy jungle en route to Tingo María and Pucallpa. Southeast from Tarma on the way to Ayacucho is more mountain terrain, where over the centuries jagged stubs of forested stone have protected great archaeological finds.

8

Huánuco market.

Updated by
Jeffrey Van
Fleet

The Central Highlands are where the massive Andes crash into the impenetrable South American rain forests and winding, cloud-covered mountain roads dip down into stark desert terrain. The way of life has changed little in hundreds of years.

Most people still depend on the crops they grow and the animals they breed—including guinea pigs and rabbits. Local festivals, traditional recipes, and craft workshops date back to before Inca ever was uttered in the region. Natural beauty abounds, with thundering rivers, winding trails, and hidden waterfalls tucked into the mountainous terrain. Lago de Junín, the country's second-largest lake, is in the north.

Despite how little daily life seems to have changed, the area has been the setting for some of the most explosive events in Peruvian history: fierce wars between the Inca and the Wanka, the most important battles for independence, and the birth of Peru's devastating terrorist movement. The region was home to the Sendero Luminoso (Shining Path) terrorists and the Tupac Amarú Revolutionary Movement for almost two decades. The Sendero Luminoso, which arose in the 1960s around Ayacucho, was finally dismantled in 1992 with the arrest of its leader, Abimaél Guzmán Reynoso. In 1999 then-president of Peru Alberto Fujimori led a successful manhunt for the leader of the Sendero Rojo terrorist faction, Oscar Alberto Ramírez Durand, shutting down the region's revolutionary stronghold for good. Now, apart from narcotrafficking and the occasional protest from coca growers the region is relatively calm.

This beautiful region is quickly gaining prominence—particularly due to tight military checkpoints that have put drug trafficking on the decline. It's one of the few truly remote regions left in the world, although improvements in road and air services have made travel here less challenging than it was even in the late 1990s.

No one knows when the first cultures settled on the *puna* (highland plains), or how long they stayed. ■TIP→ Archaeologists found what they believe to be the oldest village in Peru at Lauricocha, near Huánuco, and one of the oldest temples in the Americas, at Kotosh. Other nearby archaeological sites at Tantamayo and Garu also show that indigenous cultures thrived here long before the Inca or Spanish conquistadors ever reached the area.

When the Inca arrived in the late 1400s, they incorporated the already stable northern settlement of Huánuco into their empire. It eventually became an important stop along their route between the capital at Cusco and the northern hub of Cajamarca, and today Inca ruins are scattered along the pampas. Huánuco was officially founded by the Spanish in 1539 and the area quickly gained the attention of Spanish explorers, who turned Cerro de Pasco's buried gold, silver, copper, and coal into the center of the mining industry north of the Amazon basin. They ruled the region—and the country—until 1824, when Simón Bolívar's troops claimed Peru's autonomy by defeating the Spanish on the Quinua pampas near Huánuco.

PLANNING

WHEN TO GO

The best weather for this region is May through October, in winter and spring, when the skies are clear and daytime temperatures are moderate (nights can be frigid). The rainy season is November through April when many roads are inaccessible.

GETTING HERE AND AROUND

AIR TRAVEL

The airline LC Busre (⊕ *www.lcbusre.com.pe*) flies from Lima to Ayacucho, Huancayo, and Huánuco. Star Perú (⊕ *www.starperu.com*) flies from Lima to Ayacucho and Huánuco. Flights are often canceled in the rainy season. Always confirm your flight in good weather, too.

BUS TRAVEL

Buses from Ayacucho run to Lima, including overnight services on Los Libertadores, Ormeño, Cruz del Sur, and Expresa Molina. You can also reach Huancayo from Ayacucho (10 hours) by overnight service on Turismo Central and Expresa Molina—but prepare for a very rough road. From Huancayo, ETUCSA, Ormeño, Cruz del Sur, and Expresa Molina have many daily buses to Lima. Expresa Molina and Empresa Hidalgo have buses to Huancavelica.

CAR TRAVEL

The Central Highlands have some of the country's most scenic driving routes, and roads are paved from the capital north to Huánuco and south to Huancayo. It's five hours to La Oroya, from which a gorgeous Andes panorama stretches in three directions: north toward Huánuco, east toward Tarma, and south to Huancayo. Most sights around Huancayo in the Valle del Mantaro are accessible by car. The rugged road from Huancayo to Ayacucho, which takes around 10 hours, should be traveled only by four-wheel-drive vehicles equipped for emergencies. Except for the highway, there are mostly dirt roads in this region, so be prepared. There is no place to rent a car in this region.

8

TRAIN TRAVEL

The train journey from the capital is the most memorable travel option, but service has been cut back to about twice a month from May to November. On the route from Lima to Huancayo, the 335-km (207-mi) railway cuts through the Andes, across mountain slopes, and above deep crevasses where thin waterfalls plunge down into icy streams far below.

HEALTH AND SAFETY

Altitude sickness, or *soroche,* is a common risk in the Andes. Drink plenty of water and coca tea, move slowly, and avoid alcohol.

The Central Highlands is not the lawless region controlled by the Shining Path that it was in the 1980s and '90s. Terrorism has been eradicated and a military presence is strong. The only major concern is conflicts between the police and illegal coca growing and narco-trafficking, particularly in the area from Huánuco to Pucallpa. This has little effect on tourism; however, the occasional roadblock does occur.

Petty crime happens in cities less than on the coast. If you take the usual traveling precautions in your hotel and when walking or driving you shouldn't have any trouble. Carry your passport and other important identification at all times. Call 105 for an ambulance, the fire department, or the police.

RESTAURANTS

Dining out in the Central Highlands is a very casual experience. Restaurants are mostly small, family-run eateries serving regional fare. Breakfast is usually bread with jam or butter and juice. The midday lunch, the day's largest meal, combines soup, salad, and a rice and meat dish. You'll find snacks everywhere, from nuts and fruit to ice cream and sweet breads. Dinner is after 7 PM and extremely light. Don't worry about dressing up or making reservations. Tipping isn't customary, but waiters appreciate the extra change. All parts of the animal and almost every animal is considered. Guinea pig farming is among the more profitable occupations, so grilled *cuy* is a menu staple. Heartier fare comes in stews, which are spiced with *ají* (chili pepper) to stave off the mountain chill.

While outside influences have shaped other Andean villages, the isolation in the Central Highlands have kept recipes focused on local ingredients and traditions. Huancayo's local specialty is *papa a la huancaína* (boiled potato covered in yellow chili-cheese sauce), served cold with a sliced egg and an olive. *Pachamanca* (marinated meat, vegetables, potatoes, and spices) is wrapped in leaves, then slow-cooked on hot stones in an underground oven. Huánuco favorites include *picante de cuy* (guinea pig in hot-pepper sauce), pachamanca, fried trout, *humitas* (a tamale-like food made of ground corn and stuffed with various fillings), and sheep's-head broth. Ayacucho is famous for its filling, flavorful *puca picante* (a nutty pork-and-potato stew), served with rice and topped with a parsley sprig. The city's favorite drink is the warm *ponche* (flavored with milk, cinnamon, cloves, sesame, peanuts, walnuts, and sugar).

HOTELS

Accommodations in the Central Highlands lean toward the very basic. Only the largest properties have hot water, TVs, phones, and private baths, and almost none have (or require) air-conditioning. If you don't need pampering, and you don't expect top-quality service, you'll travel easily—and cheaply. The majority of hotels have clean, modest rooms with simple Andean motifs. Bathrooms usually have showers only, and if hot water is available it's only in the morning or evening. Most hotels have a restaurant, or at least a dining room with some type of food service. If you want a homestay experience, ask your hotel or a local travel company, who can often hook you up with hosts in the area.

Rooms are almost always available. But if you'll be traveling during the region's popular Semana Santa (Holy Week) or anniversary festivities book tours and hotels early. Also book early around the anniversary of the Battle of Ayacucho in mid-December.

WHAT IT COSTS IN NUEVO SOLES					
	¢	$	$$	$$$	$$$$
RESTAURANTS	under S/20	S/20–S/35	S/36–S/50	S/51–S/65	over S/65
HOTELS	under S/125	S/125–S/250	S/251–S/375	S/376–S/500	over S/500

Restaurant prices are per person for a main course. Hotel prices are for a standard double room, excluding tax.

HUÁNUCO SOUTH TO TARMA

8

Heading east, the road from modern, sprawling Lima climbs through the Andes, then splits north–south through the highlands. Working its way through the narrow crevasses and up the rugged hillsides of the Valle Mantaro, the northern road speeds endlessly forward at an elevation of 4,250 meters (13,940 feet) atop the Earth's largest high-altitude plains. This route north connects the mountain towns of La Oroya, Junín, Cerro de Pasco, Huánuco, and Tingo María, where local customs have been preserved even amid battles for independence and intrusions of modern technology. At an elevation of 3,755 meters (12,316 feet) by the confluence of the Río Mantaro and Río Yauli, La Oroya is a town of 36,000 and a main smelting center for the region's mining industry. From here you can head due east to Tarma or continue north by road or rail to the village of Junín. Still farther northwest along the eastern shores of Lago de Junín are Tambo del Sol and Cerro de Pasco.

At an elevation of 4,333 meters (14,212 feet), with more than 30,000 residents, Cerro de Pasco is the world's highest town of its size. It's also the main center for copper, gold, lead, silver, and zinc mining north of the Amazon basin. Coal is excavated from the Goyllarisquisga canyon 42 km (26 mi) north of town, the highest coal mine in the world. From here the road leads over pale, soggy Pampas de Quinua, where Simón Bolívar's troops outfought Spain in 1824.

About 80 km (50 mi) east of town, the Valle de Huachón provides gorgeous mountains for hiking and camping, while the trail north toward Huánuco runs along a spectacular road that plunges nearly 2,500 meters (8,200 feet) in the first 30 km (19 mi). Overlooking the land from an elevation of 1,849 meters (6,065 feet), Huánuco is a pleasant stopover between Lima and thick jungles around Pucullpa, or before heading south toward Huancayo and into the highlands. Farther north, spread between the Andean slopes and cloud forests, Tingo María is a jumping-off point for land adventures.

HUÁNUCO

365 km (226 mi) northeast of Lima; 105 km (65 mi) north of Cerro de Pasco.

At first glance Huánuco is just a picturesque collection of colonial buildings and churches along the Río Huallaga amid rocky, forested mountains: an archetypal Spanish settlement, but history runs far deeper here. Evidence of some of Peru's earliest human settlements, and some of the oldest ruins in the country, were found nearby at Lauricocha and Kotosh. Pre-Inca ruins have turned up throughout these mountains, notably at Tantamayo and Garu. Huánuco was an Inca stronghold and a convenient stopover on their route from Cusco north to Cajamarca. Thousands of Inca relics litter the surrounding pampas.

Huánuco's cool, 1,894-meter (6,212-foot) elevation makes for pleasant winter days and crisp nights, but in the rainy summer the town is just low enough to become immersed in the thick mountain fog. The Spanish-style architecture reflects the town's 1539 founding, and later buildings tell the story of Huánuco's importance as a cultural hub. Still, the original Peruvian traditions run deep, particularly during the annual Huánuco anniversary celebrations. Mountain hikes, swims in natural pools, and dips in nearby hot springs add to the area's natural appeal.

GETTING HERE AND AROUND

Most of Huánuco can be seen on foot or via short, cheap cab rides. A guide is recommended for exploring beyond the city. The area is a major coca-growing region and farmers are leery about strange characters hanging about. Tours from several agencies on the Plaza de Armas will bring you to the major sites within a few hours of the city for under S/50. David Figueroa Fernandini Airport (HUU) is 8 km (5 mi) away from Huánuco.

ESSENTIALS

Airport David Figueroa Fernandini Airport (✉ *Airport Hwy., Km 6* ☎ *062/513–066*).

Bus Expreso Huallaga (✉ *Puente Calicanto*). **León de Huánuco** (✉ *Robles 821*). **Transportes Rey** (✉ *28 de Julio 1201*). **Turismo Central** (✉ *Capac 499*).

Currency Banco de Crédito (✉ *2 de Mayo 1005, Huánuco* ✉ *Huánuco 699* ⊕ *www.viabcp.com*).

Mail Serpost (✉ *2 de Mayo 1157* ☎ *062/512–503*).

Quecha of the Andes

The Quechua are the original mountain highlands dwellers. Their traditions and beliefs have survived Inca domination, Spanish conquests, and the beginning influences of modern technology. Throughout the region, Quechua is the first language spoken and traditional costumes are still woven on backstrap looms and worn at the markets. Many Quechua make their living by farming maize and coca in the valleys or potatoes and quinoa in the higher altitudes, while other families herd llamas and alpacas on the cold, windy puna.

Walk through the narrow, cobbled streets of any village and you'll spot Quechua men by the large, patterned, fringed ponchos draped over their shoulders, their heads topped by matching tasseled cloths beneath big, cone-shape, felt hats. Knee-length pants are held up with a wide, woven belt that often has a local motif—such as the famous mountain train. Despite the cold, men usually wear rubber sandals, often fashioned from old tires.

Quechua women's attire is equally bright, with modern knit sweaters and a flouncing, patterned skirt over several petticoats (added for both warmth and puff). Instead of a poncho, women wear an *aguayo*, a length of sarong-like fabric that can be tied into a sling for carrying a baby or market goods, or wrapped around their shoulders for warmth. Hats for the women differ from village to village; some wear black-felt caps with neon fringe and elaborate patterns of sequins and beads, whereas others wear a plain brown-felt derby. Women also wear rubber sandals for walking and working in the fields, but often go barefoot at home.

The Morochuco are a unique group of formerly nomadic Quechua who live near Ayacucho on the Pampas de Cangallo. They have light skin and blue eyes, and, unlike other Quechua, many Morochuco men wear beards. Cattle breeding and horse training are the main occupations. Renowned for their fearlessness and strength, the Morochuco fought for Peru's independence on horseback with Simón Bolívar, and local lore has it that they are the descendents of the army of Diego de Almagro, a Spanish hero killed by Pizarro.

The Morochuco are first-rate horseback riders—women and children included—who use their swiftness and agility to round up bulls on the highland pampas. Women ride in long skirts and petticoats, whereas men don thick wool tights and dark ponchos. Both men and women wear *chullos*, a wool hat with earflaps, beneath a felt hat tied under the chin with a red sash.

Look for gatherings of stone or adobe-brick homes with thatched roofs as you travel through the mountains. These typical Quechua homes are basic inside and out. Food is cooked either in an adobe oven next to the dwelling or over an open fire inside. Mud platforms with llama wool or sheepskin blankets make do for beds; occasionally a family will have the luxury of a wooden bed frame and grass mattress. All members of the family work in the fields as soon as they are able. Members of the *ayllu* (extended family) are expected to contribute to major projects like harvesting the fields or building a new home.

—By Holly S. Smith

8

Iglesia La
Merced **1**
Iglesia San
Cristóbal **2**
Iglesia San
Francisco **4**
Museo de
Ciencias **3**

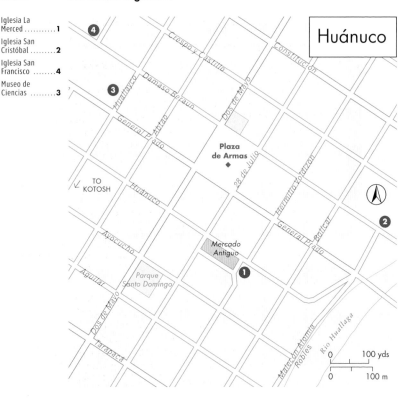

Visitor Info Oficina de Turismo (✉ *On main plaza, Prado 714* ☎ *064/512–980*). **Incas del Perú** (✉ *Av. Giraldez 652* ☎ *064/222–395*).

EXPLORING

❸ A block from the Plaza de Armas, the small **Museo de Ciencias** is a natural-history museum with multilingual displays of local crafts and weaving, shells, fossils, Inca tools, and what might be the world's largest collection of bad taxidermy. ✉ *Gen. Prado 495* ☎ *No phone* 💲 *S/2* 🕙 *Mon.–Sat. 8–noon and 3–7.*

❹ The 16th-century **Iglesia San Francisco** has Cusco School paintings and a few colonial-era antiques. Peek inside to see the spectacular gilt wall and arches behind the altar. ✉ *2 de Mayo y Beruan* ☎ *No phone* 💲 *Free* 🕙 *Daily 6–10 and 5–8.*

❶ The Romanesque **Iglesia La Merced** was built in 1600 by Royal Ensign Don Pedro Rodriguez. Colonial treasures include a silver tabernacle, paintings of the Cusco School, and the images of the Virgen Purisima and the Corazon de Jesus that were gifts from King Phillip II. ✉ *Valdizán Cuadra 4* ☎ *No phone* 💲 *Free* 🕙 *Daily 6–10 and 5–8.*

❷ Fronting a landscape of steep, grassy mountain slopes, the **Iglesia San Cristóbal**, with its three-tiered bell tower, was the first local church built by the Spanish settlers in 1542. Inside is a valuable collection of colonial-era paintings and baroque wood sculptures of San Agustín, the Virgen de la Asunción, and the Virgen Dolorosa. ☒ *San Cristóbal y Beraún* ☎ *No phone* 🖅 *Free* ⊘ *Mass time.*

★ In the Andean foothills at 1,812 meters (5,943 feet), **Kotosh**, a 4,000-year-old archaeological site, is famous for the Templo de las Manos Cruzadas (Temple of the Crossed Hands). Some of the oldest Peruvian pottery relics were discovered below one of the niches surrounding the main room of the temple, and the partially restored ruins are thought to have been constructed by one of the country's earliest cultures. Inside the temple you'll see re-created images of the crossed hands. The original mud set is dated 3000–2000 BC and is on display in Lima's Museo Nacional de Antropología, Arqueología, e Historia del Perú. ■TIP➔ The site was named Kotosh (pile) in reference to the piles of rocks found strewn across the fields. Taxi fare is S/15 for the round-trip journey from Huánuco, including a half hour to sightsee. ☒ *5 km (3 mi) west of Huánuco* ☎ *No phone* 🖅 *S/3.50* ⊘ *Daily sunrise–sunset.*

The **Pampas de Huánuco,** also called Huánuco Viejo, is a major site of Inca ruins. These fields are along the highland pampas near the town of La Unión. ☒ *10 km (6 mi) northwest of Huánuco* ☎ *No phone* 🖅 *Free* ⊘ *Daily 24 hrs.*

OFF THE BEATEN PATH

Tomayquichua. This small village was the birthplace of Micaela Villegas, a famous mestiza entertainer in the 18th century and the mistress of Viceroy Manuel de Amat y Juniet, a Spanish military hero and prominent colonial official. Also known as La Perricholi, her story was the basis of Prosper Mérimée's comic novella *Le Carrosse du Saint-Sacrement* and she was an important character along with the Viceroy in Thornton Wilder's *The Bridge of San Luis Rey.* A festival in July with parades, music, and dancing celebrates her vitality. Beautiful mountain views are the main attraction of the 2,000-meter- (6,500-foot-) high area. Sixteenth-century San Miguel Arcángel, one of the first churches built in the Huánuco area, is nearby in the village of Huacar. ☒ *18 km (11 mi) south of Huánuco.*

WHERE TO EAT AND STAY

Restaurants in Huánuco are simple and small, mostly offering local cuisine with a smattering of Chinese and continental selections. Little eateries are around the plaza and its neighborhoods, and around the markets. ■TIP➔ Most hotels have a small restaurant, but if yours does not, your host will usually fix a meal on request. Hotels are basic, with shared cold-water baths at most budget places. Spend a little more and you'll get lots more comfort, including a private bath, hot water, and a better mattress. But don't expect the Ritz.

¢

Fodor's Choice

★

Casa Hacienda Shismay. About 17 km (10.5 mi) away from the city this fortresslike colonial hacienda sits on 8,650 acres amid the stunning scenery of the Esperanza Valley. Rooms are rustic and cozy, but have brick fireplaces and an endless wood supply. Hierba Buena restaurant (¢) serves regional specialties and some basic international fare. Musicians from the nearby village of San Sebastián often come during dinner to play. The hotel will arrange horseback riding, trekking, birdwatching, and homestays in the area. **Pros:** incredible value; romantic;

lots of land. **Cons:** far from town; no public transportation; might be too rustic for some. ✉ *Amarilis* ☎ *062/96236–7734, 01/348–6216 in Lima* ⊕ *www.shismay.com* 🛏 *4 rooms* 🛠 *In-room: no a/c, no phone, no TV. In-hotel: restaurant, laundry service, parking (free)* ▭ *MC, V* ⦿ *EP.*

$ 🏨 **Gran Hotel Cusco.** Its age shows in chipped paint, squeaky pipes, and ceiling cracks, but overall this local favorite has held up okay over the decades. Rooms have the modern essentials: TV, phone, and hot shower. It's popular with visiting business travelers, so book early for weekdays. The restaurant (¢) serves tasty Peruvian grilled meats and stews, as well as salads and *tallarines* (noodles). **Pros:** decent price; modern amenities. **Cons:** showing its age; lacks frills. ✉ *Huánuco 614–616* ☎ *062/513–578* 🛏 *60 rooms* 🛠 *In-room: no a/c, Wi-Fi. In-hotel: restaurant, laundry service, Internet terminal, parking (free)* ▭ *No credit cards.* ⦿ *BP.*

$ 🏨 **Grand Hotel Huánuco.** The colonial-style building is chic, swanky, and
Fodor's Choice completely out of place in simple Huánuco, which explains the bargain
★ rate for a room. Rooms, with private baths and hot water, are modern and eclectic. Some rooms overlook the plaza, but beware of noise on mornings and weekends. Public areas are opulent yet intimate, with corners to relax in and have a quiet conversation. ■**TIP**→ **The pool, sauna, and gym provide respite for those returning from long day tours of the surrounding pampas.** The Majestuoso restaurant ($) is by far the best in town and serves everything from regional to international dishes. **Pros:** on the plaza; first-class service; good restaurant. **Cons:** some rooms are noisy. ✉ *Jr. Dámaso Beraún 775* ☎ *062/512–410* ⊕ *www. grandhotelhuanuco.com* 🛏 *32 rooms* 🛠 *In-room: no a/c, Wi-Fi. In-hotel: restaurant, room service, pool, gym, Internet terminal, parking (free)* ▭ *AE, D, DC, MC, V* ⦿ *BP.*

¢ 🏨 **Hostal Residencial Huánuco.** It's the town's favorite backpacker hang-out, where you can kick off your hiking boots and chat with new friends over a cup of *maté* (tea) in the garden. Shop the food market, then whip up your meal in the kitchen—the owners will even give cooking lessons. Hot water and laundry facilities set this hostel above other budget options. **Pros:** friendly owners and staff; easy to meet other travelers; kitchen access. **Cons:** pretty basic; can get crowded. ✉ *Huánuco 775* ☎ *062/512–050* 🛏 *23 rooms* 🛠 *In-room: no a/c, no phone, kitchen, no TV. In-hotel: laundry facilities, parking (free)* ▭ *No credit cards* ⦿ *EP.*

TANTAMAYO

158 km (98 mi) northwest of Huánuco.

The fields around Tantamayo are rich with pre-Inca ruins, some from the oldest cultures to settle in Peru. Most notable are the thick, seven-story stone skyscrapers of the Yarowilca, who flourished from AD 1200 to 1450. ■**TIP**→ **Finds at Susupio, Hapayán, Piruro, and Selmín Granero are the best-preserved.** The ruins are within easy walking distance of Tantamayo village, which has a hostel and basic restaurants; or catch a bus to Tantamayo and visit the ruins without a guide.

TINGO MARÍA

129 km (80 mi) north of Huánuco.

The warmth and humidity in the Andean foothills hit you as you descend from the Huánuco highlands. Not many travelers visit this settlement at the border between mountains and jungle, as it has gotten a bad rap for being in the midst of the country's coca-growing core. It's a shame, though, to miss Tingo María's vibrance and beauty, seen in its colorful, bustling markets and frenzied festivals. A strong military presence keeps out drug smugglers from the Río Huallaga valley to the north.

With a backdrop of mountains shaped like La Belle Durmiente (Sleeping Beauty), Tingo María is a safe haven of 21,000 residents who make their living tending the surrounding coffee, rubber, and sugarcane farms. Banana and tea plantations also wind their way up the slopes, and less than 15 km (9 mi) farther out there are hidden lakes, waterfalls, and caves to explore. Most travelers come here to visit **Parque Nacional Tingo María,** in the midst of the Pumaringri mountains. Many highland and rain-forest species live here, including parrots, primates, and bats. ■TIP➜ This is also the home of the rare, nocturnal guacharo (oilbird), a black-and-brown, owl-like bird with a hooked beak and a 1-meter (3-foot) wingspan. You can also explore the famed **Cueva de las Lechuzas** (Las Lechuzas Cave), on the skirts of the Bella Durmiente, an enormous limestone cave that shelters an important colony of guacharos (also known as *santanas*).

GETTING HERE AND AROUND

Tingo María is about three hours north of Huánuco on a paved road. You'll pass through several military checkpoints along the way, which are precautions to prevent drug trafficking and intermittent guerrilla activity. ■TIP➜ Summer and autumn rains often cause landslides, and the road is frequently under repair. Given the military checkpoints and road conditions, rural travel at night is not recommended. Léon de Huánuco provides bus service twice daily to Huánuco, the nearest metropolis of any size, with connections from there to Lima. Although Tingo María Airport has an airstrip just west of town, it presently serves only private flights.

ESSENTIALS

Tiny Tingo María has neither banks nor ATMs. Huánuco is the nearest place to stock up on cash.

Buses **León de Huanuco** ✉ *Parque Central* ☏ *062/562-030*)

WHERE TO EAT AND STAY

There are plenty of small restaurants and inexpensive hotels—most with cold water, but some with private baths and cable TV.

¢ ⊡ **Villa Jennifer Farm and Lodge.** Most international travelers stay at this excellent Danish-Peruvian-run lodge, a nine-room bird-watchers' haven on 25 acres not far from the national park. ✉ *Km 3.4, Castillo Grande* ☏ *62/96269–5059* ⊕ *www.villajennifer.net* ↵ *10 rooms* ⌂ *In-room: no a/c, no phone, no TV. In-hotel: restaurant, pool, laundry facilities, Internet terminal, parking (free)* ▭ *No credit cards* ¶⃝ *BP.*

8

VALLE YANAHUANCA

35 km (22 mi) south of Tingo María; 73 km (45 mi) north of Huancayo.

One of the longest surviving stretches of Inca road, the Qhapaq Nan, passes through the massive rocky outcrops and deep meadows of the Valle Yanahuanca. Forested hills threaded by shallow, pebbled rivers lead 4 km (2½ mi) farther to the village of Huarautambo, where pre-Inca ruins are treasures to search for in the rugged terrain. Continue along the 150-km (93-mi) Inca track and you'll pass La Union, San Marcos, Huari, Llamellin, and San Luis.

RESERVA NACIONAL JUNÍN

238 km (148 mi) south of Yanahuanca; 165 km (102 mi) north of Huancayo.

This reserve is at the center of the Peruvian puna, the high-altitude cross section of the Andes, which, at 3,900 to 4,500 meters (12,792 to 14,760 feet), is one of the highest regions in which humans live. Its boundaries begin about 10 km (6 mi) north of town along the shores of Lago de Junín, which, at 14 km (9 mi) wide and 30 km (19 mi) long, is Peru's second-largest lake after Titicaca.

Flat, rolling fields cut by clear, shallow streams characterize this cold, wet region between the highest Andes peaks and the eastern rain forest. Only heavy grasses, hearty alpine flowers, and tough, tangled berry bushes survive in this harsh climate, although farmers have cultivated the warmer, lower valleys into an agricultural stretch of orchards and plantations. The mountains are threaded with cave networks long used as natural shelters by humans, who hunted the llamas, alpacas, and vincuñas that graze on the plains. The dry season is June through September, with the rains pouring in between December and March.

The reserve is also the site of the **Santuario Histórico Chacamarca,** an important battle site where local residents triumphed over the Spanish conquistadors in August of 1824. A monument marks the victory spot. The Chacamarca Historical Sanctuary is within walking distance of Junín, and several trails lead around the lake and across the pampas. Bird fans stop here to spot Andean geese and flamingos and other wildlife on day trips from Tarma.

TARMA

350 km (217 mi) east of Lima; 25 km (16 mi) southeast of Junín.

The hidden mountain town known as "The Pearl of the Andes" has grown into a city of 155,000 whose Peruvian roots are held close in its traditions and sights. Long before the Spanish arrived, indigenous peoples built homes and temples in the hills that framed the town, the ruins of which are still being turned up by local farmers who have plowed much of the terrain into flower and potato fields, coffee plantations, and orchards. The town's look is all Spanish, though, with a small Plaza de Armas and several colonial-style churches and mansions.

Laguna de Paca lakeside resort, near Jauja.

At an elevation of 3,050 meters (10,004 feet), Tarma has a cool and breezy climate, with crisp nights all year. ■ TIP→ Get out in these nights, too, as candlelight processions are a major part of the town's many festivals—notably the Fiesta San Sebastián in January, Semana Santa in March or April, Semana de Tarma in July, and Fiesta El Señor de Los Milagros in October. Tarma is definitely not a tourist town, but a place to visit for true Peruvian traditions.

Tarma's **Oficina de Turismo,** on the Plaza de Armas, can help you find qualified local guides for sights in the region.

GETTING HERE AND AROUND

Transportes Chanchamayo, Transportes DASA, and Transportes Junín all offer daily bus service, each two or three times a day, between Tarma and Lima. Transportes Chanchamayo also offers continuing service to Huancayo.

ESSENTIALS

Bus **Transportes Chanchamayo** (✉ Callao 1002 ☎ 064/321–882). **Transportes DASA** (✉ Callao 1012 ☎ 064/321–843). **Transportes Junin** (✉ Amazonas 669 ☎ 064/321–324).

Internet **Colegio Santa Rosa** (✉ Amazonas 892 ☎ 064/321–457).

Mail **Serpost** (✉ Callao 356 ☎ 064/321–241).

Visitor Info **Oficina de Turismo** (✉ 2 de Mayo y Lima ☎ 064/321–010).

EXPLORING

Señor de Muruhuay Sanctuary. The village of Acobamba is a 10-km (6-mi) drive from town, where you can tour the El Señor de Muruhuay sanctuary. An image of the crucified Christ was said to have appeared here.

San Pedro de Cajas. About 15 km (9 mi) northwest of Tarma is the town of San Pedro de Cajas, well-known for its exquisite weaving and as an excellent place to buy good-quality, locally made wall hangings and rugs.

Gruta de Guagapo. Head northwest of Tarma 28 km (17 mi) to Palcamayo, then continue 4 km (2½ mi) west to explore the Gruta de Guagapo limestone cave system, a National Speleological Area. Guides live in the village near the entrance and can give you a basic short tour, but you'll need full spelunking equipment for deep cavern trips.

WHERE TO EAT AND STAY

¢ ✕ **Le Break Pizzeria Café.** Hidden away a few blocks from the plaza, ITALIAN   tiny Le Break is one of the town's better dining options. There's nothing Peruvian about this place, only wood-fired pizzas and pastas. It's popular with visiting Limeños. ⊠ *Callao 220* ☎ *064/323–334* ▭ *No credit cards.*

¢ ✕ **Restaurant Chavín.** This popular travelers' hangout is on the plaza. PERUVIAN   There's kitschy Andean decor—pictures of snow-covered mountains, patterned wall hangings—and lively lunchtime crowds. Hearty stews and rice dishes are the midday specials; at dinner you'll find grilled meat and even fish. ⊠ *Lima 262* ☎ *064/321–449* ▭ *MC, V.*

$ ✕ **Restaurant Señorial.** Tarma's most upscale restaurant is still casual and PERUVIAN   chic, the place where the top of the townsfolk dine with fresh-pressed attire and just-shined shoes. The chefs show off their Andean flavors in *pachamanca* (marinated, slow-cooked meat, vegetables, potatoes, and spices) and *picante de cuy* (guinea pig in hot pepper sauce). You can also order pastas and sauces, grilled meats, and seafood. ⊠ *Huánuco 138* ☎ *064/323–334* ⊙ *No dinner Sun.* ▭ *No credit cards.*

$ ⊡ **Hacienda La Florida.** Experience life at a Spanish hacienda at this Fodor's Choice   charming bed-and-breakfast that's a 10-minute drive from Tarma.
★   Rooms, which sleep up to four guests, are furnished with period pieces, local art, and handmade textiles that evoke the 18th-century aesthetic. There's even a camping section with a bathroom (S/10), and hiking trails that lead to ruins and highland villages. **Pros:** breakfast included; hiking trails lead from property. **Cons:** simple; car ride from town. ⊠ *6 km (4 mi) north of Tarma* ☎ *064/341–041; 01/344–1358 in Lima* ⊕ *www.haciendalaflorida.com* ↰ *5 rooms, 6 campsites* ⌂ *In-room: no a/c. In-hotel: restaurant, laundry service, parking (free)* ▭ *AE, MC, V* |⊙| *BP.*

¢ ⊡ **Hostal Durand.** A number of budget hotels are on Jr. Lima leading from the plaza and the Durand is the best value. The rooms are clean, new, and even have private baths, hot water, and TVs. The rooms near the street are the largest and have nice views of the plaza. **Pros:** clean, modern, cheap. **Cons:** lacks character; above a busy street and shop. ⊠ *Jr. Lima 583* ☎ *064/317–434* ⊕ *hostaldurand.blogspot.com* ↰ *18 rooms* ⌂ *In-room: no a/c, no phone. In-hotel: restaurant, laundry service, Internet terminal, no parking* ▭ *No credit cards* |⊙| *BP.*

QUECHA LESSON

Here's a small sampling of Quecha words. It won't make you fluent, but people appreciate the effort when you learn a few of words of their language.

My name is...–Nuqap...sutiymi
Good-bye–Rikunakusun
Good morning–Windía
How are you?–Ima hinalla?
Thank you–Añay

Words:
House–Wasi
Mother–Mama
Father–Papa, tayta
Son–Wawa
Daughter–Wawa
Yes–Arí
No–Mana
Please–Allichu
Hello–Rimaykullayki, napaykullayki

Phrases:
What is your name?–Imataq sutiyki?

Numbers:
Zero–Ch'usaq
One–Huq, huk
Two–Iskay
Three–Kinsa, kimsa
Four–Tawa
Five–Pishqa, pisqa, pichqa
Six–Soqta, suqta
Seven–Qanchis
Eight–Pusaq, pusac
Nine–Isqun
Ten–Chunka

$$ \quad \text{☗ } \textbf{Los Portales.} $$ Considered by locals to be the best hotel in town, this colonial-style mansion surrounded by gardens offers more warmth than grandeur. Rooms, which have modern amenities and private baths with hot water, are decorated with a mix of real and reproduction antiques that complement the elegant architecture. The staff is very helpful with advice for regional sightseeing. **Pros:** historic charm; Lima-like amenities for half the price; friendly staff. **Cons:** out of town; often filled. ⊠ *Castilla 512* ☎ *064/321–411* ⊕ *www.hotelportalestarma.com* ☎ *45 rooms* ⚲ *In-room: no a/c, refrigerator (some), Wi-Fi. In-hotel: restaurant, bar, laundry service, Internet terminal, parking (free)* ⊟ *AE, D, DC, MC, V* ⎹◎⎸ *BP.*

SAN PEDRO DE CASTA

120 km (74 mi) northeast of Lima.

This compact Andean village is a collection of mud-brick and clapboard homes and shops where you can watch craftspeople and farmers at work on the highland plains. For many visitors, the town is a starting point for the three-hour, uphill hike to the unusual rock formations at **Marcahuasi**, 3 km (2 mi) from San Pedro, where winds have worn the earth into a menagerie of animal shapes. Other hiking trails weave through the grasslands around San Pedro, but you'll need to spend at least one night to get used to the high altitude. Carry a water filtration kit to drink from the lakes. San Pedro is about 40 km (25 mi) north of Chosica, on the main highway between Lima and La Oroya. Most visit on a day trip from Tarma, about 1½ hours by car or the hourly buses.

TARMA SOUTH TO AYACUCHO

The road from Tarma continues beside the spine of the mountains, alternately cutting through high-altitude plains and winding in coils alongside steep crevasses. The thin air can be biting in the shade and scorching in the mid-afternoon sun beating down on a dry, barren landscape pounded into rough grasslands between the peaks. ■TIP➔Look for spots of black, brown, and white—wild llamas and alpacas that roam this cold, rocky range. Near Pucapampa, the road rises to 4,500 meters (14,760 feet), often causing soroche in travelers while the resident (and rare) gray alpaca remains quite comfortable.

Still the road rises, passing tiny Santa Inés and Abra de Apacheta, the latter at 4,750 meters (15,580 feet). Somehow the scenery continues to be even more spectacular, for oxides in the earth have painted the rocks and creeks in a wash of vibrant colors. One of the highest roads in the world is 14 km (9 mi) farther, the 5,059-meter (16,594-foot) pass 3 km (2 mi) north of Huachocolpa. From here the journey is downhill into the wide, windy Valle Huanta, a landscape of lakes and hot springs, caverns, and ruins.

JAUJA

280 km (174 mi) southeast of San Pedro de Casta; 60 km (37 mi) south of Tarma.

Jauja has the distinction of having been Peru's original capital, as declared by Francisco Pizarro when he swept through the region; he changed his mind in 1535 and transferred the title to Lima. ■TIP➔Jauja still has many of the ornate 16th-century homes and churches that mark its place in the country's history. The Wednesday and Sunday markets display Andean traditions at their most colorful, showing the other side of life in this mountain town. Although there are several moderately priced hotels, many travelers come here on a day trip from Huancayo. Those who stay usually head to the lakeside **Laguna de Paca** resort area 4 km (2½ mi) from town.

CONCEPCIÓN

Fodor'sChoice *15 km (9 mi) southeast of Jauja; 25 km (16 mi) northwest of Huancayo.*
★   The village of Concepción is the site of the 1725 **Convento de Santa Rosa de Ocopa.** Originally a Franciscan foundation whose role was to bring Christianity to the Amazon peoples, now the building has a reconstructed 1905 church and a massive library with more than 25,000 books—some from the 15th century. The natural-history museum displays a selection of regional archaeological finds including traditional costumes and local crafts picked up by the priests during their travels. A restaurant serves excellent, if simple, Andean food, and several spare but comfortable accommodations are in the former monks' quarters. Admission includes a guided tour. 🖻*No phone* 🖃*S/5* ☉ *Wed.–Mon. 9–1 and 3–6.*

HUANCAYO

25 km (16 mi) southeast of Concepción; 40 km (25 mi) southeast of Jauja.

It's not hard to see how the modern city of Huancayo, which has close to 260,000 residents, was once the capital of pre-Inca Huanca (Wanka) culture. In the midst of the Andes and straddling the verdant Río Mantaro valley, the city has been a source of artistic inspiration from the days of the earliest settlers, and has thrived as the region's center for culture and wheat farming. A major agricultural hub, Huancayo was linked by rail with the capital in 1908, making it an endpoint to what was once the world's highest train line (but is now in second place). Although it's a large town, its little shops, small restaurants, blossoming plazas, and broad colonial buildings give it a comfortable, compact feel.

Huancayo was also a stronghold for the toughest Peruvian indigenous peoples, including the Huanca, who out-fought both the Inca and the Spanish. Little wonder that Peru finally gained independence in this region, near Quinua, in 1824. ■TIP→ Still, the Spanish left their mark with the town's collection of hacienda-style homes and businesses, most with arching windows and fronted by brick courtyards with carefully groomed gardens. For an overview of the city, head northeast 4 km (2½ mi) on Giráldez, 2 km (1 mi) past Cerro de la Libertad park, to the eroded sandstone towers in the hillsides at Torre-Torre.

The drive from Lima to Huancayo is breathtaking, with the road rising to more than 4,700 meters (15,416 feet) before sliding down to the valley's 3,272-meter (10,731-foot) elevation. As you enter the city, four-lane Calle Real is jammed with traffic and crammed with storefronts—but look more closely and you'll see the elegant churches and colorful markets tucked into its side streets, hallmarks of local life that make the city so charming. Women with long black braids beneath black-felt hats still dress in multitiered skirts and blouses with *mantas* (bright, square, striped cloths) draped over their shoulders. Note the intricate weavings—particularly the belts with the famous train worked into the pattern.

GETTING HERE AND AROUND

Huancayo's tiny Francisco Carle Airport (JAU) is 45 km (27 mi) north of Huancayo near Jauja. Although Huancayo is big, most of the areas of interest to travelers are within walking distance of the plaza. The exceptions are the craft villages in the Mantaro Valley. Combi vans circle the city streets looking for passengers for the 20–40-minute rides to each town or you can take a comprehensive valley tour from any of the travel agencies in Huancayo S/50. Taxis are another option as they're quite economical.

> **GOOD TO KNOW**
>
> It's best to bring U.S. cash to the smaller towns of this region, as traveler's checks and credit cards usually aren't accepted. Travel agencies or larger hotels might change money if you're in a pinch.

8

Capilla de la
Merced **2**

Museo
Salesiano **3**

Parque de la
Identidad
Wanka **4**

Parque del Cerro
de la Libertad **5**

Plaza
Huamanmrca **1**

Huancayo

ESSENTIALS

Bus Cruz del Sur (✉ *Ayacucho 281* ☎ *064/235–650*). **ETUCSA** (✉ *Puno 220* ☎ *064/232–638*). **Expresa Molina** (✉ *Angaraes 334, Huancayo* ☎ *064/224–501*). **Ormeño** (✉ *Castilla 1379* ☎ *064/251–199*). **Turismo Central** (✉ *Ayacucho 274* ☎ *066/223–128*).

Currency Banco de Crédito (✉ *Real 1039* ⊕ *www.viabcp.com*).

Internet Huancayo Internet (✉ *Loreto 337* ☎ *064/233–856*).

Mail Serpost (✉ *Huamanmarca 350* ☎ *064/231–271*).

Visitor Info Oficina de Turismo (✉ *Casa de Artesana, Real 481* ☎ *064/233–251*).

EXPLORING

2 In front of the Río Shulcas, the **Capilla de la Merced** is a national monument marking where Peru's Constitutional Congress met in 1830 and the Constitution was signed in 1839. In addition to information about this historic gathering, the Chapel of Mercy also exhibits Cusqueño paintings. ✉ *Real y Ayacucho* ☎ *No phone* 🎫 *Free* ⊘ *Weekdays 9–noon and 3–6:30.*

3 The **Museo Salesiano** has more than 5,000 objects. Look for the well-preserved rain-forest creatures and butterflies from the northern jungles. Local fossils and archaeological relics are also displayed at the Salesian

CLOSE UP

Tour & Travel Agencies

Ayacucho is surrounded by archaeological ruins and natural wonders, all of which can be viewed on a package tour. Morochucos Travel Services has city excursions and routes to Huari, Quinua, Valle Huanta and Vilcashhuamán.

Around Huancayo you can hike, bike, and explore local villages with the amazing Incas del Perú, which also has a Spanish-language school, book exchange, and folk-art collection. They will also arrange volunteering and hiking throughout the Manataro Valley and high jungle, as well as music, cooking, weaving, and gourd-carving workshops. Murakami Tours and Wanka Tours are among the better options from the numerous package-tour offices in town. Dargui Tours

offers multiday tours of the region, with a focus on the archaeological ruins around Huancayo.

Max Adventures in Tarma has several tour packages, local maps, and information.

Contacts **Dargui Tours** (⊠ *Jr. Ancash 367, Ayacucho* ☎ *064/238–100*). **Incas del Perú** (⊠ *Giráldez 652, Huancayo* ☎ *064/223–303* ⊕ *www. incasdelperu.com*). **Max Adventures** (⊠ *2 de Mayo 682, Tarma* ☎ *064/323–908*). **Morochucos Travel Services** (⊠ *Constitución 14, Ayacucho* ☎ *066/912–261*). **Murakami Tours** (⊠ *Jr. Lima 354, Huancayo* ☎ *064/234–745*). **Wanka Tours** (⊠ *Real 565, Huancayo* ☎ *064/231–778*).

Museum. ⊠ *2 blocks west of Real, across Río Shulcas* ☎ 064/247–763 ✆ *S/5* ☉ *Weekdays 8–noon and 2–6.*

8

5 The **Parque del Cerro de la Libertad** is an all-in-one amusement site 1 km (½ mi) east of the city. You can picnic in the grass, watch the kids at the playground, swim in the public pool, dine at the restaurant, or stroll through the zoo. ■TIP→ Folkloric dancers and musicians perform at the Liberty Hill Park amphitheater on weekends. A 15-minute walk from the park brings you to the site of Torre Torre, a cluster of 10–30-meter rock towers formed by wind and rain erosion. ⊠ *Giráldez.*

4 The focus of the beautiful **Parque de la Identidad Wanka** *(Wanka Identity Park)* is on the pre-Inca Huanca culture, which occupied the area but left few clues to its lifestyle. Pebbled paths and small bridges meander through blossoming gardens and past a rock castle just right for children to tackle. The enormous sculpture honors the local artists who produce the city's *mates burilados* (carved gourds). ⊠ *San Antonio.*

1 When the Spanish founded Huancayo in 1572, the **Plaza Huamanmarca** was the city center and the site of the weekly *Feria Dominical* (Sunday market). Today Huamanmarca Square is fronted by the post office, the telephone agency, and the Municipal Hall. ⊠ *Calle Real between Loreto and Piura.*

OFF THE BEATEN PATH

Warvilca. This ruined temple was built by the pre-Inca Huanca culture. The closest village is Huari, which has a little museum on the main square with ceramic figures, pottery, and a few bones and skulls. ⊠ 9

CLOSE UP

High Train

The Central Highlands' Ferrocarril Central Andino once laid claim to being the world's highest rail route. With the 2006 opening of China's Qinghai-Tibet Railway, the Peru route was knocked down to second place. No matter, though: this is one of the country's most scenic areas, and tracks cut through the mountains and plains all the way from Lima to Huancayo.

On the topic of "knocking down," the line these days is a shadow of what it once was, and trains ply the route only once or twice a month between May and November, requiring some careful planning if you want the journey to be a centerpiece of your visit to Peru. (The railway's website lists departure dates, with Lima-Huancayo service operating mostly every other Friday. Trains depart the capital's Desamparados train station at 7 AM for the 12-hour journey to Huancayo. Return trips to Lima usually take place the following Sunday.

The 335-km (207-mi) route twists through the Andes at an elevation of 4,782 meters (15,685 feet). The engine chugs its way up a slim thread of rails that hugs the slopes, speeding over 59 bridges, around endless hairpin curves, and through 66 tunnels—including the 1,175-meter- (3,854-foot-) long Galera Tunnel, which, at an altitude of 4,758 meters (15,606 feet) is its highest point.

Snacks, lunch, and soft drinks are included in the price (S/178-S/324 round-trip). You can request oxygen if you get short of breath over the high passes, and the mate de coca is poured freely. The decades-old Clásico cars are okay in a pinch, but the newer Turístico cars are much more comfortable with reclining seats.

✉ *Av. José Gálvez Barrenechea 566, San Isidro, Lima* ☎ *01/226-6363* ⊕ *www.ferrocarrillcentral.com.pe*

km (6 mi) from Huancayo ☎ *No phone* 🎟 *S/15* ☉ *Ruins: daily 10–noon and 3–5; museum: daily 10–noon.*

WHERE TO EAT

The local specialty is *papa a la huancaína* (boiled potato covered in a ají-cheese sauce), served cold with an olive. Budget restaurants with set lunch menus are on Arequipa south of Antojitos, as well as along Giráldez. You can pick up a quick morning meal at the Mercado Modelo after 7 AM, and juice stands, with fresh fruit brought in daily from the high jungle, are on every street.

¢ ✕ **Antojitos.** The tasty grilled meats, wood-smoked pizzas, and hearty

PERUVIAN sandwiches at this renowned backpacker restaurant draw more than just the budget crowd. The highland sophisticates meet here for a glass of local wine, businesspeople snack on the filling lunch specials, and the live bands on weekends always draw a crowd. ✉ *Puno 599* ☎ *064/237–950* 🖃 *AE, MC, V.*

¢ ✕ **La Cabaña.** A romantic air pervades this cozy, charming restaurant

PERUVIAN that has long been a travelers' favorite. The cuisine combines Peruvian

Fodor's Choice specialties like *anticuchos* (grilled marinated beef hearts) and *calientitos*

★ ("little hotties," a hot punch made of tea, rum, and spices) with basic continental fare like pasta, pizza, and *parrillada* (grilled meats). Dine in the garden on balmy days, or around the fireplace on chilly evenings. There's live music Thursday through Saturday. ■TIP➜ The owners can arrange cooking classes, Spanish lessons, music instruction, and long-term local homestays. Two hostel rooms, a book exchange, and numerous maps are available. ⊠ *Giráldez 652* ☎ *064/223–303* ▭ *MC, V.*

$ ✕**Detrás de la Catedral.** With the cathedral only steps away, romantic is

CONTINENTAL an understatement. Stone walls and candlelit tables calm the air that's scented with the aroma of roasted lamb, grilled trout, and pastas. Call ahead for reservations or prepare to wait. ⊠ *Ancash 335* ☎ *064/212–969* ▭ *AE, MC, V.*

¢   ✕**Panadería Coqui.** Petite tables swathed in rippling cloths are arranged

CAFÉ in tea-party style in the airy dining room. It's a perfectly elegant way to sample the pretty cakes and pastries while sipping espresso. Hungrier patrons can get pizza and sandwiches. Afterward, wander into the liquor shop to check out the local specialties. ⊠ *Puno 356* ☎ *064/234–707* ▭ *MC, V.*

¢   ✕**Restaurant Olímpico.** This upmarket restaurant, open for more than 60

PERUVIAN years, still serves a downtown lunch crowd with cheap, hearty Andean

★ specials. It's popular and always crowded, but good food is guaranteed. For a basic selection of soup, salad, meat, rice, and dessert, try the daily special. Otherwise, you can order a mix of Peruvian delicacies, including cuy, from the à la carte menu. ⊠ *Giráldez 199* ☎ *064/234–181* ▭ *AE, D, DC, MC, V.*

¢   ✕**Restaurant Vegetariano Nuevo Horizonte.** Health food has arrived in

VEGETARIAN the Andes at this vegetarian spot. Pastas, soups, and rice dishes with vegetable bases are all on the menu. The kitchen whips up yogurt, soy milk, and fruit drinks as well. You can also stock up on organic products and vitamins. ⊠ *Cajamarca 379* ☎ *No phone* ▭ *No credit cards.*

WHERE TO STAY

$ 🛏**Hostal El Márquez.** It lacks the character of Hotel Turismo, but the fairly new El Márquez is the only comparable hotel in town. The rooms have been recently renovated but remain bland. There's supposed to be 24-hour hot water so if you just want a cozy place to sleep look no further. **Pros:** centrally located; recently renovated; modern comforts. **Cons:** bland; the hot water isn't always hot. ⊠ *Jr. Puno 294* ☎ *064/219–026* ⊕ *www.elmarquezhuancayo.com* ♨ *In-room: no a/c, no phone, Wi-Fi. In-hotel: restaurant, laundry service, Internet terminal, parking (free)* ▭ *AE, D, DC, MC, V* ❍❘*BP.*

¢   🛏**Hotel Olímpico.** This central hotel has more charm than its larger competitors, and it's close to the center of town. Cozy rooms with modern furniture have all the amenities, including TVs, phones, and bathrooms with hot water. **Pros:** right on the plaza; good price. **Cons:** getting run down; not all rooms created equal. ⊠ *Ancash 408* ☎ *064/214–555* ↪*32 rooms* ♨ *In-room: no a/c. In-hotel: restaurant, room service, laundry service, parking (free)* ▭ *No credit cards* ❍❘*BP.*

$ 🛏**Hotel Presidente.** The most popular lodging with visiting Limeños has the comforts of a modern hotel, and a bland 20th-century exterior to match. Rooms, with contemporary furnishings and Andean fabrics and accents, have TVs, phones, private baths with hot water—and

8

thin walls. There's a wheelchair-accessible elevator. **Pros:** great amenities; train packages. **Cons:** mostly business oriented. ✉ *Real 1138* ☎ *064/231–275* ⊕ *www.hoteles-del-centro.com* ⇱ *80 rooms* ♿ *In-room: no a/c, refrigerator (some). In-hotel: restaurant, room service, laundry service, parking (free)* ▭ *AE, D, DC, MC, V* ⊠⊙ *BP.*

$–$$ 🛏 **Hotel Turismo Huancayo.** The hacienda-style exterior of this elegant hotel gives it a worldly charm that sets it above the younger options. Public areas are ornate, with Peruvian paintings and local crafts and textiles. Rooms are sparkling clean, and many have TVs, phones, and private baths with hot water. Ask to see several different options before you agree to stay, as rooms vary in size, decor, view, and amenities. Although the neighborhood is quieter than those around the plaza, the hotel is conveniently in the middle of town. **Pros:** excellent service. **Cons:** street and plaza in front often see protests; quality of rooms vary. ✉ *Ancash 729* ☎ *064/231–072* ⊕ *www.hoteles-del-centro.com* ⇱ *53 rooms* ♿ *In-room: no a/c, no phone (some), Wi-Fi. In-hotel: restaurant, room service, laundry service, Internet terminal, parking (free)* ▭ *AE, D, DC, MC, V* ⊠⊙ *BP.*

¢ 🛏 **La Casa de la Abuela.** Hot showers, hearty Peruvian home cooking, and a sunny garden gathering spot attract budget travelers and volunteers to this old colonial mansion. Rooms have a mix of contemporary, colonial, and comfortably worn pieces; some are dorms, and some have private bathrooms. The shared laundry and kitchen are often busy. Pros: extremely friendly and helpful staff; great breakfasts. Cons: often full; not many rooms; not all rooms have bath. ✉ *Giráldez 691* ☎ *064/234–383* ⊕ *www.incasdelperu.com/casa-de-la-abuela* ⇱ *4 rooms, 3 dormitories* ♿ *In-room: no a/c, no phone, kitchen, no TV. In-hotel: laundry facilities, parking (free)* ▭ *No credit cards* ⊙ *CP.*

NIGHTLIFE

Huancayo's nightlife is surprisingly spunky. Many restaurants turn into *peñas* with dancing, live music, and folkloric performances from Friday to Sunday between 7 PM and midnight (though some may start and end earlier). If you arrive around or after the time the show begins, expect to pay a cover of about S/7. Dance clubs are usually open from about 10 PM to 2 AM and have a cover charge of S/10–S/14.

La Cabaña (✉ *Giráldez 652* ☎ *064/223–303*) has rollicking live *folklórico* and pop bands Thursday through Saturday. Video karaoke is the main attraction at the **Taj Mahal** (✉ *Huancavelica 1052*) when you're not dancing. A trendy crowd of young locals and the occasional backpacker heads to **Café Bizarro** (✉ *Puno 656* ☎ *No phone*) where the occasional live rock band plays bad '80s covers.

SHOPPING

Huancayo and the towns of the surrounding Valle del Mantaro are major craft centers. The region is famous for its mate *burilado* (large, intricately carved and painted gourds depicting scenes of local life and historic events), many of which are made 11 km (7 mi) outside of town in the villages of Cochas Grande and Cochas Chico. Silver filigree and utensils are the specialties of San Jerónimo de Tunán, and exquisite knitwear, woolen sweaters, scarves, wall hangings, and hats are produced in San Agustín de Cajas and Hualhaus.

Elegant, high-quality textiles are woven and sold at **Artesanía Sumaq Ruray** (✉ *Brasilia 132* ☎ *064/237–018*). You'll find top-quality, locally made goods near the Plaza Constitución at **Casa del Artesano** (✉ *Real 495* ☎ *No phone*), where artists sit shop-by-shop working on their various crafts. Artists' shops and stalls line the **Centro Commerical Artesanal El Manatial** (✉ *Ancash 475* ☎ *No phone*), where you can browse for clothing, textiles, ceramics, wood carvings, and many other crafts.

The city's main shopping venue is the weekend **Mercado** (✉ *Av. Huancavelica* ☎ *No phone*), which is spread down one of the city's main thoroughfares and its side streets. In particular, look for mate burilado, mantas, straw baskets, and *retablos* (miniature scenes framed in painted wooden boxes). **Mercado Mayorista** (✉ *Prolongación Ica* ☎ *No phone*), stretching around the blocks near the train station, is the daily produce market. You'll need several hours to wander through the stalls of local crafts and foodstuffs, where you'll find traditional medicines and spices among such local delicacies as gourds, guinea pigs, fish, and frogs. The **Sunday crafts market** (✉ *Calle Huancavelica* ☎ *No phone*) has textiles, sweaters, embroidery, wood carvings, and ceramics. This is a good place to shop for the carved gourds.

EN
ROUTE

Valle de Mantaro. The wide Mantaro Valley stretches northwest of Huancayo, embracing not only the Río Mantaro but also a vast area of highlands lakes and plains. Trails run along the jagged mountainsides to archaeological sites and crafts villages. By road, you'll reach Cochas Chicas and Cochas Grandes, gourd-carving centers 11 km (7 mi) north of Huancayo, with some of the most talented mate burilado artists in the country. The road west leads 10 km (6 mi) to Hualhaus, a weaving village where you can watch blankets and sweaters being crafted from alpaca and lamb's wool dyed with local plants. About 5 km (3 mi) north is San Jerónimo de Tunan, where the Wednesday market specializes in gold and silver filigree. Cross the Río Mantaro and head 10 km (6 km) west to Aco, a village of potters and ceramics artists. Group tours from Huancayo cover the valley, but the roads are good enough that you can drive on your own—although you won't have a guide or a translator. Minibuses from the Avenida Giraldez also reach these villages.

8

HUANCAVELICA

147 km (91 mi) south of Huancayo.

Spread out high in the Andes, Huancavelica was founded in the 16th century by Spanish conquistadors, who discovered the rich veins of silver and mercury threaded through the rocky hillsides. The abundant mercury was vital in the extraction of silver from mines in Peru and Bolivia, including Potosí. Although mining was difficult at 3,680 meters (12,979 feet), the Spanish succeeded in making the city an important profit center that today has grown to a population of around 40,000.

This scenic town is sliced by the Río Huancavelica, which divides the commercial district on the south and the residential area in the north.

The road is rough, but the surroundings are beautiful, a mix of quiet, clapboard-style villages fronting vast sheep pastures and snowcapped mountains. ■TIP→ If you have a good map and your own equipment, excellent hiking opportunities are in the surrounding mountains.

A lack of good roads leading to the town has kept the Andean city away from the winds of change. You'll still see traditional costumes worn by women in the markets and shops and the narrow, cobbled streets are still lined with elegant, colonial-style mansions and 16th-century churches. Residents from all over the region crowd the sprawling Sunday market, as well as the daily food market at the corner of Muñoz and Barranca.

Most crafts and clothing are made in the villages on the outskirts of Huancavelica, and you're welcome to visit the artisans' shops. Other neighboring explorations include the viewpoints from Potaqchiz, a short stroll up the hill from San Cristóbal. Thermal baths are on the hillside across from town.

GETTING HERE AND AROUND

The town is quite compact and nearly everything of interest is confined to a few short streets in the center. Few roads lead to Huancavelica; many mountain villages can only be reached by foot. A good, albeit steep, path starts from behind the rail station and has pleasant views of the city and surrounding mountains. The altitude is a common problem to visitors here, so take it slow and drink plenty of bottled water.

The best place for contacts on local culture in Huancavelica is **Instituto Nacional de Cultura** (⊠ *Plaza San Juan de Dios*), which offers language, music, and dance lessons, cultural talks, and details on historic sights and regional history. It's open Monday through Saturday 10–1 and 3–7.

ESSENTIALS

Currency **Banco de Crédito** (⊠ *Toledo 300* ⊕ *www.viabcp.com*).

Mail **Serpost** (⊠ *Pasaje Ferrúa* ☎ *067/452–750*).

Visitor Info **Ministerio de Industria y Comercio, Turismo, y Artesanías** (⊠ *Nicolás de Piérola 180*).

EXPLORING

Huancavelica's **Plaza de Armas** is the main gathering place. Across from the plaza is the restored 17th-century cathedral. ⊠ *Toledo y Segura* ☎ *No phone* ⊠ *Free* ⊘ *Daily 24 hrs.*

The **Iglesia de San Francisco** was begun in 1673 and took six more decades to complete. The dual white towers and red stone doorway—carved with regional motifs—make the San Francisco Church one of the most attractive buildings in town. ⊠ *Godos y Tagle* ☎ *No phone* ⊠ *Free* ⊘ *Mon.–Sat. 4–6.*

The Sunday **Feria Dominical** market attracts artists and shoppers from all the mountain towns. It's a good place to browse for local crafts—although you'll get better quality (and sometimes better prices) in the villages. ⊠ *Garma y Barranca* ⊘ *Sun. 8–3.*

San Cristóbal. Locals believe that these hot-spring mineral baths, found in the tree-covered slopes north of town, have healing powers. Hundreds of pilgrims come from the surrounding villages during holy days. ⊠ *5 de Agosto* 🕿 *No phone* 🛁 *S/0.50 private room, S/0.35 public area* ⊙ *Daily 6–3.*

WHERE TO EAT AND STAY

Restaurants line Barranca, Toledo, and the streets around the Plaza de Armas. All are casual and have a mix of Andean and continental cuisine. Most restaurants have an à la carte menu useful for sampling several dishes. Hotels usually have restaurants, or at least a small café or dining room.

$ 🛏 **Hotel Presidente Huancavelica.** The town's top hotel is in an attractive, Spanish-colonial building on the plaza. Rooms have bland modern furnishings, but they're sizable and comfortable, with phones and hot showers. Rooms with shared baths are cheaper. The restaurant is open for lunch and dinner when the hotel is busy; otherwise, it's open for breakfast only. **Pros:** historic building; prime plaza setting. **Cons:** mixed amenities; pretty basic for the best hotel in town. ⊠ *Carabaya y Muñoz* 🕿 *067/452-760* ⊕ *www.hoteles-del-centro.com* 🛏 *45 rooms, 40 with bath* ⚭ *In-room: no a/c, Wi-Fi. In-hotel: restaurant, laundry service, Internet terminal, parking (free)* ▭ *AE, D, DC, MC, V* ⦿⧈ *BP.*

¢ 🛏 **Mercurio.** The modestly furnished rooms at this colonial-style hotel on the plaza are spic-and-span, with private bathrooms—some with tubs—and hot water. The restaurant ($) serves hearty portions of Peruvian cuisine, as well as pasta. **Pros:** great location; can't beat the price. **Cons:** bathrooms are hit or miss; very basic. ⊠ *Torre Tagle 455* 🕿 *067/452-773* 🛏 *45 rooms* ⚭ *In-room: no a/c. In-hotel: restaurant, laundry service, parking (free)* ▭ *MC, V* ⦿⧈ *BP.*

QUINUA

37 km (23 mi) northeast of Ayachuco.

Fodor's Choice
★

The Battle of Ayacucho, the decisive battle against Spain in the Peruvian War of Independence, took place on the **Pampas de Quinua** grasslands 37 km (23 mi) northeast of the city, near the village of Quinua, on December 9, 1824. Today a white obelisk rises 44 meters (144 feet) above the pampas to commemorate how the locals firmly cemented Peru's independence here when they defeated the Spanish. You can follow the surrounding events through exhibits in the compact **Quinua museum** (⊠ *Plaza de Armas* 🛁 *S/5* ⊙ *Mon.–Sat. 10–1 and 3–5*). Come the first week in December to celebrate the town's role in Peru's democracy, when you'll see extravagant local performances, parties, parades, and crafts fairs. There's a little local market on Sunday. ■ **TIP**➔ Quinua is one of the craft centers of Peru. It's best known for its ceramics, and you'll find various examples on the windowsills and rooftops of the adobe houses. Miniature churches, delicately painted with ears of corn or flowers, are frequently-seen symbols of good luck. The ubiquitous ceramic bulls are figures once used in festivities associated with cattle-branding ceremonies. Tours from Ayacucho bring you into the workshops of the many craftsmen in the village. Among the better quality workshops are:

8

Cerámica Artística Sánchez, Rumi Wasi, Quinta, and Galería Artesanal Límaco; all on Jr. Sucre off the main plaza. Tours of Huari, Vilcashuaman, and Vischongo often include Quinua, but you can also get here by bus from Ayacucho.

AYACUCHO

114 km (71 mi) south of Huancavelica; 364 km (226 mi) northeast of Pisco.

Tucked into the folds of the Andes, 2,740 meters (8,987 feet) up on the slopes, Ayacucho is a colorful, colonial-style town. Though its looks are Spanish—all glowing white-alabaster mansions with elegant columns and arches—it's primarily an indigenous town inhabited by people who still speak Quechua as a first language and don traditional costume for their daily routine. Visitors are greeted with some amazement (and lots of warmth) in this city of 120,000 where artists are revered and celebrations like Carnaval and Semana Santa take place in a frenzy of activity and energy. Religion is a serious pursuit, too, in this city of churches, where more than 50 sanctuaries beckon worshippers at all hours.

Civilization in Peru began in the valleys around Ayacucho about 20,000 years ago. Dating back this far are the oldest human remains in the country—and perhaps in the Americas—found in a cave network at Piquimachay, 24 km (15 mi) west of the city. Over the centuries, the region was home to many pre-Hispanic cultures, including the Huari (Wari), who set up their capital of Huari 22 km (14 mi) from Ayacucho some 13,000 years ago. When the Inca arrived in the 15th century, they ruled the lands from their provincial capital at Vilcashuamán.

The Spanish came and conquered the reigning Inca, and Francisco Pizarro founded Ayacucho in 1540. First named Huamanga for the local *huamanga* (alabaster) used in handicrafts, Ayacucho grew from a small village into a broad city known for its many colonial-style churches. Nearly 300 years later it was the center of Peru's rebellion for independence from the Spanish, when the Peruvian army led by Antonio José de Sucre defeated the last Spanish at nearby Quinua on December 9, 1824. The first bells of Peru's independence were sounded at the Iglesia Santo Domingo in Ayacucho.

It took a century more before the city built its first road links west to the coast, and the road to Lima went unpaved through the 1960s. Ayacucho might have opened to tourism then, but for the influence of Abimael Guzmán, a philosophy teacher at the University of Huamanga who set up the Sendero Luminoso (Shining Path) here. From March 1982, when bombs and gunfire first sounded through the cobbled streets, thousands of Ayacuchanos fled or were killed during fighting between the Shining Path and the government. The city was nearly cut off from the rest of Peru during the early 1990s. Guzmán was finally arrested in 1992 and the Sendero Luminoso dismantled, but even with stability tourism has been slow to establish itself outside of Semana Santa and the city receives only about a thousand visitors a month.

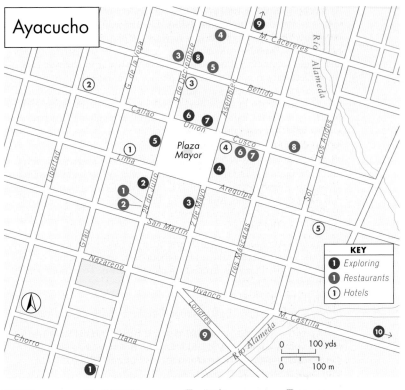

Ayacucho

KEY

1 Exploring
1 Restaurants
1 Hotels

0 — 100 yds
0 — 100 m

Exploring ▼

Casa Jaúregui **3**

Catedral **4**

Cementerio Municipal **10**

Iglesia Santo Domingo **8**

La Compañia de Jesús **2**

Museo Cáceres **1**

Museo de Arqueología y
Antropología Hipólito
Unánue **9**

Museo de Arte Popular
Joaquín López Antay **6**

Prefectura **5**

Palacio de Marqués de
Mozobamba **7**

Resturants ▼

Antonino's **6**

El Monasterio **1**

La Brasa Roja **7**

La Casona **5**

Lalo's cafe **2**

Niños **3**

Mia Pizza **4**

Restaurant Los Álamos **8**

Restaurant Urpicha **9**

Hotels ▼

Hotel Plaza Ayacucho **3**

Hotel San Francisco
de Paula **2**

Hotel Santa Mariá **5**

Hotel Santa Rosa **1**

La Colmena Hotel **4**

8

Ayacucho's resulting isolation from the modern world means that to visit is to step back into colonial days. Elegant white huamanga buildings glow in the sunlight, bright flowers spilling out of boxes lining high, narrow, wooden balconies. ■TIP➔ Beyond the slim, straight roads and terra-cotta roofs, cultivated fields climb the Andes foothills up to the snow. Electricity, running water, and phones are unreliable, if even available. Banks and businesses are hidden in 16th-century *casonas* (colonial mansions). Women in traditional Quechua shawls draped over white blouses, their black hair braided neatly, stroll through markets packed with small fruit, vegetable, and craft stalls.

GETTING HERE AND AROUND

Most of the city can be explored on foot as most tourist amenities, hotels, restaurants, and the bulk of the churches and colonial buildings are within a few blocks of the Plaza de Armas. Getting to out-of-the-way workshops in Santa Ana and La Libertad requires a quick cab ride. Basic city tours (S/20) offered at every agency depart daily and will save you much of the hassle.

Ayacucho's Alfredo Mendívil Duarte Airport (AYP) is 4 km (2½ mi) from the city. You can take a taxi (about S/4), or catch a bus or colectivo from the Plaza de Armas, which will deliver you about a half block from the airport.

ESSENTIALS

Airport Alfredo Mendívil Duarte Airport (✉ Ejército 950 ☎ 066/312–088).

Bus Ayacucho Tours (✉ Cáceres 880 ☎ 066/313–532). **Cruz del Sur** (✉ Av. Mariscal Cáceres 1264 ☎ 066/312–813). **Expreso Molina** (✉ 9 de Diciembre 459 ☎ 066/311–348). **Los Libertadores** (✉ Tres Máscaras ☎ 066/313–614). **Ormeño** (✉ Libertad 257 ☎ 066/312–495).

Currency Banco de Crédito (✉ 28 de Julio y San Martín ⊕ www.viabcp.com).

Internet Instituto Pacífico (✉ Callao 106 ☎ 066/314–299).

Mail Serpost (✉ Jr. Asamblea 295 ☎ 066/312–224).

Visitor Info La Dirección General de Industria y Turismo (✉ Jr. Asamblea 481 ☎ 066/312–548). **Ministerio de Turismo Ayacucho** (✉ Jr. Asamblea 400 ☎ 066/312–548). **iPerú** (✉ Portal Municipal 48, Plaza Mayor ☎ 066/318–305 ✉ Alfredo Mendívil Duarte Airport).

EXPLORING

❶ In Casona Vivanco on the Plaza Mayor, the 17th-century **Museo Cáceres** honors Andrés Cáceres, an Ayacucho resident and former Peruvian president best known for his successful guerrilla leadership during the 1879–83 War of the Pacific against Chile. His Cáceres Museum is one of the city's best-preserved historic mansions, which today protects a mix of military memorabilia and ancient local artifacts, including stone carvings and ceramics. Note the gallery of colonial-style paintings. ✉ 28 de Julio 508 ☎ 066/326–166 ◀S/3 ⊘ Mon.–Sat. 9–noon and 2–6.

❸ Across from the Iglesia Merced on the Plaza Mayor, you'll see the colonial-style **Casa Jaúregui**. The Jaúregui House is an art gallery with paintings, sculptures, and local crafts by Peruvian artists. ⊠ *Plaza Mayor* ☎ *066/314-299* 🎬 *S/4* ☉ *Weekdays 9-noon and 3-5.*

❷ You can't miss the ocher-color, baroque-style exterior of the Jesuit church, **La Compañia de Jesús.** The towers were added a century after the main building, which has religious art and a gilt altar. ⊠ *Jr. 28 de Julio y Lima* ☎ *No phone* 🎬 *Free* ☉ *Mass time.*

❺ The **Prefectura,** or Boza and Solís House, is tucked into a 1748, two-story *casona histórica* (historic mansion). Local independence-era heroine María Prado de Bellido was held prisoner in the Prefecture's patio room until her execution by firing squad in 1822. ⊠ *28 de Julio* ☎ *066/312-229* 🎬 *S/2* ☉ *Weekdays 8-noon and 2-6.*

❻ The **Museo de Arte Popular Joaquín López Antay,** in the Casona Chacón on the Plaza Mayor, has some of the region's best art. The exquisite and valuable collections include clay sculptures, silver filigree, retablos, and paintings. Trace the town's history, as well as the craftsmanship behind many pieces, through photo exhibits. ■**TIP→** Note the gathering of looms used to weave lamb and alpaca wool into textiles and clothing. The Museum of Popular Art shares the Casona with the Banco de Credito in one of the city's best-preserved colonial-style mansions. ⊠ *Unión 28* ☎ *066/312-467* 🎬 *Free* ☉ *Tues.-Fri. 9-12:30 and 2-5, Sat. 10-12:30.*

❽ The 1548 **Iglesia Santo Domingo** is now a national monument. The first bells ringing out Peru's independence from the Spanish after the Battle of Ayacucho were sounded from here. Byzantine towers and Roman arches mark the church's facade. ⊠ *Jr. 9 de Diciembre y Bellido* ☎ *No phone* 🎬 *Free* ☉ *Mass time.*

OFF THE BEATEN PATH

Huari. The wide plains that make up the 300-hectare (740-acre) Santuario Histórico Pampas de Ayacucho are scattered with relics of the Huari culture, which evolved 500 years before that of the Inca. Huari was its capital, thought to have once been home to 60,000 or more residents, and its surrounding fields contain a maze of tumbled stone temples, homes, and 12-meter (39-foot) walls. This is believed to have been the first urban walled settlement in the Andes, created by a civilization whose livelihood was based on such metalworking feats as bronze weapons and gold and silver jewelry. A small museum displays skeleton bits and samples of ceramics and textiles; opening times are at the whim of the workers. You can get here cheaply from Barrio Magdalena in Ayacucho via irregular buses, which continue to Quinua and Huanta for S/3. Most travel agents in town offer guided tours to the site for around S/60. ⊠ *22 km (14 mi) northeast of Ayacucho* ☎ *No phone* 🎬 *Site: free; museum: S/3* ☉ *Ruins: daily 10-5; museum: hrs vary.*

❾ On display at the **Museo de Arqueología y Antropología Hipólito Unánue,** at the Centro Cultural Simón Bolívar, are regional finds from the Moche, Nazca, Ica, Inca, Canka, Chavín, and Chimu cultures. Highlights of the Hipólito Unánue Archaeology and Anthropology Museum include ceremonial costumes, textiles, everyday implements, and even artwork from some of the area's oldest inhabitants. The museum is locally referred to as Museo INC. ⊠ *Av. Independencia* ☎ *066/312-360* 🎬 *S/4* ☉ *Mon.-Sat. 8:30-11 and 2-5.*

8

7 Built in 1550 and now the home of the Escuela de Bellas Artes (School of Fine Arts), the **Palacio de Marqués de Mozobamba** is one of the city's oldest structures. The colonial-era, baroque-style architecture includes *portales* (stone arches) in front and a monkey-shaped stone fountain in the courtyard. ■ TIP➜ Notice the Andean carvings of snakes, cougars, and lizards etched into the stone. Two Inca stone walls were discovered in 2003 during restorations. ✉ *Unión 47* ☎ *No phone* 🎫 *Free* ☼ *Weekdays 10–4.*

4 Walk through the plaza gardens and you'll immediately spot the twin brick bell towers of the 1612 Ayacucho **Catedral**, built by Bishop Don Cristóbal de Castilla y Zamora. Step inside to view the cathedral's carved altars with gold-leaf designs, a silver tabernacle, and an ornate wooden pulpit. Look for the plaque inside the entrance that quotes from Pope John Paul II's speech during his visit in 1985. The **Museo de Arte Religioso** exhibits antique objects from the sanctuary's early days, carvings of saints, and religious paintings; ask for visiting privileges if the doors are locked. During Semana Santa, the church hosts an extremely popular Palm Sunday candlelight procession with a statue of Christ transported on the back of a white donkey. ✉ *Asemblea* ☎ *No phone* 🎫 *Free* ☼ *Church: Mass time; museum: Mon., Tues., and Sat. 9–noon and 3–5, Fri. 9–noon and 4–7.*

10 At the end of the airport runway, the enormous **Cementerio Municipal** looks like a huge condo with multiple walls of crypts. Many of the sites date from the 1970s and 1980s, when the Sendero Luminoso held the region hostage. ✉ *End of airport runway.*

OFF THE BEATEN PATH

Vilcashuamán and Intihuatana. Four long hours south of Ayacucho on winding, unpaved roads is the former Inca provincial capital of Vilcashuamán, set where the north–south Inca highway crossed the east–west trade road from Cusco to the Pacific. You can still see the double-seated throne and a five-tiered platform surrounded by stepped fields once farmed by Inca. An hour's walk from Vilcashuamán (or a half-hour's walk south past the main road from Ayacucho) is Inhuatana, where Inca ruins include a palace and tower beside a lagoon. Former Inca baths, a sun temple, and a sacrificial altar are also on the grounds. Check out the unusual 17-angled boulder, one of the odd building rocks that are an Inca hallmark. Ayacucho travel agencies can organize tours of both sites (S/65), or you can catch a bus or *colectivo* (small van) from Avenida Castilla on Tuesday, Thursday, and Saturday. If you take public transport, you'll have to stay overnight, as vehicles return on alternate days.

WHERE TO EAT

Outside of a few international restaurants catering to visiting tourists Ayacucho stands by its Andean specialties. The city is famous for its filling, flavorful *puca picante* (a peanutty pork-and-potato stew), served with rice and topped with a parsley sprig. ■ TIP➜ The city's favorite drink is the hot, creamy, pisco-spiked ponche (flavored with milk, cinnamon, cloves, sesame, peanuts, walnuts, and sugar). The best time to sample this popular concoction is during Semana Santa. In the first week of November, Ayacuchanos are busy baking sweet breads shaped like horses, *caballos*, and babies, *guaguas*, to place in baskets for the spirits at the family gravesites. You'll find inexpensive restaurants where

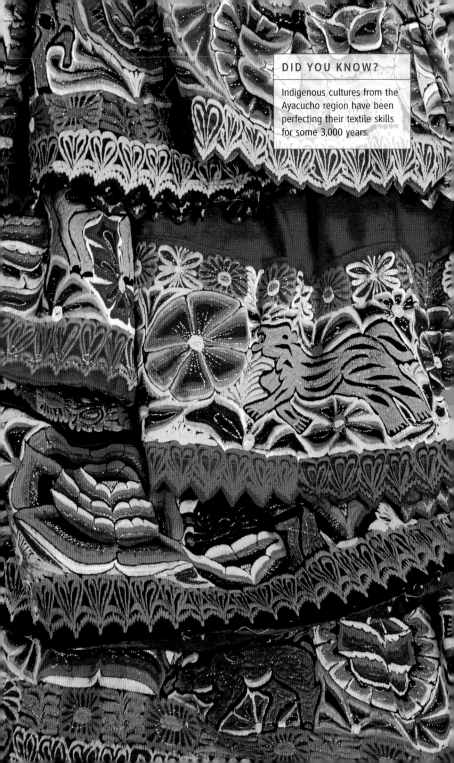

you can grab a cheap *almuerzo* (lunch) along Jirón San Martin. Many restaurants are closed on Sunday.

¢   ✕**Antonino's.** The glow of the brick oven on the rows of Chilean reds

CONTEMPORARY   bathe the small Italian restaurant with a cozy, romantic feel. Pizzas and pastas are a safe bet, especially if you've been stuck eating regional dishes for awhile. ⊠ *Cusco 144* ☎ *066/318–816* ▭ *No credit cards.*

¢   ✕**El Monasterio.** You can sit under the stars in the pleasant colonial

PERUVIAN   courtyard at the Centro Turístico San Cristóbal de Huamanga, home to several excellent restaurants and cafés, shops, and galleries. The best is El Monasterio in the near corner, which cooks up regional specialties like *puca picante* (pork-and-potato stew) and roasted cuy. ⊠ *Jr. 28 de Julio 178 int 116* ☎ *066/312–343* ▭ *V.*

¢   ✕**La Brasa Roja.** *Pollos a la brasa*, or Peruvian rotisserie chicken, is the

PERUVIAN   specialty at the tiny La Brasa Roja that's lost among the cheap hotel cafes on Jr. Cusco. Choose between a quarter, half, or whole chicken with fries and salad. ⊠ *Cusco 180* ☎ *066/312–388* ▭ *No credit cards.*

¢   ✕**La Casona.** Dining in this Spanish-style home is like attending an inti-

PERUVIAN   mate, upscale party in a fine hacienda. Soft music wafts between high

★   walls lined with paintings and woven textiles, while conversations ebb and flow at a low hum. The scent of fresh flowers decorating the glass-topped tables mixes with the delicious aromas of Peruvian specialties like *puca picante* (pork and potatoes in red sauce) and *tortas* (sweet cakes). ⊠ *Bellindo 463* ☎ *066/312–733* ▭ *MC, V.*

¢   ✕**Lalo's café.** Lalo's is a modern patio café with coffees, teas, pastries,

CAFÉ   and light meals. It's much more Parisian and much less Ayacucho, which attracts the city's well-to-do and NGO workers in the mornings and evenings. ⊠ *Jr. 28 de Julio 178* ☎ *066/311–331* ☉ *Closed Sun.* ▭ *No credit cards.*

¢   ✕**Mia Pizza.** You'll make friends at this dinner-only spot where patrons

ITALIAN   sit side by side at wooden tables to snack on Italian fare. You can't miss with the pizza, cooked in an authentic wood-burning oven. The cheesy cannelloni and hearty spaghetti are also good bets. ⊠ *Jr. Asemblea 138* ☎ *066/311–283* ☉ *No lunch* ▭ *No credit cards.*

¢   ✕**Niños.** The building is old Spanish style, but the food is modern,

CONTEMPORARY   ranging in flavors from the meaty Andean *parrillada* (grill) to pasta and sandwiches. Come on weekends to catch bands that rock the crowd. The restaurant is across the street from the Iglesia Santo Domingo. ⊠ *9 de Diciembre 205* ☎ *066/314–537* ▭ *V.*

¢   ✕**Restaurant Los Álamos.** This popular backpacker hangout begins the

PERUVIAN   day with serious breakfasts: hearty egg and meat dishes, pancakes, sweet breads, and the like. After dark, huge dinners, such as pollo a la brasa and *tallarin verdes* (noodles with pesto) are often accompanied by local bands crooning crowd favorites. ⊠ *Cusco 215* ☎ *066/312–782* ▭ *No credit cards.*

¢   ✕**Restaurant Urpicha.** Eating here feels like you're having dinner at

PERUVIAN   Grandma's. Meals are lovingly (and slowly) prepared, but worth the

Fodor'sChoice   wait. The kitchen turns out such traditional Andean specialties as grilled

★   cuy and *puca picante,* potatoes in a spicy sauce with peanuts, rice, and pork. Drop by on a weekend to hear the best local folk groups. ⊠ *Londres 272* ☎ *066/313–905* ▭ *No credit cards.*

WHERE TO STAY

$$ ⊞ **Hotel Plaza Ayacucho.** The city's most expensive hotel is in a gracious colonial building partly overlooking the Plaza Mayor. Spacious gardens and opulent sitting areas belie the modest rooms with worn carpet and nicked modern furnishings. The best (and quietest) accommodations are on the second floor, where there's a view of the terra-cotta roofs and the courtyard. You can request a balcony over the plaza, but beware the ever-present commotion outside—especially on Sunday and during festivals. **Pros:** some rooms overlook plaza; the place to stay for Semana Santa. **Cons:** room quality varies; stuffy atmosphere. ⊠ *Jr. 9 de Diciembre 184* ☎ *066/312–202* ⇨ *84 rooms* ⌂ *In-room: no a/c, Wi-Fi. In-hotel: restaurant, room service, parking (free)* ═ *AE, MC, V* ⎮◎⎮ *BP.*

$ ⊞ **Hotel San Francisco de Paula.** At this Spanish mansion, local charm is threaded throughout the winding rooms and public areas, decorated with folk-art pieces, textiles, and crafts. Antique furnishings bring the colonial era to life, but modern room amenities like TVs and refrigerators pour on 21st-century comfort. Book a room with a balcony to enjoy the street scene below, or dine at the rooftop restaurant for city and mountain views. **Pros:** nice views of city and hills; regional art everywhere. **Cons:** plain rooms; tacky bedspreads. ⊠ *Callao 290* ☎ *066/312–353* ⊕ *www.hotelsanfranciscodepaula.com* ⇨ *40 rooms* ⌂ *In-room: no a/c, refrigerator, Wi-Fi. In-hotel: restaurant, bar, laundry service, Internet terminal, parking (free)* ═ *No credit cards* ⎮◎⎮ *BP.*

$ ⊞ **Hotel Santa María.** The only bad news in this charming hotel is that it's three blocks from the plaza. Otherwise the blend of colonial style with modern features and bold colors make it one of the best options in Ayacucho. Wood floors and Andean decor flush out the guest rooms, while a contemporary theme runs throughout the hotel. **Pros:** cosmopolitan vibe; great price. **Cons:** steep walk to the plaza; doesn't feel quite like Ayacucho. ⊠ *Jr. Arequipa 320* ☎ *066/314–988* ⊕ *www.hotelesjian.com. pe* ⇨ *22 rooms* ⌂ *In-room: no a/c, Wi-Fi. In-hotel: restaurant, room service, bar, laundry service, Internet terminal, parking (free)* ═ *No credit cards* ⎮◎⎮ *BP.*

¢ ⊞ **Hotel Santa Rosa.** Near the plaza, this pleasant little hotel has a pretty courtyard with gardens and a brick walkway. Rooms have a mix of antiques, handmade fabrics, and contemporary furnishings, plus unexpected modern amenities like TVs and phones. Private bathrooms only have hot water in the morning and evening. **Pros:** beautiful courtyard; good restaurant; local charm with a modern feel. **Cons:** hot water isn't available all day; room sizes vary. ⊠ *Jr. Lima 166* ☎ *066/314–614* ⊕ *www.hotel-santarosa.com* ⇨ *26 rooms* ⌂ *In-room: no a/c, Wi-Fi. In-hotel: restaurant, room service, bar, laundry service, Internet terminal, parking (free)* ═ *No credit cards* ⎮◎⎮ *BP.*

¢ ⊞ **La Colmena Hotel.** Though the rooms are small, the quiet and pleasant courtyard makes this one of the city's most popular budget options. Rooms, with plain furniture and local art, come with or without baths; hot water runs only in the morning. Rooms in the back tend to be dingy and lack light, so try for the ones facing the street. **Pros:** great regional restaurant; close to plaza. **Con:** dingy bathrooms. ⊠ *Cusco 140* ☎ *066/311–318* ⇨ *18 rooms, 12 with private bath* ⌂ *In-room: no a/c, no TV. In-hotel: parking (free)* ═ *No credit cards* ⎮◎⎮ *BP.*

NIGHTLIFE

Peña Macha (✉ *Grau 158* ☎ *No phone*) is a disco during the week but has folkloric shows and live music on weekends. At **Taberna El Buho** (✉ *Jr. 9 de Diciembre 284* ☎ *No phone*), kick back with a pisco sour and listen to '80s rock, before getting the nerve to run upstairs to sing karaoke. Admire the local art on the walls and dozens of upside-down black umbrellas on the ceiling while grabbing a drink or pizza at the **Taberna Magía Negra** (✉ *Cáceres y Vega* ☎ *No phone*).

SHOPPING

Ayacucho is the home of many of Peru's best artists, whom you can often visit at work in their neighborhood shops or galleries. Look for retablos, the multi-tiered, three-dimensional displays of plaster characters in scenes of the city's famed religious processions and historic battles. The busy Mercado Domingo (Sunday Market) in Huanta, an hour north, is fun to visit.

Ayacucho's produce and meat market is the **Mercado Andrés Vivanco** (✉ *Jr. 28 de Julio* ☎ *No phone*), found behind the Arco del Triunfo in a one-story building; shops continue for several streets behind.

The **Santa Ana neighborhood** is a famous weaving area, where you can visit local artists and their galleries. In particular, look for complex *tejidos* (textiles), which have elaborate—and often pre-Hispanic—motifs that can take more than a half-year to design and weave. These creations, made of natural fibers and dyes, can cost $200 USD or more for high-quality work. **Familia Sulca** (✉ *Cáceres 302* ☎ *066/312–990*) is known for its beautiful carpets. **Galería Latina** (✉ *Plazuela Santa Ana 105* ☎ *066/318–315*) is the workshop of world-renowned weaver Alejandro Gallardo. Internationally famous weaver Edwin Sulca Lagos works out of **Las Voces del Tapiz** (✉ *Plazuela Santa Ana 82* ☎ *066/314–242*).

In Santa Ana, intricate alabaster, or Huamanga stone, carvings are the specialty of **Jose Gálvez** (✉ *Jeruslaén 12* ☎ *066/314–278*).Many famous retablo artists live in Ayacucho, particularly around the neighborhood known as Barrio La Libertad. **Artesanías Helme** (✉ *Bellido 463* ☎ *No phone*) has a selection of retablos and other art with delicate depictions of Andean life and religious scenes. **Artesanías Huamanguina Pascualito** (✉ *Cusco 136* ☎ *066/311–013*) has an extensive collection of carvings. The collection of retablos at **Ohalateria Artesanías** (✉ *Plaza de Armas* ☎ *No phone*), in the center of town, is a good place to begin studying the different delicately carved motifs you'll find in the area. Workshops owned by the artist family **Urbano** (✉ *Peru 308 and 330* ☎ *No phone*) are among the best places to find finely crafted retablos. In Barrio Belén, members of the **Familia Pizarro** (✉ *San Cristóbal 215* ☎ *No phone*) carve *piedra huamanga* (alabaster sculptures) and weave fine textiles. The widest selection of handicrafts in Ayacucho, from retablos to sweaters, can be found at **Mercado Artesanal Shosaku Nagase** (✉ *Plazoleta El Arco* ☎ *No phone*), about a kilometer north of the city center.

The North Coast and Northern Highlands

WORD OF MOUTH

Magnificent places to visit are Kuelap in the city of Chachapoyas (take a plane from Lima or a bus from Chiclayo) and Chavín, in Huaraz.

—llello

WELCOME TO THE NORTH COAST AND NORTHERN HIGHLANDS

TOP REASONS TO GO

★ **The Ancient World.** Along the coast, Chavín, Moche, and Chimú ruins date as far back as 3,000 BC. In the highlands are Wari sites, and Kuélap, a stunning complex built by the Chachapoyans a thousand years before Machu Picchu.

★ **Real Peru.** People are friendly, excited to talk to foreigners, and want to share their culture. The coast's warmer temperatures don't hurt either.

★ **Outdoor Adventure.** The highlands provide plenty of trekking, climbing, and rafting, especially around Huaraz, where mountains soar above 6,000 meters (19,500 feet).

★ **Colonial Architecture.** The coastal city of Trujillo is one of the best places for colonial architecture. It's like walking into a time warp, and you may feel inspired to wear a hoop skirt or starch your collar.

★ **Beaches.** The northernmost coast offers year-round sun, white-sand beaches, and a relaxed, tropical atmosphere, especially in Máncora and Punta Sal.

The National Museum of the Royal Tombs of Sipan in Lambayeque.

1 **The North Coast.** Explore almost unlimited archaeological sites, well-preserved colonial architecture, and relaxed beach towns with year-round sun and surf. Fresh seafood is abundant, the climate is warmer, and life is more relaxed.

Huaraz.

2 Huaraz and the Cordillera Blanca. Stunning snow-capped peaks, natural hot springs and incredible international food make this one of the north's most popular areas. With more than 40 peaks above 6,000 meters (19,500 feet) and the second-highest peak in all the Americas, this provides spectacular views and outdoor activities.

3 The Northern Highlands. See a landscape almost untouched by the modern world, with farm pastures, mountains, and herds of cows, goats, and sheep in Cajamarca. Head to Chachapoyas, near the border of the Amazon, for extraordinary greenery and the astonishing ruins at Kuélap, often compared to Machu Picchu, but built more than a thousand years before.

GETTING ORIENTED

Travel from one geographic region to another is quite challenging and only recommended for those without time constraints. Instead, choose a region and explore accordingly: for the North Coast, travel from archeological ruins to the beach in a south-north direction; for Huaraz and the Cordillera Blanca, use the town of Huaraz as your focal point—from there discover glaciers, snow-capped peaks, and natural hot springs; for the Northern Highlands, fly to Cajamarca to begin discovering the gateway to the Amazon.

9

Cordillera Blanca.

Updated by Jeffrey Van Fleet

The North Coast and Northern Highlands are some of the least traveled but most diverse areas of Peru. There are beaches, mountains, green fertile valleys, dry desert, and tremendous archaeological sites and museums. The region also has the least developed tourism industry and travel often requires time and patience.

Like the rest of Peru, there's incredible history behind the cities and towns you see today. First inhabited more than 13,000 years ago, the Chavín and Moche people later built colossal cities near the coast, to be replaced over time by civilizations like the Chimú and Chachapoyas. Eventually, all these were overtaken by the Inca, followed by the Spanish. Luckily, the extensive ruins and elaborate colonial-era mansions and churches are being preserved in many areas of the north.

A place of extraordinary natural beauty, the northernmost reaches of Peru have magnificent mountains, steep sea cliffs, and vast deserts. The steep, forested hills emerge from the highlands, and trekkers and climbers from around the world converge to hike the green valleys and ascend the rocky, snow-capped peaks towering more than 6,000 meters (19,500 feet) above the sea. The coast offers spectacular white-sand beaches, year-round sun, and an abundance of fresh seafood.

As Peru becomes a more popular international destination, tourism in the north is slowly awakening, but is still light years behind Machu Picchu and Lake Titicaca. Come now and explore the relatively virgin territory that provides a rich peek into the cultural, historical, and physical landscape of Peru.

PLANNING

WHEN TO GO

The weather along the north coast is always pleasant, although it's sunnier from November to May. The northern highlands weather is more capricious—rainy season is November to early May, while it's drier from mid-May to mid-September. September and October have fairly good weather, but occasional storms frighten off most mountaineers.

GETTING HERE AND AROUND

AIR TRAVEL
The easiest way to get around is by plane. You'll definitely want to fly to destinations like Piura and Cajamarca. LAN (⊕ *www.lan.com*) and Star Perú (⊕ *www.starperu.com*) fly to most cities in the region.

BUS TRAVEL
Bus service throughout the region is generally quite good. Emtrafesa (⊕ *www.emtrafesa.com*) runs all the way up the coast. Other reputable companies for the coastal communities include Cruz del Sur (⊕ *www.cruzdelsur.com.pe* ☎ *01/311–5050 in Lima*) and Expreso Chiclayo (☎ *074/233–071 in Chiclayo*). For the highlands, Móvil (⊕ *www.moviltours.com.pe*) is a good choice. Whenever possible, pay for a *bus-cama* or *semi-cama*, which gets you an enormous seat that fully reclines, and attendant service that includes at least one meal and a movie.

CAR TRAVEL
Driving can be a challenge—locals rarely obey road rules—but a car is one of the best ways to explore the region. The Pan-American Highway serves the coast. From there take Highway 109 to Huaraz and Highway 8 to Cajamarca. Small reputable rental-car agencies are in Trujillo, Chiclayo, Piura, and Huaraz. Think twice before driving to archaeological sites; some are hard to find, and it's easy to get lost on the unmarked roads. Consider hiring a driver or taking a tour. Roads in the northern highlands are always in some disrepair.

TAXI TRAVEL
Taxi rides in town centers should cost around S/3; rates go up at night. A longer ride to the suburbs or town environs costs from S/5 to S/15. Negotiate the price before you head off. Taxis hire out their services for specific places, ranging from S/15 and up depending on the distance, or around S/300 for the entire day.

HEALTH AND SAFETY
Use purified water for drinking and brushing your teeth. If you're out trekking, bring an extra bottle with you. Also, eat foods that have been thoroughly cooked or boiled. If vegetables or fruit are raw, be sure they're peeled. In the highlands, especially Huaraz, relax for a few days and drink lots of water to avoid dehydration and altitude sickness.

In the big cities on the coast, be on your guard and take simple precautions, such as asking the concierge at the hotel to get you a taxi and carrying only the cash you need. In small coastal towns or in the highlands things are more secure, but be aware of your belongings at all times.

RESTAURANTS
The north coast has excellent seafood, while simpler, but equally delicious, meat-and-rice dishes are more common in the highlands. Some of Trujillo's fancier restaurants expect you to dress up for dinner, but most spots along the coast are quite casual. Depending on the restaurant, the bill may include a 10% service charge; if not, a 10% tip is appropriate.

9

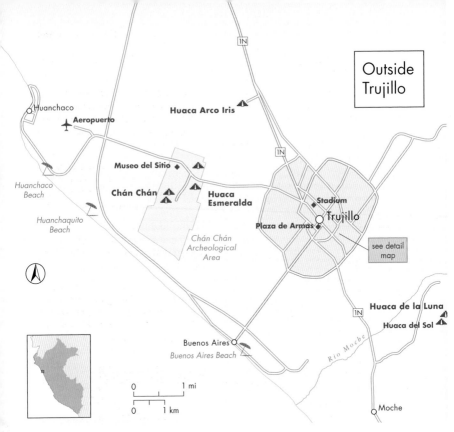

Throughout the region, *almuerzo* (lunch) is the most important meal of the day. It's eaten around 2 PM. *Cena* (dinner) is normally a lighter meal.

HOTELS

Cities along the north coast, especially Trujillo and Chiclayo, have a wide range of lodgings, including large business hotels and converted colonial mansions. The latter, usually called *casonas,* offer personalized service not found in the larger hotels. In smaller towns, such as Barranca and Casma, luxury lodgings do not exist, but you'll have no problem finding a clean and comfortable room. The highlands have excellent lodges with horse stables and hot springs; you can also find family-run inns with simple, basic rooms. Assume hotels do not have air-conditioning unless otherwise indicated.

Finding a hotel room throughout the coastal and highlands areas ought to be painless throughout the year, although coastal resorts like Máncora and Punta Sal are often jammed in summer and holiday weeks. Sports enthusiasts head to Huaraz and Cajamarca in summer so make reservations early. Plan at least two months in advance if you want to travel during Easter and Christmas, when Peruvians take their holidays.

NORTH COAST MENU

The coast serves mostly fresh seafood, often cold—a refreshing meal on a hot day. The highlander diet consists of root vegetables, like yucca and potato, and a variety of meats, where all parts of an animal are eaten. Both regions have spicy and non-spicy meals, so ask first.

Cabrito con tacu-tacu: This dish of kid with grilled rice, usually served with beans, tastes like Peruvian comfort food. It's rich in flavor, but has no spice.

Cangrejo reventado: This stew consists of boiled crab, eggs, and onions. Often served with yucca, this is a fresh, spicy dish.

Cebiche de mococho: Cebiche made of algae for adventurous eaters. You really get a taste of the sea and, so they say, lots of protein.

Cuy: Guinea pig is one of the more popular dishes in Peru. It's a good but chewy meat usually served whole so you need to decide if this is something you want to see before eating.

Shámbar: Particular to Trujillo, this bean stew is a nice, semi-spicy meat alternative.

Parrilladas: At restaurants serving *parrilladas* (barbecues) you can choose from every imaginable cut of beef, including *anticucho* (beef heart) and *ubre* (cow udder).

WHAT IT COSTS IN NUEVO SOLES

	¢	$	$$	$$$	$$$$
RESTAURANTS	under S/20	S/20–S/35	S/36–S/50	S/51–S/65	over S/65
HOTELS	under S/125	S/125–S/250	S/251–S/375	S/376–S/500	over S/500

Restaurant prices are per person for a main course. Hotel prices are for a standard double room, excluding tax.

9

THE NORTH COAST

From pyramids to sun-drenched beaches, the north coast offers great diversity in landscape, weather, and activities. The north coast was, until recently, largely ignored by foreign tourists, but all the way up this sun-drenched stretch of coastal desert you'll find plenty of places to explore and relax, including well-preserved colonial architecture, numerous ancient ruins, excellent restaurants, reasonable beach resorts, and a friendly and relaxed people.

Rich in history and filled with an astonishing number of archaeological sites, especially from Barranca to Piura, the northern coast redefines what is "old." Visit tombs, huge adobe cities, and unbelievable mummies. Explore museums filled with artifacts that date back to 3500 BC. In the far north, especially Máncora and Punta Sal, take off your watch and sink into the sand, soak up the sun, and eat up the luscious seafood.

GETTING HERE AND AROUND

Once in a city, it's extremely easy to get around via taxis or tours; however, getting from city to city requires more planning. There are flights to Tumbes, Piura, or Trujillo from Lima, but not from city to city; the best option is to start by flying into a city and either rent a car or take one of the many frequent, but long, bus rides to other towns.

BARRANCA

200 km (124 mi) northwest of Lima on Pan-American Hwy.

A nondescript town with little to visit except a large Chimú temple nearby, this is a stop for those who are either determined to see every archaeological site in Peru or do not have the time to go to Trujillo or Chiclayo, but would like to see some northern ruins.

GETTING HERE AND AROUND

To get to Barranca, head north from Lima on the Pan-American Highway through the bleak, empty coastal desert, and pass several dusty villages.

EXPLORING

With its seven defensive walls, the gigantic temple at **Paramonga** is worth a look. A small museum has interesting displays on Chimú culture. The archaeological site sits just off the Pan-American Highway, about 3 km (2 mi) north of the turnoff for Huaraz. For a few dollars you can take a taxi to the ruins from the nearby town of Barranca. ⊠ *Pan-American Hwy.* ☎ *No phone* 💲 *S/5* ⊙ *Daily 8–6.*

WHERE TO EAT AND STAY

$ ✕ **Don Goyo.** Here's the best restaurant option in Barranca, offering a
PIZZA large selection of pizza, pasta, and grilled meat dishes. On the menu is the requisite *pollo a la brasa* (rotisserie chicken), all pizzas are served with garlic bread, and regardless of what you order, it will come with a friendly smile. Fresh, homemade yogurts and cheeses are sold on the premises. ⊠ *Jr. Gálvez 506* ☎ *01/235–2378* ▭ *No credit cards.*

¢ 🛏 **Hotel Chavín.** A full-service hotel at bargain prices, this is the best deal
☾ in Barranca. The plain concrete six-story hotel provides wood-floored rooms (ask for one in the rear if noise is a concern) and a decent restaurant serving criollo food. The staff is well-trained and detail-oriented. To relax, dip into the pool and swim up to the poolside bar, the hotel's best feature. One of the few safe places to go out at night is the **Karaoke Hotel Chavín**, in back of the first floor. **Pros:** extensive facilities for a low price. **Cons:** location is on a highly-trafficked main road. ⊠ *Jr. Gálvez 222* ☎ *01/235–5025* ⊕ *www.hotelchavin.com.pe* ⤢ *72 rooms* ☾ *In-room: a/c, Wi-Fi. In-hotel: 2 restaurants, bar, pool, Internet terminal, parking (free)* ▭ *AE, MC, V.*

CASMA

170 km (105 mi) north of Paramonga.

Once known as the "City of Eternal Sun," Casma, like Lima, is now subject to cloudy winters and sunny summers. However, with its leafy Plaza de Armas and a number of pleasant parks, it makes the best base

Northern Journeys

EXPLORING THE ANCIENTS

If seeing the important archaeological sites, ruins and museums are your main priority, start your journey in Trujillo and the important Moche pyramids of the Huaca de la Luna and Huaca del Sol, as well as Chán Chán, built by the Chimú people (but be sure to take at least a day to walk around and enjoy the spectacular colonial architecture). From here, head north to Chiclayo and peer into the Tomb of Sipán and explore world-class historical museums. If you can extend your trip past a week, probably for another four to five days, take the bus from Chiclayo to Chachapoyas and visit Kuélap, a precursor to Machu Picchu built over one thousand years before.

EXPLORING THE OUTDOORS

If you want to see the spectacular mountains of the highlands, head up (and up and up) to the mountain town of Huaraz. Drink water and take a day or so to acclimatize to the altitude,

taking in the local sights and hot springs. Take a three-day trek around the Cordillera Blanca. Discuss the numerous options with your guide. If you can extend your trip past a week, head to Trujillo to enjoy the architecture and ruins (⇨ *see Exploring the Ancients*). Note: you can fly to Huaraz, but there's only one flight per week so it takes careful advance planning.

REST AND RELAXATION

If you want to take a week to relax, fly from Lima to Piura, walk around the city, eat in one of the excellent restaurants, and sleep in one of the first-rate hotels. After a relaxing breakfast at your hotel (almost always included in the price of your room), head to Máncora or Punta Sal for the next few days. Regardless of where you stay, you'll be able to relax on the beach or poolside, and—if you're inspired to get out of your beach chair—to go on a fishing trip, learn to surf or try the even more adventurous kite-surfing.

9

for visiting the nearby ruins. If you're not into the archaeology thing, you might not want to include Casma in your itinerary.

GETTING HERE AND AROUND

Casma lies about six hours north of Lima. Cruz del Sur buses stop here on their Lima–Trujillo routes. Once in town, mototaxis are the best way to get around.

EXPLORING

The origins of **Sechín**, one of the country's oldest archaeological sites dating from around 1600 BC, remain a mystery. It's not clear what culture built this coastal temple, but the bas-relief carvings ringing the main temple, some up to 4 meters (13 feet) high, graphically depict triumphant warriors and their conquered, often beheaded enemies. The site was first excavated in 1937 by the archaeologist J.C. Tello. It has since suffered from looters and natural disasters. Archaeologists are still excavating here, so access to the central plaza is not permitted. ■TIP➜A trail leading up a neighboring hill provides good views of the temple complex, and the surrounding valley. A small museum has a good collection of Chavín ceramics and a mummy that was found near Trujillo. To get to the ruins, head southeast from Casma along the Pan-American Highway for about 3 km (2 mi), turning east onto a paved road leading to Huaraz. The ruins sit about 2 km (1¼ mi) past the turnoff. ☎ *No phone* ✉ *S/6, includes admission to Pañamarca* ☉ *Daily 8–6.*

Several other ruins are near the town of Casma, but the heavily weathered Mochica city of **Pañamarca** is what to see after Sechín. Located 10 km (6 mi) from the Pan-American Highway on the road leading to Nepeña, Pañamarca has some interesting murals. If they're not visible right away, ask a guard to show you as they are often closed off. A taxi will take you to the ruins for about S/20 an hour. Negotiate the price before you leave. ☎ *No phone* ✉ *S/6, includes admission to Sechín* ☉ *Daily 8–6.*

WHERE TO EAT AND STAY

¢ ✕ **El Tío Sam.** The best restaurant in Casma, this local favorite serves just
SEAFOOD about every type of seafood imaginable. The *arroz chaufa con mariscos* (shellfish with Chinese-style fried rice) is especially good, but if you're not in the mood for seafood, try the *cebiche de pato.* This isn't traditional cebiche, but cooked duck, served with rice, yucca, and beans. Don't be put off by the cement floor—the restaurant lacks polish, but it serves good food. ⊠ *Av. Huarmei 138* ☎ *043/411–447* ▭ *MC, V.*

¢ 🏠 **El Farol.** A respite from the dusty streets, gardens surround this pleasant hotel. Although the rooms have unsightly fluorescent lights, they're comfortable and affordable. The bamboo-walled restaurant specializes in seafood and looks onto the center gardens. **Pros:** calm and natural beauty transports you away from the city. **Cons:** service is a little too calm and requires patience. ⊠ *Av. Túpac Amarú 450* ☎ *043/411–064* ⊕ *www.elfarolinn.com* ⤴ *23 rooms, 4 suites, 1 bungalow* ⚬ *In-room: a/c, no phone. In-hotel: restaurant, pool, gym, laundry service, Wi-Fi hotspot, Internet terminal, parking (free)* ▭ *V.*

PLAYA TORTUGAS

20 km (12 mi) north of Casma.

An easy drive from the Sechín area, this small beach is a more low-key base to explore the nearby ruins. ■ **TIP→** A ghost town in winter, it's much more pleasant, in terms of both weather and people, in summertime. The stony beach, in a perfectly round cove, surrounded by brown hills, looks drab and offers limited hotel and restaurant options, but with its fleet of fishing boats and pleasant lapping waves, it's a relaxing destination.

GETTING HERE AND AROUND

Playa Tortugas is most easily reached by taxi from Casma. Expect to pay S/20 for the 15-minute drive.

WHERE TO STAY

¢ 🏠 **Hospedaje Las Terrazas.** A pleasant stone walkway leads from the lobby to the bamboo-ceilinged rooms. They have basic, clean rooms, each with a terrace and view of the bay. Make sure you're around for the exhilarating sunset viewing, but also take a look at the back of the hotel, where the black hills turn an eerie orange. **Pros:** excellent views and relaxed atmosphere. **Cons:** bland furnishing and service. ⊠ *Caleta*

Tours

Condor Travel and Guía Tours both organize tours to the ruins around Trujillo. Clara Bravo and Michael White are great guides for Trujillo, and also lead trips farther afield. Sipán Tours is one of Chiclayo's best tour companies for trips to the Tomb of Señor Sipán.

There are many tour companies in Huaraz; Monttrek is among the best, arranging rafting, trekking, and mountain-climbing expeditions. Clarín Tours is said to be one of Cajamarca's best. In Piura, call Piura Tours.

In Chachapoyas, contact Vilaya Tours. The company arranges tours to Kuélap, as well as to the remote ruins of Gran Vilaya, which requires a 31-km (19-mi) hike, and to the Pueblo de Los Muertos, which requires a 23-km (14-mi) hike.

Contacts **Clara Bravo and Michael White** (✉ Cahuide 495, Trujillo ☎ 044/243–347 ⊕ www.xanga. com/trujilloperu). **Condor Travel** (✉ Jr. Independencia 553, Trujillo ☎ 044/254–763, 877/236–7199 in U.S. ⊕ www.condortravel.com). **Clarín Tours** (✉ Del Batán 161, Cajamarca ☎ 076/366–829 ⊕ www.clarintours. com). **Guía Tours** (✉ Jr. Independencia 580, Trujillo ☎ 044/245–170 ⊕ www.guiatours.com.pe). **Monttrek** (✉ Av. Luzuriaga 646, Huaraz ☎ 043/42–1121 ⊕ www.monttrekperu. com). **Piura Tours** (✉ Jr. Ayacucho 585, Piura ☎ 073/326–778). **Sipán Tours** (✉ 7 de Enero 772, Chiclayo ☎ 074/229–053 ⊕ www.sipantours. com). **Vilaya Tours** (✉ Jr. Grau 624, Chachapoyas ☎ 041/477–506 ⊕ www.vilayatours.com).

Norte, Playa Tortugas ☎ 043/94361–9042 ⊕ *www.lasterrazas.com* ⟿ 8 *rooms* ⚲ *In-room: a/c, no phone, no TV. In-hotel: restaurant, parking (free)* ⊟ V ⦿ *BP.*

TRUJILLO

561 km (350 mi) northwest of Lima on Pan-American Hwy.

The well-preserved colonial architecture, pleasant climate, and archeological sites have made Trujillo a popular tourist destination. The Plaza de Armas and beautifully maintained colonial buildings make central Trujillo a delightful place to while away an afternoon. Occupied for centuries before the arrival of the Spaniards, ruins from the Moche and Chimú people are nearby, as is a decent museum. Combine this with a selection of excellent hotels, restaurants, and cafés, and you'll see why Trujillo, officially founded in 1534, competes with Arequipa for the title of Peru's "Second City." The only serious problem for tourists is trying to fit in the time to visit all the sights—literally, since many places close from 1 to 4 for lunch.

GETTING HERE AND AROUND

Both LAN Perú and Star Perú fly from Lima to Trujillo's Aeropuerto Carlos Martínez de Pinillos (TRU), 5 km (3 mi) north of the city on the road to Huanchaco.

Almost everything is within walking distance in the center of the city and for everything else there are reasonably priced taxis. If you don't have a car, ask your hotel to arrange for a taxi for the day or to tour a specific place. For the archaeological sights, another option is to join a day tour from a travel agency.

ESSENTIALS

Currency Scotiabank (⊠ *Pizarro 314* ☎ *044/256–600* ⊕ *www.scotiabank.com. pe*).

Mail Post Office (⊠ *Av. Independencia 286* ☎ *044/245–941*). **DHL** (⊠ *Av. Pizarro 318* ☎ *044/233–630* ⊕ *www.dhl.com.pe*).

Medical Hospital Belén (⊠ *Bolívar 350* ☎ *044/245–281*).

Pharmacy Boticas Fasa (⊠ *Jr. Pizarro 512* ☎ *044/899–028*).

Rental Car Trujillo Rent-a-Car (⊠ *Prolongación Bolivia 293* ☎ *044/420–059*).

Visitor Info iPerú (⊠ *Jr. Pizarro 402* ☎ *044/294–561* ⊕ *www.peru.info*).

ARCHAEOLOGICAL SITES

Begin your archaeological exploration at the **Museo del Sitio.** The entrance fee includes admission to the museum, plus Chán Chán, Huaca Arco Iris, and Huaca Esmeralda, so hold onto your ticket (you may also go directly to the ruins and purchase the same ticket there, for the same price). ■TIP➔ This small but thorough museum has displays of ceramics and textiles from the Chimú empire. From Trujillo, take a taxi or join a tour from an agency. Each location is a significant distance from the next. Guides are available at the entrance of each site for S/10 or more (S/20 Chán Chán) and are strongly recommended, both for the information they can provide and also for safety reasons (a few robberies of visitors have occurred in the more remote sectors of the archaeological sites). At the museum, and all sites listed below, there are clean restrooms and a cluster of souvenir stalls and snack shops, but no place to buy a full meal. ⊠ *Carretera Huanchaco, 5 km (3 mi) northwest of Trujillo* ☎ *044/206–304* 🎫 *S/11, includes admission to Chán Chán, Huaca Arco Iris, and Huaca Esmeralda; ticket valid for 48 hours* ◷ *Daily 9–4.*

Fodor's Choice
★

Chán Chán. The sprawling adobe-brick capital city, whose ruins lie 5 km (3 mi) west of Trujillo, has been called the largest mud city in the world. It once held boulevards, aqueducts, gardens, palaces, and some 10,000 dwellings. Within the city were nine royal compounds, one of which, the royal palace of Tschudi, has been partially restored and opened to the public. Although the city began with the Moche civilization, 300 years later, the Chimú people took control of the region and expanded the city to its current size. While less known than the Incas, who conquered them in 1470, the Chimú were the second-largest pre-Columbian society in South America. Their empire stretched along 1,000 km (620 mi) of the Pacific, from Lima to Tumbes.

Before entering this UNESCO World Heritage Site, see the extensive photographic display of the ruins at the time of discovery and post-restoration. Then, begin at the Tschudi complex, the Plaza Principal, a monstrous square where ceremonies and festivals were held. The throne of the king is thought to have been in front where the ramp is found. The reconstructed walls have depictions of sea otters at their

Which Culture Was That Again?

CLOSE UP

The massive walls of Chan Chan, near Trujillo, once home to 10,000 dwellings.

It's a common question after a few days of exploring the extensive archaeological sites in the north. So many different civilizations were emerging, overlapping, and converging, that it can be difficult to keep track of them all.

Chavín: One of the earliest major cultures in northern Peru is the cat-worshipping Chavín. The Chavín empire stretched through much of Peru's northern highlands and along the northern and central coasts. Artifacts dating back to 850 BC tell us that the Chavín people were excellent artisans, and their pottery, with its florid, compact style, can be seen in the museums of Trujillo and Lima.

Moche: About 500 years later, a highly advanced civilization called the Moche emerged. It was their carefully planned irrigation systems, still in use today, that turned the desert into productive agricultural land. Their fine ceramics and large Moche pyramids, still standing near present-day Trujillo and Chiclayo, give us insight about

their architectural advances and daily lives. Such oddities as dragon motifs are perhaps a testament to commerce and intercultural exchange between South America and Asia. Despite voracious *huaqueros,* or looters, the tomb of the Lord of Sipán, discovered in 1987, was intact and untouched, revealing more about their complex culture.

Chimú to Inca: The Chimú came on the scene about AD 850. That civilization continued to conquer and expand until around 1470, when it, like most others in the area, was assimilated by the huge Inca empire. The awe-inspiring city of Chán Chán, built by the Chimú, sits near present-day Trujillo. Although the Inca center of power lay farther south in the Cusco–Machu Picchu area, its cultural influence stretched far beyond the northern borders of Peru and it was near present-day Tumbes that Pizarro, the Spanish pig farmer–turned-conquistador, first caught site of the glory of the Inca empire.

9

base. From here, head deep into the ruins toward the royal palace and tomb of Señor Chimú. The main corridor is marked by fishnet representations, marking the importance of the sea to these ancient people. ■TIP➔ You will also find renderings of pelicans, which served as ancient road signs, their beaks pointing to important sections of the city. Just before you arrive at the Recinto Funerario, the funeral chamber of Señor Chimú, you pass a small natural reservoir called a *huachaque*. Forty-four secondary chambers surround the funeral chamber where the king Señor Chimú was buried. In his day it was understood that when you pass to the netherworld you can bring all your worldly necessities with you, and the king was buried with several live concubines and officials and a slew of personal effects, most of which have been looted. Although wind and rain have damaged the city, its size—20 square km (8 square mi)—still impresses.

Huaca Arco Iris. Filled with intriguing and unusual symbolic carvings, and with an urban backdrop, is the restored Huaca Arco Iris or Rainbow Pyramid. Named for the unusual rainbow carving (the area rarely sees rain), it's also known as the Huaca El Dragón, or Pyramid of the Dragon, because of the central role dragons play in the friezes. ■TIP➔ This structure, built by the early Chimú, also has a repeating figure of a mythical creature that looks like a giant serpent. On the walls, mostly reconstructions, you will see what many archaeologists believe are priests wielding the knives used in human sacrifices. Half-moon shapes at the bottom of most of the friezes indicate that the Chimú probably worshipped the moon at this temple. ✉ *Pan-American Hwy., 5 km (3 mi) north of Trujillo* ☎ *No phone* 🖃 *S/11, includes admission to Chán Chán, Huaca Esmeralda, and Museo del Sitio; ticket valid for 48 hours* ☉ *Daily 9–4.*

Huaca Esmeralda. Much like the other Chimú pyramids, the ruins' most interesting aspects are the carved friezes, un-restored and in their original state. The images include fish, seabirds, waves, and fishing nets, all central to the life of the Chimú. Like other Chimú pyramids on the northern coast, the ancient temple mound of Huaca Esmeralda, or the Emerald Pyramid, is believed to have served as a religious ceremonial center. The pyramid is in an area that's dangerous for unaccompanied tourists, so go with a guide. ✉ *Huanchaco Hwy., 2 km (1 mi) west of Trujillo* ☎ *No phone* 🖃 *S/11, includes admission to Chán Chán, Huaca Arco Iris, and Museo del Sitio; ticket valid for 48 hours* ☉ *Daily 9–4.*

Fodor's Choice
★
Huaca de la Luna and Huaca del Sol. When you consider that these temples were built more than 3,000 years ago, the mud and adobe pyramids near the Pan-American Highway and Río Moche are quite impressive. The Moche people were the first to spread their influence over much of the north coast, and all subsequent civilizations, including the Chimú and Incas, built upon what this group began.

The smaller of the two pyramids—the only one you can actually tour—is the **Huaca de la Luna**, the Pyramid of the Moon. The adobe structure is painted with anthropomorphic and zoomorphic reliefs. ■TIP➔ Many of the figures picture the Moche god Ai-Apaec, whereas others depict fanciful creatures, notably dragons; the use of dragon images may point to cultural and commercial exchange between the cultures of South America and Asia. The Moche expanded the pyramid several times during their reign, covering up the exterior's original reliefs. Since 1990 archaeologists have slowly uncovered the ancient layers of the pyramid. Walk through to its very heart to glimpse some of its first facades. ■TIP➔ On most days you're able to watch archaeologists as they uncover multicolor murals. Facilities include a visitor center at the entrance, with a small craft market, cafeteria, restrooms, and parking area (free).

> ### FARMACIA VS BOTICA
>
> Pharmacies are abundant in Trujillo and Huaraz. If the sign says FARMACIA, it means that there's a licensed pharmacist; if the sign says BOTICA, it means that the products will be the same, but no actual pharmacist is there (despite the professional white coats and willingness to answer questions). Either is sufficient if you just need to buy band-aids, but go to a farmacia if you have questions.

Although the nearby **Huaca del Sol,** or the Pyramid of the Sun, sits along the same entry road, it's not yet ready for the public. Standing more than 40 meters (130 feet) high—slightly shorter than it originally stood—with more than 140 million bricks, this is the largest adobe-brick structure in the New World. Scattered around its base are what some archaeologists believe are "signature bricks," with distinctive hand, finger, and foot marks that identify the community whose labor produced the bricks for their lords. ■TIP➔ Researchers believe that the pyramid served as an imperial palace for the Moche people. Once a storehouse of untold treasures, it has been stripped clean over the centuries by huaqueros. So great were its riches that in 1610 the Spanish diverted the Río Moche to wash away the pyramid's base and lay bare the bounty within. Although many tourists wander around the base, this is not recommended as the structure may not be solid and it's possible to destory part of this important temple with a single step. ✉ 10 km (6 mi) southeast of Trujillo ☏ 044/834–901 ⊕ www.huacadelaluna. org.pe 🎫 S/11 ⌚ Daily 9–4.

EXPLORING
More than any other city in Peru, Trujillo maintains much of its colonial charm, especially inside Avenida España, which encircles the heart of the city. This thoroughfare replaced a 9-meter- (30-foot) high wall erected in 1687 to deter pirates. Two pieces of the wall stand at the corner of Estete and España.

❹ **Casa de la Emancipación.** This branch of Banco Continental is unlike any bank you've ever been in. Go through the central courtyard and up to the small art gallery on the right. Enjoy the current exhibition, anything from modern to traditional artwork, and see a scale model of Trujillo when it was a walled city. ■TIP➔ Continue to the back, taking in the chandeliers, the large gold mirrors and the small fountain, and imagine the day that, in this house, the city declared its independence from Spain on December 29, 1820. It later became the country's first capitol building and meeting place for its first legislature. ✉ Pizarro 610 ☏ 044/246–061 🎫 Free ⌚ Mon.–Sat. 9–12:30 and 4–6:30 (frequent special events may affect these hrs).

Exploring ▼

Casa de la
Emancipación ...**4**

Casa del
Mayorazgo de
Facala **1**

Casa Urquiaga ...**3**

Monasterio El
Carmen **7**

Museo
Cassinelli **9**

Museo de
Arqueología **6**

Museo del
Juguete **8**

Palacio
Iturregui **5**

Plaza de Armas ..**2**

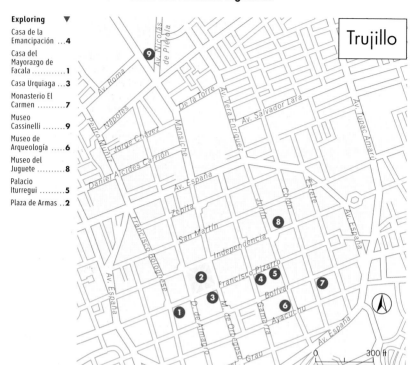

● **Casa del Mayorazgo de Facala.** The open courtyard, from 1709, is surrounded by beautiful cedar columns, greenery, and bankers—as with many colonial mansions, this one is now owned by a bank. However, Scotiabank welcomes tourists and clients into the house to see its wonderfully preserved beauty. Notice the classic brown stucco-covered thick adobe walls and Moorish-style carved-wood ceiling. The security guards are happy to answer questions about the house. ⊠ *Pizarro 314, entrance on corner of Bolognesí and Pizarro* ☎ *044/249–994* ☐ *Free* ☉ *Weekdays 9:15–12:30 and 3:30–6, Sat. 9:15–12:30.*

● **Casa Urquiaga.** The enormous, elaborately carved wooden door is a stunning entrance to this beautifully restored neoclassical mansion from the early 19th century. ■TIP➡ The house is owned by Peru's Central Bank; simply inform the guard that you'd like to go inside and look around. Don't miss the lovely rococo furniture and the fine collection of pre-Columbian ceramics. ⊠ *Pizarro 446* ☎ *044/245–382* ☐ *Free* ☉ *Weekdays 9:30–3, weekends 10–1:30.*

● **Monasterio El Carmen.** Still used as a nunnery, this handsome monastery, built in 1725, is regarded as the city's finest example of colonial art. It has five elaborate altars and some fine floral frescos. Next door is a museum, the Pinacoteca Carmelita, with religious works from the 17th and 18th centuries and an interesting exhibition on restoration techniques. ⊠ *Av. Colón at Av. Bolívar* ☎ *044/233–091* ⊟ *S/3* ⏱ *Mon.–Sat. 9–1.*

9 **Museo Cassinelli.** This private museum in the basement of a gas station has a 2,800-piece collection, mostly concerning indigenous cultures. Of note are some spectacular portrait vases from the Moche civilization and whistling pots, which produce distinct notes that mimic the calls of various birds. ⊠ *Av. Nicolás de Piérola 607* ☎ *044/246–110* ⊟ *S/6* ⏱ *Daily 9–1 and 2–6.*

6 **Museo de Arqueología.** Originally built in the 17th century, this museum displays pottery and other artifacts recovered from the archaeological sites surrounding Trujillo.

There are excellent reproductions of the colorful murals found at the Huaca de la Luna, the pyramids southeast of the city. ⊠ *Jr. Junín 682, at Jr. Ayacucho* ☎ *No phone* ⊟ *S/6* ⏱ *Mon. 9–2:30, Tues.–Fri. 9–1 and 3–6, weekends 9–4.*

8 **Museo del Juguete.** Puppets, puzzles, toys, games. What could be more fun than a toy museum? This private museum houses a large collection of toys from all over the world and shows the transformation of toys through the centuries. ■TIP→ The toys from pre-Colombian Peru are especially interesting, giving a seldom-seen view into the daily lives of ancient people. You can't play with the toys so it may not be appropriate for very young children. ⊠ *Jr. Independencia 705* ☎ *044/208–181* ⊟ *S/3* ⏱ *Mon.–Sat. 10–6, Sun. 10–2.*

NEED A BREAK?

Feel like you're part of the colonial history while enjoying delicious coffee at the **Museo Café Bar** (⊠ *Corner of Junín and Jr. Independencia* ☎ *044/297–200* ⊟ *AE, D, DC, MC, V*). With a black-and-white-checkered marble floor, a dark-wood bar, floor-to-ceiling glass cabinets, and cushioned leather seats, it's a relaxed café in the afternoon and a hopping bar in the early evening. Advice: come to soak up the atmosphere, not to satiate your appetite.

5 **Palacio Iturregui.** One look at the elaborate courtyard with its two levels of white columns, enormous tiles, and three-tiered chandeliers and you'll know why this is called a palace rather than a house. From the intricate white-painted metalwork to the gorgeous Italian marble furnishings, every detail has been carefully restored and maintained. Originally built in 1842, it's now the home of the private Club Central de Trujillo. Unfortunately, the club only allows visitors limited access. You may only enter, for a small fee, weekdays 8–10:30 AM and visit only the front courtyard 11–6. If you find these colonial-era mansions as fascinating as we do, get there early to visit the inside. The grand salon alone is worth it. ⊠ *Pizarro 688* ☎ *044/234–212* ⌨ *S/6, or free to visit courtyard only* ☉ *Inside club: weekdays 8–10:30; courtyard only: Mon.–Sat. 11–6.*

**NEED A
BREAK?**

Homemade gelato is at **De Marco** (⊠ *Pizarro 725* ☎ *044/234–251* ⊟ *AE, D, DC, MC, V*), a small bistro that also serves excellent value criollo food at lunch and sponsors occasional peñas (folklore shows) at night.

② Plaza de Armas. Brightly colored, well-maintained buildings and green grass with walkways and benches make this one of the most charming central plazas. Fronted by the 17th-century cathedral and surrounded by the colonial-era mansions that are Trujillo's architectural glory, this is not, despite claims by locals, Peru's largest main plaza, but it's one of the nicest.

WHERE TO EAT

Trujillo serves up delicious fresh seafood and a variety of excellent meat dishes. Try the cebiche made with fish or shellfish, *causa,* a northern cold casserole made of mashed potatoes and stuffed fish, tasty *cabrito al horno* (roast kid) or *seco de cabrito* (stewed kid), or *shámbar,* a bean stew tinged with mint.

$
ITALIAN
★

✕ **De Marco.** Come to this noisy but cheerful eatery for good Peruvian and Italian dishes, excellent coffee, an enormous selection of desserts, and free filtered water. Try the *seco de cabrito,* a local delicacy made of stewed goat. If you eat the freshly baked bread on the table, there's a small fee (S/0.25 each), but the special herbed butter is no extra charge. ⊠ *Pizarro 725* ☎ *044/234–251* ⊟ *AE, D, DC, MC, V.*

$
PERUVIAN

✕ **El Mochica.** It's crowded and busy, but a fun place to eat. Start with an industrial-size portion of spicy cebiche *de lenguado* (sole marinated in citrus), followed by rice smothered with *camarones* (shrimp) or *mariscos* (shellfish). Join the many other enthusiastic diners at this local spot. ⊠ *Bolívar 462* ☎ *044/224–247* ⊟ *AE, D, DC, MC, V.*

$$
PERUVIAN
★

✕ **Las Bóvedas.** This elegant restaurant in the Hotel Libertador offers diners a beautiful space and delicious food. An impressive *bóveda,* or vaulted brick ceiling, arches over the dining room and plants fill the niches. The house specialty is the local delicacy, shámbar, garnished with *canchita* (fried bits of corn). It's served only on Monday. ⊠ *Independencia 485* ☎ *044/232–741* ⊟ *AE, D, DC, MC, V.*

④
$
ECLECTIC

✕ **Romano.** Although this Trujillo establishment looks like it's seen better days in its five-plus decades, Romano still offers diners good food and friendly service. For dinner, enjoy seafood and pasta dishes, followed by excellent homemade desserts. Skip the dimly lit front and, via a long, fluorescent-lighted hallway, enter the small, cozy back room with natural light and a more congenial feeling. ⊠ *Pizarro 747* ☎ *044/252–251* ⊟ *AE, D, DC, MC, V.*

⑤
$
PIZZA

✕ **San Remo.** People come here for the best pizza in town. Select from a large list of pizzas, with every topping imaginable, or choose one of the many other dishes, mostly pasta, but also meat and poultry options. The deer head in the entryway, the stained-glass windows, and the small wooden bar add to an old-school atmosphere. There's an excellent selection of South American and European wines. ⊠ *Av. Húsares de Junín 450* ☎ *044/293–333* ▭ *AE, D, DC, MC, V* ⊗ *No lunch.*

WHERE TO STAY

❶ 🖵 **El Gran Marqués.** This upscale, $$ full-service business hotel is minutes from the city center. Most of the rooms look down on a pool surrounded by lush gardens. On the roof are a small spa and sauna, and a small pool. Rooms have maroon carpets, wood furnishings, and paisley spreads. **Pros:** very efficient service. **Cons:** caters to business travelers and can be impersonal. ⊠ *Díaz de Cienfuegos 145, Urb. La Merced* ☎ *044/249–366* ⤳ *45 rooms, 5 suites* ☖ *In-room: a/c, Wi-Fi. In-hotel: restaurant, room service, bar, pools, gym, spa, laundry service, parking (free)* ▭ *AE, D, DC, MC, V* ⊚ *BP.*

TRUJILLO TIME

Many of the museums and restaurants are closed for lunchtime from about 1 to 4 or 4:30. It can be quite hot around midday, so it's best to plan on indoor activities. It's easy to hail a taxi in Trujillo, and the in-town fare of about S/3 is quite reasonable. As always when traveling, be on your guard if you visit the market area—access your cash discreetly and keep your valuables close.

❷ 🖵 **Gran Bolívar.** A modern hotel hides behind the historic facade of this $ centrally located lodging. The spacious rooms overlook a courtyard filled with streaming sunlight. Inside the hotel is a full-service tourist agency, which offers a decent selection of local tours. Ask to see a few rooms beforehand, as some are nicer than others. **Pros:** colonial architecture; beautiful central courtyard; central location; good staff. **Cons:** some rooms have lots of light, others have very little. ⊠ *Jr. Bolívar 957* ☎ *044/222–090* ⊕ *www.perunorte.com/granbolivar* ⤳ *28 rooms, 7 suites* ☖ *In-room: a/c (some), refrigerator, Wi-Fi. In-hotel: restaurant, room service, bar, gym, spa, laundry service, parking (free)* ▭ *AE, D, DC, MC, V* ⊚ *CP.*

❸ 🖵 **Gran Hotel El Golf.** If you want to stay outside the city, this mod-$$ ern hotel is the best place to stay. The rooms face a large pool, surrounded by beautifully landscaped gardens and palm trees. It's a good choice for families since it has open areas for kids to play. There's a nearby golf course. **Pros:** quiet, attractive setting. **Cons:** can be isolating without a car. ⊠ *Los Cocoteros 500, El Golf* ☎ *044/282–515* ⊕ *www.granhotelgolftrujillo.com* ⤳ *129 rooms, 9 suites* ☖ *In-room: a/c, safe, Wi-Fi (some). In-hotel: restaurant, room service, bar, pools, gym, laundry service, Internet terminal, parking (free)* ▭ *AE, D, DC, MC, V* ⊚ *CP.*

❹ 🖵 **Hotel Libertador.** On the Plaza de Armas, this elegant, upscale hotel $$ is the best choice in Trujillo. It offers beautiful colonial architecture, ★ room details like pre-Colombian designs, locally tooled leather and wood furniture, and wrought-iron wall lamps, along with all the modern amenities. ■**TIP→** Look at your room in advance as some are smaller and don't have much natural light. If you fancy people-watching, ask for a room in the front with a small balcony facing the street. **Pros:** central location; beautiful architecture. **Cons:** some rooms are better than

9

others. ✉ *Independencia 485* ☎ *044/232–741* ⊕ *www.libertador.com. pe* ⇱ *74 rooms, 5 suites* ⚘ *In-room: a/c, refrigerator, safe, Wi-Fi. In-hotel: restaurant, room service, bar, pool, gym, sauna, laundry service, Internet terminal, parking (free)* ▭ *AE, D, DC, MC, V* ⦿ *BP.*

❺ 🛏 **Los Conquistadores.** Near the Plaza de Armas, this business hotel has
$$ large rooms with separate sitting areas. The staff is well-trained and offers a professional, no-frills hotel with quiet common areas away from the noisy street and spacious, clean rooms. The rate includes a buffet breakfast. **Pros:** excellent location; large rooms. **Cons:** bland furnishings; little natural light. ✉ *Diego de Almagro 586* ☎ *044/244–505* ⊕ *www.losconquistadoreshotel.com* ⇱ *38 rooms, 12 suites* ⚘ *In-room: a/c, refrigerator, safe, Wi-Fi. In-hotel: restaurant, room service, bar, laundry service, Internet terminal, parking (free)* ▭ *AE, D, DC, MC, V* ⦿ *BP.*

NIGHTLIFE

A venerable men's club, **Chelsea** (✉ *Estete 675* ☎ *044/257–032*) is a good place for a drink on the weekends. **Luna Rota** (✉ *Av. América Sur 2119* ☎ *044/228–877*) has live local music most evenings. The dance club and casino downstairs mainly attract a 40 and over crowd, but upstairs the disco music blasts away. In a converted mansion with a friendly vibe, **Tributo** (✉ *Almagro and Pizarro*) has live music, mainly cover or "tribute" (hence, the name) bands on weekends.

SHOPPING

Along Avenida España, especially where it intersects with Junín, stalls display locally made leather goods, particularly shoes, bags, and coats. Be wary of pickpockets during the day, and avoid it altogether after sunset. For made-to-order boots or belts, check out **Creaciones Cerna** (✉ *Bolognesi 567* ☎ *044/205–679*). **Luján** (✉ *Obregoso 242* ☎ *044/205–092*) sells stylized Peruvian jewelry. **Los Tallanes** (✉ *Jr. San Martín 455* ☎ *044/220–274*) has a wide selection of handicrafts.

HUANCHACO

12 km (7½ mi) northwest of Trujillo.

Less than half an hour away from the city, Huanchaco is a little beach community where surfers, tourists, affluent *Trujillianos,* families, and couples easily mix. With excellent restaurants, comfortable hotels and never-ending sunshine, this is a nice place to unwind for a couple of days or to live it up at one of the many annual fiestas. The Festival del Mar is held every other year during May, the Fiesta de San Pedro held every June 29, and multiple surfing and dance competitions happen throughout the year.

■ **TIP➔** Head to the beach in the late afternoon to watch fishermen return for the day, gliding along in their caballitos de totora, traditional fishing boats that have been used for more than 1,000 years. These small, unstable boats, made from totora reeds, can be seen in Moche ceramics and other pre-Columbian handiwork. The boat's name, *caballitos,* means "little horse" and comes from how fishermen kneel on them.

GETTING AROUND

Huanchaco sits well enough within the Trujillo orbit that taxiing it is the best way to get out here. The drive takes about 15 minutes and the fare runs about S/20.

MONEY

Replenish your supply of cash at any bank back in Trujillo.

EXPLORING

Although people come to Huanchaco for the beach, one of Peru's oldest churches, **El Santuario de Huanchaco**, on a hill overlooking the village, is a nice sidetrip. The Sanctuary of Huanchaco was built on a Chimú ruin around 1540. In the second half of the 16th century a small box containing the image of *Nuestra Señora del Socorro* (Our Lady of Mercy) floated in on the tide and was discovered by locals. The image, which is kept in the sanctuary, has been an object of local veneration ever since. ⊠ *At Andrés Rázuri and Unión* ☎ *No phone* 🖃 *Free* ☉ *Daily 8–6.*

THE BEACHES

The beaches around Huanchaco are popular, though the water can be rather cold.

Playa Malecón, north of the pier, is the town's most popular beach and is filled with restaurant after restaurant. Local craftspeople sell their goods along the waterfront walk. Rocky **Playa Huankarote**, south of the pier, is less popular for swimming, but there's good surfing.

WHERE TO EAT AND STAY

$ ✕**Big Ben.** Skip the first floor and head upstairs to the terrace for great
SEAFOOD views of the beach. Enjoy Huanchaquero specialties, including *cangrejo reventado* (baked crab stuffed with eggs) and cebiche *de mococho* (algae cebiche). Only open 11–6, this open-air restaurant serves lunch and sunset drinks from a special wine list or cocktail menu. ⊠ *Av. Victor Larco 836* ☎ *044/461–378* ⊕ *www.bigbenhuanchaco.com* 🖃 *AE, D, DC, MC, V* ☉ *No dinner.*

$ ✕**Club Colonial.** An excellent menu, beautifully decorated, and the abso-
SEAFOOD lute best place to watch the sunset, this is one of the finest places to
Fodor'sChoice dine in northern Peru. Club Colonial combines recipes from the Old
★ World with ingredients from the New World, coming up with wonderful combinations of fresh seafood, pasta, greens, meats, and more. ■TIP→ **There's everything from Basque-style sea bass to crepes covered with tropical fruit.** The restaurant is filled with colorful colonial artifacts and has a cozy bar and an outdoor terrace. The food and atmosphere haven't changed much over the years, but this is a new location on a newly created street, so asking for directions can be tricky. It's closer to the surfers' section of the beach than the fishermen's area. ⊠ *Av. La Rivera 171* ☎ *044/461–015* 🖃 *AE, MC, V.*

$ ✕**Estrella Marina.** This lively restaurant on Playa Huanchaco can be
SEAFOOD noisy, but the view of the ocean is superb. Dishes are typical of the region, with plenty of fresh seafood concoctions, such as cebiche marinated in citrus juice. Whatever you order, sit upstairs for the better ocean view. ⊠ *Av. Victor Larco 594* ☎ *044/461–850* 🖃 *AE, MC, V* ☉ *Closed Wed.*

9

$ ⛺ **Hostal Bracamonte.** This pleasant hotel, across the boulevard from
☺ Playa Huanchaco, is popular with Peruvian families, especially in summer, and has a pool set in beautifully landscaped grounds, a small
restaurant, a small playground, lots of grassy areas to play in, and a
good "neighborhood" feel. There's even a camping area, but it's bring-
your-own-tent. **Pros:** if you have kids, this is the place to be. **Cons:** if
you don't have kids, this is not the place for you. ⊠ *Jr. Los Olivos 503*
☎ *044/461–162* ⊕ *www.hostalbracamonte.com* ⌕ *24 rooms, 8 bun-*
galows ⚷ *In-room: a/c, Wi-Fi. In-hotel: restaurant, bar, pool, Internet*
terminal, parking (free) ▭ *AE, D, DC, MC, V.*

$ ⛺ **Las Palmeras.** Across from the tranquil Playa Los Tumbos, a beach
★ on the northern end of the waterfront, Las Palmeras is a welcoming
hotel once you get past the gated entrance. Its spotless rooms have
terraces; most have great views of the ocean. A narrow garden with a
small pool makes your stay very relaxing. Since the hotel is gated in,
there's a feeling of privacy. At this writing, the hotel is in the process of
building a new restaurant in front of the hotel. **Pros:** pristine and comfortable rooms; very quiet and relaxing. **Cons:** difficult to find behind
a closed gate; prices vary based on location of the room. ⊠ *Av. Vic-*
tor Larco 1150 ☎ *044/461–199* ⊕ *www.laspalmerasdehuanchaco.com*
⌕ *20 rooms, 1 suite* ⚷ *In-room: a/c, Wi-Fi. In-hotel: restaurant, room*
service, pool, laundry service, Internet terminal, parking (free) ▭ *V.*

NIGHTLIFE

Worth checking out, especially on the weekend, is **Sabes?** (⊠ *Larco 920*
☎ *044/461–555*). It's a laid-back place at the northern end of the main
drag with good music and drinks. A local hotspot, mainly filled with
foreign travelers, is **El Kero** (⊠ *Av. La Rivera 115* ☎ *044/461–184*), a
restaurant and pub with an extensive menu, including Peruvian and
foreign food, and loud music for the after-dinner crowd.

SIPÁN

35 km (21 mi) east of Chiclayo.

This tiny village of about 1,700 doesn't offer much, but nearby is one
of the country's major archaeological sites. Arrange for a taxi or tour
to take you to the tomb of the Lord of Sipán.

EXPLORING

The **Tumba del Señor de Sipán** *(Tomb of the Lord of Sipán)* was discovered by renowned archaeologist Walter Alva in 1987. The road to the
archaeological site, not far from the town of Sipán, winds past sugar
plantations and through a fertile valley. You'll soon reach a fissured
hill—all that remains of a temple called the Huaca Rajada. ■ **TIP**➔ The
three major tombs found here date from about ad 290 and earlier, and
together they form one of the most complete archaeological finds in the
Western Hemisphere. The tombs have been attributed to the Moche culture, known for its ornamental pottery and fine metalwork. The most
extravagant funerary objects were found in the tomb, now filled with
replicas placed exactly where the original objects were discovered. The
originals are now on permanent display in the Museo Tumbas Reales

de Sipán in Lambayeque. The Lord of Sipán did not make the journey to the next world alone—he was buried with at least eight people: a warrior (whose feet were amputated to ensure that he didn't run away), three young women, two assistants, a servant, and a child. The tomb also contained a dog and two llamas. Hundreds of ceramic pots contained snacks for the long trip. Archaeological work here is ongoing, as other tombs are still being excavated. ☎ *No phone* ✉ *S/10, S/20 for a guide (strongly recommended)* ⊙ *Daily 8–5:30.*

CHICLAYO

219 km (131 mi) north of Trujillo.

A lively commercial center, Chiclayo is prosperous and easygoing. Although it doesn't have any colonial architecture or special outward beauty, it's surrounded by numerous pre-Columbian sites. ■TIP➜ The Moche and Chimú people had major cities in the area, as did the Lambayeque, who flourished here from about 700 to 1370. Archaeology buffs flocked to the area after the 1987 discovery of the nearby unlooted tomb of the Lord of Sipán. Chiclayo is a comfortable base from which to visit that tomb as well as other archaeological sites.

GETTING HERE AND AROUND

Both LAN Perú and Star Perú connect Lima with Chiclayo's Aeropuerto José Quiñones González (CIX) just outside the city. Star Perú also flies between Chiclayo and Trujillo.

For the most part, you'll need to take a taxi around Chiclayo. Within the city limits, each ride should cost about S/3; ask for help at your hotel to negotiate anything beyond the city. Look at the map before hailing a taxi, though, because some things are within walking distance.

ESSENTIALS

Currency **Banco de Crédito** (⊕ *www.viabcp.com*).

Internet **Africa Café Web** (✉ *San José 473* ☎ *074/229–431*).

Mail **Post Office** (✉ *Elías Aguirre 140* ☎ *074/237–031*).

Medical **Clínica del Pacífico** (✉ *Av. José Leonardo Ortiz 420* ☎ *074/232–141*).

Pharmacy **Max Salud** (✉ *Av. 7 de Enero 185* ☎ *076/226–201*).

Visitor Info **iPerú** (✉ *Av. Sáenz Peña 838* ☎ *074/205–703* ⊕ *www.peru.info*).

EXPLORING

The enormous **Cathedral,** dating back to 1869, is worth a look for its neoclassical facade on the Plaza de Armas, and its well-maintained central altar. ✉ *Plaza de Armas* 🖼 *Free* ⊙ *Daily 6:30AM–1 and 3–6.*

For fresh air and a great spot for people-watching, head to the **Paseo Las Musas.** The pedestrian walk borders a stream and has classical statues depicting scenes from mythology. To enjoy this the most, look up at the statues and people walking by and ignore the excessive litter along this beautiful promenade. ✉ *La Florida and Falques.*

The closest beach to Chiclayo is in the port town of **Pimentel,** 14 km (8½ mi) west of Chiclayo. Access via taxi should cost about S/15 each way.

9

Although the beach is not so attractive, there's an interesting curved pier dating back more than a century, and many other enjoyable sights along the beach. Walk along and observe the old colonial beach houses, navy officers in white outside the maritime station, and an excessive number of young Peruvian couples walking hand in hand.

WHERE TO EAT

Much like Trujillo, Chiclayo and Lambayeque offer *cabrito, causa* and *pescado seco* (salted fish). The area is more famous for *kinkón* (pronounced much like "King Kong"), a large, crispy pastry. It's filled with *manjar blanco*, a sweet filling made of sugar, condensed milk, and cinnamon boiled down until it's thick and chewy.

❶ ⊄ ✕ **Hebrón.** A friendly staff serves a wide range of national and international specialties from 7 AM to midnight daily at this centrally located PERUVIAN ☺ eatery. There's an excellent breakfast menu, free Wi-Fi, big corner windows for good people-watching, and a playground, "Hebrónlandia," in the back. Families could easily spend half a day here. There are "children's options" on the menu, but the whole menu is pretty kid-friendly and the size/price is no different. ⊠ *Av. Balta 605* ☎ *074/222–709* ⊟ *AE, D, DC, MC, V.*

❷ ⊄ ✕ **La Parra.** Despite the bland decorations, this restaurant serves delicious grilled meats. La Parra specializes in parrilladas, with an extensive PERUVIAN menu including every imaginable part of the cow. The *anticuchos* (beef heart) and *ubre* (cow udder) are well-prepared house specials. If this sounds unappetizing, you can always get grilled steak or head to the *chifa* (Chinese) restaurant next door, run by the same people. ⊠ *Manuel María Izaga 752* ☎ *074/227–471* ⊟ *AE, D, DC, MC, V.*

❸ $ ✕ **Marakos Grill.** Come here for the best barbecue in Chiclayo. The grilled-to-perfection *parrillas* (barbecue) combinations are the best STEAK options, serving groups ranging from two to seven, and including steak, ★ ribs, chorizo sausages and more—plus your choice of side dishes. For the more adventurous eaters, try the tender *anticucho* (beef heart) or *avestruz* (ostrich). There are two locations on the same block, both owned by the same family, one by the parents, the other by their son. Although the menus are the same, the restaurant at 696 has a more family-friendly atmosphere while the one at 490 is smaller and more intimate. ⊠ *Av. Elvira Garcia y Garcia 490* ⊠ *Av. Garcia y Garcia 696* ☎ *074/232–840* ⊕ *www.marakosgrill.com* ⊟ *AE, D, DC, MC, V.*

❹ $ ✕ **Nueva Venecia.** Fantastic pizza, served on a wooden block fresh from the oven, is why this hugely popular Italian restaurant is busy every PIZZA night. The list of toppings is extensive and there are some pasta choices. You might have to wait on the street to get in, and once inside you'll feel almost-stifling heat from the pizza ovens, but you're guaranteed good food and old-country charm. ⊠ *Av. Balta 365* ☎ *074/233–384* ⊟ *AE, D, DC, MC, V* ☺ *Closed Sun.*

❺ $$ ✕ **Típico Fiesta.** Well-known for its excellent food, the Chiclayo location of this Peruvian-owned restaurant group lives up to its reputation. Start PERUVIAN with the "Fiesta Hot Round," an appetizer sampler, and order *comida norteña* (typical food of northern Peru), including sumptuous *cabrito* (kid), or other carefully prepared dishes such as imported salmon with capers. Try the special breakfast on weekends 8–11 and sit upstairs for the best ambience. ✉ *Salaverry 1820* ☎ *074/201–970* ▭ *AE, D, DC, MC, V* ⊗ *No dinner Sun.*

WHERE TO STAY

①
$$
⌁ **Garza Hotel.** Don't be fooled by the bland exterior: inside there's a poolside bar and outdoor fireplace for cool nights, an admirable restaurant serving regional cuisine, efficient staff, and excellent accommodation. Enjoy the traditional artwork throughout the hotel, as well as your welcome cocktail, free breakfast, cable TV, and air-conditioning. **Pros:** first-rate service and accommodation; central location. **Cons:** nothing makes it Peruvian, you could be anywhere in the world. ✉ *Bolognesi 756* ☎ *074/228–172* ⊕ *www.garzahotel.com* ⌁ *91 rooms, 3 suites* ⌁ *In-room: a/c, refrigerator, Wi-Fi. In-hotel: 2 restaurants, room service, bar, pool, gym, spa, laundry service, Internet terminal, parking (free)* ▭ *AE, D, DC, MC, V* ⊙|*BP.*

②
$$
★
⌁ **Gran Hotel Chiclayo.** Come for a high standard of everything from the well-trained staff, spacious rooms, and extra hotel amenities, including a pool, casino, restaurant, gym, and spa. An in-house travel agency can help you do everything from arrange a tour to rent a car. For this reason, the hotel is as popular with executives in town for a meeting as travelers here to see the ancient ruins. Rooms have large windows that let in a lot of light and some rooms have balconies. A buffet breakfast is included in the rate. **Pros:** central location; first-rate accommodation and amenities. **Cons:** occasionally large business groups overtake the hotel. ✉ *Av. Federico Villareal 115* ☎ *074/234–911* ⊕ *www.granhotelchiclayo.com. pe* ⌁ *129 rooms, 16 suites* ⌁ *In-room: a/c, Wi-Fi. In-hotel: 2 restaurants, room service, bar, pool, gym, spa, laundry service, Internet terminal, parking (free)* ▭ *AE, D, DC, MC, V* ⊙|*BP.*

③
$
⌁ **Inti Hotel.** With newly refurbished rooms and noise-proof glass for street-side rooms, this hotel offers you one of the best deals in Chiclayo. Rooms are clean, the staff is professional, and the hotel feels busy, but not hurried. Inti Hotel is a new name. The original name was Inca Hotel, but after losing a legal battle with Cusco, a city that believes they have exclusive right to all things Inca, the hotel was forced to change its name. **Pros:** quality rooms at a low price. **Cons:** dimly lighted hallways; mediocre hotel restaurant. ✉ *Av. Luis Gonzales 622* ☎ *074/235–931* ⊕ *www.intihotel.com.pe* ⌁ *62 rooms, 2 suites* ⌁ *In-room: a/c, Wi-Fi. In-hotel: restaurant, room service, bar, laundry service, Internet terminal, parking (free)* ▭ *AE, D, DC, MC, V* ⊙|*CP.*

④
$
⌁ **Las Musas.** People stay here for the view of the Paseo Las Musas. The hotel has standard accommodation and services, but each room overlooks the promenade. Other nice features include a waterfall and tiny koi pond at the entrance, a sixth-floor restaurant with great views of the entire city, and one suite with an enormous heart-shape Jacuzzi. **Pros:** location and views. **Cons:** rooms are very average. ✉ *Los Faiques 101, Urb. Santa Victoria* ☎ *074/239–884* ⊕ *www.lasmusashotel.com.pe* ⌁ *41 rooms, 5 suites* ⌁ *In-room: a/c, Wi-Fi. In-hotel: restaurant, room service, bar, laundry service, Internet terminal, parking (free)* ▭ *AE, D, DC, MC, V* ⊙|*CP.*

9

NIGHTLIFE AND THE ARTS

A favorite pastime of Chiclayans is karaoke. One of the hottest places to show your vocal skills is the Gran Hotel Chiclayo's discotheque and bar **Solid Gold** (✉ *Av. Federico Villarreal 115* ☎ *074/234–911*).

If singing in front of strangers doesn't sound like fun, try **Bali Lounge** (✉ *Av. José L. Ortiz 490* ☎ *074/235–932*) for an extensive menu of high-level, expensive Peruvian and Japanese-Peruvian fusion options, top shelf liquors, imported beers, and an exuberant crowd. Starting around 11, the line for **Ozone Disco** (✉ *Av. José L. Ortiz 490* ☎ *074/235–932*), just next door, begins. At this discotheque, people in their early twenties to early fifties revel in the (excessively) loud music and good cocktails. The first-floor bar and dance floor costs S/10 to enter.

SHOPPING

Chiclayo's indoor **Central Market** on Avenida Balta is no longer the city's main market. Once famed for its ceramics, weavings, and charms made by local *curanderos* (folk healers), now there's mainly fresh food for sale, and a nice little "food court" in the back. Head over to the larger, more popular **Outdoor Market** beginning at the intersection of Avenida Balta and Avenida Arica. This vast market has fresh meat, vegetables, and fruit from local farms, as well as clothing, pirated DVDs and CDs, handbags, and more. You can also ask at any of the stalls to point you to a shaman for immediate help or to make an evening appointment. Wander around and enjoy, but don't lose each other in the crowd. For the best handicrafts in the area, go to **Mercado Artesanal de Monsefú**, about 14 km (9 mi) south of Chiclayo. You can buy straw hats, baskets, cotton weavings, embroidery, clay pots, wall hangings, all kinds of delicious snacks, and more. It's well worth the trip (round-trip taxi from Chiclayo, including waiting for you to shop, costs about S/35).

LAMBAYEQUE

12 km (7 mi) north of Chiclayo.

This small town has some well-preserved colonial-era buildings but the reason to come is for the outstanding museums. The museums exhibit details about the Moche civilization, and the original artifacts from the tomb in Sicán.

GETTING HERE AND AROUND

The town is small enough to walk around from place to place or you can take an inexpensive taxi (S/3 within town) to the different museums. To get here from Chiclayo, you can easily hire a taxi or rent a car.

EXPLORING

Fodor's Choice
★

Go to the **Museo Arqueológico Nacional Brüning** to see how the different pre-Incan civilizations lived on a daily basis. Covering the Moche, Lambayeque, and other pre-Inca cultures such as the Cupisnique, Chavín, Chimú, and Sicán, there are excellent interpretive displays, showing how people fished, harvested, kept their homes. There's also a wonderful photography exhibit of the archaeologist Hans Heinrich Brüning and his experiences in Peru beginning in the late 1800s. Descriptions are in Spanish, so an English-speaking guide is recommended. ✉ *Huamachuco* *and Atahualpa* ☎ *074/282–110* ⊕ *www.museobruning.com* 💳 *S/10, S/20 for a guide* ⊗ *Daily 9–5.*

The impressive **Museo Nacional Tumbas Reales de Sipán**, which ranks among the country's best museums, displays the real artifacts from the tomb of the Lord of Sipán, one of the greatest archaeological finds of recent years. (Why the real artifacts are not actually in Sipán is a question no one was able to answer.) The stunning exhibits detail where every piece of jewelry, item of clothing, or ceramic vase was found. ■ TIP→ English-speaking guides are available to help with the Spanish-only descriptions and confusing order of exhibits. All bags, cameras, and cell phones must be checked before you can enter the museum. ⊠ *Av. Juan Pablo Vizcardo and Guzmán* ☎ *074/283–977* ⊕ *www.tumbasreales.org* 💳 *S/7, S/20 for a guide* ⊗ *Tues.–Sun. 9–5.*

FERREÑAFE

18 km (11 mi) northeast of Chiclayo.

Although it's produced more winners of the Miss Peru contest than any other town, Ferreñafe has other charms. The Iglesia Santa Lucia, begun in 1552, is a good example of baroque architecture. However, most visitors come to visit its excellent new museum.

EXPLORING

Although the **Museo Nacional Sicán** offers insight into the culture of the Sicán people, there are also unique exhibits on such topics as the *El Niño* effect and where the pre-Incan civilizations fit into world history. Visual timelines hammer home just how far back Peruvian history goes. See the exhibits introducing the Sicán (also known as the Lambayeque), including everything from common eating utensils to ceremonial burial urns, models of what their homes might have looked like, and a central room full of treasures from this coastal culture renowned for its amazing headdresses and masks. ⊠ *Av. Batán Grande* ☎ *074/286–469* ⊕ *sican.perucultural.org.pe* 💳 *S/8* ⊗ *Tues.–Sun. 9–5.*

9

PIURA

269 km (167 mi) north of Chiclayo.

The sunny climate, friendly people, and good food make Piura a delightful stop on your way north. Since most of the major flight and bus routes to the north-coast beaches travel through Piura, stopping here is not just easy, it's often required.

As a central commercial hub and the country's fifth-largest city (population 380,000), it's hard to believe how relaxed and friendly the city is to tourists. Historically, however, it's a community used to transitions. Founded in 1532 by Francisco Pizarro before he headed inland to conquer the Incas, the community changed locations three times before setting down on the modern-day location along the banks of the Río Piura.

GETTING HERE AND AROUND

LAN Perú flies between Lima and the Aeropuerto de Piura (PIU), 2 km (1 mi) east of the city.

Adobe Pyramids

In Túcume, 35 km (21 mi) north of Chiclayo, you can see an immense pyramid complex, including Huaca Larga, one of the largest adobe pyramids in South America, as well as dozens of smaller ones spread across a dry desert. Go first to the small museum, **Museo de Sitio**, and take a tour with an English-speaking guide to learn about the history of the nearby ruins. Then, follow your guide and climb 10 minutes to see the 26 giant pyramids, surrounded by the smaller ones, and the areas in between, which have yet to be excavated.

The rugged desert landscape, sprinkled with hardy little *algarrobo* (mesquite) trees, is probably very similar to what it looked like when—so the legend goes—a lord called Naymlap arrived in the Lambayeque Valley, and with his dozen sons founded the Lambayeque dynasty and built the pyramids we see today. ☎ *076/422–027* ✉ *S/10* ☉ *Daily 8–5.*

The best way to get around Piura is to walk. However, inexpensive and safe taxis are available from the street if you have heavy bags or are ready for a siesta.

ESSENTIALS

Currency Banco de Crédito (⊕ *www.viabcp.com* ✉ *Av. Grau 133* ☎ *073/336–822*).

Medical Hospital Cayetano Heredia (✉ *Av. Independencia s/n, Urb. Miraflores* ☎ *073/303–208*).

Visitor Info iPerú (✉ *Av. Ayacucho 377* ☎ *073/320–249* ⊕ *www.peru.info*).

EXPLORING

On the city's main square, the **Catedral de Piura** is worth a visit. Built in 1588, it's one of the country's oldest churches. Inside you'll find an altarpiece dedicated to the Virgen de Fátima dating back more than 350 years. ✉ *Plaza de Armas* ✉ *Free.*

WHERE TO EAT AND STAY

$ ✕ **Capuccino.** This modern Peruvian restaurant has an extensive menu.
PERUVIAN Traditional rice and meat dishes, as well European-inspired salads,
★ sandwiches, and entrées mix local and imported ingredients. Whether you choose the Thai salad or lomo saltado, expect to savor your meal. Relax in the serene dining room and don't forget to order dessert along with the delicious cappuccino. ✉ *Calle Tacna 786* ☎ *074/301–111* ▬ *AE, MC, V* ☉ *Closed Sun.*

¢ ✕ **El Arrecife.** If you couldn't tell by the name—which means "the reef"—
SEAFOOD the rope chairs and tanks filled with tropical fish should inform you that this is a seafood restaurant. Choose from 14 different cebiches at this local lunch-only establishment and if you still have room, there are countless other fresh fish dishes to sample. ✉ *Jr. Ica 610* ☎ *074/313–161* ▬ *No credit cards.*

$ ▨ **Hotel Costa Del Sol.** This business hotel offers modern rooms and facilities, along with excellent service. In addition to the small kidney-shape pool in the central terrace, local artwork is displayed in the common areas and every room looks out onto a simple atrium. The completion of new rooms and an upgraded hotel bar will only improve this already excellent hotel. **Pros:** catering to business travelers means better all-around service. **Cons:** the modern architecture lacks charm; some rooms have little natural light. ⊠ *Av. Loreto 649* ☎ *074/302-864* ⊕ *www. costadelsolperu.com* ↰ *58 rooms, 10 suites* ♿ *In-room: a/c, safe, refrigerator, Wi-Fi. In-hotel: restaurant, room service, bar, pool, gym, laundry service, Internet terminal, parking (free)* ▭ *AE, D, DC, MC, V* |◯| *CP.*

$$ ★ **Los Portales.** A venerable hotel on the tree-shaded Plaza de Armas, Los Portales has charming colonial architecture. In the center of its small courtyard, you'll find a fountain and umbrella-shade tables. Nearby, the pool has its own waterfall and palm-dotted island, along with a decent in-hotel café and restaurant. Rooms are spacious, though the bathrooms are small and dimly lighted. **Pros:** beautiful colonial architecture; all the modern amenities one could want. **Cons:** some rooms are better than others. ⊠ *Libertad 875* ☎ *074/321-161* ⊕ *www.hotelportalespiura.com* ↰ *33 rooms, 2 suites* ♿ *In-room: a/c, Wi-Fi. In-hotel: restaurant, room service, bar, pool, laundry service, parking (free)* ▭ *AE, D, DC, MC, V* |◯| *BP.*

SHOPPING

The tiny pueblo of **Catacaos,** 12 km (7 mi) southwest of Piura, is famous for its textiles, gold and silver figurines, and excellent pottery. The small market, filled with street stalls and shops, is open daily until 6 PM. Look around as much as you like, but to get the best price, only closely examine what you really want to buy. To get to Catacaos, take the Pan-American Highway. A taxi should cost around S/30 round-trip.

In Piura, **Artesanías Lucas** (⊠ *Jr. Comercio 629*) does not offer the selection and prices that Catacaos has, but there is a respectable assortment of artisanal goods.

9

MÁNCORA

229 km (142 mi) north of Piura.

This laid-back beach destination, famous for its sunshine and white-sand beaches, has excellent waves for surfing, fishing, and diving. Although the relaxed but dusty town has tourist offices, restaurants, and small shops, the real draw are the hotels about 2 km (1¼ mi) south along **Las Pocitas,** a lovely beach with rocky outcrops that hold tiny pools of seawater at low tide.

GETTING HERE AND AROUND

Comfortable Cruz del Sur buses ply the long 14-hour route between Lima and Máncora. If you wish to fly, LAN Perú connects Lima with the Aeropuerto de Tumbes (TBP), about an hour away. Taxis at the airport charge about S/100 for the trip to Máncora or Punta Sal. Once you arrive at Máncora, mototaxis are the best way to get around.

WHERE TO STAY

$$$ ⌐ **Las Pocitas.** This full-service, family-friendly hotel has a large pool, restaurant, bar, game area, and a beautiful beach. Relax in a hammock on your room's terrace or join other guests at one of the many hotel facilities. If you want to explore more than just the beach, the staff can arrange horseback riding, surfing lessons, a sailing trip, massages, and tours of nearby mangroves. **Pros:** larger spaces than most hotels; good options for activities. **Cons:** if all you want is the beach, you can stay somewhere else for less. ⌧ *Km 1162, Pan-American Hwy.* ☎ *073/258–432* ⊕ *www.laspocitasmancora.com* ⌐ *21 rooms* ⌂ *In-room: a/c, refrigerator, Wi-Fi. In-hotel: 2 restaurants, bar, pool, beachfront, laundry service, parking (free)* ⊟ *AE, MC, V* ⦿*CP.*

HOLD ON!

As a general rule, taxis are abundant, cheap, and safe throughout Peru. Enter the mototaxi, a three-wheeled motorcycle, attached to a double-seat, covered by an awning. No metal, no glass, nothing between you, the road and the other cars. The good news? Mototaxis often are slower and go only short distances. Whenever possible, take a regular taxi in a car. However, for those places—especially Máncora and Punta Sal—in which mototaxis are the main source of travel, hold on and enjoy the ride!

$ ⌐ **Los Corales.** Directly on the beach with very reasonable rates, this little
★ lodging is one of the best deals in Máncora. The bamboo furnishing, tiled floors, colorful bedspreads, and terraces with hammocks give the rooms a tropical theme. Enjoy the tranquil seating areas, full-service restaurant, pool, and lovely stretch of beach connected to the hotel. **Pros:** offers the same beachside location and service at a lesser cost. **Cons:** with only 15 rooms, reservations are difficult to get. ⌧ *Km 1215, Old Pan-American Hwy.* N ☎ *073/258–309* ⊕ *www.loscoralesmancora.com* ⌐ *15 rooms* ⌂ *In-room: no a/c, no phone, safe, no TV. In-hotel: restaurant, bar, pool, beachfront, laundry service, Wi-Fi hotspot, parking (free)* ⊟ *AE, MC, V* ⦿*CP.*

PUNTA SAL

25 km (15 mi) north of Máncora, 70 km (43 mi) south of Tumbes.

Sit on the beach, go for a swim, and relax in the afternoon sun—just what you want from a beach resort. That's probably why Punta Sal has become a popular vacation spot in recent years. A few kilometers north of the Pan-American Highway, hotels and resorts abound in this area, tourists and vacationing Limeños flock here for the blond-sand beach, comfortable ocean breezes, and a sunny climate.

WHERE TO STAY

$$ ⌐ **Hotel Caballito de Mar.** This top-notch beach resort has tropical bungalows with private terraces, an excellent fresh seafood restaurant and beach access. Arrange for a surfing-, diving-, or other excursion, play in the ocean waves, or just relax in one of the comfortable lounge chairs around the small seahorse-shape pool. All meals are included in the standard room price, or you can opt for the cheaper breakfast-only

Fodor's Choice
★

Surfers take to the waves at Máncora, the north's hotspot beach destination.

plan. **Pros:** First-rate service, larger family bungalows available, reasonable rates. **Cons:** Only the suites have air-conditioning and minibar; prices nearly double during peak holidays. ⊠ *Punta Sal, Km 1187, Pan-American Hwy. N* ☎ *072/540–058* ⊕ *www.hotelcaballitodemar. com* ⤳ *25 rooms* ⌂ *In-room: a/c (some), no phone, refrigerator (some), Wi-Fi. In-hotel: restaurant, bar, pool, beachfront, laundry service, Internet terminal, parking (free)* ☰ *AE, MC, V* ⑩ *BP, FAP.*

9

$ ⑪ **Punta Sal Club Hotel.** Offering a variety of bungalows, rooms, and beach areas, this upscale, all-inclusive resort is the place to go for luxury and relaxation. You'll enjoy the sparkling beach, excellent service, delicious food, and extensive activity choices, which are guaranteed to make you forget that stress was ever a part of your life. Bungalows are significantly better than the regular rooms so shell out the extra soles. **Pros:** top-quality hotel. **Cons:** regular rooms are nothing special; rates vary by season. ⊠ *Punta Sal, Km 173, Sullana-Tumbes Hwy.* ☎ *072/540–088* ⊕ *www.puntasal.com.pe* ⤳ *12 rooms, 15 bungalows* ⌂ *In-room: a/c, Wi-Fi. In-hotel: restaurant, bar, pool, gym, spa, beachfront, laundry service, Internet terminal, parking (free)* ☰ *AE, MC, V* ⑩ *CP.*

THE PERU-ECUADOR BORDER

About an hour's drive north of the beach resorts of Máncora and Punta Sal is Tumbes, the last city on the Peruvian side of the Peru-Ecuador border. Tumbes played a major role in Peruvian history: it was here that Pizarro first saw the riches of the vast Inca empire. In the past, tensions were high—it wasn't until 1941 that Tumbes became part of

CLOSE UP

Discover Nature

Some of the most incredible flora and fauna live in protected areas near Máncora and Punta Sal. Luckily, we can visit these important ecological areas, but only through a reputable hotel and experienced guide. Do not believe it if someone tells you they can bring you there and back in an hour. Most trips involve extensive driving, as well as hiking and camping. Including these areas in your itinerary isn't always possible, but the experience will leave you inspired and amazed.

Santuario Nacional Los Manglares de Tumbes: Crocodiles and a diverse collection of birds live in this mangrove reserve. Accessible only by unmotorized boat, this swamp forest is where the ocean water and river water meet, providing some of the most productive ecosystems on the planet.

Parque Nacional Cerros de Amotape: This area was created to protect the equatorial dry forest and its inhabitants. Living in this area are the condor, puma, boa constrictor, and approximately 100 other species of mammals, reptiles, and birds.

Zona Reservada de Tumbes: The dry forest and humid forest exist together in this protected zone, making it one of the more interesting areas to explore. As much of the flora and fauna in this area are in danger of extinction, this is also an extremely important area.

Peru following a military skirmish. Tensions are now minimal. Other than its geographical and historical importance, Tumbes doesn't offer much to tourists. While good hotels are in the city, there is little charm and few sights. Include Tumbes in your itinerary only if you plan to enter Ecuador via the land-border crossing here. If you go, be extra aware of your personal belongings. Tumbes, like many border towns, has its fair share of counterfeit money, illegal goods, and scams to get money from foreigners.

HUARAZ AND THE CORDILLERA BLANCA

The Cordillera Blanca is one of the world's greatest mountain ranges. The soaring, glaciated peaks strut more than 6,000 meters (19,500 feet) above sea level—only Asia's mountain ranges are higher. Glaciers carve their lonely way into the green of the Río Santa valley, forming streams, giant gorges, and glorious gray-green alpine lagoons. On the western side of the valley is the Cordillera Negra. Less impressive than the Cordillera Blanca, its steep mountains have no permanent glaciers and are verdant and brooding. A drive along the paved stretch of road through the valley offers spectacular views of both mountain ranges. You'll find an abundance of flora and fauna in the valley and in the narrow gorges that come snaking their way down from the high mountains. Deer, *vizcacha* (rodents resembling rabbits without the long ears), vicuñas, puma, bear, and condors are among the area's inhabitants. You'll also find the 10-meter-tall (32-foot-tall) *puya raimondii* (the world's largest bromeliad), whose giant spiked flower recalls that of a century plant.

Continued on page 415

BIG MOUNTAINS
of the Cordillera Blanca

by Oliver Wigmore

The lofty ice-clad peaks of Cordillera Blanca soar above 6,000 meters (20,000 feet) and stretch for over 100 kilometers (62 miles) north to south across the Andes. These mountains, worshipped by Andean peoples for thousands of years, are now the idols of global adventure tourism.

Explore ancient ruins, ascend icy summits at the crack of dawn, hike isolated alpine valleys, be absorbed by the endless azure blue of glacial lakes, or put your feet up at a mountain lodge.

The formation of the present Andean mountain chain began as the Nazca plate collided with and was forced beneath the South American plate, driving the ocean floor up to produce the world's longest exposed mountain range. This resulted in the formation of the Pacific coastal desert, the highland puna, and the verdant Amazon basin. Since then the Andes have been the bridging point between these diverse environmental and ecological zones. The Cordilleras Blanca, Negra and Huayhuash, and the Callejón de Huaylas Valley were formed 4 to 8 million years ago, producing spectacular peaks and many distinct ecological niches.

The May to September dry season brings the most stable weather—and the big crowds. Increasingly people are battling the rain and snow for the isolation that comes with the off-season.

Peruvians cross a log bridge in the Jancapampa Valley, as the Cordillera Blanca looms before them.

DID YOU KNOW?

Inca legend tells of Huascarán, a wife who castrated her adulterous husband and fled with her favorite child on her back and the rest in tow. Coming to rest, the Cordillera Blanca was formed by their bodies. Their tears created the Santa and Marañón rivers.

CORDILLERA BLANCA

Taulliraju Mount, Cordillera Blanca, Huascaran National Park, Peru.

The Cordillera Blanca encompasses the mighty Huascarán, Peru's highest peak at 6,767m (22,204ft), and Alpamayo 5,947m (19,511ft), once proclaimed the most beautiful mountain in the world by UNESCO. Most of the Cordillera Blanca is within the Huascarán National Park, for which an entry ticket is required. Valid for one day or one month, these can be purchased at the entry gates or from the park headquarters in Huaraz.

Thanks to the newly paved road, the glacial lakes are now a popular day trip from Huaraz. Their beauty is still worth the trip.

HIGH POINTS

1. The Santa Cruz Trek: You ascend the Santa Cruz valley, crossing the Punta Union pass at 4,760m (15,617ft) beneath the breathtaking peaks, then descend to the spectacular azure blue of the Llanganuco Lakes. One of Peru's most popular alpine treks, it's often overcrowded, with litter and waste becoming a serious problem. For pristine isolation, look elsewhere.

2. Pastoruri Glacier: You can walk on a tropical glacier, ice-climb, ski, and witness the impacts of climate change. Popular day tours from Huaraz often combine the trip here with a visit to see the impressive Puya raimondii trees.

3. Chavín de Huántar: On the eastern side of the cordillera is Chavin de Huantar, where in around 900 BC the first pan-Andean culture developed. The Chavin culture eventually held sway over much of central Peru. The site can be visited on a long day trip from Huaraz.

4. Olleros to Chavín Trek: A short three-day trek across the Cordillera terminates at Chavin de Huantar. Guiding companies in Huaraz offer this trek with llama hauling your gear.

5. Quilcayhuanca and Cojup Valley Loop: This trek is becoming popular due to its relative isolation and pristine condition. It explores two spectacular high alpine valleys, crosses the 5,000m (16,404ft) Pico Choco Pass, passing beautiful glacial lakes, one of which caused the 1941 destruction of Huaraz city in a flood of mud, rocks, and ice.

6. Laguna 69: Spectacular glaciers encircle the lake and give it deep turquoise color. It can be seen on a long day hike from Huaraz. However, spending the night allows you to explore, and you will likely have the lake to yourself once the day trippers leave. This is an ideal acclimation trek.

7. Alpamayo Basecamp: An arduous week-long trek takes you on a northern route through the Cordillera, passing the spectacular north face of Nevado Alpamayo (5947m/19,511ft).

8. Huascarán: Peru's highest peak is one of the Cordillera's more challenging summits.

Climbing: Relatively easy three to five day guided summit climbs of Ishinka (5,550m/18,208ft), Pisco (5,752m/18,871ft) and Vallunaraju (5,684m/18,648ft) are arranged at any of the guiding outfitters in Huaraz. Prices and equipment vary—get a list of what's included. Many smaller companies operate purely as booking agencies for the larger companies.

1 The Santa Cruz Trek

Huaicayan

Cashapampa

Huaripampa

7 Alpamayo
5,947m
(19,511ft)

Artesonraju

Pirámide

Caraz

Pisco
5,752m
(18,871ft)

0 ——— 3 mi
0 ——— 3 km

Laguna 69 6

Huandoy

Chacraraju

Yanama

Caraz

C O R D I L L E R A (H U A S C A R Á N)

Chopicalqui

Contrahierbas

Pueblo Libre

Yungay

Huascarán
6,768m
(22,204ft) 8

Chacas

Utla

Musho

Huaypan

Hualcan

Pompey

Mancos

Copa

Shilla

Huaicán

Copa

Carhuaz

Copá Chico

Vicos

Bayoraju

Paqcharaju

Ranrahirca
Marcará

Vicos

Kekepatipa

Akilpo

C O R D I L L E R A   N E G R A

Anta

Pashpa

Joncopampa

Toellaraju

9

Palcaraju

Taricá

Coltón

Ishinka
5,550m
(18,208ft)

Pucaranra

Jangas

Ranrapaica

Pico Choco

Vallunaraju
5,684m
(18,648ft)

COJUP
VALLEY

Churup

Monterrey

Wilkawain

Quilcayhuánca and
Cojup Valley Loop 5

Pitec

QUILCAYHUÁNCA
VALLEY

Huaraz

Huahulac

Macashca

Río Santa

A llama—member of the camelid
family and provider of wool for
Andean weavers—Chavín, Cordillera Blanca.

Chavin de
Huántar 3

Pastoruri
Glacier 2

Olleros 4

Agocancha

GOOD TO KNOW

CLIMBING HISTORY

The first climbers in the region were probably pre-Colombian priests, attempting difficult summits to perform sacred rituals atop icy summits. This climbing tradition was continued by the Spanish conquistadors who wanted to exploit the rich sulphur deposits atop many of Peru's volcanic cones, and to show their dominance over Mother Nature. Modern climbing in the region took off in 1932 when a German-Austrian expedition completed many of the highest summits, including Huascarán Sur. Since then the peaks of the Cordillera Blanca and Peru have attracted climbers from around the world for rapid-summit sport climbs and solo summits. Extended duration expeditions and large support crews are less common here than in the Himalayas.

SAFETY TIPS

This area is a high alpine environment and weather patterns are unpredictable. Be prepared for all weather possibilities. It's not uncommon to experience snow storms and baking sun over the course of a single day, and at night temperatures plummet. Sunburn, dehydration, exhaustion, and frostbite are all potential problems, but by far the major issue is *soroche* (altitude sickness). It's extremely important to pace yourself and allow enough time for acclimatisation before attempting any long-distance high-altitude treks or climbs.

(above) Cullicocha; (below) Sheperds hut, Huaraz.

ENVIRONMENTAL CHANGE

The warming climate is producing alarming rates of retreat in glacial water reserves of the Cordillera Blanca. The heavily populated Pacific coast relies almost exclusively on seasonal runoff from the eastern Andes for water supplies and hydroelectricity. The feasibility of transporting water across the Andes from the saturated Amazon basin is now being debated.

MAPS

For serious navigation, get the Alpenvereinskarte (German Alpine Club) topographic map sheets, which cover the Cordillera Blanca over two maps (north and south). They are sold by Casa de Guías and the gift store below Café Andino. Many local expedition outfitters sell an "officially illegal" copy with a little persuasion.

The valley between the Cordillera Blanca and the Cordillera Negra is often called the Callejón de Huaylas. It's named after the town of Huaylas in the northern part of the valley. ■TIP➡ The town is possibly the most important climbing and trekking destination in South America. From here, arrange to go white-water rafting; head out on a 10-day trek through the vast wilderness; or stay closer to home, taking one-day excursions to the 3,000-year-old ruins at Chavín de Huántar, local hot springs, a nearby glacier, and an alpine lagoon. Climbers come during the dry season to test their iron on the more than 40 peaks in the area exceeding 6,000 meters (19,500 feet). The 6,768-meter (21,996-foot) summit of Huascarán is the highest in Peru and is clearly visible from Huaraz on sunny days. To the south of Huaraz, the remote and beautiful Cordillera Huayhuash offers numerous trekking and climbing excursions as well. The outdoor options are limitless.

The area has been inhabited since pre-Inca times, and Quechua-speaking farmers still toil on the land, planting and harvesting crops much as they did thousands of years ago. The land in the valley is fertile, and corn and oranges are abundant. Up above, potatoes and other hearty crops grow on the steep terrain. The goddess *Pachamama* has always provided, but she can be iron-willed and even angry at times; every now and then she will shake her mighty tendrils and a section of one of the glaciers will crumble. The resulting rock and ice fall, called an *aluvión*, destroys everything in its path. In 1970 one such aluvión resulted from a giant earthquake, destroying the town of Yungay and almost all of its 18,000 inhabitants. Most of the towns throughout the area have suffered some damage from the numerous earthquakes, so not much colonial architecture survives. What remains are friendly, somewhat rugged-looking towns that serve as excellent jumping-off points for exploration of the area's vast wilderness and mountain ranges, hot springs, and 3,000-year-old ruins.

9

HUARAZ

400 km (248 mi) north of Lima.

Peru's number-one trekking and adventure-sports destination, Huaraz is an easy starting point for those wishing to explore the vast wilderness of the Cordillera Blanca. Unfortunately, the town has been repeatedly leveled by natural disasters. In the later part of the 20th century three large earthquakes destroyed much of Huaraz, claiming more than 20,000 lives.

Despite the setbacks and death toll, Huaraz rallied, and today it's a pleasant town filled with good-natured people. Being the most popular tourist destination in northern Peru, Huaraz also has a great international scene; while the town has few sights, the restaurants and hotels are some of the best in the region. ■TIP➡ Many businesses close between September and May, when the town practically shuts down without its hoards of climbers and trekkers. It can be hard to find an outfitter at this time; call ahead if you plan a rainy-season visit.

GETTING HERE AND AROUND

Huaraz is a small town and you can walk almost everywhere. Or, if you've just arrived and are feeling a little breathless from the altitude, take a taxi for S/5. To enjoy any of the nearby treks and sights, hire a guide as it's not safe to go alone.

ESSENTIALS

Currency Banco de Crédito (⊠ Av. Luzuriaga 691 ☎ 043/421–170 ⊕ www. viabcp.com). **Scotiabank** (⊠ José de Sucre 760 ☎ 043/721–500 ⊕ www. scotiabank.com.pe).

Mail Post Office (⊠ Av. Luzuriaga 702 ☎ 043/421–030).

Medical Hospital Victor Ramos Guardia (⊠ Av. Luzuriaga, Cuadra 8 ☎ 043/421–861).

Rental Car Monte Rosa (⊠ Jr. José de la Mar 691 ☎ 043/421–447).

Visitor Info iPerú (⊠ Pasaje Atusparia ☎ 043/428–812 ⊕ www.peru.info).

EXPLORING

❷ Every few years, as a new mayor is elected, the town gets an updated **Plaza de Armas**, which is on the corner of Luzuriaga, the town's main drag, and José Sucre. Thanks to the current mayor, who removed a gigantic, towering statue of Christ, the plaza provides nice views of the surrounding mountains. There are several *ferias artesanales* (artisanal kiosks) bordering the plaza.

❶ The small **Museo Arqueológico de Ancash** displays some very unique items, including a mummified baby and teenager, created by covering the dead with salt, *muña* (wild mint), *quinua* (a corn-like plant), and *izura* (pink earth). ■TIP→ Upstairs numerous skulls bear the scars (or rather holes) from trepanation, the removal of bone from the skull. Additionally, the museum has Chavín textiles and ceramics, and a delightful little park accessible through the bottom floor. Here you'll find original carved stones, benches, and a little café. ⊠ Av. Luzuriaga 762 ☎ 043/421–551 ⊕ www.huaraz.com/museo ☑ S/5, includes a guide ☉ Mon.–Sat. 9–5, Sun. 9–1.

❸ For a pungent look at Andean culture, head to the **Mercado Central**. At this market you'll see fruits and vegetables grown only in the highlands as well as cuy, chickens, ducks, and rabbits, which you can purchase alive or freshly slaughtered. ⊠ Entrance at Jr. de la Cruz Romero and Av. Cayetano Requena.

❹ To see Huaraz's colonial remnants, head to **Jirón José Olaya**, a pedestrian-only street where several houses with handsome facades still stand. It's best to visit on Sunday when there's a weekly *Feria de Comida Típica*, a regional street festival with typical food and craft stalls. ⊠ East of town center on right-hand side of Raimondi and a block behind Confraternidad Inter Este.

❺ The **Mirador de Retaquenua** lookout point has an excellent view of Huaraz, the Río Santa, and the surrounding mountains. It's a 45-minute walk up, but the directions are complicated so it's best to hire a guide or just take a taxi. ⊠ Av. Confraternidad Inter Sur and Av. Confraternidad Inter Este.

Jirón José
Olaya **4**

Mercado
Central **3**

Mirador de
Retaquenua **5**

Museo
Arqueológico de
Ancash **1**

Plaza de
Armas **2**

Wilcahuaín **6**

Huaraz

6 North of the city is a small archaeological site called **Wilcahuaín.** The Wari temple, dating back to AD 1100, resembles the larger temple at Chavín de Huántar. Each story of the crumbling three-tiered temple has seven rooms. There's a small museum and recently built basic bathroom facilities and a limited restaurant. Trained and knowledgeable local students will be your guide for a small tip (suggested minimum tip: S/15). ⊠ *8 km (5 mi) north of Huaraz* ☎ *No phone* 🖃 *S/5* ⊘ *Daily 6–6.*

**OFF THE
BEATEN
PATH**

Glaciar Pastoruri. A popular day trip from Huaraz is a visit to the Glaciar Pastoruri, where you can hike around the glacier and visit a glowing blue-ice cave. ■ TIP➜ On this trip you'll ascend to well above 4,000 meters (13,000 feet), so make sure you're used to the high altitude. Wear warm clothing, sunscreen, and sunglasses, as the sun is intense. Drink lots of water to avoid altitude sickness. The easiest and safest way to get here is with a tour company from Huaraz. The tour costs about S/20 to S/30 and takes eight hours. Admission to the glacier is S/5. You can also hire diminutive horses to take you up to the glacier from the parking lot for about S/15. It's not the most spectacular glacier in the world, but if you've never seen one up close, it's worth the trip. The glacier is south of Huaraz, off the main highway at the town of Recuay.

WHERE TO EAT AND STAY

$ ✕ **Creperie Patrick.** With a breezy terrace upstairs and a cozy bistro
FRENCH downstairs, this French eatery is an excellent choice. There's couscous
Fodor'sChoice and fondue, as well as hard-to-find local dishes such as grilled alpaca.
★ Don't miss the sumptuous dessert crepes and good wine selection. After
two decades in Peru, chef and owner Patrick now makes homemade
delicacies including his own liquors, jams, mustards, granola, and more.
⊠ *Av. Luzuriaga 422* ☎ *043/426–037* ▭ *No credit cards* ☽ *No lunch
Oct.–Apr.*

$ ✕ **El Horno.** With a terrace area for sunny afternoons and a recently
ITALIAN expanded dining room for the evenings, El Horno is a good stop any
★ time. ■TIP➡ Here you'll find some of the finest pizzas in Huaraz—baked
by a Frenchman, no less. The doughy crusts are superb and the service
faultless. Excellent salads, sandwiches, pastas, and barbecued meats
are also on the menu. If you are, by some chance, looking for French
books, there is a French-only book exchange here as well. ⊠ *Parque
del Periodista 37* ☎ *043/424–617* ▭ *No credit cards* ☽ *Closed Sun.,
no lunch Oct.-Apr.*

$ ✕ **Piccolo Ristorante.** Walk straight to the outdoor patio in the back to
ITALIAN enjoy your meal in the peaceful Parque del Periodista. The Italian eatery specializes in pastas and pizza, but the international specialties like
filete de trucha a la piamontesa (trout in herb sauce) and filet mignon
round out the menu nicely. The breakfasts are especially good, as is
the freshly brewed coffee. ⊠ *Jr. Julián de Morales 632* ☎ *043/509–210*
▭ *AE, MC, V.*

$$ ✕ **Siam de Los Andes.** Thai food high in the Peruvian Andes—who would
THAI have thought? Siam de Los Andes is a true anomaly in the land of tacu-
★ tacu and pollo a la brasa. The light, delicate, and at times extremely
spicy food is the real deal; from the chicken satay to the shredded pork,
it's very good. The Thailand-born owner's secret? He takes regular trips
to the homeland, importing those hard-to-find ingredients. Closed dur-
ing the low season. ⊠ *Augustin Gamarra 560* ☎ *043/428–006* ▭ *No
credit cards* ☽ *No lunch. Closed Oct.–Apr.*

$$ ⌂ **Hotel Andino.** A Swiss-style chalet set high on the hill above Huaraz,
Hotel Andino is one of the town's best lodging. There are several types
of clean, modern rooms, each with carefully planned details. Some
have terraces with excellent views of the mountains, others look out
on the wonderfully green interior garden; some suites have fireplaces,
DVD players, and separate kitchens. Each floor has a computer with
Internet access and the main floor has different seating areas, including
one with a fireplace, to enjoy this tranquil hotel. **Pros:** the best views
in Huaraz. **Cons:** it's just outside the heart of central Huaraz. ⊠ *Pedro
Cochachín 357* ☎ *043/421–662* ⊕ *www.hotelandino.com* ⤳ *60 rooms*
△ *In-room: DVDs (some), safe. In-hotel: restaurant, laundry service,
Internet terminal, parking (free)* ▭ *AE, D, DC, MC, V.*

$ ⌂ **Hotel Colomba.** Here is the best hotel to come to if you—or your
☺ kids—are high-energy and want activities. In addition to a beautiful
garden setting around this hacienda-turned-hotel, there's a rock-climb-
ing wall, soccer field, basketball court, game room, gym, and playground. The staff is well-trained and friendly. **Pros:** family friendly; lots

of activities. **Cons:** some rooms are better than others, but all cost the same (ask for a room in the back with parquet floors). ⊠ *Jr. Francisco de Zela 210, Independencia* ☎ *043/421–501* ⊕ *www.huarazhotel.com* ↝ *20 rooms* ⌂ *In-room: refrigerator (some), safe (some), Wi-Fi. In-hotel: restaurant, room service, gym, laundry service, Internet terminal, parking (free)* ⊟ *AE, D, DC, MC, V* ⊙ *BP.*

$
★ ⊞ **Hotel San Sebastián.** Perched on the side of a mountain, this hotel has great views of the Cordillera Blanca. Many rooms have small balconies and shady terraces are scattered about the hotel. Built in the Spanish-colonial style, the hotel exudes rustic charm with plenty of pine furniture and natural sunlight. The owner is Selio Villón, a mountain guide with more than 20 years of experience. **Pros:** reasonable rates with first-rate accommodation. **Cons:** hotel keeps expanding, losing some of its "family" charm. ⊠ *Jr. Italia 1124* ☎ *043/426–960* ⊕ *www. sansebastianhuaraz.com* ↝ *30 rooms, 1 junior suite* ⌂ *In-room: no phone, Wi-Fi. In-hotel: restaurant, room service, bar, laundry service, Internet terminal, parking (free)* ⊟ *V.*

NIGHTLIFE

Café Andino (⊠ *Jr. Lucar y Torre 530, 3rd floor* ☎ *043/421–203*) is a funky café offering light snacks, hot and cold beverages, and a seemingly endless supply of newspapers and books in English. To warm yourself up at night, enjoy one of the many cool bars and dance clubs. The ever-popular **el Tambo** (⊠ *José de la Mar 776* ☎ *043/423–417*) has low ceilings and curvy walls. There's a large dance floor where you can get down to salsa music. Just down the street from el Tambo is **Makondo's** (⊠ *José de la Mar and Simón Bolívar* ☎ *043/423–629*). The music here tends to be pop. To relax with the backpacker circuit, head to **Vagamundo** (⊠ *Julián de Morales 753* ☎ *043/509–063*). Join other vagabonds for a game of foosball, a movie, or dancing. For strong cocktails and loud rock music head to **X-treme Bar** (⊠ *Gabino Uribe and Luzurriaga* ☎ *043/423–150*).

OUTDOOR ACTIVITIES

BIKING If you're an experienced mountain biker, you'll be thrilled at what the area offers along horse trails or gravel roads, passing through the Cordilleras Blanca and Negra. **Mountain Bike Adventures** (⊠ *Jr. Lucar and Torre 530* ☎ *043/424–259* ⊕ *www.chakinaniperu.com*) rents bikes and has experienced guides to take you to the good single-track spots.

CLIMBING AND TREKKING If dreams of bagging a 6,000-meter (19,500-foot) peak or trekking through the wilderness haunt your nights, Huaraz is the place for you. Huaraz sits at a lofty 3,090 meters (10,042 feet), and the surrounding mountains are even higher. Allowing time to acclimatize is a life-saving necessity. Drinking lots of water and pacing yourself help avoid high-altitude pulmonary edema (commonly known as altitude sickness). ■TIP➔ The climbing and trekking season runs from May through September—the driest months. You can trek during the off-season, but drudging every day through thick rain isn't fun. Climbing during the off-season can be downright dangerous, as crevasses get covered up by the new snow. Even if you're an experienced hiker, you shouldn't venture into the backcountry without a guide.

9

The guided treks in the region vary by the number of days and the service. You can opt for smaller one-, two-, and three-day hikes, or an expedition of 10 to 20 days. Most guided treks provide donkeys to carry your equipment, plus an emergency horse. So many outfitters are in the area that looking for a qualified company can become overwhelming. Visit a few places, talk with the guides, and make sure you're getting what you really want. **Casa de Guías** (✉ *Parque Ginebra 28/G* ☎ *043/421–811* ⊕ *www.casadeguias.com.pe*) is an association of certified freelance guides who offer excellent advice and personalized trips, including mountaineering and trekking as well as rock- and ice-climbing courses.

WHITE-WATER
RAFTING

There's good rafting on the Río Santa with Class 3 and 4 rapids. The freezing cold glacial river water brings heart-pumping rapids. The most-often-run stretch of river is between Jangas and Caraz. The river can be run year-round, but is at its best during the wettest months of the rainy season, between December and April. Be prepared with the right equipment; the river is cold enough to cause serious hyperthermia. **Monttrek** (✉ *Av. Luzuriaga 646, upstairs* ☎ *043/421–124* ⊕ *www.monttrekperu. com*) is one of the best rafting outfitters in Huaraz. The company also has friendly and experienced guides for trekking and mountaineering.

SHOPPING

Craft booths on either side of the Plaza de Armas have tables piled high with locally woven textiles. If you arrive and find that you need some gear, **Tatoo Adventure Gear** (✉ *Jr. Simón Bolívar 26* ☎ *043/422–066* ⊕ *www.tatoo.ws*) has a large selection of quality gear, mainly imported.

CHAVÍN DE HUÁNTAR

110 km (68 mi) southeast of Huaraz.

★ Although the ruins appear unimpressive at first—most of the area was covered by a huge landslide in 1945—underground you'll discover a labyrinth of well-ventilated corridors and chambers. ■TIP➔ They're illumined by electric lights that sometimes flicker or fail altogether—it's wise to bring your own flashlight. Deep inside the corridors you'll come upon the **Lanzón de Chavín.** This 4-meter-high (13-foot-high) dagger-like rock carving represents an anthropomorphic deity (complete with fangs, claws, and serpentine hair); it sits elegantly at the intersection of four corridors. Built by the Chavín, one of the first civilizations in Peru, little is known about this ancient culture, although archaeologists believe they had a complex religious system. The main deity is always characterized as a puma or jaguar. Lesser deities, represented by condors, snakes, and other animals, were also revered.

This is a fascinating archaeological site that you can day-trip to from Huaraz. Chavín de Huántar sits on the southern edge of Chavín, a tiny village southeast of Huaraz. On the drive from Huaraz you get good views of two Andean peaks, Pucaraju (5,322 meters/17,296 feet) and Yanamarey (5,237 meters/17,020 feet). Construction on the road may delay your journey—check on conditions before setting out. Tours from Huaraz visit the ruins, a small on-site museum, and the alpine Laguna de Querococha during the 8-hour tour. The tour costs about S/30 per person, not including the entrance fee to the ruins. If you'd prefer to get here on your own, regular buses run between Huaraz and Chavín, and you can hire a guide at the entrance to the ruins. ☎ *No phone* ✉ *S/11* ⊙ *Daily 8–4.*

GETTING HERE AND AROUND

If you have a car—and an excellent map and good sense of direction—you can head out and explore the windy, confusing roads. For all others, simply hiring an inexpensive taxi when needed will ensure you arrive where you need to safely. Major trips and treks should be arranged with experienced, certified guides.

MONTERREY

5 km (3 mi) north of Huaraz.

This area provides a quiet and attractive alternative to Huaraz. For some, it can feel isolating: there isn't a town center, just hotels and restaurants spread about. There are local hot springs and a nice hiking trail just behind Hotel Monterrey that leads across a stream and up into the hills, eventually taking you to the Wilcahuaín Ruins. And you're just a 15-minute drive from Huraz.

GETTING HERE AND AROUND

To get to the Monterrey area, head north from Huaraz on what is popularly called the Callejón de Huaylas, passing attractive little villages and taking in spectacular scenery from the comfort of your car.

EXPLORING

Popular with locals, **Los Baños Termales de Monterrey** is a large public bathing area where you can soak your troubles away. Although the facilities could use some refreshing, a dip in the sulfur-rich waters is quite relaxing. For a more tranquil bath, as it can get very crowded on the weekends, you can rent a private tub. Didn't bring your bathing suit on your hiking trip? Don't worry, you can buy (or rent!) one here. ✉ *Av. Monterrey s/n, at Hotel Monterrey* ☎ *043/427–690* ✉ *S/3.50* ⊙ *Daily 6–5.*

WHERE TO EAT AND STAY

$$

PERUVIAN

★

✕ **El Cortijo.** This outdoor restaurant has the absolute best barbecue around, from steaks to ribs. The plastic patio furniture, placed around the grass and centered on the large barbecue pit, add to the "down-home" feeling. Or maybe it's the swing set in the front. Either way, El Cortijo is a great place to spend part of a sunny afternoon—or perhaps the entire afternoon, as the food is plenty and the service can be slow. ✉ *Carretera Huaraz–Caraz* ☎ *043/423–813* ⊙ *Daily 8–7* ▤ *AE, D, DC, MC, V* ⊙ *No lunch Oct.–Apr.*

$

Fodor's Choice

★

▦ **El Patio de Monterrey.** A lovely hacienda built in the colonial style, El Patio is a great lodging option for those wishing to stay in the country. It's only 6 km (4 mi) from Huaraz, making it a feasible alternative for those wishing to stay near the city. Whitewashed walls, wooden beams, hand-painted tiles, greenery and flowers everywhere, and a delightful stone patio make this one of the area's loveliest lodgings. The antiques-filled rooms have a clean, provincial look. There's a small chapel here, as

9

CLOSE UP

Life in the Andes

This region of the Andes has sustained some 12,000 years of cultural development. From Guitarrero Cave through the Chavín, Huari, and Inka cultures to the present day.

The highland puna has been the breadbasket for countless generations of Andean communities. Fertile glacial plains and mineral-rich rivers provide the nutrients for the rigorous growing cycles of traditional highland crops such as potatoes, while lower elevations allow the production of grains including quinoa, oats, barley, wheat, and corn. The region also provides pasture for wild and domestic herds

of llamas, alpacas, and vicuñas. Various species of bird and waterfowl also inhabit the area and sightings of the enormous condor are possible.

To this day traditional life remains a struggle. Indigenous populations continue to eke a meager existence from the land, while attempting to keep up with the rapidly changing face of a modernizing Peru. Increasingly young people are moving away from traditional life to find employment in the cities, mines, or Peru's booming tourism industry.

—Oliver Wigmore

priests originally built the hacienda. A taxi from here to Huaraz is only S/8 so a car is not a necessity. **Pros:** close to the city; luxurious country-estate. **Cons:** you may not see much else while you're here. ⊠ *Carretera Huaraz–Caraz, Km 206* ☎ *043/424–965* ⊕ *www.elpatio.com.pe* ➴ *25 rooms, 4 cabañas* ⚬ *In-room: no a/c Wi-Fi (some). In-hotel: restaurant, room service, bar, laundry service, Wi-Fi hotspot, Internet terminal, parking (free)* ▭ *AE, D, DC, MC, V* ⦿ *CP.*

CARHUAZ

35 km (22 mi) north of Huaraz.

A small, laid-back village, less touched by recent earthquakes, Carhuaz is a popular stop along the Callejón de Huaylas. A bright spot is the ice-cream shop, which scoops up excellent homemade *helado*. The town comes alive with bullfights, fireworks, dancing, and plenty of drinking during its festival honoring the Virgen de la Merced, held every year September 14–24. This is one of the best festivals in the region.

WHERE TO EAT

¢ ✕ **Heladería El Abuelo.** You won't want to miss this ice-cream shop,
CAFE mostly for the fantastic flavors such as pisco sour and beer. The owner is a good source for information about the region; he also rents nice rooms in a lodge near town. ⊠ *Merced 727* ☎ *043/494–149* ▭ *No credit cards.*

YUNGAY

59 km (37 mi) north of Huaraz.

On May 31, 1970, an earthquake measuring 7.7 on the Richter scale shook loose some 15 million cubic meters of rock and ice that cascaded down the west wall of Huascarán Norte. In the quiet village of Yungay, some 14 km (8½ mi) away, people were going about their normal activities. Some were waiting for a soccer game to be broadcast on the radio, others were watching the Verolina Circus set up in the stadium. Then the debris slammed into town at a speed of more than 200 mi per hour. Almost all of Yungay's 18,000 inhabitants were buried alive. The quake ultimately claimed nearly 70,000 lives throughout Peru.

The government never rebuilt in Yungay, but left it as a memorial to those who had died. They now call the area **Campo Santo,** and people visit the site daily. ■TIP➔ Walking through the ruined town, you'll see upturned buses, the few remaining walls of the cathedral, and, oddly, a couple of palm trees that managed to survive the disaster. There's a large white cross at the old cemetery on the hill south of town. It was here that 92 people who were tending the graves of friends and relatives were on high-enough ground to survive. You pay a nominal S/2 to enter the site.

New Yungay was built just beyond the aluvión path—behind a protective knoll. It serves as a starting point for those visiting the spectacular Laguna Llanganuco.

LAGUNAS DE LLANGANUCO

Fodor's Choice ★ Make sure your camera memory card is empty when you go to see these spectacular glaciers, gorges, lakes, and mountains. Driving through a giant gorge formed millions of years ago by a retreating glacier, you arrive at Lagunas de Llanganuco. The crystalline waters shine a luminescent turquoise in the sunlight; in the shade they're a forbidding inky black. ■TIP➔ Waterfalls of glacial melt snake their way down the gorge's flanks, falling lightly into the lake. There are many *quenual* trees (also known as the paper-bark tree) surrounding the lakes. Up above, you'll see treeless alpine meadows and the hanging glaciers of the surrounding mountains. At the lower lake, called Lago Chinancocha, you can hire a rowboat (S/3 per person) to take you to the center of the lake. A few trailside signs teach you about local flora and fauna. The easiest way to get here is with an arranged tour from Huaraz (about S/25 plus S/5 entrance fee). The tours stop here and at many other spots on the Callejón de Huaylas, finishing in Caraz.

EXPLORING

Laguna Llanganuco is one of the gateways to the **Parque Nacional Huascarán,** a 340,000-hectare park created in 1975 to protect and preserve flora and fauna in the Cordillera Blanca. ■TIP➔ This incredible mountain range has a total of 663 glaciers and includes some of the highest peaks in the Peruvian Andes. Huascarán, which soars to 6,768 meters (21,996 feet), is the highest in Peru. The smaller Alpamayo, 5,947 meters (19,327 feet), is said by many to be the most beautiful mountain in the world. Its majestic flanks inspire awe and wonder in those lucky enough to get a glimpse. The monstrous Chopicalqui and Chacraraju rise above 6,000 meters (19,500 feet).

Within the park's boundaries you'll find more than 750 plant types. There's a tragic scarcity of wildlife in the park—most have been decimated by hunting and the loss of natural habitats. Among the 12 species

Cordillera Huayhuash

While much smaller than the Cordillera Blanca, the main chain of the Cordillera Huayhuash is known for its isolation and pristine environment. For years the area remained essentially off limits to foreign tourism as it was a major stronghold for the Shining Path movement that wracked much of Peru's central highlands with terrorism throughout the 1980s. Today this isolation is what makes the region so special. Treks in this region are measured in weeks not days with road access and tourist infrastructure almost nonexistent. The opportunities to spot rare Andean wildlife are much greater here and the chances of meeting tour groups next to nothing.

Cordillera Huayhuash Circuit: The major draw here is the Cordillera Huayhuash circuit. This taxing trek can take up to two weeks, passing some of the region's most spectacular mountain scenery. Access to this trail was traditionally via Chiquián but the road has now been extended to Llamac. Tours and supplies are best organized in Huaraz although Chiquián does provide some limited facilities and porters and mules can be arranged here.

Wildlife: The isolation and pristine nature of the Cordillera Huayhuash make it an ideal place to see many of the region's rare species.

Siula Grande (6,344 meters, 20, 813 feet): See the mountain made famous by Joe Simpson in his gripping tale of survival in *Touching the Void.*

Yerupaja (6,617 m, 21,709 ft): The second-highest mountain in Peru.

—Oliver Wigmore

of birds and 10 species of mammals in the park, you're most likely to see wild ducks and condors. With a great deal of time and an equal amount of luck you may also see foxes, deer, pumas, and viscachas.

The giant national park attracts campers, hikers, and mountain climbers. Myriad treks weave through the region, varying from fairly easy 1-day hikes to 20-day marathons. Within the park, you can head out on the popular **Llanganuco–Santa Cruz Loop,** a three- to five-day trek through mountain valleys, past crystalline lakes, and over a 4,750-meter-high (15,437-foot-high) pass. Other popular hikes include the one-day Lake Churup Trek, the two-day Quilcayhuanca–Cayesh trek, and the two-day Ishinca Trek. Check with guide agencies in Huaraz for maps, trail information, and insider advice before heading out.

Although experienced hikers who know how to survive in harsh mountain conditions may want to head out on their own, it's much safer to arrange for a guide in Huaraz. You can opt to have donkeys or llamas carry the heavy stuff, leaving you with just a daypack. The most common ailments on these treks are sore feet and altitude sickness. Wear comfortable hiking shoes that have already been broken in, and take the proper precautions to avoid altitude sickness (drink lots of water, avoid prolonged exposure to the sun, and allow yourself time to acclimatize before you head out). The best time to go trekking is during the dry season, which runs May through September. July and August are the driest months, though dry season doesn't mean a lack of rain or even snow, so dress appropriately.

Some hikers decide to enter the park at night to avoid paying the hefty S/65 for a multiday pass (from 2 to 30 days). The money from these fees goes to protect the wonders of the Andes; consider this before you slip in during the dead of night. (Nighttime safety is a concern, too.) You can purchase a pass at the Huaraz office of Parque Nacional Huascarán, at the corner of Rosas and Federico Sal. ⊠ *Federico Sal y Rosas 555* ☎ *043/422–086* 🖃 *S/5 day pass, S/65 multiday pass* ☉ *Daily 6–6.*

CARAZ

67 km (42 mi) north of Huaraz.

One of the few towns in the area with a cluster of colonial-era architecture, Caraz is at the northern tip of the valley—only a partly paved road continues north. North of Caraz on the dramatic road to Chimbote is the Cañon del Pato, the true northern terminus of the Callejón de Huaylas. Caraz is an increasingly popular alternative base for trekkers and climbers. While in town be sure to try the ultra-sweet *manjar blanco* frosting.

WHERE TO EAT AND STAY

¢ 🏠 **Chamanna.** This cluster of cabañas among beautifully landscaped gardens is the town's best lodging. Benches let you admire mountain streams and towering peaks. Although not all the cabañas have private bathrooms, they are nonetheless stylish, with interesting murals and hand-hewn furniture. The restaurant (¢) serves excellent French and international cuisine. The German owner is affable and helpful. **Pros:** the distance provides peacefulness and calm. **Cons:** hiring taxis and traveling means less time to enjoy the great outdoors. ⊠ *Av. Nueva Victoria 185* ☎ *044/689–257* ⊕ *www.chamanna.com* 🛏 *10 cabañas, 5 with bath* ⚒ *In-room: no a/c, no phone, no TV. In-hotel: restaurant, laundry service, Internet terminal* 🖃 *AE, D, DC, MC, V* ⧖ *EP.*

Fodor's Choice ★

9

THE NORTHERN HIGHLANDS

The green valleys and high mountaintops that comprise the northern highlands are certainly one of the area's biggest draws, as is the area's rich history. But few travelers venture here; it's hard to reach and far from the more popular destinations of Cusco, Puno, and Machu Picchu.

Several major archaeological sites are in the northern highlands. ■ TIP➡ **The pre-Inca fortress of Kuélap, near Chachapoyas, is one of the region's best-preserved ruins.** The region's largest town, Cajamarca, is the center for exploration and was the site of one of history's quickest and wiliest military victories. It was here in 1532 that Pizarro and his meager force of 160 Spaniards were able to defeat more than 6,000 Inca warriors and capture Atahualpa, the new king of the Inca empire. Without a king, the vast empire quickly crumbled. In and around Cajamarca you'll find a handful of Inca and pre-Inca sites. There are also chances for horseback riding and hiking in the green valleys and hills.

CAJAMARCA

865 km (536 mi) northeast of Lima; 304 km (188 mi) northeast of Trujillo.

Cajamarca is the best place to stay if you want to explore the lovely landscape and rich history of the northern highlands; from here there are a number of daylong excursions to nearby ruins and hot springs.

The largest city in the northern highlands, it's a tranquil town of more than 150,000 people. It sits in a large green valley surrounded by low hills. The name Cajamarca means "village of lightning" in the Aymara language. It's fitting, for the ancient Cajamarcans worshipped the god Catequil, whose power was symbolized by a bolt of lightning. ■TIP→ The area around town was first populated by the Cajamarcan people, whose major cultural influence came from the cat-worshipping Chavín, 3,000 years ago. The Inca conquered the region in about 1460, assimilating the Chavín culture. Cajamarca soon became an important town along the *Capac Ñan* or Royal Inca Road.

The arrival of the Spanish conquistador Pizarro and his quick-witted defeat of the Incas soon brought the city and much of the region into Spanish hands. Few Inca ruins remain in modern-day Cajamarca; the settlers dismantled many of the existing structures to build the churches that can be seen today. The town's colonial center is so well preserved that it was declared a Historic and Cultural Patrimony Site by the Organization of American States in 1986.

GETTING HERE AND AROUND

LAN Perú flies daily between Lima and the Aeropuerto de Cajamarca (CJA), 3 km (2 mi) east of town.

Most places are within walking distance, but taxis are abundant if you feel a little breathless from the altitude or want to go somewhere a little outside of the city center. If you like your taxi driver, arrange a pickup another day. For major exploration outside of the city, the best option is to join a tour for the day. Cajamarca is 2,650 meters (8,612 feet) above sea level. Although not very high by Andes standards, it's still quite high. Take your time, wear sunscreen, and drink plenty of water to avoid altitude sickness.

ESSENTIALS

Currency Banco de Crédito (✉ *Jr. Apurimac 717* ☎ *076/362–742* ⊕ *www. viabcp.com*). **Scotiabank** (✉ *Jr. Amazonas 750* ☎ *076/827–101* ⊕ *www. scotiabank.com.pe*).

Mail Post Office (✉ *Jr. Amazonas 443* ☎ *076/82406–52045*).

Medical Hospital de Cajamarca (✉ *Av. Mario Urtega 500* ☎ *076/822–557*).

Visitor Info iPerú (✉ *Av. 13 de Julio s/n* ☎ *076/823–042* ⊕ *www.peru.info*).

EXPLORING

❼ Baños del Inca. About 6 km (4 mi) east of Cajamarca are these pleasant hot springs offering several public pools and private baths. The central bath, Poza del Inca, is an intact Incan pool with a system of aqueducts built by the Incas and still in use today. Despite the large size of the

Baños del Inca ..**7**

Catedral **1**

Cerro Santa
Apolonia **6**

El Complejo de
Belén **5**

El Cuarto del
Rescate **4**

Iglesia de San
Francisco **3**

Plaza de Armas ..**2**

complex, it's quite relaxing and popular with the locals. ⊠ *Av. Manco Cápac* ☎ *076/348–563* 🖼 *S/6* 🕙 *Daily 5–8.*

❶ **Catedral de Cajamarca.** Originally known as the Iglesia de Españoles (because only Spanish colonialists were allowed to attend services), this cathedral on the Plaza de Armas was built in the 17th and 18th centuries. It has an ornate baroque facade that was sculpted from volcanic rock. Like many of the town's churches, the cathedral has no belfry; the Spanish crown levied taxes on completed churches, so the settlers left the churches unfinished, freeing them from the tight grip of the tax collector. ⊠ *Jr. Del Batán and Amalia Puga* ☎ *No phone* 🖼 *Free* 🕙 *Daily 3–6.*

❻ **Cerro Santa Apolonia.** At the end of Calle 2 de Mayo are steps leading to this hilltop *mirador,* or scenic lookout, to see a bird's-eye view of the city. At the top are many carved bricks dating to pre-Columbian times. ■ **TIP→** One of the rocks has the shape of a throne and has been dubbed the Seat of the Inca. According to local legend, it was here that Inca kings would sit to review their troops. You'll find pretty gardens and great views of the town. You can either walk or go by taxi (round-trip S/5). ⊠ *End of 2 de Mayo* ☎ *No phone* 🖼 *S/2* 🕙 *Daily 8–6.*

9

Ventanillas de Otuzco. One of the oldest cemeteries in Peru, the Ventanillas de Otuzco (Otuzco Windows) dates back more than 3,500 years. The ancient necropolis, 8 km (5 mi) northeast of Cajamarca, is comprised of several large burial niches carved into a cliff. From afar the niches look like windows, hence the area's name. On closer inspection you see that many of the burial niches have carved decorations. Sadly, the site is slowly being eroded by wind and rain. If you're incredibly inspired by this cemetery, you can go about 30 km (18 mi) from Combayo, in the same direction, and visit the better-preserved Ventanillas de Combayo. A three-hour guided tour to Ventanillas de Otuzco costs around S/25.

⑤ **El Conjunto de Belén.** Built in the 17th century, this large complex, origi-
★ nally a hospital, now houses the city's most interesting museums and a colonial church. At the **Museo Arqueológico de Cajamarca**, the town's archaeological museum, are exhibits of Cajamarcan ceramics and weavings. The pre-Inca Cajamarcans were especially famous for their excellent patterned textiles that were often dyed vivid shades of blue. The **Museo Etnográfico** has a few displays of everyday bric-a-brac—there's even an old saddle and a dilapidated coffee grinder—dating back to pre-colonial times. The **Iglesia de Belén** is a charming church with a polychrome pulpit and cupola. ⊠ *Jr. Belén and Jr. Junín* ☎ *076/362–903* ✉ *S/5, includes admission to entire Conjunto de Belén and El Cuarto del Rescate* ☉ *Mon., Wed.–Fri. 9–1 and 3–6; weekends 9–1.*

④ **El Cuarto del Rescate.** The Ransom Chamber is the only Inca building still standing in Cajamarca and, although the big stone room itself isn't much to look at, the history is enough to make this worth a visit. Legend has it that after Pizarro and his men captured Atahualpa, the Inca king offered to fill the chamber once with gold and twice with silver. The ransom was met, but the war-hardened Spaniards killed Atahualpa anyway. ⊠ *Jr. Amalia Puga 750* ☎ *044/922–601* ✉ *S/5, includes admission to Cunjunto de Belén* ☉ *Mon., Wed–Fri. 9–1 and 3–6; weekends 9–1.*

③ **Iglesia de San Francisco.** Built in the 17th and 18th centuries, the Church of San Francisco sits proudly on the Plaza de Armas in front of the main cathedral. The church's two bell towers were begun in republican times and finished in 1951. The church was called the Iglesia de Indios (Church of the Indians) as indigenous peoples were not allowed to attend services at the main cathedral. ■TIP→ Inside you'll find catacombs and a small religious-art museum. To the right of the church, the Capilla de la Virgen de Dolores is one of Cajamarca's most beautiful chapels. A large statue of Cajamarca's patron saint, La Virgen de Dolores, makes this a popular pilgrimage destination for local penitents. ⊠ *Northeast corner of Plaza de Armas* ☎ *No phone* ✉ *S/3 for museum* ☉ *Daily 3–6.*

② **Plaza de Armas.** Like all main colonial cities, this is the main square and includes a fountain, benches, and street vendors, making it a nice place to hang out. Built on roughly the same spot as the great plaza where the Atahualpa was captured and later killed, Cajamarca's Plaza de Armas no longer shows any sign of Inca influence, but it's good to remember. ⊠ *Av. Lima and Arequipa.*

OFF THE BEATEN PATH

Cumbe Mayo. This pre-Inca site, 23 km (14 mi) southwest of Cajamarca, is surrounded by a large rock outcropping, where you'll find various petroglyphs left by the ancient Cajamarcans. There are also petroglyph-adorned caves so a guided tour is highly recommended. This site, discovered in 1937 by the famous Peruvian archaeologist J.C. Tello, also includes some of the most notable aqueducts in the Andes. Constructed around 1000 BC, the aqueduct was designed to direct the ample water from the Andes into the drier area of Cajamarca, where there was a large reservoir. Amazingly, more than 8 km (5 mi) of the ancient aqueduct are intact today. Guided tours cost around S/25 and take about four hours.

OUTDOOR ACTIVITIES

A number of hikes are in the area around Cajamarca, from the rivers of the region, to past Inca and pre-Inca ruins. Most follow the *Capac Ñan* or Royal Inca Road, that ran from Cusco all the way north to Quito. One of the most popular walks is to the pre-Inca necropolis of **Combayo.** To get to the trailhead, drive 20 km (12 mi) north of the Baños del Inca. The hike takes around four or five hours. The **Ruta del Tambo Inca** takes you to an old Inca *tambo*, or resting point. It's difficult to find this trailhead and roads sometimes get washed out during the rainy season, so ask in town to confirm the following: Drive 46 km (28 mi) from Cajamarca on the road to Hualgayoc. Near Las Lagunas turn onto a dirt road and follow the road to the milk depository at Ingatambo. The trail begins here. The 16-km (10-mi) trip takes about eight hours. The best time to go trekking is during the dry season, May through September.

The **Association for the Rescue of the Cajamarcan Ecosystem** (✉ *Av. Manco Cápac 1098* ☎ *076/894–600 Ext. 360* ⊕ *www.aprec.org*) publishes an excellent guide with maps and route descriptions of many other hikes in the region. The goal is to create sustainable ecotourism in a place where the mining companies control the local economy. Their office is in the Hotel Laguna Seca. **Clarín Tours** (✉ *Jr. Del Batán 161* ☎ *076/366–829*) offers trips, with English-speaking guides, to many of the ruins in and around Cajamarca.

WHERE TO EAT AND STAY

❶
¢–$
CONTINENTAL

✕ **Cascanuez.** This is the place in Cajamarca for decadent desserts and delicious coffee. Casanuez translates to "The Nutcracker," and Sugar Plum Fairies would approve of the extensive homemade pastries, tortes, and other tempting treats. There's also a small dinner and lunch menu with highland staples such as potato soup and grilled meats, but the desserts are their mainstay and important not to miss. ✉ *Av. Puga 554* ☎ *076/366–089* ▭ *MC, V.*

❷
$$
PERUVIAN
★

✕ **El Batán.** Although the food is excellent, the real feast is the visual one: the restaurant building is a beautifully restored 18th-century mansion. The patio dining area, including a stained-glass roof, has iron chairs and a stone floor. In addition to picturesque surroundings, this criollo restaurant has specialty meat dishes, a menu in Spanish and English, a small art gallery upstairs, and live music on the weekends. ✉ *Jr. Del Batán 369* ☎ *076/366–025* ▭ *AE, D, DC, MC, V* ☉ *No dinner Sun.*

9

❸ ✕ **El Querubino.** Here gourmet food
$ is paired with slow service. Ask for
CONTINENTAL the chef's daily specials or enjoy a
★ large selection of dishes, such as
fettucini with pesto sauce, gnocchi
with herbed-sauce, roasted duck
or *causa de langostinos*, mashed
potatoes with shrimp. To complement your meal, choose from the
most extensive wine list in Cajamarca and enjoy the nice details,
such as the monogrammed plates
in pastel hues and walls painted
a soft Tuscan yellow. ⊠ *Av. Puga
589* ☎ *076/340–900* ⊟ *AE, D, DC,
MC, V.*

> ### DRINKING THE AGUARDIENTES
>
> *Aguardientes* (homemade liqueurs) are common throughout the region. They're made in sundry flavors, including *mora* (black-berry), *maracuyá* (passion fruit), *café* (coffee), and *leche* (milk). Unfortunately, there's no place that offers tourists a sample, so if you want to try one of these strong, home-brewed liqueurs, you'll have to convince a Peruvian to take you home and share his private collection.

❹ ✕ **Salas.** Across from the Plaza de
$ Armas, this is where to get typi-
PERUVIAN cal food from the area. Open 7–10 daily, the menu includes authentic
regional specialties such as cuy, *perico* (a lake fish), and Spanish-style
tortillas. There's also an extensive selection of piscos, top-shelf liquors,
and wines. Although the furnishings and staff look like they have been
there since the restaurant opened in 1947, the food is fresh and delicious. ⊠ *Av. Puga 637* ☎ *076/362–867* ⊟ *AE, D, DC, MC, V.*

$ ⛫ **El Portal del Marqués.** If you want to stay in Cajamarca's historic
district, this lovely casona is an excellent choice. Surrounding two
sunny courtyards, the rooms have a modern style while the common
areas have hand-woven rugs and antique colonial furniture. The beds
are narrow and soft. **Pros:** in the heart of Cajamarca city. **Cons:** the
city can be noisy. ⊠ *Jr. de Comercio 644* ☎ *076/343–339* ⊕ *www.
portaldelmarques.com* ⤬ *31 rooms, 2 suites* ⚬ *In-room: no a/c, refrigerator (some), DVDs, safe, Wi-Fi. In-hotel: restaurant, bar, laundry
service, Internet terminal, parking (free)* ⊟ *AE, D, DC, MC, V* ⊠*BP.*

$ ⛫ **Hotel El Ingenio.** The best bargain in Cajamarca. Like all the other
hotels, this is in a renovated hacienda with extensive grounds. There's a
lovely central courtyard with a giant orange tree, well-kept gardens, and
a charming wooden bar. Each room is simply decorated with antique-
looking hardwood furniture and large, comfy beds. **Pros:** the same quality service at a very reasonable price. **Cons:** some rooms are better than
others. ⊠ *Av. Via de Evitamiento 1611–1709* ☎ *076/368–733* ⊕ *www.
elingenio.com* ⤬ *33 rooms, 6 suites* ⚬ *In-room: no a/c, refrigerator,
safe, Wi-Fi. In-hotel: restaurant, room service, bar, laundry service,
Internet terminal, parking (free)* ⊟ *AE, D, DC, MC, V* ⊠*BP.*

$$ ⛫ **Hotel Laguna Seca.** Come here to pamper yourself. This refurbished
Fodor's Choice hacienda, which has well-manicured garden areas throughout its exten-
★ sive grounds, offers private and public baths from the nearby natural
thermal hot springs—in fact, each room has a large tub and direct access
to this water. ■TIP➔ Try a massage or other spa treatment, relax in the
Jacuzzi, or tour the grounds on horseback. Decorated with antique-look-
ing hardwood furniture and large, comfy beds, every detail of this hotel

was chosen to help guests do one thing: relax. **Pros:** in-room natural hot spring water. **Cons:** outside of the city limits. ⊠ *Av. Manco Cápac 1098, Baños del Inca* ☎ *076/584–300* ⊕ *www.lagunaseca.com.pe* ⇄ *37 rooms, 5 suites* ⟳ *In-room: no a/c, Wi-Fi. In-hotel: restaurant, room service, bars, pools, spa, bicycles, laundry service, Internet terminal, parking (free)* ⊟ *AE, D, DC, MC, V.*

$ ★ ☪ ⊡ **La Posada del Puruay.** In the countryside, this hacienda is far from the noise of Cajamarca and has extensive gardens, a trout hatchery, and green hills for horseback riding and hiking. The hacienda was constructed in 1914, so the rooms have authentic touches like vaulted wood-beam ceilings. Large rosaries adorn the walls. It feels like you're visiting well-to-do relatives for a summer holiday. **Pros:** transported to another time and place; reasonable price. **Cons:** small number of rooms can be a drawback if you don't like the other guests. ⊠ *Carretera Porcón, Km 4.5* ☎ *076/367–028* ⇄ *7 rooms, 6 suites* ⟳ *In-room: no a/c, Wi-Fi (some). In-hotel: restaurant, room service, bar, laundry service, parking (free)* ⊟ *AE, D, DC, MC, V* �†⊙⊦ *BP.*

NIGHTLIFE

Los Frailones (⊠ *Av. Perú 701* ☎ *076/364–113* ⊕ *www.losfrailones.com*) has an air of sophistication not often found in these parts. This beautifully renovated casona has antiques throughout. The waiters dress in monks' robes. The house has several levels, where you'll find a grill, a dance floor, and a cozy pub. There are peñas on weekends and sometimes during the week. **Up & Down** (⊠ *Tarapacá 782* ☎ *No phone*) has a dance floor in the basement with overwhelmingly loud salsa and pop music. **Cowboy Pub** (⊠ *Amalia Puga 212* ☎ *076/365–529*) is a local watering hole, popular with the town's miners.

SHOPPING

The town of **Llacanora**, 13 km (8 mi) from the city on the road to the Baños del Inca, is a typical Andean farming community, now a cooperative farm, famous for agriculture and making reed bugles. People come to see the traditional village, but there are also several shops around town to buy locally produced goods.

CHACHAPOYAS

460 km (285 mi) east of Chiclayo.

At the *ceja de la selva* (jungle's eyebrow), Chachapoyas is the capital of Peru's Amazonas department. ■ **TIP→ The town is a good jumping-off point for exploring some of Peru's most fascinating and least-visited pre-Inca ruins.** The giant fortress at Kuélap, and the ruins of Purunllacta and Gran Vilaya, are nearby. Despite the Amazonas moniker, there's nothing jungle-like about the area around Chachapoyas. The surrounding green highlands constitute what most people would call a highland cloud forest. Farther east, in the region of Loreto (won by Peru in the 1942 border dispute with Ecuador), you'll find true jungle.

Chachapoyas is a sleepy little town of 20,000. It has a well-preserved colonial center and one small archaeological museum. Chachapoyas—difficult to reach because of the poor roads through the mountains—is

The circular structures at the pre-Inca city of Kuélep.

most easily accessed from Chiclayo. Infrequent flights arrive here from Lima as well.

GETTING HERE AND AROUND

In town, everything is close and within walking distance. There are plenty of taxis, but you'll have little chance of needing one. To get to the archaeological sites, you must go with a guide. The most enjoyable and cost-effective way of doing this is with a tour. There's no public transportation and you cannot hire a guide once at the sites.

ESSENTIALS

Currency Banco de Crédito (✉ Jr. Ortiz Arrieta 576 ☎ 041/477–430 ⊕ www. viabcp.com).

Medical Hospital Chachapoyas (✉ Jr. Triunfo, Cuadra 3 ☎ 044/477–354).

Visitor Info iPerú (✉ Jr. Ortiz Arrieta 588 ☎ 041/477–292 ⊕ www.peru.info).

EXPLORING

The **Iglesia Santa Ana** is the town's oldest church. It was one of Peru's first "Indian churches," where indigenous people were forced to attend services. The church was built in the 17th century and is on a small square of the same name. ✉ Av. Santa Ana.

Showing artifacts from the area's ancient civilizations, a small display of Chachapoyan ceramics is at the **Museo Arqueologíco**. You'll also find a ghoulish display of mummies lying in the fetal position. ✉ Jr. Ayacucho 504 ☎ 041/477–045 ✉ Free ☉ Weekdays 8–1 and 2–4:45.

This small, rocky natural hot spring a few blocks west of the Plaza de Armas at the **Pozo de Yanayacu** isn't much, but is nice to look at. It's said the spring magically appeared during a visit from Saint Toribio de Mogrovejo. ⊠ *Jr. Salamanca, 2 blocks west of Jr. Puno.*

OFF THE BEATEN PATH

Purunllacta. About 35 km (22 mi) southeast of Chachapoyas are the ruins of Purunllacta, a good place for hiking. With pre-Inca agricultural terraces, dwellings, ceremonial platforms, and roads extending for more than 420 hectares, but few tourists, this can be peaceful and also boring as you have no explanation of what you're seeing. To get here, drive to the town of Cheto. From the town it's a one-hour walk uphill to the site. Few people know about this or go, so ask in Cheto for directions to the trailhead, and don't be alarmed if you have to ask more than one person. There's no entrance fee.

> **CERAMIC STOP**
>
> About 10 km (6 mi) north of Chachapoyas is the tiny pueblo of Huancas, whose citizens are well-known for their pottery; this is a good place to buy artisanal goods and locally made ceramics.

WHERE TO EAT AND STAY

¢ ✕**El Tejado.** With windows overlooking the town's Plaza de Armas, this
PERUVIAN is one of the most elegant eateries in Chachapoyas. The criollo food is serviceable, and the staff is most attentive when the *dueña* (owner) is around. ⊠ *Jr. Santo Domingo 424* ☎ *041/477–592* ▭ *No credit cards* ⊗ *No dinner Sun.*

¢ ✕**La Tushpa.** Probably the best eatery in town, La Tushpa has good
CONTINENTAL grilled steaks served with homemade *chimichuri* (a green sauce made with herbs, garlic, and tomatoes). There are also pizzas and other items from the on-site bakery. Though the place feels institutional, the restaurant is more welcoming than most in the region, thanks to an extremely friendly waitstaff. Make sure to look at the Andean textiles hanging on the walls. Ask to see the owner's orchard garden, which he keeps above the restaurant. ⊠ *Jr. Ortiz Arrieta 769* ☎ *041/477–478* ▭ *V.*

¢ 🏨**Gran Hotel Vilaya.** A pleasant, if slightly antiseptic, hotel in the center of Chachapoyas, the Gran Hotel Vilaya has rooms with simple wooden furnishings. The service is quite friendly, and there's a good in-house travel agency. **Pros:** good service. **Cons:** unattractive concrete building. ⊠ *Jr. Ayacucho 755* ☎ *041/477–664* ⊕ *www.hotelvilaya.com* ⤴ *19 rooms, 1 suite* ⚬ *In-room: no a/c, no phone, safe. In-hotel: bar, laundry service* ▭ *No credit cards* ⊘*BP.*

$ 🏨**Hostal Casa Vieja.** This colorful old house, with its bougainvillea-filled
★ courtyard and pleasant terraces, is the finest in Chachapoya. There's a charming salon with a fireplace and upright piano. The rooms vary greatly; ask to see a handful before you decide. No. 3, with its large sitting area and chimney, is the nicest. **Pros:** amazing old house with modern touches. **Cons:** some rooms are better than others. ⊠ *Jr. Chincha Alta 569* ☎ *041/477–353; 512/466–7211 in U.S.* ⊕ *www.casaviejaperu. com* ⤴ *11 rooms, 3 suites* ⚬ *In-room: no a/c, Wi-Fi. In-hotel: restaurant, room service, laundry service, Internet terminal, parking (free)* ▭ *V.*

¢ 🏨**Puma Urco.** Simple, clean rooms and friendly staff make this a good budget alternative. Most rooms have large beds with flowers painted over the headboards. However, the walls are paper-thin. This is a good choice if all other options are full. **Pros:** good location. **Cons:** very basic

9

rooms. ⊠ *Jr. Amazonas 833* ☏ *041/477–871* ↝ *20 rooms* ⌂ *In-room: no a/c, no phone. In-hotel: laundry service* ═ *MC, V* ⦿ *BP.*

NIGHTLIFE

La Reina (⊠ *Jr. Ayacucho 727* ☏ *041/477–618*) has a large selection of local *aguardientes* (locally distilled liquors) in flavors that range from *leche* (milk) to *mora* (blackberry). **La Estancia** (⊠ *Jr. Amazonas 861* ☏ *041/478–432*) is a friendly pub. The owner loves to chat with the customers about the region's history and natural beauty.

KUÉLAP

72 km (45 mi) south of Chachapoyas.

★ The most impressive archaeological site in the area is the immense pre-Inca city of Kuélap. Most visitors to this region come solely to see the grand city. Little is known about the people who built it; archaeologists have named them the Chachapoyans or Sachupoyans. They were most likely a warlike people, as the city of Kuélap is surrounded by a massive defensive wall ranging from 6 to 12 meters (20 to 40 feet) high. The Chachapoyans left many cities and fortresses around the area. In 1472 they were conquered by the Inca Huayna Capac. ■ TIP→ If you've been to Machu Picchu, or just seen photographs, you'll recognize many similarities in this complex, built almost a thousand years before.

A visit to Kuélap is an all-day affair. The city sits at a dizzying 3,100 meters (10,075 feet) above sea level, high above the Río Utcubamba. The oval-shape city has more than 400 small, rounded buildings. The city's stonework, though rougher than that of the Inca, has geometric patterns and designs, adding a flight of fancy to a town seemingly designed for the art of war. The most interesting of the rounded buildings has been dubbed El Tintero (the Inkpot). Here you'll find a large underground chamber with a huge pit. ■ TIP→ Archaeologists hypothesize that the Chachapoyans kept pumas in this pit, dumping human sacrifices into its depths.

It's best to visit Kuélap with a tour group from Chachapoyas. The trip costs around S/60 per person. Vilaya Tours, in the Grand Hotel Vilaya, is highly recommended. Remember to bring a hat for protection from the sun. Take frequent rests and drink lots of water to avoid altitude sickness. ⊠ *72 km (45 mi) south of Chachapoyas* ☏ *No phone* ☞ *S/11.20* ☽ *Daily 6–6.*

Bolivia

WORD OF MOUTH

"I would describe Bolivia as the country of contrasts . . . jungle and desert and rich and poor in the same geographical site . . . Indians with their cultures accepting the Christian and mixed in a colorful syncretism . . . it is beautiful."

—flintstones

WELCOME TO BOLIVIA

TOP REASONS TO GO

★ **Water, water everywhere.** Carnival in Oruro may seem like the biggest frat-house water fight in the world, but it's also a stunning realization of Bolivian folklore and dance.

★ **Flipper of the Forest.** Yes, friends, that *was* a pink dolphin you just saw in the Beni River—and no, you didn't have too much *chicha* to drink. The Amazonian basin is home to an astonishing array of wildlife, including caimans, Amazonian catfish the size of Volkswagens, sloths, jaguars, and the famed pink dolphins.

★ **No salt added.** The Salar de Uyuni, the giant salt desert that borders Chile, is an impressive, barren, and unique landscape.

★ **On top of the world.** The Isla de Sol, sitting pretty in the middle of Lake Titicaca, not only has the best views of the mountains of the Royal Range and the sacred waters of the lake itself, but it also has sparkling white beaches.

1 **La Paz.** La Paz and its surroundings are what many people expect Bolivia to be: poor, high, desolate, and cold. However, drop down the other side of the city and you are in the subtropical Yungas in an hour, and the farther you go the deeper and darker the Amazon becomes.

2 **Lake Titicaca.** Lake Titicaca embodies all the mysteries of Bolivia's ancient and not so ancient indigenous societies, and the sacred character of this vast body of water is understandable. Its stunning islands and mountain backdrop give you a real opportunity to step back and reflect.

3 **Central Bolivia.** The center of the country is the home of the two "other" cities, Cochabamba and Santa Cruz, and each is distinct and in its own way the capital of its region. Go to the permanent spring of Cochabamba to relax and live well, and to Santa Cruz's oil-rich territories to experience a cowboy boomtown grown very big.

4 **Southern Bolivia.** The jewel of the south, and some would say Bolivia, is the Salar de Uyuni, the vast otherworldly salt flats, but to appreciate the great tragedies of Bolivia's past and the torments of its present, you need to go to Potosí, the skeleton of a once hugely wealthy city.

GETTING ORIENTED

From the altiplano to the Amazon basin, Bolivia borders five countries and comprises nearly every microclimate and ecosystem imaginable. It's most famous for the Andes, which take up a large chunk of the west. Also well known are the vast jungle regions of Amazonia, which extend all the way east into Brazil. But Bolivia has a surprisingly varied series of ecosystems within those two major regions. Mountain areas vary from cool and dry (as in the high-altitude cities of La Paz and Potosí), to temperate (the cities of Cochabamba and Sucre), to warm and pleasant almost year-round (in the fertile, grape-growing lands near the southern city of Tarija). Jungle areas also vary: from very humid and warm, as in Santa Cruz, to the more temperate climates in the northwest province of Pando. In the northeast province of Beni, encompassing the city of Trinidad, the hot, wet climate is occasionally broken by cold spells called *surazos*.

Guaporé River
iso Firme

BRAZIL

San Ignacio
San Rafael
San Matias
Lago Conception
San Jose
Robore
Puerto Quijarro
Puerto Suarez

PARAGUAY

10

Updated by
Marlise Kast

"ROOFTOP OF THE WORLD" is how people describe Bolivia. The dizzying altitude of parts of this country is almost always mentioned. Bolivia's second largest city, La Paz, is the world's highest capital, at 3,640 meters (11,942 feet). The city's Aeropuerto Internacional El Alto, at 4,057 meters (13,310 feet), is the world's highest commercial airport. Lake Titicaca is the highest navigable lake in the world. They play football on top of mountains.

But these high-flying statistics don't reveal much about the country or the people. Bolivia is larger than Texas and California combined, but most of its 8 million people are concentrated in a handful of urban centers—La Paz, Santa Cruz, Cochabamba, and Sucre—making it a very easy place to get to know. Off the beaten track—and onto the very unbeaten—Bolivia contains every type of terrain, from tropical lowlands to parched desert to rugged mountain peaks. It has the second-largest range of natural environments in the world, after Mexico. Although generally considered an Andean nation, nearly two-thirds of the country sweats it out in the steamy Amazon Basin—remote, overlooked, and as inhospitable as it is soul-stirring. On Bolivia's wildest frontier, indigenous tribes live as they have for centuries, unimpressed, it seems, by the displays of the modern world. In the provinces of Beni and Santa Cruz, near the border of Brazil, tribes still hunt with bows and arrows.

To the west of these tropical lowlands, just beyond Cochabamba and Santa Cruz, the Andes rise sharply to form the backbone of South America's Pacific coast. This two-prong mountain range shelters between its eastern and western peaks a long, rambling plain. Known as the altiplano, this high, cold plateau may seem bleak, but for the adventurous traveler there are treasures to be found, including the mountains themselves, the deep-blue waters of Lake Titicaca, the staggering views of the Salar de Uyuni, and the ancient and bloodstained city of Potosí.

Centuries of Spanish dominion have left their mark, but Bolivia remains a land of indigenous farmers, ranchers, and artisans. On the windswept Andean plateaus you will still see local weavers toting their crafts and red-cheek children to weekly markets. By the time the sun has risen, the brightly dressed Aymara are in place, ready to sell textiles and ponchos, not to mention vegetables, fruits, and medicinal herbs. On city streets you'll see business executives in the latest designer fashions shouting into mobile phones as they buy flowers from bowler-hatted indigenous women. These ladies will also be shouting into mobile phones, but through a mouth-full of coca leaves. And here is the root of Bolivia's magic: the ancient and the modern are conjoined here, and, as far as the passing traveler is concerned, seamlessly.

PLANNING

WHEN TO GO

With its extremes of terrain, altitude, and climate, Bolivia has something to appeal to nearly every traveler. During the rainy season from November to March, heavy downpours make overland traveling difficult and dangerous, as many smaller roads are virtually impassable. If you plan to travel this way, it's best to go between April and October, when winter skies mean endless sun and perfect light. Expect hazy views between July and September when farmers burn entire hillsides to clear the land for cultivation.

CLIMATE

In high-altitude cities like La Paz and Potosí the weather can get very chilly, particularly at night. Lowland cities like Santa Cruz, sitting in the Amazon basin, are hot and humid most of the year. Cochabamba, dubbed the "City of Eternal Spring," enjoys a mild Mediterranean climate year-round.

The following are the average monthly maximum and minimum temperatures for La Paz. Remember, this is not indicative of the country as a whole, and that almost all other regions are more temperate.

10

AVERAGE HIGHS AND LOWS								
Jan.	64F	18C	May	66F	19C	Sept.	72F	17C
	43	6		35	2		38	3
Feb.	64F	18C	June	60F	16C	Oct.	65F	18C
	43	6		36	2		40	4
Mar.	64F	18C	July	61F	16C	Nov.	67F	20C
	43	6		34	1		42	6
Apr.	66F	19C	Aug.	62F	17C	Dec.	64F	18C
	40	4		35	2		43	6

HOLIDAYS

During Carnaval and many of Bolivia's other holidays the country virtually shuts down, sometimes for a couple of days before and after. Don't plan to travel on the holiday itself, as transit is practically nonexistent. Major holidays are New Year's Day; Carnaval (weekend prior to start of Lent); Good Friday (April); Labor Day (May 1); Independence Day (August 6); All Saints' Day (November 2); Christmas.

GETTING HERE AND AROUND

Those coming from Peru can catch one of LAN Perú's four daily flights from Lima or Arequipa to Aeropuerto Manco Cápac in Juliaca, the closest airport to Puno on Lake Titicaca. From here, buses for Bolivia depart daily at 7:30 AM from the Puno Bus Terminal and take about three hours to the border. After visa and passport inspections, passengers continue twenty minutes to the charming town of Copacabana, the hub of transportation, where they continue on either by boat to Isla del Sol or by bus to Bolivia's main cities and towns. Buses from Puno to Copacabana are available through Tour Peru and cost S/20.

Traveling around Bolivia is an enjoyable experience if you savor unpredictability, display huge amounts of patience, and have lots of time to hang around in airports, bus stations, and on the wrong side of landslides. Flying is often the best way to go, as it is relatively cheap in-country and fast. Bus services between cities and to the border can be excellent, but dangerous if they are overnight, or during national holidays. Car rental is expensive, and you need to be a confident and assertive driver to manage Bolivian highways and the off-road experience of minor roads. Renting a taxi for a day is a viable option, but settle on a price first and only pay 50% up front.

AIR TRAVEL

All international and domestic flights to La Paz arrive at El Alto airport, which is on the altiplano in the city of El Alto, 12 km (7 mi) from downtown. Many stop first at Santa Cruz's airport, Viru Viru, which also serves as an international hub. American Airlines has daily flights between Miami, Santa Cruz, and La Paz. AeroSur, Bolivia's domestic airline, flies to most major cities in Bolivia, and TAM, the military airline, can offer very good value. Amazonas airline (☎ 02/222–0848) connects La Paz to Cobija, Santa Cruz, Trinidad, and other eastern points.

Domestic flights can be heavily booked, so always reconfirm your reservation a day or so in advance. If you do not, your reservation may be canceled. Travelers coming from Peru who want to explore Lake Titicaca can fly into Aeropuerto Manco Cápac in Juliaca near Puno and then continue three-hours by bus into Bolivia. This is a very economical option. LAN Perú has four daily flights from Lima or Arequipa to Juliaca for around $150 USD.

Airlines AeroSur (☎ 03/336–4446 Santa Cruz, 02/244–4930 La Paz ⊕ www. aerosur.com). **American Airlines** (☎ 02/235–1360, 03/334–1314⊕ www. aa.com). **Aerolineas Argentinas** (☎ 03/333–9776/9777 ⊕ www.aerolineas. com.ar). **LAN** (☎ 800/100–521 or in the U.S. 866/435–9526 ⊕ www.lan.com).

CLOSE UP

Modern Politics

Bolivia's government, under its new, official name, The Plurinational State of Bolivia, is currently headed by President Evo Morales, the nation's first indigenous President. Initially elected in 2005, President Morales won a recall referendum in August 2008 and was reelected to a five-year term in 2010. A member of the *Moviemiento al Socialism* (MAS) party, Morales' main initiatives as a candidate were renegotiating natural gas prices with international companies and rewriting the Bolivian Constitution. After a highly disputed revisionary process, the new Constitution was approved by 60% of the electorate in 2009. Morales also kept his campaign promise to nationalize most of Bolivia's natural gas fields. Acknowledging the multicultural ethnicity of the nation, the Law of Autonomy and Decentralization (LAD) was enacted in July 2010, giving increased political and financial rights to indigenous Bolivians. The 2010–2015 Plurinational Legislative Assembly is controlled in both bicameral houses by MAS. The government consists of an executive, a legislative, a judicial, and an electoral branch. Bolivia has nine Administrative Departments or geographical states, each with representative Prefects (governors), elected every five years. Mayors and members of local City Councils are also selected by popular vote. After a stormy, and often bloody, history with nearly 200 heads of state in a brief 175-year period, Bolivia appears to have entered a period of relative political stability.

BUS TRAVEL

Private bus companies connect Bolivia's major cities. Because of the often poor roads, bus journeys can be very slow—a trip from La Paz to Santa Cruz, for example, can take more than 24 hours. Securing a seat is usually no problem, though you should reserve at least a day in advance for the long and tedious rides between La Paz, Sucre, Potosí, and Santa Cruz. The best way to do this is either through an agency or by going to the bus terminals themselves.

From Copacabana to La Paz, Turisbus has buses departing daily at 1:30 and the cost is (Bs)25 for the three-hour trip. There are also public buses and white minivans departing from Plaza Sucre in Copacabana every hour, but they are uncomfortable, make multiple stops along the way, and take nearly four hours. It is safer to buy a ticket from one of the agencies on Plaza Sucre that operate tourist buses rather than pay less for one of the public buses that are prone to crime.

Bus Companies Expreso Mopar (☎ 02/228–4585 ⊕ www.mopar.com.bo). **Trans Copacabana** (☎ 02/237–7894 ⊕ www.transcopacabana.com.bo). **Turisbus** (☎ 02/862–2160 ⊕ www.turisbus.com).

CAR TRAVEL

It takes confidence and a thick skin to drive in Bolivian cities, courage to use the big highways between them, and special 4x4 skills to manage the smaller roads; in most cases, it's easier to use public transport or hire a taxi. In the city, drive defensively and assume that vehicles around you

10

are going to do the stupidest thing possible, especially at traffic lights. Before driving outside the city, inquire about the conditions around your proposed destination. Most roads are unpaved and poorly maintained. During the rainy season many are subject to flash floods and landslides, so prepare for long delays. If you can, hire a driver familiar with the area so that you can enjoy the scenery without frazzling your nerves. Avoid driving at night outside built-up areas, especially on the highways—it's terrifying.

Renting a car can be very expensive in Bolivia, particularly because you need a four-wheel-drive vehicle to reach many destinations. The rate for a four-wheel-drive vehicle is $300–$700 USD per week. Compact cars suitable for short trips cost $150–$250 USD per week. The minimum age for most car rentals in Bolivia is 25 years. You need a passport, driver's license (some rental companies require an International Driver's License), and a credit card.

The national oil company, YPFB, maintains service stations on most major roads. Many are open 24 hours a day and gas is cheap, approximately $1.70 USD per gallon. Away from the main roads, GASOLINA signs alert you to private homes where fuel is sold (make sure they filter the gasoline for impurities when they fill your tank). Unleaded gasoline is available at some service stations.

TRAIN TRAVEL

Bolivia's great train services all died years ago, and the country is now crisscrossed only by rusty rails. There is still transport between Oruro and towns near the border like Uyuni, Tupiza, and Villazon. There's also occasional service from Uyuni to Calama, Chile, though it's a long, rough, high, and cold ride. The classic ride from La Paz to Arica on the coast of Chile stopped running many years ago. Check what's going on at ⊕ *www.fca.com.bo.*

ESSENTIALS
ELECTRICITY

Bolivia's electric current is 110/220 volts AC in La Paz and 220 volts AC in the rest of the country. You'll need adapters for two-pronged outlets, which are used for both types of current. Be very careful to make sure your appliance can take a 220 voltage (usually stated somewhere on the casing) before you plug it in.

ENTRY REQUIREMENTS

American citizens must have a tourist visa, which can be purchased before arriving or at ports of entry. Requirements are fairly complex, so the latter is not recommended. At the time of this writing, Americans entering Bolivia must pay $150 USD for a tourist visa and are required to receive the yellow fever vaccine. If you want to stay longer than your 30 days, you have the option of overstaying your visa and being fined (Bs)10 for each extra day you stay, purchasing a 30-day extension for (Bs)150, or hopping across the border into Peru and back with a new visa. Citizens of Australia, Canada, Switzerland, the United Kingdom, and New Zealand need only a valid passport, and receive a free 30-day visa upon arrival in Bolivia (it doesn't hurt to ask if they will extend it to 90).

HEALTH AND SAFETY

ALTITUDE Due to the high altitude in La Paz and Potosí, you may suffer from *soroche,* or altitude sickness, when you arrive. Symptoms include dizziness, fatigue, and shortness of breath. Avoid alcohol and coffee, drink lots of water, and rest as much as you can in the first few days. It is also recommended that you eat less than usual prior to and upon arrival. Do not take the soroche pills sold in pharmacies within Bolivia—they are a dangerous mix of chemicals banned in the United States and Europe. Symptoms usually disappear within a week. If they do not, consult a doctor, especially if you have a history of high blood pressure. *Mate de coca,* an herbal (and completely legal) tea made from coca leaves, can be very effective. Some higher-end hotels will administer oxygen to guests upon arrival. If you suffer from heart or lung diseases, or are pregnant, consult your doctor before traveling.

FOOD AND DRINK Although the higher areas of Bolivia are relatively free of bacteria, lower altitudes harbor some really dangerous strains. To play it safe, do not drink tap water and order beverages without ice. Avoid eating food from street vendors. You can find most of the things you want to try in restaurants and cafés for a slightly higher price. If you buy on the street or from a market, take the U.S. Center for Disease Control and Prevention's advice: "Boil it, cook it, peel it, or forget it."

OTHER PRECAUTIONS At present, only Americans are required to receive the yellow fever vaccine, costing approximately $150 USD and valid for 10 years. Don't get one from the health centers in Bolivia—they are not recognized internationally. The northern and eastern areas of the country, especially jungle regions, are more prone to yellow fever epidemics. No other shots or vaccination certificates are required for entering Bolivia, although all travelers will need a yellow fever vaccine if moving on to countries such as Brazil. If you'll be spending time in remote areas, ask your doctor about typhoid, hepatitis A and B, and tetanus vaccinations. If you're headed for the Amazon, consider antimalarial prophylactics.

Bring plenty of sunblock—the high altitudes feel cool, but the sun will burn you within minutes due to the thin atmosphere. Wear sunglasses and a hat as much as possible. The trek across Isla del Sol can be particularly brutal since the open landscape is void of shade. In the winter, humidity in La Paz can drop to 0%, and your skin and eyes can get very uncomfortable, so use moisturizing cream and drops if necessary.

Be careful with dogs—in the cities they are friendly, but be very wary in rural areas. Usually picking up a stone is enough to warn them off. Rabies is a real risk in Bolivia, so if you're bitten by anything see a doctor immediately.

SAFETY Crime is not a major problem in Bolivia compared to other Latin American countries, but it's increasing both in frequency and seriousness. In larger cities such as La Paz, Cochabamba, Sucre, and Santa Cruz, street crime—including pickpocketing, mugging, and purse-snatching—is on the rise. Avoid wearing flashy jewelry and watches, and be aware of your surroundings at all times, especially in busy plazas and on jam-packed buses. Carry only as much cash as necessary when in the city, especially in crowded market areas. When walking through busy cities

10

such as La Paz, carry a copy of your passport rather than the original since passport theft is common. Exercise special caution around bus terminals, where there have been several kidnappings and even murders of tourists. Don't trust any "policemen" who ask to see your papers: be assertive, don't let them search you, and walk away fast. Never take an unmarked taxicab, especially in the Cementario area of La Paz. For public transport, use "radio taxis" (they have a telephone number on a sign on the roof), public buses and minibuses, or the fixed-route, shared *trufis*. For further advice, the best sources are the British Embassy's Travel Advice at ⊕ *www.fco.gov.uk* and the U.S. Department of State's Country Specific Information at ⊕ *www.travel.state.gov*.

LANGUAGE

Spanish is the predominant language in the cities, and Bolivian Spanish is one of the easiest on the continent to understand. Quechua and Aymara are spoken by highlanders who may or may not also speak Spanish, while Guaraní is spoken in some parts of the Amazonian basin. Hotel staffs usually have some knowledge of English, French, or German. Learning a few words of Spanish will go down well—in many places people will assume you can speak it.

MONEY MATTERS

The unit of currency is the boliviano, which can be divided into 100 centavos. Bolivianos come in bills of 5, 10, 20, 50, 100, and 200. Coins come in denominations of 10, 20, and 50 centavos and 1, 2 and 5 bolivianos. At this writing, the exchange rate was (Bs)7 to the U.S. dollar. Bolivians frequently refer to their currency as *pesos*.

You can change U.S. dollars and European currency in banks, *casas de cambio* (house of change), and on the street (not recommended). Most banks in Bolivia's larger cities have ATMs, but muggings at these have become more common, so be careful and never withdraw cash alone or at night.

Most major credit cards are accepted in most cities and towns in Bolivia, but only in established retail chains, hotels, and restaurants. American Express is generally unpopular. If you are traveling in a rural area, make sure to bring along enough cash and carry it in a variety of small denominations (coins and notes lower than 10 Bolivianos).

PHONES

The international code for Bolivia is 591. Dial the country code, then the departmental area code, then the seven-digit number. If you are calling from abroad, drop the "0" from the area code. Local codes for the departments are as follows: La Paz, Oruro, Potosí, 2; Santa Cruz, Beni, Pando, 3; Cochabamba, Tarija, Chuquisaca (Sucre), 4. To call a Bolivian mobile phone from abroad, use 591 and the mobile number.

Long-distance and international calls can be made from local offices of Entel, Cotel, and AXS. You'll find their offices everywhere. The least-expensive place to make international calls is at an Internet café through Skype or by purchasing a prepaid phone card.

Courtyard of Casa Real de Moneda in Potosi.

TAXES

Throughout Bolivia, a 13% value-added tax (IVA) is added to hotel and restaurant prices and to items purchased in some stores. If you are charged IVA, you should also be given a receipt or *factura*. It's worth asking for a price *sin factura* (without a receipt) if you are bargaining, as this may mean paying less. Street vendors work strictly in cash.

TIPPING

Bolivia is not a tipping culture, but expect to pay for small favors and "help" everywhere. In restaurants, a tip of 5% to 10% is in order if you are happy with the service. Taxi drivers do not expect tips unless you hire them for the day, in which case 10% is appropriate. Airport porters expect (Bs)5 per baggage cart they handle. Shoeshine boys, who pop up out of the cracks in the pavement on every corner, will try to charge you 10 times the going rate of (Bs)1—their roguish smiles may persuade you to tip more. If someone offers to watch your car, best to accept or they will steal it instead—again, (Bs)1 is standard for this "service."

RESTAURANTS AND HOTELS

CUISINE Bolivia is one of the least-expensive countries in South America for travelers. A meal at a basic restaurant should cost no more than (Bs)20, and even at the most elegant restaurants you can eat well for less than (Bs)50.

Bolivian cuisine is healthy, wholesome, and satisfying, if lacking the finer touch. Cheaper eateries go for quantity as much as quality, so avoid over-ordering. Soups make a complete meal in themselves, loaded with meat, potatoes, vegetables, and quinoa. Look out for the peanut soup—it'll change your ideas about nuts. Fresh trout from Lake Titicaca is fried, stuffed, steamed, grilled, spiced, or covered in a rich sauce. Another excellent, delicate fish from the lake is *pejerrey,* which is especially good in *cebiche,* a cold marinated fish dish often eaten midmorning. Set lunch—*almuerzo* or *almuerzo executivo*—is always good value, whether it's in a fancy restaurant or from a market stall. Many meals are served with a spicy sauce called *llajwa,* made from the local hot peppers. It comes in various shades, and you'll soon be addicted.

In the highlands, where carbohydrates are the dietary mainstay, they freeze-dry potatoes, then soak them overnight and boil them. The result, *chuño* and *tunta,* is then used to accompany main dishes. Other traditional fare includes *asado de* llama, roast llama, and *pique macho,* beef grilled with hot peppers, chopped tomatoes, and onions, often served with fried potatoes and gravy. Snacks include *saltenas* and *tucumanas,* pastries filled with meat, chicken, or vegetables. Eating these without having them explode all over your clothes takes skill, so watch how the locals do it. Over your Sunday newspaper you can try *api,* a delicious hot grain drink served with deep-fried pastries.

ACCOM-
MODATIONS
With growing competition for tourist dollars, there has been a push to upgrade older hotels, and, where possible, to build new ones. The style, however, remains very Bolivian, and unless you are paying top dollar you need to be flexible and, to a certain extent, accept what you get. There is now a wider range of accommodations, from cozy guesthouses to luxury resorts. Eco-resorts are on the rise, although you may form your own opinion about how green some of them really are. There are also growing numbers of backpacker hostels, mostly run by foreigners; the standards may be better, but you may not appreciate the frat-house atmosphere. Many hotels have two pricing systems—one for Bolivians and one for foreigners. Even if you are in the latter category, good accommodations can be found for $15 USD or less, particularly away from the cities. The most expensive luxury hotels are more pricey, at $120–$150 USD per night for a double. Do not be afraid to ask to see the room in advance—it's common practice in Bolivia—and take your time when you do. Unless you are staying in a warmer climate area such as Coroico, air conditioning is pretty much unheard of. Make sure your room has a heater instead.

WHAT IT COSTS IN BOLIVIANOS				
	¢	$	$$	$$$	$$$$
Restaurants	under (Bs)10	(Bs)10–(Bs)20	(Bs)21–(Bs)50	(Bs)51–(Bs)90	over (Bs)90
Hotels	under (Bs)30	(Bs)30–(Bs)100	(Bs)101–(Bs)300	(Bs)301–(Bs)700	over (Bs)700

Restaurant prices are based on the median main course price at dinner. Hotel prices are for two people in a standard double room with bathroom in high season.

VISITOR INFORMATION

At this writing there are no official tourist information offices outside La Paz. The InfoTur offices—a new state initiative—are well stocked with information, leaflets, and brochures. You can find them at the airports in La Paz (☎ *02/211–2008*), Santa Cruz (☎ *03/336–9595*), and Uyuni (☎ *02/262–2102*). You can also check out the growing range of dedicated Web sites, such as ⊕ *www.bolivianet.com* or ⊕ *www. bolivianweb.com*.

LA PAZ

Perched on the edge of the altiplano, La Paz overlooks a landscape of great—if stark—beauty. If you fly into Aeropuerto Internacional El Alto, the plateau breaks without warning and reveals the deep, jagged valley that cradles the town. At dusk, as the sun sets on the bare flat-lands that surround La Paz, a reddish glow envelops the city's greatest landmark: the towering, snow-capped peaks of Illimani.

The city is nestled in a bowl-shape valley and ranges in altitude from 10,168 to 13,450 feet above sea level. The altitude might make things difficult at first, but it also ensures that La Paz is free of heat and humidity, and devoid of mosquitoes and other pesky insects.

Nearly half of La Paz's 1.3 million residents and most of its indigenous inhabitants live in poorly constructed adobe and brick homes on a barren plateau called El Alto, which has grown so much it is now a separate city with 800,00 residents. Downtown La Paz is more cosmopolitan, and the south of the city, the Zona Sur, is extremely European in flavor.

GETTING HERE AND AROUND

Taxis are the quickest alternative for getting to and from the airport. The current going rate for the 30- to 45-minute journey is around (Bs)50—use a taxi from the rank and you won't be overcharged. Mini-buses also service the airport. The cost is approximately (Bs)3.8, but it's rather a rough introduction to La Paz.

Within the city, taxis and *trufis* (shared route taxis), identifiable from the destination sign lodged in the windshield, are cheap and plentiful and can be found lining up in the cemetery district. Expect to pay less than (Bs)3 for most trips within the city center. Terminal de Buses (the main terminal) is located just north of La Paz at Plaza Antofagasta on Avenida Uruguay and offers transportation to areas south and east of the city. Newer radio taxis, identified by the illuminated sign on the roof, are the safest option for tourists. Rates are fixed at (Bs)8 to (Bs)20, depending on the length of your journey. Cheaper are *micros*, 12-seat minivans that travel roughly the same bus routes. They're quicker and more comfortable, especially if you get the front seat. Listen carefully before you board, as destinations are shouted out the window as the vehicles roll through the city. Better yet, ask a local to help you locate the right one. Both trufis and micros do regular routes and stop at request if hailed down.

10

GREAT ITINERARIES

It is possible to see many of the most memorable sites in Bolivia in 15 days, but you need to fly at certain stages due to the huge distances, and it's best to start low and work your way up so that you minimize the effects of altitude.

Start in Santa Cruz. From here fly northeast to the jungle town of Trinidad for a three-day float trip on the Río Mamoré aboard the flotel Reina Enin. The flotel is essentially a large barge with cabins on it; during the day, as you drift, you stop at little villages along the river. Return to Santa Cruz and then fly on to the colonial town of Sucre. Spend the fifth day touring its well-ordered colonial streets and museums. Make sure to visit the market in nearby Tarabuco if you're there on a Sunday. On your sixth day, take a bus southwest to the colonial mining town of Potosí. Remember to take it easy when you get here, as it's very high up. Take a walking tour of the city and visit its churches and museums. On Day 7, take a bus to Oruro. Don't hang about here, but take the overnight train to the Salar de Uyuni. Drive out onto the Salar and stay the night in the salt hotel, then retrace your

steps back to Uyuni, Oruro, and then on to La Paz. On your 10th day, visit La Paz's outdoor markets in the morning and then head out to see the Valley of the Moon in the afternoon, or just amble along the Prado avenue and people-watch. Visit the fascinating ruins of Tiwanaku on the 11th day, then the same day head to Huatajata on Lake Titicaca and spend the night at one of the hotels there. On the 12th day, catch the early hydrofoil to Isla del Sol to see its sparkling beaches and Inca ruins and spend the night. Wake up for the dawn if you can. On the 13th day, catch the boat back to Copacabana. Have a look at the church, grab a final view of the lake from the Cavalry, then get a bus back to La Paz.

For those coming to Bolivia for a side trip from Peru, the most convenient areas to visit are La Paz and Lake Titicaca's villages and islands. From Puno (on the Peru side of Lake Titicaca) travel three hours by bus across the border into Bolivia. Copacabana makes a good base. You can catch a boat to Isla del Sol and Lake Titicaca's surrounding villages. La Paz is 71 km (44 mi) east.

Because La Paz is so compact, visiting the city's main sights would seem easy; however, add time if you're walking or climbing the hills and taking frequent breaks to assuage the effects of the altitude. You'll need a couple of days for a thorough exploration, but don't worry about getting lost—if you do, just go down the hill and you'll reach the main avenue eventually.

SAFETY AND PRECAUTIONS

Safety never used to be a problem in La Paz, but things are changing, and unfortunately a lot of crime now is directed at tourists. This is unlikely to go any further than opportunistic theft, especially bag-snatching or pickpocketing, but at night and in certain areas it can be worse, particularly around large concentrations of tourists. Be especially careful around Sagárnaga and San Francisco church, and at the Cementario bus terminal, where there have been several cases of kidnappings of tourists. In general, avoid obvious shows of wealth and tourist status such as expensive cameras, keep an eye on your bags at all times, look like you know where you are going, and be aware of what is happening around you. Never visit ATMs alone. A common scam is for somebody to surreptitiously spray something on you, then help you clean it off, taking everything you have in the process. The latest scheme is for thieves dressed as police to demand your passport and money. Do not walk around town with your passport and only carry the amount of money you plan to spend while you're out. Leave valuables at the hotel and only carry photocopies of official documents. Be very cautious when using taxis at night—always look for radio taxis or trufis (⇨ *see the section on safety earlier in the chapter*). This said, La Paz remains in general a safe city and a relief for travelers arriving from other South American countries; a few basic precautions just make this all the more enjoyable.

ESSENTIALS

Buses Trans El Dorado (✉ *Terminal de Buses* ☎ *02/235-9153*). **Transporte 20 de Octubre** (✉ *Calle Yanacachi 1434* ☎ *02/231-7391*).

Bus Terminal Terminal de Buses (✉ *Av. Perú* ☎ *02/236-7275*).

Embassies United States (✉ *Av. Arce 2780, Casilla 425, La Paz* ☎ *02/216-8000* ⊕ *www.usembassy.gov*). **British** (✉ *Av. Arce 2732, La Paz* ☎ *02/243-3424*).

Mail Federal Express (✉ *Calle Capitán Ravelo 2401* ☎ *02/244-3437*). **La Paz Post Office** (✉ *Av. Mariscal Santa Cruz at Calle Oruro*).

Rental Cars Hertz (✉ *Av. Heroes del Km 7 #777* ☎ *02/280-0675*). **Kolla Motors Ltda.** (✉ *Calle Rosendo Gutierrez 502* ☎ *02/241-9141*). **Imbex** (✉ *Av. Montes 522* ☎ *02/231-6895*).

Taxis Servisur (☎ *02/279—9999*). **Magnifico del Sur** (☎ *02/275—1212*). **Uriarte** (☎ *777-60666*).

Train National Railroad Line (✉ *Fernando Guachilla 494, La Paz* ☎ *02/241-6545* ⊕ *www.fca.com.bo*).

Tour Operators America Tours SRL (✉ *Av. 16 de Julio 1490* ☎ *02/237-4204* ⊕ *www.america-ecotours.com*). **Fremen Tours** (✉ *Calle Pedro Salazar 537* ☎ *02/241-7062* ⊕ *www.andes-amazonia.com*). **Magri Turismo** (✉ *Calle Capitán Ravelo 2101* ☎ *02/244-2727* ⊕ *www.magriturismo.com*). **Turisbus** (✉ *Ave. Illampu #704, La Paz* ☎ *02/245-1341* ⊕ *www.turisbus.com*).

10

EXPLORING

Heading into La Paz from the airport, the city's main thoroughfare changes names several times: Avenida Ismael Montes, Avenida Mariscal Santa Cruz, El Prado, Avenida 16 de Julio, and Avenida Villazón. The street, a colorful blur of trees, flowers, and monuments, is often clogged with pedestrians and vendors, especially on weekends. On Sunday it's blocked off to traffic completely. At the end of the Prado, the street splits into Avenida 6 de Agosto and Avenida Arce, which lead to the residential areas of San Jorge and Sopocachi, where many of La Paz's

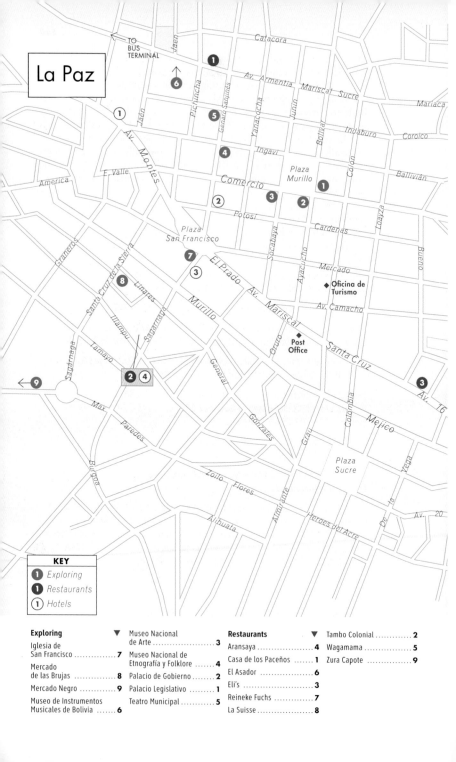

La Paz

KEY
- ① *Exploring*
- ① *Restaurants*
- ① *Hotels*

Exploring ▼

Iglesia de
San Francisco **7**

Mercado
de las Brujas **8**

Mercado Negro **9**

Museo de Instrumentos
Musicales de Bolivia **6**

Museo Nacional
de Arte **3**

Museo Nacional de
Etnografía y Folklore **4**

Palacio de Gobierno **2**

Palacio Legislativo **1**

Teatro Municipal **5**

Restaurants ▼

Aransaya **4**

Casa de los Paceños **1**

El Asador **6**

Eli's **3**

Reineke Fuchs **7**

La Suisse **8**

Tambo Colonial **2**

Wagamama **5**

Zura Capote **9**

0   350 yards

0   350 meters

Pando

Corrales

Plaza Uyuni

Panama

Av. Carrasco

Busch

Olympic Stadium

Pinilla

Av. Illimani

Av.

Romero

Saavedra

Saracho

Av. Simón Bolívar

Parque

J. Manuel Loza

Río

Central

Choqueyapu

Roosevelt

de Julio

⑥
⑤

Plaza Del Estudiante

Zapata

④ ⑦

Cinemateca ◆

Cap Ravelo

de Octubre

Av. 6 de Agosto

Av. Arce

Guachalla

⑥ – ⑨
⑧   ⑨

➎

TO VALLE DE LA LUNA →

Av. Ecuador

TO ZONA SUR ↘

Hotels   ▼

The Adventure Brew Hostel **1**

Camino Real Suites **8**

Casa Grande **9**

Hostal Naira **3**

Hotel Europa **6**

Hotel Gloria **2**

Hotel Plaza **5**

Hotel Rosario **4**

Radisson Plaza Hotel **7**

bars and restaurants are located. Continue down the hill on 6 de Agosto and you will eventually reach Obrajes and the Zona Sur.

PLAZA MURILLO

Plaza Murillo and the streets that surround it in the downtown area of the city are steeped in history and easy to cover in a morning of wandering. The original square dates from 1549, the year after the city was founded. Renovated in 1870, the charm of the plaza makes it fun just to sit and watch the world—and the occasional marching band—go by. Nearby you'll find the city's grand governmental buildings and some of its most beautiful churches, as well as the picturesque Calle Jaén.

TOP ATTRACTIONS

⑥ Museo de Instrumentos Musicales de Bolivia. This museum, founded by local musician Ernesto Cavour, is the most complete collection of musical instruments in the nation; if you think it's all *charangos* and *quenas*, you haven't seen half of what Bolivian music has to offer. Seven rooms feature percussion, string, and wind instruments used in the various regions of Bolivia. There is a special section where children can play ancient instruments made from such materials as wood, bone, turtle shells, and toucan beaks. ⊠ *Calle Jaén 711, Casa de la Cruz Verde* ☎ *02/240–8177* ⌸ *(Bs)5* ⊙ *Daily 9:30–1, 2:30–6:30.*

Fodor'sChoice
★
☾

③ Museo Nacional de Arte. Commissioned by a Spanish noble in 1775, the National Art Museum holds three stories of paintings and sculpture. The first floor is devoted to contemporary foreign artists; the second to works by Melchor Pérez Holguín, considered to be the master of Andean colonial art; and the third to a permanent collection of Bolivian artists. You can also relax in the central courtyard beside the lovely alabaster fountain. ⊠ *Plaza Murillo at Calle Comercio, Zona Central (Downtown)* ☎ *02/240–8600* ⊕ *www.mna.org.bo* ⌸ *(Bs)10* ⊙ *Tues.– Sat. 9–12:30 and 3–6:30, Sun. 9:30–12:30.*

④ Museo Nacional de Etnografía y Folklore. Housed in an ornate 18th-century building, the National Museum of Ethnography and Folklore exhibits feathers, masks, and weavings from indigenous peoples. It has permanent displays on the Ayoreos, who live in the Amazon region, and the Chipayas, who come from the surrounding altiplano. ⊠ *Calle Ingavi 916, Zona Central* ☎ *02/240–8640* ⊕ *www.musef.org.bo* ⌸ *(Bs)15* ⊙ *Tues.–Fri. 9–12:30 and 3–7, Sat. 9–4:30, Sun. 9–12:30.*

② Palacio de Gobierno. The imposing Presidential Palace was guarded by tanks and machine gun-toting soldiers until 1982, when the constitutional government was restored following a 1979 coup and three years of military rule. Presidential guards now watch the front door instead. In front of the palace is a statue of former president Gualberto Villarroel. In 1946 a mob stormed the building and dragged Villarroel to the square, where he was hanged from a lamppost. The structure, which is closed to the public, is also known as Palacio Quemado (Burned Palace), because it has twice been gutted by fire. ⊠ *Plaza Murillo, Zona Central (Downtown).*

CLOSE UP

Beverages of Bolivia

Even if you're just after a tipple, sipping a glass of wine or having a cool one at high altitude can have a cost. Nonetheless, once you are acclimatized, there are some interesting beverages to sample.

BEER

Each major city still has its own brewery, generally founded by Germans who emigrated here at the same time as they came to the United States, and microbreweries have started to pop up. There's also the CBN, the national beer company. As well as their standard brew, Paceña in La Paz often has special labels, which are always worth trying. Sureña in Sucre is a good bet. Avoid the Carnival beer, Bock—it has more alcohol than Carnival spirit.

LIQUOR

For something a little different, try *singani,* the local liquor. It's best in the potent pisco sour made with lime juice or the slightly smoother *chuflay,* made with ginger ale. *Chicha* is a grain alcohol locals concoct by chewing maize, spitting out the resulting mash, adding water, and allowing the mixture to ferment. The sweet, rather cloudy result is drunk mainly in the lowland valleys in and around Cochabamba, and tastes a lot better than it sounds, once you forget how it's made.

WINE

Tarija, in the Andean foothills near the Argentine border, is Bolivia's wine-growing area. Grapes grow here at 2,000 meters above sea level and the wines have been produced since the early 17th century. The major producers are La Concepcion and Kohlberg, although you can also buy good unlabeled wines in the *bodegas.* Tarija's Malbec and Cabernet Sauvignon have won international medals.

WORTH NOTING

1 **Palacio Legislativo.** The meeting place for Bolivia's Congress, the Legislative Palace was built in 1905. This imposing classical structure has a visitor's gallery where you can observe the legislators in session, which is more entertaining that it sounds. Not all meetings are open to the public and you must show your passport to enter. ⊠ *Plaza Murillo, Zona Central (Downtown)* 🎫 *Free* ⊙ *Weekdays 9–noon and 2:30–5.*

5 **Teatro Municipal.** A handsome building both inside and out as a result of an extensive restoration, the Municipal Theater regularly stages traditional dance and music, as well as classical music performances and theater. Check the sign outside the theater or the newspaper for upcoming events. ⊠ *Calle Genaro Sanjinés 629, Zona Central (Downtown)* 📞 *No phone.*

PLAZA SAN FRANCISCO

This broad plaza just south of Avenida Mariscal Santa Cruz is the city's cultural heart. Indigenous people come to hawk all sorts of handicrafts, as well as more prosaic goods, such as CDs, watches, and electrical gadgets. If you're lucky, you'll see a wedding at the beautiful Iglesia de San Francisco. Behind this plaza is a network of narrow cobblestone

10

Bolivian History

Almost everywhere in Bolivia you'll stumble across reminders of the country's long, eventful, and tragic history. A civilization said to be more advanced than the Inca thrived in Bolivia sometime between 1600 BC and AD 1200 in an area 74 km (46 mi) west of La Paz called Tiwanaku. It's considered by many to be the "cradle of the American civilizations." When the Inca arrived, the city was already in ruins, destroyed by a drought. Spanish conquistadors conquered the Inca civilization in the 1500s—their stay has left its mark, particularly in Sucre and Potosí.

From its earliest days, Bolivia's fortunes have risen and fallen with its mineral wealth. Centuries ago it was the Inca and Aymara who dug deep for precious silver. In the 17th century, Spain's colonization of South America was fueled largely by the vast amounts of silver hidden deep in Cerro Rico, the "Rich Hill" that towers over Potosí in southern Bolivia. Cerro Rico's seemingly inexhaustible lode, first discovered in 1545, quickly brought thousands of prospectors to what was at the time the greatest mining operation in the New World. During the 17th and 18th centuries Potosí was the most populous and wealthiest city in the Americas. For

the Spanish, the phrase *"vale un Potosí"* ("worth a Potosí") became a favorite description for untold wealth. But there's a darker side to the story. Some 8 million indigenous Quechua people died in the mines after being forced to stay inside the airless tunnels for as long as six months. Even today, men who work in the mines have far shorter than average life spans and suffer the same fate as their ancestors.

Bolivia was named in honor of its liberator, Simón Bolívar, who proclaimed the country's independence from Spain in 1825; until then, it had been simply called Alto Peru. The country was once much, much larger than it is today, but losing wars has been a costly habit. It originally extended to the Pacific, but after rich deposits of nitrates were discovered in the Atacama Desert, Chile began to eye the region. During the War of the Pacific that broke out in 1879, Chile captured Bolivia's short stretch of coastline, leaving the country landlocked. Bolivia stubbornly believes that someday it will once again have a seaport. In addition, Bolivia lost 38,000 square miles when Brazil annexed a large part of the Amazon basin in 1903, then twice as much again after a dispute with Paraguay in 1935.

streets full of tourism agencies, craft shops, the Mercado de las Brujas (Witches' Market), bars, and hostels. Try to do your shopping away from Sagárnaga Street, the heart of backpacker land.

❼ **Iglesia de San Francisco.** Considered one of the finest examples of Spanish-

Fodor's Choice colonial architecture in South America, the carved facade of the 1549

★ Church of San Francisco is adorned with birds of prey, ghoulish masks, pinecones, and parrots—a combination of Spanish and Indian motifs created by local artisans who borrowed heavily from the style then popular in Spain. Crafts stalls line the church wall; most days you'll find colorful weavings and handmade musical instruments. Climb the

narrow stairs to the roof for great views of downtown La Paz, or stay grounded in the café inside the church. ⊠ *El Prado at Calle Sagárnaga.*

8 Mercado de las Brujas. On Calle Linares, just off bustling Calle Sagárnaga, you'll find the Witches' Market, where indigenous women in tall bowler hats sell lucky charms, curses, medicinal herbs, and ingredients for powerful potions. You can have your fortune told through the reading of coca leaves, or if you are building a new house, you can buy a dried llama fetus to bury in the yard for good luck. Although this market is internationally recognized, it is not the best place to find gifts for the folks back home.

9 Mercado Negro. Near the intersection of Calle Max Paredes and Calle Graneros, the streets are filled with peddlers hawking clothing, handcrafts, and household goods. Tucked into alleys and courtyards are *tambos* (thatch or tin roof structures meaning "place of rest") where you can purchase oranges, bananas, and coca leaves. The leaf is chewed by farmers and miners (and tourists) to ward off hunger and the effects of the altitude.

WHERE TO EAT

La Paz restaurants are becoming increasingly cosmopolitan, and though there is still a lack of sophistication in dining out, the range is improving. Alongside a vast array of establishments serving traditional Bolivian fare, you can now choose between a small but excellent handful of sushi restaurants, get thoroughly carnivorous at one of the many Argentinean grill houses, go upmarket with new Swiss/Bolivian cuisine, or splash out on traditional dishes from the old country, Spain. The area around Plaza del Estudiante and the residential neighborhood of Sopocachi have a good selection of cheap eating. For a more international and expensive experience, head down to the southern area of the city, where you will also find the café-terrace set lounging around. Wherever you go, look out for the *almuerzo* if you're after a good-value set lunch.

$$$$
LATIN AMERICAN
Fodor'sChoice
★
✗**Aransaya.** From its location on the penthouse floor of the Radisson Plaza Hotel, this upscale, formal restaurant gives diners spectacular views of the city. The presentation of the Bolivian and international cuisines is excellent, and so is the service, but be prepared to wait for your dinner. One of the most requested dishes is the milanesa de lagostinos. This is a great place to impress your guests. ⊠ *Av. Arce 2177* ☎ *02/244–1111* ⊟ *AE, MC, V.*

$$
LATIN AMERICAN
✗**Casa de los Paceños.** Get the real Bolivian eating experience at this fancier version of all those cheap restaurants you see downtown. Tucked inside a colonial building, this traditional eatery serves such daring dishes as *ranga* (cow's stomach) and *ají de lengua* (cow's tongue with chili sauce). For something a bit more familiar, request the grilled chicken, pork, or steak. Unfortunately the real Bolivian experience here includes the service, which is dismal. Be patient, because the food, especially the *chairo* soup, is very good. For live music and patio seating, visit their second location in South La Paz. ⊠ *Av. Sucre 856* ☎ *02/228–0995* ⊟ *AE, MC, V.*

$$$
ARGENTINE

✗ **El Asador.** Eat anything you can cut off a cow at this Argentine-owned grill in the south of the city. There's also chicken, fish, and pork, all served on sizzling hot plates. Fast, efficient service, generous portions, and cheap prices, which include side dishes, make this a popular weekend eatery. ⊠ *Av. Montenegro 740, Zona Sur* ☎ *02/279–1962* ▤ *MC, V.*

$$
AMERICAN

✗ **Eli's.** There are branches of this cheap and cheerful American-style diner all over the city but the oldest, opened in 1942, is inside the Monje Campero cinema. You may not spot James Dean huddled over a coffee in a booth, but he'll certainly be up on the wall with a thousand other stars, none of them as old as the waiters. This is a great spot to grab an ice cream Sunday after strolling down Avenida El Prado or catching a movie next door. The huge menu features pasta, sandwiches, and desserts and the prices are extremely reasonable. ⊠ *Av. El Prado 1495* ☎ *02/239–295* ▤ *MC, V.*

$$$
LATIN AMERICAN

✗ **La Suisse.** Don't be fooled by the Swiss-chalet frontage and the name, this is modern Bolivian cuisine at its best. It may feel like you're sitting inside a cuckoo clock, but the dining is excellent. Try sticking with the starters and get a range of things to try, or fork out on a llama steak and a fondue (cheese, meat, and chocolate) to follow. They also serve rösti (Swiss potato dish) and paella. It's the place to go for birthdays, anniversaries, and funerals, so book your table. ⊠ *Av. Muñoz Reyes 1710* ☎ *02/279–3160* ▤ *MC, V.*

$$$
GERMAN

✗ **Reineke Fuchs.** Monster sausages, spaetzle, mustard, and brown bread, towering glasses of *weisbier*—you'll get the whole German experience at this popular restaurant, with branches in the center and the south of the city. Imbibe cautiously: the drinks will leave you with a sore head, and wallet. ⊠ *Pasaje Jauregui 2241 (Downtown)* ☎ *02/277–2103* ⊕ *www.reinekefuchs.com* ▤ *AE, MC, V.*

$$$
LATIN AMERICAN
Fodor's Choice
★

✗ **Tambo Colonial.** Located on the second floor of Hotel Rosario, this cozy restaurant means "a place to gather and barter local products." In this case, the bartering means reasonable prices for exceptional cuisine including almond-crusted trout with orange rice or grilled llama served with a creamy mustard sauce. Meals begin with a salad bar of fresh vegetables, which is somewhat of a rarity in the city. The presentations are beautiful and the portions just right. Romantics might want to sit in the candlelit brick room at the back of the restaurant. Bring your camera (and sweet tooth) for the chocolate mousse with sorbet—it's truly a work of art. ⊠ *Av. Lllampu 704, Hotel Rosario La Paz* ☎ *02/2451 658* ⊕ *www.hotelrosario.com* ☾ *No lunch* ▤ *MC, V.*

$$$$
JAPANESE

✗ **Wagamama.** The specialty is fresh trout from Lake Titicaca cooked Japanese style, but the sushi and noodle dishes are excellent, too, and the hot plate is noisy fun. The chicken teriyaki is highly recommended. ⊠ *Pasaje Pinilla 2557, off Av. Arce, 1 block downhill from Plaza Isabel la Católica* ☎ *02/243–4911* ▤ *MC, V* ☾ *Closed Sun.*

$$$
SPANISH

✗ **Zurracapote.** You'd think you were back in the old country at this high-concept Spanish restaurant, and that includes the prices. The wine menu is probably the best in La Paz. Avoid the main dishes—which can be insipid—and choose a selection of tapas and a good Chilean or Argentinean wine. The octopus in garlic butter is a memorable starter, as are the stewed squid and *sopa marinera* (seafood in coconut milk).

10

Save room for the mouthwatering Crema Catalana, the Catalan version of crème brûlée. ⊠ *Calle Federico B., 28B* ☎ *02/211–9788* ☰ *MC, V.*

WHERE TO STAY

Although the number of rooms in La Paz increases every year, hotels are often booked solid during holidays and festivals. Make reservations at least a month in advance when possible. Inexpensive hotels and hostels tend to be located near Calle Sagárnaga.

$$ ☷ **The Adventure Brew Hostel.** Probably the most notable of the recent crop of backpacker hostels staggering drunkenly onto the Bolivian hotel market, this well-run establishment just down from the bus station offers good services—including an on-site microbrewery—and the usual crop of free offers. Tasty food includes a pancake breakfast and nightly barbecues on the rooftop. You do need to pay for a room in advance by credit card if booking through hostelworld.com, which may not be entirely convenient. **Pros:** really well-informed staff; Saya microbrew and rooftop bar; social setting. **Cons:** located on a very busy road; private rooms often full; endless partying. ⊠ *Av. Montes 533* ☎ *02/246–1614* ⊕ *www.theadventurebrewhostel.com* ⚡ In-room: no a/c. In-hotel: restaurant, bar, Wi-Fi hotspot, laundry facilities ☰ *MC, V* ⦙◉⦙ *BP.*

$$ ☷ **Camino Real Suites.** Located in the quieter south zone, this hotel is situated at a lower elevation (3,200 meters/10,500 feet above sea level) than downtown La Paz, which makes adjusting to the altitude somewhat more bearable. Unlike many La Paz hotels that claim a five-star rating, here you'll find true luxuries like soundproof windows, free Wi-Fi, air-conditioned rooms, a large spa, and a beautiful breakfast buffet. Rooms are modern and spacious, each with a plasma TV and workstation. Since the hotel is circular in shape, every room has a panoramic view of the Andes Mountains and surrounding neighborhood. The hotel also has its own fleet of taxis that will take you to the center of La Paz (20 min drive) for (Bs)15. **Pros:** excellent service; great dinner menu; lower elevation. **Cons:** slightly outside of downtown; circular lobby can get noisy due to the acoustics. ⊠ *Av. Ballivian 369 and Calle 10, Calacoto, Zona Sur* ☎ *02/279–2323* ⊕ *www.caminoreal.com.bo* ⚡ *70 rooms* ⚡ In-room: a/c, safe, Wi-Fi (some). In-hotel: restaurant, room service, bar, gym, pool, spa, laundry service, Internet terminal, Wi-Fi hotspot, parking (free) ☰ *AE, MC, V* ⦙◉⦙ *BP.*

$$$$ ☷ **Casa Grande.** Prepare for pampering at this luxury property complete
Fodor's Choice with oxygen tanks, a golf course, personal laptops and cell phones, and
★ a staff of 60 to attend to just 36 rooms. Each apartment-like room has a small kitchen, lounge area, dining room, flat-screen TV, and iPod docking station. Refrigerators are stocked full of goodies and there's a wonderful grocery store across the street if you feel the urge to cook. The Jacuzzi-bathtubs are fantastic after a long day of traveling. **Pros:** airport shuttle; exceptional staff; great bathrooms. **Cons:** no central heating; outside of downtown La Paz. ⊠ *Av Ballivian No 1000; Calacoto 1132, Zona Sur* ☎ *02/279–5511* ⊕ *www.casa-grande.com.bo* ⚡ *36 rooms* ⚡ In-room: no a/c, safe, kitchen, refrigerator, DVD, Wi-Fi. In-hotel: res-

taurant, room service, bar, golf course, pool, gym, spa, laundry service, Internet terminal, Wi-Fi hotspot, parking (free) = *AE, MC, V* |O| *BP.*

$$ 🍴**Hostal Naira.** This charming and consistently popular hostel, whose bright, cheerful rooms surround a central courtyard, sits above the famous Peña Naira, where groups perform traditional folk music. There's always hot water—a luxury at this price range—and the service is excellent. This is the best deal in town with such amenities as cable TV, on-site computers, and a travel agency to organize your daily excursions. Rooms 204–207 have great views of Iglesia de San Francisco. **Pros:** gracious staff; clean rooms; on-site travel agency. **Cons:** the tourist-intense neighborhood can be tiring. ⊠ *Sagárnaga 161* ☎ *02/235–5645* ⊕ *www.hostalnaira.com* ↪ *22 rooms* ♿ *In-room: no a/c, safe, Wi-Fi. In-hotel: restaurant, room service, laundry facilities, Internet terminal, Wi-Fi hotspot* = *MC, V* |O| *BP.*

$$$$ 🍴**Hotel Europa.** The view of snowcapped Mt. Illimani from the rooftop garden sets this downtown hotel apart. There's original artwork by Gaston Ugalde on display in the lobby, and the restaurant does great breakfasts. Rooms have heated floors, flat-screen TVs, and large desks. Aside from that, it's a standard five-star range of facilities. Floors 6–9 are nonsmoking, and even-numbered rooms tend to be quieter since they are away from the neighboring school. The fitness center and pool are popular with expats. **Pros:** the crepes; the bar. **Cons:** tricky access; endless wedding receptions. ⊠ *Calle Tiahuanacu 64* ☎ *02/231–5656* ⊕ *www.hoteleuropa.com.bo* ↪ *110 rooms* ♿ *In-room: no a/c, safe, Wi-Fi. In-hotel: 2 restaurants, room service, bars, pool, gym, laundry service, Internet terminal, parking (free)* = *AE, MC, V* |O| *BP.*

$$$ 🍴**Hotel Gloria.** This friendly hotel a block from Plaza San Francisco has an inexpensive rooftop restaurant that specializes in national dishes and a ground-level restaurant that caters to vegetarians. Rooms are small but comfortable and have televisions mounted from the ceiling. Built in 1977, the hotel could use a renovation and soundproof windows, but if you are looking for a central location, this is the place. It also has a tour desk in the lobby. **Pros:** friendly staff; good location. **Cons:** street noise; some rooms smell of cigarette smoke; mediocre breakfast. ⊠ *Calle Potosí 909* ☎ *02/240–7070* ⊕ *www.hotelgloria.com.bo* ↪ *88 rooms, 2 suites* ♿ *In-room: no a/c, safe, Wi-Fi. In-hotel: 2 restaurants, bar, laundry service, Wi-Fi hotspot, parking (free)* = *AE, MC, V* |O| *BP.*

$$$$ 🍴**Hotel Plaza.** The rooftop restaurant and bar of this luxurious but now aging business hotel have excellent views of La Paz and the Andes. Ask for a room facing Mt. Illimani; besides good views, you'll have less noise from the street. **Pros:** as central as you can get. **Cons:** now rather aged; staff can be pretentious; hard to justify its five-star status. ⊠ *Av. 16 de Julio 1789* ☎ *02/237–8311* ⊕ *www.plazabolivia.com.bo* ↪ *175 rooms, 10 suites* ♿ *In-room: no a/c, Wi-Fi. In-hotel: 2 restaurants, bars, pool, gym, laundry service* = *AE, MC, V* |O| *CP.*

$$$ 🍴**Hotel Rosario.** This charming, Spanish-style hotel has had a complete makeover and expansion. The sunny courtyard has a fountain surrounded by clay pots overflowing with flowers and there is an Internet café on the third floor. Rooms are on the small side, but most

Fodor's Choice
★

10

Corruption

Like most developing countries, Bolivia has a serious corruption problem. Despite government efforts to take a hard line, the problem continues to run throughout society, from a traffic cop's request for "collaboration" to a government minister's filling up his offshore accounts with federal reserve. You may not notice anything if you are traveling light, but stay any length of time and you will have to deal with it.

You need to decide where you stand. Refuse to cooperate and pay nothing, and you will waste huge amounts of time wrestling with Bolivian bureaucracy—and you can never win against Bolivian bureaucracy. Dig into your pocket whenever you need to, and this will mean digging really deep once people realize you are ready to do this. You can take the middle ground—the average traffic policeman makes less than $200 a month, and your (Bs)1 "fine" for going the wrong way up a one-way street will help him put food on the table. It's your choice, but be aware of the impact either way.

have private baths and all are clean and bright; many have spectacular views of Chacaltaya. The restaurant serves excellent Bolivian dishes and offers a complimentary buffet breakfast. The travel agency, Turisbus, has an office in the lobby. **Pros:** the architecture; the no-smoking policy (unusual in La Paz); transportation to/from the sister hotel at the Lake. **Cons:** rough towels; limited toiletries; street noise. ⊠ *Calle Illampu 704* 📷 *02/245–1658 or 02/245–6634* ⊕ *www.hotelrosario.com* 🛏 *41 rooms, 1 suite* ⌂ *In-room: no a/c, safe, Wi-Fi. In-hotel: restaurant, laundry service* ▭ *AE, MC, V* ⏀ *BP.*

$$$$ 📺 **Radisson Plaza Hotel.** Yet another luxury hotel with great views. The focus at this high-rise business hotel not far from Plaza de los Estudiantes is on luxury and service. Upper-floor rooms have excellent views of the city and the surrounding mountains, as does the rather upscale rooftop restaurant. **Pros:** the genuine focus on clients; airport shuttle. **Cons:** rather antiseptic atmosphere and not very Bolivian. ⊠ *Av. Arce 2177* 📷 *02/244–1111, 800/333–3333 in U.S.* ⊕ *www.radisson.com/ lapazbo* 🛏 *239 rooms, 7 suites* ⌂ *In-room: no a/c, safe, Wi-Fi. In-hotel: 2 restaurants, bar, pool, gym, laundry service, Wi-Fi hotspot, parking (free)* ▭ *AE, MC, V.*

NIGHTLIFE

Bars and clubs open and close in La Paz in the blink of a llama's eyes, but some have stood the test of more than a couple of months of existence and are worth visiting, especially for live music. To check what's going on and what's still open, pick up a free weekly culture and nightlife guide, such as *Mañana Seguro* or *Afuera*.

BARS

Even if you are not a party animal, we recommend visiting a bar or two in La Paz. Most have a mixed, friendly crowd, play great music—often live—and are lots of fun. People go to socialize, dance, and celebrate the weekend, even if it's Monday.

Sopocachi, southeast of the Plaza de los Estudiantes, has the largest concentration of bars, many around Plaza Aboroa. Avoid spending too much time in the plaza, especially late at night—it gets a bit rough after midnight. **Mongo's Rock Bottom Cafe** (⌧ *Hermanos Manchego 2444* ☎ *02/244–0714*) has been around for years, but is still one of the most popular bars in town thanks to the music, often live, and the friendly mixed crowd of locals and tourists. It also has one of the most interesting menus in the city. Reserve first to avoid the squeeze. **RamJam** (⌧ *Presbiterio Medina 2421* ☎ *02/242–2295*) is newer, but with a similar vibe for a yuppy crowd: you can mix air with your liquor at the oxygen bar on the second floor of the bar.

Traffic (⌧ *Av. Arce 2549* ☎ *02/211–8033*) is probably the hippest bar in town once the music—techno, trance, and ambient—kicks off after 10. It attracts a young, relaxed dance crowd. **Diesel Nacional** (⌧ *Av. 20 de Octubre 2271* ☎ *02/242–3477*) is a high-concept bar up from Aboroa with friendly service and a quirky menu. You can remember your bohemian roots and gawk at La Paz's hippies at lovely old **Boca y Sapo** (⌧ *Indaburo 654*).

Well-to-do thirtysomethings hole up with '60s, '70s, and '80s music videos and pricey beer at **Capotraste** (⌧ *Av. Montenegro/Calle 18 San Miguel* ☎ *02/277–2856*). Take a look at their menus—every one is a classic rock album.

DANCE CLUBS

Forum (⌧ *Calle Víctor Sanjinés 2908* ☎ *02/232–5762*) is a cavernous club two blocks from Plaza España. It's frequented mainly by the under-20 set and American Marines. **Mongo's** (⌧ *Hermanos Manchego 2444* ☎ *02/235–3914*) turns into a lively club in the evening Thursday through Saturday, playing a blend of Latin dance and modern house and disco. Get there early or expect a long wait. This place is popular with tourists.

LIVE MUSIC

Almost every bar in La Paz plays live music, but if you want to see what's happening on the modern scene, try **Equinoccio** (⌧ *Av. Sanchez Lima 2191* ☎ *706–12413*). There is live jazz and a real jazz vibe almost every night at **Thelonius** (⌧ *20 de Octubre 2172* ☎ *02/242–4405*).

PEÑAS

Peñas are nightclubs that showcase traditional Bolivian music and dance. The energetic live performances—as popular with Paceños as they are with tourists—cost from $8 to $20 USD per person. Dinner is usually included. For authentic Bolivian music, **Peña Huari** (⌧ *Sagarnaga 339* ☎ *02/231–6225*) is one of the best. The cover is $15 USD and does not include dinner.

10

The most famous peña is **Peña Naira** (✉ *Sagarnaga 161* ☎ *02/232–5736*), near Plaza San Francisco. Shows are a bargain at $5 USD. **Casa del Corregidor** (✉ *Murillo 1040* ☎ *02/236–3633*) has performances most evenings.

THE ARTS

For concert, theater, and cinema listings, pick up a copy of the Spanish-language *La Prensa, La Razón,* or *El Diario.* Or grab a copy of one of the free weekly culture and nightlife guides, such as *Mañana Seguro* or *Afuera.* You'll find these in most bars and restaurants, and cultural centers such as the *Alliance Française* or the *Goethe-Institut.*

CINEMA

La Paz has a small selection of cinemas showing mainstream releases, but the best place to see both these and art-house stuff is at the **Cinemateca** (✉ *Calle Oscar Soria, casi esq. Rosendo Gutierrez* ☎ *02/244–4090* ⊕ *www.cinematecaboliviana.org*). As well as having the most comfortable seats and best equipment, it's also a library of Bolivian film and an exhibition space, the whole thing housed in a stunning new building.

GALLERIES

The **Galería Emusa** (✉ *Av. 16 de Julio 1607* ☎ *02/375–042*), in El Prado, hosts rotating exhibits of Bolivian sculpture and art. **Arte Unico** (✉ *Av. Arce 2895* ☎ *02/232–9238*) mounts varied exhibits. For modern work, try the **Arte Espacio Caf** (✉ *Av. Arce 2915* ☎ *02/243–3333*).

THEATER

The **Teatro Municipal** (✉ *Calle Genaro Sanjinés 629* ☎ *02/237–5275*) stages folk events and traditional music and dance concerts. It's worth going just to see the refurbished building. Check listings for upcoming events.

SHOPPING

MARKETS

Calle Sagárnaga, near Plaza San Francisco, is a good place to look for local handicrafts, Aymara embroidered shawls, and wool. Prices start at $15 USD and peak at more than $200 USD for those made of buttery-soft vicuña wool. Colorful *polleras,* the traditional skirts worn by indigenous women, are priced between $50 and $100 USD; bowler hats start at around $20 USD. Along the tiny streets that lead off to the right and left are numerous crafts shops. On Calle Linares, just off Calle Sagárnaga, you'll find the **Mercado de las Brujas**. The Witches' Market is where you'll find folk remedies and herbal treatments. For contemporary clothes, try the **Mercado Negro** on Calle Max Paredes. For the ultimate flea-market experience, visit the Feria 16 de Julio in El Alto on Thursday or Sunday. As one of the largest markets in the world, here you can buy anything from a forklift truck to a Kalishnikov rifle. There's no address, as it covers almost the whole city. Don't carry anything at all with you: pickpocketing is rife.

Shoppers peruse Mercado Uyustus in La Paz.

SPECIALTY SHOPS

Before you begin bargain hunting for alpaca sweaters, visit one or two stores to get an idea of what to look for. High-quality hand-knit designs that sell for around $100 USD here fetch three times that amount in the United States. The shops along Calle Sagárnaga, near Plaza San Francisco, are a good place to compare quality and price, but also venture into the streets above for better bargains.

Artesanías Sorata (⊠ *Calle Linares 862* ☎ *02/231–7701* ⊕ *www.artesaniasorata.com*) carries traditional alpaca knitwear with ethnic designs. **Casa Fisher** (⊠ *Av. Mariscal, Handal Center* ☎ *02/239–2946* ⊕ *www. casafisher.com*) is known for high-quality knits. One of the best places in town to buy reasonably priced *chompas,* colorful jackets made with traditional textiles, is **Coral** (⊠ *Calle Linares 836* ☎ *02/234–2599*).

If you are interested in Bolivian and South American art, music, and literature, then **Escaparate** (⊠ *Calle 21, 8446* ☎ *02/277–5700* ⊕ *www. boliviacultural.com*) is the best place in La Paz, if not the country. The collection is excellent, and there is usually an art exhibition in the store, too. They'll let you sit around for hours, and the owner speaks English.

10

SPORTS

SOCCER

Bolivians would be lost without their weekly soccer fix. Even the poorest, most remote villages have a playing field. Games are usually played on the only flat piece of land in town, so sheep and cows often graze on the field when there's not a match, and through-traffic may interrupt

Bolivian Crafts

Bolivia's rich selection of crafts includes silver jewelry, handwoven rugs, intricate embroidery, and traditional musical instruments such as the *quena* (flute) and *charango* (mandolin). You'll also find sweaters, gloves, scarves, and ponchos made from alpaca or llama wool. Both materials make for excellent fabrics. Crafts shops, like other types of business in Bolivia, are usually grouped together. In La Paz, for instance, most can be found on Calle Sagárnaga. It's always worth looking for cooperatives outside the capital, however. These sell traditional textiles made in rural areas, especially in the provinces of Chuquisaca and Potosí. The shawls, hats, and skirts worn by highland women are sold in most of the local markets and in some stores in La Paz, but shopkeepers sometimes refuse to sell some types of traditional garments to foreigners. However, the felt bowler hats are for sale everywhere, and make an interesting fashion statement back home. Due to the low level of tourism, souvenirs tend to be realistically priced. Although bargaining is expected in rural markets, many sellers will drop their prices only by small amounts, typically 5% to 10%. In general, stores are open from 10 AM to 7 PM Monday through Saturday, while street vendors can be found selling goods seven days a week. It is forbidden by law to export original pre-Columbian pieces, colonial silver plates, and colonial paintings.

proceedings. La Paz has three teams: Bolívar, La Paz FC, and the Strongest. All compete in the **Estadio Hernando Siles** (⊠ *Plaza de los Monolitos* ☎ *02/235–7342*), in the Miraflores district. The spectacle is always very entertaining, although the soccer can be terrible. You can also watch an entire stadium full of people trying to sit in the shade. Check local press or TV for games.

TIWANAKU

72 km (44 mi) west of La Paz.

An hour's drive west of La Paz, Tiwanaku (also spelled Tiahuanacu) is Bolivia's most important archaeological site. Partial excavations have revealed the remains of five different cities, one built on top of the other. The site's most impressive monument is the 10-ton La Puerta del Sol (Gate of the Sun), an imposing stone fixture believed to be a solar calendar built by a civilization that surfaced around 600 BC and mysteriously disappeared around AD 1200. The gate is part of an elaborate observatory and courtyard that contain monoliths and a subterranean temple. Although the site lacks the sweep and splendor of Peru's Machu Picchu, it does provide a glimpse into the ancestry of the Aymara, who still farm the ingeniously constructed terraces built centuries ago.

Start your visit with the museum next to the ruins. It displays artifacts found at the sight, the most spectacular of which is a 20-ton, 7.3-meter- (24-foot-) tall monolithic statue sculpted out of red sandstone. The monolith was discovered by an American, Wendell C. Bennett, during

Tiwanaku ruins outside of La Paz.

excavations in 1934, and since then had been on display in an open-air garden museum in La Paz, where it was being seriously eroded by weather. It was returned to Tiwanaku when the new indoor museum opened in 2002. Admission to the ruins and the museum is around (Bs)140 and guides are available at the entrance for (Bs)70.

Bring a warm sweater or poncho—the area is frequently windy and cold, as there are no trees to break the wind. If you are in La Paz in June, go out to the site for dawn on the day of summer solstice; it's a moving experience.

GETTING HERE AND AROUND

Buses to Tiwanaku leave daily from the Cementario bus terminal in La Paz and cost around $2 USD. The near two-hour ride is scenic, offering nice views of Volcano Huayna Potosi in the distance. Local guides are usually available outside the ruins for (Bs)70, but it's best to book one through a reputable tour company in La Paz. Most travel agencies offer half-and-full day trips to Tiwanaku, leaving at 8 AM and returning around 4 PM. Rates—usually around (Bs)300—include lunch near the main square, a guide, transportation, and entrance to the Tiwanaku ruins and museum.

The Tiwanaku ruins are located next to the village of Tiwanaku on Highway 3 heading west from La Paz to Lake Titicaca. Be sure to ask about the return bus schedule so you don't get stuck there.

ESSENTIALS

Tour Operator **Turisbus** (✉ Ave. Illampu #704 at Hotel Rosario, La Paz ☎ 02/245–1341 ⊕ www.turisbus.com).

WHERE TO STAY

$$ ☂ **Akapana Hotel.** Named for the pyramid at the Tiwanaku ruins, this five-star hotel is one of the few places to stay in the area. The large property has a restaurant, library, gym, swimming pool, coffee shop, game room, and relaxation garden. Single, double, and executive suites are available; request one of the larger rooms with a fireplace and balcony. For cultural music and exotic drinks, visit the Folkloric Peña "Wiracocha," open Thursday, Friday, and Saturday. City tours can be booked through the hotel's travel agent. **Pros:** coca baths at Spa Putini; hotel is close to the ruins; live music at Wiracocha. **Cons:** on-site conference centers make this more of a business hotel. ⊠ *Av. Manco Kapac No. 20 esq. Calle del Alambrado, Tiwanaku* ☎ *02/289–5104 or 7354–5206* ⊕ *www.hotel-akapana.com* ⇱ *30 rooms* △ *In-room: no a/c, safe, Wi-Fi. In-hotel: restaurant, bar, pool, gym, spa, laundry service, Wi-Fi hotspot, parking (free)* ⊟ *AE, MC, V* ⊺⊙⊢ *BP.*

COROICO

70 km (43 mi) northeast of La Paz.

Your first glimpse of the small resort town of Coroico will be unforgettable as you come around one of the numerous bends in the road on the long descent down from the Andes. People come here to see Los Yungas, an astounding subtropical region, as well as for an excellent break from the city of La Paz. If you really want to earn your sunbed by the pool, hitch onto a bicycle tour down the old "Road of Death."

GETTING HERE AND AROUND

Between 6 AM and 5 PM, buses for Coroico depart every half hour from "El Ex-Gasolinera" at Villa Fatima in La Paz, (Bs)30. Arrival and departures in Coroico take place at Coroico's main plaza. Public minivans to La Paz, (Bs)20, are also available from the Coroico bus station next to the main market. Alternatively you can book an all inclusive downhill mountain bike tour to Coroico through Gravity Assisted Mountain Biking.

Private transportation to Coroico (by way of the old or new road in a four-wheel drive) can be arranged through Turisbus.

ESSENTIALS

■TIP➜ Coroico does not have ATMs and most proprietors do not accept credit cards. Bring enough cash.

Banks **Prodem Bank** ⊠ *Plaza Principal; C. Julio Zuazo Cuenca* ☎ *02/289–5522).*

Internet **Internet** ⊠ *Across from church, next to Fie Bank* ☎ *02/740–19621 or 740–19602).*

Tour Operator **Gravity Assisted Mountain Biking** (☎ *02/231–3849* ⊕ *www.gravitybolivia.com).* **Mauricio Suarez Guzman** (☎ *591/156–6242).* **Turisbus** (⊠ *Ave. Illampu #704 at Hotel Rosario, La Paz* ☎ *02/245–1341* ⊕ *www.turisbus.com).* **Vagantes Canyoning** (☎ *02/241–3065* ⊕ *www.elvagante.com).* **Zipline Bolivia** (⊠ *Yolosa, 7 km from Coroico* ☎ *02/231–3849* ⊕ *www.ziplinebolivia.com).*

Festivals

The two-week **Feria de Alasitas** takes place in La Paz beginning January 24. It's an orgy of wishful thinking, as everybody buys miniature versions of the things they long for, including cars, houses, visas to the U.S., wads of euros, and gigantic penises, and get them blessed by the Pachamama. Even the newspapers are published in tiny editions. The creativity is dazzling, and it's a great souvenir opportunity.

February brings **Carnival**, a weeklong celebration that includes music and dancing all over the country. The biggest bash is held in the mining town of Oruro, 225 km (140 mi) southeast of La Paz. It's a pre-Lenten tradition, started more than 200 years ago, when workers, dressed as devils, danced to honor the Virgin in a festival called La Diablada. Although the Saturday before Ash Wednesday is the biggest day for the huge groups of Bolivian dancers, festivities last for a week. Away from the religious spectacle, Carnival is an excuse for some serious partying and can get very rowdy.

Pujllay is a colorful festival commemorating the 1816 victory by the Tarabucan people over the Spanish (a rare event in South American history); it takes place the week following Carnival in the village of Tarabuco.

Carnival in Oruro

The battle is re-created, but without the hand-to-hand fighting, steel claws, and bloodshed. Nonetheless, the spectacle of drunken, sweating warriors marching down the streets to the battleground is still stirring, as is the sight of all the tourists being overcharged for handicrafts.

Easter and especially **Good Friday** celebrations, characterized by candlelit religious processions by masked supplicants, are held all over the country, but are particularly impressive in Copacabana on Lake Titicaca. They are preceded by the arrival of pilgrims who have walked from La Paz over the preceding three or four days. Book early if you want to stay in the town over the Easter period, and get there a couple of days before; the pilgrims move quicker than the traffic jams on Good Friday itself.

June 24, the **Fiesta de San Juan** in La Paz, is traditionally regarded as the coldest day of the year. It's warmed up with bonfires, hot drinks, and hot dogs, and huge firework displays all over the city—many using suborbital-size rockets and enough dynamite to bring down the government. Get a view from high up and enjoy the show.

El Día de Todos los Santos (All Saints' Day) and **El Día de los Muertos** (All Souls' Day) take place all over Bolivia on November 1 and 2. On November 1 families prepare breads shaped in the form of things that hold importance—and at exactly noon the dead descend on the table. They remain there for 24 hours, then on All Soul's Day they are gone. Many families then go to the cemetery and party around—and on top of—the graves of their ancestors late into the night.

10

EXPLORING

Fodor'sChoice
★
El Camino de la Muerte. You might say your chances are just as good biking to Coroico from La Paz as they are taking a bus down what the UN once proclaimed "the world's most dangerous road," and you'd probably be right. This North Yungas Road, commonly known as "El Camino de la Muerte" (Road of Death), was built in the 1930s during the Chaco War by Paraguayan prisoners. Dotting the 69 km (43 mi) narrow trek are crosses honoring the estimated 300 travelers killed along the road each year. Although vehicles are still permitted to drive on the old road, most public transport now goes down the newer South Yungas Road (Chulumani Road). Unfortunately this paved highway cuts through Cotapata National Park, home to monkeys, parrots, the spectacled bear, and oropendolas, known for their woven basket-nests and bright yellow tails. **Turisbus** offers guided tours along the old road in comfortable four-wheel-drive vehicles, although most travelers prefer to explore the area by bike so it's just you, the subtropics, and some terrifying drops. Choose your agency carefully, make sure your bike has good brakes before you set off, and don't look down. The oldest, safest, and best (and most expensive; $100 USD) is **Gravity Assisted Mountain Biking.** Their English-speaking guides utilize the latest model of U.S. mountain bikes and carry all the rescue and first-aid equipment you hope not to use when biking down.

No matter how you travel, prepare yourself for drastic changes in temperature since you'll be dropping from 4,700 meters/15,400 feet (at Pampa Larama Lake beside the Statue of Jesus Christ) to 800 meters/2,624 feet (just outside of Coroico at the Santa Barbara Bridge).

WHERE TO EAT AND STAY

$$
GERMAN
✕ **Back Stube.** Just off the main square, this colorful restaurant—with a flowered trellis and yellow walls—has a large terrace overlooking the valleys below. German owner, Detlev Vois, has lived in Bolivia more than 13 years yet still hangs onto his European roots through such dishes as sauerbraten, filet with spaetzle, and the sweet *rollo de canela*. The menu also features vegetable curry, omelets, and sandwiches. ✉ *Calle Adalid Linares, Coroico* ☎ *719–54991* ▭ *No credit cards* ☉ *Closed Mon. and Tues.*

$$$
▣ **El Viejo Molino.** This beautiful Spanish-style resort hotel is perched high above the valley, among clusters of sugarcane and banana trees heavy with fruit. Relax by the pool or play a few games of tennis. There is also a large garden area with a children's playground. At the tour office you can make arrangements for a rafting trip on a nearby river. The grilled steak in the restaurant is one of the excellent entrées. **Pros:** good service in a stunning location; sauna for relaxing. **Cons:** overpriced for this jungle location. ✉ *On hwy into Coroico, Camino Santa Barbara, Km 1* ☎ *02/289–5506* ⊕ *www.hotelviejomolino.com* ⟿ *28 rooms* △ *In-room: a/c, safe. In-hotel: restaurant, room service, bar, gym, pool, laundry service* ▭ *MC, V* ⚙ *BP.*

$$
▣ **Hotel Esmeralda.** From the sunny patio at this unpretentious hotel up the hill from Coroico's central plaza you'll get astounding views of the valley below and, if you biked, the road you came down. The hotel is also surrounded by gardens and there are plenty of activities to keep you

North Yungas Road, commonly known as "El Camino de la Muerte" (Road of Death).

busy including a sauna, swimming pool, foosball, and billiards. Most rooms have balconies with private baths. If you don't have transportation, you can catch a taxi from town and the hotel will reimburse you the expense. The restaurant, with a charcoal pizza oven, is good, but get there early to beat the scramble for the barbecue dinner. From the hotel you can arrange hiking tours of nearby Parque Nacional Madidi. **Pros:** the gardens and their views. **Cons:** the walk up to the hotel will finish you off if you've been hiking; the shared bathrooms can be grim. ⊠ *5 ms uphill from plaza* ☎ *02/213–6017* ⊕ *www.hotelesmeralda.com* ↘ *32 rooms* ☐ *In-room: no a/c. In-hotel: restaurant, pool, laundry service, Wi-Fi hotspot, parking (free)* ⊟ *MC, V* ◯ *BP.*

$$$$ 🔲 **Hotel Rio Selva.** Probably the best hotel in the Yungas, and it can get ☾ very busy as a result. Go during the week to unwind and do very little except listen to the river, slide down a tube into a pool or two, and slap bugs. At this resort-style property, you can choose from a wide range of room types including cabañas, apartments, studios, and standard rooms. The property spans three acres with such offerings as racquetball courts, a movie theater, soccer field, and game room. There is even an on-site chapel where mass is held. Of the eleven swimming pools, several double as aqua-discos with music blaring throughout the day. This resort is a great place to practice your Spanish since the clientele and staff are predominately Bolivians. **Pros:** complimentary child care; plenty of activities; the orchid garden. **Cons:** insects; the loud pool areas; property is showing signs of age. ⊠ *Carretera Cota Pata Santa Barbara, Km 90* ☎ *02/289–5559, 02/289–5571* ⊕ *www.rioselva.com.bo* ↘ *112 rooms* ☐ *In-room: a/c. In-hotel: restaurant, pools, spa, laundry service, gym, Wi-Fi hotspot* ⊟ *MC, V* ◯ *AI.*

$$ ⚲ **La Senda Verde.** This refuge for abused and mistreated animals is set in a subtropical jungle 7 km (4 mi) from the town of Coroico. There are five small cabins where you can overnight, although you won't find any luxuries here (no Internet, no a/c, no cell reception). Most guests come to relax by the pool, enjoy a meal at the restaurant, and spend time with the rescued monkeys. **Pros:** jungle setting; animal rescue. **Cons:** no luxuries. ⊠ *Yungas, 7 Km from Coroico, close to the village of Yolosa, Yungas* ☎ *02/213–9996* ⊕ *www.sendaverde.com* ⌂ *5 rooms* ⌂ *In-room: no phone, no a/c, no TV. In-hotel: restaurant, pool, parking (free)* ⊟ *No credit cards* ⎮⊘⎮ *CP.*

RURRENABAQUE

410 km (254 mi) from La Paz.

Labeled the "Pearl of Beni River," the small town of Rurrenabaque is the gateway to the Amazon Basin and the launching point for jungle and pampas tours along the Yucuma River. Prices are generally the same for both day trips and can be booked 24 hours in advance from tour companies in Rurrenabaque. Allow more time for the pampas tour since it involves three hours in a jeep followed by a three-hour canoe ride, compared to the jungle tour, which takes just three hours by boat.

The town itself has less than 8,000 permanent residents, most of which are Tacana natives and still speak the native language. Rurrenabaque, which translates to "Ravine of Ducks," is a haven for backpackers who are drawn to the areas eco-lodges and activities.

Nature is abundant here with more than 1,000 species of birds and 300 types of mammals and reptiles. Prepare yourself for the mosquitoes though, especially if you take the pampas tour.

GETTING HERE AND AROUND

Two airlines—Amazonas and Aerocon—offer flights from La Paz and Santa Cruz to Rurrenabaque. Agencies Trans-Totaï and Palmeras in Coroico sell bus tickets to Rurrenabaque for about (Bs)70. This rate includes transport in a minibus to the neighboring town of Yolosita where passengers transfer to another bus for Rurrenabaque. Minibuses depart from Coroico at 1 AM and depart from Yolosita between 2 and 3 PM. The trip takes about 14 hours.

ESSENTIALS

■**TIP→** There are no ATMs in Rurrenabaque and few places accept credit cards.

Currency Exchange Prodem Bank (⊠ *Av Avaroa esq Jose Manuel Pando* ☎ *03/892-2616 or 711-30759*).

Airlines Aerocon (☎ *03/351-1010* ⊕ *www.aerocon.bo*). **Amaszonas** (☎ *02/222-0848* ⊕ *www.amaszonas.com*).

WHERE TO STAY

$$$ ⚲ **Chalan Ecolodge.** This eco-lodge in Madidi National Park offers a
Fodor's Choice great chance to experience Bolivia's rain forest. The lodge, owned and
★ operated by the Quechua-Tacana community of San José de Uchupi-amonas, immerses you in a culture that has lived in the tropical rain

forest for 300 years. The property offers three types of accommodation; luxurious cabins with private bath, twin/triple rooms with private bath, and twin rooms with shared bath. All are equipped with mosquito nets, balconies and hammocks where you can relax and read. While you're here, be on the lookout for hundreds of species of birds, troops of monkeys, herds of wild peccaries, and the elusive jaguar. You reach the park from Rurrenabaque by a five-hour canoe trip and a 30-minute walk through the rain forest to your thatch-roof cabin facing Lago Chalalan. A five-day/four-night package, with three nights at Chalalan, is available for around $470 USD per person, but plan to spend more with the airfare ($186 USD round-trip). For information, contact **America Tours SRL**. **Pros:** jungle setting; private guide; great food. **Cons:** difficult to reach; expensive; cold-water showers. ⊠ *Calle Comercio, media cuadra de la Plaza Principal, Rurrenabaque* ☎ *03/892–2419, 02/237–4204* ⊕ *www.chalalan.com* ⟿ *14 rooms* ⟡ *In-room: no phone, no a/c, no TV. In-hotel: restaurant, bar* ☰ *MC, V* ⟡❙ *CP.*

Mamore River. Fremen Tours' four-day riverboat expedition from Trinidad offers you the opportunity to take a shortcut into the heart of the Amazon basin. Fly from La Paz to Trinidad in the Beni region, then it's a short drive (if it's the dry season) to the river. The program includes opportunities for day and nighttime animal-spotting, and treks into the jungle itself. The boat is small but has a good kitchen, and the service is excellent. If you risk it in the rainy season, you'll find a smaller group of travelers accompanying you, which is better—it can get claustrophobic and noisy on board. For information, contact **Fremen** in La Paz. (⊕ *www.andes-amazonia.com*).

OFF THE
BEATEN
PATH

LAKE TITICACA

At an altitude of 12,506 feet, Titicaca is the world's highest navigable lake and also one of the largest. It covers an area of 7,988 square km (3,963 square mi) in the altiplano, shared between Peru and Bolivia. Some of the highest peaks in the Andes rise along the northeastern shore. The lake is actually two bodies of water joined by the narrow Estrecho de Tiquina (Strait of Tiquina). The smaller section, Lago Huiñaymarca, is the easiest to reach from La Paz. To see the much larger Lago Chucuito, travel on to Peru (⇨ *see Chapter 4*). To visit the islands, which are the highlight of the lake, include Copacabana on your itinerary.

Considered sacred by the Aymara people who live on its shores, Lake Titicaca was also revered by the Tiwanaku and Inca civilizations. Here you'll find Isla del Sol (Sun Island) and Isla de la Luna (Moon Island), each with ruins in varying states of decay. According to legend, Isla del Sol is where the Inca Empire was founded when Manco Kapac and Mama Ojllo, son and daughter of the Sun God Inti, came down to Earth to improve the life of the altiplano people. This, some might say, is taking some time—tourism has brought few benefits, and life, clawed out of the barren landscape, continues to be hard for the Aymara Indians who inhabit this area.

10

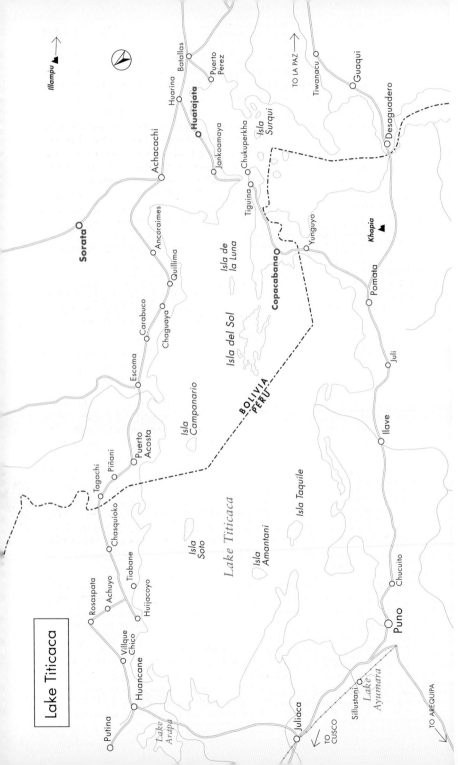

Major archaeological discoveries continue both around and in the lake, but for the traveler the real attraction is the beauty of the area, and the undeniable power and energy that emanates from it. Few who visit Titicaca fail to be impressed.

GETTING HERE AND AROUND

Renting a car and driving yourself is an excellent way to get to Lake Titicaca. Take the El Alto Highway northwest from La Paz. The road is paved between La Paz, Huatajata, the strait at Tiquina, and Copacabana, and barring heavy traffic, takes less than four hours. If it's your own vehicle, get it blessed at the church while you are there.

Minibuses run regularly from the gates of El Viejo Cementerio in La Paz to destinations along Lake Titicaca, including Batallas, Huatajata, and Tiquina. One-way tickets are about $1. Private bus companies that collect passengers at their hotel charge roughly $10 round-trip to Copacabana (four hours) and $15 to Sorata (six hours). Companies are at the bus terminal in La Paz.

ESSENTIALS

Tour Operators Crillón Tours (✉ *Av. Camacho 1223* ☎ *02/213–6612* ⊕ *www. titicaca.com*). **Diana Tours** (✉ *Calle Sagárnaga 328* ☎ *02/235–0252* ⊕ *www. diana-tours.com*). **TransTur** (☎ *02/237–3423*). **Turibus** (✉ *Calle Illampu* ☎ *02/232–5348 or 02/236–9542* ⊕ *www.turisbus.com*).

HUATAJATA

85 km (53 mi) from La Paz.

This popular weekend escape for Paceños is a regular stop on the guided-tour circuit and the easiest way to experience the beauty of the lake. Huatajata is a practical base for exploring the area, and there is a succession of cheap and not so cheap trout restaurants along the road. The fish is fresh in all of them. For picnics, you can try the tree-lined but heavily littered pebble-strewn beach at Chúa, the village beyond Huatajata.

GETTING HERE AND AROUND

To reach Huatajata, take any bus heading to Copacabana. Buses depart every 30 minutes from the Cementario bus terminal in La Paz and cost (Bs)15. Private transportation to and from Huatajata also can be arranged by Crillón Tours.

ESSENTIALS

■ TIP→ The nearest banks and medical facilities are located in La Paz.

Shuttle Service Crillón Tours (✉ *Av. Camacho 1223, La Paz* ☎ *591/233–7533* ⊕ *www.titicaca.com*).

EXPLORING

Andean Roots Eco Village. Part of the Inca Utama Hotel & Spa is this small but charming museum and exhibition on the culture and history of the region. Replicas of mud houses that many of the Chipaya people of the surrounding altiplano still live in are outside the museum, along with some disgruntled and very shaggy llamas. Probably the most interesting things are the replicas of the *tortora* (reed) boats used by explorer Thor

10

Heyerdahl for his expeditions across the Pacific and Atlantic oceans. The real ones were built just down the coast. The Limachi brothers who built these, and who served in the crew for some of these epic journeys, are often here and happy to talk to you for the price of a postcard. The replicas themselves are not only technically impressive but also rather beautiful. ⊠ *Off hwy. from La Paz to Copacabana (Km 80), Huatajata* ☎ *02/233-7533, 800/488-5353 in U.S.* ⊕ *www.titicaca.com* ✉ *Free with purchase of food or drink from Inca Utama Hotel* ☉ *Daily 9–6.*

WHERE TO STAY

$$$$ 🏨 **Inca Utama Hotel.** This expensive hotel on the Lake includes the
🕓   Andrean Roots Eco Village, a cultural museum, an observatory, a rather basic spa and gym, and a small children's park. Hydrofoils depart daily from the dock alongside the hotel to the Sun and Moon islands, Copacabana, and Puno (on the Peruvian side of the lake). You can make reservations at the hotel or with Crillón Tours' office in La Paz. The restaurant serves fine international cuisine and is a popular destination for Paceños for Sunday lunch. Your receipt will get you into the **Andean Roots Eco Village** and the **Museo del Altiplano.** A boardwalk extends out onto the lake to the Choza Nautica thatch-roof restaurant, which we have never seen open. **Pros:** the setting; herb garden; good restaurant. **Cons:** flavorless decor and service style; property is looking aged; slow Internet connection. ⊠ *Off hwy from La Paz to Copacabana (Km 80), Huatajata* ☎ *02/233-7533, 800/488-5353 in U.S.* ⊕ *www.titicaca.com* ⤢ *65 rooms, 4 suites* ⚅ *In-room: no a/c. In-hotel: 2 restaurants, bar, gym, spa, Wi-Fi hotspot, parking (free)* ▭ *AE, MC, V* ☉⚈ *CP.*

COPACABANA

79 km (49 mi) from Huatajata.

Copacabana, a pleasant, if touristy town, provides easy access to the lake, the islands and the surrounding countryside. It is also a major pilgrimage destination for devout Bolivians at Easter and lost South American hippies all year. A highlight is watching the sunset over the water from the Stations of the Cross, the highest point of Copacabana.

GETTING HERE AND AROUND

You can get a bus to Copacabana from the Cementario in La Paz or organize your trip through an agency in town. Tourist buses, (Bs)40, are usually booked a day in advance and will pickup passengers around 8 AM at most central La Paz hotels. Public buses to Copacabana depart from the bus station but schedules are not reliable. From the cementario zone, minibuses depart every hour from 6:30 AM to 4:30 PM, but this area is not very safe. The route to Copacabana will pass Huatajata and continue on the El Alto Highway to the Strait of Tiquina where you can see the handful of patrol boats that stubbornly persist from what was Bolivia's navy. This narrow strait (2,790 feet across) joins the upper lake, Lago Chicuito and the lower lake, Lago Pequeno of Lake Titicaca. At this crossing point, your bus or car is loaded onto a small and very unstable raft, which chugs slowly across the strait, while you speed across in a small motorboat. Ask the Navy conscripts manning the crossing for permission if you wish to stay with your vehicle, though you may decide against it once you've seen the rafts. From here it's a 90-minute drive to Copacabana. If you're starting in Peru, Tour Peru has buses departing from the main terminal in Puno at 7:30 AM for S/20. The most enjoyable option is to rent a car and drive—it takes about three hours from La Paz and the roads are good, as are the views.

In the center of Copacabana's main plaza, the tourist information booth is the place to find information about the area.

ESSENTIALS

Bank **Prodem** (⊠ Av 6 de Agosto s/n entre Calles Oruro y Pando ☎ 02/862–2183 or 02/862–2530 ⏱ Closed Mon.).

Bus Transportation **Tour Peru** (⊠ Jr Tacna 285 Ofc 103, Puno ☎ 951–676600).

Internet Internet Café (⊠ Ave 6 de Agosto, Copacabana).

Pharmacy **Farmacia** (⊠ Northwest corner of Plaza 2 de Febrero, Copacabana ☎ 795–42606 or 701–07978 ⏱ 8 am–10 pm).

Police (⊠ Plaza 2 de Febrero, north end, Copacabana ☎ 02/222–5016 or 800–108–687 ⊕ www.policiaturistica.gov.bo).

Post Office **Copacabana Post Office** (⊠ Plaza de Febrero).

Visitor Info **Centro de Informacion Turistica** (⊠ Av. 16 de Julio, esq Av 6 de Agosto ⏱ Wed.–Sun. 8–noon and 2–6).

EXPLORING

Cerro Calvario. Marking the highest point of Copacabana are The Stations of the Cross, built in the 1950s for the thousands of pilgrims who summit the hill for prayer and penance on Good Friday. For many tourists, these stone monuments serve as the ideal spot to admire the city and watch the sunset. ⊠ *Trail begins near the red chapel at the end of Calle Destacamento 211, Copacabana.*

Copacabana Cathedral. The town's breathtaking Moorish-style cathedral, built between 1610 and 1619, is where you'll find the striking sculpture of the Virgin of Copacabana. There was no choice but to build the church, because the statue, carved by Francisco Yupanqui in 1592, was already drawing pilgrims in search of miracles. If you see decorated cars lined up in front of the cathedral, the owners are waiting to have them blessed for safe travel. Walk around to a side door on the left and light a candle for those you wish to remember, then admire the gaudy glitter and wealth of the church interior itself. Throngs of young Paceños do the three-day walk to Copacabana from La Paz to pay homage to the statue with a candlelight procession on Good Friday. You can combine your visit with the semi-scramble up past Cerro Calvario (Calvary Hill) on the point above the town. If the climb doesn't knock you out, the view will.

Horca del Inca. Dating back to 14th century BC, this structure was originally built by the pre-Inca Chiripa culture as an astronomical observatory. Four of the seven horizontal rock slabs were later destroyed by the Spanish who believed gold was hidden inside. The remains of the ruins show signs of vandalism, yet still warrant a visit for those wanting to blend culture and exercise. The slope is steep and rather challenging,

10

but the view of Lake Titicaca will help alleviate the pain. ⊠ *Southeast part of Copacabana* 🖾 *(Bs)10* ⏱ *7–6.*

WHERE TO EAT

Copacabana has a wide array of hotels, hostels, international cafés, bars and pizza joints, which reflects its popularity as a weekend destination from La Paz and as the crossing point for travelers from Peru. There's a lot of competition, so most are good value—the best thing to do for lunch or dinner is wander along the two main streets and window-shop first. You can find the famous trout dishes everywhere.

$
CAFÉ

✕ **Condor and The Eagle Café.** If you are dying for a decent cup of coffee, this is the place to get your caffeine fix. This cozy spot operates as a bookstore, Internet café, and breakfast house. Power up with a bowl of muesli mixed with natural yogurt, fresh fruit, and honey, or grab a cappuccino and brownie to go. They have a wide variety of American classics for sale as well as handmade arts and crafts. ⊠ *Corner of Ave. 6 de Agosto and Bolivar St, across from Plaza Sucre, Copacabana* ☎ *No phone* ⊕ *www.facebook.com/elcondoryelaguilacafe* ⊟ *No credit cards* ⏱ *Closed Wed.*

$$
VEGETARIAN

✕ **Kala Uta.** Good things come to those who wait at this "slow cooking movement" restaurant. Homemade pizza, pasta, and salad are all on the menu, as is trout prepared twenty different ways. Main courses come with quinoa, corn, or sweet potatoes. For dessert, take your pick from flan, crepes or flambé. ⊠ *Av 6 Agosto, across from Plaza Sucre, Copacabana* ☎ *749–01288* ⊟ *No credit cards.*

$$
SEAFOOD

✕ **Snack 6 de Agosto.** Although it serves various entrées, this place is best known for its trout, fresh from Lake Titicaca. There's also a selection of vegetarian dishes including a flavorful quinoa soup. ⊠ *Av. 6 de Agosto* ☎ *02/0862–2040* ⊟ *MC, V.*

$$
VEGETARIAN

✕ **Sujna Wasi.** This Spanish-owned restaurant is tiny, with seating for fewer than two-dozen people. It's the place to come in Copacabana for vegetarian food. They also serve trout with quinoa and great breakfasts from 7–11 daily. The restaurant has a small library with books, maps, and travel information. ⊠ *Calle General Gonzalo Jaúregui 127* ☎ *02/7486–1624* ⊟ *No credit cards.*

WHERE TO STAY

$$

🛏 **Ambassador Hotel.** This hotel near the lake is aligned with a youth hostel, which means it offers special rates for students. Although rooms are somewhat small and dated, they are brightly painted and have hardwood floors and floral bedding. Request one of the nine rooms with a lake view. If you can get past the fake fireplace and swan shrine in the lobby, head to the rooftop restaurant for an incredible view. **Pros:** right on the beach. **Cons:** rubbish from the lake close by; no Internet; somewhat tacky decor in the lobby. ⊠ *Calle General Gonzalo Jaúregui, Plaza Sucre* ☎ *02/862–2216* 🛌 *42 rooms* ⚬ *In-room: no a/c. In-hotel: restaurant, laundry service* ⊟ *No credit cards* ⏱◯ *CP.*

$$
Fodor'sChoice
★

🛏 **Hotel La Cupula.** It's worth staying on in Copacabana just to enjoy this alternative-style hotel tucked below the hills at one corner of the bay. Breakfast, costing (Bs)25, is exceptional, especially if you're a vegetarian. The recent addition of five kitchen-equipped bungalows with tranquil lake views, creative natural designs, and a separate reception area make it all the more interesting. You can relax in a garden-hammock or curl up with a book in the library. There is also a communal kitchen and a TV room with a selection of more than 130 DVDs. The charming upstairs restaurant is open to the public. **Pros:** alternative vibe; great vegetarian breakfasts; the penthouse room—if you can get it. **Cons:** breakfast not included; no Internet; hotel is often full; staff can be hard to locate. ⊠ *Michel Pérez 1–3* ☎ *02/862–2029* ⊕ *www. hotelcupula.com* ↪ *17 rooms, 6 suites* ⌂ *In-room: no a/c, kitchen (some). In-hotel: restaurant, room service, laundry service* ▭ *MC, V* ⋈ *EP.*

$$$ 🛏 **Hotel Rosario Del Lago Titicaca.** One of the nicest accommodations in

Fodor's Choice   Copacabana, this colonial-style hotel is a few blocks from the main

★   plaza. Its clean, homey rooms, including a spacious suite that sleeps six, have excellent views of the shore. Recently renovated rooms include balconies, flat-screen TVs, and glass-walled bathrooms that look onto the water. Restaurant Kota Kahuana ("View of the Lake") specializes (like every eatery in town) in trout caught in Lake Titicaca, as well as international fare. The small on-site museum, Taypi, is worth a visit. **Pros:** friendly staff; good buffet breakfast; the view of the sunset from any of the rooms; heaters in the rooms. **Cons:** no closets; no Wi-Fi in the rooms; lack of toiletries. ⊠ *Calle Rigoberto Paredes and Av. Costanera* ☎ *02/862–2141, 02/245–1341 in La Paz* ⊕ *www.hotelrosario.com/lago* ↪ *29 rooms, 1 suite* ⌂ *In-room: no a/c. In-hotel: restaurant, room service, bar, laundry service, Internet terminal, Wi-Fi hotspot* ▭ *AE, MC, V* ⋈ *BP.*

ISLA DEL SOL AND ISLA DE LA LUNA

12 km (7½ mi) north of Copacabana.

Fodor's Choice   The largest of Lake Titicaca's islands, **Isla del Sol** is the best place to

★   visit and stay on the lake. The views of the Cordillera Real mountains are amazing, especially at dawn and dusk, and the island has beautiful white sandy beaches and an extraordinary terraced landscape. There are ruins, including the Inca palace of Pilkokaina and a strange rock formation said to be the birthplace of the sun and moon, and an excellent Inca trail across the island. Some travelers take a boat to the northern community of Challa Pampa and then hike 3–4 hours to the southern community of Yumani where most accommodations (and the main "village") can be found. Although rewarding, the island trail is void of shade with only three spots to buy water along the way. If your goal is to just laze around and soak up the cosmic energy, then be sure to disembark at the southern boat port of Yumani, unless you are staying at one of the few hotels on the north side. One of the best beaches on Isla del Sol is located on the north end, directly behind the museum. Regardless of your destination, plan on hiking at least 30 minutes uphill from the boat port. Nearly every property is staggered high on the slope, which means that both altitude and fitness should be taken into consideration.

10

En route to Isla del Sol, boats sometimes stop at **Isla de la Luna,** where the ruins of Iñacuy date back to the Inca conquest. You'll find an ancient convent called Ajlla Wasi (House of the Chosen Women). Stone steps lead up to the unrestored ruins of the convent.

GETTING HERE AND AROUND

The most expensive—and comfortable—way to get here is by hydrofoil from the **Inca Utama Hotel** in Huatajata, but cheaper boats leave from Copacabana at 8:30 AM and 1:30 PM and return from Isla del Sol south port at 8:30 AM, 10:30 AM and 3:30 PM. The journey from Copacabana takes about two hours and costs (Bs)20. Once you are on the island, it's walking all the way, unless a mule has been organized through your hotel ahead of time. The tourist office, located on the northern side of Isla del Sol, offers private guides for (Bs)90 or (Bs)10 per person when booking groups of 10.

ESSENTIALS

Boat Transportation **Andes Amazonia** (⊠ *Av 6 de Agosto, Esq Plaza Sucre, Copacabana* ☎ *02/862-2616* ⌂ *(Bs)10* ⊗ *9:30–12 and 3–6).*

Visitor Information **Asociacion Turismo Comunitario** (⊠ *Isla del Sol, north end, North port, Isla del Sol* ☎ *719-15544 or 735-89580).*

SAFETY AND PRECAUTIONS

You may be asked to pay (Bs)10 to get onto the Inca trail on the island, and then again at various points along it. The initial payment (from either the north or sound end) seems legitimate, and justified, but none of the others do, so be firm.

WHERE TO STAY

You will be amply rewarded for your climb up the steps from the port—the higher you go, the cheaper the hostels or *posadas.* They are almost all good, if basic. The north side of the island is more barren but also has attractive options, including a place on the beach itself.

$ **Hostal Pacha-Mama.** Located at the north end of the island, this low-budget hostel is a bit unkempt, but it's right on the beach and has hot showers. In 2010, six new rooms were built at the back of the property. Although they lack a view, they're much cleaner and come with private baths. Breakfast, lunch, and dinner are offered, along with laundry service. **Pros:** cheap as they come; the hot water is a novelty. **Cons:** be prepared to rough it in the rooms; on a very busy road; the payment policy; endless partying. ⊠ *Isla del Sol North, Playa* ☎ *02/735–30261* ⌂ *20 rooms* ☖ *In-room: no a/c. In-hotel: restaurant, laundry* ☱ *No credit cards* ❏❶ *EP.*

$$ **Hostal Puerta del Sol.** This budget option at the south end of the island has rooms with private baths, shared baths, and spacious cabañas. Standard rooms are colorfully decorated with floral duvets and throw rugs atop hardwood floors. Most rooms open onto a grass terrace with tables and chairs where you can waste away the day. There are excellent views of the Peruvian side of the lake, and the restaurant is good. **Pros:** great location; unobstructed views. **Cons:** simple accommodation. ⊠ *On ridge of Isla del Sol, South Side* ☎ *735–06995, 719–55181*

◥ *21 rooms, 2 cabañas* ⊘ *In-room: no a/c. In-hotel: restaurant, laundry service* ▭ *No credit cards* ❚⊘❙ *CP.*

$$$$ ⛫ **La Estancia Ecolodge.** Staggered on a hillside, each bungalow (named for flora) has an unobstructed view of Lake Titicaca, making it the perfect place to watch the sunrise. The ecolodge uses alternative energy, recycles water back into the garden and takes garbage off the island. All 14 palapa-adobe buildings have hot-water showers warmed by solar power, and Trombe walls that heat the rustic-European-style rooms with stone floor bathrooms and beamed ceilings. Three-course meals are served at a set time in a common dining area, and both breakfast and dinner are included in the rate, which is significantly cheaper if booked through the office in La Paz. **Pros:** excellent views; great showers; dinners integrate local flavors. **Cons:** unlit paths at night; arrangements must be made through La Paz office. ⊠ *South end of Isla del Sol* ☎ *02/244–2727* ⊕ *www.ecolodge-laketiticaca.com* ◥ *14 rooms* ⊘ *In-room: no a/c, no TV. In-hotel: restaurant, bar, water sports, laundry service* ▭ *AE, MC, V* ❚⊘❙ *MAP.*

$$$
Fodor's Choice
★

⛫ **La Posada del Inca.** Your stay at this lovely posada begins with a 30-minute mule ride (a llama carries your luggage) from the boat dock to the garden-lobby where fruit trees shade handmade reed couches. Rooms in this beautifully restored colonial-style hacienda on the south end of Isla del Sol are attractively furnished with reclaimed wood, and all have private baths. Hot-water showers, wall heaters and electric blankets are all powered with solar energy. The hillside location offers sweeping views of the lake. Before dinner, guests gather around the fire in the cozy bar where three flavors of oxygen are available for those acclimating to the altitude. The restaurant serves meals family-style in the dining room; most of the ingredients come from the on-site greenhouse. Rooms must be booked as part of a hydrofoil tour with Crillón Tours in La Paz, making this one of the more expensive options on the island. **Pros:** high standard of service; good food; pleasant garden setting. **Cons:** the pricing; slightly out of place on the island. ☎ *02/233–7533* ⊕ *www.titicaca.com* ◥ *21 rooms* ⊘ *In-room: no a/c. In-hotel: restaurant, bar* ▭ *AE, MC, V* ❚⊘❙ *MAP.*

10

SORATA

45 km (28 mi) north of Huatajata.

Sorata lies nearly 8,200 feet above sea level in a tropical valley at the foot of Mt. Illampu. This is a starting point for serious hikers to climb the snowcapped mountain or tackle the arduous, weeklong trek along the Camino del Oro (Trail of Gold) to the gold-mining cooperatives. Others just come to soak up the scenery and sleep in the shade of the mountains for a while. If you're not a hiker, don't expect too much else in the way of attractions. The deteriorating town is centered around the main square, Plaza General Enrique Penaranda, where Sorata's annual fiesta is held on September 14.

During your stay, you might only see one or two other tourists, which many say is a lingering result of the September 2003 protests. At that

Trekking Around Sorata

The Camino de Oro and the Illampu Circuit are the two classic treks starting from Sorata, but they are long, arduous, and can be dangerous. Less strenuous undertakings are the two-day trek to the Laguna Chalata or a stunning three-day hike to the Laguna Glacier. Official guides can be found in the office opposite the Residential Sorata. Prices vary depending on what's included, but you should pay around (Bs)300 for a one-day trip and (Bs)600 for a two-day (one night) trip, including meals and guide. Hiring sleeping bags and tents will cost you more. The most spectacular trip leaving from Sorata is the five-day bike and boat journey to Ruhrenabaque.

Andean Epics (☎ *591/712–76685, 591/712–76685* ⊕ *andeanepics.com*) provides a fully provisioned trip with good bikes into the Bolivian rain forest, where you pick up a boat for a river trip to the jungle town. It costs around $350 USD per person depending on group size.

A good day walk from Sorata is the San Pedro cave, a three-hour walk around a winding mountain road to the caves, where there is a (Bs)15 entry fee. No guides are needed for this relatively flat hike, which takes in some spectacular views from high above the Sorata River and the valley it has carved in the mountains.

---

time, gunfire with Bolivian police and roadblocks left dozens of foreign travelers trapped in the town for days. Despite efforts to rebuild tourism in Sorata (a new road was built between Achacachi and Sorata in 2007) the town never fully recovered. Today it serves as a getaway for La Paz weekenders and the occasional foreign explorer.

GETTING HERE AND AROUND

Buses depart half-hourly or when full from the Cementerio in La Paz, and cost about (Bs)15. Use caution when waiting for transportation at the Cementerio in La Paz since this area is prone to theft and can be dangerous for travelers. The buses arrive in and depart from Sorata's main plaza. Minibuses from Sorata to La Paz leave every hour from the main square and operate between 3 AM and 6 PM. From Copacabana you can take any bus to La Paz, get off in Huarina, and flag a bus to Sorata. The drive from La Paz to Sorata takes around three hours, and from Huatajata to Sorata approximately two hours. Landslides during rainy season are common. For private transport and tours to Sorata from La Paz or Huatajata, contact Net Traveller.

ESSENTIALS

■TIP➔ Sorata does not have ATMs and the vast majority of places do not accept credit cards. Bring enough cash if you plan to stay awhile.

Banks **Prodem Bank** (✉ *Plaza Enrique Penaranda N 139, Sorata town center* ☎ *02/213–6679*).

Buses **Trans Unificada** (☎ *02/238–1693*).

Pharmacies **Farmacia** (✉ *Plaza Enrique Penaranda, beside the church, Sorata town center*).

Tour Operators **Net Traveller** (☎ 591/795–90817 or 591/712–17515 ⊕ *www. bolivianettraveller.com*).

Visitor Info **Association de Guias Turisticas Sorata** (✉ *Calle Sucre, across from Hostel Residential Sorata, Sorata town center* ☎ 715–94612).

WHERE TO EAT AND STAY

$$

ECLECTIC

✕ **Pete's Place.** Tucked away on a side street inside a hostel, don't let the awkward location of this restaurant put you off. This colorful place, owned by an Englishman, is probably the best place to eat in Sorata. The menu has something for everyone, meat lover or vegetarian, and the restaurant's owner is a good source of tips and information about Sorata and surroundings. Power up with one of Pete's hearty breakfasts or try the chicken curry for lunch or dinner. The restaurant is often closed on Tuesday when the owner heads to La Paz. ✉ *Hostal Don Julio Sorata, Plaza Principal.*

$$$

Fodor's Choice

★

🏠 **Altai Oasis.** The bumpy road, 15 minutes from Sorata's main square, truly does lead to paradise. Meandering through manicured gardens are stone pathways leading to your choice of cabins, dorms, or campsites. At this riverside refuge, campsites are set in a grassy knoll and include fire pits, a common kitchen, eco-toilets and hot-water showers. Perched above the valley is an open-air restaurant that serves organic dishes prepared with ingredients from the property's farm. Rooms have skylights, beamed ceilings, hardwood floors, stone showers, and comfy duvets. Request "Tower #1" for the best views, or book one of the cabins for groups of three or more. The 7-acre property also has a kiosk, playground, movie room, swimming pool, and garden with rescued animals. Owner Johny Resnikowski speaks English, German, Spanish, French, and Italian. **Pros:** manicured gardens; beside the river; friendly owners. **Cons:** if you're not an animal lover, the rescued pets might be a bother; steep climb from the river to the restaurant. ✉ *Pass the school, beyond the soccer field, and follow the signs to Altai Oasis. Turn left before Café Illampu, Sorata* ☎ 715–19856 or 712–26927 ⊕ *www.altaioasis. com* ⇗ *13 rooms, 2 cabins, 60 tent sites* ⌂ *In-room: no a/c, safe, kitchen (some). In-hotel: restaurant, bar, pool, laundry facilities, Wi-Fi hotspot, parking (free), some pets allowed* ▭ *AE, MC, V* �🍽 *CP.*

$$$

🏠 **Gran Hotel Sorata.** This hotel's charm lies in the outdoor garden and lovely views across the valley. On-site is an Internet café and game room, as well as a large swimming pool open to nonguests for a small fee. Rooms at this 1940s hotel were renovated in 2007, however the bathrooms could use a face-lift. The restaurant specializes in the traditional dishes of the region. If you are coming from La Paz, the hotel is on the main highway 1 km (½ mi) from Sorata's central square. Make sure you notify the hotel of your upcoming arrival since the managers often lock the doors and head to La Paz for supplies. **Pros:** lovely setting; out of town slightly, so quieter. **Cons:** slow service; management not always on premises. ✉ *Carretera Principal Sorata* ☎ 02/289–5003, 02/735–20356 ⊕ *www.granhotelsorata.com* ⌂ *In-room: no a/c. In-hotel: restaurant, pool, bar, Internet terminal* ▭ *AE, MC, V* �🍽 *CP.*

10

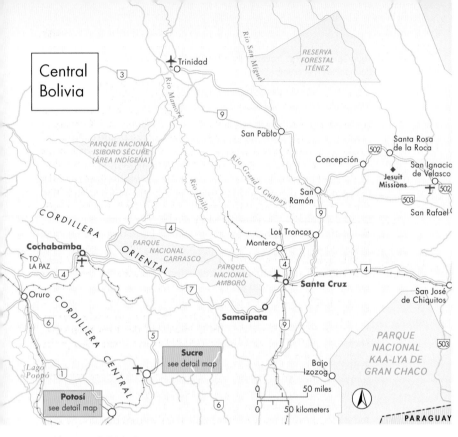

TOURS

You'll get a much clearer idea of the quality of tour operators by looking in Sorata itself than in La Paz. You'll also get a better deal. Below are some recommendations if you want to organize things before you get there:

America Tours normally organizes jungle trips, and is very good at it, but they also go to the Laguna Glacier during the April to October climbing season. (✉ *Office 9, ground floor, 1490 Edificio Av., Av. Prado, La Paz* ☎ *02/237–4204* ⊕ *www.america-ecotours.com*).

Bolivian Mountains offers four-day trekking trips to the Laguna Glacier, as well as to most of the peaks in Bolivia. They have very competent guides—a rarity in the mountains of Bolivia—and can organize any routes you'd care to try. (✉ *Rigoberto Paredes 1401 y Colombia, La Paz* ☎ *02/248–2767* ⊕ *www.bolivianmountains.com*).

Climbing South America offers climbing, trekking, biking, and cultural tours around Bolivia. (✉ *Calle Murillo #993, 1st Floor Office A, La Paz* ☎ *02/215–2232* ⊕ *www.climbingsouthamerica.com*).

CENTRAL BOLIVIA

The two major cities in central Bolivia, Cochabamba and Santa Cruz, are both southeast of La Paz—but here ends all similarity. Cochabamba, the country's third-largest city, is in a fertile valley in the foothills of the Andes. Often referred to as the "Granero de Bolivia," (Granary of Bolivia) Cochabamba produces a large share of the country's fruit and vegetables, and much of its meat and dairy products. Nestled in the eastern foothills of the Andes, it is known for its mild, sunny weather. Hot and humid Santa Cruz, Bolivia's largest city, is on the edge of the Amazon basin. In addition to agriculture, its economy is fueled by lumber, gas, and oil; the booms of the last few decades have resulted in its being a real economic and political powerhouse.

GETTING HERE AND AROUND

The drive between Cochabamba and Santa Cruz takes 10 hours on the Nuevo Camino (New Road). It may be new, but don't try this route without a four-wheel-drive vehicle. You can break the trip into almost equal parts by staying overnight at Villa Tunari.

SAFETY AND PRECAUTIONS

Take the normal health precautions for tropical regions when traveling in this area—drink only bottled water, and don't eat from street stands where food is sitting around. Make sure to bring along plenty of mosquito repellent.

COCHABAMBA

400 km (250 mi) southeast of La Paz.

Nestled in the valleys of central Bolivia, Cochabamba is considered the "The Garden City" due to its year round spring-like climate. This bustling metropolis is one of the oldest cities in Bolivia, and many buildings from the 16th century stand along its narrow streets. Near the city's main plaza are small cafés and elaborate cathedrals. On weekends, locals find bargains at La Cancha, Cochabamba's main market, or head to one of the hole-in-the-wall eateries for *chicharrón de chancho*, the local pork specialty.

GETTING HERE AND AROUND

From La Paz, drive 190 km (118 mi) south to Caracollo, one of the few villages along the way with a gas station, and then head east toward Cochabamba. The drive takes about five hours. By bus, the trip takes closer to seven hours; tickets cost between $10 and $25 USD. To avoid standing in the aisle for the entire journey, book tickets at least a day in advance. Many companies have buses that leave several times a day.

AeroSur flies daily from La Paz and Sucre to Aeropuerto Jorge Wilsterman in Cochabamba. The airport is 10 km (6 mi) from downtown. A taxi into town is about $5 USD.

Built on the traditional grid pattern, the central part of Cochabamba is divided into quadrants beginning at the intersection of Avenida de las Heroínas and Avenida Ayacucho. Streets are labeled *norte* (north), *sur*

10

(south), *este* (east), and *oeste* (west). The quadrant is included as an abbreviation in the address; for example, Hotel Aranjuez is located at Calle Buenos Aires E-0563.

ESSENTIALS

Air Travel AeroSur (⊕ www.aerosur.com). Aeropuerto Jorge Wilsterman (☎ 04/422-6548).

Bus Depot Terminal de Cochabamba (✉ Av. Ayacucho at Av. Aroma).

Currency Exchange Banco Mercantil (✉ Calle Calama E-0201, Cochabamba ☎ 04/425-1865). Banco Nacional (✉ Calle Nataniel Aguirre S-0198, Cochabamba ☎ 04/425-1860).

Internet Café Center Internet (✉ Av. de las Heroínas E-0267, Cochabamba ☎ 04/423-3423).

Post Office Cochabamba (✉ Av. de las Heroínas and Av. Ayacucho).

Rental Cars A. Barron's (✉ Calle Sucre E-0727, Cochabamba ☎ 04/422-2774). Toyota (✉ Av. Libertador Bolívar 1567, Cochabamba ☎ 04/428-5703).

Taxis Radio Taxi (✉ Lanza N-579, Cochabamba ☎ 04/422-8856).

Visitor Info Cochabamba (✉ Calle General Achá ☎ 04/422-1793 ☾ Weekdays 9–noon and 2:30–5).

EXPLORING

Many of the sights in Cochabamba, a colonial town founded in 1571, are scattered around the palm-lined **Plaza 14 de Septiembre,** where magnolias and jacarandas bloom and pigeons cruise for crumbs. Facing the main square is the **Catedral de Cochabamba,** which was started in 1571 but took more than 150 years to complete. One block southeast from the main square is a church called the **Templo de San Francisco,** a colonial masterpiece built in 1581 but thoroughly renovated in 1782 and again in 1926. Inside the Temple of St. Francis are elaborately carved wooden galleries and a striking gold-leaf altar.

El Cristo de la Concordia. A gleaming white statue of Christ with his arms outstretched stands watch on a hilltop overlooking Cochabamba. Slightly larger than The Statue of Christ in Rio de Janeiro, this is where many people come to get a perspective on this city with a population of more than half a million.

La Heroínas de la Coronilla. This monument honors women who died during Bolivia's protracted War of Independence. There are outstanding views of Cochabamba from La Coronilla, a hill on the outskirts of the city where the monument is located.

Museo Arqueológico. This excellent museum is one of the more comprehensive and interesting collections of artifacts outside of La Paz. On display in the Museum of Archaeology are pre-Columbian pottery, silver and gold work, and strikingly patterned handwoven Indian textiles. ✉ *Jordán and Aguirre* ☎ *No phone* ✍ *(Bs)20* ☾ *Weekdays 8:30–6:30, Sat. and Sun. 9–12.*

Palacio Portales. Across the Río Rocha, this palace was built but never occupied by Simón Patiño, a local tin baron who amassed one of the world's largest fortunes. The mansion and 10-acre gardens reflect his predilection for French Renaissance style. One of the chambers on the upper floor mimics Italy's Sistine Chapel. The mansion, a five-minute taxi ride from the center of town, is now a cultural and educational center. ⊠ *Av. Potosí 1450* ☎ *04/424–3137* ✉ *(Bs)10* ☉ *Tours weekdays at 5* PM *and Sat. at 11* AM.

WHERE TO EAT

Eating out and eating big is even more important in Cochabamba than the rest of the country; there may not be international dishes, but for traditional Bolivian fare the city is unrivaled. Leave yourself lots of time and don't eat breakfast first. If you are after something lighter—or resting between lunch and dinner—there are plenty of places for coffee and cakes, especially in El Prado near Plaza Colon, and in Calle España and its side streets.

$$$
BRAZILIAN
✕ **Bufalo Rodizio.** At this Brazilian-style eatery, all the meat you can eat is carved at your table by waiters dressed as gauchos. The traditional *Feijoada* (bean stew with beef and pork) is considered the house specialty. There's also an excellent salad bar and a variety of pasta dishes. Reserve a table on Sunday; they are usually packed with diners enjoying great views of the city. ⊠ *Edificio Torres Sofer, Av. Oquendo N-0654, 2° piso* ☎ *04/425–1597* ⊕ *www.bufalosrodizio.web.bo.*

$$
LATIN AMERICAN
✕ **Casa de Campo.** This informal and lively restaurant serves traditional Bolivian dishes—grilled meats and a fiery *picante mixto* (grilled chicken and beef tongue). Servings are large enough for two, so come with an appetite if you order local favorites like *Pollo Borracho* (chicken cooked in alcohol), pork in orange sauce, or grilled *conejo* (guinea pig). The *pique lobo* soup is extremely flavorful. Food is served outdoors on a shaded patio. ⊠ *Av. Aniceto Padilla and Av. Bolívar* ☎ *04/424–3937* 🖃 *AE, MC, V.*

$$
CHINESE
✕ **Chifa Lai Lai.** This *chifa,* or Chinese restaurant, has the kind of service usually found only in more expensive places. The food is tasty and the wines are reasonably priced. Start with the crispy spring rolls followed by one of their Ecuadoran shrimp dishes. Most selections, like sweet and sour chicken or pork, come with a side of rice or noodles. ⊠ *Av. Aniceto Padilla* ☎ *04/424–0469* 🖃 *AE, MC, V.*

$$
IRISH
Fodor's Choice
★
✕ **Na Cunna.** This Irish pub and restaurant on Avenida Salamanca (near Lanza) has a wide selection of dishes, a very friendly atmosphere, and an active role in the city's music scene. A main meal costs about (Bs)30. It's open Tuesday to Saturday from 7:30 PM to about 2:30 AM, with bands on Friday or Saturday. The live music makes it popular with young travelers who enjoy blending entertainment with a pint of Guinness. ⊠ *Av. Salamanca 577* ☎ *04/452–1982* 🖃 *MC, V.*

WHERE TO STAY

$$$
🛏 **Gran Hotel Cochabamba.** Most of the simple but comfortable rooms at this two-story hotel overlook the gazebo in the center of the plant-filled courtyard. Although rather small, the rooms have all the modern amenities including a 32-inch flat-screen TV with DVD player. The adjoining Restaurante Carillón serves a tasty pique macho and an excellent Sunday buffet. The hotel is located 1 km from the train station and

10

3 km from the city center. **Pros:** reasonable prices and good service. **Cons:** see the rooms first—away from the courtyard they're rather dark. ⊠ *Plaza Ubaldo Anze* ☎ *04/448–9520* ⊕ *www.granhotelcochabamba. com* ↪ *43 rooms, 5 suites* ⚿ *In room: no a/c, safe, DVD, Internet. In-hotel: restaurant, bar, tennis court, pool, laundry service, Wi-Fi hotspot* ⊟ *AE, MC, V* ⦿*BP.*

$$$ 🛏 **Hotel Aranjuez.** This elegant hotel is noted for its lovely gardens overflowing with bougainvillea. The well-appointed rooms are spacious and comfortable; most have baths attached. A live jazz band plays in the lobby bar most weekends. Although the hotel was renovated in 2010, it still retains the feeling of an old hacienda. **Pros:** beautiful gardens; holistic massage salon; welcoming for kids. **Cons:** rather pricey for the city. ⊠ *Av. Buenos Aires E-0563* ☎ *04/428–0076 or 04/428–0077* ⊕ *www.aranjuezhotel.com* ↪ *30 rooms, 3 suites* ⚿ *In room: no a/c, safe, DVD, Internet. In-hotel: restaurant, bar, pool, laundry service, Wi-Fi hotspot, parking (free)* ⊟ *AE, MC, V* ⦿*BP.*

$$$ 🛏 **Hotel Portales.** In a quiet residential area in the northern part of the city, this Spanish-colonial-style hotel surrounded by lush gardens is Cochabamba's most luxurious accommodation. It has numerous recreation facilities, from a racquetball court to two heated pools. It's a short taxi ride from the center of town, and local swing bands play in the bar. **Pros:** nice gardens; good restaurants. **Cons:** the rooms can be rather dilapidated; no elevator—not good if you are on the top floor. ⊠ *Av. Pando 1271* ☎ *04/428–5444* ⊕ *www.hotel-portales.com* ↪ *98 rooms, 8 suites* ⚿ *In-room: a/c. In-hotel: 2 restaurants, bar, pools, gym, laundry service, Wi-Fi hotspot* ⊟ *AE, MC, V* ⦿*BP.*

$$ 🛏 **Hotel Union.** You'll appreciate this hotel's location—a block from the main square. The rooms are simple and clean. Mostly business travelers stay here so don't expect much in the way of pampering and amenities. Ask for an upper-floor room away from noisy Avenida de las Heroínas. **Pros:** very central. **Cons:** service can be indifferent; no Internet. ⊠ *Calle Baptista S-0111* ☎ *04/450–9144* ↪ *30 rooms, 2 suites* ⚿ *In-room: a/c. In-hotel: restaurant, bar, laundry service* ⊟ *AE, MC, V* ⦿*CP.*

SHOPPING

Cochabamba is well known for its alpaca sweaters and leather goods, but don't expect prices much lower than in La Paz. Plaza Colón marks the start of **El Prado** (sometimes called Avenida Ballivián), a shop-lined avenue that stretches north to the Río Rocha. The local market, **La Cancha,** is open daily near Avenida Aroma. It's a good place to browse for less expensive crafts.

Asarti (⊠ *Calle México and Av. Ballivián* ☎ *04425–0455*) sells high-quality knits. They also have a showroom at the Radisson Hotel in La Paz. **Casa Fisher** (⊠ *Calle Ramorán Rivero 0204* ☎ *04/428–4549*) sells beautiful alpaca sweaters. **Tipay** (⊠ *Calle Jordán E-0732* ☎ *04/425–1303*) is a clothing cooperative of local women who sell handmade knits in alpaca and cotton.

SANTA CRUZ

900 km (560 mi) southeast of La Paz.

Just 30 years ago, oxen pulled carts through the muddy streets of Santa Cruz and cowboys rode in to wash off the dust and raise some more. Now this is the largest city in Bolivia and the most westernized. Exploitation of massive reserves of natural gas and oil have made the department of Santa Cruz the richest in the country. Add the temperatures to the mix (average 30°C, 86°F) and you have a very different proposition from the altiplano and La Paz. The people are different, too, more Brazilian in spirit and behavior (especially during Carnival), and the beauty of the women is legendary. Nonetheless, Santa Cruz, with more than 1.3 million inhabitants, hasn't been completely transformed—you can still find traces of its colonial past in the architecture of the city center. And don't be put off by the discos, country clubs, and burger joints—there are many good reasons to make the trip down, including the Jesuit Missions of Chiquitos, two exceptional national parks (Amboro and Noel Kempf Mercado), and the ancient fortress of Samaipata.

GETTING HERE AND AROUND

International flights stop at Aeropuerto Internacional Viru-Viru in Santa Cruz before continuing to La Paz. Similarly, flights from La Paz stop in Santa Cruz on their way out of the country. The airport is about 15 km (9 mi) north of the city. Buses to the center of town depart every 20 minutes and cost about (Bs)8. Taxis run about (Bs)50. The bus ride from La Paz takes about 20 hours and cost between (Bs)69 and (Bs)174.

Santa Cruz is a driver's town, but taxis are readily available on the streets; exercise caution and always use radio taxis.

SAFETY AND PRECAUTIONS

Crime in Santa Cruz is generally not focused on tourists as much as it is in La Paz, for example, but there is more of it, and it's dangerous. Armed robbery, kidnapping, and car theft are more common, and you should take necessary precautions. The best advice is to forget the relative safety of other Bolivian cities and behave as if you are in an average South American city.

ESSENTIALS

Air Travel Aeropuerto Internacional Viru-Viru (☎ *03/334–4411*).

Bus ServicesTerminal de Santa Cruz (✉ *Av. Cañoto at Av. Irala*). **Expreso Mopar** (☎ *02/237–7443*). **Trans Copacabana** (☎ *02/237–7894*).

Currency Exchange Banco Mercantil Santa Cruz (✉ *René Moreno at Suárez de Figueroa, Santa Cruz* ☎ *03/334–5000*). **Banco Nacional** (✉ *René Moreno 258, Santa Cruz* ☎ *03/336–4777*).

Internet Café Café Internet (✉ *Calle Sucre 673* ☎ *03/335–2161*).

Post Office Santa Cruz (✉ *Between Junín and Florida*).

Rental Cars A. Barron's (✉ *Av. Alemana 50, Santa Cruz* ☎ *03/342–0160*). **Imbex** (✉ *Calle Monseñor Peña 320, Santa Cruz* ☎ *03/353–3603*).

10

Taxis Radio Taxi Equipetrol (⊠ *Av. General Martínez 338, Santa Cruz*
☎ *03/335–2100*).

Visitor Info Santa Cruz (⊠ *Casa de la Cultura 1st fl., on Plaza* ☎ *03/333–2770*
⊙ *Weekdays 8:30–noon and 2:30–6*).

EXPLORING

Basílica Menor de San Lorenzo. Built between 1845 and 1915 on the ruins
of a 17th-century cathedral, this imposing church, on Plaza 24 de Septiembre, holds a small museum displaying colonial-era religious icons,
paintings, and sculptures. ⊠ *Plaza 24 de Septiembre* ☎ *03/332–7381*
⊠ *(Bs)10* ⊙ *Tues., Thurs. and Sun. 10–noon and 4–8.*

Casa de la Cultura. Cultural exhibits, recitals, and concerts, in addition
to a permanent exhibit of crafts made by indigenous people are all
housed here. ⊠ *Plaza 24 de Septiembre* ☎ *03/345–5000* ⊠ *Free* ⊙ *Daily*
9–noon and 3–6.

Fodor'sChoice
★
Jesuit Missions of Chiquitos. In the Chiquitania region of Santa Cruz, Jesuit
priests in the 17th century built this church for local Christianized Indians. The 10 churches that remain are beautiful examples of a merging
of Catholic and local religious influences of that period, as well as the
venue of an international festival of Baroque and Renaissance music.
It's also a UNESCO World Heritage Site. Ask about tours to the area
in agencies in the city.

WHERE TO EAT

There is a smaller range of hotels in Santa Cruz than in La Paz, but a
wider range of restaurants—both are generally more expensive, reflecting the fact that this is the most business-oriented region of the country.

$$$
FRENCH
✗ **El Candelabro.** International food and a very elegant ambience are
provided at this upmarket establishment split into two spaces: a piano
bar with live music (weekends only) and a restaurant. Treat yourself
to one of the many seafood dishes like salmon carpaccio, linguini with
shrimp or the sushi platter. Paella de Mariscos is a house favorite. The
menu also features chicken, risotto, llama, and a variety of vegetar-
ian specialties. ⊠ *Calle 7 Oeste Equipetrol* ☎ *03/337–7272* ⊕ *www.
restaurantecandelabro.com* ▭ *MC, V.*

$$$
BOLIVIAN
Fodor'sChoice
★
✗ **La Casa del Camba.** Big and always busy, this restaurant is one of the
best places to eat regional dishes. Popular selections include *picante de
gallina* (spicy chicken) or *chicharrón* (boiled pork ribs seasoned with
garlic, oregano, and lemon). Most plates are big enough for two. The
kitchen and service are excellent. If you happen to stop by on a weekend, you'll be treated to live music. The restaurant has a branch out
in the countryside, too. ⊠ *Av. Cristóbal de Mendoza* ☎ *03/342–7864*
▭ *AE, MC, V.*

$$$
ARGENTINE
✗ **Los Hierros.** Barbecue beef is the order of the day, and it's of the
finest cuts. Other mouthwatering options include pork loin, shrimp
kebab, salmon with capers, or catfish filet. Add one of their delicious
salads to your plate, and if you're brave, an antipasto first. The grilled
provolone is a great way to start your meal, and the wine list is huge.
Request a table on the second-floor terrace. ⊠ *Av. Monseñor Rivero 300*
☎ *03/337–1309* ⊕ *www.los-hierros.com* ▭ *AE, MC, V.*

Bolivian breakfast.

$$$
ECLECTIC
✕ **Makhassan.** Tasty food, good service, and kind people are what you'll find at this more affordable alternative to Yorimichi (⇨ *see review below*). The food is European–Asian fusion and includes Thai orange chicken, honey-glazed tuna, and coconut curry langostino. The lobster and salmon are prepared a variety of ways. The restaurant only offers sushi at night. ⊠ *Av. Las Americas 71* ☎ *03/332–2323* ⊕ *www.makhassan.com* ▭ *AE, MC, V.*

$$$$
JAPANESE
✕ **Yorimichi.** One of the most expensive restaurants in the city, and the service is dreadful, but the sushi is excellent. The combo platter of temaki, sashimi, nigiri, and California rolls will set you back less than $20 USD. Be prepared for the 15% service charge added to your bill. ⊠ *Av. Busch 548* ☎ *03/334–7717* ▭ *AE, MC, V.*

WHERE TO STAY

$$$
🛏 **Gran Hotel Santa Cruz.** This family-owned hotel dating from the 1930s is a few blocks south of Plaza 24 de Septiembre and is one of the few five-star hotels in the commercial center of Santa Cruz. Rooms are like comfortable dens; those that overlook the pool have small private balconies. The restaurant serves very good international cuisine. **Pros:** very comfortable; children under 12 are free; ATM in front of hotel. **Cons:** bad coffee; rooms next to the pool can get noisy. ⊠ *Calle Pari 59* ☎ *03/334–8811* ⊕ *www.granhotelsantacruz.com* ⤴ *70 rooms, 12 suites* ⌂ *In-room: a/c, safe, Internet. In-hotel: 2 restaurants, bars, pool, gym, laundry service, parking (free)* ▭ *AE, MC, V* ⦿ *BP.*

$$$$
🛏 **Hotel Camino Real.** A free-form pool meanders through the tropical gardens at this low-rise, high-class hotel in a residential neighborhood on the outskirts of Santa Cruz. The Tranquera restaurant serves

good international fare. The hotel offers guests cell phones and laptops upon request. Every room has a balcony and all the amenities you'd expect from an international five-star hotel. **Pros:** babysitting service; spacious rooms; heaters in rooms. **Cons:** far from the center of town; slow room service. ⊠ *Calle K 279, Equipetrol Norte* ☎ *03/342–3535* ⊕ *www.caminoreal.com.bo* ⊷ *121 rooms, 8 suites* ♿ *In-room: a/c, safe, Wi-Fi. In-hotel: 2 restaurants, pool, gym, spa, room service, laundry service, parking (free)* ▭ *AE, MC, V* ⦿ *BP.*

$$$$ ☷ **Hotel Los Tajibos.** This sprawling resort hotel on the edge of the city and 15 minutes from the airport is a series of low-slung buildings surrounded by lush gardens. It is frequented by business travelers who utilize the on-site convention center. El Papagayo restaurant serves excellent seafood. **Pros:** huge gardens; clean rooms; almost all rooms on the ground floor. **Cons:** long walk to the dining area; no outside food or drink allowed; street noise. ⊠ *Av. San Martín 455* ☎ *03/342–1000* ⊕ *www.lostajiboshotel.com* ⊷ *178 rooms, 6 suites* ♿ *In-room: Wi-Fi, no a/c. In-hotel: 2 restaurants, pool, gym, spa, parking (free), Wi-Fi hotspot, Internet terminal* ▭ *AE, MC, V* ⦿ *BP.*

$$ ☷ **Hotel Paititi.** This comfortable budget option is the sister hotel to the Viru Viru in Cochabamba. Air-conditioned rooms are available, or for a slight discount, you can request a room with a fan. **Pros:** good value. **Cons:** canned music; thunderous a/c; single rooms feel like cells. ⊠ *Av. Cañoto 450* ☎ *03/355–9167* ⊕ *www.hotelviruviru.com/hotelpaititi* ⊷ *40 rooms, 12 suites* ♿ *In-room: a/c (some). In-hotel: Internet terminal* ▭ *AE, MC, V* ⦿ *CP.*

$ ☷ **Jodanga.** This is one of the growing number of backpacker hostels in Bolivia, and a bit more civilized than others. The features are fairly standard for this kind of stay: free beers, Skype address, open kitchen, etc., but they include as much friendly help as they can give you. They even give Spanish classes and organized tours. There is a comfy lounge area with a TV and more than 100 DVDs to choose from. On Saturday night, stay for the open bar and all-you-can-eat barbecue for (Bs)45. The proximity to the bus station and airport make this a popular place, so book ahead. **Pros:** lively environment; airport pickup (unusual for a hostel); committed staff. **Cons:** late-night drinking in the Jacuzzi; laundry service is pricey. ⊠ *El Fuerte No. 1380* ☎ *03/339–6542* ⊕ *www.jodanga.com* ⊷ *37 beds, 4 private rooms* ♿ *In-room: a/c. In-hotel: pool, laundry service, Wi-Fi hotspot* ▭ *AE, MC, V* ⦿ *CP.*

$$$$ ☷ **Yotaú.** The spacious accommodations in this all-suite hotel are more like apartments, complete with kitchens and washing machines. Just outside of Santa Cruz in the suburb of Barrio Equipetrol, this strikingly modern hotel has a landscaped garden. Babysitting service and holistic massages are available upon request. Special rates are available for guests that stay three nights or more. **Pros:** babysitting service; wide range of facilities including gym, car rental, and medical care. **Cons:** expensive option if you are not with family or friends; large rooms; architecture is not to all tastes. ⊠ *Av. San Martín 7* ☎ *03/336–7799* ⊕ *www.yotau.com.bo* ⊷ *100 suites* ♿ *In-room: no a/c. In-hotel: restaurant, bar, pool, gym, laundry, Wi-Fi hotspot, parking (free)* ▭ *AE, MC, V* ⦿ *BP.*

Central Bolivia Tours

Recommended day trips in the department of Santa Cruz include the ancient site of Samaipata and Amboro National Park—both are close to the city itself and they can be combined. You can also stay overnight at Amboro and venture a bit deeper into this excellent park to see its cloud forests and birds. Noel Kempf Mercado Park, on the northeastern border with Brazil, offers a great opportunity to stay in real Amazon jungle, and has a good range of services for tourists. It's best to take five or six days for this and camp in the park. The Jesuit Missions are another highlight of this area, but their distance from the city of Santa Cruz means it's a good idea to have a few days free to visit the churches.

There are numerous tour operators for this area. When looking, make sure the agency you choose is legitimate and worth the money by checking with the municipal tourism authority (☎ 03/378–493) or the tourist office at the airport.

TOUR OPERATORS

Rosario Tours offers trips to all the main attractions of central Bolivia and has an excellent reputation (✉ Are-nales 193, Santa Cruz ☎ 03/336–9656 ⊕ www.rosariotours.com).

Forest Tours covers all the main destinations, but with a clear ecotourism focus (✉ Cuellar, 22, between 24 de Septiembre and Libertad, Santa Cruz ☎ 03/337–2042 ⊕ www.forestbolivia. com).

Magri Turismo covers all of Bolivia and is a well-established company with offices in many cities. In Santa Cruz you will find them at (✉ Guarnes, esq. Potosí, Santa Cruz ☎ 03/334–5663 ⊕ www.magriturismo.com).

Viru Viru Travel has a particularly good range of ecotourism tours for the national parks of Santa Cruz, and also covers the baroque music festival at the Jesuit Missions (✉ Edificio Oriente, Local 1, Calle Chuquisaca esq. Ballivián, Santa Cruz ☎ 03/336–4040 ⊕ www.viruvirutravel.com).

Ruta Verde covers all the main tourist destinations in Bolivia, including the big-three national parks and a trip retracing Che Guevara's last steps. It's Dutch-run, and has a good reputation. (✉ Calle 21 de Mayo 318, Santa Cruz ☎ 03/339–6470 ⊕ www. rutaverdebolivia.com).

10

NIGHTLIFE

Dress to impress and take your credit cards if you're going out in the center of Santa Cruz or in the neighborhood of Equipetrol—most of the bars are exclusive and pricey. Nonetheless, it can be very entertaining watching the young and beautiful flaunt it all at one of the high-concept establishments. Have a walk along Avenida San Martín in Equipetrol and take your pick.

SHOPPING

Santa Cruz is not the best place to pick up your handcrafted and hard-bargained-for indigenous piece of art, as most shops are focused on modern creature comforts, but you'll find crafts shops and street vendors scattered around Plaza 24 de Septiembre. **Artecampo** (✉ Calle Monseñor Salvatierra 407 ☎ 03/334–1843) is a cooperative with a colorful selection of handmade hammocks made from locally grown cotton. There are also mobiles and intricate hand-painted woodwork.

SAMAIPATA

120 km (74 mi) southwest of Santa Cruz.

Located 2½ hours east of Santa Cruz, Samaipata is situated near the national park Amboró between the Andes foothills. Best known for the pre-Colombian ruins El Fuerte, this lush hideaway is also home to waterfalls Las Cuevas and La Pajcha and serves as the gateway to the Cruceño Valleys where historic cave paintings are found. Unpaved village roads are lined with shops selling fresh bread, organic vegetables, local honey, and various types of cheese and sausage. Framing the main Plaza Principal are art galleries and a small museum explaining the region's history. Samaipata still lacks an independent tourist office and money exchange so bring enough Bolivianos if you plan on staying awhile. Between April and September, south winds make for cold nights.

GETTING HERE AND AROUND

From Santa Cruz city, minibuses depart daily for Samaipata at 5 PM from Avenida Omar Chávez Ortiz on the corner of Soliz de Olguin. You can also catch a 4 PM bus departing from Plaza Oruro at Avenida Grigota. The ride takes 2½ hours and costs approximately (Bs)15. Private taxis from Santa Cruz will cost you about (Bs)25 per person.

ESSENTIALS

Taxi **Expresso Samaipata** (☎ *03/333–5067*).

EXPLORING

El Fuerte. Lurking in the valleys 200 km (124 mi) from the city of Santa Cruz, *El Fuerte* (the fort) of Samaipata was once the center of a huge pre-Colombian civilization; there is now some doubt that it had any military purpose, but it still impresses. The massive sculptured rock at the heart of the site, best seen from a distance, is a unique monument to Andean culture and development, and one of the largest carved stones in the world. The best way to get to the site is by road from Santa Cruz to the town of Samaipata (about two hours), then hire a taxi to the fort itself, which is 7 km (4 mi) away. 🖼 *(Bs)20* ⊙ *Daily 9–5.*

WHERE TO EAT AND STAY

$ ✕ **La Ranita.** This French bakery and teahouse has many choices of excel-
CAFÉ lent pastries and bread; get there early when the loaves are still warm. Late risers can enjoy happy hour from 6–7 PM and sample the delectable chocolate brownies. ⊠ *Calle Arce, half a block off the town square* ☎ *03/944–6390* ▬ *MC, V* ⊙ *Closed Tues. and Wed.*

$$ ✕ **Tierra Libre.** Set in a beautiful garden near the town square, this eatery
BOLIVIAN offers excellent Bolivian and International food. The tapas-like *Tablitas* are great for sampling a variety of flavors. Vegetarian dishes are prepared with organic, locally grown ingredients and the lemonade is squeezed just before it reaches the table. Owner-Chef "Alex" from Cochabamba, is considered one of the best in the region. Live music is occasionally featured on weekends. ⊠ *Calle Sucre* ☎ *726–022729* ▬ *MC, V* ⊙ *Closed Wed.*

Sunday Market Foray

If you are in Sucre over a weekend, take a full-day excursion to the village of Tarabuco to experience its famous Sunday market. About 64 km (40 mi) east of Sucre, here you will see indigenous women wearing tri-cornered hats fringed with coins, and men with brightly colored ponchos and leather helmets resembling those worn centuries ago by the Spanish conquistadors. Like many towns in the region, Tarabuco is filled with vendors from end to end selling finely woven belts and *charangos*, a stringed instrument made from armadillo shells. In mid-March Tarabuco is the location of one of South America's liveliest traditional festivals, Pujilay.

$$ ☷ **Andoriña Hostel.** Two blocks from the main square, this rustic hostel doubles as an art gallery with more than 200 framed photographs on the walls. The Dutch-Bolivian owners offer local transportation, Tai Chi workshops, movie night, live music, and a hearty pancake breakfast. Packed lunches are available for hikers, and if you'd like local insight, the owners can provide guided tours to hidden waterfalls at no cost. Communal areas include a cozy lounge and a rooftop Jacuzzi overlooking the valley. If you happen to fall in love with the place, the hostel welcomes volunteers for six weeks at a time. **Pros:** common areas with book exchange; comfy beds. **Cons:** most rooms have bunks with ladders; no Internet. ⊠ *Calle Campero s/n, opposite 'El Deber' 2 blocks before Main square* ☎ *03/944–6333* ⊕ *www.andorinasamaipata. com* ➴ *5 rooms* ⚐ *In-room: no a/c. In-hotel: bar* ▭ *AE, MC, V* ❖❘ *BP.*

SOUTHERN BOLIVIA

10

There are some major contrasts in the south of Bolivia, partly because it is so huge. Potosí, steeped in history, most of it bloody, is high, cold, and barren. Tarija, up against the Argentinian border, is warm, friendly, and easygoing. Sucre is somewhere in the middle, an earnest university town and the capital of Bolivia. The Salar de Uyuni is, quite simply, out of this world.

GETTING HERE AND AROUND

Although the highways aren't the best, driving can be a nice way to see some areas of southern Bolivia. When visiting Potosí it's best to fly to Sucre and drive from there. You should also consider hiring a car and driver or taking a tour through a travel agency. The highway is good between Sucre and Potosí, but plan to overnight, as it passes through mountains and is not lighted. The best way to get to the wine country of Tarija is by flying direct from La Paz or Santa Cruz.

SUCRE

740 km (460 mi) southeast of La Paz.

Sucre has had many names since it was founded by the Spanish in 1538. The town's first official name was La Plata, but it was just as often called Charcas. In 1776, after splitting the region from Peru, the Spanish changed the name to Chuquisaca. Locals now refer to Sucre as *la ciudad blanca* (the white city)—no wonder, since by government edict all buildings in the center of the city must be whitewashed each year.

It was in Sucre that the region declared its independence from Spain in 1825. The country was named for its liberator, Simón Bolívar. Sucre was the country's original capital, but the main government functions were transferred to La Paz in the late 1800s, leaving the Corte Suprema de Justicia (Supreme Court) as Sucre's main governmental function.

Although its population now tops 200,000, Sucre—with its ornate churches, cobblestone streets, and broad plazas—retains the feel of a colonial town. Its moderate year-round climate and friendly people make it a pleasant if somewhat dull place to stay while taking side trips to Tarabuco or Potosí, or checking out the dinosaur prints outside of town.

GETTING HERE AND AROUND

Sucre's Aeropuerto Juana Azurduy de Padilla (☎ *064/454–445*)—about 5 km (3 mi) north of Sucre—has regular flights to La Paz on AeroSur. A taxi ride into town should cost about (Bs)15. Buses bound for Potosí and Sucre leave La Paz daily. The 19-hour trip to Sucre costs less than (Bs)100. Buses between Sucre and Potosí depart approximately every hour. The trip takes about three hours and costs about (Bs)40.

ESSENTIALS

Bus Contacts Sucre (✉ *Calle Ostria Gutiérrez* ☎ *04/644–1292*).

Currency Exchange Banco Santa Cruz (✉ *Calle San Alberto and España* ☎ *04/645–5400*).

Post Office Sucre (✉ *Av. Argentina 50*).

Rental Cars Imbex (✉ *Serranoí 165, Sucre* ☎ *04/646–12222*).

Taxis Exclusivo (✉ *Jaime Mendoza 960, Sucre* ☎ *064/451–414*). **Sucre** (✉ *Playa 25 de Mayo, Sucre* ☎ *064/451–333*).

Visitor Info Sucre Oficina de Turismo (✉ *Nicolás Ortiz 182* ⊘ *Weekdays 8–noon and 2–6*).

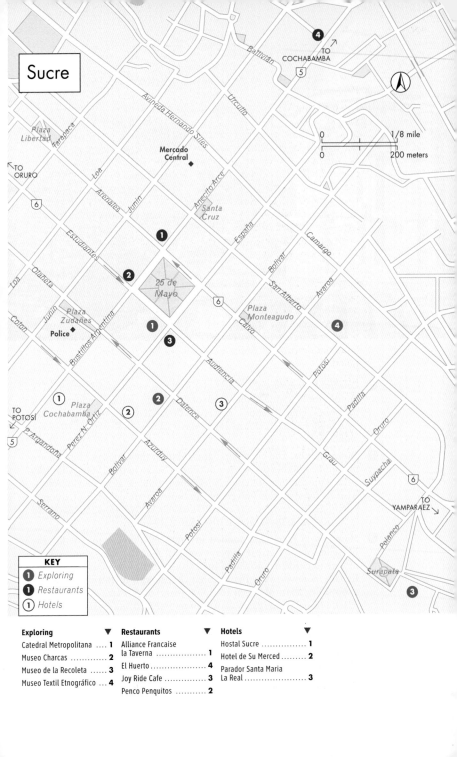

Sucre

Mercado Central ◆

Plaza Libertad

← **TO ORURO**

Plaza Zudáñez

Police ◆

Plaza Cochabamba

← **TO POTOSÍ**

25 de Mayo

Plaza Monteagudo

Santa Cruz

TO COCHABAMBA

TO YAMPARAEZ →

Surapata

0 — 1/8 mile
0 — 200 meters

Exploring ▼	Restaurants ▼	Hotels ▼
Catedral Metropolitana **1**	Alliance Francaise la Taverna **1**	Hostal Sucre **1**
Museo Charcas **2**	El Huerto **4**	Hotel de Su Merced **2**
Museo de la Recoleta **3**	Joy Ride Cafe **3**	Parador Santa Maria La Real **3**
Museo Textil Etnográfico ... **4**	Penco Penquitos **2**	

KEY
① Exploring
① Restaurants
① Hotels

The city of Potosí is a UNESCO World Heritage site.

EXPLORING

① Catedral Metropolitana. Started in 1559, this neoclassical cathedral is famous for its statue of the Virgin of Guadalupe, which is adorned with diamonds, gold, emeralds, and pearls donated during the 17th century by mining barons. ⊠ *Plaza 25 de Mayo* ⊠ *Free* ⊗ *Weekdays 10–noon and 3–5, Sat. 10–noon.*

② Museo Charcas. The most popular exhibits at the Charcas Museum are mummified bodies discovered outside of Sucre in the 1960s. Curators believe the centuries-old mummies were entombed as human sacrifices. Also featured at this university-run museum are galleries of colonial paintings and textiles. ⊠ *Calle Bolívar 698* ☎ *04/645–3285* ⊠ *(Bs)20* ⊗ *Mon.–Fri. 8:30–12 and 2:30–6, Sat. 2:30–6.*

③ Museo de la Recoleta. Founded in 1601 by Franciscan monks, the Museum of the Retreat displays colonial religious works in a setting of serene gardens known as the "Courtyard of the Orange Trees." Equally noteworthy is the restored chapel with its intricately carved choir stalls, many of which are 1,000 years old. ⊠ *Plaza Pedro Anzures* ☎ *04/645–1987* ⊠ *(Bs)10* ⊗ *Weekdays 9–11:30 and 3–5:30.*

④ Museo Textil Etnográfico. This museum is housed in the colonial Caserón de la Capellanía. The Textile and Ethnographic Museum preserves the 4,000-year-old weavings and tapestry art of the Andean world, especially communities around Tarabuco. A display of costumes showcases regional fiesta garb; there are also loom demonstrations. ⊠ *Calle San Alberto 413* ☎ *04/645–3841* ⊠ *(Bs)16* ⊗ *Mon.–Sat. 8:30–12:30 and 2:30–6.*

WHERE TO EAT

Sucre's large student population keeps its many inexpensive restaurants in business. Around Plaza 25 de Mayo, many offer a *menú del día* or *almuerzo* (meal of the day) for $2 or $3 USD. If you're not a fan of spicy food, avoid dishes prefaced with the words *ají* (pepper) or *picante* (spicy).

$$ ✕ **Alliance Française la Taverna.** You may not have come to Sucre to eat

FRENCH crepes, but they're excellent at this restaurant in the French Cultural Center. The menu also includes delicious ratatouille or beefsteak with Roquefort sauce. Entrees come with salad, fries and a beverage. Seating is available in the dining room or outside in the courtyard. The reasonable prices and location, near Plaza 25 de Mayo and the Universidad San Francisco, make it a popular spot. ⊠ *Calle Aniceto Arce 35* ☎ *04/645–5719* ▭ *No credit cards.*

$$ ✕ **El Huerto.** At this restaurant near the municipal park, adventurous

LATIN AMERICAN carnivores should try a traditional Bolivian entrée, such as *picante de lengua* (spicy tongue). For something a bit more familiar, order filet mignon or one of the many pasta dishes like lasagna Bolognese. The chef's specialty is the Paella Andina prepared with quinoa and seafood. There's plenty on the menu for vegetarians, too. The outdoor patio has a beautiful garden, and is a pleasant place to linger over a long meal. Bring a sweater at night, as it gets a bit chilly. ⊠ *Ladislao Cabrera 86* ☎ *04/645–1538* ⊕ *www.elhuertorestaurante.com* ▭ *MC, V.*

$ ✕ **Joy Ride Cafe.** As the name suggests, a backpacker café with all that it

CAFÉ involves, but they also run mountain biking and hiking trips. The café serves tapas and a great range of Belgian beers, too. Grab a seat on the patio or in the upstairs lounge where films are shown every evening. ⊠ *Nicolás Ortiz 14* ☎ *04/642–5544* ⊕ *www.joyridebol.com* ▭ *MC, V.*

$ ✕ **Penco Penquitos.** For pocket change you can have a sandwich or nibble

CAFÉ on an impressive selection of fresh pastries, from éclairs to empanadas, at this café near the university. Omelets make for a good brunch or you can satisfy your sweet tooth with a slice of lemon meringue pie. ⊠ *Calle Estudiantes 66* ☎ *04/644–3946* ▭ *No credit cards.*

WHERE TO STAY

Sucre has many small hotels and hostels, almost all of which are comfortable, clean, and friendly. Most include breakfast.

$$$ ▥ **Hostal de Su Merced.** When you notice the colorful wood ceiling in the reception room—a reproduction of the original painted by a Jesuit priest—you know instantly that this family-owned hotel is a gem. Built as a private home in the late 17th century, the gleaming white colonial structure with a handsome rooftop terrace has large, airy rooms with sunlight streaming in through the tall windows. There is a lovely courtyard and from the sundeck you get excellent views of the entire city. **Pros:** colonial architecture; on-site Spanish courses; good breakfast. **Cons:** slightly run-down rooms; unfriendly service; pricey. ⊠ *Calle Azurduy 16* ☎ *04/644–2706, 04/644–2706, or 04/644–5150* ⊕ *www. desumerced.com* ⇥ *14 rooms, 2 suites* ⚙ *In-room: no a/c. In-hotel: restaurant, room service, laundry, Wi-Fi hotspot* ▭ *AE, MC, V* ⎢⎥ *BP.*

10

$$ ☐ **Hostal Sucre.** This colonial-style place, just two blocks from Plaza 25 de Mayo, is built around two inner courtyards—which means the rooms are all quiet. A restaurant serves light meals and snacks. **Pros:** a nice old building; lovely courtyards; helpful staff. **Cons:** hotel interior could use renovation; rooms are cold at night. ⊠ *Calle Bustillos 113* ☎ *04/645–1411* ⊕ *www.hostalsucre.com.bo* ↪ *33 rooms* △ *In-room: no a/c. In-hotel: restaurant, Wi-Fi hotspot* ⊟ *AE, MC, V* ⊠ *CP.*

$$$ ☐ **Parador Santa Maria La Real.** Although expensive by Bolivian stan-
Fodor's Choice dards, this 18-century villa is definitely worth the splurge. Inside are
★ stunning courtyards, a small museum, and 23 rooms, each adorned with antiques and works of art. Owner Sonia Pascual is a former art professor who has decorated the hotel colonial style, and has restored sections to its original state including the beautiful blue patio. The rooftop terrace offers views across Sucre, making it the perfect spot to read a book or gaze at the stars. Although the hotel lacks a restaurant, room service is available throughout the day. Discounts are offered to those who stay a minimum of three nights. **Pros:** heaters in the rooms; comfortable beds; close to city center; great breakfast. **Cons:** staff can be unfriendly; voices echo in the courtyard. ⊠ *Calle Bolivar 625* ☎ *04/643–9592* ⊕ *www.parador.com.bo* ↪ *19 rooms, 4 suites* △ *In-room: no a/c, safe, refrigerator, Wi-Fi. In-hotel: room service, gym, spa, laundry service, Wi-Fi hotspot, parking (free)* ⊟ *AE, MC, V* ⊠ *BP.*

POTOSÍ

169 km (105 mi) southwest of Sucre.

Potosí has a split and tragic personality. Its soaring churches and opulent mansions call to mind a time when this was the wealthiest city in South America. The sagging roofs and crumbling facades make it difficult to put the town's painful past and difficult present out of your mind.

Silver, tin, and zinc from nearby Cerro Rico made fortunes for the mineral barons who built their grand homes along Potosí's winding cobblestone streets. Tens of thousands of people flocked here hoping to make a little money. In 1650, with a population topping 160,000, Potosí was the largest and most prosperous city, first on the continent and then in the world, and the Spanish even now describe things of great value as "worth a potosí." But that wealth came from the labor of more than 8 million indigenous people forced to work in the mines, most of whom died there.

There's another old saying that puts all this wealth into perspective: "Bolivia had the cow, but the other countries got the milk." Potosí is now one of Bolivia's poorest cities. Depleted mines, outdated machinery, and an inhospitable terrain—Potosí sits on a windy plain at 13,452 feet above sea level—are not leading to prosperity. But as more and more buildings are restored (some as an act of contrition by the Spanish), more people are being drawn to one of Bolivia's most interesting cities.

GETTING HERE AND AROUND

Potosí has no direct flights from La Paz, but you can get here directly from La Paz by bus. The journey, via Oruro, takes about nine hours, and is bearable with an overnight Bus Cama (bus with a bed). A better

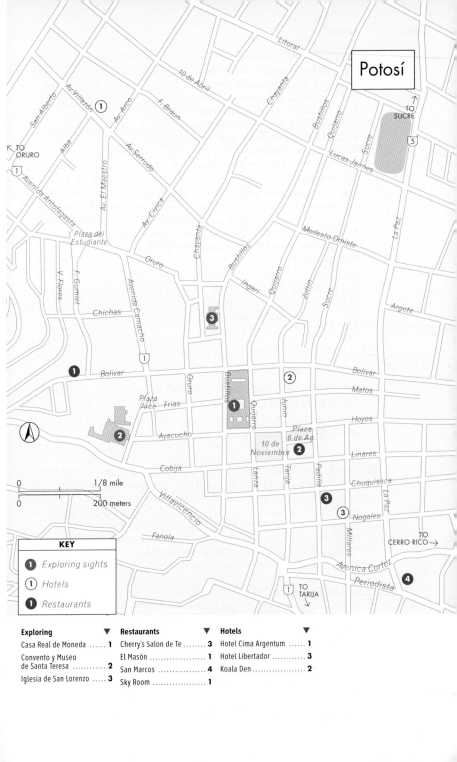

Potosí

TO SUCRE

TO ORURO

TO CERRO RICO →

TO TARIJA

KEY

1 Exploring sights

1 Hotels

1 Restaurants

0   1/8 mile

0   200 meters

Exploring ▼	**Restaurants** ▼	**Hotels** ▼
Casa Real de Moneda **1**	Cherry's Salon de Te **3**	Hotel Cima Argentum **1**
Convento y Museo de Santa Teresa **2**	El Masón **1**	Hotel Libertador **3**
Iglesia de San Lorenzo **3**	San Marcos **4**	Koala Den **2**
	Sky Room **1**	

alternative is to come via Sucre, as the road is better and the journey is short (164 km/three hours). If you're coming from Santa Cruz, daily flights are available through AeroSur, BOA, and TAM, and take about 45 minutes. You could also fly from La Paz to Sucre (40 minutes) and then catch a three-hour bus to Potosí.

> **TIP**
>
> Potosí is very high up, so take precautions. Don't come directly here from sea level, take it easy once you are here, and bring a lot of warm clothing.

The only way to get around Potosí itself is to walk. The steep, winding streets and sidewalks are narrow, so pedestrian traffic can often be more of a problem than cars. To visit the museums and historic buildings you'll need a guide. English-speaking guides aren't always available, so consider arranging a tour through a travel agency in La Paz or Santa Cruz.

ESSENTIALS

Airlines AeroSur (✉ *Av. Irala #616, Santa Cruz* ☎ *03/336-7400* ⊕ *www. aerosur.com*). **BOA** (✉ *Prolongación Aroma #20 Edificio Casanova PB of. 7 Azona Palacio de Justicia., Santa Cruz* ☎ *03/312-1343* ⊕ *www.boa.bo*). **TAM** (☎ *800/570-5700* ⊕ *www.tam.com.br*).

Buses Potosí Bus Terminal (✉ *Av. Universitaria* ☎ *02/624-3362*).

Post Office Potosí (✉ *Av. Lanza 13*).

Taxis I.N.N. (✉ *Calle Frias 58* ☎ *062/222-606*). **Potosí** (✉ *Zona San Clemente 125* ☎ *062/225-257*).

Visitor Info Potosí Oficina de Turismo (✉ *Cámara de Minería, Calle Quijarro* ☎ *02/225-288* ⊘ *Weekdays 9–noon and 3–6*).

EXPLORING

❶ Casa Real de Moneda. The showpiece of Potosí is the Royal Mint, built

Fodor'sChoice ★ in 1773 at a cost of $10 million USD. This massive stone structure, where coins were once minted with silver from nearby Cerro Rico, takes up an entire city block. It now holds Bolivia's largest and most important museum. On display are huge wooden presses that fashioned the strips of silver from which the coins were pressed, as well as an extensive collection of the coins minted here until 1953. There's also an exhibit of paintings, including works by Bolivia's celebrated 20th-century artist, Cecilio Guzmán de Rojas. A guard accompanies all tours to unlock each room as it's visited. The building is cool, so bring along a sweater. To see everything will take about three hours. ✉ *Ayacucho at Lanza* ☎ *04/622-2777* ⊕ *www.casanacionaldemoneda. org.bo* ⊡ *(Bs)20* ⊘ *Tues.–Sat. 9–noon and 2:30–7, Sun. 9–12.*

Fodor'sChoice ★ **Cerro Rico.** Five thousand tunnels crisscross Cerro Rico, the "Rich Hill," which filled Spain's coffers until the silver reserves were exhausted in the early 19th century. Today tin is the primary extract, though on the barren mountainside you still see miners sifting through the remnants of ancient excavations. If you don't mind tight spaces, take a tour through one of the mines that are still active. You'll descend into the dark, humid tunnels where hundreds of workers strip down to next to nothing because of the intense heat. ■TIP➔ Keep in mind that these mines are muddy, and wear clothes you don't mind getting dirty. Hard hats, raincoats, boots, and carbide lamps are provided, but take along a flashlight to get a better look at things. The extremely narrow entrance to the mine may scare you off, but go in far enough to give *El Tío* (a statue of a small, grinning devil) a cigarette and add more coca leaves to the pile around his feet. The miners say he brings safety and prosperity.

② Convento y Museo de Santa Teresa. The Convent and Museum of St. Theresa displays a strange mix of religious artifacts. In one room are sharp iron instruments once used to inflict pain on penitent nuns, as well as a blouse embroidered with wire mesh and prongs meant to prick the flesh. Other rooms contain works by renowned colonial painters, including Melchor Pérez Holguín. ⊠ *Calle Chicas* ☎ *02/622–3847* ✉ *(Bs)21* ⊙ *Weekdays 9–noon and 2–6.*

③ Iglesia de San Lorenzo. Potosí's most spectacular church, built between 1728 and 1744, has some of the finest examples of baroque carving in South America. Elaborate combinations of mythical figures and indigenous designs are carved in high relief on the stone facade. If the front doors are locked, try to get in through the courtyard. ⊠ *Calle Bustillos* ☎ *No phone.*

WHERE TO EAT

Potosí is not known for its food, but one thing worth trying is the delicious *kala'purka* soup, made with maize flour and cooked using volcanic stones. You'll be full for days.

$
CAFÉ
✕**Cherry's Salon de Te.** At this delightful coffee shop you can sip a cup of refreshing mate de coca while you ponder the delicious selection of cakes and strudels. To start off your day, order the pancake stack or a healthy bowl of muesli. ⊠ *Calle Padilla 8* ☎ *02/622–2969* ▬ *No credit cards.*

$$
LATIN AMERICAN
✕**El Mesón.** Potosí's most exclusive restaurant has a quiet dining room set inside an old bookstore on the corner of the town plaza. Here you can get traditional Bolivian food with a French influence including trout, steak, and pasta prepared a variety of ways. ⊠ *Calle Tarija at Calle Linares* ☎ *02/622–3087* ▬ *MC, V.*

$$
LATIN AMERICAN
✕**San Marcos.** Potosí's most unusual restaurant occupies a former silver processing plant. Each piece of ancient machinery has been put to use—the bar, for example, is a platform where stones were once washed. Both local and international dishes are served, including *trucha al gusto* (trout broiled with lemon, garlic, and pesto sauce) and *filete flambé San Marcos* (steak doused with cognac and set aflame). The llama steak is served in a light sauce of butter, lemon, and mint. There's live music every Friday night. ⊠ *La Paz and Betanzos* ☎ *02/622–2781* ▬ *MC, V.*

$$
LATIN AMERICAN
✕**Sky Room.** You'll be treated to fine sunset views from this aptly named rooftop restaurant. The service can be indifferent, but the restaurant serves good traditional dishes, such as *pichanga* (various types of meats served with salad). The *Milanesa de Pollo* (breaded chicken), served with soup, salad and dessert, will run you about (Bs)25. ⊠ *Edif. Matilde, Calle Bolívar 701* ☎ *02/622–0138* ▬ *MC, V.*

10

WHERE TO STAY

$$$ ⬚ **Hotel Cima Argentum.** Near the Santa Teresa Convent and six blocks from the Casa de Moneda, this is one of Potosí's more modern hotels. The large rooms and nine suites are spread over three floors, with balconies overlooking a courtyard under a glass dome. The rooms are rather somberly decorated but comfortable. The restaurant is open from 7 AM to 11 PM. **Pros:** heaters in rooms; modern design and service standards. **Cons:** rather gloomy and chilly rooms; street noise; far from downtown. ⊠ *Av. Villazon 239* 🕾 *02/622–9538* ⊕ *www.hca-potosi.com* ↩ *20 rooms, 9 suites* ⚱ *In-room: no a/c, Wi-Fi. In-hotel: restaurant, room service, laundry service, Internet terminal, Wi-Fi hotspot, parking (free)* ▭ *MC, V* ⦵|*BP.*

$$$ ⬚ **Hotel Libertador.** Artwork by local Potosí painters brightens hallways and rooms in this centrally located hotel, probably the best in the city, although you may find this designation relative. There's a small patio on the top floor where you can risk a little sun. The big plus here is central heating. **Pros:** heaters in the rooms. **Cons:** indifferent service and facilities for the price. ⊠ *Millares 58* 🕾 *02/622–7877* ⊕ *www. libertadorpotosi.com.bo* ↩ *23 rooms, 2 suites* ⚱ *In-room: no a/c, Wi-Fi. In-hotel: bar, Wi-Fi hotspot, parking (free)* ▭ *MC, V* ⦵|*BP.*

$$ ⬚ **Koala Den.** This backpacker hostel is a bit pricey for this bracket, but the staff is helpful, the rooms are heated, and you can have your own bathroom. Added bonuses include a book exchange, hot showers, public kitchen, and a communal lounge where TV and Wi-Fi are available. A bunk in a dorm room will run you (Bs)53, compared to (Bs)150 for a private room for two. The hostel is also very central. **Pros:** quieter than average; friendly staff; good breakfast. **Cons:** run-down on the outside; slow Internet connection. ⊠ *Junin 56* 🕾 *02/622–6467* ⚱ *In-room: no a/c. In-hotel: bar, Wi-Fi hotspot* ▭ *No credit cards* ⦵|*CP.*

SHOPPING

Despite Potosí's rich mineral wealth, don't expect bargains on handcrafted silver jewelry. Brass and low-grade silver items can be found at the **Mercado Central** at Bustillos and Bolívar. The **Mercado Artesenal**, on the corner of Sucre and Omiste, has locally produced crafts.

SALAR DE UYUNI

219 km (136 mi) southwest of Potosí.

Fodor's Choice One of Bolivia's most spectacular sites, the Salar de Uyuni is the world's
★ highest salt flat, at 3,650 meters (11,975 feet) above sea level, and also the largest, at 10,582 square km (4086 square mi). Once part of a prehistoric salt lake covering most of southwestern Bolivia, it still extends through much of the departments of Potosí and Oruro. As well as the vast expanse of salt, you'll find a series of eerie, translucent lagoons tinted green and red due to high copper and sulfur contents. Living on the lagoons are flamingos (also tinted green and red), rheas, vicuñas, and foxes. Driving across the salt flat, whether in the dry or rainy season, is a unique experience.

Southern Bolivia Tour Operators

Candelaria Tours in Sucre organizes trips to Potosí and to nearby Tarabuco for the Sunday market. In Potosí, Sin Fronteras and Hidalgo Tours organize excursions around the city as well as to the Cerro Rico mines. Fremen Tours in La Paz arranges wine tours of the Tarija area.

It is best to organize a trip on the Salar while you are still in La Paz—local agencies in Uyuni are unreliable, to say the least, and this is no place to get stuck. Toñito Tours specializes in tours in southwestern Bolivia. It has a major commitment to the local community in Uyuni, and its hotel does an excellent pizza. Trips to the Salar de Uyuni are usually for four days and cost about $30 USD a day, including accommodations, a car and driver, and a cook who prepares three meals a day.

Tour Companies Candelaria Tours (✉ *Calle Audiencia 1, Sucre* ☎ *064/461–661* ⊕ *www. candelariatours.com*). Altamira Tours (✉ *Av. del Maestro 50, Sucre* ☎ *04/645–3525* ⊕ *www. altamiratoursbolivia.com*). Fremen Tours (✉ *Plaza Abaroa, La Paz* ☎ *02/232–7073* ⊕ *www.frementours. com*). Hidalgo Tours (✉ *Av. Bolívar at Av. Junín, Potosí* ☎ *062/222–5186* ⊕ *www.hidalgotours.net*). Magri Turismo (✉ *Calle Capitán Ravelo 2101, La Paz* ☎ *02/244–2727* ⊕ *www.magriturismo.com*). Sin Fronteras (✉ *Calle Bustillos 1092, Potosí* ☎ *062/224–058*). Toñito Tours (✉ *Sagárnaga 189, La Paz* ☎ *02/233–6250* ✉ *Av. Ferroviaria 152, Uyuni* ☎ *02/693–3186* ⊕ *www. bolivianexpeditions.com*). Zig Zag Eco Tours and Treks (✉ *Calle Illampu 867, La Paz* ☎ *02/2457814 or 71522822* ⊕ *www.zigzagbolivia.com*).

GETTING HERE AND AROUND

It takes four to five hours of travel on very rough roads to reach Uyuni from Potosí and twice that from La Paz, but there is a new road, which makes this more viable, and takes you right to the edge of the Salar at Tahua. Most people choose to make arrangements with a travel agency, such as Fremen Tours or Zig Zag Eco Tours and Treks. Another option is to get a bus to Oruro and take the train from there to Uyuni, which takes about seven hours for the train portion alone. Buses from La Paz to Oruro take three hours, or you can book an overnight bus leaving La Paz at 9 PM and arriving in Uyuni at 7 AM. Although traveling by railway is cheaper, faster and more comfortable than traveling by bus, the schedules are limited to 3:30 on Tuesday and Friday with Expreso del Sur and 7 PM Wednesday and Sunday with Wara Wara.

The site of Uyuni is remote, and can be extremely cold, with night temperatures falling to -25°C (-13°F). While the area is accessible year-round, the most popular time to go is from March to December, when the Salar should be dry. If you battle through during the rainy season, you will be rewarded with an extraordinarily vivid mirror effect from the shallow water covering the flats. Whenever you go, take plenty of sunblock, sunglasses (with side panels if possible), and lots of warm

10

clothing. In addition, if you are sleeping on the Salar in the salt hotel, take a good sleeping bag.

SAFETY AND PRECAUTIONS

If you are driving, avoid the temptation to cross without a good guide: the flats can be treacherous and can hide huge sinkholes. Take a lot of spare fuel for unexpected detours. One of the most common causes of accidents on the flats is drivers making sharp turns and rolling their vehicles.

ESSENTIALS

Buses Todo Turismo (☎ 02/211–9418 ⊕ www.touringbolivia.com).

Tour Operators Fremen Tours (✉ Plaza Abaroa, La Paz ☎ 02/232–7073 ⊕ www.frementours.com). Zig Zag Eco Tours and Treks (✉ Calle Illampu 867, La Paz ☎ 02/245–7814 ⊕ www.zigzagbolivia.com).

EXPLORING

The **Salar** is the obvious draw, and best seen and appreciated by a drive across it. In the middle of the flats you will find the Isla del Pescado (Fish Island) or Incahuasi, which has great views of the vast expanse of white and the distant hills, framed by the gigantic cactus that grow here. You can't stay here, but there is a restaurant run by the owners of Mongo's in La Paz.

This trip is enough in itself, but many people combine it with (and most tours include) a visit to the grotto Galaxy Cave, formed by the explosion of hot lava into a freezing lake and a detour down to the Laguna Colorada (Red Lake) and Laguna Verde (Green Lake) close to the Chilean border. It's well worth it. The two lakes, in the Eduardo Aboroa Reserve, are a haven for birds, and provide some of the most striking scenery in Bolivia. Get there in the afternoon for the full, colorful, effect.

WHERE TO STAY

There are few places to stay on the Salar itself, including the salt hotel (a hotel made of salt), which is a frequent overnight (and very cold) stop on the numerous tours out of Uyuni. In the town, there are several options catering to the large numbers of travelers using Uyuni as a base from which to explore. There is an interesting hotel in the village of Tahua, on the northern side of the flats if you are coming directly from La Paz by car.

$$$ Fodor'sChoice ★
🏨 **Hotel de Sal.** This newer hotel and community project is in Tahua, a small village right on the edge of the northern side of the flats under the volcano Thunupa. It's more upscale than other hotels in the region, as reflected in the locally crafted furniture, arty design, and, impressively, Wi-Fi. An extension of its natural environment, the hotel has stone floors and walls made of salt blocks. Most rooms have views of the surrounding dessert. It also has the great advantage of being at the end of the new road from La Paz and 20 minutes from the Isla del Pescado, meaning you can avoid Uyuni entirely. **Pros:** modern facilities; staggering location; serious commitment to the community. **Cons:** you need a car to get here; cold at night. ☎ 02/720–20069, 02/693–2987 ⊕ www. taykahoteles.com ⤵ 20 rooms ⚬ In-room: no a/c. In-hotel: restaurant, bar, parking (free), Wi-Fi hotspot ▭ MC, V ⎥⊙⎢ BP.

The "Salt Hotel," entirely built of salt blocks, in Salar de Uyuni.

$$ ⊞ **Hotel Toñito.** This whitewashed colonial hotel is just two blocks from the colorful Plaza 10 de Noviembre. Many rooms overlook the hotel's two courtyards. Ask to see one of the more spacious modern rooms with solar heated showers. Don't miss the pizza in their restaurant. The hotel is part of the Toñito group, which can organize tours onto the Salar from the office just down the road from the hotel. They also have a serious commitment to supporting the local community. The power has been known to go out on occasion and there's no backup generator, so pack a flashlight for emergencies. **Pros:** pizza restaurant; good coffee. **Cons:** rooms can be claustrophobic; noise from the central courtyard. ⊠ *60, Av. Ferroviaria* ☎ *02/693–3186, 02/693–3186 in La Paz* ⊕ *www.bolivianexpeditions.com* ⇄ *40 rooms* ⌂ *In-room: no a/c, Internet. In-hotel: restaurant, laundry service, Wi-Fi hotspot, parking (free)* ▭ *No credit cards* ⦿⊙ *CP.*

10

TARIJA

570 km (354 mi) south of Sucre.

Tarija is where you go when you've had enough of Bolivia, not just because it's on the way out of the country to Argentina or Paraguay, but also because it's different. The people, the climate, the food, and the culture all have more in common with those of neighboring countries than they do with the surrounding Bolivian territory. It's also different because you may be the only tourist in the entire city. Add to this the excellent weather and the fact it is Bolivia's wine-producing region, and you have an ideal getaway destination.

GETTING HERE AND AROUND

You can fly direct to Tarija from La Paz or Santa Cruz, or if you are already in the neighborhood in Sucre then it's a day's bus trip. The overland journey from La Paz is epic, and not recommended. Once you are in the city, walking is a good option. It's not large, and you won't have the inconveniences of La Paz's altitude or Santa Cruz's heat.

ESSENTIALS

Visitor Info **Secretaría del Turismo** (✉ *Calle 15 de abril entre Sucre y Daniel Campos*).

EXPLORING

The best thing to do in Tarija is nothing, but before the easygoing vibes get you take the opportunity to visit one of the many **wine cellars**, or *bodegas*, dotted around the city. Among the best are Concepcion's **Valle de Concepción**, (✉ *60, Av. Ferroviaria* ☎ *66/51514*) and Kohlberg's **Francisco Lazcano Barrio San Jorge II**, (✉ *Carretera Panamericana* ☎ *66/663–0002 or 66/663–6366*).

WHERE TO STAY

$$$$ ⛑ **Los Parrales.** Spacious, clean, and comfortable rooms are what you'll get at this large resort located beside Guadalquivir River. City and mountain views from the restaurant are stunning, and the manicured gardens and large swimming pool are great for relaxing. The center of town is about 3.5 km (2.17 mi) from the hotel, so expect to pay around (Bs)15 for a taxi. Most of the staff members only speak Spanish, but the service is excellent and friendly. **Pros:** good breakfast; clean rooms; children under 10 stay free. **Cons:** hot water takes a few minutes to warm up; spa could use renovating. ✉ *Urbanizacion El Carmen de Aranjuez Km 3.5* ☎ *04/664–8444* ⊕ *www.losparraleshotel.com* ⇆ *36 rooms* ᕚ *In-room: a/c, safe, refrigerator, Wi-Fi. In-hotel: restaurant, room service, bar, gym, spa, laundry service, Wi-Fi hotspot, parking (free)* ▭ *AE, MC, V* ᕧ *CP.*

UNDERSTANDING PERU

English–Spanish
Vocabulary

SPANISH VOCABULARY

ENGLISH	SPANISH	PRONUNCIATION

BASICS

Yes/no	Sí/no	see/no
Please	Por favor	pore fah-**vore**
May I?	¿Me permite?	may pair-**mee**-tay
Thank you (very much)	(Muchas) gracias	(**moo**-chas) **grah**-see-as
You're welcome	De nada	day **nah**-dah
Excuse me	Con permiso	con pair-**mee**-so
Pardon me	¿Perdón?	pair-**dohn**
Could you tell me?	¿Podría decirme?	po-dree-ah deh-**seer**-meh
I'm sorry	Lo siento	lo see-**en**-toh
Good morning!	¡Buenos días!	**bway**-nohs **dee**-ahs
Good afternoon!	¡Buenas tardes!	**bway**-nahs **tar**-dess
Good evening!	¡Buenas noches!	**bway**-nahs **no**-chess
Goodbye!	¡Adiós!/¡Hasta luego!	ah-dee-**ohss**/**ah** -stah **lwe**-go
Mr./Mrs.	Señor/Señora	sen-**yor**/sen-**yohr**-ah
Miss	Señorita	sen-yo-**ree**-tah
Pleased to meet you	Mucho gusto	**moo**-cho **goose**-toh
How are you?	¿Cómo está usted?	**ko**-mo es-**tah** oo-**sted**
Very well, thank you	Muy bien, gracias	**moo**-ee bee-**en**, **grah**-see-as
And you?	¿Y usted?	ee oos-**ted**
Hello (on the telephone)	Diga/ Aló	**dee**-gah/ ah-**loh**

NUMBERS

1	un, uno	oon, **oo**-no
2	dos	dos
3	tres	tress
4	cuatro	**kwah**-tro
5	cinco	**sink**-oh

6	seis	saice
7	siete	see-**et**-eh
8	ocho	**o**-cho
9	nueve	new-**eh**-vey
10	diez	dee-**es**
11	once	**ohn**-seh
12	doce	**doh**-seh
13	trece	**treh**-seh
14	catorce	ka-**tohr**-seh
15	quince	**keen**-seh
16	dieciséis	dee-es-ee-**saice**
17	diecisiete	dee-es-ee-see-**et**-eh
18	dieciocho	dee-es-ee-**o**-cho
19	diecinueve	**dee**-es-ee-new-**ev**-eh
20	veinte	**vain**-teh
21	veinte y uno/veintiuno	**vain**-te-oo-**oo**-noh
30	treinta	**train**-tah
32	treinta y dos	train-tay-**dohs**
40	cuarenta	kwah-**ren**-tah
43	cuarenta y tres	kwah-**ren**-tay-**tress**
50	cincuenta	seen-**kwen**-tah
54	cincuenta y cuatro	seen-**kwen**-tay **kwah**-tro
60	sesenta	sess-**en**-tah
65	sesenta y cinco	sess-**en**-tay **seen**-ko
70	setenta	set-en-tah
76	setenta y seis	set-en-tay **saice**
80	ochenta	oh-**chen**-tah
87	ochenta y siete	oh-**chen**-tay see-**yet**-eh
90	noventa	no-**ven**-tah
98	noventa y ocho	no-**ven**-tah-**o**-choh
100	cien	see-**en**

101	ciento uno	see-**en**-toh **oo**-noh
200	doscientos	doh-see-**en**-tohss
500	quinientos	keen-**yen**-tohss
700	setecientos	set-eh-see-**en**-tohss
900	novecientos	no-veh-see-**en**-tohss
1,000	mil	meel
2,000	dos mil	dohs meel
1,000,000	un millón	oon meel-**yohn**

COLORS

black	negro	**neh**-groh
blue	azul	ah-**sool**
brown	café	kah-**feh**
green	verde	**ver**-deh
pink	rosa	**ro**-sah
purple	morado	mo-**rah**-doh
orange	naranja	na-**rahn**-hah
red	rojo	**roh**-hoh
white	blanco	**blahn**-koh
yellow	amarillo	ah-mah-**ree**-yoh

DAYS OF THE WEEK

Sunday	domingo	doe-**meen**-goh
Monday	lunes	**loo**-ness
Tuesday	martes	**mahr**-tess
Wednesday	miércoles	me-**air**-koh-less
Thursday	jueves	hoo-**ev**-ess
Friday	viernes	vee-**air**-ness
Saturday	sábado	**sah**-bah-doh

MONTHS

January	enero	eh-**neh**-roh
February	febrero	feh-**breh**-roh
March	marzo	**mahr**-soh

April	abril	ah-**breel**
May	mayo	**my**-oh
June	junio	**hoo**-nee-oh
July	julio	**hoo**-lee-yoh
August	agosto	ah-**ghost**-toh
September	septiembre	sep-tee-**em**-breh
October	octubre	oak-**too**-breh
November	noviembre	no-vee-**em**-breh
December	diciembre	dee-see-**em**-breh

USEFUL PHRASES

Do you speak English?	¿Habla usted inglés?	**ah**-blah oos-**ted** in-**glehs**
I don't speak Spanish	No hablo español	no **ah**-bloh es-pahn-**yol**
I don't understand (you)	No entiendo	no en-tee-**en**-doh
I understand (you)	Entiendo	en-tee-**en**-doh
I don't know	No sé	no seh
I am American/ British	Soy americano (americana)/ inglés(a)	soy ah-meh-ree-**kah**-no (ah-meh-ree-**kah**-nah)/in-**glehs(ah)**
What's your name?	¿Cómo se llama usted?	koh-mo seh **yah**-mah oos-**ted**
My name is . . .	Me llamo . . .	may **yah**-moh
What time is it?	¿Qué hora es?	keh **o**-rah es
It is one, two, three . . . o'clock.	Es la una/Son las dos, tres . . .	es la **oo**-nah/sohn lahs dohs, tress
Yes, please/No, thank you	Sí, por favor/No, gracias	**see** pohr fah-**vor**/no **grah**-see-us
How?	¿Cómo?	**koh**-mo
When?	¿Cuándo?	**kwahn**-doh
This/Next week	Esta semana/ la semana que entra	**es**-teh seh-**mah**-nah/lah seh-**mah**-nah keh **en**-trah
This/Next month	Este mes/el próximo mes	**es**-teh mehs/el **proke**-see-mo mehs

This/Next year	Este año/el año que viene	es-teh **ahn**-yo/el **ahn**-yo keh vee-**yen**-ay
Yesterday/today/ tomorrow	Ayer/hoy/mañana	ah-**yehr**/oy/mahn-**yah**-nah
This morning/ afternoon	Esta mañana/ tarde	es-tah mahn-**yah**-nah/ **tar**-deh
Tonight	Esta noche	es-tah **no**-cheh
What?	¿Qué?	keh
What is it?	¿Qué es esto?	keh es **es**-toh
Why?	¿Por qué?	pore **keh**
Who?	¿Quién?	kee-**yen**
Where is . . . ? the train station?	¿Dónde está . . . ? la estación del tren?	**dohn**-deh es-**tah** la es-tah-see-on del trehn
the bus stop?	la parada del autobus?	la pah-**rah**-dah del ow-toh-**boos**
the post office?	la oficina de correos?	la oh-fee-**see**-nah deh koh-**rreh**-os
the bank?	el banco?	el **bahn**-koh
the hotel?	el hotel?	el oh-**tel**
the store?	la tienda?	la tee-**en**-dah
the cashier?	la caja?	la **kah**-hah
the museum?	el museo?	el moo-**seh**-oh
the hospital?	el hospital?	el ohss-pee-**tal**
the elevator?	el ascensor?	el ah-**sen**-sohr
the bathroom?	el baño?	el **bahn**-yoh
Here/there	Aquí/allá	ah-**key**/ah-**yah**
Open/closed	Abierto/cerrado	ah-bee-**er**-toh/ ser-**ah**-doh
Left/right	Izquierda/derecha	iss-key-**er**-dah/ dare-**eh**-chah
Straight ahead	Derecho	dare-**eh**-choh
Is it near/far?	¿Está cerca/lejos?	es-**tah sehr**-kah/ **leh**-hoss
I'd like . . .	Quisiera . . .	kee-see-ehr-ah
a room	una habitación	**oo**-nah ah-bee-tah-see-**on**
the key	la llave	lah **yah**-veh
a newspaper	un periódico	oon pehr-ee-oh-**dee**-koh
a stamp	un sello de correo	oon **seh**-yo deh koh-**reh**-oh

I'd like to buy . . .	Quisiera comprar . . .	kee-see-**ehr**-ah kohm-**prahr**
cigarettes	cigarrillos	ce-ga-**ree**-yohs
matches	cerillos	ser-ee-ohs
a dictionary	un diccionario	oon deek-see-oh-**nah**-ree-oh
soap	jabón	hah-**bohn**
sunglasses	gafas de sol	**ga**-fahs deh sohl
suntan lotion	loción broceadora	loh-see-**ohn** brohn-seh-ah-**do**-rah
a map	un mapa	oon **mah**-pah
a magazine	una revista	**oon**-ah reh-**vees**-tah
paper	papel	pah-**pel**
envelopes	sobres	so-brehs
a postcard	una tarjeta postal	**oon**-ah tar-**het**-ah post-**ahl**
How much is it?	¿Cuánto cuesta?	**kwahn**-toh **kwes**-tah
It's expensive/ cheap	Está caro/barato	es-**tah kah**-roh/ bah-**rah**-toh
A little/a lot	Un poquito/ mucho	oon poh-**kee**-toh/ **moo**-choh
More/less	Más/menos	mahss/**men**-ohss
Enough/too much/too little	Suficiente/ demasiado/ muy poco	soo-fee-see-**en**-teh/ deh-mah-see-**ah**-doh/ **moo**-ee poh-**koh**
Telephone	Teléfono	tel-**ef**-oh-no
Telegram	Telegrama	teh-leh-**grah**-mah
I am ill	Estoy enfermo(a)	es-**toy** en-**fehr**-moh(mah)
Please call a doctor	Por favor llame a un medico	pohr fah-**vor ya**-meh ah oon **med**-ee-koh

ON THE ROAD

Avenue	Avenida	ah-ven-**ee**-dah
Broad, tree-lined boulevard	Bulevar	boo-leh-**var**
Fertile plain	Vega	**veh**-gah
Highway	Carretera	car-reh-**ter**-ah
Mountain pass	Puerto	poo-**ehr**-toh
Street	Calle	**cah**-yeh

Waterfront promenade	Rambla	**rahm**-blah
Wharf	Embarcadero	em-bar-cah-**deh**-ro

IN TOWN

Cathedral	Catedral	cah-teh-**dral**
Church	Templo/Iglesia	**tem**-plo/ee-**glehs**-see-ah
City hall	Casa de gobierno	kah-sah deh go-bee-**ehr**-no
Door/gate	Puerta/portón	poo-**ehr**-tah/por-**ton**
Entrance/exit	Entrada/salida	en-**trah**-dah/sah-**lee**-dah
Inn, rustic bar, or restaurant	Taberna	tah-**behr**-nah
Main square	Plaza principal	plah-thah prin-see-**pahl**
Market	Mercado	mer-**kah**-doh
Neighborhood	Barrio	**bahr**-ree-o
Traffic circle	Glorieta	glor-ee-**eh**-tah
Wine cellar, wine bar, or wine shop	Bodega	boh-**deh**-gah

DINING OUT

Can you recommend a good restaurant?	¿Puede recomendarme un buen restaurante?	**pweh**-deh rreh-koh-mehn-**dahr**-me oon bwehn rrehs-tow-**rahn**-teh?
Where is it located?	¿Dónde está situado?	**dohn**-deh ehs-**tah** see-**twah**-doh?
Do I need reservations?	¿Se necesita una reservación?	seh neh-seh-**see**-tah **oo**-nah rreh-sehr-bah-**syohn**?
I'd like to reserve a table . . .	Quisiera reservar una mesa . . .	kee-**syeh**-rah rreh-sehr-**bahr** oo-nah **meh**-sah . . .
for two people	para dos personas	**pah**-rah dohs pehr-**soh**-nahs
for this evening	para esta noche	**pah**-rah **ehs**-tah **noh**-cheh

for 8:00 PM	para las ocho de la noche	**pah**-rah lahs **oh**-choh deh lah **noh**-cheh
A bottle of . . .	Una botella de . . .	**oo**-nah bo-**teh**-yah deh
A cup of . . .	Una taza de . . .	**oo**-nah **tah**-thah deh
A glass of . . .	Un vaso de . . .	oon **vah**-so deh
Ashtray	Un cenicero	oon sen-ee-**seh**-roh
Bill/check	La cuenta	lah **kwen**-tah
Bread	El pan	el pahn
Breakfast	El desayuno	el deh-sah-**yoon**-oh
Butter	La mantequilla	lah man-teh-**key**-yah
Cheers!	¡Salud!	sah-**lood**
Cocktail	Un aperitivo	oon ah-pehr-ee-**tee**-voh
Dinner	La cena	lah **seh**-nah
Dish	Un plato	oon **plah**-toh
Menu of the day	Menú del día	meh-**noo** del **dee**-ah
Enjoy!	¡Buen provecho!	bwehn pro-**veh**-cho
Fixed-price menu	Menú fijo o turistico	meh-**noo** **fee**-hoh oh too-**ree**-stee-coh
Fork	El tenedor	el ten-eh-**dor**
Is the tip included?	¿Está incluida la propina?	es-**tah** in-cloo-ee-dah lah pro-**pee**-nah
Knife	El cuchillo	el koo-**chee**-yo
Large portion of savory snacks	Raciónes	rah-see-**oh**-nehs
Lunch	La comida	lah koh-**mee**-dah
Menu	La carta, el menú	lah **cart**-ah, el meh-**noo**
Napkin	La servilleta	lah sehr-vee-**yet**-ah
Pepper	La pimienta	lah pee-me-**en**-tah
Please give me	Por favor déme	pore fah-**vor** **deh**-meh
Salt	La sal	lah sahl
Savory snacks	Tapas	**tah**-pahs
Spoon	Una cuchara	**oo**-nah koo-**chah**-rah
Sugar	El azúcar	el ah-**thu**-kar

| Waiter!/Waitress! | ¡Por favor Señor/Señorita! | pohr fah-**vor** sen-**yor**/sen-yor-**ee**-tah |

EMERGENCIES

Look!	¡Mire!	**mee**-reh!
Listen!	¡Escuche!	ehs-**koo**-cheh!
Help!	¡Auxilio! ¡Ayuda! ¡Socorro!	owk-**see**-lee-oh/ ah-**yoo**-dah/ soh-**kohr**-roh
Fire!	¡Incendio!	en-**sen**-dee-oo
Caution!/Look out!	¡Cuidado!	kwee-**dah**-doh
Hurry!	¡Dése prisa!	**deh**-seh pree-sah!
Stop!	¡Alto!	**ahl**-toh!
I need help quick!	¡Necesito ayuda, pronto!	neh-seh-**see**-toh ah-**yoo**-dah, **prohn**-toh!
Can you help me?	¿Puede ayudarme?	**pweh**-deh ah-yoo-**dahr**-meh?
Police!	¡Policía!	poh-lee-**see**-ah!
I need a policeman!	¡Necesito un policía!	neh-seh-**see**-toh oon poh-lee-**see**-ah!
It's an emergency!	¡Es una emergencia!	ehs **oo**-nah eh-mehr-**hehn**-syah!
Leave me alone!	¡Déjeme en paz!	**deh**-heh-meh ehn pahs!
That man's a thief!	¡Ese hombre es un ladrón!	**eh**-seh **ohm**-breh ehs oon-lah-**drohn**!
Stop him!	¡Deténganlo!	deh-**tehn**-gahn-loh!
He's stolen my . . .	Me ha robado . . .	meh ah rroh-**bah**-doh . . .
pocketbook	la cartera	lah kahr-**teh**-rah
wallet	la billetera	lah bee-yeh-**teh**-rah
passport	el pasaporte	ehl pah-sah-**pohr**-teh
watch	el reloj	ehl rreh-**loh**
I've lost my . . .	He perdido	eh pehr-**dee**-doh
suitcase	mi maleta	mee mah-**leh**-tah
money	mi dinero	mee dee-**neh**-roh
glasses	los anteojos	lohs ahn-teh-**oh**-hohs
car keys	las llaves de mi automóvil	lahs **yah**-behs deh mee ow-toh-**moh**-beel

TELLING TIME AND EXPRESSIONS OF TIME

What time is it?	¿Qué hora es?	keh **oh**-rah ehs?
At what time?	¿A qué hora?	ah keh **oh**-rah?
It's . . .	Es . . .	ehs . . .
one o'clock	la una	lah **oo**-nah
1:15	la una y cuarto	lah **oo**-nah ee **kwahr**-toh
1:30	la una y media	lah **oo**-nah ee **meh**-dyah
It's . . .	Son las . . .	sohn lahs . . .
1:45	dos menos cuarto	dohs **meh**-nos **kwahr**-toh
two o'clock	dos	dohs
morning	la mañana	Lah mah-**nyah**-nah
afternoon	la tarde	lah **tahr**-deh
It's midnight	Es medianoche	ehs **meh**-dyah **noh**-cheh
It's noon	Es mediodía	ehs meh-dyoh-**dee** ah
In a half hour	En media hora	ehn **meh**-dyah **oh**-rah
When does it begin?	¿Cuándo empieza?	**kwahn**-doh ehm-**pyeh**-sah?

PAYING THE BILL

How much does it cost?	¿Cuánto cuesta?	**kwahn**-toh **kwehs**-tah?
The bill, please	La cuenta, por favor	lah-**kwen**-tah pohr fah-**bohr**
How much do I owe you?	¿Cuánto le debo?	**kwan**-toh leh **deh**-boh?
Is service included?	¿La propina está incluida?	lah proh-**pee**-nah ehs-**tah** een-kloo-ee-dah?
This is for you	Esto es para usted	**ehs**-toh ehs pah-rah oos-**tehd**

GETTING AROUND

Do you have a map of the city?	¿Tiene usted un mapa de la ciudad?	**tyeh**-neh oos-**tehd** oon **mah**-pah deh lah syoo-**dahd**?
Could you show me on the map?	¿Puede usted indicármelo en el mapa?	**pweh**-deh oo-**stehd** een-dee-**kahr**-meh-loh ehn ehl **mah**-pah?
Can I get there on foot?	¿Puedo llegar allí a pie?	**pweh**-doh yeh-**gahr** ah-**yee** ah pyeh?
How far is it?	¿A qué distancia es?	ah keh dees-**tahn**-syah ehs?
I'm lost	Estoy perdido(-a)	ehs-**toy** pehr-**dee**-doh(-dah)
Where is . . .	¿Dónde está . . .	**dohn**-deh ehs-**tah** . . .
the Hotel Rex?	el hotel Rex?	ehl oh-**tehl** rreks?
. . . Street?	la calle . . .?	lah **kah**-yeh . . .?
. . . Avenue?	la avenida . . .?	lah ah-beh-**nee**-dah . . .?
How can I get to . . .	¿Cómo puedo ir a . . .	**koh**-moh **pweh**-doh eer ah . . .
the train station?	la estación de ferrocarril?	lah ehs-tah-**syon** deh feh-rroh-cah-**rreel**?
the bus stop?	la parada de autobuses?	lah pah-**rah**-dah deh ow-toh-**boo**-ses?
the ticket office?	la taquilla?	lah tah-**kee**-yah?
the airport?	el aeropuerto?	ehl ah-eh-roh-**pwehr**-toh?
straight ahead	derecho	deh-**reh**-choh
to the right	a la derecha	ah lah deh-**reh**-chah
to the left	a la izquierda	ah lah ees-**kyehr**-dah
a block away	a una cuadra	ah **oo**-nah **kwah**-drah
on the corner	en la esquina	ehn lah ehs-**kee**-nah
on the square	en la plaza	ehn lah **plah**-sah
facing, opposite	enfrente	ehn-**frehn**-teh
across	al frente	ahl **frehn**-teh
next to	al lado	ahl **lah**-doh

near	cerca	**sehr**-kah
far	lejos	**leh**-hohs

ON THE BUS

I'm looking for the bus stop	Estoy buscando la parada de autobuses	ehs-**toy** boos-**kahn**-doh lah pah-**rah**-dah deh ow-toh-**boo**-sehs
What bus line goes . . .	¿Qué línea va . . .	keh **lee**-neh-ah bah . . .
north?	al norte?	ahl **nohr**-teh?
south?	al sur?	ahl soor?
east?	al este?	ahl **ehs**-teh?
west?	al oeste?	ahl oh-**ehs**-teh?
What bus do I take to go to . . .	¿Qué autobús tomo para ir a . . .	keh ow-toh-**boos** toh-moh **pah**-rah eer ah . . .
Can you tell me when to get off?	¿Podría decirme cuándo debo bajarme?	poh-**dree**-ah deh-**seer**-meh **kwan**-doh **deh**-boh bah-**hahr**-meh?
How much is the fare?	¿Cuánto es el billete?	**kwahn**-toh ehs ehl bee-**yeh**-teh?
Should I pay when I get on?	¿Debo pagar al subir?	**deh**-boh pah-**gahr** ahl soo-**beer**?
Where do I take the bus to return?	¿Dónde se toma el autobús para regresar?	**dohn**-deh seh **toh**-mah ehl ow-toh-**boos** pah-**rah** rreh-greh-**sahr**?
How often do the return buses run?	¿Cada cuánto hay autobuses de regreso?	**kah**-dah **kwahn**-toh ahy ow-toh-**boo**-sehs deh rreh-**greh**-soh?
I would like . . .	Quisiera . . .	kee-**syeh**-rah . . .
a ticket	un billete	oon bee-**yeh**-teh
a receipt	un recibo	oon reh-**see**-boh
a reserved seat	un asiento numerado	oon ah-**syehn**-toh noo-meh-**rah**-doh
first class	primera clase	pree-**meh**-rah **klah**-seh
second class	segunda clase	seh-**goon**-dah **klah**-seh
a direct bus	un autobús directo	oon ow-toh-**boos** dee-**rehk**-toh

| an express bus | un autobús expreso | oon ow-toh-**boos** ehks-**preh**-soh |
| ticketed luggage | equipaje facturado | eh-kee-**pah**-heh fahk-too-**rah**-doh |

ACCOMMODATIONS

I have a reservation	Tengo una reservación/ una reserva	**tehn**-goh oo-nah rreh-sehr-vah-**syohn**/. . . oo-nah rre-**sehr**-vah
I would like a room for . . .	Quisiera una habitación por . . .	kee-**syeh**-rah oo-nah ah-bee-tah-**syohn** pohr . . .
one night	una noche	**oo**-nah **noh**-cheh
two nights	dos noches	dohs **noh**-chehs
a week	una semana	**oo**-nah seh-**mah**-nah
two weeks	dos semanas	dohs seh-**mah**-nahs

How much is it . . .	¿Cuánto es . . .	**kwahn**-toh ehs . . .
for a day?	por día?	pohr **dee**-ah?
for a week?	por una semana?	pohr **oo**-nah seh-**mah**-nah?

| Does that include tax? | ¿Incluye impuestos? | een-**kloo**-yeh eem-**pwehs**-tohs? |

Do you have a room with . . .	¿Tiene una habitación con . . .	**tyeh**-neh oo-nah ah-bee-tah-**syohn** kohn . . .
a private bath?	baño privado?	**bah**-nyoh pree-**bah**-doh?
a shower?	una ducha?	**oo**-nah **doo**-chah?
air-conditioning?	aire acondicionado?	**ay**-reh ah-kohn-dee-syoh-**nah**-doh?
heat?	calefacción?	kah-leh-fak-**syohn**?
television?	televisor?	teh-leh-bee-**sohr**?
hot water?	agua caliente?	**ah**-gwah kah-**lyehn**-teh?
a balcony?	balcón?	bahl-**kohn**?
a view facing the street?	vista a la calle?	**bees**-tah ah lah **kah**-yeh?
a view facing the ocean?	vista al mar?	**bees**-tah ahl mahr?

Does the hotel have . . .	¿Tiene el hotel . . .?	**tyeh**-neh ehl oh-**tehl** . . .?
a restaurant?	un restaurante?	oon rrehs-tow-**rahn**-teh?
a bar?	un bar?	oon bahr?

a swimming pool?	una piscina?	**oo**-nah pee-**see**-nah
room service?	servicio de habitación?	sehr-**bee**-syoh deh ah-bee-tah-**syohn**?
a safe-deposit box?	una caja de valores/ seguridad?	**oo**-nah **kah**-hah deh bah-**loh**-rehs/ seh-goo-ree-**dahd**?
laundry service?	servicio de lavandería?	sehr-**bee**-syoh deh lah-vahn-deh-**ree**-ah?

I would like . . .	Quisiera . . .	kee-**sye**-rah . . .
meals included	con las comidas incluidas	kohn lvahs koh-**mee**-dahs een-**kluee**-dahs
breakfast only	solamente con desayuno	soh-lah-**men**-teh kohn deh-sah-**yoo**-noh
no meals included	sin comidas	seen koh-**mee**-dahs
an extra bed	una cama más	**oo**-nah **kah**-mah mahs
a baby crib	una cuna	**oo**-nah **koo**-nah
another towel	otra toalla	**oh**-trah **twah**-yah
soap	jabón	hah-**bohn**
clothes hangers	ganchos de ropa	**gahn**-chohs deh **rroh**-pah
another blanket	otra manta	**oh**-trah **mahn**-tah
drinking water	agua para beber	**ah**-gwah **pah**-rah beh-**behr**
toilet paper	papel higiénico	pah-**pehl** ee-**hye**-nee-koh

This room is very . . .	Esta habitación es muy . . .	**ehs**-tah ah-bee-tah-**syohn** ehs mue . . .
small	pequeña	peh-**keh**-nyah
cold	fría	**free**-ah
hot	caliente	kah-**lyehn**-teh
dark	oscura	ohs-**koo**-rah
noisy	ruidosa	rruee-**doh**-sah

The . . . does not work	No funciona . . .	noh foon-**syoh**-nah . . .
light	la luz	lah loos
heat	la calefacción	lah kah-leh-fahk-**syohn**
toilet	el baño	ehl **bah**-nyoh
the air conditioner	el aire acondicionado	ehl **ay**-reh ah-kohn-dee-syo-**nah**-doh
key	la llave	lah **yah**-beh
lock	la cerradura	lah seh-rah-**doo**-rah
fan	el ventilador	ehl **behn**-tee-lah-

		dohr
outlet	el enchufe	ehl ehn-**choo**-feh
television	el televisor	ehl teh-leh-bee-**sohr**

May I change to another room?	¿Podría cambiar de habitación?	poh-**dree**-ah kahm-**byar** deh ah-bee-tah-**syohn**?

Is there . . .	¿Hay . . .	ahy . . .
room service?	servicio de habitación?	sehr-**bee**-syoh deh ah-bee-tah-**syohn**?
laundry service?	servicio de lavandería?	sehr-**bee**-syoh deh lah-vahn-deh-**ree**-ah?

EMAIL AND THE INTERNET

Where is the computer?	¿Dónde está la computadora?	**dohn**-deh eh-**stah** lah kohm-poo-tah-**doh**-rah

I need to send an email	Necesito enviar un correo electrónico	neh-seh-**see**-toh ehn-**byahr** oon koh-**reh**-yoh eh-lehk-**troh**-nee-koh

Can I get on the Internet?	¿Puedo conectarme con el internet?	**pweh**-doh koh-nehk-**tahr**-meh ahl **een**-tehr-net?

Do you have a Web site?	¿Tiene página web?	**tyeh**-neh **pah**-hee-nah web?

BARGAINING

Excuse me	Perdón	pehr-**dohn**

I'm interested in this	Me interesa esto	meh een-teh-**reh**-sah **ehs**-toh

How much is it?	¿Cuánto cuesta?	**kwahn**-toh **kwehs**-tah?

It's very expensive!	¡Es muy caro!	ehs muee **kah**-roh!

It's overpriced (It's not worth so much)	No vale tanto	noh **vah**-leh **tahn**-toh

Do you have a cheaper one?	¿Tiene uno más barato?	**tyeh**-neh **oo**-noh mahs bah-**rah**-toh?

This is damaged— do you have another one?	Está dañado, ¿hay otro?	ehs-**tah** dah-**nyah**-doh, ahy **oh**-troh?

What is the lowest price?	¿Cuál es el precio mínimo?	**kwahl** ehs ehl **preh**-syoh **mee**-nee-moh?
Is that the final price?	¿Es el último precio?	ehs ehl **ool**-tee-moh **preh**-syoh?
Can't you give me a discount?	¿No me da una rebaja?	noh meh dah **oo**-nah rreh-**bah**-hah?
I'll give you . . .	Le doy . . .	leh doy . . .
I won't pay more than . . .	No pago más de . . .	noh **pah**-goh mahs deh . . .
I'll look somewhere else	Voy a ver en otro sitio	voy ah behr ehn **oh**-troh **see**-tyoh
No, thank you	No, gracias	noh, **grah**-syahs

TOILETRIES

toiletries	objetos de baño	ohb-**jeh**-tohs deh **bah**-nyoh
a brush	un cepillo	oon seh-**pee**-yoh
cologne	colonia	koh-**loh**-nyah
a comb	un peine	oon **pay**-neh
deodorant	desodorante	deh-soh-doh-**rahn**-teh
disposable diapers	pañales desechables	pah-**nyah**-lehs deh-seh-**chah**-blehs
hairspray	laca	**lah**-kah
a mirror	un espejo	oon ehs-**peh**-hoh
moisturizing lotion	loción humectante	loh-**syohn** oo-mehk-**tahn**-teh
mouthwash	enjuague bucal	ehn-**hwah**-geh boo-**kahl**
nail clippers	cortaúñas	kohr-ta-**oo**-nyahs
nail polish	esmalte de uñas	ehs-**mahl**-teh deh **oo**-nyahs
nail polish remover	quitaesmalte	kee-tah-ehs-**mahl**-teh
perfume	perfume	pehr-**foo**-meh
sanitary napkins	toallas sanitarias	toh-**ah**-yahs sah-nee-**tah**-ryahs

shampoo	champú	chahm-**poo**
shaving cream	crema de afeitar	**kreh**-mah deh ah-fay-**tahr**
soap	jabón	hah-**bohn**
a sponge	una esponja	**oo**-nah ehs-**pohn**-hah
tampons	tampones	tahm-**poh**-nehs
tissues	pañuelos de papel	pah-**nyweh**-lohs deh pah-**pehl**
toilet paper	papel higiénico	pah-**pehl** ee-**hyeh**-ee-koh
a toothbrush	un cepillo de dientes	oon seh-**pee**-yoh deh **dyehn**-tehs
toothpaste	pasta de dientes	**pahs**-tah deh **dyehn**-tehs
tweezers	pinzas	**peen**-sahs

Travel Smart Peru

WORD OF MOUTH

"Note about altitude—we suffered minor issues but not until reaching Cusco and Puno. We drank tons of water, rested, avoided alcohol but refused to give up caffeine (we drank Coke daily). I had a minor headache a few times but it was nothing some Tylenol couldn't cure. I'm not a tea drinker, so did not drink the coca tea or chew coca leaves. For my sister and I, water was the wonder drug."
—3sistahs

GETTING HERE AND AROUND

Because of the long distances involved, most travelers choose to fly between the major cities of Peru. The good news is that domestic flights can be reasonable, sometimes less than $100 USD per segment.

TRAVEL TIMES FROM LIMA		
To	By Air	By Car/Bus
Cusco	1 hour	24 hours
Puno	2 hours	19 hours
Arequipa	1¼ hours	15 hours
Trujillo	1 hour	9 hours

■TIP➜ Ask the local tourist board about hotel and local transportation packages that include tickets to major museum exhibits or other special events.

▌ BY AIR

Almost all international flights into Peru touch down at Aeropuerto Internacional Jorge Chávez, on the northwestern fringe of Lima. Flying times are for nonstop flights to Lima: from Miami 5 hours 45 min; Houston 6 hours 45 min; Los Angeles 8 hours 35 min; and New York 7 hours.

Departure taxes on international flights from Lima are $31 USD and domestic flights $6.82 USD. These taxes, usually paid after you check in for your flight—although your airline may already include the tax in your ticket price—must be paid in cash, either in U.S. dollars or Peruvian nuevos soles. If you're paying in dollars, try to have the exact amount ready, as you'll be given change in local currency. It's a good idea to wait to convert your nuevos soles back to dollars until after you pay the departure tax.

The least expensive airfares to Peru are priced for round-trip travel. Airlines generally allow you to change your return date for a fee; most low-fare tickets, however, are nonrefundable.

Airlines and Airports Airline and Airport Links.com (⊕ *www.airlineandairportlinks.com*) has links to many of the world's airlines and airports.

Airline Security Issues Transportation Security Administration (⊕ *www.tsa.gov*) has answers for almost every question that might come up.

AIRPORTS

Peru's main international point of entry is Aeropuerto Internacional Jorge Chávez (LIM), on the northwestern fringe of Lima. It's a completely modern facility with plenty of dining and shopping options, and flights that arrive and depart 24 hours a day. There are ATMs and currency exchange offices in the main terminal and the arrivals terminals. These are nowhere to be found in the departures terminal, so do your banking before heading through security.

Airport Information Aeropuerto Internacional Jorge Chávez (⊠ *Av. Faucett s/n* ☏ *01/517-3100* ⊕ *www.lap.com.pe*).

GROUND TRANSPORTATION

If your hotel doesn't offer to pick you up at the airport, you'll have to take a taxi. Arrange a ride with one of the official airport taxis whose companies have counters inside the arrivals area of the terminal. A taxi to most places in the city should cost no more than $25–30 USD. It's a 20-minute drive to El Centro, and a 30-minute drive to Miraflores and San Isidro.

FLIGHTS

Dozens of international flights touch down daily at Lima's Aeropuerto Internacional Jorge Chávez, mostly from other Latin American cities. But there are also plenty from the U.S. American flies from Miami, Continental flies from Houston and Newark. Delta has daily flights from Atlanta, and Spirit flies from Fort Lauderdale. The South American–based airline LAN flies from Los Angeles, Miami, and

New York's JFK. Air Canada flies from Toronto.

If you're flying from other Latin American cities, you have a wide range of regional carriers at your disposal. LAN has flights from most major airports in the region, as does Taca. Brazil's TAM flies from Sao Paulo. Copa, affiliated with Continental, flies from its hub in Panama City. Aeroméxico flies from Mexico City, Aerolineas Argentinas flies from Buenos Aires, Avianca from Bogota, and Taca from San José, Costa Rica.

DOMESTIC

With four mountain ranges running through Peru plus a large swath of the Amazon jungle, flying is the best way to travel from Lima to most cities and towns. LAN Perú, the carrier with the most national flights, departs several times each day for Arequipa, Cajamarca, Chiclayo, Cusco, Iquitos, Juliaca, Piura, Pucallpa, Puerto Maldonado, Tacna, Tarapoto, Trujillo, and Tumbes. LC Busre flies to Andahuaylas, Ayacucho, Cajamarca, Huancayo, Huánuco and Huaraz. Peruvian Airlines flies to Arequipa, Cusco, Iquitos, and Tacna. Star Perú flies to Arequipa, Ayacucho, Chiclayo, Cusco, Huánuco, Iquitos, Juliaca, Pucallpa, Puerto Maldonado, Tarapoto, and Trujillo. Taca flies to Cusco.

LAN Perú operates the majority of domestic flights within the country, frequently with service several times a day between major destinations, but its fares skew higher than the competition. LAN Perú does offer lower fares—and you can see them on its Web site—but only residents of Peru are eligible to use them.

Airline Contacts Aerolineas Argentinas (✆ 800/333–0276 in North America, 01/513–6575 in Lima ⊕ www.aerolineas.com.ar). **Aeroméxico** (✆ 800/237–6639 in North America, 01/705–1111 in Lima ⊕ www.aeromexico.com). **Air Canada** (✆ 888/247–2262 in North America, 01/241–1457 in Lima ⊕ www.aircanada.com). **American Airlines** (✆ 800/433–7300, 01/211–7000 in Lima ⊕ www.aa.com). **Avianca** (✆ 800/284–2622 in North America, 01/440–4104 in Lima ⊕ www.avianca.com). **Continental Airlines** (✆ 800/231–0856, 01/712–9230 in Lima ⊕ www.continental.com). **Copa** (✆ 800/359–2672 in North America, 01/610–0808 in Lima ⊕ www.copaair.com). **Delta Airlines** (✆ 800/241–4141, 01/211–9211 in Lima ⊕ www.delta.com). **LAN** (✆ 866/435–9526 in North America, 01/213–8200 in Lima ⊕ www.lan.com). **Spirit Air** (✆ 800/772–7117, 01/517–2536 in Lima ⊕ www.spiritair.com). **Taca** (✆ 800/400–8222 in North America, 01/511–8222 in Lima ⊕ www.taca.com). **TAM** (✆ 888/235–9826 in North America, 01/202–6900 in Lima ⊕ www.tam.com.br).

Domestic Airlines LAN Perú (✆ 01/213–8200 ⊕ www.lan.com). **LC Busre** (✆ 01/619–1313 ⊕ www.lcbusre.com.pe). **Peruvian Airlines** (✆ 01/716–6000 ⊕ www.peruvianairlines.pe). **Star Perú** (✆ 01/705–9000 ⊕ www.starperu.com. **Taca** (✆ 01/511–8222 ⊕ www.taca.com).

▌ BY BUS

The intercity bus system in Peru is extensive, and fares are quite reasonable. Remember, however, that distances between cities can be daunting. It's best to use buses for shorter trips, such as between Lima and Ica or between Cusco and Puno. That way you can begin and end your trip during daylight hours. If you stick with one of the recommended companies, like Cruz del Sur, you can usually expect a comfortable journey.

Second-class buses (*servicio normal*) tend to be overcrowded and uncomfortable, whereas the more expensive first-class service (*primera clase*) is more comfortable and much more likely to arrive on schedule.

Bus fares are substantially cheaper in Peru than they are in North America or Europe. Competing bus companies serve all major and many minor routes, so it can pay to shop around if you're on an extremely tight budget. Always speak to the counter clerk, as competition may mean fares are cheaper than the official price posted on the fare board.

For the 15-hour journey between Lima and Arequipa, Cruz del Sur's fares for its top service, called *Cruzero*, are $32–$46 USD. Its less-expensive service, called *Imperial,* is $27 USD. Inka Express, which promotes itself to tourists rather than the local market, uses large, comfortable coaches for the popular eight-hour journey between Cusco and Puno. Tickets are $30 USD and the trip includes snacks and brief rest stops at points of interest along the way.

Tickets are sold at bus-company offices and at travel agencies. Be prepared to pay with cash, as credit cards aren't always accepted. Reservations aren't necessary except for trips to popular destinations during high season. Summer weekends and major holidays are the busiest times. You should arrive at bus stations early for travel during peak seasons.

Bus Information Cruz del Sur (⊠ *Av. Javier Prado 1109, San Isidro, Lima* ☎ *01/311–5050* ⊕ *www.cruzdelsur.com.pe*). **Inka Express** (⊠ *Av. La Paz C-23, Cusco* ☎ *084/247–887* ⊕ *www.inkaexpress.com*).

▌ BY CAR

In general, it's not a great idea to have a car in Peru. Driving is a heart-stopping experience, as most Peruvians see traffic laws as suggestions rather than rules. That said, there are a few places in Peru where having a car is a benefit, such as between Lima and points south on the Pan-American Highway. The highway follows the Pacific Ocean coastline before it cuts through the desert, and stops can be made along the way for a picnic and a swim. The highway is good, and although there isn't too much to see along the way, it's nice to have the freedom a car affords once you get to your destination.

If you rent a car, keep these tips in mind: outside cities, drive only during daylight

hours, fill your gas tank whenever possible, and make sure your spare tire is in good repair. In some areas, drivers caught using a cell phone while driving receive a hefty fine, especially on the coastal highway following the cliff along the Pacific Ocean between Lima and Miraflores, and San Isidro.

Massive road-improvement programs have improved highways. But elsewhere, including some parts of Lima, roads are littered with potholes. Outside of the cities, street signs are rare, lighting is nonexistent, and lanes are unmarked. Roads are straight along the coast, but in the mountains they snake around enough to make even the steadiest driver a little queasy.

And then there are the drivers. When they get behind the wheel, Peruvians are very assertive. Expect lots of honking and last-minute lane switching when you're in a city. On the highways you'll encounter constant tailgating and passing on blind curves. Take our word for it and leave the driving to someone else if you can. Consider hiring a car and driver through your hotel, or making a deal with a taxi driver, for some extended sightseeing. Drivers often charge an hourly rate regardless of the distance traveled. You'll have to pay cash, but you'll often spend less than you would for a rental car.

The major highways in Peru are the Pan-American Highway, which runs down the entire coast, and the Carretera Central, which runs from Lima to Huancayo. Most highways have no names or numbers; they're referred to by destination.

CAR RENTALS

If you plan to rent a car it's best to make arrangements before you leave home, and book through a travel agent who will shop around for a good deal. If you plan to rent during a holiday period, reserve early.

The minimum age for renting a car in Peru is 25. All major car-rental agencies have branches in downtown Lima as well as branches at Jorge Chávez International

Airport that are open 24 hours. You can also rent vehicles in Arequipa, Chiclayo, Cusco, Tacna, and Trujillo.

The cost of rental cars varies widely, but is generally between $20 and $30 USD for a compact, $40 to $65 USD for a full-size car. A daily $10–$20 USD collision damage waiver is usually added to your bill. Always make sure to check the fine print, as some companies give you unlimited mileage whereas others give you between 200 and 240 km (124 and 150 mi) free, then charge you a hefty 25 to 60 cents for every kilometer you drive above that. Many rental firms include in your contract a statement saying you may not take the vehicle on unpaved roads, of which there are many in Peru. Many also forbid mountain driving for certain types of vehicles in their fleets.

Always give the rental car a once-over to make sure that the headlights, jack, and tires (including the spare) are in working condition. Note any existing damages to the car and get a signature acknowledging the damage, no matter how slight.

GASOLINE
Gas stations are almost never found in the middle of the large cities. Most are on the outskirts, and are often difficult to find. Make sure to ask your rental company where they're located. Stations along the highways are few and far between, so don't pass up on the chance to gas up. Many stations are now open 24 hours.

PARKING
If you have a rental car, make sure your hotel has its own parking lot. If not, ask about nearby lots. In the cities, guarded parking lots that charge about $1 USD an hour are common.

ROADSIDE EMERGENCIES
The Touring y Automóvil Club del Perú will provide 24-hour emergency road service for members of the American Automobile Association (AAA) and affiliates upon presentation of their membership cards. (Towing is free within 30 km [18 mi] of several urban areas.) Members of AAA can purchase good maps at low prices.

Emergency Services Touring y Automóvil Club del Perú (✉ *Av. Trinidad Morán 698, Lince, Lima* ☎ *01/614-9999* ⊕ *www. touringperu.com.pe*).

RULES OF THE ROAD
In Peru your own driver's license is acceptable identification, but an international driving permit is good to have. They're available from the American and Canadian automobile associations and, in the United Kingdom, from the Automobile Association and Royal Automobile Club. These international permits, valid only in conjunction with your regular driver's license, are universally recognized; having one may save you a problem with local authorities.

Speed limits are 25 kph–35 kph (15 mph–20 mph) in residential areas, 85 kph–100 kph (50 mph–60 mph) on highways. Traffic tickets range from a minimum of $4 USD to a maximum of $40 USD. The police and military routinely check drivers at roadblocks, so make sure your papers are easily accessible. Peruvian law makes it a crime to drive while intoxicated, although many Peruvians ignore that prohibition.

▌ BY TRAIN

Trains run along four different routes: between Cusco and Machu Picchu, between Ollantaytambo and Machu Picchu, between Urubamba and Machu Picchu, and between Cusco and Lake Titicaca. In addition there's a line between Puno and Arequipa that's operated for groups only. Tickets can be purchased at train stations, through travel agencies, or on the Internet. During holidays or high season it's best to get your tickets in advance.

Three companies offer train service to Machu Picchu. PeruRail, which has run the route since 1999, is operated by Orient-Express, the same company that runs one of the most luxurious and famous trains in the world, the Venice Simplon Orient Express between London and Venice. It operates service to Machu Picchu from Cusco (technically from the nearby town of Poroy, about 20 minutes outside the city) and the Sacred Valley towns of Ollantaytambo and Urubamba. New for 2010 and 2011, respectively, Inca Rail and Andean Railways run service between Ollantaytambo and Urubamba and Machu Picchu. Foreigners are prohibited from riding the very inexpensive local trains that travel the route. The Machu Picchu station is not at the ruins themselves, but in the nearby town of Aguas Calientes. ⇨ *See Chapter 6 for more information about these trains.*

Three or four PeruRail trains a week, depending on season, take passengers on the 10-hour trip between Cusco and Puno on Lake Titicaca. The plush Andean Explorer is $156 USD one-way.

Note that there are two different train stations in Cusco. Estación San Pedro serves the Machu Picchu route, and Estación Wanchaq serves the Lake Titicaca route.

Reserve and purchase your ticket as far ahead as possible, especially during holidays or high season. Reservations can be made directly with PeruRail through its Web site, or through a travel agency or tour operator.

Reservations Andean Railways (☏ 084/221–199, 01/613–5288 *in Lima* ⊕ *www.machupicchutrain.com*). **Inca Rail** (☏ 084/233–030, 01/613–5288 *in Lima* ⊕ *www.incarail.com*). **PeruRail** (☏ 084/581–414, 01/517–1884 *in Lima* ⊕ *www.perurail. com*).

Train Stations Estación Wanchaq (Cusco–Lake Titicaca route) (✉ *Av. Pachacutec 503* ☏ 084/238–722).

ESSENTIALS

▮ ACCOMMODATIONS

It's always good to take a look at your room before accepting it, especially if you're staying in a budget hotel. If it isn't what you expected, there might be several other rooms from which to choose. Expense is no guarantee of charm or cleanliness, and accommodations can vary dramatically within a single hotel. Many older hotels in some of the small towns in Peru have rooms with charming balconies or spacious terraces; ask if there's a room *con balcón* or *con terraza* when checking in.

If you ask for a double room, you'll get a room for two people, but you're not guaranteed a double mattress. If you'd like to avoid twin beds, you'll have to ask for a *cama matrimonial* (no wedding ring seems to be required).

The lodgings we list are the cream of the crop in each price category. We always list the available facilities, but we don't specify whether they cost extra; when pricing accommodations, always ask what's included and what costs extra. Properties are assigned price categories based on a standard double room at high season (excluding holidays).

▮ TIP → Assume that hotels operate on the European Plan (EP, no meals) unless we specify that they use the Breakfast Plan (BP, with full breakfast), Continental Plan (CP, Continental breakfast), Full American Plan (FAP, all meals), Modified American Plan (MAP, breakfast and dinner) or are all-inclusive (AI, all meals and most activities).

APARTMENT AND HOUSE RENTALS

Apartment rentals are not a viable option in most parts of Peru. However, they're becoming more popular in Lima. One company that has proven reliable is Inn Peru, which rents apartments in the neighborhood of Miraflores. You can get a roomy two- or three-bedroom apartment for less than you'd pay for a shoebox-size hotel room.

Contacts Home Away (☎ 512/493–0382 ⊕ www.homeaway.com). **Inn Peru** (☎ 945/607–2173 in U.S., 01/99857–8350 ⊕ www.innperu.com). **Villas International** (☎ 415/499–9490 or 800/221–2260 ⊕ www.villasintl.com).

BED-AND-BREAKFASTS

Bed-and-breakfasts are a popular option all over Peru, but especially in tourist areas like Cusco, Arequipa, and Puno. Many are in charming older buildings, including colonial-era homes built around flower-filled courtyards. Breakfast ranges from a roll with butter and jam to a massive buffet.

Reservation Services Bed and Breakfast. com (☎ 512/322–2710 or 800/462–2632 ⊕ www.bedandbreakfast.com) also sends out an online newsletter. **Bed & Breakfast Inns Online** (☎ 310/280–4363 or 800/215–7365 ⊕ www.bbonline.com).

HOME EXCHANGES

With a direct home exchange you stay in someone else's home while they stay in yours. Some outfits also deal with vacation homes, so you're not actually staying in someone's full-time residence, just their vacant weekend place.

Exchange Clubs Home Exchange.com (☎ 800/877–8723 ⊕ www.homeexchange.com); $119 for a one-year online listing.

HOTELS

Peru uses a rating system of one to five stars for its accommodations. A hotel can have one to five stars, an apart-hotel (a hotel with apartment-like rooms) three to five, and a hostel one to three. Lodgings with fewer stars are not necessarily inferior—they may only be missing an amenity or two that may not be important to you, such as telephones or television in the rooms. The name of a hotel does not necessarily have anything to do with its luxuriousness. A *posada*, for example, can be at the high, middle, or low end.

■ COMMUNICATIONS

INTERNET

Email has become a favorite way to communicate in Peru. Lima, Cusco, and other larger cities have dozens of Internet cafés. (Look for a sign with an @ symbol out front.) Even on the shores of Lake Titicaca you can stop in a small shop and send an email message back home for about $1 USD. And many of the country's airports, including Lima's Jorge Chávez International Airport and Cusco's Teniente Alejandro Velasco Astete International Airport, offer free wireless connections if you're traveling with your own laptops or wireless device. Even hotels that don't have wireless in their rooms will probably have a strong signal in the public areas.

Computer keyboards in South America are not quite the same as ones in English-speaking countries. Your biggest frustration will probably be finding the @ symbol to type an email address. On a PC, you have to type ALT+164 with the NUMBERS LOCK on or some other combination. If you need to ask, it's called *arroba* in Spanish.

If you're traveling with a laptop, carry a converter if your computer isn't dual voltage. (Most are these days.) Carrying a laptop could make you a target for thieves. Conceal your laptop in a generic bag, and keep it close to you at all times.

Contacts Cybercafes (⊕ *www.cybercafes. com*) lists more than 4,000 Internet cafés worldwide.

PHONES

The good news is that you can now make a direct-dial telephone call from virtually any point on earth. The bad news? You can't always do so cheaply. Calling from a hotel is almost always the most expensive option; hotels usually add huge surcharges to all calls, particularly international ones. In some countries you can

phone from call centers or even the post office. Calling cards usually keep costs to a minimum, but only if you purchase them locally. And as expensive as international mobile phone calls are, they are still usually a much cheaper option than calling from your hotel.

To call Peru direct, dial 011 followed by the country code of 51, then the city code, then the number of the party you're calling. (When dialing a number from abroad, drop the initial 0 from the local area code.)

CALLING WITHIN PERU

To get phone numbers for anywhere in Peru, dial 103. For an operator dial 100, and for an international operator dial 108. To place a direct call, dial 00 followed by the country and city codes. To call another region within the country, first dial 0 and then the area code.

To reach an AT&T operator, dial 0–800–50288. For MCI, dial 0–800–50010. For Sprint, dial 0–800–50020.

CALLING OUTSIDE PERU

For international calls you should dial 00, then the country code. (For example, the country code for the U.S. and Canada is 1.) To make an operator-assisted international call, dial 108.

Access Codes AT&T Direct (☎ *800/225–5288*). **MCI WorldPhone** (☎ *800/444–4444*). **Sprint International Access** (☎ *800/793–1153*).

LOCAL DO'S AND TABOOS

CUSTOMS OF THE COUNTRY

Peru is one of South America's most hospitable nations. Even in the overburdened metropolis of Lima, people are happy to give directions, chat, and ask a question you'll hear a lot in Peru, *¿De dónde viene usted?* (Where are you from?) Peruvians are quite knowledgeable and proud of the history of their country. Don't be surprised if your best source of information isn't your tour guide but your taxi driver or hotel desk clerk.

GREETINGS

In the cities, women who know each other often greet each other with a single kiss on the cheek, whereas men shake hands. Men and women often kiss on the cheek, even when being introduced for the first time. Kissing, however, is not a custom among the conservative indigenous population.

SIGHTSEEING

To feel more comfortable, take a cue from what the locals are wearing. Except in beach towns, men typically don't wear shorts and women don't wear short skirts. Bathing suits are fine on beaches, but cover up before you head back into town. Everyone dresses nicely to enter churches. Peruvian women wearing sleeveless tops often cover their shoulders before entering a place of worship.

OUT ON THE TOWN

Residents of Lima and other large cities dress up for a night on the town, but that doesn't necessarily mean a jacket and tie. Just as in Buenos Aires or Rio de Janiero, you should dress comfortably, but with a bit of style. In smaller towns, things are much more casual. You still shouldn't wear shorts, however.

LANGUAGE

Spanish is Peru's national language, but many indigenous languages also enjoy official status. Many Peruvians claim Quechua, the language of the Inca, as their first language, but most also speak Spanish. Other indigenous languages include the Tiahuanaco language of Aymará, which is spoken around Lake Titicaca, and several languages in the rain forest. But English is now routinely taught in schools, and many older people have taken classes in English. In Lima and other places with many foreign visitors, it's rare to come across someone without a rudimentary knowledge of the language.

A word on spelling: since the Inca had no writing system, Quechua developed as an oral language. With European colonization, words and place-names were transcribed to conform to Spanish pronunciations. Eventually, the whole language was transcribed, and in many cases words lost their correct pronunciations. During the past 30 years, however, national pride and a new sensitivity to the country's indigenous roots have led Peruvians to try to recover consistent, linguistically correct transcriptions of Quechua words. As you travel you may come across different spellings and pronunciations of the same name. An example is the city known as Cusco, Cuzco, and sometimes even Qosqo. Even the word Inca is frequently rendered as the less-Spanish-looking Inka.

A bit of terminology, too: The word *Indio* (Indian) is considered pejorative in Peru and Latin America. (We use the word only to describe an Indian restaurant.) To avoid offense, stick with *indígena* (indigenous) to describe Peru's Inca-descended peoples. Likewise, the words *nativo* (native) and *tribú* (tribe) rub people here the wrong way and are best left to old Tarzan movies.

CALLING CARDS

Public phones use phone cards that can be purchased at newsstands, pharmacies, and other shops. These come in denominations ranging from S/3 to S/40. Your charges will appear on a small monitor on the phone, so you always know how much time you have left. Instructions are usually in Spanish and English.

MOBILE PHONES

If you have a multiband phone (some countries use different frequencies than what's used in the United States) and your service provider uses the world-standard GSM network (as do T-Mobile, AT&T, and Verizon), you can probably use your phone abroad. Roaming fees can be steep: 99¢ a minute is considered reasonable. And overseas you normally pay the toll charges for incoming calls. It's almost always cheaper to text message than to make a call, since text messages have a very low set fee.

If you just want to make local calls, consider buying a new SIM card (note that your provider may have to unlock your phone for you to use a different SIM card) and a prepaid service plan in the destination. You'll then have a local number and can make local calls at local rates. If your trip is extensive, you could also simply buy a new cell phone in your destination, as the initial cost will be offset over time.

■TIP➜ If you travel internationally frequently, save one of your old mobile phones or buy a cheap one on the Internet; ask your cell phone company to unlock it for you, and take it with you as a travel phone, buying a new SIM card with pay-as-you-go service in each destination.

Contacts **Cellular Abroad** (☎ 800/287–5072 ⊕ www.cellularabroad.com) rents and sells GMS phones and sells SIM cards that work in many countries. **Mobal** (☎ 888/888–9162 ⊕ www.mobal.com) rents mobiles and sells GSM phones (starting at $49 USD) that will operate in 190 countries. Per-call rates vary throughout the world. **Planet Fone** (☎ 888/988–4777 ⊕ www.planetfone.com)

rents cell phones, but the per-minute rates are expensive.

▌ CUSTOMS AND DUTIES

You're always allowed to bring goods of a certain value back home without having to pay any duty or import tax. But there's a limit on the amount of tobacco and liquor you can bring back duty-free, and some countries have separate limits for perfumes; for exact figures, check with your customs department. The values of so-called "duty-free" goods are included in these amounts. When you shop abroad, save all your receipts, as customs inspectors may ask to see them as well as the items you purchased. If the total value of your goods is more than the duty-free limit, you'll have to pay a tax (most often a flat percentage) on the value of everything beyond that limit.

When you check through immigration in Peru put the white International Embarkation/Disembarkation form you filled out in a safe place when it's returned to you. You will need it when you leave the country. If you lose it, in addition being delayed, you may have to pay a small fine. You may bring personal and work items; a total of 3 liters of liquor; jewelry or perfume worth less than $300 USD; and 400 cigarettes or 50 cigars into Peru without paying import taxes. After that, goods and gifts will be taxed at 20% their value up to $1,000 USD; everything thereafter is taxed at a flat rate of 25%.

U.S. Information U.S. Customs and Border Protection (⊕ www.cbp.gov).

▌ EATING OUT

Most smaller restaurants offer a lunchtime *menú*, a prix-fixe meal ($3–$5 USD) that consists of an appetizer, a main dish, dessert, and a beverage. Peru is also full of cafés, many with a selection of delicious pastries. Food at bars is usually limited to snacks and sandwiches.

The restaurants we list are the cream of the crop in each price category.

⇨ *For information on food-related health issues, see Health below.*

MEALS AND MEALTIMES

Food in Peru is hearty and wholesome. Thick soups made of vegetables and meat are excellent. Try *chupes*, soups made of shrimp and fish with potatoes, corn, peas, onions, garlic, tomato sauce, eggs, cream cheese, milk, and whatever else happens to be in the kitchen. Corvina, a sea bass caught in the Pacific ocean, is superb, as is a fish with a very large mouth, called *paiche*, that is found in jungle lakes and caught with spears. Or try piranha—delicious, but full of bones. *Anticuchos* (marinated beef hearts grilled over charcoal) are a staple. Peru's large-kernel corn is very good, and it's claimed there are more than 100 varieties of potatoes, served in about as many ways. And there is always *cebiche*, raw fish marinated in lemon juice and white wine then mixed with onions and red peppers and served with sweet potatoes, onions, and sometimes corn.

Top-notch restaurants serve lunch and dinner, but most Peruvians think of lunch as the day's main meal, and many restaurants open only at midday. Served between 1 and 3, lunch was once followed by a siesta, though the custom has largely died out. Dinner can be anything from a light snack to another full meal. Peruvians tend to dine late, between 7 and 11 PM.

Unless otherwise noted, the restaurants listed in this guide are open daily for lunch and dinner.

RESERVATIONS AND DRESS

Peruvians dress informally when they dine out. At the most expensive restaurants, a jacket without a tie is sufficient for men. Shorts are frowned upon everywhere except at the beach, and T-shirts are appropriate only in very modest restaurants.

In this book we only mention reservations specifically when they are essential or when they are not accepted. For popular restaurants, book as far ahead as you can (often 30 days), and reconfirm as soon as you arrive. We mention dress only when men are required to wear a jacket or a jacket and tie.

WINES, BEER, AND SPIRITS

Peru's national drink is the pisco sour, made with a pale grape brandy—close to 100 proof—derived from grapes grown in vineyards around Ica, south of Lima. Added to the brandy are lemon juice, sugar, bitters, and egg white. It's a refreshing drink and one that nearly every bar in Peru claims to make best. Tacama's Blanco de Blancos from Ica is considered the country's best wine. Ica's National Vintage Festival is in March.

Peruvian beer (*cerveza*) is also very good. In Lima, try Cristal and the slightly more upscale Pilsen Callao, both produced by the same brewery. In the south it's Arequipeña from Arequipa, Cusqueña from Cusco, and big bottles of San Juan from Iquitos, where the warm climate makes it taste twice as good. In Iquitos locals make Chuchuhuasi from the reddish-brown bark of the canopy tree that grows to 100 feet high in the Amazon rain forest. The bark is soaked for days in *aguardiente* (a very strong homemade liquor) and is claimed to be a cure-all. However, in Iquitos, it has been bottled and turned into a tasty drink for tourists.

▋ ELECTRICITY

The electrical current in Peru is 220 volts, 50 cycles alternating current (AC). A converter is needed for appliances requiring 110 voltage. U.S.-style flat prongs fit most outlets.

Consider buying a universal adapter, which has several types of plugs in one lightweight, compact unit. Most laptops and mobile phone chargers are dual voltage (i.e., they operate equally well on 110 and 220 volts), so require only an adapter. These days the same is true of small appliances such as hair dryers. Always check labels and manufacturer instructions to be sure. Don't use 110-volt outlets marked FOR SHAVERS ONLY for high-wattage appliances such as hair dryers.

Contacts Global Electric & Phone Directory (⊕ www.kropla.com) has information on electrical and telephone plugs around the world. **Walkabout Travel Gear** (⊕ www.walkabouttravelgear.com) has good coverage of electricity under "adapters."

▌ EMERGENCIES

The fastest way to connect with the police is to dial 105. For fire, dial 116. The Tourism Police, part of the National Police of Perú, exists for the security and protection of travelers. Officers are usually found in around hotels, archaeological centers, museums, and any place that is frequently visited by tourists. They almost always speak English.

Foreign Embassies Canada (⊠ Bolognesi 228, Miraflores ☎ 01/319-3200 ⊕ www.peru.gc.ca). **New Zealand** (⊠ Av. Los Nogales 510, San Isidro ☎ 01/422-7491). **United Kingdom** (⊠ Av. José Larco 1301, Miraflores ☎ 01/617-3000 ⊕ ukinperu.fco.gov.uk). **United States** (⊠ Av. La Encalada, Cuadra 17, Monterrico ☎ 01/618-2000 ⊕ lima.usembassy.gov).

▌ HEALTH

The most common illnesses are caused by contaminated food and water. Especially in developing countries, drink only bottled, boiled, or purified water and drinks; don't drink from public fountains or use ice. You should even consider using bottled water to brush your teeth. Make sure food has been thoroughly cooked and is served to you fresh and hot; avoid vegetables and fruits that you haven't washed (in bottled or purified water) or peeled yourself. If you have problems, mild cases of traveler's diarrhea may respond to Imodium (known generically as loperamide) or Pepto-Bismol. Drink plenty of fluids; if you can't keep fluids down, seek medical help immediately.

Infectious diseases can be airborne or passed via mosquitoes and ticks and through direct or indirect physical contact with animals or people. Some, including Norwalk-like viruses that affect your digestive tract, can be passed along through contaminated food. If you are traveling in an area where malaria is prevalent, use a repellent containing DEET and take malaria-prevention medication before, during, and after your trip as directed by your physician. Speak with your physician and/or check the CDC or World Health Organization Web sites for health alerts, particularly if you're pregnant, traveling with children, or have a chronic illness.

Medical Insurers International Medical Group (☎ 800/628-4664 ⊕ www.imglobal.com). **International SOS** (⊕ www.internationalsos.com). **Wallach & Company** (☎ 800/237-6615 or 540/687-3166 ⊕ www.wallach.com).

SHOTS AND MEDICATIONS

No vaccinations are required to enter Peru, although yellow fever vaccinations are recommended if you're visiting the jungle areas in the east. It's a good idea to have up-to-date boosters for tetanus, diphtheria, and measles. A hepatitis A inoculation can prevent one of the most common intestinal infections. Those who might be around animals should consider a rabies vaccine. As rabies is a concern, most hospitals have anti-rabies injections. Children traveling to Peru should have their vaccinations for childhood diseases up-to-date.

According to the Centers for Disease Control and Prevention (CDC), there's a limited risk of cholera, typhoid, malaria, hepatitis B, dengue, and Chagas' disease. Although a few of these you could catch anywhere, most are restricted to jungle areas. If you plan to visit remote regions or stay for more than six weeks, check with the CDC's International Travelers Hot Line.

Health Warnings **Centers for Disease Control & Prevention** (*CDC* ☎ *877/394–8747 international travelers' health line* ⊕ *www. cdc.gov/travel*). **World Health Organization** (*WHO* ⊕ *www.who.int*).

SPECIFIC ISSUES IN PERU

The major health risk in Peru is traveler's diarrhea, caused by viruses, bacteria, or parasites in contaminated food or water. So watch what you eat. If you eat something from a street vendor, make sure it's cooked in front of you. Avoid uncooked food, food that has been sitting around at room temperature, and unpasteurized milk and milk products. Drink only bottled water or water that has been boiled for several minutes, even when brushing your teeth. Order drinks *sin hielo,* or "without ice." Note that water boils at a lower temperature at high altitudes and may not be hot enough to rid the bacteria, so consider using purification tablets. Local brands include Micropur.

Mild cases of traveler's diarrhea may respond to Imodium, Pepto-Bismol, or Lomotil, all of which can be purchased in Peru without a prescription. Drink plenty of purified water or tea—chamomile (*manzanilla*) is a popular folk remedy.

The number of cases of cholera, an intestinal infection caused by ingestion of contaminated water or food, has dropped dramatically in recent years, but you should still take care. Anything raw, including cebiche, should only be eaten in the better restaurants.

Altitude sickness, known locally as *soroche,* affects the majority of visitors to Cusco, Puno, and other high-altitude locales in the Andes. Headache, dizziness, nausea, and shortness of breath are common. When you visit areas over 10,000 feet above sea level, take it easy for the first few days. Avoiding alcohol will keep you from getting even more dehydrated. To fight soroche, Peruvians swear by *mate de coca,* a tea made from the leaves of the coca plant. (If you are subject to any type of random drug testing through your workplace, know that coca tea can result in a positive test for cocaine afterwards.) Some travelers swear by the prescription drug acetazolamide (brand name, Diamox). Whether that's an appropriate course is for you and your health-care professional to decide.

Spend a few nights at lower elevations before you head higher. If you must fly directly to higher altitudes, plan on doing next to nothing for the first day or two. Drinking plenty of water or coca tea or taking frequent naps may also help. If symptoms persist, return to lower elevations. If you have high blood pressure or a history of heart trouble or are pregnant, check with your doctor before traveling to high elevations.

Mosquitoes are a problem in tropical areas, especially at dusk. Take along plenty of repellent containing DEET. You may not get through airport screening with an aerosol can, so take a spritz bottle or cream. Local brands of repellent are readily available in pharmacies. If you plan to spend time in the jungle, be sure to wear clothing that covers your arms and legs, sleep under a mosquito net, and spray bug repellent in living and sleeping areas. You should also ask your doctor about antimalarial medications. Do so early, as some vaccinations must be started weeks before heading into a malaria zone.

Chiggers are sometimes a problem in the jungle or where there are animals. Red, itchy spots suddenly appear, most often *under* your clothes. The best advice when venturing out into chigger country is to use insect repellent and wear loose-fitting clothing. A hot, soapy bath after being outdoors also prevents them from attaching to your skin.

OVER-THE-COUNTER REMEDIES

Over-the-counter analgesics may curtail soroche symptoms, but consult your doctor before you take these, as well as any other medications you may take regularly. Always carry your own medications with you, including those you would ordinarily take for a simple headache, as you will usually not find the same brands in the local *farmacia* (pharmacy). However, if you forgot, ask for *aspirina* (aspirin). Try writing down the name of your local medication, because in many cases, the pharmacist will have it or something similar.

▮ HOLIDAYS

New Year's Day; Easter holiday, which begins midday on Holy Thursday and continues through Easter Monday (March or April); Labor Day (May 1); St. Peter and St. Paul Day (June 29); Independence Day (July 28); St. Rosa of Lima Day (August 30); Battle of Angamos Day, which commemorates a battle with Chile in the War of the Pacific, 1879–81 (October 8); All Saints' Day (November 1); Immaculate Conception (December 8); Christmas.

▮ MAIL

Letters sent within the country cost S/3 for less than 20 grams; letters and cards up to 20 grams sent to the United States and Canada cost S/7.20. Bring packages to the post office unsealed, as you must show the contents to postal workers. Mail service has been improving, and a letter should reach just about anywhere in a week from any of the main cities. For timely delivery or valuable parcels, use FedEx, DHL, or UPS.

DHL, FedEx, and UPS all have offices in Peru. Because of the limited number of international flights, overnight service is usually not available.

▮ MONEY

Peru's national currency is the nuevo sol (S/). Bills are issued in denominations of 10, 20, 50, 100, and 200 soles. Coins are 1, 5, 10, 20, and 50 céntimos, and 1, 2, and 5 soles. (The 1- and 5-céntimo coins are rarely seen.) At this writing, the exchange rate was S/2.75 to the U.S.

dollar. Peru is not one of those "everybody takes dollars" places—many businesses and most individuals are not equipped to handle U.S. currency—so you should try to deal in soles.

You'll want to break larger bills as soon as possible. Souvenir stands, craft markets, taxi drivers, and other businesses often do not have change.

Currency Conversion Google (⊕ *www.google.com*). **Oanda.com** (⊕ *www.oanda.com*). **XE.com** (⊕ *www.xe.com*).

▪**TIP➜** If you're planning to exchange funds before leaving home, don't wait 'til the last minute. Banks never have every foreign currency on hand, and it may take as long as a week to order. For the best exchange rates you're better off to wait until you get to Peru to change dollars into local currency.

ATMS AND BANKS

Your own bank will probably charge a fee for using ATMs abroad; the foreign bank you use may also charge a fee. Nevertheless, you'll usually get a better rate of exchange at an ATM than you will at a currency-exchange office or even when changing money in a bank. And extracting funds as you need them is a safer option than carrying around a large amount of cash.

▪**TIP➜** PIN numbers with more than four digits are not recognized at ATMs in many countries. If yours has five or more, remember to change it before you leave.

ATMs (*cajeros automáticos*) are widely available, especially in Lima, and you can get cash with a Cirrus- or Plus-linked debit card or with a major credit card. Most ATMs accept both Cirrus and Plus cards, but to be on the safe side bring at least one of each.

ATM Locations MasterCard Cirrus (☏ *800/424-7787* ⊕ *www.mastercard.com*). **Visa Plus** (☏ *800/843-7587* ⊕ *www.visa.com/atm*).

CREDIT CARDS

Throughout this guide, the following abbreviations are used: **AE**, American Express; **D**, Discover; **DC**, Diners Club; **MC**, MasterCard; and **V**, Visa.

It's a good idea to inform your credit-card company before you travel. Otherwise, the credit-card company might put a hold on your card owing to unusual activity—not a good thing halfway through your trip. Record all your credit-card numbers—as well as the phone numbers to call if your cards are lost or stolen—in a safe place, so you're prepared should something go wrong. Both MasterCard and Visa have general numbers you can call (collect if you're abroad) if your card is lost, but you're better off calling the number of your issuing bank, since MasterCard and Visa usually just transfer you to your bank; your bank's number is usually printed on your card.

Although it's usually cheaper (and safer) to use a credit card abroad for large purchases (so you can cancel payments or be reimbursed if there's a problem), note that some credit-card companies *and* the banks that issue them add substantial percentages to all foreign transactions, whether they're in a foreign currency or not. Check on these fees before leaving home, so there won't be any surprises when you get the bill.

■ TIP➜ Before you charge something, ask the merchant whether or not he or she plans to do a dynamic currency conversion (DCC). In such a transaction the credit-card processor (shop, restaurant, or hotel, not Visa or MasterCard) converts the currency and charges you in dollars. In most cases you'll pay the merchant a 3% fee for this service in addition to any credit-card company and issuing-bank foreign-transaction surcharges.

Dynamic currency conversion programs are becoming increasingly widespread. Merchants who participate in them are supposed to ask whether you want to be charged in dollars or the local currency, but they don't always do so. And even if they do offer you a choice, they may well avoid mentioning the additional surcharges. The good news is that you *do* have a choice. And if this practice really gets your goat, you can avoid it entirely thanks to American Express; with its cards, DCC simply isn't an option.

For costly items, try to use your credit card whenever possible—you'll come out ahead, whether the exchange rate at which your purchase is calculated is the one in effect the day the vendor's bank abroad processes the charge or the one prevailing on the day the charge company's service center processes it at home.

Major credit cards, especially MasterCard and Visa, are accepted in most hotels, restaurants, and shops in tourist areas. If you're traveling outside major cities, always check to see whether your hotel accepts credit cards. You may have to bring enough cash to pay the bill.

Before leaving home make copies of the back and front of your credit cards; keep one set of copies with your luggage, the other at home.

Reporting Lost Cards American Express (☎ 800/528–4800 in U.S., 336/393–1111 collect from abroad ⊕ www.americanexpress. com). **Diners Club** (☎ 800/234–6377 in U.S., 303/799–1504 collect from abroad ⊕ www. dinersclub.com). **Discover** (☎ 800/347–2683 in U.S., 801/902–3100 collect from abroad ⊕ www.discovercard.com). **MasterCard** (☎ 800/627–8372 in U.S., 636/722–7111 collect from abroad ⊕ www.mastercard.com). **Visa** (☎ 800/847–2911 in U.S., 410/581–9994 collect from abroad ⊕ www.visa.com).

CURRENCY AND EXCHANGE

You can safely exchange money or cash traveler's checks in a bank, at your hotel, or at *casas de cambio* (exchange houses). The rate for traveler's checks is usually the same as for cash, but many banks have a ceiling on how much they will exchange at one time.

■ TIP➜ Even if a currency-exchange booth has a sign promising no commission, rest assured that there's some kind of huge, hidden fee. (Oh . . . that's right. The sign didn't say no fee). Rates are always better at an ATM or a bank.

PACKING

For sightseeing, casual clothing and good walking shoes are desirable and appropriate, and most cities don't require formal clothes, even for evenings. If you're doing business in Peru, you'll need the same attire you would wear in U.S. and European cities: for men, suits and ties; for women, suits for day wear, and for evening, depending on the occasion—ask your host or hostess—a cocktail dress or just a nice suit with a dressy blouse.

Travel in rain-forest areas will require long-sleeve shirts, long pants, socks, sneakers, a hat, a light waterproof jacket, a bathing suit (if you want to swim), sunscreen, and insect repellent. You can never have too many large resealable plastic bags (bring a whole box), which are ideal for storing film, protecting official documents from rain and damp, and quarantining stinky socks.

If you're visiting the Andes, bring a jacket and sweater, or acquire one of the hand-knit sweaters or ponchos crowding the marketplaces. Evening temperatures in Cusco are rarely above 50°F. For beach vacations, you'll need lightweight sportswear, a bathing suit, a sun hat, and lots of sunscreen. Peruvians are fairly conservative, so don't wear bathing suits or other revealing clothing away from the beach.

Other useful items include a travel flashlight and extra batteries, a pocketknife with a bottle opener (put it in your checked luggage), a medical kit, binoculars, and a calculator to help with currency conversions. A sarong or light cotton blanket can have many uses: beach towel, picnic blanket, and cushion for hard seats and, most important, always travel with tissues or a roll of toilet paper as sometimes it's difficult to find in local restrooms.

Weather Accuweather.com (⊕ *www. accuweather.com*). **Weather.com** (⊕ *www. weather.com*)

PASSPORTS AND VISAS

Visitors from the United States, Canada, the United Kingdom, Australia, and New Zealand require only a valid passport and return ticket to be issued a 90-day visa at their point of entry into Peru.

Make two photocopies of the data page of your passport, one for someone at home and another for you, carried separately from your passport. While sightseeing in Peru, it's best to carry the copy of your passport and leave the original hidden in your hotel room or in your hotel's safe. If you lose your passport, call the nearest embassy or consulate and the local police. Also, never, ever, leave one city in Peru to go to another city (even for just an overnight or two) without carrying your passport with you.

GENERAL REQUIREMENTS FOR PERU	
Passport	Valid passport required for U.S. residents
Visa	Not necessary for U.S. residents with a valid passport
Vaccinations	Yellow fever vaccination required for those visiting infected areas
Driving	Driver's license required
Departure Tax	$31 USD for international flights; $6.82 USD for domestic flights; payable in cash only

RESTROOMS

In Lima and other cities, your best bet for finding a restroom while on the go is to walk into a large hotel as if you're a guest and find the facilities. The next best thing is talking your way into a restaurant bathroom; buying a drink is a nice gesture if you do. Unless you're in a large chain hotel, don't throw toilet paper into the toilet—use the basket provided, as unsanitary as this may seem. Flushing paper can clog the antiquated plumbing. Always carry your own supply of tissues or toilet paper, just in case.

Public restrooms are usually designated as *servicios higiénicos*, with signs depicting the abbreviation SS.HH.

Find a Loo The Bathroom Diaries (⊕ *www.thebathroomdiaries.com*) is flush with unsanitized info on restrooms the world over—each one located, reviewed, and rated.

▌SAFETY

Be street-smart in Peru and trouble generally won't find you. Money belts peg you as a tourist, so if you must wear one, hide it under your clothing. If you carry a purse, choose one with a zipper and a thick strap that you can drape across your body; adjust the length so that the purse sits in front of you. Carry only enough money to cover casual spending. Keep camera bags close to your body. Note that backpacks are especially easy to grab or open secretly. Finally, avoid wearing flashy jewelry and watches.

Many streets throughout Peru are not well lighted, so avoid walking at night, and certainly avoid deserted streets, day or night. Always walk as if you know where you're going, even if you don't.

Use only "official" taxis with the company's name emblazoned on the side. Don't get into a car just because there's a taxi sign in the window, as it's probably an unlicensed driver. At night you should call a taxi from your hotel or restaurant.

Do not let anyone distract you. Beware of someone "accidentally" spilling food or liquid on you and then offering to help clean it up; the spiller might have an accomplice who will walk off with your purse or your suitcase while you are distracted.

Women, especially blondes, can expect some admiring glances and perhaps a comment or two, but outright come-ons or grabbing are rare. Usually all that is needed is to ignore the perpetrator and keep walking down the street.

■ TIP➔ Distribute your cash, credit cards, IDs, and other valuables between a deep front pocket, an inside jacket or vest pocket, and a hidden money pouch. Don't reach for the money pouch once you're in public.

Contact Transportation Security Administration (*TSA* ⊕ *www.tsa.gov*).

▌TAXES

A 19% *impuesto general a las ventas* (general sales tax) is levied on everything except goods bought at open-air markets and street vendors. It's usually included in the advertised price and should be included with food and drink. If a business offers you a discount for paying in cash, it probably means they aren't charging sales tax (and not reporting the transaction to the government).

By law restaurants must publish their prices—including taxes and sometimes a 10% service charge—but they do not always do so. They're also prone to levy a cover charge for anything from live entertainment to serving you a roll with your meal. Hotel bills may also add taxes and a 10% service charge.

Departure taxes at Lima's Aeropuerto Internacional Jorge Chávez are $31 USD for international flights—some airlines already include the tax in their ticket prices, so ask—and $6.82 USD for domestic flights.

▌TIME

Peru is on Eastern Standard Time (GMT-0500) year-round, with no daylight saving time observed. From November to March, the time in Peru is the same as in New York and Miami. The rest of the year, when the United States does observe daylight saving time, Peru is one hour behind the U.S. East Coast.

▌TOURS

Many people visiting Peru do so as part of a tour package. Nothing wrong with that, especially for those who don't speak Spanish or are unaccustomed to foreign travel. On the other hand, do you really want to see the same sights as everyone else? There's no reason that you can't book your own tour. It's easy to arrange a custom itinerary with any travel agent.

Several Lima-based companies can arrange trips around the city as well as around the country. Long-established Lima Tours offers tours of the city and surrounding area as well as of the rest of the country. Lima Vision has some excellent tours, some of which include lunch at a traditional restaurant or a dinner show.

Recommended Companies Lima Tours (✉ Jr. de la Unión 1040, El Centro ☎ 01/619-6900 ⊕ www.limatours.com.pe). **Lima Vision** (✉ Jr. Chiclayo 444, Miraflores ☎ 01/447-0482 ⊕ www.limavision.com).

▌VISITOR INFORMATION

ONLINE TRAVEL TOOLS

Andean Travel Web, an independent Web site, has great information about regional destinations. Assisting travelers is iPerú, which has English- and Spanish-language information about the city and beyond. The Web site, in English and Spanish, is extremely helpful in planning your trip.

The most thorough information about Peru is available at South American Explorers. This nonprofit organization dispenses a wealth of information. You can also call ahead with questions, or just show up at its clubhouses in Lima (Miraflores) or Cusco (as well as Quito and Buenos Aires) and browse through the lending library and read trip reports filed by members. It costs $60 USD to join, and you can make up for that with discounts offered to members by hotels and tour operators.

All About Peru Andean Travel Web (⊕ www.andeantravelweb.com). **iPerú** (☎ 01/574-8000 in Peru ⊕ www.peru.info). **South American Explorers** (☎ 01/444-2150 in Peru, 800/274-0568 in U.S. ⊕ www.saexplorers.org).

INDEX

A

Accommodations, 535–536
Adobe pyramids, 404
Agua Calientes, 276–277, 295–297, 300, 302
Aguas Termales, 273, 277
Air travel, 530–531
Amazon Basin, 308, 313
Bolivia, 440, 470, 486, 489, 502
Central Highlands, 343, 346, 368
Cusco and the Sacred Valley, 213, 216
Lima, 51
luggage, 294
North Coast and Northern Highlands, 381
Southern Andes and Lake Titicaca, 149
Southern Coast, 134
Airports, 530
Al Frio y al Fuego ✕, 331
Alpaca 111 (shop), 99
Alpaca clothing, 99, 245
Alpacas, 164
Altai Oasis 🛏, 483
Altitude sickness, 12, 15, 214, 443
Amantani Island, 201
Amazon Basin, 10, 303–338
dining, 309, 330, 331–332
emergencies, 309
Iquitos and environs, 304, 326–338
lodging, 309, 313–314, 319–323, 324–325, 332–333, 336–338
Madre de Dios, 304, 309–310, 312–314, 319–325
nightlife and the arts, 333
shopping, 334
sports and the outdoors, 304
Amazon Yarapa River Lodge 🛏, 337
Amusement parks, 359
Anapia Island, 203–204
Andahuaylillas, 251–252
Andean Roots Eco Village, 473–474
Andes culture, 422
Apartment and house rentals, 535
Aransaya ✕, 456
Archaeological ruins, 24. ⇨ See also Museums
Bolivia, 475–476

Central Highlands, 349, 351, 352, 356, 357, 359–360, 366
Cusco, 227–228, 246–248, 249–251, 252, 261, 262, 268
Lima, 62, 65, 69–70
Machu Picchu and the Inca Trail, 272, 273, 278–294
North Coast and Northern Highlands, 384, 385–386, 388–391, 417, 420–421, 427, 428, 429, 433, 434
Southern Andes and Lake Titicaca, 152, 155, 202, 205–206
Southern Coast, 111, 112–113, 134
Arequipa, 146, 167–186
Astrid y Gaston ✕, 79
Asunción, 206
ATMs, 542
Ausangate, 265
Awamaki, 268
Awana Kancha, 253
Ayacucho, 341, 366–374

B

Bahuaja-Sonene National Park, 314, 319–323
Baños del Inca, 23, 426–427
Barranca, 384
Bars and pubs
Amazon Basin, 333
Bolivia, 461
Central Highlands, 362
Cusco and the Sacred Valley, 240–241
Iquitos, 333
Lima, 95–96
North Coast and Northern Highlands, 396, 398, 402, 419, 431, 434
Southern Andes and Lake Titicaca, 184
Basilica Menor de San Lorenzo, 490
Beaches
North Coast and Northern Highlands, 386, 397
Southern Andes and Lake Titicaca, 152, 153, 154–155
Southern Coast, 117–118
Bed & breakfasts, 535
Bicycling, 419
Boat and ferry travel
Amazon Basin, 308

Bolivia, 480
Southern Andes and Lake Titicaca, 203, 208
Bodega El Carmen, 124
Bodega El Catador, 125
Bodega Hacienda Tacama, 125
Bodega Lazo, 125, 128
Bodega Vista Alegre, 128
Bolivia, 435–510
Central Bolivia, 437, 485–495
dining, 445–446, 456–458, 468, 476, 483, 487, 490–491, 494, 499, 503
entry requirements, 442
lodging, 445–446, 458–460, 466, 468–471, 474, 476–477, 480–481, 483, 487–488, 491–492, 495, 499–500, 504, 508–509, 510
nightlife and the arts, 460–462, 493
outdoor activities and sports, 463–464
Southern Bolivia, 437, 495–510
shopping, 462–463, 488, 493–494, 495, 504
Bolivia side trip, 206–208
Boquerón del Diablo, 108
Border crossings, 157, 207, 407–408
Bus travel, 531–532
Amazon Basin, 308
Bolivia, 441, 449, 475, 482, 486, 489, 496, 502, 508
Central Highlands, 343, 346, 351, 353, 358, 368
Cusco and the Sacred Valley, 214, 216
Lima, 51–52
Machu Picchu and the Inca Trail, 274–275
North Coast and Northern Highlands, 381
Southern Andes and Lake Titicaca, 149, 188, 208
Southern Coast, 106, 115, 134
Butterfly farm, 330

C

Cahuachi Pyramids, 134
Cajamarca, 426–431
Camaná, 152–154
Campo Santo, 108
Candelabra, 118, 120
Capilla de la Merced, 358
Capilla St. Ignatius, 172

Capuccino ✕ , *404*
Car travel and rentals,
  532–533
*Bolivia, 441–442, 449, 486,
  489, 496*
Central Highlands, 343
*Cusco and the Sacred Valley,
  214, 216*
Lima, 52
*North Coast and Northern
  Highlands, 381, 388, 416*
*Southern Andes and Lake Titi-
  caca, 149, 170*
Southern Coast, 106
Caral, *24, 70*
Caraz, *425*
Carhuaz, *422*
Casa Andina ✕▥ , *143*
Casa Andina Private Collection
  Arequipa ▥ , *181*
Casa Andina Private Collection
  Suasi ▥ , *193*
Casa Andina San Blas ▥ , *236*
Casa Arequipa ▥ , *181, 183*
Casa de Fierro, *328*
Casa de Garcilaso, *228*
Casa de la Cultura, *490*
Casa de la Emancipación, *391*
Casa de la Literatura
  Peruana, *60*
Casa del Mayorazgo de
  Facala, *392*
Casa del Moral, *170*
Casa Goyeneche, *60, 173*
Casa Grande ▥ , *458–459*
Casa Hacienda Shismay ✕▥ ,
  349–350
Casa Jaúregui, *368–369*
Casa-Museo Maria Reiche,
  134, 141
Casa Real de Moneda, *502*
Casa Riva-Agüero, *55*
Casa Torre Tagle, *58, 60*
Casa Tristan del Pozo, *173*
Casa Urquiaga, *392*
Casma, *384–386*
Casona Iriberry, *173–174*
Cataratas de Sipia, *158*
Catedral (Arequipa), *170, 172*
Catedral (Ayacucho), *370*
Catedral (Cusco), *220–221*
Catedral (Lima), *55*
Catedral (Puno), *190*
Catedral de Cajamarca, *427*
Catedral de Cochabamba, *486*
Catedral de Piura, *404*
Catedral Metropolitana, *498*
Cathedral (Chiclayo), *399*
Caves, *249, 288, 351, 354*

Ceiba Tops ▥ , *337*
Cementerio de Chauchilla, *141*
Cementerio Municipal, *370*
Cemeteries, *141, 370, 428*
Central Highlands, *10,
  339–374*
dining, *344, 345, 349, 354,
  360–361, 370, 372*
*Huánuco south to Tarma, 340,
  345–355*
lodging, *345, 349–350, 351,
  354–355, 361–362, 365, 373*
nightlife, *362, 374*
shopping, *362–363, 374*
*Tarma south to Ayacucho, 341,
  356–374*
Centro de Producción Artesa-
  nias Andina, *264*
Centro de Rescate Amazónico,
  328
Cerrito de Huajsapata, *190*
Cerro Azul, *110–111*
Cerro Calvario, *475*
Cerro Rico, *502–503*
Cerro San Cristóbal, *60*
Cerro Santa Apolonia, *427*
Chachapoyas, *431–434*
Chala, *151–152*
Chalan Ecolodge ▥ , *470–471*
Chamanna ▥ , *425*
Chán Chán, *22, 24, 388, 390*
Chavín de Huántar, *412,
  420–421*
Chi Cha ✕ , *176*
Chiclayo, *399–402*
Children's attractions
Amazon Basin, 335
Bolivia, 452
Central Highlands, 359
Lima, 57, 68
*North Coast and Northern
  Highlands, 393*
*Southern Andes and Lake Titi-
  caca, 173*
Chincha, *112*
Chinchero, *264, 267*
Chinchero-Huayllabamba, *265*
Chivay, *160–163, 165–167*
Choquequirau, *24, 265*
Chucuito, *205–206*
Churches.➪ See also Monaster-
  ies and convents
*Bolivia, 454, 456, 475, 486,
  490, 498, 503*
*Central Highlands, 348–349,
  356, 358, 364, 369, 370*
*Cusco and the Sacred Valley,
  220–221, 222, 223, 228,
  251–252, 264*

Lima, 55, 57, 60–61
*North Coast and Northern
  Highlands, 397, 399, 404,
  427, 428, 432*
*Southern Andes and Lake
  Titicaca, 170, 172–173, 174,
  190–191, 205, 206*
Southern Coast, 113, 123–124
Cicciolina ✕ , *234*
Cinema, *462*
Climate, *27, 439*
Climbing, *412, 414, 419–420*
Club Colonial ✕ , *397*
Coca leaves, *294*
Cochabamba, *485–488*
Coco K'intu ✕ , *192*
Colca Canyon, *22, 25, 161–162*
Colcampata, *226*
Common Area, *285*
Communications, *536, 538*
Concepcíon, *356*
Conde de Lemos Balcony, *190*
Connectivity, *12*
Convento de la Recoleta, *174*
Convento de Santa Catalina de
  Siena, *222*
Convento de Santa Rosa de
  Ocopa, *356*
Convento de Santo
  Domingo, *60*
Convento y Museo de Santa-
  Teresa, *503*
Convents.➪ See Monasteries
  and convents
Copacabana, *474–477*
Copacabana Cathedral, *475*
Cordillera Blanca, *23, 408–414*
Cordillera Huayhuash, *424*
Coroico, *466, 468–470*
Correo Central, *55*
Cotahuasi Canyon, *23, 158*
Cotahuasi Village, *155,
  157–160*
Country Club Lima Hotel ▥ ,
  62, 93
Credit cards, *7, 543*
Cruz del Condor, *162*
Cueva de las Lechuzas, *351*
Cuisine, *15*
Amazon Basin, 333
Bolivia, 453
*Cusco and the Sacred Valley,
  230, 235*
Lima, 71–75
*North Coast and Northern
  Highlands, 383*
*Southern Andes and Lake Titi-
  caca, 156*
Cumbe Mayo, *429*

Currency, *543–544*
Cusco and the Sacred Valley, 10, *209–270*
dining, *230–235, 254, 256, 268–269*
lodging, *230, 236–240, 254–256, 263–264, 267, 269–270*
nightlife and the arts, *240–241, 243*
Sacred Valley of the Inca, *211, 252–270*
shopping, *243–246, 264*
side trips, *210, 246–252*
Southeastern Urubamba Valley, *210*
Customs, *538*

D

Dance, *21, 96, 241, 461*
De Marco ✕ , *394*
Dédalo (shop), *100*
Dining, *538–539.* ⇨ *See also* under specific cities, towns and areas; Cuisine
price categories, *70, 107, 150, 230, 276, 309, 345, 383, 446*
Distrito de Belén (Iquitos), *328, 330*
Duties, *538*

E

Economy, *16, 18*
El Batán ✕ , *429*
El Camino de la Muerte, *468*
El Conjunto de Belén, *428*
El Cortijo ✕ , *421*
El Cristo de la Concordia, *486*
El Cuarto del Rescate, *428*
El Dorado Plaza Hotel 🛏 , *332*
El Estaquería, *141*
El Faro de la Marina, *65–66*
El Hauchachinero 🛏 , *131–132*
El Horno ✕ , *418*
El Patio de Monterrey 🛏 , *421–422*
El Querubino ✕ , *430*
El Santuario de Huanchaco, *397*
El Yavari, *190*
Electricity, *13, 442, 539–540*
Embassies, *449*
Emergencies, *540*
Estación de Desamparados, *60*
Etiquette and behavior, *15, 537*

F

Fallen Angel ✕ , *234*
Feria Dominical, *364*
Ferreñafe, *403*

Ferry travel. ⇨ *See* Boat and ferry travel
Festivals and seasonal events, *20, 27, 146, 188, 393, 467*
Film, *19*
Fitzcarrald, *331*
Floating Islands, *200*
Folklore, *241*
Fortress of Ollantaytambo, *262, 268*
Fory Fay Cevicheria ✕ , *178*
Fountains, *285*
Funeral Rock, *282*

G

Gay and lesbian clubs, *96–97, 184, 241*
Glaciar Pastoruri, *417*
Government, *18*
Gran Hotel Chiclayo 🛏 , *401*
Grand Hotel Huánuco 🛏 , *350*
Great River Amazon Raft Race, *332*
Greens ✕ , *231*
Gruta de Guagapo, *354*
Guardhouse, *282*

H

Hacienda La Florida 🛏 , *354*
Handicrafts, *100, 340, 464*
Health and safety, *12, 14–15*
Amazon Basin, *308, 313, 328*
Bolivia, *443–444, 448–449, 475, 480, 482, 485, 489, 508*
Central Highlands, *344*
Cusco and the Sacred Valley, *215, 216*
Lima, *52*
Machu Picchu and the Inca Trail, *275*
North Coast and Northern Highlands, *381, 388, 391, 399, 404, 416, 426, 432*
Southern Andes and Lake Titicaca, *150, 169, 170, 188, 189*
Southern Coast, *106, 115, 134*
Hiking
Cusco and the Sacred Valley, *265*
Machu Picchu and the Inca Trail, *294*
North Coast and Northern Highlands, *419–420, 429*
Southern Andes and Lake Titicaca, *158–159, 163*
History, *39–46*
Holidays, *440, 542*
Home exchanges, *535*

Homestays, *167, 200*
Horca del Inca, *475–476*
Hostal Casa Vieja 🛏 , *433*
Hot springs
Central Highlands, *365*
Machu Picchu and the Inca Trail, *277*
North Coast and Northern Highlands, *421, 426–427, 432–433*
Hotel Antigua Miraflores 🛏 , *90*
Hotel Caballito de Mar ✕🛏 , *406–407*
Hotel de Sal 🛏 , *508*
Hotel La Cupula 🛏 , *476–477*
Hotel Laguna Seca 🛏 , *430–431*
Hotel Libertador 🛏 (Trujillo), *395–396*
Hotel Monasterio 🛏 , *237*
Hotel Nazca Lines 🛏 , *144*
Hotel Pakaritampu ✕🛏 , *270*
Hotel Palacio, *330*
Hotel Paracas Libertador 🛏 , *120*
Hotel Rosario 🛏 , *459–460*
Hotel Rosario Del Lago Titicaca 🛏 , *477*
Hotel San Sebastián 🛏 , *419*
Hotels, *7, 535–536.* ⇨ *See also* Lodging
price categories, *87, 107, 150, 230, 276, 309, 345, 383, 446*
Huaca Arco Iris, *390*
Huaca de la Luna, *390–391*
Huaca del Sol, *390, 391*
Huaca Esmeralda, *390*
Huaca Huallamarca, *62*
Huaca Pucllana, *65*
Huaca Pudlana ✕ , *81*
Huacachina, *130–132*
Huancavelica, *363–365*
Huancayo, *341, 357–363*
Huanchaco, *396–398*
Huánuco, *340, 346, 348–350*
Huaraz, *415–420*
Huari, *369*
Huascarán National Park, *25, 412*
Huatajata, *473–474*
Huayna Picchu, *288*
Huaytara, *113*
Huiñay Huayna, *288*

I

Ica, *103, 122–125, 128–130*
Iglesia de Belén, *428*
Iglesia de Jesús, María y José, *60–61*

Iglesia de La Compañía, *172–173, 222*
Iglesia de la Merced, *55, 57*
Iglesia de San Francisco (Arequipa), *174*
Iglesia de San Francisco (Cajamarca), *428*
Iglesia de San Francisco (Huancavelica), *364*
Iglesia de San Francisco (La Paz), *454, 456*
Iglesia de San Francisco (Lima), *57*
Iglesia de San Lorenzo, *503*
Iglesia de San Pedro, *57*
Iglesia La Merced, *348*
Iglesia San Cristobal, *348–349*
Iglesia San Francisco (Huánuco), *348*
Iglesia San Francisco (Ica), *123–124*
Iglesia San Juan Bautista, *190–191*
Iglesia San Pedro, *228*
Iglesia Santa Ana, *432*
Iglesia Santa Clara, *228*
Iglesia Santo Domingo (Ayacucho), *369*
Iglesia y Convento de Santo Domingo, *174*
Iglesia y Plazoleto de San Blas, *223*
Inca Bridge, *288*
Inca ruins. ⇨ *See* Archaeological ruins
Inca Trail, *22, 268, 272, 278–281, 287, 290–294*
Incahuasi ruins, *111*
Indio Feliz ✕ , *295*
Inkaterra Machu Picchu ✕▢ , *300*
Internet, *12, 536*
Bolivia, 466, 486, 489
Central Highlands, 353, 358, 368
Cusco and the Sacred Valley, 244
North Coast and Northern Highlands, 399
Southern Andes and Lake Titicaca, 170, 189
Southern Coast, 123, 134
Intihuatana (Central Highlands), *370*
Intihuatana (Machu Picchu), *285*
Intipunku, *288*
Iquitos and environs. ⇨ *See* Amazon Basin

Isla de la Luna, *202, 477, 480–481*
Isla de los Monos, *335*
Isla del Sol (Bolivia), *202, 477, 480–481*
Islas Ballestas, *118*
Islas Los Uros (Floating Islands), *200*
Itineraries, *32–38, 448*

J

Jauja, *356*
Jesuit Missions of Chiquitos, *490*
Jirón José Olaya, *416*
Juli, *206*
Julio Tello Museum, *120*
Jungle lodges, *320*

K

Kayaking, *160*
Kotosh, *349*
Kuélap, *434*
Kusikay, *243*

L

La Asunción, *205*
La Cabaña ✕ , *360–361*
La Casa del Camba ✕ , *490*
La Casa del Corregidor, *190*
La Casona ✕ , *237–238*
La Casona ✕ (Ayacucho), *372*
La Compañia de Jesús, *369*
La Heroinas de la Coronilla, *486*
La Mansión del Fundador, *174*
La Mar ✕ , *82*
La Merced, *228, 230*
La Miel, *153*
La Nueva Palomino ✕ , *178*
La Paz, Bolivia, *447–471*
La Posada del Inca ▢ , *481*
La Posada del Puruay ▢ , *431*
La Punta, *153*
Lago Sandoval, *319*
Lago Valencia, *319*
Laguna de Paca, *356*
Lagunas de Llanganuco, *423–425*
Lagunilla, *120*
Lake Titicaca, *22–23, 196–204, 437, 471–484*
Lambayeque, *402–403*
Language, *14, 355, 444*
Spanish vocabulary, 512–528
Lanzón de Chavín, *420*
Lares Valley, *265*
Las Casitas del Colca ▢ , *166–167*

Las Palmeras ▢ , *398*
Lectures, *243*
Lighthouses, *65–66*
Lima, *24, 47–100*
Barranco, 48, 66–68, 76–77, 87–88
dining, 68, 69, 70, 76–86
El Centro, 48, 54–62, 77–79, 88–89
emergencies, 53
lodging, 86–94
Miraflores, 48, 63–66, 79–84, 89–93
nightlife and the arts, 94–98
Pueblo Libre, 48, 68–69, 87
San Isidro, 48, 62, 84–86, 93–94
shopping, 98–100
Literature, *19*
Llachon Peninsula, *204*
Llamas, *164*
Llosa, Mario Vargas, *16–17*
Lodging, *535–536.* ⇨ *See also* under specific cities, towns and areas
price categories, 87, 107, 150, 230, 276, 309, 345, 383, 446
Los Baños Termales de Monterrey, *421*
Los Corales ▢ , *406*
Los Portales ▢ , *405*
Luggage, *294*
Lunahuaná, *111–112*

M

Machu Picchu and the Inca Trail, *10, 17, 22, 271–302*
dining, 275, 295–296
Inca Trail, 272, 278–281, 287, 290–294
lodging, 275–276, 296–297, 300, 302
Madre de Dios. ⇨ *See* Amazon Basin
Mail, *542*
Amazon Basin, 313, 328
Bolivia, 449, 475, 486, 489, 496, 502
Central Highlands, 346, 353, 358, 364, 368
Cusco and the Sacred Valley, 216, 256
Machu Picchu and the Inca Trail, 277
North Coast and Northern Highlands, 388, 399, 416, 426
Southern Andes and Lake Titicaca, 170, 189
Southern Coast, 123, 134

Malecón Tarapacá, *330*
Malls, *98*
Mamore River, *471*
Máncora, *24, 405–406*
Manu Biosphere Reserve, *323–325*
Markets, *99, 261*
Marakos Grill ✕, *400*
Marcahuasi, *355*
Meal plans, *7*
Mejia Lagoons, *154*
Mercado Artesanal, *277, 295*
Mercado Central (Huaraz), *416*
Mercado de las Brujas, *456*
Mercado Negro, *456*
Mercado San Camilo, *174–175*
Mirador de Retaquenua, *416*
Mirador los Lobos, *120*
Miraflores Park Plaza ▦ , *92*
Molino de Sabandía, *175*
Mollendo, *154–155*
Monasteries and convents
Bolivia, 503
Central Highlands, 356
Cusco and the Sacred Valley, 222
Lima, 60
North Coast and Northern Highlands, 392–393
Southern Andes and Lake Titicaca, 173, 174
Monasterio de Santa Catalina, *173*
Monasterio El Carmen, *392–393*
Money matters, *15, 542–544*
Amazon Basin, 313, 328
Bolivia, 444, 466, 470, 475, 482, 486, 489, 496
Central Highlands, 346, 358, 364, 368
Cusco and the Sacred Valley, 216, 256, 268
Machu Picchu and the Inca Trail, 277
North Coast and Northern Highlands, 388, 397, 399, 404, 416, 426, 432
Southern Andes and Lake Titicaca, 153, 170, 188
Southern Coast, 115, 123, 134
Monterrey, *421–422*
Moray, *267*
Mototaxis, *406*
Municipalidad de Lima, *61*
Museo Amano, *66*
Museo Amazónico, *330*
Museo Antonini, *141*

Museo Arqueologico (Chachapoyas), *432*
Museo Arqueológico de Ancash, *416*
Museo Arqueológico de Cajamarca, *428*
Museo Arqueológico Nacional Brüning, *402–403*
Museo Arqueológico Rafael Larco Herrera, *68*
Museo Cabrera, *124*
Museo Cáceres, *368*
Museo Carlos Dreyer, *191*
Museo Cassinelli, *393*
Museo Charcas, *499*
Museo de Arqueología, *393*
Museo de Arqueología y Antropología Hipólito Unánue, *369*
Museo de Arte Contemporáneo, *230*
Museo de Arte de Lima, *25, 57–58*
Museo de Arte Italiano, *61*
Museo de Arte Popular Joaquín López Antay, *369*
Museo de Arte Precolombino, *226*
Museo de Arte Religioso, *370*
Museo de Arte Religioso del Arzobispado, *226–227*
Museo de Ciencias, *348*
Museo de Instrumentos Musicales de Bolivia, *452*
Museo de la Coca and Costumbres, *191*
Museo de la Electricidad, *68*
Museo de la Inquisición, *58*
Museo de la Nación, *69*
Museo de la Recoleta, *498*
Museo del Juguete, *393*
Museo de Oro, *69*
Museo de Sitio, *404*
Museo de Sitio Manuel Chávez Ballón, *295*
Museo del Sitio ,*388*
Museo Etnológico, *428*
Museo Hilario Mendívil, *223*
Museo Histórico Regional (Ica), *124*
Museo Inka, *223, 226*
Museo Nacional de Antropología, Arqueología, e Historia del Perú, *68–69*
Museo Nactional de Arte, *452*
Museo Nacional Sicán, *23, 403*
Museo Nacional de Etnografía y Folklore, *452*

Museo Nacional Tumbas Reales de Sipán, *403*
Museo Pedro de Osma, *66–67*
Museo Rafael Larco Herrera, *25*
Museo Salesiano, *358–359*
Museo Santuarias de Andinos, *173*
Museo Santuary, *25*
Museo Textil Etnográfico, *498*
Museums, *25*
Amazon Basin, 330
Amazon culture, 330
anthropology, 66, 68–69, 134, 141, 173, 369, 452
archaeology, 62, 65, 68–69, 70, 113, 141, 175, 191, 223, 226, 358–359, 369, 385, 388, 393, 402–403, 404, 416, 428, 432, 498
Bolivia, 452, 498, 503
Central Highlands, 348, 356, 358–359, 368, 369, 370
Cusco and the Sacred Valley, 223, 226–227, 228, 230, 243
history, 60, 68–69, 124, 141, 228, 295, 368, 370, 393, 428, 503
Lima, 57–58, 60, 61, 62, 65, 66–67, 68, 69, 70
Machu Picchu and the Inca Trail, 295
natural history, 348, 356
Nazca culture, 124, 134, 141
North Coast and Northern Highlands, 384, 385, 388, 393, 402–403, 404, 416, 428, 432
Southern Andes and Lake Titicaca, 173, 175, 191
Southern Coast, 113, 120, 124, 134, 141
Music, *19, 95, 97–98, 185, 461*

N

Na Cunna ✕ , *487*
National parks and reserves, *25*
Amazon Basin, 314, 319–325, 336
Central Highlands, 351, 352
North Coast and Northern Highlands, 408
Southern Coast, 118, 120
Southern Andes and Lake Titicaca, 153, 154, 175, 197
Nazca, *132–144*
Nazca Lines, *23, 135–139, 141–142*

Nightlife and the arts. *See* under specific cities, towns and areas
Nobel Laureate, 16–17
North Coast and Northern Highlands, 10, 375–434
dining, 381–382, 383, 384, 386, 393, 394–395, 397, 400–401, 404, 418, 421, 422, 429–430, 433
Huaraz and the Cordillera Blanca, 377, 408–425
lodging, 382–383, 384, 386–387, 395–396, 398, 401, 404–405, 406–407, 418–419, 421–422, 425, 430–431, 433–434
nightlife and the arts, 378, 380, 384, 402, 414, 417
shopping, 396, 402, 405, 420, 431
sports and the outdoors, 376, 385, 419–420, 429

O

Obelisco, 313
Ollantaytambo, 262, 267–270
Ottantaytambo, 24

P

Pacha Papa ✕, 233
Pachacámac, 69–70
Packing, 26, 544
Palace of the Princess, 285
Palacio de Gobierno, 58, 452
Palacio de Inca Roca, 227
Palacio de Marqués de Mozo-bamba, 370
Palacio Iturregui, 393–394
Palacio Legislative, 453
Palacio Portales, 486–487
Paladar 1900 ✕, 179–180
Pampas de Huánuco, 349
Pampas de Quinua, 365
Pañamarca, 386
Parador Santa Maria La Real ⬒, 500
Parcas Peninsula, 117–118, 120–122
Paragliding, 66
Paramonga, 384
Parks. *See also* National parks and reserves
Central Highlands, 359
Lima, 61–62, 65, 67
North Coast and Northern Highlands, 423–424
Southern Peru, 108–110

Parque de la Exposición, 61–62
Parque de la Identidad Wanka, 359
Parque del Amor, 65
Parque del Cerro de la Liber-tad, 359
Parque El Olívar, 62
Parque Miraflores, 65
Parque Municipal, 67
Parque Nacional Cerros de Amotape, 408
Parque Nacional Huascarán, 423–424
Parque Nacional Tingo María, 351
Paseo Las Musas (Chiclayo), 399
Passports and visas, 544
Pastoruri Glacier, 412
Peñas, 97, 179, 461–462
Peruvian Amazon, 334–338
Petroglyphs, 155
Pikillacta, 250–251
Pilpintuwasi Butterfly Farm, 330
Pimentel, 399–400
Pisac, 253–255, 261
Pisco, 98, 114–117
Piura, 403–405
Playa Grande, 152
Playa Tortuga, 386–387
Plaza de Armas (Cajamarca), 428
Plaza de Armas (Cusco), 220–222
Plaza de Armas (Huaraz), 416
Plaza de Armas (Huancavel-ica), 364
Plaza de Armas (Trujillo), 394
Plaza de Armas (Lima), 58
Plaza e Iglesia de San Fran-cisco (Cusco), 230
Plaza 14 de Septiembre, 486
Plaza Huamanmarca (Huancayo), 359
Plaza Murillo, 452–453
Plaza San Francisco, 453–456
Plaza San Martin (Lima), 58
Pomata, 206
Port Bellavista Nanay, 330
Posada Amazonas ⬒, 321
Potosí, 500–504
Pozo de Yanayacu, 432–433
Prefectura, 369
Price categories
Amazon Basin, 309
Bolivia, 446
Central Highlands, 345

Cusco and the Sacred Valley, 230
dining, 70, 107, 150, 230, 276, 309, 345, 383, 446
Lima, 70, 87
lodging, 87, 107, 150, 230, 276, 309, 345, 383, 446
Machu Picchu and the Inca Trail, 276
North Coast and Northern Highlands, 383
Southern Andes and Lake Titicaca, 150
Southern Coast, 107
Pucusana, 108
Puente Colgante, 113
Puente de los Suspiros, 67
Puerto Chicama, 24
Puerto Inca, 152
Puerto Maldonado, 310, 312–314
Puka Pukara, 249
Puno, 186, 188–196
Punta Sal, 406–407
Punta Sal ✕, 83
Purunllacta, 433

Q

Qenko, 248–249
Qorikancha, 227–228
Quecha language, 355
Quechua people, 347
Quinua, 365–366

R

Rafting, 159–160, 163, 165, 420
Raqchi, 252
Religion, 18–19
Reserva Nacional Allpahuayo Mishana, 336
Reserva Nacional de Paracas, 118, 120
Reserva Nacional Junin, 352
Reserva Nacional Pacaya Samiria, 336
Reserva Nacional Pampas Galeras, 153
Reserva Nacional Salinas y Aguada Blanca, 175
Restaurant Olimpico ✕, 361
Restaurant Urpicha ✕, 372
Restaurants, 7, 538–539. *See also* Dining under specific cit-ies, towns and areas; Cuisine
price categories, 70, 107, 150, 230, 276, 309, 345, 383, 446
Restrooms, 544–545

Ribereños, *310*
Rio Abiseo National Park, *25*
Ruins. ⇨ *See* Archaeological ruins
Rumicolca, *251*
Rurrenabaque, *470–471*

S

Sacred Rock, *285*
Sacsayhuamán, *23, 246–248*
Safety. *See* Health and safety
Salapunco, *249*
Salar de Uyuni, *504–505, 508–509*
Salcantay trek, *265*
Salineras, *267*
Samaipata, *494–495*
San Blas (Cusco), *222–223*
San Cristóbal, *365*
San Juan de Letrán, *206*
San Pedro de Cajas, *354*
San Pedro de Casta, *355*
San Pedro Mártir, *206*
Sand boarding, *102, 133*
Sandoval Lake Lodge ⊞ , *322*
Santa Cruz, *489–494*
Santa Cruz de Jerusalén, *206*
Santiago Apóstol de Nuestra Señora del Rosario, *206*
Santo Domingo, *205*
Santuario Histórico Chacamarca, *352*
Santuario Nacional Lagunas de Meíji, *154*
Santuario Nacional Los Manglares de Tumbes, *408*
Sechin, *385–386*
Second Home Peru ⊞ , *87–88*
Señor de Muruhuay Sanctuary, *354*
Siam de Los Andes ✕ , *418*
Sillustani, *204–205*
Sipán, *398–399*
Soccer, *58, 463–464*
Sonesta Hotel El Olivar ⊞ , *94*
Sonesta Posada del Inca Valle Sagrado ✕⊞ , *256*
Sorata, *481–484*
Southeastern Urubamba Valley, *210*
Southern Andes and Lake Titicaca, *10, 145–208*
Arequipa, *146, 167–186*
Canyon Country, *146, 155, 157–167*
crossing the border, *157, 207*
dining, *150, 153, 155, 165, 176–180, 191–192*

Far Southern Coast, *146, 151–155*
Islands of Lake Titicaca, *197–202*
lodging, *150, 152, 153–154, 155, 165–167, 181, 183–184, 192–195, 206*
nightlife and the arts, *179, 184–185, 195–196*
Puno and Lake Titicaca, *147, 186–208*
shopping, *185–186, 196*
sports and outdoor activities, *158–160, 162–163, 165*
Southern Coast, *10, 101–144*
dining, *106, 115–117, 120, 129, 131, 142*
Ica and Nazca, *103, 122–144*
lodging, *107, 108, 110–112, 115, 117, 120–122, 129–130, 131–132, 143–144*
north of Pisco, *102, 107–113*
Pisco and the Paracas Peninsula, *103, 113–122*
shopping, *130*
Spanish vocabulary, *512–528*
Sports and the outdoors, *19*
⇨ *Also* under specific cities, towns and areas; specific activities
Storage Houses, *282*
Sucre, *496–500*
Sucusuri Biological Reserve, *336*
Sumaq Hotel ✕⊞ , *302*
Surfing, *109*
Symbols, *7*

T

Tallera de Artesania de Andres Calle Flores, *142*
Tambo Colonial ✕ , *457*
Tambo Colorado, *112–113*
Tambomachay, *249–250*
Tambopata National Reserve, *314, 315, 319–323*
Tambopata Research Center ⊞ , *322–323*
Tanta ✕ , *79*
Tantamayo, *350*
Taquile Island, *201*
Taray, *253*
Tarija, *509–510*
Tarma, *352–355*
Taxes, *445, 545*
Taxis
Amazon Basin, *328*
Bolivia, *449, 486, 490, 494, 496, 502*

Cusco and the Sacred Valley, *214, 216*
Lima, *521*
North Coast and Northern Highlands, *381*
Southern Andes and Lake Titicaca, *149, 170, 189*
Teatro Municipal, *453*
Telephones, *12, 444, 536, 538*
Temple of Raqchi, *252*
Temple of the Condor, *285*
Temple of the Sun, *282*
Templo de Inca Uyu, *205–206*
Templo de San Francisco, *486*
Theater, *243, 462*
Three Windows, *285*
Ticonata Island, *204*
Time, *12, 545*
Timing the visit, *27*
Tingo María, *25, 351*
Tipón, *250*
Tipping, *13, 169, 445*
Titilaka ⊞ , *195*
Tiwanaku, *464–466*
Tomayquichua, *349*
Toro Muerto, *155*
Totora reeds, *205*
Tours and travel agencies, *28–31, 546*
Amazon Basin, *311, 328, 335*
Bolivia, *449, 465, 466, 473, 483, 484, 493, 505, 508*
Central Highlands, *359, 387*
Cusco and the Sacred Valley, *224–225*
Lima, *53*
Machu Picchu and the Inca Trail, *287, 294, 301*
North Coast and Northern Highlands, *387*
Southern Andes and Lake Titicaca, *158, 165, 203, 208*
Southern Coast, *111, 117, 119*
Train travel, *533–534*
Bolivia, *442, 449*
Central Highlands, *344, 360*
Cusco and the Sacred Valley, *214, 220*
Machu Picchu and the Inca Trail, *275, 298–299*
Southern Andes and Lake Titicaca, *149–150, 189*
Transportation, *14, 16, 530–534*
Travel times, *530*
Trekking. ⇨ *See* Hiking
Trujillo, *387–396*
Túcomo, *404*
Tumba del Señor de Sipán, *398–399*

U

Urubamba, 256, 263–264

V

Vaccines, 26, 540–541
Valle de Mantaro, 363
Valle del Sur, 250–252
Valle Yanahuanca, 352
Valley of the Volcanoes, 160
Ventanillas de Otuzco, 428
Via La Encantada ✕, 142
Vicunas, 164
Vilcashuamán, 370
Visas, 544
Visitor information, 546
Amazon Basin, 313, 328
Bolivia, 447, 475, 480, 483, 486, 490, 496, 502, 510

Central Highlands, 348, 353, 358, 364, 368
Cusco and the Sacred Valley, 215, 220
Lima, 53
Machu Picchu and the Inca Trail, 299
North Coast and Northern Highlands, 388, 399, 404, 416, 426, 432
Southern Andes and Lake Titicaca, 170, 189
Southern Coast, 123

W

Warvilca, 359–360
Wasai Tambopata Lodge , 323

Weather, 27
Web sites, 546
Wilcahuaín, 417
Wildlife, 315–318, 408
Wineries, 111, 124–125, 128

Y

Yanahuara, 175–176
Yucay, 255–256
Yungay, 422–423
Yura, 175
Yuspique Island, 203–204

Z

Zona Reservada de Tumbes, 408

PHOTO CREDITS

onandia/Shutterstock. 200, JTB Photo Communications, Inc./Alamy. 201 (top), GARDEL Bertrand/ age fotostock. 201 (bottom), Danita Delimont/Alamy. 202 (top), Harry Papas/Alamy. 202 (bottom), Ian Nellist/Alamy. 207, FOTOPANORAMA /age footstock. Chapter 5: Cusco & The Sacred Valley: 209, Kevin Schafer/age fotostock. 210, Robert Fried/Alamy. 211 (top), Bjorn Svensson/age fotostock. 211 (bottom), Jon Arnold Images Ltd/Alamy. 212, Stephen H. Taplin. 218-219, Digital Vision/Super-Stock. 229, Mark Titterton/Alamy. 242, Kevin Schafer/Alamy. 251, Stephen H. Taplin. 257, Klaus Lang/Alamy. 258-259, Gonzalo Azumendi/age fotostock. 260 (top), Guylain Doyle/age fotostock. 260 (center), Ozimages/Alamy. 260 (bottom), Danita Delimont/Alamy. 261 (top), GARDEL Bertrand/age fotostock. 261 (bottom), Danita Delimont/Alamy. 262 (top), Gail Mooney-Kelly/Alamy. 262 (bottom), Bjorn Svensson/age fotostock. 265, James Brunker/Alamy. 266, David Noton Photography/Alamy. Chapter 6: Machu Picchu & the Inca Trail: 271 and 273 (top), Tim Jarrell. 273 (center), Andrew Holt/ Alamy. 273 (bottom), Bryan Busovicki/Shutterstock. 274, SuperStock/age fotostock. 278-279, Robert Fried/Alamy. 280, Melvyn Longhurst/Alamy. 281, The Granger Collection, New York. 282 (left and right), Tim Jarrell. 282 (bottom), Stephen H. Taplin. 283 (left), Tim Jarrell. 283 (right), Fabricio Guzmán. 284 (top left), Robert Harding Picture Library Ltd/Alamy. 284 (top right), Rachael Bowes/ Alamy. 284 (bottom), Christine McNamara. 285 (top left), Jordan Klein. 285 (top right), Tim Jarrell. 285 (bottom), Nick Jewell/Flickr. 286, SouthAmerica Photos/Alamy. 287, Christine McNamara. 288, Ozimages/Alamy. 289, Melvyn Longhurst/Alamy. 290-291, Pep Roig/Alamy. 290 (left), Jason Scott Duggan/Shutterstock. 290 (right), Christine McNamara. 291 (left), Stephen H. Taplin. 291 (right), Robert Fried/Alamy. 292-293, Stephen H. Taplin. 297, Orient-Express Hotels. Chapter 7: The Amazon Basin: 303, Hemis /Alamy. 304, infocusphotos.com/Alamy. 305 (top), Michael Doolittle/Alamy. 305 (bottom), Papilio/Alamy. 306, Michele Falzone/Alamy. 315, Mark Jones/age fotostock. 316-317, Steffen Foerster/iStockphoto. 316 (top), Mark Bowler Amazon-Images/Alamy. 316 (2nd from top), Mark Jones/age fotostock. 316 (3rd fom top), Kevin Schafer/VIREO. 316 (4th from top), Andoni Canela/age fotostock. 316 (bottom), infocusphotos.com/Alamy. 317 (top), Robert E. Barber/Alamy. 317 (3rd from top), Holt/VIREO. 317 (4th from top), Mathew Tekulsky/VIREO. 317 (bottom), Andoni Canela/age fotostock. 318, Andoni Canela/age fotostock. 329, Hemis /Alamy. Chapter 8: The Central Highlands: 339 and 340, SouthAmerica Photos/Alamy. 341, Bert de Ruiter/Alamy. 342, Bert de Ruiter/Alamy. 353, Corey Wise/Alamy. 371, Joam Boam/Alamy. Chapter 9: The North Coast & Northern Highlands: 375, Pavan Aldo/SIME/eStock Photo. 376, Marion Kaplan/Alamy. 377 (top), Pep Roig/Alamy. 377 (bottom), Galen Rowell/Mountain Light/Alamy. 378-379, Corey Rich/Aurora Photos. 380, Emmanuel LATTES/Alamy. 389, Chris Howey/Shutterstock. 407, John Warburton-Lee Photography/Alamy. 409, Galen Rowell/Mountain Light/Alamy. 410-411, Tolo Balaguer/age fotostock. 412, Tolo Balaguer/age fotostock. 413, J Marshall/Tribaleye Images/Alamy. 414 (top), Galen Rowell/Mountain Light/Alamy. 414 (bottom), Alun Richardson/Alamy. 432, Endos/Alamy. Chapter 10: Bolivia:435, Nacho Calonge / age fotostock. 436, Harald Toepfer/Shutterstock. 437(top), James Harris/Flickr. 437(bottom), Mathieu Crete/iStockphoto. 438, Dirk Ercken/Shutterstock. 445, Florian Kopp / age fotostock. 455, José Fuste Raga / age fotostock. 463, roberto contini / age fotostock. 465, Laurent Guerinaud / age fotostock. 467, gary yim/Shutterstock. 469, giovanni mereghetti / age fotostock. 478-479, Christophe Boisvieux / age fotostock. 491, Ozimages / Alamy. 498, ESCUDERO Patrick / age fotostock. 506-507, HEINTZ Jean / age fotostock. 509, Bjorn Svensson / age fotostock.

ABOUT OUR WRITERS

Freelance journalist and consultant David Dudenhoefer lives in Chaclacayo, Peru, in the foothills east of Lima. He has worked on various Fodor's guides over the years, including Costa Rica and Panama. For this guide, he updated the Experience Peru, Lima, and Amazon Basin chapters.

Writer and photographer Nicholas Gill, who updated the Southern Coast and the Southern Andes and Lake Titicaca chapters, lives in Lima, Peru and Brooklyn, New York. Visit his personal website (www.nicholas-gill.com) or his ezine on Latin American food and travel (www.newworldreview.com) for more information.

Michelle Hopey is a Boston-based writer who has lived, worked, and traveled extensively throughout South America. She has authored, updated, and contributed to several guidebooks on the region. For our guide, she updated the Cusco and the Sacred Valley, and Machu Picchu and the Inca Trail chapters.

As a freelance journalist and author, Marlise Elizabeth Kast has contributed to more than 50 publications including *Forbes*, *Surfer*, *San Diego Magazine*, and *New York Post*. Her passion for traveling has taken her to 65 countries and led her to establish short-term residency in Switzerland, Dominican Republic, Spain, and Costa Rica. Marlise updated the Lake Titicaca and Bolivia chapters. For more information, visit www.marlisekast.com.

Ruth Anne Phillips (Nazca Lines feature) earned her Ph.D. in Art History with a specialization in the Pre-Columbian Andes in May 2007. She has taught at various colleges in and around New York City. She has published on the relationship between Inca structures and the sacred landscape.

Paul Steele (Visible History feature) has a PhD on Inca culture history from the University of Essex in England that looked at the Inca myth-stories of origin. He is the author of the *Handbook of Inca Mythology*.

Mark Sullivan (Food in Peru feature) is a former Fodor's editor who has traveled extensively in South America. He has also written and edited for Fodor's South America and Central America books.

After picking up a B.A. and Postgraduate degree in English Literature from Otago University in New Zealand, Katie Tibbetts moved to Seoul, South Korea to work as an ESL teacher. She eventually made a break for South America where she picked up work in Quito, Ecuador. For our guide, she updated the Cusco and the Sacred Valley, and Machu Picchu and the Inca Trail chapters. Currently, Katie is back to living and teaching in Seoul.

San Jose, Costa Rica-based writer and pharmacist Jeffrey Van Fleet divides his time between Latin America and his native Wisconsin, and never passes up a chance to partake of the diversity that is Peru. He has contributed to Fodor's guides to Costa Rica, Honduras, Guatemala, Panama, Mexico, Los Cabos and Baja California, Chile, Argentina, and Central and South America. Jeff updated the Central Highlands, North Coast and Northern Highlands, and Travel Smart chapters for this edition.

Doug Wechsler (The Jungle Life feature) has studied and photographed wildlife in the Amazon and tropical forests around the world. He is Director of VIREO, the world's most comprehensive collection of bird photographs, at The Academy of Natural Sciences in Philadelphia. Wechsler (www.dougwechsler. com) has authored 22 children's books about nature.

After completing degrees in Archaeology, Geography, and Marine Science in New Zealand, Oliver Wigmore (Big Mountains feature) went walkabout. Between ski seasons in Canada and archaeological digs in Belize and Ecuador, Oliver has spent much time exploring South and Central America. Falling in love with the magic and diversity of Peru, he can't stay away from the place.